LONDON ACCESS®

ACCESS®PRESS does not solicit individuals, organizations, or businesses for inclusion in our books, nor do we accept payment for inclusion. We welcome, however, information from our readers, including comments, criticisms, and suggestions for new listings. Send all correspondence to: ACCESS®PRESS, 10 East 53rd Street, Fifth Floor, New York, NY 10022

P9-EEJ-049

Orientation

A provincial settlement on the edge of the civilized world; a trading district dominated by merchants and aldermen; a royal stronghold; a center of politics, power, and culture . . . London has had almost as many faces as it has years of history. England's capital and Britain's seat of government has evolved over the centuries from an area covering just 677 acres into a vast 620-square-mile metropolis along the north and south banks of the **River Thames**, home to seven million citizens.

Indeed, London is not one but several cities coexisting in the same space. Look up at **Big Ben** on a bright autumn morning, or stroll along the **Embankment** on a warm summer evening at sunset and you'll find the London of film sets, complete with red double-decker buses, chunky black cabs, and umbrella-toting politicians. Look closer, and catch a glimpse of local London, comprising 32 highly individual boroughs, each with its own mayor and council, not to mention its own special quirks and charms. An elegant town house atmosphere permeates **Mayfair**, for example, while the literary legacy of Virginia Woolf's era clings to **Bloomsbury**. To the east, finance still dominates the original **City**, or **Corporation, of London**; meanwhile, law and politics rule sober **Westminster**.

Of course, there is also historic London, seat of cathedrals and kings. The city was established roughly 2,000 years ago, first as a Celtic settlement, then as **Londinium**, a lonely Roman outpost that eventually grew into the hub of an empire extending around the globe. The city is a survivor, having outlasted a whole series of catastrophes: Queen Boadicea of the Celts burned the city to the ground in AD 61, but within a few years it had risen from the ashes; the Great Plague swept through in 1665, followed by the Great Fire of 1666, but neither disaster nor the 20th-century Blitz could annihilate the city's collective soul or the souls of its inhabitants past and present. Famous ghosts from every epoch cohabit here—in just one day you may happen upon Henry VIII or Anne Boleyn in the **Tower of London**, William Shakespeare in **Southwark**, and Charles Dickens in **Tavistock Square**. Even modern redevelopment plans have failed to tarnish London's grandeur: **St. Paul's Cathedral** retains its majesty, despite the cheerless and now derelict glass-and-steel structures that now crowd it on **Paternoster Square**.

But no city thrives on its past alone. Modern London stands tall, in the space-age **Lloyd's of London Building**, in the high-tech **Docklands** developments, and in the best of con-temporary art and theater, as well as in the fast-food

joints that have cropped up on various corners. "Modern British" describes the inventive, eclectic cooking of a new generation of chefs who base their dishes on British ingredients but draw on the best of international food and flavor combinations, using such seasonings as lemongrass, coriander, white truffle oil, and pairing quail with foie gras and wild mushrooms or monkfish with herb risotto and tomato confit. Trendy restaurants are booming, and the fashion scene is rated the most exciting in the world by international designers who have opened their flagship stores here. But, to be honest, London also possesses a dark side, with an undercurrent of racial tension in the **East End**; a class system that produces its own special problems, including stereotypes perpetuated by something as simple as an accent or dialect; the homeless, who huddle under railway bridges; and, of course, crime. The infamous pea-soup fogs have disappeared, but they've been replaced by noxious exhaust fumes and grime—mostly from cars jamming narrow streets and alleyways never meant to cope with modern-day traffic.

For all its problems, however, the magic of London acts as an elixir for tourists: 27.7 million of them visited in 1998 alone. Some come for the **West End** musicals; some for the fashion of **Bond Street** and **Knightsbridge;** some to wander the spacious parks and meet history face-to-face; others to explore the modern street culture that thrives in tiny art galleries and pulsates in clubs and discos. Whatever the reason, visitors to London share an affection for a city that is at once ancient and modern, reserved and tempestuous— an ever-changing kaleidoscope of a metropolis.

How To Read This Guide

LONDON ACCESS® is arranged so you can see at a glance where you are and what is around you. The numbers next to the entries in the following chapters correspond to the numbers on the maps. The text is color-coded according to the kind of place described:

Restaurants/Clubs: Red   **Hotels:** Blue
Shops/ Outdoors: Green   **Sights/Culture:** Black

Rating the Restaurants and Hotels

The restaurant star ratings take into account the quality, service, atmosphere, and uniqueness of the restaurant. An expensive restaurant doesn't necessarily ensure an enjoyable evening; however, a small, relatively unknown spot could have good food, professional service, and a lovely atmosphere. Therefore, on a purely subjective basis, stars are used to judge the overall dining value (see the star ratings at right). Keep in mind that chefs and owners often change, which sometimes drastically affects the quality of a restaurant. The ratings in this guidebook are based on information available at press time.

The price ratings, as categorized at right, apply to restaurants and hotels. These figures describe general price-range relationships among other restaurants and hotels in the area. The restaurant price ratings are based on the average cost of a dinner entrée for one person, including tax (VAT) but excluding tip. Hotel price ratings reflect the base price of a standard room for two people for one night during the peak season. At press time, the exchange rate was 62p to $1.

Restaurants

★	Good
★★	Very Good
★★★	Excellent
★★★★	An Extraordinary Experience
$	The Price Is Right (less than $12)
$$	Reasonable ($12-$16)
$$$	Expensive ($17-$20)
$$$$	Big Bucks ($21 and up)

Hotels

$	The Price Is Right (less than $100)
$$	Reasonable ($105-$175)
$$$	Expensive ($180-$250)
$$$$	Big Bucks ($255 and up)

Map Key

• City/Town	M30 Motorway A50 'A' Road
	A3 Primary Route B603 'B' Road
■ Point of Interest	Highway] Tunnel [
	Tube Station Main Road
1 Entry Number	Secondary Road
	Trail/Pedestrian Path
British Rail Station	Railway

To call London from the US, dial 011-44, followed by the city code and local number. When calling from inside Great Britain, dial 0, the city code, and the local number. The city code for inner London is 207; for outer London, 208. In this chapter, the city code is included in all phone numbers. Note: These new city codes, replacing the more familiar 171 and 181 respectively, were expected at press time to be fully operational by April 2000; the old codes should continue to be usable for some months after that.

Getting to London

Two major airports serve London from North America: **Heathrow,** roughly 15 miles west of the city's center, and **Gatwick,** some 28 miles to the south.

Airports

Heathrow Airport

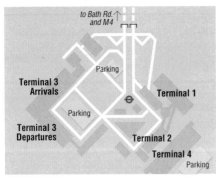

to Bath Rd. and M4

Parking

Terminal 3 Arrivals

Terminal 1

Parking

Terminal 3 Departures

Terminal 2

Terminal 4

Parking

Heathrow is the world's busiest airport, and the closest to London proper. Most major North American airlines (with the exception of **Delta**) fly into **Heathrow**'s four terminals; US transatlantic arrivals and departures generally use **Terminal 3,** although **British Airways** uses **Terminal 4.** Each terminal has its own **Travel Information Centre,** bank, currency exchange bureau, drugstore (or "chemist," as the English say), post office, and hotel booking desk. Each terminal has trained medical staff as well, and there is a 24-hour **Medical Centre** located in the **Queen's Building** between **Terminals 1** and **2.** The **London Tourist Board** (open daily; 207/932.2020 for hotel reservations only) has an office at the **Underground** station serving **Terminals 1** through **4;** ask for free travel and tourist information.

Airport Services Each of the four terminals has its own facilities and services, so to minimize confusion there is one number to call that will connect you to the right department (specify which terminal), no matter what information you require, from parking to immigration control: 208/759.4321. But for all **Medical Emergencies**, the number is 208/745.7047.

Airlines

Air Canada	208/897.1331
	800/776.3000 (toll free in US)
American	345/789789
	800/433.7300 (toll free in US)
British Airways	345/222111
	800/247.9297 (toll free in US)
KLM Royal Dutch Airlines	208/750.9200
United	1426/915500
	800/538.2929 (toll free in US)
Virgin Atlantic	1293/747747
	800/862.8621 (toll free in US)

Getting to and from Heathrow Airport

By Bus **Airbus** (208/400.6655) offers two buses that connect **Heathrow** with central London: the **A1** goes to **Victoria Station** via **Hyde Park Corner,** and the **A2** goes to **Russell Square** via **Euston Station.** Both buses run daily from 6AM to 11:50PM, depart every 30 minutes, and stop at each terminal. Bus transport costs more than the tube (subway) and usually takes a lot longer (75 to 100 minutes, depending on traffic), but if you can keep from nodding off after the long flight, you can sightsee along the way.
National Express (990/808080) offers frequent service to central London.

By Car To get to London from **Heathrow Airport,** take the **M4** east to the **A4,** which leads into the center of the city. To get to the airport from the city, take the A4 west to the M4. There is long- and short-term parking at each terminal. There are no tolls in either direction; depending on the traffic, the drive takes from 30 to 45 minutes.

Rental Cars The following rental car companies have counters at Heathrow Airport:

Alamo	208/759.6200
	800/327.9633 (toll free in US)
Avis	990/900500, 800/331.1212 (toll free in US)
Budget	208/759.2216
	800/427.3325 (toll free in US)
Europcar	208/897.0811
	800/227.7368 (toll free in US)
Hertz	990/996699, 800/654.3001 (toll free in US)

By Subway The **Underground** system has two tube stations at the airport: one serving **Heathrow Central (Terminals 1-3),** the other serving **Terminal 4.** Both are on the **Piccadilly Line** and are the quickest and cheapest way to go between central London and the airport. Trains leave approximately every 10 minutes Monday through Saturday from 5:08AM to 11:49PM (5:26AM-11:33PM in **Terminal 4**), and on Sunday from 5:58AM to 10:57PM (5:52AM-10:46PM in **Terminal 4**); operation is more frequent during peak hours (weekdays 7-9:30AM and 4:30-7PM). The trip takes 40 to 55 minutes, depending upon the destination. For more information about schedules and fares, call 207/222.1234.

By Train With the inauguration of the **Heathrow Express** in 1998 it is now possible to reach Central London by train. The **Heathrow Express** runs from all **Terminals 1-4** nonstop to **London Paddington** every 15 minutes daily (5:10AM-11:40PM). The journey takes 15 to 20 minutes. For more information on the service, call 845/600.1515.

By Taxi Taxis wait for passengers at the authorized ranks located outside each terminal; it takes about 50 minutes to travel from the airport to the center of town. Fares can be steep, however (£45/$72 to Piccadilly, for example), so it's best to share a cab with other travelers. To book a private car (limo) in advance call **Capital Airways** (208/933.8899; in the US 805/482.8210); cost, £25/$40.

Gatwick Airport

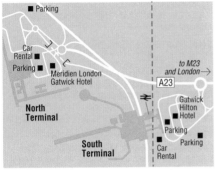

Besides serving many major North American airlines, **Gatwick** also receives the bulk of charter flights into its **North** and **South Terminals**, which are linked by a free rapid-transit system that runs every three minutes. Both terminals have 24-hour information desks located in the international arrivals concourse. Each terminal operates banks, exchange bureaus, post offices, and hotel booking desks.

Airport Services

Airport information/emergencies
  (specify which terminal) 1293/567675
Currency Exchange (Thomas Cook)
  North Terminal 1293/567197
  South Terminal 1293/568800
Customs and Excise 208/910.3744
Lost and Found/Lost Luggage 1293/503463
Parking
  NCP Flightpath......800/128128 (toll free in Britain)
  APCOA Parking Express 800/626671
  ....(toll free in Britain)
Police 1293/531122
Business Service Centers
  Meridien London Gatwick Hotel, North Terminal....
  ....1293/567070
Gatwick Hilton Hotel, South Terminal ..1293/518080
Traveler's Aid.......................................1293/504283

Airlines

American 345/789789,
  ....800/433.7300 (toll free in US)
British Airways 208/759.2525, 800/776.3000
  ....(toll free in US)
Canadian Airlines.....................................345/616767
Continental 1293/535353, 800/525.0280
  ....(toll free in US)

Delta.......................800/414767 (toll free in Britain),
  ....800/221.1212 (toll free in US)
Northwest 900/516000, 800/447.4747
  ....(toll free in US)
TWA ......345/333333, 800/221.2000 (toll free in US)
Virgin Atlantic 1293/747747, 800/862.8621
  ....(toll free in US)

Getting to and from Gatwick Airport

By Bus **Flightline 777** (990/747777) operates a daily bus service between **Gatwick** and **Victoria Coach Station;** buses run from 5:20AM to 11PM and leave both terminals approximately every hour; travel takes at least an hour and 20 minutes. Unlike the other transportation options from the airport, **Flightline** accepts American and Canadian dollars as payment. **Flightlink** (1293/502359) offers luxury bus service to the center of London; travel time is about 90 minutes.

By Car To get from **Gatwick** to London, take the **M23** north to the **M25,** which circles the city and links with several roads leading into the center, including the **A23,** the **A316,** and the **A20.** To get to the airport from the city, take the M25 to the M23 heading south. There is long- and short-term parking at the **North** and **South Terminals.** The drive takes an hour to 90 minutes, depending on traffic.

Rental Cars The following rental car companies have counters at **Gatwick Airport:**
Alamo ....1293/567790, 800/327.9633 (toll free in US)
Avis........990/900500, 800/331.1212 (toll free in US)
Budget....1293/540141, 800/427.3325 (toll free in US)
Europcar 01293/531062, 800/227.7368
  ....(toll free in US)
Hertz ......990/996699, 800/654.3001 (toll free in US)

By Train The fast, convenient **Gatwick Express** (345/484950) train leaves the **South Terminal** for **Victoria Station** every 15 minutes from 5:20AM to 9:50PM (then every 30 minutes to 12:50PM); travel time runs about half an hour. Another option is the **Thameslink** (345/484950) train service, which runs from Gatwick to **London Bridge, Blackfriars,** and **King's Cross** stations every 15 minutes from 3:34AM to 12:05PM. The trip takes about 35 minutes.

By Taxi Cabs are lined up at taxi stands outside both terminals. The trip takes about 1.5 hours (depending on traffic) and costs about £65 (about $114). To book a car service in advance, call **Capital Airways** (208/933.8899); cost, £40/$64.

Getting Around London

A word of advice for surviving urban London: Don't hesitate to carry a map—even Londoners do! The *A-Z* series (National Geographers A-Z Ltd., in various sizes and prices), is by far the best; you can pick up a copy at most newsstands and bookstores.

The best sources for tourist information are the **London Tourist Board Information Centre** in **Victoria**

Station and the **British Travel Centre** (see **Visitors' Information Centers,** page 14).

Bicycles

Bicycling around London is only for the truly adventurous, seasoned cyclist. The amount of traffic makes conditions extremely dangerous even if you *do* remember to stay on the left side of the street. Try to avoid major roads, where you will be subjected to traffic fumes as well as lorries (trucks) thundering past, often too close for comfort. It's a good idea to wear a helmet for protection.

Still, bicycling is one of the most enchanting ways to explore the city—the pace is slow enough to allow you to take in the beauty of the architecture and green spaces and find hidden paths through the back streets. It's also much easier to park a bike than a car; always lock your bike when you leave it.

Bicycles can be rented from **Mountain Bike & Ski** (18 Gillingham St, between Wilton Rd and Guildhouse St, 207/834.8933) and **Bikepark** (9 Macklin St, between Drury La and Newton St. 207/430.0083). You will have to leave a hefty deposit (about £200/$320 on a credit card).

Double-Decker Buses

The only way to become a bona fide Londoner—even temporarily—is to use public transport. Mastering the tube or the bus eases the pressure on the wallet and orients you in a way that taxi rides never will.

If speed is not a priority, take a London bus. The view from the top is unbeatable, and just riding the bus—with its roller-coaster movements and friendly atmosphere—offers a quintessential London experience. Because many routes are handled by private companies, some buses may not be the traditional red color; however, all have "London Transport Board Service Bus" written on the side. All stops have signs indicating the numbers of the buses that stop there and most show outlines of the route. The destination is written in the window at the front of the bus, and you need to know which direction you are going. For most buses, have your fare or **Travelcard** (for information about **Travelcards,** see **Underground** on page 10) ready to show the driver as you board at the front. However, some red "Routemaster" buses (mostly in central London) have a doorless opening at the back; for these, enter, get a seat (if you can), and show your pass or pay your fare when the conductor comes around. As on the tube, the fare is tied to zones, but the bus is generally cheaper. Strange but true: The bus driver cannot sell you a one-day bus pass; look for the passes at newsstands and in tube stations. Hang on to your bus ticket, as inspectors make occasional spot checks.

Bus Etiquette

- Don't cut in the bus line, or "queue," as it's called here; doing so may annoy the locals.

- You may be the only person at the stop waiting for your particular bus, so keep your eyes open. Buses do sail past, even when they're supposed to stop. Don't feel silly flagging your bus down; you'll have to in any case if the stop is marked "Request."

- Smoking is not permitted on any bus.

- There is no standing on the upper deck or on the platform.

- Even though the English do it, don't jump on or off a moving bus.

- Avoid buses at rush hour (weekdays 8AM-9:30AM, 4:30-7PM), it may be a long wait before you get one.

- Some of the larger one-man buses (without a conductor) can be very dangerous, as they travel fast and brake suddenly. If possible, stay in your seat, and hold on tight at all times, as people can get thrown around.

Scenic Bus Routes

Route numbers are displayed on the front of the bus.

8—Victoria, Mayfair, Oxford Circus, Holborn, Bank, Liverpool Street. This bus affords views into **Buckingham Palace** gardens and includes most of the **Oxford Street** shopping area. It's the only bus that goes through **Berkeley Square** and **Bond Street.**

11—King's Road, Sloane Square, Victoria Coach Station, Victoria, Westminster Cathedral, Westminster Abbey, Westminster, Whitehall, Horse Guards, Trafalgar Square, National Gallery, The Strand, Law Courts, Fleet Street, St. Paul's Cathedral.

12—Bayswater, Hyde Park, Marble Arch, Oxford Street, Oxford Circus, Regent Street, Piccadilly Circus, Trafalgar Square, National Gallery, Horse Guards, Whitehall, Westminster, Millbank, Tate Gallery, Vauxhall Bridge.

15—Paddington, Marble Arch, Oxford Street, Oxford Circus, Regent Street, Piccadilly Circus, Trafalgar Square, The Strand, Aldwych, Fleet Street, St. Paul's Cathedral, Tower of London.

53—Oxford Circus, Regent Street, Piccadilly Circus, National Gallery, Trafalgar Square, Whitehall, Horse Guards, Westminster, Westminster Bridge, Imperial War Museum, Elephant and Castle.

Night Buses

Special night buses (marked with an "N") run from London to the suburbs all night until 6AM (unlike ordinary buses, which run until midnight or 1AM). Buses leave from **Trafalgar Square** and the restaurant, theater, and cinema districts in central London. The **London Visitor Travelcard** is not valid on these buses; exact change is required.

Driving

If you can avoid driving in London, by all means do so. If you're determined to try it, however, remember that driving in the UK is a left-hand/ left-lane experience. Given that London traffic is also becoming increasingly aggressive and more congested, and that city parking is nearly nonexistent during working hours, you could be in for some hair-raising moments. Also bear in mind that gasoline (called "petrol" on this side of the Pond) is much more expensive than it is in the US: a liter (which equals a little more than a quart) costs about 60p/90¢.

That said, here are some tips to make the ride smoother: As long as you have been driving for at least a year, and are over the age of 18 (21 in some cases), your US or Canadian driver's license is valid for 12 months in the UK. However, getting an

International Driving Permit—available for a small fee through the **American Automobile Association (AAA)** or the **Canadian Automobile Association (CAA)**—isn't a bad idea since it could help placate the police if you're unlucky enough to have an accident. It is mandatory in Britain to wear seat belts—both in front and back seats. Speed limits in urban areas are technically 30 mph, but most Londoners tend to ignore this. When approaching a "roundabout," a circular junction that is the bane of those who are unfamiliar with it, *always, always* yield to the traffic approaching from *your right.*

Car Rental Renting a car in Britain isn't cheap (£169/$272 and up per week for a midsize car), but rental companies such as **Avis, Budget,** and **Hertz** frequently offer sizable discounts if you arrange to rent a car when purchasing your airline ticket. The charges usually include unlimited mileage, insurance, and temporary **Automobile Association (AA)** membership, but be sure you understand exactly what type of insurance is included in the package (and waive the coverage if your credit card already provides rental car insurance). If you want a car simply to take you *out* of London, then hold off and rent one from a local company rather than from the bigger, more expensive names at the airports.

Parking Unless you want to carry a hefty supply of change and risk having your wheel clamped or your car towed away, look for one of the multistory **National Car Parks (NCPs)** sprinkled around central London; some are marked on the larger-scale city maps. These car parks may be more expensive than meters, but they save hassles, headaches, and a lot of precious time.

Chauffeur Services For the fainthearted (and the wise), chauffeur-driven cars may be an appealing alternative. Most major car-rental agencies, including those listed below, offer this service.

Avis 207/581.1023

Carey Camelot 207/235.0234

Europcar...207/834.6701

Hertz..207/284.9900

By Taxi Who has not been in love at one time or another with a black London cab? Capacious, timeless, and honorable, these shiny vehicles—nearly all are Austins—are icons of British dependability and integrity. (They still are referred to as "black cabs," even though they're not always black these days.) Taxi ranks can be found in front of hotels and popular tourist areas; otherwise, flag down a cab if its yellow "For Hire" sign is lit. If your destination is under six miles away and within London boundaries, drivers are obligated to take you where you want to go. This city's taxi drivers are the best and most knowledgeable ones around by virtue of having learned a huge amount of London geography and then passing an incredibly tough exam to prove it. To book a black cab 24 hours a day (for an additional fee), call 207/272.0272. If you have any problems with a particular driver, contact the **Taxi Drivers' Association** (207/286.1046).

While minicabs (ordinary cars) are another option, it's wise to rely on recommendations from hotels or friends, since these cabs must be ordered by telephone. Many "bucketshop" drivers also operate a cheaper service in the central London area, but they are often unlicensed, underinsured, and, because they haven't had to take the exam, frequently get lost.

Tours The best way to see London (especially on a warm, sunny day) is by boat. You can cover 28 twisting miles of the Thames from **Hampton Court** to **Greenwich Palace** on one of the passenger boats that spend their days cruising up- and downstream from central London, with the pilot providing commentary along the way. For general information, call 891/505471 (premium rate call); for information on trips from **Westminster Pier** to **Greenwich,** call 207/930.4097; for the **Tower of London,** 207/930.9033; to the **Thames River Barrier,** 207/930.3373; to **Hampton Court,** 207/930.4721; and to **Kew Gardens,** 207/930.2062. There are also boats from **Charing Cross Pier** to the **Tower** and Greenwich, 207/987.1185.

A good way to get a sense of the city on dry land is via a bus tour. There are two basic types: the panorama, which is an 18- to 20-mile nonstop sight-seeing excursion; and full- or half-day guided tours, which typically cover **Westminster Abbey** and the Changing of the Guard (if it's being held) in the morning, and **St. Paul's** and the **Tower of London** in the afternoon. The grande dame of coach excursions is the **Original London Sightseeing Tour** (operated by **London Coaches;** 208/877.1722), which runs a 1.5-hour tour through the city on a traditional red double-decker bus (open-topped in summer). From 10AM to 5PM Easter-October (10AM-4PM November-Easter), tours depart every half hour from **Piccadilly Circus, Victoria,** and **Baker Street Stations.** There's no need to book; just show up and wait. **Harrods** offers two-hour bus tours that include tea, coffee, biscuits, and commentary (given daily at 10:30AM, 1:30PM, and 4PM), as well as an extensive, full-day excursion (given Thursday only) that features **Westminster Abbey, St. Paul's Cathedral,** Changing of the Guard, and the **Tower of London.** Lunch, tea, coffee, and biscuits are included in the full-day trips. The tours leave the store approximately at 8:45AM; 207/581.3603.

Note: For those who love castles, abbeys, palaces, stately homes, gardens, and historic sites, a **Great British Heritage Pass** will give you access to 600 of them dotted around the country—many of which are accessible on day trips from London (see **Day Trips,** page 216). Available for 3-, 7-, and 15-day lengths, the pass can be purchased at the **British Travel Centre** (see Visitors' Information Centers, page 14), at the **Tourist Information Centres** at **Heathrow** and **Gatwick Airports,** at the **London Tourist Board Information Centre** at **Victoria Station,** or through your travel agent or **British Tourist Authority (BTA)** offices in the US and Canada. The **London White Card,** a 3-day or 7-day pass (for individuals and families) to 15 major attractions in the city, mostly museums, is also sold at **BTA** offices in the US and Canada, at top London hotels, at tourist information centers, or at the attractions themselves.

By Train Trains are a great, civilized way to travel. The whole country is linked to London via a rail network that used to be called **British Rail;** however, the railways and their related services have been privatized, so you will now see many different logos at the various rail stations. A circular network of stations (including **Charing Cross, Euston, King's Cross, Liverpool Street, Paddington, Victoria,** and **Waterloo**) fans out into the suburbs (some lines go farther out into the English countryside as well). If you want to get to the Continent from London, either take the train from **Victoria Station** to the ferry at Folkestone, or head to **Waterloo Station,** where you can pick up the **EuroStar** (0345/303030) train that goes to Paris or Brussels via the Channel Tunnel. Most long-distance trains have buffet or restaurant facilities, but check when you buy your ticket. All have toilets and all are at least somewhat accessible to those with disabilities, but some of the stations are more difficult to negotiate than others. On some routes you might need to change trains (which can be nightmarish), so find out beforehand.

One of the best ways to enjoy cheap train fares is to get a **BritRail** pass (available from travel agents), which you must purchase before you arrive in Britain. Both first-class and standard tickets are valid for periods of 4, 8, 15, and 22 days, and for one month. They include versions for 16-to-25-year-olds (Youth Pass) and over-60-year-olds (Senior Pass). Railway personnel maintain that if you take three trips out of London to big cities or major attractions, you will cover the cost of the pass. **BritRail** passes allow you to travel on any train, although on busy routes, such as London to Edinburgh, you should reserve a seat. Check when you book the ticket.

On long-distance intercity journeys, book **Apex** tickets from rail stations (seven days before departure) or buy a **Saver** or **Super Saver** ticket on the day you plan to travel. Those who buy **Savers** or **Super Savers** will find there are early morning and some evening travel restrictions, and Fridays, summer Saturdays, Easter, and bank holiday weekends are blacked out. Children under 16 pay half price and those under 5 ride free when accompanied by an adult.

Even without a pass or a discount ticket, however, you can sometimes find good train fares. To get the cheapest fare (this depends on how full the train is likely to be, not on your bargaining skills) for rail travel in Britain, and rail and sea journeys to the Continent and Ireland, visit the **British Travel Centre** (see **Visitors' Information Centers,** page 14) or one of these main line station travel centers: **Charing Cross, Euston, King's Cross, Liverpool Street, Paddington, Waterloo,** or **Victoria.**

London has nine major rail train stations, each of which serves a different part of Britain and is accessible by tube or bus. For information about trains and schedules, there is one number to call: 345/484950 (24-hour service).

Underground The tube, as the Underground system is familiarly called, is by far the easiest, the most efficient, and the most economical way to get around London. It is fast, fairly clean, and relatively safe; however, as in any city, always be alert late at night. You can pick up a free visitors' guide at the **London Transport Information & Travel Centre,** at the following tube stations: **Charing Cross, Euston, Heathrow Central, King's Cross/St. Pancras, Liverpool Street, Oxford Circus, Piccadilly Circus, St. James's Park,** and **Victoria.** Tube stations are marked by circular red and blue **London Transport** signs. There are 11 lines (or routes), each designated by a different name and color. An extension of the gray *Jubilee Line* is under construction and was scheduled to open as we went to press. Large-scale maps of the Underground network are displayed in each station, and each compartment of the train *should* have a map of the train's route. You can also pick up a free map at any tube station. Be forewarned: Some trains, such as those on the *District* and *Circle Lines*, use the same platforms, so check the lighted platform signs and the destination board on the front of the train before boarding. Smoking is not permitted anywhere on the Underground.

Service runs from 5:30AM to sometime between 12:30 and 1AM, Monday through Saturday; from 7AM to around midnight on Sunday and bank holidays. If you travel after 9:30AM on weekdays, you'll save heaps with a one-day **Travelcard,** which is good for unlimited travel on the tube, the buses, the **Docklands Light Railway,** and the southeast rail system throughout the Greater London area. There is a **Weekend Travelcard** valid for Saturday and Sunday that is 25 percent cheaper than buying two separate **One Day Travelcards.** There is also a **Family Travelcard,** valid for Saturday and Sunday, for a group consisting of two adults traveling with one child or up to four children; however, the family must travel together at all times with this ticket.

Alternatively, if you have a passport-size photograph, you can purchase a weekly or monthly (or for other periods up to a year) **Season Travelcard**—a cheaper option if you plan to travel extensively. London is divided into six travel zones, and all tube tickets and **Travelcards** are sold according to zone; most major attractions are located in zones 1 and 2. If you know you are going to stay only within zone 1, you can buy **Carnet Tickets,** a booklet of 10 single tube tickets for zone 1 only, valid for up to 12 months.

You can now purchase tickets and **Travelcards** from ticket machines in most Underground stations, as well as from the usual ticket counters, but you need to know which zones you want to visit beforehand. Study the display boards outlining the zones (if in doubt, ask a friendly native). Be sure to hold on to your ticket: You'll need it to pass through the entry/exit turnstiles, and once in a while, a plainclothes inspector may ask to see it during your journey. If you cannot show a valid ticket, you are liable for an on-the-spot fine (£5/$3.10 on the buses; £10/$6.20 on the tube). In London, 24-hour travel information about the Underground is available at 207/222.1234.

ondon Transport also offers a special **London Visitor Travelcard,** which you must buy in the JS. The advantages are that you won't need a photograph and you won't have to buy a new one every day or week. Although it is slightly more expensive, the **London Visitor Travelcard** (available for three, five, or seven days) offers a discount on standard tube fares, as well as on tickets to major tourist attractions. It allows you to travel central Underground and bus routes, the **Docklands Light Railway,** and some suburban train services, such as **Network Southeast.**

Walking You can only really get to know and love a city through your eyes and feet, and London offers marvelous rewards to the walker. Such distinguished feet as those of Daniel Defoe, Samuel Johnson, James Boswell, John Gay, Thomas Carlyle, and Sir Anthony Hopkins have made walking the streets of London part of their life's work. Some advice: In addition to regular traffic, there's the added hazard (and one not to be underestimated) of cyclists cutting swaths through pedestrians on the pavement. Walking tours are listed in the *Times* and in the weekly *Time Out* magazine, and include such topics as "The City," "The Great Fire and Plague," and "The London of the Romans, Victorians, Shakespeare, and Dickens." It is now possible to walk from the **Thames Flood Barrier** back to the river's source in the **Cotswolds**—a very long walk, indeed! Pick up a special free leaflet, *The Thames Path,* at the main tourist information centers.

FYI

Accommodations In addition to hotels, there are other kinds of accommodations in London. Bed-and-breakfast establishments are available in a variety of price ranges, and staying in one allows visitors to make contact with local people and get a sense of the city's everyday life. The organization **Uptown Reservations** (207/351.3445) puts visitors in touch with stylish host homes in **Chelsea.** Another option is to rent an apartment (which the British call a "flat") or cottage. The cheapest lodgings (probably best suited to young people) are at youth hostels. They offer only the most basic accommodations, and you must be prepared to share rooms and facilities. These fill up quickly; call ahead to check if there is space. The best two (in terms of location) are **Holland House** (Holland Walk, between Kensington High St and Holland Park Ave, 207/937.0748), in **Holland Park** in **Kensington,** and **City of London** (36 Carter La, at Deans Ct, 207/236.4965), right by **St. Paul's.** For information on these and other youth hostels, contact **Central London Booking Service,** 207/248.6547.

London is a popular place to visit year-round, so it is always a good idea to make reservations before you come (and reservations are absolutely necessary during high season—from April through October).

Business Services Almost every hotel and an increasing number of shops and newsstands offer fax and photocopy services for a charge. Sending a

fax to the US, however, will cost a minimum of £3.50 (about $5.25) per page. **Chesham Executive Centre** (150 Regent St, between Regent's Pl and Beak St, 207/439.6288) has fax, telex, and photocopy facilities.

Climate Believe it or not, London's climate is relatively moderate and mild, although it is prone to change at a moment's notice. Whatever the season, you'd be well advised to bring sweaters and jackets for evenings, as well as raincoats, umbrellas, and, above all, shoes that are kind to the feet and can endure the occasional puddle.

Months	Average Temperature (°F)
January-March	36-45
April-June	40-56
July-September	56-72
October-December	45-58

Customs and Immigration All foreign visitors to the UK must have a valid passport, which will be stamped by immigration officials at each entry point. Although there is rarely a problem, it might help speed things along if you can provide the address where you'll be staying while in the UK.

Drinking The pub (short for "public house") is to Britain what cafes are to France. To complete the British experience, you should have at least one drink, and preferably a meal, in a pub. The minimum age for drinking in the UK is 18. Pubs are usually open from 11AM to 11PM Monday through Saturday, and from noon to 10:30PM on Sunday. Ten minutes before closing time, you'll usually hear the barman call for "last orders." Although many pubs are getting more adventurous, your best bet is to opt for standards in terms of drinks: beer, ale, or lager, all served by the half (pint) or pint. There is no waiter service, even in pubs that serve food (unless they have set aside a restaurant-style area or room).

Most pubs worth their salt now serve a variety of dishes, including vegetarian meals, but some traditional terminology is worth noting: "bangers" are sausages; "bangers and mash" are sausages with mashed potatoes; "chips" are french fries, while "crisps" are potato chips; "Cornish pasties" consist of meat and vegetables wrapped in dough; a "ploughman's lunch" is a cheese and salad plate; a "pork pie" is chopped spiced pork wrapped in dough; "sausage rolls" are tiny sausages rolled up in dough; and "shepherd's pie" consists of ground lamb covered in mashed potatoes.

Embassies and Consulates
Australian High Commission (Australia House, Strand, at Aldwych, 207/379.4334, 891/600333).

Canadian High Commission (Macdonald House, Grosvenor Sq, between Grosvenor and Brook Sts, 207/258.6600).

US Embassy (24 Grosvenor Sq, between Upper Grosvenor and Upper Brook Sts, 207/499.9000, 891/200290).

Hours Most shops and businesses in London are open Monday through Saturday from 9AM to 5 or 6PM; more and more shops now operate on Sunday, usually from noon to 5 or 6PM. Opening and closing times for shops and attractions are listed by day(s) only if they open between 8 and 11AM and close between 4 and 7PM. In all other cases, specific hours will be given (e.g., 6AM-2PM, daily 24 hours, noon-5PM).

Medical Care Because the US and the UK have no reciprocal health agreement, be sure to take out medical insurance before leaving home. If you should become ill, you will be treated at a London hospital or doctor's office without question, but you'll be charged at the private patient rate, which can be expensive. In emergencies, dial 999, and you will be connected to an operator who will inquire about the nature of the problem, then arrange for an ambulance, police, or a fire engine. Although patients who arrive at a hospital by ambulance get priority, horror stories about delays abound. If possible, head for the nearest hospital "casualty department" (i.e., emergency room), then be prepared to have someone make a fuss until you're seen by a doctor; otherwise, you could be in for a long wait.

The following London hospitals have 24-hour emergency rooms: **Charing Cross Hospital** (Fulham Palace Rd, at St. Dunstan's Rd, 208/846.1234), **Guy's Hospital** (St. Thomas St, at Great Maze Pond, 207/955.5000), **Royal Free Hospital** (Pond St, between Fleet Rd and Rosslyn Hill, 207/794.0500), and **University College Hospital** (Gower St, at University St, 207/387.9300). **St. Bartholomew's Hospital** (W Smithfield, between Little Britain and Giltspur St, 207/601.8888) treats patients (for minor injuries only) from 8AM to 8PM.

There are no 24-hour pharmacies ("chemists" in Britspeak) per se in London; night duty rotates, and the places that are closed display the name and address of the evening's all-night drugstore in the window. **Bliss Chemist** (5-6 Marble Arch, between Cumberland Pl and Edgware Rd, 207/723.6116) is open daily 9AM-midnight. **Boots** has two locations that keep long hours: one in the center of Piccadilly Circus (207/734.6126), which is open Monday through Friday 8:30AM-8PM, Saturday 9AM-8PM, and Sunday noon-6PM; and one at 114 Queensway, between Inverness Pl and Porchester Gardens (207/229.1183), which is open Monday through Saturday 9AM-10PM and Sunday noon-6PM.

Money The basic unit of British currency is the pound sterling. There are 100 pence to the pound. Two-pound coins are the largest and are silver with a golden center, pound coins are small, thick, and golden; 50p coins are silver and hexagonal, while the 20p coin is similar but smaller; the 10p coin is small, silver, and round; and the 5p coin is minuscule; tuppences (two-penny pieces) and pennies are both copper. The color of £5 notes is greenish blue; £10, orange; £20, light purple; and £50, greenish gold. Credit cards are used as in the US, the most popular being VISA and MasterCard (which used to be known in Britain as Access).

Banks are open Monday through Friday 9AM to 4:30PM, and many branches are open on Saturday from 9AM to noon as well. Traveler's checks in US dollars can be exchanged for British currency at large banks (such as **Barclays, Lloyds, Midland,** and **National Westminster**) during their normal operating hours, or at the **American Express Travel Service Office** (102-104 Victoria St, between Artillery Row and Carlisle Pl, 207/828.7411) Monday through Friday 9AM-5:30PM and Saturday 9AM-4PM. This office also allows you to cash personal checks for up to $1,000, depending on the type of AMEX card you have. In addition, large post offices, such as the **Trafalgar Square Post Office** (see below), now change traveler's checks. Avoid changing your money at exchange bureaus and hotel cashiers, as they charge a higher commission.

While inflation has been brought under control for the time being, some things in London—hotels, gasoline, and good restaurants, for example—still seem hideously expensive. The exchange rate varies daily, and is listed in major newspapers such as the *Times* or *Financial Times.*

Personal Safety Keep a close eye on your bags and valuables at all times. Many pickpockets operate around the Underground system, in the main rail stations, and on the busiest tourist streets. If possible, women should use a closed or zipped purse—and hang on to it. Some pickpockets travel in gangs during the summer, so be particularly careful when people are crowding onto buses or tubes.

Steer clear of the many accommodations hustlers who work the areas around the main train stations, especially **Victoria;** most of the places offered by these room touts are overcrowded, uninsured, and have little or no fire protection—and they're usually pretty dreadful as well. It's better to consult the **Tourist Information Centre** at the station or find your own accommodations.

Post Office The **Trafalgar Square Post Office** (24 William IV St, between Adelaide St and St. Martin's La, 207/930.9580) offers full postal service and collectors' items, such as stamps, coins, and cards; it also changes traveler's checks. It's open Monday through Saturday 8AM-8PM (until 8:30PM on Friday). Local post offices, which are often within newsstands or corner grocery shops, are usually open Monday through Friday 9AM-5PM, and Saturday 9AM-noon.

Publications Of London's many newspapers, the *Times,* the *Guardian,* the *Independent,* and the *Daily Telegraph* (all dailies), and the *Sunday Times* and the *Observer* (Sunday only) are most useful to visitors. For up-to-date news about the nightclub and entertainment scene, consult *Time Out,* which is published every Wednesday; the *Guardian* also has a good entertainment section in its Friday edition. The *Evening Standard,* published Monday through Friday, is London's only "local" newspaper. On Thursday the *Standard* publishes a comprehensive listings magazine called *Hot Tickets* which is given away free with the newspaper. All are available at newsagents and bookstores throughout the city.

Public Holidays In addition to the Christmas and Easter holidays, Britain rests on Boxing Day (26 December), Easter Monday, Good Friday, May Day (first Monday in May), Spring Bank Holiday (last Monday in May), and August Bank Holiday (last Monday in August). These are called "bank holidays" because banks close on those days. Many other businesses stay open, but you'll never know which ones unless you call ahead or happen to wander past.

Restaurants In general, reservations are not necessary except at the most expensive restaurants, although making them may prevent a wait in some establishments. Most of the time, casual dress is acceptable, although some of the more elegant places do require that men wear jackets and ties.

Rest Rooms As in many cities around the world, there never seem to be enough public toilets (or "loos," as they're often called here), especially when you need one. However, all public buildings, including museums and department stores, have them, and if you're poised and surreptitious, you can take advantage of those in the larger hotels. Pubs and restaurants generally expect you to be a customer for the privilege. For the daring, there are automated, French-style toilets, located in public parks; these, however, can often be a chilling experience.

Services for Travelers with Disabilities

Artsline (54 Chalton St, London NW1 1HS, 207/388.2227; fax 207/383.2653) advises on theater, cinema, museum, and other arts and entertainment center access for those with disabilities and special needs. Most cinemas, theaters, and public places try to accommodate disabled patrons, although doing so is not mandated by law as it is in the US. Always call and check when booking or visiting, as this ensures special help when you arrive and an appropriate seat. A monthly magazine, *Disability Arts in London,* is available free to any disabled person in the UK; call 207/916.6351. Free at theaters is *The Disabled Access Guide to London's West End Theatres,* published by the **Society of London Theatre (SOLT)** (Bedford Chambers, The Piazza, Covent Garden, London WC2E 8HQ, 207/557.6700; fax 207/557.6799).

Evan Evans (26-28 Paradise Rd, Richmond, Surrey TW9 1SE, 208/930.2377), which runs daily coach tours of London, takes a number of disabled passengers as long as each one is accompanied by an able-bodied person. Tours leave from its office (26 Cockspur St on the southwest side of Trafalgar Sq). Call ahead to book a reservation, specifying the nature of the disability.

Holiday Care Service (Second floor, Imperial Buildings, Victoria Road, Horley, Surrey RH6 7PZ, 1293/774535; fax 1293/784647) is a charity offering free information and advice on vacations for people with special needs, such as the elderly and the disabled. Call or write explaining your special needs and what sort of holiday you are looking for, and provide a rough estimate of your budget. Though it is not a booking service, the organization has details on inclusive or specialized holidays, accommodations, transportation, publications, and guides for UK destinations. In addition, it can connect you with car and driver hire services, if desired. **Tripscope** (208/994.9294; fax 208/994.3618) is another service that offers free advice about local and long-distance journeys from London.

London Transport (55 Broadway, London SW1H 0BD, 207/918.3312) runs a daily **Stationlink** bus service catering to people with disabilities. Beginning at 8:30AM, two circular routes cover all the main line rail stations (except **Charing Cross** and **Cannon Street**). **SL1** goes clockwise; **SL2** goes counterclockwise; both connect with the wheelchair-accessible **Airbus** services to **Heathrow Airport** at **Victoria** and **Euston.** These are fully accessible, low-fly buses, and the drivers are well trained in handling the needs of people with disabilities. You also can call **London Transport** for advice on public transport.

The **National Trust** (36 Queen Anne's Gate, between Petty France and Dartmouth St, 207/222.9251; fax 208/809.1754), which owns places of historic interest or natural beauty all over the country, publishes a free annual booklet, *Information for Visitors with Disabilities,* showing those sights accessible to people with disabilities, including scented gardens for the blind. And for further information, contact the **Royal Association for Disability Rehabilitation (RADAR;** 250 City Rd, London EC1V 8AF, 207/250.3222; fax 207/250.0212).

Shopping London is truly a shopper's paradise, whether you're a serious buyer or just looking. Some of the city's most upscale shopping streets, with a mixture of tony department stores, antiques shops, and high-fashion clothiers, include **Old** and **New Bond Street; St. Christopher's Place; Regent, Sloane,** and **Jermyn Streets; Knightsbridge;** and **King's Road.** Burlington Arcade, Piccadilly Arcade, and **Princes Arcade** offer a wide selection of fashionable stores as well, and **Savile Row** is *the* place to go for custom-made menswear. **Oxford Street** is the main shopping place for a mixed variety of shops and department stores, mostly mid-range and low-cost. Also be sure to check out at least one of London's many street markets, which offer everything from kitschy collectibles to priceless antiques; the best are **Portobello Road, Camden Passage, Piccadilly Market,** and the **Covent Garden** area.

Smoking Smoking is not allowed in rail or Underground stations; otherwise, it depends on the individual establishment. Most restaurants have a no-smoking section; ask when booking a table.

Telephones Telephone boxes accept a variety of change: 10p, 20p, 50p, and £1 coins. **British Telecom (BT)** cards, which are used like credit cards to make calls at specially marked phone boxes, can be obtained from most newsstands and sweet shops in units of 10 to 200. If you'll be making a lot of calls, dial after 6PM or during weekends, when the rates are cheapest. Some numbers are referred to as "premium rate"; this means that you'll pay up to 50p per minute for a call, usually for recorded information (similar to 900 numbers in the US). Most premium rate numbers have a special prefix, such as 891. Telephoning from hotels is expensive, so stick to the British Telecom boxes (and ignore the occasional privately run phone boxes); if you'll be making a long-distance call, have a phone card or lots of change on hand. Many booths now take credit cards, too. Direct-dial to the US can be made by dialing 001, followed by your area code and number.

Tickets Beware of the ubiquitous ticket touts (scalpers), who operate along theater queues and from supposedly reputable ticket offices scattered throughout the city. Most of the time, the tickets they sell are grossly overpriced—and some may not even be genuine. Aim instead to get a normal price and standby tickets directly from theater box offices, your hotel, or the **Society of London Theatre** half-price–ticket booth in **Leicester Square;** at the latter, you'll have to stand in line on the day of the performance, but it's worth it to get a legitimate seat at a reasonable price. Also, be adventurous: Some excellent performances at lower prices can be found at smaller theaters outside the **West End,** as well as in the larger arts complexes such as the **Barbican** or **South Bank;** check *Time Out* for details.

Tickets for concerts and sporting events can be ordered by phone from **Ticketmaster** (207/344.4444) and **First Call** (207/420.0000), as well as from the individual box offices.

Time Zone London is in the Greenwich Mean Time zone, which is five hours later than New York and eight hours later than Los Angeles. Like the US, Britain observes daylight saving time, turning their clocks ahead an hour in the spring and back an hour in the fall, although the two countries don't do it on the same date. British timetables use a 24-hour clock to denote time; for example, 1:30PM would be written as "13:30."

Tipping In restaurants, check whether service is included or not, especially if you find the amounts you are expected to pay left blank on the credit card slip (as it quite often is) because they just want a bit more money. If service is not included and the service and food have been good, then go ahead and tip between 10 and 15 percent. When you collect your bill at your hotel, again check whether service has been included. Taxi drivers hope for between 10 and 15 percent. Porters, cloakroom attendants, and hairdressers also expect a small tip.

Value Added Tax (VAT) At 17.5 percent of the marked price, the Value Added Tax (VAT) can be substantial. But if you are leaving the UK within three months, you can claim back the VAT on many of the items you buy if you have spent more than a certain amount in one shop (the total varies). Make sure the store operates the over-the-counter export scheme, which involves filling out a VAT 707 form. (The shop will give it to you along with a stamped, addressed envelope.) You must carry as hand luggage the goods for which you intend to collect a VAT refund and present them to UK customs as you leave the country. Customs will stamp the forms, which you will then mail back to the shop before leaving the country. If you forget and pack the goods, or simply cannot carry them, then you have to show them to the officials when you arrive in the US, get the form stamped there, and mail it to the shop. You can get your refund as a check in pounds sterling (which can cost a lot to process through your bank), or, if you've paid with a credit card, as a credit to your account. The refund process takes about six weeks.

Visitors' Information Centers

The **London Tourist Board (LTB) Information Centre** in the front court of **Victoria Station** (Terminal Pl, between Wilton and Buckingham Palace Rds; daily) offers free information on travel within London and the UK, theater, concert, and tour bookings, and accommodations, as well as good maps and guidebooks for sale. It charges a nominal fee for arranging a place to stay.

Other information centers are at the **Liverpool Street Underground Station**; at **Waterloo International Terminal** (inside **Waterloo** rail station); at **Hay's Galleria** (Tooley St, at Battle Bridge La, 403.8299; daily mid-Mar–Oct; M-Sa 11AM-4PM, Su noon-4PM Nov–mid-Mar); at **Heathrow Airport** (at the Underground station concourses for **Terminals 1, 2** and **3** and at the arrivals concourse for **Terminal 4**); and at **Gatwick Airport** (at the arrival concourse of the **South Terminal**). For hotel and bed-and-breakfast reservations, call 0207/824.8844 (credit card holders only).

The **British Tourist Authority (BTA) (British Travel Centre),** 1 Regent St, (at Charles II St) also runs an information center that gives free comprehensive information for all of Britain. There is a theater booking desk, a rail information and booking desk, a bookshop, and an accommodations service.

Phone Book

Emergencies

Ambulance/Police/Fire 999

Dental Emergencies 208/677.6363

Drugstores

    Bliss Chemist 207/723.6116

    Boots 207/734.6126, 207/229.1183

Emergency Road Services (for members)

    Automobile Association (AA).............800/919595
    ....(toll free in Britain)

    RAC ....800.550550 (toll free in Britain)

Hospitals

    Charing Cross Hospital 208/846.1234

    Guy's Hospital 207/955.5000

    Royal Free Hospital.........................207/794.0500

    St. Bartholomew's Hospital 207/601.8888

    University College Hospital 207/387.9300

Lost or Stolen Credit Cards

    American Express...........................207/222.9633

MasterCard	1268/298168
VISA	800/895082 (toll free in Britain)

Visitors' Information

British Hotel Reservation Centre	207/828.2425
Directory Information	192
Disabled Visitors' Information	1293/774535
	208/994.9294
International Operator	155
International Telegrams	800/190190
	(toll-free in Britain)
London Transport	
Lost Property	207/486.2496
Travel Information	207/222.1234
Travel Update (traffic flow)	207/222.1200
Millennium Events Info Line	891/663344
Operator Services	100

Recorded tourist information, premium rate (dial 839/123, then the following numbers):

Changing of the Guard	411
Current Exhibitions	403
Day Trips	484
Museums	429
Palaces	481
River Trips/Boats for hire	432
Sporting Events	442
Sunday in London	407
What's on this Week	440
Time check	123
US and International Directory Information	153
US Customs/US Passport Office	207/499.9000
Weather	839/500951

The London Ledger of Annual Events

For the traveler who wishes to take in more than just the sights, the following is a calendar of the most interesting events in London. For more information about what's happening in the city, consult listings in magazines or visit any tourist information center.

January

London Parade Led by the Lord Mayor of Westminster, beginning at noon on 1 January, a parade complete with marching bands, floats, classic cars, and clowns makes its way from **Parliament Square** along **Whitehall** to **Trafalgar Square,** then west along **Cockspur Street** and **Pall Mall,** north along **Lower Regent Street** to **Piccadilly Circus,** west along **Piccadilly,** then north along **Berkeley Street** to finish in **Berkeley Square.** A gala performance is usually held at the **Royal Albert Hall, Kensington Gore,** in conjunction with the festivities.

International Boat Show This 10-day display of all types of boats and boating equipment, including a specially created indoor harbor, takes place at the **Earl's Court Exhibition Centre** the first week of January. For details, call 207/385.1200.

Commemoration Ceremony of Charles the Martyr At 11:30AM on the last Sunday of the month, the **King's Army** (members of the English Civil War Society in period dress) progresses from **St. James's Palace** to **Banqueting House.** There, at noon, a wreath is laid beneath the window through which Charles I stepped onto the scaffold. The parade continues to **Trafalgar Square** to the base of the statue of the ill-fated king, then returns through **Admiralty Arch** back to **St. James's Palace.**

February

Chinese New Year In late January or early February, usually on the Sunday closest to the actual date of Chinese New Year, celebrations, including the famous Dragon Dance (where as many as 12 performers wear a huge, brightly colored dragon costume and dance through the streets), take place mostly in Chinatown. The best places to watch the festivities include the areas around **Gerrard Street** in **Soho,** where streets are decorated with streamers and garlands, and **Leicester Square.** For further information, call 207/734.5161.

Fine Art and Antiques Fair This is held annually at the end of the month at **Olympia** exhibition halls in **Earl's Court.** About 350 antiques and fine art dealers from all over Britain and Europe display their wares. For details, call 207/603.3344.

March

Head of the River Race Held on the **Thames** around 20 March, this race is a processional contest for eight-oared racing shells. The course extends from **Mortlake** to **Putney;** 420 crews—one behind the other—start at 10-second intervals, and the one that returns in the fastest time wins. The best place for viewing is from the **Surrey** bank, just above **Chiswick Bridge.** Arrive about 30 minutes before the race begins (approximately 12:30PM), then walk along the towpath toward Putney.

Oxford and Cambridge Boat Race The two universities first raced on the Thames in 1829, and have competed annually since 1845. The race takes place around the last week of March, and its course

15

is from the **University Stone,** Putney, to Mortlake. Starting time varies due to tides; check newspapers for details. Good views can be had from the Putney and Chiswick Bridges, from the **Dove Inn** (19 Upper Mall between Rivercourt and Weltje Rds, Hammersmith), or from the **Ship Inn** (10 Thames Bank, Mortlake, by Chiswick Bridge).

April

London Harness Horse Parade Easter Monday presents a rare opportunity to see working horses of all kinds compete for prizes at **Battersea Park** in south London. Festivities begin around 10:30AM with a veterinary inspection, followed by a parade, a judging of classes (such as Heavy Horses and Single Horsed Commercial Vans), and a Grand Parade of Winners between noon and 1PM. For other Easter events, call 839/123418.

London Marathon More than 25,000 runners compete in this grueling 26-mile race, which takes place in mid-April. It begins 9-9:30AM at **Blackheath/Greenwich** and ends at the Mall. For details call 161/620.4117.

May

Football Association Cup Final The top prize event in the British soccer world, it takes place mid-month at **Wembley Stadium.** For details, call 208/902.0902 (see "The Sporting Life," page 77).

Chelsea Flower Show *The* event for gardeners the world over takes place at the **Royal Hospital Grounds, Chelsea,** for four days during the last week of May. Plants, flowers, garden furniture, tools, theme gardens, and greenhouses are all on display. The first 2.5 days are reserved for members of the **Royal Horticultural Society** only; the last 2 are for the public (excluding children under five years of age). Advance tickets may be purchased by phone with a credit card (call 207/344.4343).

June

Derby Day Held on the first Saturday of the month at **Epsom Racecourse, Epsom,** Surrey, this is one of the greatest horse-racing events in the world. The main race, called the Derby, is held at 3:45PM. Tickets can be ordered starting in January by writing to **The Racing Department, Sandown Park Racecourse, Esher, Surrey, KT10 0AJ;** call 1372/470047 for more information.

Beating the Retreat Mounted bands, trumpeters, massed bands (several bands performing as one group), and pipes and drums of the Household Division display their marching and drilling prowess at 9:30PM at **Horse Guards Parade.** The event occurs at the beginning of the month. Tickets go on sale at the end of February; call 207/839.5323.

Sounding Retreat: Light Division During the second week of the month, Horse Guards Parade stages a follow-up to Beating the Retreat. The Sounding Retreat display takes place over three consecutive

nights beginning at 6:30PM. See **Beating the Retrea** above for ticket details.

Royal Academy Summer Exhibition The **Royal Academy of Arts** hosts the largest contemporary art show in the world, featuring works by painters, sculptors, printmakers, and architects—well-known alongside the undiscovered. The show begins in earl June and lasts through mid-August.

Trooping the Colour Also known as the **Queen's Birthday Parade,** this ceremony celebrates the sovereign's official (but not actual) birthday on the second or third Saturday. The queen leaves **Buckingham Palace** at around 10:30AM and travels down the **Mall** to Horse Guards Parade, where massed bands greet her with the national anthem an a gun salute in **Green Park.** After the queen's troop inspection, the parade begins. At 12:30PM, Her Majesty returns to **Buckingham Palace,** where she appears on the balcony with other members of the Royal Family to witness the Royal Air Force fly past at 1PM. Tickets for outdoor seats on Horse Guards Parade (behind the **Horse Guards Building**) are available by ballot only, and are limited to two per person. If you can't get ceremony tickets, try for tickets to one of the two rehearsals (without the queen). Apply in writing before the end of February to the **Brigade Major (Trooping the Colour), Household Division HQ, Horse Guards, Whitehall, London SW1A 2AX.** Do not send money—instead, include a self-addressed envelope with two international reply coupons (the equivalent of British stamps). For recorded information, call 839/123413.

Royal Ascot This famous mid-June horse race at **Ascot Racecourse** in **Berkshire** (roughly 25 miles west of London), immortalized in *My Fair Lady,* is well known for the fashions—especially the hats—of those who attend. The queen and other members of the Royal Family arrive from **Windsor** each day in open carriages. They then drive down the course at 2PM before the first race begins. Admission to the Grandstand for the four-day event is by ticket only; write well in advance to the **Secretary, Grand Stand, Ascot Racecourse, Berkshire SL5 7JN;** call 1344/22211 for details.

Wimbledon Lawn Tennis Championships Top players from all over the world converge on the **All England Club** in **Wimbledon** (about six miles southwest of central London) from the last week of June to the beginning of July to compete for one of the most coveted titles in tennis. Though some tickets are available on the day of play, it's advisable to apply for them between August and December. Send a self-addressed envelope with international reply coupons to the **All England Lawn Tennis & Croquet Club, PO Box 98, Church Road, Wimbledon, SW19 5AE,** or call 208/946.2244. The **London Tourist Board** provides information starting in June; call 839/123417.

July

Hampton Court Palace International Flower Show Almost as well established as the show at Chelsea, this one is held during the second week in July at **Hampton Court.** The show also features musical entertainment and crafts displays. Call 207/344.4333 for details.

BBC Henry Wood Promenade Concerts The "Proms" have taken place at the **Royal Albert Hall** every year since they were begun in 1895 by Sir Henry Wood. The nightly concerts, which range from jazz to classical music, begin in mid-July and run until mid-September. Season and individual tickets are available in advance from the **Royal Albert Hall;** call 207/589.8912 for details. In addition, inexpensive standing-room tickets may be had on the day of the performance. You can purchase the *Proms Guide,* available early May, at major newsstands.

August

Notting Hill Carnival The carnival—a sort of midsummer Mardi Gras—takes place on the Sunday and Monday of the last weekend of August (a bank holiday) in **Notting Hill,** a London area with a strong Caribbean tradition. Lovers of steel bands and *soca* (a fusion of soul and Calypso music that originated in the West Indies) will be in their element. There are fabulous costume parades and hundreds of street vendors sell food and crafts from all over the globe. Festivities kick off at noon.

September

Great River Race At the end of the month, more than 150 traditional boats sail 22 miles on the Thames, from **Richmond** to the **Docklands.** The flotilla includes gigs, skiffs, Chinese dragon boats, Hawaiian war canoes, Irish curraghs, and whalers. The race begins just below **Ham House,** Richmond, at 10AM and finishes at **Greenwich Pier** around 1PM.

October

Pearly Kings and Queens Harvest Festival Cockney fruit and vegetable hawkers, known as costermongers, have a reputation for being snappy dressers. The leading costermongers were called "the Pearly Kings and Queens," in recognition of their characteristic pearl-button–studded outfits. This religious service, held around 3 October at 3PM at **St. Martin-in-the-Fields Church** (207/930.1862), is probably the only place you'll see their sartorial splendor. The altar is arrayed with fruits and vegetables, and a Pearly King or Queen reads from the Bible.

Horse of the Year Show Top names in equestrian circles compete in show jumping, dressage, shire, hunter, and hacks at **Wembley Arena, Wembley,** in northwest London. The event is usually held during the first week of the month. Call the box office at 208/902.0902 for ticket information.

Trafalgar Day Parade On or around 21 October, the anniversary of Lord Nelson's victory at the Battle of Trafalgar in 1805 is commemorated with a parade and service performed by Sea Cadets (boys and girls aged 12-18) from all over the country. A wreath is laid at the foot of **Nelson's Column,** and Nelson's Prayer is read by a young cadet. The ceremony starts at 11AM in Trafalgar Square.

November

Bonfire Night On 5 November 1605, Guy Fawkes was arrested as one of the conspirators in the Gunpowder Plot to kill King James I and blow up Parliament. Since then, fireworks and bonfires have been lit throughout the country on this date. For details of displays in the London area, call 839/123410.

London to Brighton Car Run Held on the first Sunday of November, this gathering attracts more than 400 entrants from all over the world, who subject their veteran and classic cars to a grueling 58-mile stretch of road. Cars leave from **Hyde Park Corner** between 7:30 and 9AM and follow the **A23** to **Brighton,** where they begin arriving at **Madeira Drive** around 10:45AM.

Lord Mayor's Show This tradition, which dictates that the Lord Mayor ride in the gilded State Coach to the **Law Courts** for the declaration of office, dates from the 13th century. Today, there's also a parade featuring floats, military bands, and units of the armed services, and fireworks on the Thames. The event is usually slated for the second Saturday of the month. For more information, call 839/123413.

Remembrance Sunday On a date near 11 November, a memorial service is held at the **Cenotaph,** Whitehall, to honor all those in the military who gave their lives in the two World Wars and other conflicts. The queen arrives at 10:59AM, and a two-minute silence begins at 11AM, ended by a gun fired from Horse Guards Parade. The queen lays a wreath at the **Cenotaph,** and the Bishop of London conducts a short service.

Christmas Lights Christmas lights are switched on daily from dusk to midnight in **Bond, Jermyn, Oxford,** and **Regent Streets** from mid-November until Twelfth Night (6 January). For more information, call the **London Tourist Board**'s Christmas Service at 839/123418.

December

Trafalgar Square Christmas Tree Since 1947, the city of Oslo, Norway, has presented London with a Norwegian Christmas spruce in gratitude for help given by the British during World War II. The tree is set up in Trafalgar Square in early December and decorated with white lights. It is lit daily from noon to midnight until Twelfth Night (6 January), and carols are sung each evening until Christmas Eve.

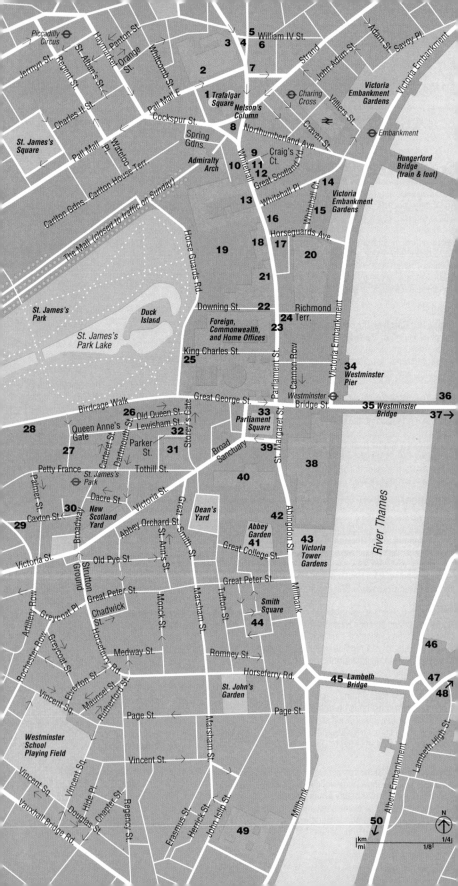

Westminster

A walk through the City of Westminster forms a kind of pilgrimage, a journey that parallels the **River Thames**, covers one-and-a-half acres of hallowed ground, embraces 900 years of history, and provides a first-rate view of history in the making. Westminster is Britain's seat of power: Kings and queens are still crowned here, and the process of democracy continues to unfold before public scrutiny. The **Palace of Westminster**, better known as the **Houses of Parliament**, is where the **House of Commons** and the **House of Lords** conduct the sometimes tempestuous, sometimes snoozy, day-to-day business of government. Neighboring **Westminster Abbey** occupies the seat of spiritual power and, with its sepulchres of famous Britons, serves as a reminder of the ultimate end to all struggles—death. Your tour of **Westminster Abbey** could be delayed by a wedding or a funeral, as this is not a museum; people make vows, pray, and mourn the dead here.

About a mile north of **Westminster Abbey** is **Trafalgar Square**, where London's citizens regularly gather (like so many excitable pigeons) to celebrate or protest; through it all, this English *grande place* casts an impartial eye on the legislation passed down the road by Parliament and administered next door by officials in **Whitehall.**

The **National Portrait Gallery** is a who's who of English history, the **National Gallery** surveys European art dating from the 1200s to the turn of this century, while the splendid **Tate Gallery** revels in British art as well as in modern international works. After perusing the collections, contemplate the Thames with London as a backdrop, a scene that could have been painted by the pre-Raphaelites or Whistler. You may also decide to stop for a concert at **St. John's in Smith Square** or sample English ale in a pub next to an MP or two.

The ideal time to visit this area is Monday through Friday, when Parliament is in session. On weekends, Westminster and Whitehall are all but abandoned—MPs return to their constituencies, civil servants stay home, and many of the restaurants, pubs, and shops that exist primarily to serve the governing elite are closed. On Sunday, the most interesting parts of **Westminster Abbey** are closed.

For the best views of Westminster, cross over the Thames to **Lambeth,** a south London district whose main attractions, **Lambeth Palace** and the **Museum of Garden History**, cluster beside the river.

City code 207 unless otherwise noted.

1 Trafalgar Square A testament to the Battle of Trafalgar, England's decisive victory over Napoléon's fleet off the coast of Spain in 1805, this square (pictured on page 20) is London's grandest place. It is even more monumental testimony to the defeat of anything like Napoleonic vision in town planning. If this were Paris, Haussmann's ruthlessness would have you looking down heart-stopping vistas of **Buckingham Palace** and **Westminster Abbey**; broad avenues would connect the square to Regent Street and the **British Museum;** and the square itself, instead of sunken and treeless, would be green, elevated, and uniform.

Until 1830, the site was occupied by the **Royal Mews,** when mews were reserved for mewing: the molting of birds of prey. Edward I (ruler from 1272 to 1307) kept his hawks here, and Richard II (who reigned from 1377 to 1399) kept his falcons and goshawks, a rather distinguished legacy for the famous pigeons and starlings who mew monotonously in the square today. By the reign of Henry VII (1485 to 1509), horses were kept in the **Royal Mews.** In 1732, landscape gardener, architect, and painter William Kent built the **Royal Stables** on this site, then known as "Great Mews," "Green Mews," and "Dunghill Mews." The stables stood until 1830, when the site was leveled to construct the square and **Nelson's Column.** The original idea of the square came from architect **John Nash,** who had already brought elegance and grandeur to London with Regent Street, **Regent's Park,** and **Marble Arch,** under the aegis of the prince regent, later George IV. With Regent Street, **Nash** provided the first north-south axis to connect London's three main east-west routes (Oxford Street, Piccadilly, and the Strand). In his early sketches of Trafalgar Square, **Nash** saw the site as the medieval turning point in the road leading from **Westminster Abbey** to **St. Paul's Cathedral.** There was no open space, only a widening where the bronze statue of Charles I had stood since 1675, marking the spot where the three roads met. **Nash** designed the area as a grand axis connecting government (Parliament), finance (the City), and aristocracy (St. James's and the Royal Parks). Parliament accepted **Nash**'s site but unfortunately rejected his designs.

Trafalgar Square, as it appears today, is largely the work of **Sir Charles Barry,** the distinguished architect of gentlemen's clubs, including the **Reform Club** and the **Traveller's Club** in Pall Mall, and that club of clubs, the **Houses of Parliament. Barry** favored the Italian palazzo style for this war memorial. Four octagonal oil lamps, which have been converted to electricity, occupy the corners of the square; they are reputedly from Nelson's flagship, *HMS Victory*. Every year on 21 October, the anniversary of the Battle of Trafalgar, a parade and service are held in the square by members of the Royal Navy. Officers from modern ships of the fleet lay wreaths at the bottom of the column, and descendants of those who fought at Trafalgar contribute an anchor of laurels. Nelson, a genius for naval battle, was a hero with a gift for inspiring devotion.

The highlights of the year in the square are Christmas and New Year's Eve. An enormous Christmas tree, a gift from Norway, is erected, and carols are sung most December evenings. On New Year's Eve, thousands congregate in the square and welcome in the New Year to the chimes of nearby **Big Ben.** ♦ Bounded by the Strand and Pall Mall E, and Whitehall and Charing Cross Rd. Tube: Charing Cross

At Trafalgar Square:

Nelson's Column Born in 1758, Horatio Nelson entered the service of his country at the age of 12, suffered from seasickness all his life, and lost his right eye at the Battle of Calvi, his right arm at Santa Cruz, and his life at Trafalgar. The hero now stands atop William Railton's 170-foot-high granite column, erected in 1843. The statue of Lord Nelson by E.H. Bailey is 17 feet high and his sword measures 7 feet, 9 inches. Altogether, the monument is as tall as an 18-story building, a fine tribute to a man who stood just five feet, four inches in real life.

Almost 40 years went by after Nelson's funeral at **St. Paul's** in 1805 until his column was raised in Trafalgar Square. Railton's design of a massive Corinthian column won the competition for the monument in 1837. The capital is of bronze cast from cannons recovered from the wreck of the *Royal George.* On the sides of the pedestal are four bronze bas-reliefs cast from the metal of captured French cannons, representing incidents in the battles of St. Vincent, Aboukir, Copenhagen, and Trafalgar.

Trafalgar Square

Guarding the column are four vast (20 feet by 11 feet) and lovable lions by Queen Victoria's favorite animal painter, Sir Edwin Landseer. Late arrivals (they were installed in 1868), these magnificent, tender-faced creatures give the square its vitality. When Landseer died in 1871, the public put wreaths around the lions' necks.

Statue of George IV Standing out among the statues is George IV (king from 1820 to 1830), who worshiped Nelson (though the feeling was not mutual) and under whose auspices **John Nash** first conceived the square. After the Battle of Trafalgar had established Britain's command of the seas, George IV commissioned Turner's great battle piece, *The Battle of Trafalgar* (hanging in the **National Maritime Museum** in Greenwich). But George IV's obsession was architecture. As prince regent he built the **Royal Pavilion** in Brighton; as king he rebuilt **Buckingham Palace** and transformed **Windsor** into the finest of all the royal castles. An expert horseman, he commissioned most of the equestrian paintings by George Stubbs in the **Royal Collection.** Although it seems odd that this statue by Sir Francis Chantrey shows the king in Roman dress, riding a horse bareback without stirrups, it is in keeping with the 18th-century predilection for classical poses and costumes.

Statues of James II and George Washington Facing the square from the north are two contrasting statues: On the west is James II, in Roman dress, sculpted by the 17th-century artist Grinling Gibbons; on the east is George Washington, a 1921 bronze replica of Jean Antoine Houdon's original, which stands in Richmond, Virginia. (Perhaps Washington is honored because he had an English grandfather.) James II, who reigned from 1685 to 1688, was impulsive and bullheaded. He annoyed Parliament because of his pro-Catholic wife and politics, was succeeded by his Protestant daughter, Queen Mary II, and spent the last 11 years of his life in exile in France.

Other Statues The naval influence in Trafalgar Square includes busts in the terrace walls of Admirals Beatty and Jellicoe of World War I and Admiral Cunningham of World War II. Carved into the stone of the north wall between Jellicoe and Cunningham are the Imperial Standards for length, showing the exact measurements of an imperial inch, foot, yard, rod, chain, pole, and perch.

Fountains In a city famous for rain, fountains are few. **Sir Charles Barry**'s original fountains and their large pools were part of a design to break up the large, unruly crowds that the government of the day was perceptive enough to realize would meet in the square. Even with the fountains and their pools, however, 50,000 people can and do congregate here when the cause of democracy calls. The original fountains designed by **Barry** now face Parliament in Ottawa, Canada; the fountains in the square today were designed by **Sir Edwin Lutyens** to commemorate Admirals Jellicoe and Beatty. They have first-rate water power, and every morning at 10AM the mermaids and mermen respond to the repetitive booms of **Big Ben** by democratically christening nearby Londoners and visitors, people and pigeons.

Buildings The late Sir John Betjeman, poet laureate and passionate defender of Victorian architecture, saw the weighty stone buildings that surround Trafalgar Square as a historic backdrop. Looking left in the direction of Whitehall are **Herbert Baker**'s **South Africa House,** built in 1935, its somber classical facade indifferent; the rounded **Grand Buildings** and **Trafalgar Buildings,** designed by **Frederick** and **Horace Francis** and built in 1878 and 1881, respectively; **George Aitchison**'s **Royal Bank of Scotland,** erected in 1885; **Reginald Blomfield**'s **Uganda House,** built in 1915; and **Canada House,** the most handsome building on the square, designed by **Sir Robert Smirke** and completed in 1827. Originally the **Royal College of Physicians,** this building of warm Bath stone has suffered from conversion and extension of the upper parts but nonetheless remains a dignified presence.

THE NATIONAL GALLERY

2 National Gallery Built in 1838 by **William Wilkins**, the most important building in Trafalgar Square anchors the north side. Architects complain that the scale of the Neo-Classical building is weak in relation to the square, but the blame should fall on a parsimonious Parliament, which compelled Wilkins to use columns from the demolished Carlton House in the portico. The original building was only one room deep, more a facade than a gallery. But the gallery's size at its debut had little effect on its destiny: today, it is home to one of the most comprehensive surveys of Western European art in the world.

Unlike most of the great national galleries of Europe, this one is not built upon the foundations of a former royal collection, nor did it inherit a nationally based collection. In fact, it began late; in 1824, George IV persuaded the government to buy 38 paintings from the collection of Russian émigré and marine insurance underwriter John Julius Angerstein. The government paid

£57,000 for the pictures—which included five paintings by Claude Lorraine, Hogarth's *Marriage à la Mode* series, and works by Raphael, Reynolds, and Van Dyck—then opened the gallery to the public in Angerstein's former town house at 100 Pall Mall. Two other collectors, Sir George Beaumont and the reverend William Holwell Carr, promised important paintings to the nation if a suitable building were provided to house them. In 1838, the National Gallery opened, and the Beaumont and Holwell Carr paintings, along with Angerstein's, formed the nucleus of the national collection.

As the gallery's collection grew, so did its building. The dome and additional rooms were added in the 1870s, followed by the central staircase and further additions in 1911. In 1975, the excellent northern extension was added, and the innovative **Sainsbury Wing** opened in 1991. The 2,200-plus pictures in the gallery are predominantly by the old masters. They represent one of the finest histories of Western European painting in existence, from Duccio in 14th-century Italy to Cézanne at the beginning of the 20th century, from 1260 to 1900. The masterpieces of Holbein, Van Dyck, and Velázquez displayed here are finer than those that can be seen in their native countries. The cutoff date that divided the two collections was originally 1920, but an agreement recently made between the National Gallery and the Tate changed the date to 1900. This has resulted in an exchange of relevant 19th- and 20th-century works between the two galleries.

It's not the first time such an exchange has taken place. When the Tate Gallery opened in 1897, it took on the dual role of modern art museum and home of British art. Many British paintings in the National Gallery were transferred to the Tate, leaving the National with a small but choice collection that consists of 2 paintings by Stubbs, The *Milbanke* and *Melbourne Families;* 6 by Reynolds, including *General Banastre Tarleton,* a portrait of the general during the American War of Independence; 5 by Constable, including *The Hay Wain;* 10 by Gainsborough, including *Mr. and Mrs. Andrews* and *The Morning Walk;* and 7 by Hogarth, 6 of which are part of the *Marriage à la Mode* series.

There is no substitute for beholding the original paintings, and one of the bonuses of a free museum is being able to look at only a few works at a time, guiltlessly. No one has to see it all in one visit, and no one should try. A lifetime spent looking at these paintings seems to be about right, starting with old favorites and acquiring new loves along the way. If you are daunted by the size of the collection, use a portable "Gallery Guide" on compact disc (available for a donation), which provides introductions to each section of the gallery and commentary on each work. Free one-hour guided tours are offered twice daily; three times on Wednesday.

The gallery has also made a kind of "Hit Parade" of the 20 most famous pictures. The *Twenty Great Paintings* booklet, available in the **National Gallery Shops** (see page 23), describes them and is worth the price. Check with room guards or the information desks if you can't find a painting listed here. (Also, the top 20 may change to include Hans Holbein's *Ambassadors,* now returned after conservation treatment.) The 20 masterpieces:

The Wilton Diptych, English or French school (circa 1395). ♦ Room 53

The Battle of San Romano, Paolo Uccello (1397-1475). ♦ Room 55

The Arnolfini Marriage, Jan van Eyck (1395?-1441). ♦ Room 56

The Baptism of Christ, Piero Della Francesca (1420?-92). ♦ Room 66

Cartoon: The Virgin and Child with Saint John the Baptist and Saint Anne, Leonardo Da Vinci (1452-1519). ♦ Room 51

The Doge Leonardo Loredan, Giovanni Bellini (1430?-1516). ♦ Room 61

A Lady with a Squirrel and a Starling, Hans Holbein the Younger (1498-1543). ♦ Room 4

Bacchus and Ariadne, Titian (1488?-1576). ♦ Room 9

Le Chapeau de Paille (The Straw Hat), Peter Paul Rubens (1577-1640). ♦ Room 28

Equestrian Portrait of Charles I, Anthony Van Dyck (1599-1641). ♦ Room 30

The Toilet of Venus (The Rokeby Venus), Diego Velázquez (1599-1660). ♦ Room 29

Self Portrait aged 63, Rembrandt (1606-69). ♦ Room 27

Landscape With Psyche Outside the Palace of Cupid (The Enchanted Castle), Claude Gellée (Le Lorrain) (1604/5-82). ♦ Room 19

A Young Woman Standing at a Virginal, Johannes Vermeer (1632-75). ♦ Room 16

The Stonemason's Yard, Canaletto (1697-1768). ♦ Room 38

The Fighting Temeraire, J.M.W. Turner (1775-1851). ♦ Room 34

The Hay Wain, John Constable (1776-1837). ♦ Room 34

Madame Moitessier, Jean-Auguste-Dominique Ingres (1780-1867). ♦ Room 41

Bathers at La Grenouillère, Claude Monet (1840-1926). ♦ Room 45

Bathers at Asnières, Georges Seurat (1859-91). ♦ Room 44

On the lower floor of the gallery stacks of minor masterpieces sit alongside paintings by great artists as an overflow from the main displays above.

The *National Gallery Mosaics,* by Russian-born artist Boris Anrep, on the floors of the vestibules and halfway landing, are works of art that usually go unnoticed. In the west vestibule, the theme is *The Labors of Life,* with 12 mosaics completed in 1928, including *Art,* which shows a sculptor at work; *Sacred Love,* which depicts a father, mother, child, and dog; and *Letters,* which shows a child's slate with two favorite children's books, *Robinson Crusoe* and *Alice in Wonderland.* In the north vestibule, the theme is *The Modern Virtues,* with 15 mosaics completed in 1952. *Compassion* shows the Russian poet Anna Akhmatova being saved by an angel from the horrors of war; *Compromise* has the actress Loretta Young filling a cup with wine to symbolize American and British friendship; *Defiance* portrays Winston Churchill on the cliffs of Dover, confronting an apocalyptic beast in the shape of a swastika; and *Leisure* is T.S. Eliot contemplating both the Loch Ness monster and Einstein's formula.

In the east vestibule are 11 mosaics completed by Boris Anrep in 1929 representing *The Pleasures of Life,* including *Christmas Pudding; Conversation,* with two girls gossiping; *Mudpie,* with mud pies, a bucket, and a spade; and *Profane Love,* showing a man and two girls with a dog. In the landing is *The Awakening of the Muses,* illustrating London's beau mondes in the 1930s. It portrays the Honorable Mrs. Bryan

Guinness (one of the Mitford girls and later Lady Diana Mosley) as Polyhymnia, Muse of Sacred Song; Christabel, Lady Aberconway as Euterpe, Muse of Music; Clive Bell as Bacchus, God of Wine; Virginia Woolf as Clio, Muse of History; Sir Osbert Sitwell as Apollo, God of Music; and Greta Garbo as Melpomene, Muse of Tragedy.

Special exhibitions include the *Making and Meaning* series, which provides an in-depth analysis and presentation of a major work in the collection. Guided tours leave twice a day Monday through Saturday; also Wednesday evening. There are free lunchtime lectures Tuesday through Friday at 1PM and on Saturday at noon. Free films are shown Monday at 1PM. ♦ Free. M-Tu; W 10AM-8PM; Th-Sa; Su noon-6PM. On the north side of Trafalgar Sq (between St. Martin's Pl and Whitcomb St). 389.1785. Tube: Charing Cross, Leicester Square

Within the National Gallery:

National Gallery Shops The main shop, in the **Sainsbury Wing,** carries a full range of gallery publications, a splendid collection of art books, and specially commissioned gifts from top designers, including picture frames, velvet scarves, and fancy hats inspired by artists. In full-color and reasonably-priced, *The National Gallery Companion Guide,* by Erika Langmuir, is excellent. The gallery also publishes short, introductory guides exploring such major themes as *The Care and Conservation of Paintings; Frames; Still Life;* and *Allegory.* Also for sale are color slides and black-and-white photographs. The smaller **Room 3 Shop,** at the top of the entrance to the main gallery, carries a more limited selection. ♦ M-Sa; Su noon-5:30PM. 839.3321

National Gallery

Pret a Manger Cafe ★$ Located on the lower level of the main gallery, this cheerful self-service eatery offers healthy soups and salads, hot meals, cheeses, tarts, cakes, wine, coffee, and tea. ♦ Cafe ♦ M-Sa breakfast, lunch, and tea; Su lunch and tea. 839.3321

Sainsbury Wing Though from the outside it may appear to be a separate building, it is in fact linked with the main gallery. When the wing was first proposed, Prince Charles, always outspoken about architecture, complained that the designs for this extension, incorporating an office block, were "a monstrous carbuncle on the face of a much-loved and elegant friend." People listened; plans were dropped. Enter the supermarket barons Lord Sainsbury of Preston Candover and Simon and Timothy Sainsbury, who funded this new design and construction. A second architectural competition was held and won by the Philadelphia firm **Venturi, Scott Brown & Associates.** The result is a modern architectural success (Charles himself laid the foundation stone in 1988). The **Sainsbury Wing** is also faced with Portland stone so that the facade evolves before your eyes from the Neo-Classical architecture of the original gallery to a clean, ultramodern style that suits Trafalgar Square perfectly. Displayed here is the **National Gallery**'s early collection. The 250 Early Renaissance paintings, from 1260 to 1510, include Duccio's *The Virgin and Child* triptych **(Room 52),** *The Battle of San Romano* by Uccello **(Room 55),** van Eyck's *The Arnolfini Marriage* **(Room 56),** and *The Ansidei Madonna* by Raphael **(Room 60).** ♦ M-Tu; W 10AM-8PM; Th-Sa; Su noon-6PM.

Within the Sainsbury Wing:

Micro Gallery Don't miss this free and fascinating computerized visual information system that offers background information on every painting in the collection as well as on the artists, periods, subjects, and genres. The system is easy to use and requires no particular knowledge of computers or art history.

Brasserie ★$ After nourishing the soul with the works of the masters, drop by this brasserie for its à la carte menu of light entrées and snacks. The menu changes with the season and features a weekly special. Entrées might include Cajun-spiced salmon with potatoes, lamb casserole, omelettes, or pasta. Often the dishes reflect the theme of an exhibition, such as Italian-style dishes during an Italian Baroque exhibition. Traditional afternoon tea is served as well. ♦ Brasserie ♦ M-Tu, Th-Su lunch, tea, and snacks; W lunch, tea, snacks, and dinner to 7:30PM. 839.3321

Restaurants/Clubs: Red   **Hotels:** Blue

Shops/ 🌳 Outdoors: Green   **Sights/Culture:** Black

3 National Portrait Gallery (NPG) After getting your bearings in Trafalgar Square, this is the place to begin a day in London, a stay in England, or a trip to Europe. Built in 1895 by **Ewan Christian** and **J.K. Colling,** this museum is not a typical art gallery. Here the subject overshadows the artist. More eloquent than words, the faces in the portraits tell the history of Britain: history as poetry, biography, and prophecy. Begin on the top floor. (A floor plan of the museum is pictured on page 25.)

The great age of portraiture began with the Tudors when Hans Holbein became court painter to Henry VIII. Brought to England from Holland by Erasmus, Holbein was the greatest 16th-century artist to work in England. His portraits show a profound perception of character, powerfully direct and full of nuance. Through Holbein, Henry VIII is fixed in the viewer's mind, although unfortunately for Henry, the artist arrived in England after the king was no longer young, thin, and handsome.

The most celebrated, acclaimed, and painted monarch of all time is Elizabeth I, who was virtually an icon during her reign (1558-1603). In many of her portraits, even the decorations on her clothes are emblematic—an ermine on a sleeve symbolizes chastity, pearls represent purity. Elizabeth I's ability to rule was enhanced by her being a living idol to her people, in essence a work of art.

Alongside the kings and queens are the writers who captured the ages in words: A portrait of Shakespeare (1564-1616), attributed to John Taylor, is the best existing likeness of the playwright. While Elizabeth I was proclaiming herself Gloriana (more than mortal), Donne wrote of a heaven "where there shall be no darkness nor dazzling, but one equal light; no noise or silence, but one equal music; no fears nor hopes, but one equal possession; no ends nor beginnings, but one equal eternity." As the paintings in the 25 rooms make brilliantly clear, England would not come close to such a heaven on earth for several hundred years.

Don't miss:

The portrait of Elizabeth I, by Marcus Gheeraedts the Younger, which was completed soon after the defeat of the Spanish Armada. The queen is standing triumphantly on her kingdom of England, storm clouds behind and a brilliant sky before her. ♦ Top floor, Room 1

Charles I and Sir Edward Walker after the campaigns in the West Country in 1644-45, by an unknown painter. A look of serenity and sadness shows on the face of the king, as though to presage the tragic future. ♦ Top floor, Room 2

Oliver Cromwell with an unknown page, by Walker (circa 1649). The painting shows a man aware of the tragedy around him. ♦ Top floor, Room 2

Admiral Horatio Viscount Nelson, an unfinished study for a full-length commission, is a brilliant portrait painted from life by Sir William Beechey in 1800-01, showing all the passion and fire of the hero who destroyed Napoléon's sea power and of the man, brave, tender, and honest. ♦ Top floor, Room 12

Portraits of visionary poet/artist William Blake, born in 1757, painted by Thomas Phillips in 1807; John Keats, one of England's most beloved poets who died in Rome of tuberculosis at age 25, painted by his friend Joseph Severn in 1821-23; and finally, Lord Byron, that ultimate Romantic, painted by Thomas Phillips in 1835. Born in 1788, Byron captured the poetic imagination of the age, and died in Greece in 1824, fighting for Greek independence. ♦ Top floor, Room 13

A tiny drawing of Jane Austen (1775-1817), by her sister, Cassandra, is displayed in a leather-covered glass case. This is the only existing likeness of this beloved and acute observer of the human heart. ♦ Top floor, Room 15

The Holbein cartoon of Henry VIII in black ink and colored washes on paper, part of a wall painting for **Whitehall Palace** (now lost). Still visible are the hundreds of tiny pinpricks the artist used to transfer his designs to the wall. ♦ Top floor landing

Anne, Emily, and Charlotte Brontë (circa 1834) are here, looking young and serious. The ghost in the background is their brother, Branwell, who painted himself out of the portrait. Also by Branwell is the beautiful, cracked portrait of Emily Brontë. ♦ First floor, Room 20

Elizabeth Barrett and Robert Browning, painted by Gordigiani in 1858, occupy the same room as a portrait by Ballantyne of the artist Landseer sculpting the lions now in Trafalgar Square. ♦ First floor, Room 21

Charles Darwin (1809-82), painted by John Collier in 1883. The artist created a haunting, spiritual portrait of the man who used science to destroy the myth of creation. ♦ First floor, Room 22

Henry James (1843-1916), the American writer who loved London and settled in England, was painted by John Singer Sargent on his 70th birthday in 1913. The American artist lived in London and became the most fashionable portrait painter of his generation. ♦ First floor, Room 25

The **First Floor Landing** has the controversial portrait *Queen Elizabeth, the Queen Mother*, painted by Alison Watt. The work has received a decidedly mixed response. Other portraits include Prince Charles wearing his polo clothes and the late Princess Diana when she was plump and girlish. The most recently revamped galleries are the **Victorian** and **Early 20th Century Portraits** on the first floor, with works dating from 1837 to 1960. The **Victorian** section boasts such unusual display techniques as a "cascade" of busts representing the great figures of the era and some portraits hanging on clear glass walls. The **NPG** also has the **Clore Education Centre and Studio Galleries,** the **Heinz Archive and Library** (entrance on Orange Street), the **Wolfson Gallery** (a space devoted to temporary exhibitions), a **Photography Gallery,** and the **Late 20th-Century Galleries.** At press time, a new wing designed by **Jeremy Dixon** and **Edward Jones,** featuring additional space for the permanent collection and a new rooftop restaurant, was scheduled for completion in spring 2000. ♦ Free; occasional charge for special exhibitions. M-Sa; Su noon-6PM. 2 St. Martin's Pl (at Trafalgar Sq). 306.0055. Tube: Charing Cross

NATIONAL PORTRAIT GALLERY

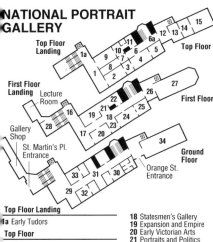

Top Floor Landing
1a Early Tudors

Top Floor
1 Mary I and Elizabeth I
2 James I and Charles I
3 17th-Century Arts and Sciences
4 Charles II and James II
5 William & Mary and Queen Anne
6 Early 18th-Century Arts and Sciences
6a The Jacobites
7 The Kit-Cat Club
8 George I and George II
9 18th-Century Arts
10 The Struggle for America
11 Britain Overseas
12 Britain at War 1793-1815
13 The Romantics
14 Science and the Industrial Revolution
15 The Regency

First Floor
16 The Royal Family
17 Queen Victoria

18 Statesmen's Gallery
19 Expansion and Empire
20 Early Victorian Arts
21 Portraits and Politics
22 Science and Technology
23 Portraits by G.F. Watts
24 Late Victorian Arts
25 The Turn of the Century
26 The First World War
27 The Armistice to the New Elizabethans

First Floor Landing
28 The Royal Family

Ground Floor
29 Politics and the Establishment from 1960
30 Photography Gallery
31 Public Figures
32 Science, Technology, and Business
33 Late 20th-Century Arts
34 Wolfson Gallery

Within the National Portrait Gallery:

National Portrait Gallery Bookshop
The best-selling postcard continues to be the melancholy portrait of Virginia Woolf. All the heroes and heroines upstairs are down here in alphabetical order, many of them also featured in biographies. ♦ Ground floor

4 Statue of Edith Cavell Behind Trafalgar Square stands a monument to Edith Cavell, a nurse accused by the Germans of spying and helping some 200 Allied prisoners to escape to neutral Holland during World War I; she was executed in 1915. The statue was created by Sir George Frampton and unveiled in 1920 by Queen Alexandra. Four years later Cavell's famous last words were added: "Patriotism is not enough." ♦ St. Martin's Pl and William IV St

5 The Chandos ★★$ A full English breakfast (try the kippers!) is served in the comfortable, Victorian-style **Opera Room** on the first floor of this handsome pub across the street from the **Trafalgar Square Post Office.** The eatery offers the usual pub grub (cottage pie and ploughman's lunches). ♦ Pub ♦ M-Sa breakfast, lunch, and dinner; Su lunch and dinner. 29 St. Martin's La (at William IV St). 836.1401. Tube: Charing Cross

6 Trafalgar Square Post Office Built in the 1960s, it stays open later than any other post office in the city. Like other main post offices, it now has a *bureau de change* and souvenir shop. ♦ M-Th, F to 8:30PM; Sa to 8PM. 24 William IV St (between Adelaide St and St. Martin's La). 930.9580. Tube: Charing Cross

7 St. Martin-in-the-Fields John Nash's design for Trafalgar Square was never realized, but his role in it endures because of his idea to open up the vista that brings this church into the square. The church, where Charles II was christened and his mistress, Nell Gwyn, was buried, is not actually part of the square but is its single source of pure loveliness. Built in 1726 by **Sir Christopher Wren**'s disciple, **James Gibbs,** the church boasts a steeple that soars to 185 feet, almost the same height as **Nelson's Column.** The steeple, which was added in 1824, has been an inspiration for many American churches. The interior is light and airy, with a lovely ceiling of Italian plasterwork. The porch offers shelter to passersby on rainy days, and the steps provide a resting place for tired tourists. On Monday, Tuesday, and Friday at 1:05PM and Thursday through Saturday at 7:30PM,

you can enjoy concerts of chamber or choral music in the church. ♦ Daily. Trafalgar Sq and Duncannon St. Concert bookings 839.8362. Tube: Charing Cross

Within St. Martin-in-the-Fields:

Cafe in the Crypt ★★$ Hidden within the church's crypt is this restaurant still known by the cognoscenti as **Fields.** It's used by actors for private parties and by office workers to meet their friends for lunch. The floors (gravestones), the walls (16th-century stone), and the black furniture are made less sepulchral by the strains of Bach. ♦ Cafe ♦ M-Sa lunch and snacks to 8PM; Su lunch and snacks. 839.4342

Brass Rubbing Center Here, you can rub effigies of medieval brasses (facsimiles), creating your own knight in shining armor or damsel in a gown. If you feel pressed for time, buy one ready-made. Children love creating effigies, and the center adjoins the **Cafe in the Crypt,** so you can enjoy a coffee while keeping an eye on the kids. ♦ M-Sa; Su noon-7:30PM 930.9306

8 Statue of Charles I Whitehall physically begins on the south side of Trafalgar Square with this equestrian statue of Charles I, who reigned from 1625 to 1649. The statue, created in 1633 by Hubert Le Sueur, shows the monarch gazing toward the scene of his tragic execution at **Banqueting House** on 30 January 1649, with Parliament looming in the distance. It was his quarrel with Parliament that led to his downfall. In 1642, civil war erupted between the Parliamentarians (the Roundheads, led by Oliver Cromwell) and the Royalists (known as the Cavaliers) over Parliament's demand to approve the king's choice of ministers. Charles was tried for treason to the realm and died on the scaffold.

Now stranded in an islet, unreachable except by the most intrepid pedestrian, this is one of the oldest, finest, and certainly most poignant statues in London. The horse's left hoof bears the date 1633 and the sculptor's signature. When the Civil War broke out in 1642, the statue was hidden in the churchyard of **St. Paul's, Covent Garden.** After the king's execution, Cromwell sold the statue for scrap to a resourceful brazier named John Rivett, who kept the statue intact but enjoyed a brisk trade in candlesticks, thimbles, spoons, and knife handles supposedly created from it. This Charles I souvenir shop thrived until the Restoration, when the statue miraculously reappeared. Charles II rewarded the brazier with £1,600. The statue finally found its home here in 1675. Note that Whitehall is the name of the street and of the immediate area, as well as a nickname for governmental bureaucracy and red tape (thanks to all the official ministries and departments here). ♦ Trafalgar Sq and Whitehall. Tube: Charing Cross

WALKERS
OF WHITEHALL

9 Walkers of Whitehall ★$$ To find a civilized setting for a drink, lunch, or snack, turn into tiny Craig's Court and enter this pub/wine bar on the left. You can try cask-conditioned ales or premium lagers with a smoked salmon sandwich, or, if you prefer, a glass of wine with a platter of pâté. ♦ Pub/Wine bar ♦ M-F lunch and dinner. Craig's Ct (off Whitehall). 976.1961. Tube: Charing Cross

10 Whitehall Theatre On the opposite side of the street to Craig's Court stands this theater, built in 1930 on the site of a tavern. **Edward Stone**'s clean, simple Art Deco lines led one newspaper to comment that the theater made the nearby government buildings look as if they needed a shave. The venue, which seats 646, usually stages farces and comedies, and its air-conditioning makes the laughter flow more easily in summer. ♦ M-Sa. Whitehall (between Downing St and The Mall). 367.1735. Tube: Charing Cross

11 Silver Cross ★★$$ Charles I licensed this establishment as a brothel and pub in 1647. The facade is Victorian, but the building dates to the 13th century, with a barrel-vaulted ceiling, ancient walls sheathed in lead, and, in the bar, a plaster ceiling embossed with vine leaves, grapes, and hops made while Charles I was still living down the street. A warm, special place, it serves home-cooked food. On its upper floors purportedly lives a ghost, said to be that of the Tudor maiden whose portrait hangs over the fireplace. ♦ Pub ♦ Daily lunch and dinner. 33 Whitehall (between Great Scotland Yd and Craig's Ct). 930.8350. Tube: Charing Cross

12 Clarence ★★$ A Whitehall institution since the 18th century, this pub has great atmosphere: leaded windows, gaslights, oak beams overhead, and wooden tables and pews. This is a good choice for connoisseurs of real ale, which can be enjoyed with full bar meals. Medieval theme nights can be arranged for parties of 12 or more. ♦ Pub ♦ Daily lunch and dinner. 53 Whitehall (between Great Scotland Yd and Craig's Ct). 930.4808. Tube: Charing Cross

13 Old Admiralty The **Robert Adam** stone screen adorned with sea horses that leads into the cobbled courtyard is all that can be seen of the place that ruled the waves for 200 years. The building was designed in 1725 by **Thomas Ripley.** In the **Board Room** upstairs is a wind dial dating from 1708 that still records each gust over the roof, even though no one waits here anymore for a sign that the wind will carry the French across the English Channel. The present Admiralty, or Royal Navy, still meets in the building. Smoking has never been allowed here, a rule even Churchill humbly obeyed. Here Nelson both took his orders and returned five years later to lie in state, awaiting his funeral at **St. Paul's.** Bailey's original model for Nelson's statue in Trafalgar Square is kept here. ♦ Whitehall (between Downing St and The Mall). Tube: Charing Cross

14 Royal Horse Guards Hotel $$$$ Once the apartments of the influential, the 280 rooms and suites, some featuring panoramic views of the Thames, are now for the affluent. The reception rooms and restaurant have the feel of an elegant country house, the lobby is light and airy, and the guest rooms are grand—some of them even have marble bathrooms! The outdoor courtyard overlooks an ornamental garden. ♦ 2 Whitehall Ct (at Whitehall Pl). 839.3400, 800/181716; fax 925.2263. Tube: Embankment

At the Royal Horse Guards Hotel:

Granby's ★★★$$$$ Just off the lobby, this dining room is decorated in traditional English style, with comfortable leather armchairs, dark wallpaper, and mahogany tables. The menu features Modern British cooking, with such elegant specialties as grilled turbot medaillons, halibut served on cabbage leaves with caviar, and sautéed pigeon. The restaurant is a popular lunchtime choice with civil servants from the nearby **Ministry of Defence.** In summer, there's outdoor seating overlooking the **Victoria Embankment Gardens.** ♦ Modern British ♦ Daily lunch and dinner. 839.3400

15 Whitehall Court This massive Victorian attempt at a French château was originally a grand apartment building, constructed in 1887 by **Archer and Green.** It was designed by the great Victorian architect **Alfred Waterhouse,** who also built the cathedral-like **Natural History Museum.** Both H.G. Wells and George Bernard Shaw had flats here, and it was the home of several clubs, including the **Farmers'** and the **Liberal Club.** It still houses the **National Liberal Club,** but much of the building is now rented for functions. ♦ Whitehall Ct (at Horseguards Ave). Tube: Embankment

16 Ministry of Defence In this more peaceful age, the **Old War Office,** built in 1898 by **William Young & Son,** is now called the **Ministry of Defence.** Inevitably, it lacks the romance of the **Old Admiralty** across the street, but the Baroque domes above its corner towers, visible from Trafalgar and Parliament Squares as well as from **St. James's Park,** have a certain grandeur. ♦ Whitehall (at Horseguards Ave). Tube: Charing Cross

17 Banqueting House On a bitter winter's day in 1649, a small procession left **St. James's Palace** and walked through the park to Whitehall. The king of England was going to his execution. Crossing Whitehall, Charles I may have had his first glimpse of the scaffold built outside the central windows of this building, which is now all that is left of the fabulous **Whitehall Palace** on this site. It would be his last look at the perfectly proportioned Palladian building commissioned by his father, James I, for grand dining occasions. **Banqueting House** and the fate of Charles I are inextricably bound. The proportions of the hall, one of the grandest rooms in England, create a perfect double cube at 110 feet long and 55 feet high. This design, created by **Inigo Jones** in 1622, represents the harmony of the universe, of peace, order, and power—the virtues of divine kingship instilled in Charles I by his father.

The building, possibly London's first with a facade of Portland stone, so inspired writer Horace Walpole that he dubbed it "the model of the most pure and beautiful taste." The magnificent ceiling, which Charles commissioned from Peter Paul Rubens, represents the glorification of James I, a statement of James's belief in the absolute right and God-given power of kings. If you follow the panels from the far end of the room, you see James rising up to heaven, having created peace on earth by his divine authority as king: peace reigns, the arts flourish, and the king is defender of his realm, the faith, and the church.

When Charles I tried to impeach five members of Parliament, civil war broke out between the Parliamentarians and the Royalists. Seven years later he was tried in **Westminster Hall** and convicted of treason to the realm. On the day of the execution, Charles wore a second shirt so that he would not shiver in the cold and have his subjects believe he was afraid. He was a sad and courageous king in death: "I go from a corruptible to an incorruptible crown where no disturbances can be."

With one blow, England was without a king, and severed with Charles's head was the belief in the divine right of kings. Until this moment, kings were the chosen representatives of God on earth. But now monarchs were just men and women—powerful, perhaps, but not all-powerful.

Despite being one of the most important buildings in English architecture, it is almost always empty. Empty, but not haunted; there is no feeling that the ghost of Charles I lingers in the place of his execution. A bust of Charles I over the staircase entrance (added by Wyatt in 1798) marks the site of the window through which he climbed onto the scaffold. ♦ Admission. M-Sa. Whitehall (at Horseguards Ave). 930.4179. Tube: Embankment

MICHAEL STORRINGS

18 Horse Guards William Kent, George II's chief architect, designed this long, picturesque—if uninspired—building (shown above) as the headquarters of the king's military General Staff. It replaced a similar dilapidated structure, dating from the reign of Charles II, which had been built on the site of Henry VIII's tiltyard. Begun in 1750, the building was completed in 1758 by **John Vardy**, who took over the design project after **Kent**'s death. Today, it's a favorite attraction for young visitors, who come to watch the pair of mounted sentries within the central archway.

The two troopers, who change duty every two hours, are drawn from the Cavalry Regiments of the Household Division, which protects the sovereign, better known to military buffs as the Life Guards, and the Blues and Royals. They sit, magnificent and impassive, on their horses, their uniforms elegant compositions of tunics and plumes. (The red tunics and white plumes belong to the Life Guards, while the blue tunics and red plumes belong to the Blues and Royals.)

In addition to the sentries in the archway, the entire Household Division is on daily duty, and the guards are changed each day in a ceremony many Londoners and visitors prefer to that which takes place at **Buckingham Palace**. At approximately 10:30AM (9:30AM on Sunday), the new guard of the Household Division leaves **Hyde Park Barracks** to ride down Pall Mall, arriving at **Horse Guards** about half an hour later, at which point the old guard returns. This was an entrance to the long-gone **Whitehall Palace.** The soldiers are not allowed to talk, but once they are in position—if you don't touch their swords or their mounts—you can take photos or be photographed with them. ♦ Whitehall (between Downing St and The Mall). Recorded information 0891/505452 (premium rate call). Tube: Charing Cross

19 Horse Guards Parade Go through the arch at **Horse Guards** to enter this parade ground with its splendid, white stone Palladian building boasting arches, pediments, and wings, architecturally one of the finest buildings in London. The parade ground used to be the **Whitehall Palace** tiltyard. In 1540,

Henry VIII invited knights from all over Europe to compete in a tournament on this site.

Every year on the second or third Saturday in June, the queen leaves **Buckingham Palace** in her carriage to drive down Horse Guards Parade in the Trooping the Colour ceremony. This is the most spectacular military display of the year in a country that has no rival in matters of pomp. An annual event dating back to medieval times, it was originally an exercise to teach soldiers to recognize their regimental flags, called "the colours." Now it marks the sovereign's official birthday—ceremonial acceptance that English weather does not guarantee a successful outdoor occasion before June. Crowds line The Mall to watch the procession, but it is possible to get tickets; see "The London Ledger of Annual Events," page 15. ♦ Behind Horse Guards. Tube: Charing Cross

20 New Ministry of Defence Designed by **Vincent Harris** just after World War II and completed in 1959, these vast buildings were placed behind Whitehall on Horseguards Avenue out of respect for the scale and proportions of the **Banqueting House.** This ministry is where the real problems of war and peace are handled—with a few exceptions. In the basement is all that survives of the original **Whitehall Palace:** Henry VIII's wine cellar. The Tudor brick-vaulted roof is 70 feet long, 30 feet wide, and weighs 800 tons. Because the wine cellar interfered with the line of the new building, it was moved 43 feet to one side, lowered 20 feet, and then pushed back to its original site. A huge excavation was made, a mausoleum of concrete and steel built around the cellar to protect it, and a system of rollers devised to shift the cellar a quarter of an inch at a time until it had completed its journey. The whole operation cost £100,000, a vast sum at the time. ♦ Horseguards Ave (off Whitehall). Tube: Embankment

21 Cabinet Office From 1733 to 1844, several great architects had a hand in the design of this building, including **William Kent, Sir John Soane,** and **Sir Charles Barry.** The lengthy facade exudes Victorian self-confidence and weightiness. At the north end is the office of the Privy Council, the queen's private council comprising "princes of the blood," high officers of the state, and members of Parliament appointed by the Crown. It seems fitting that a statue of Sir Walter Raleigh, created in 1959 by William Macmillan, looks on from across the road. Once a member of Elizabeth I's Privy Council, he was executed at Whitehall for conspiring against James I. Raleigh exhibited a very stiff upper lip on the scaffold. Testing the sharpness of the ax, he remarked, "This is a sharp medicine, but it will cure all diseases." The building is not open to the public. ♦ Whitehall (between Downing St and The Mall). Tube: Westminster

22 Downing Street History and television have made this street one of the most famous and familiar in the world. But politics and terrorism have caused it to be shut off from the public; it can be viewed only through a wrought-iron gate. Named after its first owner, Sir George Downing, the street retains a quiet, residential air. In 1735, **No. 10** became the official residence of the first prime minister, Sir Robert Walpole. (The prime minister now also has an official country house called Chequers.) **No. 11** is the residence of the Chancellor of the Exchequer. However, Prime Minister Tony Blair and his family have switched residences with Chancellor Gordon Brown, a bachelor, because **No. 11** has more bedrooms. **No. 12** is the office of the Chief Party Whip, the title for the member of Parliament responsible for stirring up party support for bills and issues. ♦ Between Whitehall and Horse Guards Rd. Tube: Westminster

23 Cenotaph Rising in the center of Whitehall is **Sir Edwin Lutyens**'s austere memorial to "The Glorious Dead" of World Wars I and II. Erected in 1920, the simple structure of Portland stone shows no sign of imperial glory or national pride or religious symbolism; it is not a monument to victory but a monument to loss. Between the wars, men would take off their hats whenever they passed. Now hats have gone out of style and memories have faded, but once a year, on Remembrance Sunday (the second Sunday of November), an impressive service and parade is held to remember the dead of these wars. It is attended by the queen and the royal family, the prime minister, representatives of the Army and Navy, and leading statesmen and leaders of Commonwealth countries and the colonies. Wreaths are placed, and at 11AM, a two-minute silence is observed. ♦ Whitehall (between King Charles and Downing Sts). Tube: Westminster

24 Richmond House This building, which houses the Department of Health and Social Security, was built in 1988 by **William Whitfield** and is an example of how a clever architect can create a modern structure that blends into a historic area. Note the stone-mullioned windows and the cluster effect of the yellow brick–and–gray granite columns, neatly set back from the street. Like other government buildings, it is not open to the public. ♦ 79 Whitehall (at Richmond Terr, facing the Cenotaph). Tube: Westminster

24 Red Lion ★★★$ This is the MPs' pub. The original was built in 1733 and visited by Dickens when he was only 11—the author found it memorable enough to bear mention in *David Copperfield*. After being torn down, the pub was rebuilt in 1899 and has hardly changed since. The bar walls are covered with drawings, cartoons, and photographs of famous politicians. There's a nice old-fashioned dining room upstairs serving old-fashioned English food while the bar serves typical pub food such as burgers and fries and a ploughman's lunch. Both bar and restaurant have division bells (these signal a vote is taking place on a bill being debated in Parliament) and the Parachute Regiment has its annual reunions here. ♦ Pub ♦ Pub: daily lunch and dinner. Dining room: daily lunch. 48 Parliament St (at Derby Gate). 930.5826. Tube: Westminster

CABINET WAR ROOMS

25 Cabinet War Rooms Winston Churchill masterminded the British war effort from this complex 17 feet underground. The public can visit 21 of these rooms, including the one where the War Cabinet met in 1940 and 1945. The control room is still crammed with phones and maps covered with marker pins showing the positions of military defenses. Churchill made many of his stirring wartime broadcasts from the room marked "Prime Minister." It is amazing to think that he brilliantly conducted a global war from these cramped underground rooms. ♦ Admission. Daily. Clive Steps, King Charles St (at Horse Guards Rd). 930.6961. Tube: Westminster

26 The Two Chairmen ★★$$ The 18th-century pub takes its name from the chair carriers who brought customers to the Royal Cockpit, where cockfights were staged for the entertainment of the king and his court, and which stood on the adjacent Cockpit Steps until 1810. (To reach the pub, climb up Cockpit Steps off Birdcage Walk to Dartmouth Street.) In the "Sedan Room" (the chairs were called sedans) you can lunch on steak-and-ale pie or fish-and-chips. ♦ Pub ♦ M-F lunch and dinner. 39 Dartmouth St (at Queen Anne's Gate). 222.8694. Tube: St. James's Park

27 Queen Anne's Gate This lovely street is lined with wonderful 18th-century houses; note that the doors are wide enough to allow passage of the popular sedan chairs of the period, as well as crinolined ladies. You'll also see boot scrapers, the occasional torchlight snuffer, and a statue of Queen Anne at **No. 15.** Beyond the statue, the houses (dating from 1704) have doorways topped by lacy-looking wooden canopies. ♦ Between Petty France and Dartmouth St. Tube: St. James's Park

28 Guards Museum If you would like to learn more about the five regiments of foot soldiers who take part in the Changing of the Guard ceremony, this is the place to visit. You'll find lots of memorabilia, the scarlet uniforms and bushy helmets, tableaux, and displays explaining the history of the regiments and their duties. There's also a shop. ♦ Admission. Daily Feb–mid-Dec. Wellington Barracks, Birdcage Walk (between Queen Anne's and Buckingham Gates). 739.9893. Tube: St. James's Park

29 Blew Coat School, National Trust This delightful shop is chock-full of English country-house accessories and gifts, such as tea towels, tea cozies, diaries, candles, fragrances, and books. Many items display designs inspired by the palatial properties under the care of the National Trust, the organization that maintains stately homes as well as much of the English countryside and coastline. This building is historic in its own right. Erected in 1709, it once served as a school for poor children. Notice the little statues of a boy and girl at the back of the building. ♦ M-F. 23 Caxton St (at Buckingham Gate). 222.2877. Tube: St. James's Park

STAKIS LONDON ST. ERMIN'S

30 Stakis St. Ermin's Hotel $$$ The exterior is unprepossessing, but inside this property recalls the elegance of Edwardian days, with a superb Baroque staircase and wood-paneled bedrooms. All 290 rooms come with en suite facilities, color TV, radio, and refreshments. The **Cloisters Brasserie** (formerly the **Carving Table**) is so popular with lords and MPs that the Parliament division bell sounds within the building so that the politicians know when to get back to cast important votes. Try the haggis, haddock, or porridge at the full English breakfast served at the **Brasserie** (the other restaurant here is the **Caxton Grill**). ♦ Caxton St (at Broadway). 222.7888; fax 222.6914. Tube: St. James's Park

31 Westminster Central Hall This domed historic hall, an international headquarters for Methodism, was built by **E.A. Rickards** and **H.V. Lancester** in 1912; the dome is the third-largest in London, after those of **St. Paul's** and the **Reading Room** of the **British Library.** In addition to being a place of worship, the hall hosts concerts and exhibitions. ♦ Chapel: daily. Services: Su 11AM, 6:30PM. Storey's Gate and Tothill St. 222.8010. Tube: St. James's Park.

Within Westminster Central Hall:

The Cafe ★$ Head to this downstairs eatery for a full English breakfast. Soup and sandwiches are offered for lunch. It's a simple but welcome respite from the abbey crowds. ♦ Cafe ♦ M-Sa breakfast and lunch. 222.8010

32 Westminster Arms ★★$ Home-cooked steak, kidney pie, and real ale make this pub popular with journalists and MPs for whom the division bell is rung in the bar. There's a pleasant restaurant upstairs and a wine bar downstairs. ♦ Pub ♦ Pub: M-F lunch and dinner; Sa-Su lunch. Restaurant: daily lunch. 9 Storey's Gate (between Parker and Lewisham Sts). 222.8520. Tube: St. James's Park

33 Parliament Square Sir Charles Barry conceived this square as a kind of garden foreground to his new **Houses of Parliament**, and it was thus laid out in 1850. Today, it forms an open-air sculpture gallery for prime ministers and other statesmen, although they are suffering in the interests of progress (the square is now a construction site for the **Jubilee** Underground line, which has experienced a number of delays but is expected to be completed in the near future). A 12-foot bronze sculpture by Ivor Robert Jones shows a determined-looking Winston Churchill standing on the corner gazing at the **House of Commons,** where he was once a leader. Among the many other brooding statesmen here are Disraeli (Lord Beaconsfield), erected in 1883 by Raggi, and Abraham Lincoln, tall and rumpled. His statue is a copy of the one by Augustus St. Gaudens in Lincoln Park, Chicago. ♦ Bounded by Bridge and Great George Sts, and St. Margaret's and Parliament Sts. Tube: Westminster

34 Westminster Pier Perhaps the only thing better than seeing London by foot is seeing London from the river. This pier is the main launching point for boat trips, either downstream to the **Tower,** Greenwich, and Thames Barrier, or upstream to the delights of **Kew Gardens,** Richmond, and **Hampton Court Palace.** There are daily cruises upstream from April through October, and downstream year-round; call the pier for more information. ♦ Victoria Embankment (just north of Westminster Bridge). 0891/505471. Tube: Westminster

34 Queen Boadicea This symbol of liberty, depicting the Celtic queen looking out onto the **Houses of Parliament** from her chariot, is well placed. In AD 61, a savage revolt broke out in the newly conquered province of Britain when Roman soldiers forced their way into her palace in east England. They flogged the recently widowed queen for refusing to surrender the lands of the Iceni and raped her two daughters. In her fury, Boadicea led a fierce rebellion, massacring the inhabitants of the Roman capital at Colchester, then turning southeast to the undefended port of Londinium. No mercy was shown, and the flourishing town was quickly destroyed. Some 70,000 people lost their lives. But the revenge of the Queen of the Iceni was short-lived. The Romans annihilated the tribe. Boadicea is alleged to have poisoned herself. In this bronze statue, erected in 1902 by Thomas Thorneycroft, Boadicea has her two half-naked daughters at her side. ♦ Westminster Bridge and Victoria Embankment. Tube: Westminster

35 Westminster Bridge Designed by **Thomas Page,** who rebuilt it to complement **Barry**'s **Houses of Parliament,** this bridge is one of the best-loved vantage points in the whole of London. You really must walk out on it to enjoy the greatest view of the seat of British government. The Gothic buildings, rising almost vertically from the Thames, are an inspiration for poets and painters alike. The 810-foot cast-iron bridge is not the one that inspired Wordsworth to write his sonnet, but the view surpasses by far what Wordsworth noted that early morning in 1803. He would not have seen the highly wrought **Houses of Parliament** with the imposing **Victoria Tower,** nor could he have set his watch by the clock lovingly, if inaccurately, called **Big Ben.** ♦ Between York Rd and Bridge St. Tube: Westminster

36 County Hall Look across the Thames from **Westminster Pier,** and you're sure to be taken aback by the palatial sweep of crescent-shaped **County Hall**—well, the *former* **County Hall.** Designed by **Ralph Knott** for the London County Council, and built between 1911-22 and 1931-33, the building eventually formed the headquarters of the Greater London Council (known as the GLC) in 1965. In 1986, the GLC was abolished by the Tory government, and the 2,390 rooms and 10 miles of corridors became empty. Since then, the **London Aquarium** (see below), and two hotels have opened here, and at press time, there were plans to establish a Chinese restaurant, a leisure center with virtual reality computer games, and a monorail ride. Trivia buffs will be interested to learn that in the early 18th century, a stoneworks on the site of **County Hall** took out a patent on a particular type of terra-cotta, which was later improved by a woman named Eleanor Coade and thus was named Coade stone. Strong, appealing, and amazingly weatherproof, Coade stone was used to build the **Royal Opera House, Somerset House,** and the **Bank of England,** among other structures. Yet when the stone yard closed in 1840, the secret of Coade stone died with it, and subsequent attempts to analyze its composition failed. ♦ Belvedere Rd (at Westminster Bridge). Tube: Waterloo, Westminster

Within County Hall:

London Aquarium This three-story, £25-million attraction, now Europe's largest aquatic exhibition, features high-tech and showy displays of exotic fish species from around the world. There's a riverside restaurant as well as a shop. ♦ Admission. Daily. Restaurant: daily breakfast, lunch, and dinner; Shop: daily; to 9PM June-Aug. 967.8000

36 London County Hall Travel Inn Capital
$$ Within this modern building are 312 smart, spacious rooms suitable for families or business travelers. Each room features two double beds along with a coffee maker and direct-dial phones. ♦ 902.1600; fax 902.1619

36 London Marriott Hotel County Hall
$$$$ Superior accommodations and facilities plus an enviable location on the River Thames opposite the **Houses of Parliament** put this newly opened hotel high on the list of London's best. Many of the 200 rooms (5 of which are suites) have river views. The decor is strictly "English traditional." Within the hotel is the **County Hall Restaurant** offering a contemporary British menu; the **Leaders** cocktail bar, which is adorned with historical memorabilia of County Hall; an indoor swimming pool; a fitness center; and access

to **The Club**—one of the most exclusive health clubs in London. ♦ 928.5200; fax 928.5300

36 South Bank Lion The 12-foot-high lion that guards the southern end of **Westminster Bridge** was originally created for the long-gone **Lion Brewery.** The regal beast, made of Coade stone, weighs in at 13 tons. ♦ Westminster Bridge Rd (at Westminster Bridge)

37 Florence Nightingale Museum
Devoted to the famous "lady of the lamp," who transformed nursing into a proper, disciplined profession, this museum is appropriately sited at **St. Thomas's Hospital,** where, in 1860, Florence Nightingale inspired the founding of Britain's first school of nursing. (The hospital is still in use, having been rebuilt after suffering damage during World War II.) The museum features tableaux of her time in the Crimea, plus personal belongings, including her medicine bag and the famous lamp. There are also photographs and documents portraying the development of health care as pioneered by this illustrious lady, who died at the age of 90 in 1910. ♦ Admission. Tu-Su. 2 Lambeth Palace Rd (at Westminster Bridge Rd). 620.0374. Tube: Westminster, Waterloo

38 Houses of Parliament To the modern world, no single view so powerfully symbolizes democracy as this assemblage of Gothic buildings (shown below), which look as if they have been here throughout the 900 years that this area has served as the site of British government. In fact, these buildings have been standing for less than 170 years, but their Gothic style powerfully represents the aspirations and traditions of those nine centuries. The "Symbol of Democracy" and the "Mother of Parliaments" remains a royal palace; it is officially called the **New Palace of Westminster,** a name that goes back to the 11th century, when this was the site of the **Palace of Westminster.** First occupied by Edward the Confessor, the palace was the principal London residence of the monarchs until 1512, when Henry VIII moved down the

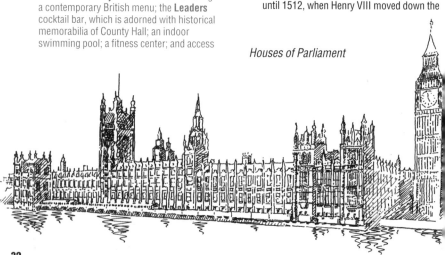

Houses of Parliament

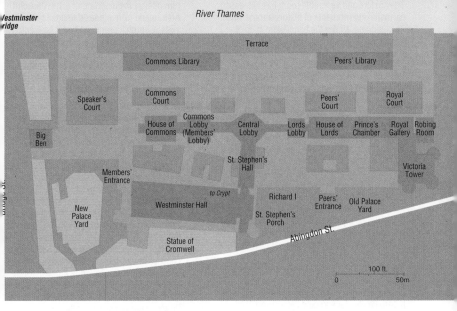

street to **Whitehall Palace.** Now the resident is a commoner, the Speaker of the **House of Commons,** who has a grand apartment here. (Currently, it's Betty Boothroyd, the first woman Speaker.) Parliament sat here until the palace burned to the ground in the disastrous fire of 1834. All that is left of the ancient **Palace of Westminster** is the crypt and cloisters of **St. Stephen's Chapel,** the **Jewel Tower,** and **Westminster Hall,** the long Norman hall that is the greatest window into the history of Britain's parliamentary heritage.

After the fire, **Sir Charles Barry** and **Augustus Pugin** won a design competition for a new and enlarged **Houses of Parliament** building (to occupy the same site) in either the Gothic or Tudor style. **Barry** gave the buildings an almost classic body; **Pugin** created a meticulous and exuberant Gothic design. Built between 1840 and 1860, the **Houses of Parliament** are laid out on an axial plan that reflects the hierarchical nature of British society: **House of Commons, Commons Lobby, Central Lobby, Lords Lobby, House of Lords, Prince's Chamber,** and **Royal Gallery** (a detailed map of the area is depicted above). The complex of buildings covers an area of eight acres and has 11 courtyards, 100 staircases, almost 1,200 rooms, and two miles of passages. The **House of Commons** is in the northern end (MPs enter from New Palace Yard on the corner of Bridge Street and Parliament Square) and the **House of Lords** is in the southern end. (The Peers' entrance is in Old Palace Yard, where Guy Fawkes was hanged, drawn, and quartered in 1606 for trying to blow up the king and Parliament, and where Sir Walter Raleigh was beheaded in 1618.) British citizens can arrange for a tour of the Houses of Parliament through the members representing their constituencies in the House of Commons; foreigners must obtain a permit for a tour, generally on Friday afternoons or when Parliament is not in session, by writing (it is recommended that you do this at least two weeks in advance) to **Parliamentary Education Unit, Norman Shaw Building (North),** London SW1A 2TT; 219.2105; edunit@parliament.uk. It is possible, though not always easy, for anyone to attend a debate in the "Mother of Parliaments"; see **House of Commons** and **House of Lords** below for details. ♦ Bridge St and Parliament Sq. Tube: Westminster

Within the Houses of Parliament:

Westminster Hall Built in 1097 by King William Rufus (William II), son of William the Conqueror, this vast, barnlike room is where Parliament began and where Simon de Montfort marched in and enforced it. At the end of the 14th century, Richard II had the hall rebuilt by **Henry Yevele,** who added the massive buttresses that support 600 tons of oak roof. The hall contains the oldest surviving example of an oak hammer beam roof, created by Hugh Herland; it was a miracle of engineering in its day, marking the end of supporting piers.

"If voting changed anything, they would have abolished it."

Ken Livingstone, Member of Parliament,
The Oxford Dictionary of Political Quotations

The austere and venerable room has witnessed earthshaking moments of history almost since its beginning. Under the benevolent eyes of the carved angels in the arches of the beams, Richard II was deposed the year the work was completed, and Henry IV was declared king. In 1535, Sir Thomas More, former Speaker of the **House of Commons,** stood trial here for treason against his former friend and tennis partner, Henry VIII, and was beheaded on Tower Hill. Seventy years later, on 5 November 1605, England's most famous terrorist, Guy Fawkes, was captured and subsequently tried and convicted for the crime of trying to blow up King James I and Parliament. Charles I stood trial in his own hall in 1649 and was convicted of treason. Oliver Cromwell, the most formidable parliamentarian who ever lived, signed the king's death warrant and had himself named Lord Protector here in 1653. After the restoration of Charles II to the throne, Cromwell was brought back to the hall—or rather his skull was cut from his skeleton and stuck on a spike on one of the oak beams, where it rattled in the wind for 25 years before finally blowing down in a storm. And it was here that Churchill lay in state while a grateful nation paid its last respects.

Crypt/St. Mary's Undercroft Though once abused and desecrated, and even used as the Speaker's coal cellar, the chapel was richly restored by **E.M. Barry** and has a wonderful pre-Raphaelite feeling. The main walls, vaulting, and bosses have withstood at least five fires. Members of both Houses of Parliament use the chapel for weddings and christenings.

St. Stephen's Porch The public enters the **Houses of Parliament,** whether for a guided tour or to sit in one of the **Stranger's Galleries,** through this porch and hall. Be prepared for the airport-style security check, with metal-detecting arches right next to **Westminster Hall,** an understandable though inglorious entrance to the **Central Lobby.**

Central Lobby The crossroads of the **Palace of Westminster** connects the **House of Commons** with the **House of Lords**. Citizens meet their MPs in this octagonal vestibule. The ceiling, 75 feet above the floor, contains 250 carved bosses with Venetian mosaics that include the patron saints of England, Ireland, Scotland, and Wales. Above the ceiling is the central spire of the palace, a feature imposed on **Sir Charles Barry's** original plans by one Dr. Reid, a ventilation expert who insisted that it be built as a shaft to expel "vitiated" air.

Members' Lobby Off the **Central Lobby** is the Piccadilly Circus of Commons life, where members gossip and talk to the lobby journalists. Also known as the **Commons Lobby,** it is architecturally rather bleak (most often described as "Neo-Gothic"), and was never fully restored after the 1941 German bombing that left it in ruins. A moving reminder of the destruction is the **Churchill Arch,** made from stones damaged in the fire 1941. Churchill proposed that it be erected in the lobby in memory of those who kept the bridge during the dark days of the war. Above the main door of the **Commons Chamber** hangs the family crest of Airey Neave, placed here after he was assassinated by terrorists in New Palace Yard in 1979.

House of Commons Each day the **House** opens with a procession in which the Speaker enters (wearing a long black gown), preceded by the sergeant-at-arms, who carries a mace (the symbol of authority), and followed by the train-bearer, chaplain, and secretary. The day begins with prayers, and no strangers (journalists or visitors) are ever admitted. When praying, MPs face the seats behind them—an extraordinary sight—because in the days when they wore swords it was impossible to kneel on the floor; therefore, they turned to kneel on the benches behind them. Every member has to swear loyalty to the Crown (a problem for the occasional MP from Northern Ireland), although no monarch has been allowed to enter the **House of Commons** since 1642, when Charles burst in to arrest his parliamentary opponents.

The **House of Commons** was completely destroyed in the air raid of 10 December 1941, and was rebuilt in 1950 by **Sir Giles Gilbert Scott,** simply and without decoration and, under Churchill's influence, in the exact proportions of the prewar building. It is impressively small: Only 436 of the 659 members can actually sit down at any one time; the rest often can be seen crowding around the door and the Speaker's chair or sitting on the steps. The lack of space is considered to be fundamental to the sense of intimacy and conversational form of debate that characterize the House. Equally important is the layout of the Chamber, with the party in office (called the Government) and the Opposition facing each other, their green leather benches two sword lengths apart and separated by two red lines on the floor, which no member is allowed to cross while addressing the Chamber.

The **Press Gallery** and the **Stranger's Gallery** are located at opposite ends of the Chamber. Theoretically, anyone may attend a session of the **House** by waiting in the queue outside **St. Stephen's Entrance,** but the **Stranger's Gallery** seats only about 200, so you are likely to have to wait an hour or two in line, or, particularly during "question times," not get in at all; for a better chance, apply to your embassy or (for Commonwealth visitors) high commission in the UK for a "card of introduction." ♦ Sessions: M, Tu, Th 3:30PM-closing (often late); W and F from 9:30AM; Prime Minister's question time: W 3-3:30PM. 219.4272

House of Lords This is the most elaborate part of **Sir Charles Barry's** design and **Augustus Pugin's** ultimate masterpiece:

Victorian, romantic, and stunning. At 80 feet long, it is not grand in size, but it is extravagantly ornate. Stained-glass windows cast a dark red light, and 18 statues of the barons of the Magna Carta stare down from the walls. Their saintlike demeanor emphasizes the sacred look of the room, but the long red-leather sofas on either side suggest a chapel of sorts. Between the two sofas is the "Woolsack" (the traditional seat of the Lord Chancellor), a huge red pouf stuffed with bits of wool collected from all over the Commonwealth. Under an immense gilded canopy is the ornate throne reserved for the queen. Because the doings in the **House of Lords** are considerably less crucial to the nation than those in the **Commons,** it is generally not difficult to get a seat in the **Stranger's Gallery** here; just get in the correct line at **St. Stephen's Entrance.** ♦ Sessions: M-W 2:30PM-closing; Th 3PM-closing; and some Fridays 219.3107; fax 219.5979

Outside the Houses of Parliament:

Big Ben Here is the most beloved image in all of London, towering 320 feet over the Thames and lighting up the sky (see illustration on page 4). Every guidebook will tell you that **Big Ben** refers to the bell, not the clock; however, in people's hearts, the **Clock Tower** (officially known as **St. Stephen's Tower**), is, and always will be, **Big Ben.** The clock's four dials are 23 feet wide. The hands are each as tall as a red London double-decker bus. The pendulum, which beats once every two seconds, is 13 feet long and weighs 685 pounds. Besides being endearing, the clock is a near-perfect timekeeper. After an extensive restoration a few years ago, the **Clock Tower** emerged several shades lighter and glistening—4,000 books of gold leaf were used to regild the gold surfaces. The initial plan had been to restore the hands to their original color, but when it was found that they were blue (the color of the Conservative party), it was felt that **Big Ben** could not be partisan and they were painted black instead (or so some people say). The hours are struck on the 13.5-ton bell, which was named **Big Ben** allegedly after Sir Benjamin Hall, the first Commissioner of Works when the bell was hung. Since 1885, a light has been shining in the tower at night when Parliament is sitting.

Victoria Tower **Sir Charles Barry** saw the **Palace of Westminster** as a legislative castle and this was to be its great ceremonial entrance. When it was built in 1860, the 336-foot tower was the tallest in the world—taller than early American skyscrapers—and it is still the world's highest square masonry tower. The tower's gateway is the entrance the queen uses for the richly ceremonial State Opening of Parliament each November. It is now an archive of more than three million parliamentary documents dating back to 1497, including the death warrant of Charles I

and a master copy of every Act of Parliament since 1497. During the day, the Union Jack flies when Parliament is sitting, and the Royal Standard is raised when the queen is present.

Statue of Cromwell The godlike statue of Oliver Cromwell caused so much controversy when Sir Hamo Thornycroft finished it in 1899 that Parliament refused to pay for it (mainly due to protests from the Irish Party). Eventually, Lord Rosebery, who was prime minister at the time, paid for the statue personally. Ironically, Cromwell looks straight across the street at the bust of the man he helped do away with—the executed Charles I, whose face is sculpted into the top of the doorway of **St. Margaret's** church.

39 St. Margaret's A few of this church's historical highlights: Sir Walter Raleigh, who was beheaded out front in 1618, is actually buried beneath the altar; Samuel Pepys married a vivacious 15-year-old here in 1655 (he was 22); John Milton married here a year later; and Winston Churchill married here in 1908. The structure was designed in 1523 by **Robert Stowell** (the tower was added in the 18th century), and has been the parish church of the **House of Commons** since 1614. The magnificent Flemish glass window was commissioned by Ferdinand and Isabella of Spain to celebrate the engagement of their daughter Catherine of Aragon to Prince Arthur, the older brother of Henry VIII. By the time the window arrived, Henry had become king and married Catherine—by then his brother's widow. Only Henry VIII is depicted in the window. Almost anywhere else, all this would be quite enough to get one's attention, but this church has the bad luck of being wedged in between the **Houses of Parliament** and **Westminster Abbey,** which steal its thunder a bit.

Treasures in the church include the font, created by Nicholas Stone in 1641; stained-glass windows in the south aisle, completed by artist John Piper in 1967; the west windows, given to the church by Americans; and the Milton window, portraying the blind poet dictating to his daughter. A memorial window to Sir Walter Raleigh, the colonizer of Virginia, quotes the American poet John Greenleaf Whittier: "The New World honours him whose lofty plea/For England's freedom made her own more sure"; and a tablet near the altar urges: "Reader—Should you reflect on his errors/Remember his many virtues/And that he was a mortal."

William Caxton, the father of modern printing, is buried somewhere here; ironically, his grave is unmarked. ♦ M-Sa; Su 1-5PM. St. Margaret St (at Parliament Sq). Tube: Westminster

40 Westminster Abbey This is one of the finest French/English Gothic buildings in the world. Officially called the **Collegiate Church of St.**

Peter, it is also the most faithful and intimate witness of British history. The abbey (depicted below) has survived the Reformation, the Blitz, and, requiring even more miraculous tenacity, nine centuries of visitors, pilgrims, worshipers, wanderers, and tourists.

It is almost impossible to see the abbey without being surrounded by thousands of tourists, either moving aimlessly down the aisles or purposefully following a raised umbrella beneath which a voice reels off *Abbey Highlights.* If possible, come here for a service, when the abbey empties of gawkers and regains some of its serenity. (Note that visitors may not walk around the abbey during services.) In any case, try to avoid it in the morning—unless you attend the blissfully quiet 8AM communion service—when all the guided bus tours in London visit **Westminster Abbey** (even more hectic because they combine a stop here with the Changing of the Guard spectacle).

Once upon a time, this really was an abbey, a monastic community designed for a life of self-sufficient contemplation, with cloisters, refectory, abbot's residence, orchards, workshops, and kitchen gardens. According to legend, the first church was built in the seventh century by Sebert, King of the East Saxons, and St. Peter himself appeared at the consecration. A Benedictine abbey was also founded; it was called **Westminster** ("west church") because it was west of the City of London. The existence of the abbey as it appears today is credited to the inspired determination of Edward the Confessor, who in 1050 set to work on a great monastery to promote the glory of God. In order to supervise the progress of the abbey and efficiently preside over his kingdom of England, he moved his palace next door— hence, the **Palace of Westminster**—and established the bond between church and state that has endured ever since.

Edward the Confessor was brought up in Normandy and built his abbey in a Norman style, advanced far beyond anything that had ever been seen in England. Ill and unable to attend the consecration of his church, which took place on 28 December 1065, the king died a week later. No one knows if his successor, Harold, was crowned here or at **St. Paul's,** but after Harold's death at the Battle of Hastings, William the Conqueror was crowned here on Christmas Day 1066. The ceremony procedure was written down in the 14th century and remains unchanged to this day. Since 1066,

the kings and queens of England have all been crowned here, with two exceptions: Edward V presumed murdered; and Edward VIII, who ascended to the throne upon his father's death but was never crowned, having abdicated because of his relationship with the divorced Wallis Simpson.

In 1245, Henry III rebuilt the now-canonized **St. Edward's Church** in a more magnificent style. Influenced by the French Gothic style of the cathedrals of Amiens and Reims (La Sainte Chapelle in Paris was being built at the same time), Henry started to build, at his own expense, the soaring and graceful church that is here today. The king's architect **Henry de Reyn** (i.e., "of Reims"), worked with great speed in cathedral terms. By 1259, the chancel, transepts, part of the nave, and the chapter house were complete, giving the medieval church a remarkable unity of style. The nave, continued in the late 14th century by **Henry Yevele** (the master mason who built **Westminster Hall**), was built in the style

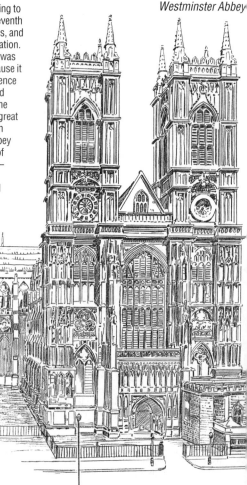

Westminster Abbey

originally planned by **Henry de Reyn.** The only important additions to Henry III's church have been the **Henry VII Chapel,** begun in 1503 and believed by many to be the most beautiful and most perfect building in England, and the towers on the west front, built in the 18th century from the designs of **Wren** and **Nicholas Hawksmoor.** The best way to enter the abbey is under the towers by the **West Door,** where you can take in the majestic height of the roof: 102 feet to the exalted vault, the pale stone touched with gold and tinted by the colored glass of the aisle windows. The eye is pulled upward by the sheer beauty of it all, then immediately distracted by the white-marble figures. (For a general floor plan of the abbey, see page 38.)

Standing at the entrance, you see the impressive length of the stone-flagged nave and the decorated choir screen in front of the nave (some say too gold, too gaudy, too late; it was created by Edward Blore in 1834). Above are 16 Waterford chandeliers presented by the Guinness family in 1965 to mark the 900th anniversary of the consecration of the abbey.

Immediately in front of you, beside the green marble slab honoring Winston Churchill, is the **Tomb of the Unknown Warrior,** a nameless British soldier brought to the abbey from France on 11 November 1920. The flag that covered the coffin hangs nearby, alongside the Congressional Medal of Honor. The poppy-covered coffin contains earth and clay from France, a terrible and moving reminder of a whole generation lost. His was the last full-bodied burial in the abbey.

To your right is **St. George's Chapel,** the **"Warrior's Chapel,"** with an altar by Sir Ninian Comper and a tablet on the west wall commemorating the one million men from the Empire and the Commonwealth who died in World War I. A memorial to Franklin D. Roosevelt hangs here. Just outside the chapel is a haunting portrait of the young Richard II. It is the first genuine portrait of a king painted in his lifetime. The sad brevity of Richard's life seems to show in his face. Looking toward the abbey center, Blore's choir screen jolts a bit. Its bright gold drains the color from Lord Stanhope and Sir Isaac Newton, who are framed within the arches. Near Newton, a bevy of scientists are gathered, including Charles Darwin, who used science to destroy the myth of creation, and Lord Rutherford, who unsettled creation by splitting the atom.

Behind the screen is the choir. The choir stalls are Victorian, but the choir itself has been in this position since Edward the Confessor's own abbey stood on the site. The organ was installed in 1730, but it has been uplifted, rebuilt, and enlarged. Organists at the abbey have been quite distinguished, including Orlando Gibbons, John Blow, and his pupil, the great composer Henry Purcell.

Because the **North Transept** has **Solomon's Porch,** one of the main entrances to the abbey, it is usually thronging with people. Still, persevere until you reach **St. Michael's Chapel** in the east aisle and Roubilliac's monument to Lady Elizabeth Nightingale (no relation to Florence). The poor woman was frightened by lightning and died of a miscarriage. She collapses into her husband's arms, while he, frantic and helpless with fear, watches Death, a wretched skeleton, aim its spear at her. A little beyond this chapel, beside the Blore screen, is the paying entrance to the rest of the abbey, including the royal chapels, the sanctuary, the **Lady Chapel,** and **Poets' Corner.** Kings and queens have been crowned in the sanctuary itself since the time of Richard II in 1377. A platform is created under the central space (the lantern) between the choir and the sanctuary. The **Coronation Chair** is brought from the **Confessor's Chapel** and placed in front of the high altar. Since the coronation of Charles I, the anthem "I was glad when they said unto me/We will go into the House of the Lord" is begun as soon as the sovereign enters the **West Door.** When Queen Elizabeth entered the choir for her coronation in 1953, under the eyes of God and the television cameras, a chorus of "Vivat, vivat, vivat regina Elizabetha" rang out from the voices of **Westminster School**'s scholars. There was an elaborate ceremony of oath taking, a service of holy communion, and anointment with special oil. Then, robed in gold and delivered of ring, scepter, and orb, the queen was crowned by the Archbishop.

To the north are the three finest medieval tombs in the abbey: Edmond Crouchback, Earl of Lancaster and youngest son of Henry III, and his wife, the rich and pretty Aveline of Lancaster. Theirs was the first marriage in the new abbey in 1269. The third grave belongs to Amyer de Valence, Earl of Pembroke.

Behind the high altar is the **Shrine of Edward the Confessor.** This is the most sacred part of the abbey, the destination of pilgrims, particularly on St. Edward's Day (13 October). The Purbeck marble tomb contains the body of the king-turned-saint. Beside him lie Henry III, who built the church in homage to the Confessor; Henry's son Edward I, the first king to be crowned in the present building; and his beloved Queen Eleanor of Provence, for whom he set up what became known as the Eleanor Crosses (the original Charing Cross was one). The crosses marked the places where her funeral cortège stopped to rest along the way from Lincoln to the abbey.

The **Coronation Chair,** when not in use for coronations, stands behind the high altar. Built in 1300, the wooden chair was designed to incorporate the **Stone of Scone** (pronounced *Skoon*) but there is an empty space there now. In 1996, the stone—which had been part of the Scottish throne since the ninth century but

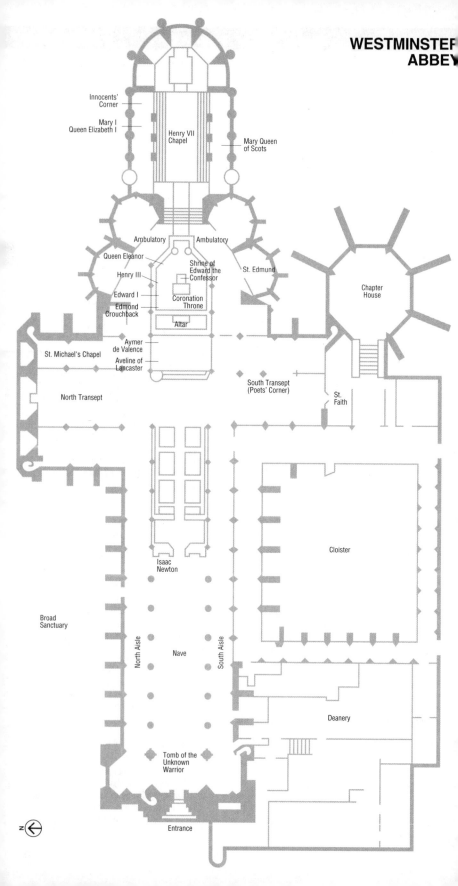

WESTMINSTER ABBEY

Innocents' Corner

Mary I / Queen Elizabeth I

Henry VII Chapel

Mary Queen of Scots

Ambulatory

Ambulatory

Queen Eleanor

Shrine of Edward the Confessor

St. Edmund

Henry III

Edward I

Coronation Throne

Edmond Crouchback

Chapter House

Altar

Aymer de Valence

St. Michael's Chapel

Aveline of Lancaster

South Transept (Poets' Corner)

North Transept

St. Faith

Isaac Newton

Cloister

Broad Sanctuary

North Aisle

South Aisle

Nave

Deanery

Tomb of the Unknown Warrior

Entrance

N

was spirited out of Scotland by Edward I in 1297 and placed in the chair—was ceremoniously returned and is now on display in Edinburgh Castle. The Stone in the Throne represented the union of the two countries, a union that, even 600 years later, is not without resistance. (The stone was even stolen from the abbey for a few weeks by Scottish nationalists in 1952.) The graffiti on the throne is blamed on 18th-century schoolboys from **Westminster School**. A truly wonderful part of the abbey is the **Henry VII Chapel** (officially, the **Lady Chapel**). Except in high summer, the chapel is quieter and less crowded than the rest of the building—a blessing, as this is one of the most beautiful places you may ever see. Notice the exquisite tracery of the fan vaulting, intricacies, and ecstasies of stone, Matisse-like in their exuberance; the high, wooden choir stalls that line the nave—and their misericords (carvings located beneath the seats), including a woman beating her husband, and mermaids, mermen, and monkeys; the black-and-white marble floor; and throughout, the royal badges, a kind of illustrated Shakespeare of Tudor roses, leopards of England, the fleur-de-lys of France, the portcullis of the Beauforts, greyhounds, falcons, and daisy roots. This is the Renaissance in England, and Heaven is on Earth in a world alive with confidence, harmony, beauty, and art. The chapel is the grand farewell to the great Gothic style, and forms the perfect setting for flags of the Order of the Bath, the chivalrous knights whose tradition dates back to 1399.

In the aisles on both sides of the chapel are a few unforgettable tombs. In the south aisle rests the effigy of Lady Margaret Beaufort, created by Torrigiani. The mother of Henry VII, she was a remarkable Renaissance woman devoted to education, the arts, and the journey of her soul. Her effigy, one of the finest in the abbey, shows a delicately lined face with gentle sensitivity. "Having restored religion to its original sincerity, established peace, restored money to its proper value . . ." Most world leaders would give anything to merit an epitaph like that, but it seems rather an understatement for Queen Elizabeth I. Her four-poster tomb in the north aisle reflects Gloriana gloriously, although ironically she is buried with her half-sister, Mary I, who imprisoned her in the **Tower of London**. (And as if that weren't enough, Mary, Queen of Scots, who was beheaded at Elizabeth's order, is buried nearby, too. Her tomb is directly across the way on the south side of the chapel.)

In **Innocents' Corner**, at the end of the aisle, are effigies of the two infant daughters of James I: Sophia, under her velvet coverlet, died at birth; and Mary, leaning on one elbow, died at age two. Both look like small dolls. Close by lie the bones of two children found in the **Tower** and brought here by order of Charles II in 1674. They are believed to be

Edward V and his brother Richard, sons of Edward IV and allegedly murdered by their uncle Richard III in 1483.

In 1889, Henry James came to **Westminster Abbey** for the memorial service of Robert Browning, whose ashes were being consigned to **Poets' Corner**. Afterward he wrote that Browning stood for "the thing that, as a race, we like best—the fascination of faith, the acceptance of life, the respect for its mysteries, the endurance of its charges, the vitality of will, the validity of character, the beauty of action, the seriousness, above all, of the great human passion." James's testimony to Browning seems a perfect testimony to Anglo-Saxon England, **Westminster Abbey,** and above all, to its **Poets' Corner,** where the recognition is the greatest a generous nation has to confer. Despite its name, this section is not a corner (it fills an entire transept on the south side of the nave), nor is it exclusively devoted to poets (it pays tribute to other writers, musicians, and performing artists).

All those honored here are not buried here, although Charles Dickens is (against his wishes), as is Thomas Hardy (but his heart is buried in his beloved Dorset). The honored include Geoffrey Chaucer, Edmund Spenser, Ben Jonson (who is buried upright elsewhere in the abbey!), William Shakespeare, John Milton, John Dryden, Dr. Samuel Johnson, Thomas Gray, Richard Brinsley Sheridan, Oliver Goldsmith, William Blake, William Wordsworth, Samuel Taylor Coleridge, Percy Bysshe Shelley, John Keats, Thomas Babington Macaulay, Jane Austen, the Brontë sisters, Sir Walter Scott, William Makepeace Thackeray, Henry Wadsworth Longfellow, John Ruskin, Rudyard Kipling, Lord Byron, George Eliot, Dylan Thomas, W.H. Auden, D.H. Lawrence, Lewis Carroll, Gerard Manley Hopkins, and Henry James. One of the newest stones, a memorial to the writers of World War I, was unveiled on 11 November 1985. Among those mentioned are Rupert Brooke, Robert Graves, Herbert Read, Siegfried Sassoon, and William Owen. Above the dates 1914-1918 is a quotation from Owen: "My subject is War, and the pity of War. The poetry is in the pity." And the ashes of Lord Olivier, one of the finest British actors, were interred in 1990—a fitting tribute to this well-loved artist.

Ninety-minute Supertours of the nave, choir, **Statesman's Aisle, Poets' Corner, Royal Chapels**, and **Coronation Chair** are offered Monday through Friday at 10AM, 11AM, 2PM, and 3PM and Saturday at 10AM, 11AM, and 12:30PM. (The **Jericho Parlour** and **Jerusalem Chamber** can be seen only on this tour.) Reservations should be made in the south aisle of the nave. *Note: Photography is not allowed in the abbey.* ◆ Admission for tours. Tours: M-Sa. Services: M-F 7:30AM, 8AM, 12:30PM, 5PM; Sa 8AM, 9:20AM, 3PM;

Su 8AM, 10AM, 11:15AM, 3PM, 6:30PM. The Sanctuary (off Broad Sanctuary). 222.7110. Tube: Westminster, St. James's Park

Within Westminster Abbey:

Abbey Bookshop Just inside the main entrance, to the right, is the official abbey shop, where you can buy books, postcards, drawings—and even **Westminster Abbey** fudge. ◆ M-Sa. 222.5565

Chapter House From 1257 until Henry VIII's reign, this exquisite octagon with a Purbeck marble roof (completed in 1250) served as the **Parliament House** for the Commons. ◆ Admission. Daily. 222.5897

Pyx Chamber Built circa 1090 and once the monastery treasury, this structure passed to the Crown during the Dissolution. Today, it contains the oldest altar in the abbey, dating from circa 1240. The word "pyx" referred to the large wooden chests that once held the standard gold and silver pieces against which coins were annually tested. ◆ Admission. Daily. 223.0019

Great Cloister The courtyard offers a breathtaking view of the flying buttresses on the south side of the **Lady Chapel.** There is a coffee stall and a brass-rubbing center. ◆ M-Sa. 930.9306

Abbey Museum The wax and wooden effigies in this 11th-century holy equivalent of **Madame Tussaud's** were used for lyings-in-state and funerals. In fact, the clothes are not costumes but the real thing, including Nelson's famous hat with its green eye patch. ◆ Admission. Daily. 223.0019

Beside Westminster Abbey:

Dean's Yard This is the point where Parliament meets public school. You can go through the iron gate to the charming tree-shaded yard behind the abbey. The yard and the buildings of **Westminster School** are also in **Little Dean's Yard,** which can be viewed through an arch on the square's east side, and are not normally open to the public; however, visits may be arranged (but are limited during term time). Write well in advance to The Domestic Bursar, Westminster School, Dean's Yard, London SW1P 3PF. The gate at the back of **Dean's Yard** leads to tranquil Great College Street, dating from 1722.

Broad Sanctuary The west entrance of **Westminster Abbey** (the usual entrance for visitors) faces an area known as **Broad Sanctuary.** This takes its name from the section surrounding the west side of the abbey, which gave fugitives a safe haven from civil law in the Middle Ages. The most famous asylum seeker was probably Elizabeth Woodville, wife of Edward IV, who came here with her sons, the sad and tragic Little Princes. ◆ Between Parliament Sq and Victoria St. Tube: Westminster

41 Abbey Garden This quiet and simply laid-out 900-year-old garden (said to be the oldest cultivated garden in England) is known for its lavender. In July and August, there are lunchtime band concerts. ◆ Nominal admission. Tu, Th. Great College St and College Mews. Tube: Westminster, St. James's Park

42 Jewel Tower In 1365-66, Edward III had the tower built, probably by **Henry Yevele,** to hold his jewels, silver and gold vessels, clothes, and furs—a sort of glorified warehouse. This surviving part of the original royal **Palace of Westminster** has a chunky look with narrow, round-arched windows—this is also how the abbey looked before it was rebuilt in the Gothic style we see today. It houses the permanent exhibition, *Parliament Past and Present.* ◆ Admission. Daily. Closed 1-2PM Nov-March. Abingdon St (at Old Palace Yd). 222.2219. Tube: Westminster

43 Victoria Tower Gardens These gardens overlooking the Thames are ideal for a picnic lunch or an afternoon nap. Two varying principles of heroism can be found in the sculpture: A.G. Walker's statue of Emmeline Pankhurst, the leader of the women's suffrage movement, who lived from 1858 to 1928 and was often imprisoned for her beliefs; and a replica (1915) of Rodin's *Burghers of Calais* (1895), a monument to those who surrendered to Edward III in 1347 rather than see their town destroyed. ◆ Off Millbank (between Lambeth Bridge and Abingdon St). Tube: Westminster

44 St. John's, Smith Square Itzhak Perlman and Yo-Yo Ma have given lunchtime concerts in this church, along with the **Allegri, Endymion,** and **Amadeus Quartets** and the **Academy of London Orchestra.** The musical reputation is high indeed. The church was built in 1728 by **Thomas Archer** and is original, idiosyncratic, and personal. After near destruction by bombs in 1941, it was rebuilt in 1965-69 by architect **Marshall Sisson.** ◆ Smith Sq (bounded by Dean Stanley and Dean Trench Sts, and Dean Bradley and Lord North Sts). 222.2168, box office 222.1061. Tube: St. James's Park, Westminster

Within St. John's, Smith Square:

Footstool ★★$$ Hidden in the brick-built crypt of **St. John's** is a pleasant, cozy restaurant where you can observe the parliamentary lobbyists at rest and at play, as well as the powers behind the political parties lunching or nibbling quiche at the self-service wine bar. ◆ Continental ◆ M-F lunch; dinner on concert evenings. 222.2779

45 Lambeth Bridge Built in 1929-32, this ornate bridge replaced the one erected in 1861. Before any bridge spanned the Thames here, there was a ferry to carry horses across the river, with the money going to the Archbishop of Canterbury. However, his moneymaking operation came to a halt when the first **Westminster Bridge** opened downriver in 1750—by an act of Parliament, he was compensated for his loss of income in the amount of £2,205. ♦ Between Lambeth Palace Rd and Millbank. Tube: Westminster

46 Lambeth Palace The London home of the Archbishop of Canterbury, the religious head of the Church of England for 800 years, the palace is mostly hidden behind high walls. However, visible from the riverfront are some 14th- and 15th-century towers. The most important, **Lollard's Tower,** was where, during the reign of Cromwell, the royalist poet Sir Richard Lovelace was imprisoned and wrote the famous line "Stone walls do not a prison make, nor iron bars a cage." Facing **St. Mary's** church nearby is **Morton's Tower and Gate,** dating from 1485 and an outstanding example of an early Tudor brick building; it is still used as the main entrance to the palace. The palace is not open to the public. ♦ Lambeth Palace Rd (between Lambeth Rd and Royal St). Tube: Westminster, Lambeth North

47 Museum of Garden History This unusual museum, which opened in 1979 in the deconsecrated 14th-century church of **St. Mary's-at-Lambeth,** next to **Lambeth Palace,** features an exhibition on the origins of domestic, decorative gardening. The subject is of avid interest to most English householders, whether they have a flower-bedecked London balcony or a country cottage garden. During the 17th century, plant pioneers John Tradescant and his son brought back such specimens as spiderwort, larch, and jasmine among rare beauties gathered during their world travels. Father and son are buried in the graveyard, which boasts a knot-garden devoted to the plants they acquired. As it happens, Captain William Bligh of *Bounty* fame, who was a local resident, is also buried here; it seems appropriate because he, too, searched for plants—his ship was carrying breadfruit when the mutiny occurred in 1789.

The museum has expanded down the road with the **Garden at the Ark** (named for the Tradescants' home), a stylish landscaped site where modern gardening and landscaping techniques are displayed. ♦ Free. Museum of Garden History: M-F, Su Mar-Dec. The Garden at the Ark: W and the first Sunday Apr-Oct. Lambeth Palace Rd (at Lambeth Rd). 401.8865. Tube: Westminster, Lambeth North

48 Imperial War Museum Despite its formidable name, this huge museum devoted to the warfare of the 20th century also features interesting exhibits about the social and domestic aspects of the wars: fashions, cooking, morale boosting, and propaganda. The *Blitz Experience* lives up to its name, re-creating the noise, smoke, and blaring searchlights during the bombings as Londoners sheltered in the Underground. Aircraft, tanks, and artillery are on display plus photographs and paintings. There's an airy, cheerful cafe and a shop with some amusing cards and souvenirs. ♦ Admission. Daily. Lambeth Rd (between St. George's and Kennington Rds). 416.5321. Tube: Lambeth North

TateGallery

49 Tate Gallery This wonderful gallery (pictured on page 42) remains accessible and welcoming despite its vast collection of more than 4,000 paintings, 50,000 prints and unique works on paper, and over 1,000 sculptures, not to mention 200 new acquisitions annually. Unable to show all its works at once, the **Tate** rotates the displays so that those in storage are made available and there is always something different to discover. The gallery's threefold collection comprises international 20th-century art, British art from 1550 to the present, and the **Turner Bequest** or **Collection.** Happily, an enormous amount of extra gallery space was being created as we went to press at the new **Tate Gallery of Modern Art** at Bankside (see end of this entry).

The **Tate Gallery** began life through the generosity of Sir Henry Tate (of the sugar manufacturer Tate & Lyle), who donated his collection of 70 "modern" British paintings and sculptures and offered to pay for a building to house it. A vacant lot on the River Thames at Millbank was acquired (it had been previously occupied by the Millbank Penitentiary, a so-called model prison based on the ideas of the philosopher and social reformer Jeremy Bentham). The wedding-cake building with a majestic entrance, designed by **Sidney J.R. Smith,** opened in 1897. Its formative years were spent as a kind of annex of the **National Gallery,** but a formal, albeit friendly, divorce took place in 1955, and the **Tate** became independent. In 1979, the northwest extension was created by **Michael Huskstepp.** Although the **Tate**'s collection used to overlap with that of the **National Gallery,** that problem was solved with a formal agreement in September 1996. The directors of the two galleries decreed that the principal dividing date between their respective collections of foreign art would be 1900, and the galleries exchanged the relevant paintings to reflect this dateline.

The **Tate**'s foreign collection now focuses firmly on the 20th century, while its French Impressionist works have been transferred to the **National Gallery.** In turn, from the **National** the **Tate** received post-1900 works, including Cézanne's *Grounds of the Château Noir;* Gustav Klimt's *Portrait of Hermine Gallia;* Matisse's *Portrait of Greta Moll;* Monet's *Water-Lilies;* Picasso's *Fruit Dish, Bottle and Violin;* Pissarro's *The Louvre under*

Snow; and Renoir's *Dancing Girl with Tambourine.* Additional 20th-century art here includes works by Kokoschka, Léger, Masson, Edvard Munch *(The Sick Child),* Kandinsky, Mondrian, and Malevich. Rodin's large marble carving, *The Kiss,* made a few years after the version in the Musée Rodin, is one of the most popular pieces in the gallery. Abstract, Expressionist, and Figurative developments in art include works by American artists from the 1940s and 1950s such as de Kooning, Newman, Pollock, and Rothko. From the 1960s are such Pop Art icons as Andy Warhol's *Marilyn Diptych* and Lichtenstein's *Whaam!* The **Tate**'s British collection will always include the great names: William Blake, William Hogarth, Joshua Reynolds, Thomas Gainsborough, John Constable, George Stubbs, David Hockney, and the Pre-Raphaelites, who are the most popular painters here. The large, elegant central galleries, which usually contain sculpture, draw crowds when the exhibits for the Turner Prize are on display. Featuring primarily controversial young artists, works include sculpture, painting, and photography.

The **Turner Bequest** is among the great treasures London offers its citizens and visitors, and one of the truly remarkable collections of the work of a single artist. At his death in 1851, J.M.W. Turner left his personal collection of nearly 300 paintings and 20,000 watercolors and drawings to the nation, with the request that they be kept together. His wish was only partially fulfilled, with some rooms devoted to his oil paintings. Now the entire collection is housed in the **Clore Gallery,** designed in 1987 by **James Stirling** and **Michael Wilford & Associates** and situated next door to the main building. The paintings are top-lit with natural daylight—the kind of light, with all its varied and changeable qualities, in which the artist expected his pictures to be exhibited. Works on paper (watercolors and drawings) hang in galleries where daylight is kept out in order to prevent the fading of the images. Not only have the architects taken great care to see that the art is sympathetically displayed and scientifically preserved, they have also made it possible for visitors to glimpse the River Thames as they stroll past the pictures. The Thames played a prominent part in Turner's life and art—he painted it, and he lived and died on its banks in Chelsea.

As of May 2000 the present building at Millbank will be renamed the **Tate Gallery of British Art,** adding new exhibition space for major artists such as Hogarth, Blake, Constable, Bacon, and Spencer, while the entire foreign collection, together with much 20th-century British art, moves to the South Bank, and the new **Tate Gallery of Modern Art.** The new building, converted from **Sir Giles Gilbert Scott**'s **Bankside Power Station** by Swiss firm **Herzog & de Meuron** is at 25 Sumner Street (between Holland and Park Sts), 401.7302

Audio guides to new displays and to the **Turner Bequest** are available. *Tate Gallery: An Illustrated Companion*, by Simon Wilson, describes 300 works. The **Tate**'s 1997 centenary sparked off other publications, including *An Illustrated History of the Tate Gallery* by Frances Spalding.
♦ Free. Admission for certain exhibitions. Daily. Millbank (at Atterbury St). 887.8000; www.tate.org.uk. Tube: Pimlico

Tate Gallery

Within the Tate Gallery:

Tate Gallery Restaurant ★★★$$

This restaurant is known for two things: the romantic and beautiful Rex Whistler mural *Expedition in Pursuit of Rare Meats*, painted in 1926-27, and the wine list, which still retains its reputation for good vintages at good prices. It is definitely not a place to rush lunch. Order a rare vintage to go with your terrine of duck foie gras with a green bean salad followed by roasted chicken with morels. ♦ British ♦ M-Sa lunch. Reservations required. 887.8877; fax 887.8902

Tate Gallery Shop On sale here are superbly printed postcards, excellent books, T-shirts with depictions of the museum's masterpieces, canvas bags, prints, posters, and specially commissioned items. Framing is also done on the premises. ♦ M-Sa; Su 2-5:40PM. 887.8876

Coffee Shop ★$ This self-service eatery features good game pies, pâtés, salads, and wine. The cakes, pastries, coffee, and tea make this a popular place; expect to share your table. ♦ Coffee shop ♦ Daily lunch, tea, and early dinner. 887.8000

50 Vauxhall Cross As you leave the **Tate Gallery,** if you look diagonally across the Thames, next to Vauxhall Bridge, you'll see an extraordinary yellow-and-green building that appears to be a modern fortress. It is, in fact, the headquarters of MI6, one of the government's secret service departments (James Bond was MI5). Notice how well its concrete facade fits its role, from the bunker effect of the lower floors to the menacing spiked windows higher up. Designed by **Terry Farrell** and completed in 1993, it has an impenetrable look with no hint of human activity inside. The building is closed to the public. ♦ Albert Embankment (at Vauxhall Bridge). Tube: Pimlico

Bests

Peter Conway
Chief Executive, Restaurateurs Association of Great Britain

The **Theatre Museum** in **Covent Garden** will cost less than the shops.

Hogarth's *Rake's Progress* sequence of paintings in **Sir John Soane's Museum** will take your breath away.

Apsley House has the capital's smartest address (at No. 1 London) but now houses the **Wellington Museum** at **Hyde Park Corner.**

Florence Nightingale's brave exploits are on display in the undercroft of **St. Thomas' Hospital.**

The **Wallace Collection** in **Hertford House** includes the famous canvas *The Laughing Cavalier.*

The **Bank of England Museum** tells why London is such an important financial capital.

The **National Portrait Gallery** is a kaleidoscope of British royal history and the personalities on the throne.

Join the congregation at **St. Bartholomew the Great** in **Smithfield** (founded 1123), the oldest church in London (except for the chapel in the **Tower** itself).

Drop in at **St. Martin-in-the-Fields,** James Gibbs's masterpiece overlooking **Trafalgar Square.**

Temple Church in the **Inns of Court**—the round church—is exceptional both in its design and history.

Sir Thomas More is the leading figure connected with **Chelsea Old Church,** but a tablet has been raised to Henry James.

St. Margaret's Westminster stands next to the **Abbey** and has been the venue of many society weddings, including Winston Churchill's. Wonderful service on Christmas Eve.

London is now recognized as the "eating out capital" of Western Europe—even by the French. Styles of cuisine available are too numerous to list and dozens of guides and magazine articles compete for the customer's attention.

Simpsons-in-the-Strand offers the typical British breakfast—in all its variety—cooked to perfection.

For tea, the **Waldorf-Astoria** (Aldwych) and the **Ritz** (Piccadilly) are the best in town. At the weekend the **Waldorf** excels by offering an organized tea dance—probably the only one left in the capital.

Harvey Nichols has taken over as the spot for "ladies who lunch."

The **Crypt** of **St. Paul's Cathedral** now offers a splendid cafeteria. Ideal place to relax before heading to the **Tower of London** in the afternoon.

Smollensky's on the Strand is a convenient venue for ravenous teenagers after the sight-seeing circuit begins to pall.

Still a firm favorite for steak and chips, **Chez Gérard** in **Charlotte Street** came top of the poll held by the *Evening Standard* in March 1997.

Libby MacNamara
Director, Association of British Orchestras

The best thing about London is the extraordinary richness and diversity of its music. The **Royal Festival Hall, Royal Albert Hall, Barbican,** and so many other venues are host to our five world-class symphony orchestras, a whole range of chamber orchestras, specialist groups, and ensembles. London is the music capital of the world. On any night of the week, all year round, you have a choice of concerts; and the **BBC** Proms each summer at the **Royal Albert Hall** are a legend! Anyone who loves music can't fail to love London.

St. James's

St. James's (pronounced by Londoners with two syllables as "Jameses") is all about mystery and history, royalty and aristocracy, pomp and civilized circumstance, and kings, queens, gentlemen, and ladies. In this elegant, anachronistic enclave, time seems to have stood still. Gentlemen still go to their clubs, an unchallenged English custom; shoes are still made with painstaking care for royal feet and hats sewn seamlessly for aristocratic heads; and when the queen is home at **Buckingham Palace**, the royal standard flies. This neighborhood provides one of the most agreeable walks in London, where visitors can gaze around at a portrait of England and Englishness utterly unchanged by war, development, mass production, pollution, or the European Community. It's the England of history books and literature, heroes and heroines, George Meredith and Oscar Wilde, and fashionable Edward VII.

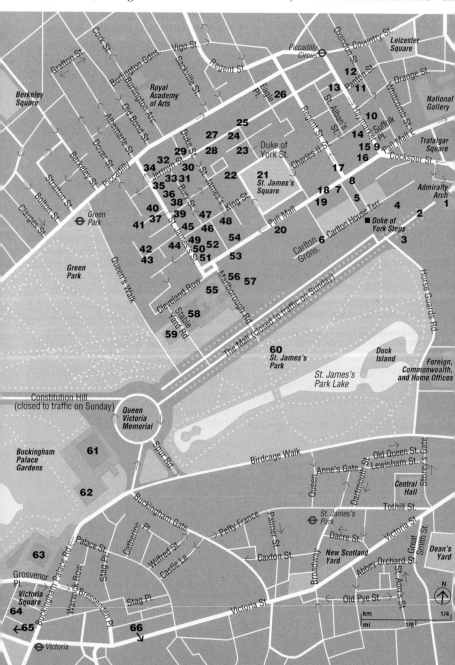

Amid the Champagne and syllabub, however, egalitarians and feminists will perceive two ancient phenomena: the segregation of the classes and the segregation of the sexes (although a few enlightened "gentlemen's clubs" have begun accepting women as members).

You can begin the journey at a monument to the uppermost echelon of society, **Admiralty Arch**, designed as a tribute from Edward VII to his mother, Queen Victoria. Proceed to **Jermyn Street**, where window-shopping is like viewing museum exhibits and the prices can reach old master figures. In an area no larger than a football field, you can have a pair of shoes especially made to fit your feet, purchase the most handsome and most expensive pipe you'll ever own, and have a tailor take your measurements for custom-made shirts (with a minimum order of six and a minimum wait of six weeks). You can buy cheddars, stiltons, wensleydales, and caerphillys in **Paxton & Whitfield**, a shop that may convince you the French are only the second-best cheese producers in the world. You can choose wild hyacinth bath oil from a famous perfumery **(Floris)** or Ajaccio Violet cologne from a regal perfumery/barbershop **(Trumper's)**, drink excellent ale in a truly Victorian pub (the **Red Lion**), or dine in one of the trendy restaurants that have infiltrated this bastion of tradition **(Quaglino's, The Avenue).** You'll see where kings and queens lived before they moved to **Buckingham Palace** and gaze at the windows of **St. James's Palace**, where Prince Charles resides. Afterward, have a look at some of the treasures from the **Royal Collection** (displayed at **Buckingham Palace** and the **Queen's Gallery**), check out the royal horses and coaches, and end the day beside the shimmering lake in **St. James's Park**, London's oldest and perhaps most romantic greensward, where Charles II walked his spaniels.

St. James's on a Saturday feels like a Sunday. The streets are empty, despite the fact that most of the shops are open. If you want to watch the Changing of the Guard ceremony at **Buckingham Palace**, call for the schedule (0839/123411) and get there half an hour early. There are few places for visitors to wait out drizzles near the royal palaces, so bring your umbrella if the sky looks threatening. The ceremony is canceled in very rainy weather.

City code 0171 unless otherwise noted.

1 Admiralty Arch The inglorious car race around Trafalgar Square doesn't prepare you for this grand Corinthian structure in Portland stone, which is actually a screen with five arches: the center arch, whose iron gates open only for ceremonial processions; two side arches for automobile traffic; and two smaller arches for pedestrians. Created by **Sir Aston Webb** in 1910, its very monumentality is a surprise because it is so un-London. This structure marks the first part of the royal processional route from **Buckingham Palace** to **St. Paul's Cathedral**. The structure was part of Edward VII's tribute to his mother, Queen Victoria, although the king himself died before the memorial was completed. ♦ The Mall (between Trafalgar Sq and Horse Guards Rd). Tube: Charing Cross

2 The Mall Two double rows of plane trees line this royal processional (pronounced to rhyme with "pal") road, which sweeps theatrically to a monumental climax. Laid out after the Restoration in 1660, the stretch from Trafalgar Square to **Buckingham Palace** was originally an enclosed alley for playing *paille maille* (a French game similar to croquet, called "pell mell" by the English). It was transformed to give a formal vista of **Buckingham Palace** by **Sir Aston Webb** in 1910 as part of a memorial to Queen Victoria. The present Mall runs just south of the original promenade, now used as a bridle path. On Sunday, the Mall partially closes to traffic, so strolling is more pleasant. ♦ Between Trafalgar Sq and Buckingham Palace. Tube: Charing Cross, Piccadilly Circus

3 The Citadel The enveloping ivy generates an air of mystery around what is actually a bomb shelter, built in 1940 for naval officers. Scrupulously maintained by the Parks Department, which mows the acre of grass on top, it serves as a reminder of the past era, before bomb technology made shelters like this obsolete. ♦ The Mall (at Horse Guards Rd). Tube: Charing Cross, Piccadilly Circus

Restaurants/Clubs: Red   Hotels: Blue

Shops/🌳 Outdoors: Green   Sights/Culture: Black

4 Carlton House Terrace These creamy white, glossy buildings on this little street parallel to the Mall are among the last contributions **John Nash** made to London before his death in 1835. Actually, it's the graceful backs of the buildings that face **The Mall.** The 1,000-footlong terrace is a stately confection of Corinthian columns and human-scale arches; the former were evidently inspired by **Jacques-Ange Gabriel**'s buildings in the Place de la Concorde. The clean outline, intercepted in the center by the **Duke of York Steps,** is a splendid contribution to **The Mall:** an impressive backdrop for royal processions by day, a royal wedding cake when floodlit at night.

Erected between 1827 and 1832, **Carlton House Terrace** replaced **Carlton House,** the palatial home purchased in 1732 by Frederick, Prince of Wales, who died before his father, George II. It was subsequently owned by George III, and then by his son, the prince regent, who transformed it at staggering expense into what was considered the most beautiful mansion in England. But after being crowned King George IV, he and **Nash** agreed to demolish **Carlton House** and convinced Parliament to allocate funds for the conversion of **Buckingham House** into **Buckingham Palace.** The columns were saved and recycled into the portico of the **National Gallery,** and **Nash** was asked to design the buildings seen today. Originally, the terrace was to line both sides of **The Mall,** providing grand town houses for the aristocracy; only one side was built, leaving **St. James's Park** on view. ♦ The Mall (between Trafalgar Sq and Duke of York Steps). Tube: Charing Cross, Piccadilly Circus

Within Carlton House Terrace:

MALL
GALLERIES

Mall Galleries These rooms exhibit traditional paintings by members of the Royal Society of Portrait Painters and the Federation of British Artists. Here is one of the few London venues to show work by well-established British artists such as Tom Coates and Claire Spencer alongside that of up-and-coming students and young unknown painters. There are regular workshops and demonstrations. ♦ Admission. Daily. 930.6844

At the dissolution of the monasteries, Henry VIII seized Hyde Park from the monks of Westminster and converted it into a hunting park.

Institute of Contemporary Arts (ICA) Founded in 1947, this lively arts center has an industrious, avant-garde atmosphere. Its three galleries exhibit British and foreign photography, architectural drawings, paintings, and event art, among other works. In the evening, interesting foreign and cult movies are shown in the cinema, while experimental films, videos, and works by new filmmakers are screened in the **Cinémathèque**, and cutting-edge plays are performed in the theater. There is always a buzz of artistic activity here, although some of the programs have been cut back due to budget constraints. Even if you don't take in a performance here, visit the first-rate bookshop, which has all the latest art books as well as magazines, postcards, and recent works by avant-garde novelists.

In order to see the exhibitions or even to have a drink at the bar or a cup of coffee at the **ICA Cafe** (see below), you must buy a day membership for a nominal fee. The exhibitions are known for highlighting new, provocative artists; the galleries featured the first solo show of Damien Hirst well before he won the **Tate**'s Turner Prize. ♦ Admission. Arts center: M noon-11PM; Tu-Sa noon-1AM, including the bar; Su noon-11PM, bar to 9PM. Galleries: M-Th, Sa-Su noon-7:30PM; F noon-9PM. Bookshop: Daily noon-9PM. 930.0493, bookshop 925.2434, box office 930.3647

Within the Institute of Contemporary Arts (ICA):

ICA Cafe ★$ Enjoy an Italian or vegetarian meal with a cold beer (such as Rolling Rock, Becks, or Pils) at the bar upstairs while you indulge in a spot of people watching or listen to the arty talk from the nearest table. ♦ Italian/Vegetarian ♦ Daily lunch and dinner. 930.8535

Royal Society Formed in the 1640s and formalized by King Charles II in 1660, this society is one of the most distinguished scientific bodies in the world. In the 17th century, it was a hub of scientific discovery, where Newton, Halley, Dryden, and Pepys chatted about inventions, although Pepys, then president, never understood Newton's *Principia.* Past presidents include Sir Christopher Wren, Davy, Huxley, Thomson, Rutherford, and Fleming. Today, the society gives medals annually for original research in many scientific fields; however, it is closed to the public. ♦ 6 Carlton House Terr. 839.5561

5 Waterloo Place One of the few pieces of town planning in London is also one of the most impressive. **John Nash** designed it in

1816 to commemorate the Duke of Wellington's triumph over the French the previous year. It marks the beginning of **Nash**'s triumphal route to **Regent's Park. Carlton House Terrace** frames Waterloo Place, which intersects Pall Mall on its way north into lower Regent Street and Piccadilly Circus. ♦ Between Carlton House Terr and Pall Mall. Tube: Charing Cross, Piccadilly Circus

At Waterloo Place:

Duke of York Steps and Duke of York Monument

Benjamin Dean Wyatt's dramatic column, built in 1834, dominates Waterloo Place. The seven-ton bronze monument here, dedicated to Frederick, the second son of George III, was financed by withholding one day's pay from all soldiers. Made by Sir Richard Westmacott, the statue of the duke stands on a pedestal that soars 137 feet into the sky; since the duke died owing £2 million, some quipped that the pink-granite column was meant to keep him out of reach of his creditors.

Statue of Edward VII

In front of the **Duke of York Steps** and facing **Waterloo Place** is Edward VII, looking hale and beefy, as Sir Bertram MacKennal immortalized him in 1921. Because of the long life of his mother, Queen Victoria, the king reigned for only 9 of his 69 years, but in that short time he inspired the Edwardian Age: a secure, elegant period for the rich and aristocratic, a world where to amuse and be amused were raisons d'être. He contributed color and pageantry to the monarchy, but he also brought a sense of serious commitment to such issues as the quality of workers' lives and the treatment of Indians by English officials. Edward was aware that beyond Europe lay his empire, the largest the world had ever known. As king, he created the entente cordiale with France and used his considerable diplomatic skill and charm to ease the conflicts between Germany and England, conflicts that were tragically too deep for any monarch to resolve. However, he is best remembered for his voracious appetite: at his last formal dinner at **Buckingham Palace,** on 5 March 1910, he made his way through nine dishes, including salmon steak, grilled chicken, saddle of mutton, and several snipe stuffed with foie gras. He died two months later. To this day, souvenirs of the Edwardian Age are still tucked away in the small streets nearby.

6 Carlton Gardens During World War II, the Free French occupied **No. 4,** where de Gaulle's message to his countrymen is inscribed on a plaque. ♦ Off Pall Mall. Tube: Charing Cross, Piccadilly Circus

7 Athenaeum Club This most august of the gentlemen's clubs occupies one of the most distinguished buildings in London. Completed in 1830, it was designed by **Decimus Burton,** the man who gave London **Constitution Arch** and the screen at the entrance to **Hyde Park.** The cream stucco facade has pure architectural dignity. A Wedgwood-like frieze wraps around the building above the first-floor windows; it is worth noting because it is a reconstruction of the one that adorned the Parthenon (the extraordinary original remnants are in their own display room at the **British Museum**). A large gilded figure of Pallas Athena, goddess of wisdom, practical skills, and prudent warfare, graces the porch and accurately sets the standards for those who enter—bishops, scientists, and the top brains of the Civil Service and Foreign Office.

Inside, the atmosphere is one of intimidating sagacity. A portrait of member Charles Darwin broods over the living. The Royal Society's Dining Society, an elite group within the formidably elite Royal Society, meets here, and those within that clever and select circle are de facto members of the **Athenaeum,** which was named after the emperor Hadrian's university in Rome. The club is not open to the public. ♦ 107 Pall Mall (at Waterloo Pl). Tube: Charing Cross, Piccadilly Circus

8 Institute of Directors The **United Service Club,** known as the **Senior,** was founded in 1815 for the triumphant officers of the Napoleonic wars and inhabited this structure for 150 years. The first building commissioned by a club, it was originally designed by **John Nash** in 1828, but most noticeable are the alterations carried out by **Decimus Burton:** the Doric columns and the Corinthian portico. The granite mounting block outside on **Waterloo Place** was put there by Wellington to help short men mount their horses.

The **Senior** collapsed in 1974. Today it is a business center for the Institute of Directors but it still has the 19th-century furniture designed for the club (including a 15-foot chandelier presented by George IV to commemorate the Battle of Waterloo), and it retains an inimitably masculine atmosphere of mahogany and leather. It is closed to visitors. ♦ 116 Pall Mall (at Waterloo Pl). 839.1233. Tube: Charing Cross, Piccadilly Circus

9 Haymarket A 17th-century market that supplied the horses of the Royal Mews, when the mews were on Trafalgar Square, gave this street its name. The market was placed here after Lord St. Albans was ordered to move it from Mayfair because of the filth that resulted from the cattle and sheep for sale. A market of some kind remained at Haymarket until the early 1800s. ♦ Between Pall Mall and Coventry St. Tube: Piccadilly Circus, Charing Cross

10 Theatre Royal Haymarket The theater has been officially named the **Theatre Royal Haymarket** since the 1760s, when it acquired its royal license. Built in 1720, it was known affectionately as the "Little Theatre in the Haymarket" in the 1730s. Henry Fielding, whose first satire, *Tom Thumb,* ran here in 1730, was one of its managers—and the principal reason Lord Chamberlain instituted powers of censorship in 1737, some of which were not lifted until 1968. After **John Nash** rebuilt it in 1820, the theater hosted performers such as Ellen Terry and Samuel Phelps. **Nash**'s exterior remains fairly intact, but the interior, redesigned first in 1904 by **C. Stanley Peach,** has been altered several times since and seats 888 people today. The theater is certainly elegant, but some people find the seats uncomfortable. ♦ Haymarket (between Suffolk Pl and Orange St). 930.8890. Tube: Piccadilly Circus, Charing Cross

10 Burberrys This raincoat manufacturer, famous for high quality and its signature plaid, has been protecting the British from the elements for more than 150 years. Aviator Sir John Alcock kept himself warm and dry in **Burberrys** gabardine on his first flight across the Atlantic, and soldiers in World War I wore **Burberrys** trench coats. When the liveried attendant opens the door today, you enter a world of old-fashioned charm and grace. ♦ M-Sa; Su noon-6PM 18-22. Haymarket (between Suffolk Pl and Orange St). 930.3343. Tube: Piccadilly Circus, Charing Cross. Also at: 165 Regent St (at New Burlington St). 734.4060. Tube: Piccadilly Circus, Oxford Circus; 3 Brompton Rd (at Knightsbridge). 581.2151. Tube: Knightsbridge

11 Comedy Theatre Thomas Verity built this theater in 1881; when it was restored in 1955 many of its Victorian decorative features were retained. This intimate 794-seat venue is well suited to the modern productions it usually mounts. ♦ Panton St (at Oxendon St). 367.1731. Tube: Piccadilly Circus

Café Fish

12 Café Fish ★★$$$ If you dream of oysters in tomato and coriander sauce and long to breath in the rich aromas of steamed bream, come devour your fishy fantasy. This restaurant has most every kind of edible sea creature you could possibly desire. The eatery is popular with businesspeople, thanks to friendly service in both the restaurant, which has a pianist in the evening, and the basement wine bar. (The wine bar has a shorter menu and can get hectic.) ♦ Seafood ♦ Restaurant: M-F lunch and dinner to 11:30PM; Sa dinner to 11:30PM. Wine bar: M-Sa lunch and dinner to 11PM. Reservations recommended. 39 Panton St (between Oxendon St and Haymarket). 930.3999. Tube: Piccadilly Circus

13 Football Football ★$$ Soccer fans were thrilled when London's theme-restaurant boom included this jolly place, featuring memorabilia galore and video screen showings of great soccer moments. Burgers, steaks, pizza, pasta, and such English specialties as bangers and mash (sausages and mashed potatoes) make this eatery popular with families. ♦ American/English ♦ Daily lunch and dinner. 57-60 Haymarket (at Norris St). 930.9970. Tube: Piccadilly Circus

14 Her Majesty's Theatre This 1,219-seat theater changes its name to fit the gender of the sovereign of the day—hence it's *Her* Majesty's, for now. The current building was erected in 1897 for Sir Herbert Beerbohm Tree by **C.J. Phipps** (who also built the **Savoy**), but a theater has stood on this site since 1705. The first opera by Handel to be produced in England was performed here, as was the first Handel oratorio. Jenny Lind made her English debut here; so did Beethoven's *Fidelio.* And the **Royal Academy of Dramatic Art (RADA)** started here. Now the theater is best known as the venue for Andrew Lloyd Webber's *Phantom of the Opera,* playing here since 1986. It's always sold out, but you can stand in line at the box office on the day of the show to see if anyone has turned in tickets. ♦ Haymarket (at Charles II St). 494.5400. Tube: Piccadilly Circus, Charing Cross

15 The Sports Cafe ★$$ Every sport imaginable is shown on 120 TV sets served by 150 satellite channels. The place is loud and cavernous with acres of gleaming wooden floors and smart display cases of sports memorabilia. The ground floor is for drinking and watching sports events and for dancing to taped music provided by a DJ Monday through Saturday at 11PM. Upstairs, the bar overlooks dark-wood tables and chairs, and diners tuck into burgers, club sandwiches, pasta dishes, and salads. ◆ American ◆ M-Th lunch and dinner to 2AM; F-Sa lunch and dinner to 3AM; Su lunch and dinner to midnight. 80 Haymarket (between Pall Mall and Charles II St). 839.8300. Tube: Piccadilly Circus, Charing Cross

15 New Zealand House This 18-story glass-and-concrete building is a veritable skyscraper in this area, and among the first to represent London's move toward modern architecture. It was built in 1963 by **Robert Matthew** for the New Zealand government. Note the interesting plaque, which says that Ho Chi Minh worked at the **Carlton Hotel,** which opened on this site in 1899 and closed in 1939. ◆ 80 Haymarket (between Pall Mall and Charles II St). Tube: Piccadilly Circus, Charing Cross

16 Farlow's Hunting and fishing enthusiasts come to this upmarket shop for its reeds, rods, game guns, and accessories as well as the weatherproof country clothes that go with them. It's located in the **Royal Opera Arcade,** London's first shopping mall, which still boasts pure Regency shop fronts from 1816, including this shop itself. The arcade's name harks back to the era when opera was being produced around the corner at **Her Majesty's Theatre.** ◆ M-Sa. 5 Pall Mall (between Haymarket and Regent St). 839.2423. Tube: Piccadilly Circus, Charing Cross

17 Crimean War Memorial Florence Nightingale is one of the few women represented in this masculine part of London; in this statue, she holds her famous lamp. Standing next to her is Sidney Herbert, secretary of war during the Crimean campaign. "Honor" is cast from captured Russian cannons. The memorial was created by John Bell in the 1850s. ◆ Waterloo Pl and Pall Mall. Tube: Charing Cross, Piccadilly Circus

18 Pall Mall Americans pronounce it like the brand of cigarettes, but the upper-class English who have their clubs here say "Pell Mell." Named after *paille maille,* the ball game that was played in The Mall, which runs parallel, this is part of the ancient route from the City to St. James's. Pall Mall is lined with gentlemen's clubs and a few appropriately exclusive shops, but its residential character has given way almost entirely to offices. It is a stately boulevard by day, a windy, monumental wasteland by night. ◆ Between Haymarket and St. James's St. Tube: Piccadilly Circus, Charing Cross

19 Travellers' Club This club was cofounded in 1819 by the Duke of Wellington, though the present building, designed by **Sir Charles Barry,** dates from 1832. One of the requirements for membership was to have

traveled at least 500 miles from London. Today, the candidates' book reveals that the present membership has gone somewhat farther afield. The special handrail on the staircase was put there to assist Napoléon's disabled foreign minister, Talleyrand, up the stairs. The club is closed to the public. ◆ 106 Pall Mall (between Waterloo Pl and Carlton Gardens). 930.8688. Tube: Charing Cross, Piccadilly Circus

19 Reform Club Members must subscribe to the Reform Bill of 1832 (which gave the vote to middle-class men) in order to be accepted into this absolutely stunning club, another **Sir Charles Barry** creation, completed in 1841. This is the club of economists, members of the Treasury, and, increasingly, writers and television executives, and reform is enough of a concern here that women have been allowed to join. The design, inspired by Rome's Palazzo Farnese, is Italian Classicism without bound. The silent interior includes a huge indoor courtyard with marble pillars and balconies, a vast library with leather chairs, library tables, and real fires in the enormous fireplaces. It looks like a film set, and indeed it has been the location for a few films, but so great is the discretion (or indifference) that no one who belongs knows which films. Like most London clubs, it is not open to the public. ◆ 104-5 Pall Mall (between Waterloo Pl and Carlton Gardens). 930.9374. Tube: Charing Cross, Piccadilly Circus

20 Royal Automobile Club Here is a club that takes members more readily than most. The opulent Edwardian building, built in 1911 by **Mewes and Davis** with **E. Keynes,** contains rooms designed in grand Louis XVI style. More enticing, however, are the squash courts, Turkish baths, solarium, and marble swimming pool, which is the most beautiful in London, its Doric columns covered in fish-scale mosaics. Unlike other clubs, no one seems to know anyone else, which probably explains why upper-crust spies Guy Burgess and Donald MacLean met here just before defecting to Russia in the 1950s. Despite its democratic outlook, the only women allowed here are wives and daughters of members. It, too, is closed to the public. ◆ 89 Pall Mall (between Carlton Gardens and Marlborough Rd). 930.2345. Tube: Green Park, Piccadilly Circus

21 St. James's Square This fine square was begun in 1665 by Henry Jermyn, first Earl of St. Albans and allegedly the secret husband of Henrietta Maria, widow of Charles I and mother of Charles II. While Charles II was in exile in France, he gave the land to the earl in gratitude for his "faithful devotion." The square was designed with mansions on all sides for the nobility who wanted or needed to be near the palace.

Celluloid London

With its long history, an abundance of architectural masterpieces, and an atmosphere that suggests mystery, tragedy, and comedy all at the same time, London makes an ideal film location. And over the years, many motion pictures have been set in this city—from historical dramas to Hollywood musicals to the great Ealing Studios comedies to grittier contemporary films. The following movies can start you on your cinematic tour of the English capital.

Alfie (1966) Michael Caine became a major star acting the title role of a callous Cockney playboy cruising the streets of 1960s London to pick up girls. Also a photographer, Alfie uses such background settings as **Big Ben,** the **Houses of Parliament,** and **Tower Bridge.**

An American Werewolf in London (1981) In a queasy mix of horror and satire, an American student is transformed into a werewolf after a gory attack in the Yorkshire moors. Some of the action takes place in London locations, including **Regent Park,** the **Tottenham Court Road** tube station, **Trafalgar Square,** and **Piccadilly Circus.**

A Christmas Carol (1956) There have been many film adaptations of this most famous Dickens tale, but none has been as highly acclaimed as this one. In a memorable performance, Alastair Sim plays the miserly, ill-tempered, misanthropic Scrooge, and again, Victorian London is evocatively portrayed.

A Fish Called Wanda (1988) Jamie Lee Curtis, Kevin Kline (who won the Best Supporting Actor Oscar), John Cleese, and Michael Palin star in this funny farce about double- and triple-crossing jewel thieves. The British legal system, class distinctions, and cultural conflicts between England and America are lampooned with dead-on accuracy. Several scenes of the film, directed by Charles Crichton, were shot in the **Law Courts,** the **Hatton Garden** diamond district, and the **Docklands** area.

Four Weddings and a Funeral (1994) Hugh Grant became an international star thanks to this stylish romantic comedy about a confirmed English bachelor who falls for a freewheeling American (Andie MacDowell). Backdrops include the **Royal Naval College** in **Greenwich** and the atmospheric, ancient church of **St. Bartholomew the Great** in **Smithfield.**

Gaslight (1944) The archetypical fog and mist of Victorian London provides an eerie backdrop for the classic tale of a man (Charles Boyer) trying to drive his wife (Best Actress Oscar winner Ingrid Bergman) insane. Angela Lansbury, playing a surly housemaid, makes her film debut.

Great Expectations (1946) One of several Dickens novels to be adapted to the screen. Director David Lean expertly tells the story of a poor orphan boy in Victorian London who is elevated in society by a mysterious patron.

The Krays (1990) This atmospheric, sometimes shockingly violent biography tells the story of Ronnie and Reggie Kray, the psychotic twins who dominated London gangland in the 1960s, virtually running everything in the **East End.** The twisted relationship the twins had with their smothering mother (played by Billie Whitelaw, who knew the real-life Krays) is disturbingly portrayed.

The Lavender Hill Mob (1951) Timid bank clerk Alec Guinness dreams up the perfect way to rob his employers of a fortune in gold—and then everything goes hilariously wrong in this classic Ealing comedy directed by Charles Crichton.

Looking for Richard (1996) In a witty and incisive documentary, Al Pacino describes his quest to produce a meaningful film version of Shakespeare's *Richard III.* His research includes visits to the **Tower of London** and the construction site of the rebuilt **Globe Theatre.**

The Madness of King George (1994) The film version of Alan Bennett's play *The Madness of George III* deals with the struggle for power in the court of King George as he begins to exhibit strange behavior. It is also a satirical look at the politics, class struggles, and medical "advances" of the time. Nigel Hawthorne and Helen Mirren give compelling performances as the king and queen. Several scenes were filmed in London area locations, including **Eton College, Syon House, Kew,** and the **Royal Naval College, Greenwich** (but *not* **Windsor Castle,** where much of the action is set).

The Man Who Knew Too Much (1956) This Alfred Hitchcock thriller about a man whose son is kidnapped to prevent him from revealing an assassination plot stars James Stewart and Doris Day. The climactic scene takes place in the **Royal Albert Hall.**

Mona Lisa (1985) Small-time hood Bob Hoskins, hired to drive a call girl around, begins to fall for her in this movie about London gangland. Michael Caine costars as a vicious mob boss. London locations include the neighborhoods of **Soho** and **Hampstead** and the **Ritz Hotel.**

My Fair Lady (1964) In a lavish cinematic version of the Lerner and Loewe musical, Professor Henry Higgins (Rex Harrison) bets that he can turn Cockney flower girl Eliza Doolittle (Audrey Hepburn) into a well-mannered, upper-class lady within a month. The first scene is set in front of the **Royal Opera House, Covent Garden.** Both the movie and Rex Harrison won Academy Awards.

Oliver Twist (1948) Another David Lean interpretation of a Dickens tale, this film about a down-and-out lad who gets involved with a gang of thieves features Alec Guinness as Fagin and Anthony Newley as the Artful Dodger. In 1968, the story was made into the Oscar-winning musical *Oliver!*

101 Dalmatians (1996) The live-action remake of the famous Disney cartoon feature stars Glenn Close as the delightfully malevolent Cruella deVil, who wants to skin a litter of puppies so she can have a fur coat. The movie was filmed on location in central London. One dazzling sequence shows a cyclist careening through the **Burlington Arcade** in **Mayfair** and ending up in Trafalgar Square.

The gardens in the square's center are open to the public (which is unusual in London, where only residents may use most neighborhood squares). The handsome bronze statue by John Bacon the Younger of William III on horseback includes the molehill on which the horse stumbled, throwing the king in a fatal accident. During World War I, a rustic building resembling a country inn was erected at the square's center to quarter American officers. Called the **Washington Inn,** it stood until 1921. At **No. 32,** the allied commanders under General Eisenhower launched the invasions of North Africa in 1942 and of northwest Europe in 1944. On the north side of the square is **Chatham House,** the residence of three prime ministers: the Earl of Chatham, otherwise known as Pitt the Elder; the Earl of Derby; and W.E. Gladstone. Wellington's dispatch announcing his victory at Waterloo was delivered to **No. 16** by the bloodstained Major Percy to the prince regent, who was dining with his foreign secretary, Lord Castlereagh. Included with the dispatch were the captured French eagle standards, now in Wellington's **Apsley House** at **Hyde Park Corner.** St. James's Square became famous overnight when the Libyan People's Bureau at **No. 5** was besieged on 17 April 1984. Gunmen within the building fired on demonstrators outside, killing a young police officer named Yvonne Fletcher. Because diplomatic immunity made it impossible for police to enter the building, the siege went on for 10 days, and the suspects were deported instead of arrested. Fresh flowers are placed on a memorial opposite **No. 5** year-round in honor of Fletcher. ♦ At Charles II, King, and Duke of York Sts. Tube: Green Park, Piccadilly Circus

22 London Library "It is not typically English. It is typically civilized," wrote E.M. Forster in an essay on this private subscription library, founded in 1841 by Thomas Carlyle but built in the 1760s by **James Stuart.** The interior looks rather run down, with worn leather chairs in the reading room, Victorian portraits on the walls, and high windows overlooking the square. Past members include Lord Tennyson, W.E. Gladstone, Henry James, Thomas Hardy, H.G. Wells, Aldous Huxley, Virginia Woolf, and Edith Sitwell. Current members are historians, biographers, critics, novelists, philosophers, playwrights, and scriptwriters, who all come to use some of the library's million-plus books; however, memberships are hard to obtain. The library is not open to the general public but its windows give a fine glimpse inside. ♦ 14 St. James's Sq (between King and Duke of York Sts). 930.7705. Tube: Green Park, Piccadilly Circus

23 Colombina ★$$ The Neapolitan chef at this refreshingly simple and inexpensive trattoria prepares delicious deep-fried mozzarella in bread crumbs and good fish dishes and grills. ♦ Italian ♦ M-Sa lunch and dinner. 4-6 Duke of York St (at Ormond Yd). 930.8279. Tube: Green Park, Piccadilly Circus

24 Red Lion Pub ★★★$ Dating from around 1880, this Victorian jewel has mahogany paneling and beautiful old mirrors, each engraved with a different British flower. Have a sandwich with your pint of bitter; on Friday and Saturday you can enjoy homemade fish-and-chips. Note that this small pub can be crowded and smoky. ♦ Pub ♦ M-Sa lunch. 2 Duke of York St (at Ormond Yd). 930.2030. Tube: Green Park, Piccadilly Circus

24 Harvie & Hudson These third-generation shirtmakers use the finest cotton poplin, which is designed, colored, and woven just for them. Their tweed jackets and overcoats are reasonably priced. ♦ M-Sa. 97 Jermyn St (at Duke of York St). 839.3578 Tube: Green Park, Piccadilly Circus. Also at: 77 Jermyn St. (at Duke of York St) 930.3949. Tube: Green Park; 55 Knightsbridge (at Wilton Pl). 235.2651. Tube: Knightsbridge

25 Jermyn Street Named after the Earl of St. Albans, Henry Jermyn, this narrow street is only a few blocks long and the architecture isn't remarkable (the west end of the street was badly damaged during the 1940 raids, when all but one of the buildings between Duke and Bury Streets were destroyed). But it's the essence of St. James's, an exclusive shopping enclave for well-to-do Englishmen who dress as the Duke of Edinburgh and Prince Charles do. ♦ Between Haymarket and St. James's St. Tube: Green Park, Piccadilly Circus

There's actually a serious organization in London called the Society of Psychical Research that lists 1,000 ghosts which people claim to have seen in stately homes, manor houses, and inns.

Charles I, whose last word was *Remember*, is remembered every year at 11AM on the Sunday nearest to 30 January, the date of his death. Hundreds of cavaliers in full dress, members of the English Civil War Society, march to Banqueting House, where they lay a wreath at noon outside the window where Charles climbed through onto the scaffold.

26 Trumper's With a lovely atmosphere and a legendary reputation, this shop offers top-quality hairbrushes, shaving brushes, soaps, hair tonics, and aftershaves. The Ajaccio Violet men's cologne smells like violets, comes in old-fashioned bottles, and is used by both sexes. There is also a renowned traditional barbershop on the premises where you can get facials, manicures, and even moustache curls. ◆ M-F, Sa 9AM-1PM. 20 Jermyn St (between Regent St and Eagle Pl). 734.1370. Tube: Piccadilly Circus. Also at: 9 Curzon St (between Clarges and Queen Sts). 499.1850. Tube: Green Park

26 Bates the Hatter This tiny gentlemen's hat shop is undaunted by the bareheaded 20th century, and time seems to be on its side. Hats are beginning to reappear. You will pay less here than at **Lock & Co** (see page 59). Be sure to admire Binks, the huge tabby cat who lived here from 1921 to 1926; he was so beloved that a taxidermist him was enlisted after his death to preserve him for all time. ◆ M-Sa. 21A Jermyn St (between Regent St and Eagle Pl). 734.2722. Tube: Piccadilly Circus

27 Hilditch & Key The shop specializes in made-to-measure shirts for men and women, including royals and politicians—but of course these tailors are far too discreet to name names. All shirts are cut by hand: the bodies with shears, the collars with a knife. The collars, considered the most important part of a shirt, are turned by hand and have removable stiffeners that must be taken out before laundering. The buttons are never synthetic—they're made from real shells. Besides the fine English cotton poplins, there's a solid selection of Viyella, a soft, warm equal mix of cotton and wool. The women's shirts come in many of the same colors and fabrics as the men's but with additional choices of bright colors

created by the shop's own designers. The nightshirts (for men and women) and pajamas are wonderful. ◆ M-Sa. 37 Jermyn St (at Princes Arcade). 734.4707. Tube: Green Park, Piccadilly Circus. Also at: 73 Jermyn St (at Bury St). 930.2329. Tube: Green Park

28 Paxton & Whitfield At any one time you can find 200 cheeses from Britain and Europe inside this shop, which occupies a house built in 1674. Mr. Paxton and Mr. Whitfield opened the shop 200 years ago, when the public predilection was for French cheeses. Now English cheeses are finally being acknowledged for their outstanding quality and for being ideal partners with wine. The salespeople here are generous with samples, so go ahead and taste the golden cheddars, the peach- and ivory-colored cheshires, the russet leicester, the marbled green sage derby, and the blue-veined stilton. Also available are fabulous game pies, hams, and pâtés, plus crackers and bread to accompany the cheese. The shop also sells wine. ◆ M-Sa. 93 Jermyn St (between Duke of York and Duke Sts). 930.0259. Tube: Green Park, Piccadilly Circus

Established 1730

28 Floris Since 1730, members of the Floris family, now in its eighth generation, have been creating aromatic perfumes, bath oils, and soaps from the flowers of the English garden. In this pretty, evocative shop, the jasmine, rose, gardenia, lily of the valley, and wild hyacinth all smell fresh and clean and as close to the real thing as you can imagine. New scents are continually being developed as well. You will also find large natural sponges, fine English brushes, antique objects for *la toilette,* and a line of scents for men. Both Queen Elizabeth and Prince Charles have bestowed their Royal Warrants on the shop, and it's popular with other famous people as

Jermyn Street Shopping

HAYMARKET

Cafe Sogo	Royal Bank of Scotland
	Figaro Five *cafe*
	Ceylon Tea Centre
department store Lillywhites	Air Lanka

REGENT STREET

Barclays Bank	Plaza Cinema
Spaghetti House	Baskin Robbins Ice Cream
Jermyn Street Theatre	
menswear Herbie Frogg	
hairdresser/perfumer Trumper's	
menswear Herbie Frogg	
Bates the Hatter	Rowley's *British restaurant*
Hotel 22 Jermyn St.	Van Heusen *men's shirts*
shirtmakers Hawes & Curtis	Church's *men's shoes*

EAGLE PLACE   **BABMAES STREET**

National Westminster Bank	People's Mobile Phones
	T.M. Lewin & Sons *shirtmakers*
Simpson	Coles *shirtmakers*
CHURCH PLACE	Von Posch *porcelain/gifts*
	Kensington Carpets

DUKE OF YORK STREET

JERMYN STREET

	Harvie & Hudson *shirtmakers*
	Russell & Bromley *men's shoes*
St. James's Church	Links of London *jewelry*
The Wren Wholefood Café	Paxton & Whitfield *cheesemongers*
	Blazer *menswear*
shirtmakers Hilditch & Key	John Lobb *shoes*
PRINCES ARCADE	Floris *perfumers*
antiques/art Mayorcas	James Bodenham *gifts*
	Hackett *menswear*
toiletries Czech & Speake	Pink *shirtmakers*
nightclub Tramp	Fisher & Son *men's shoes*
	S. Franses *tapestries*
Fortnum & Mason	Cavendish Hotel
	S. Franses *antique tapestries*

DUKE STREET

clothing/tobacco dunhill	John Bray *menswear*
	Harvie & Hudson *shirtmakers*
	Trevor Philip *scientific antiques*
shirtmakers New & Lingwood	Fabri *menswear*
PICCADILLY ARCADE	
menswear New & Lingwood	Waterman *fine art*
menswear Favourbrook	Taylor of Old Bond St. *hairdressers*
	Hilditch & Key *shirtmakers*
British restaurant Wilton's	**BURY STREET**
Victor Franses Gallery	Turnbull & Asser *menswear*
paintings Daniel Katz	
menswear Vincci	Vincci *menswear*
Mokaris Espresso Bar	R.E. Tricker *shoes*
Italian restaurant Franco's	Vincci *menswear*
	Davidoff *tobacco*

ST. JAMES'S STREET

well, including Nancy Reagan. ♦ M-Sa. 89 Jermyn St (between Duke of York and Duke Sts). 930.2885. Tube: Green Park, Piccadilly Circus

dunhill

29 dunhill It was on this very site in 1907 that Alfred Dunhill opened his small tobacconist shop; his philosophy was that everything must be "the best of its kind"—which, coincidentally, is also the motto of a new generation of consumers. The shop has expanded to include leather goods, pens, watches, fragrances, umbrellas, and all sorts of accessories to complement men's and women's clothes and complete the ever-so-smart **dunhill** look. There is still a tobacconist area, a humidor room, and a wall display of "museum" pieces. ♦ M-Sa. 30 Duke St (at Jermyn St). 290.8602. Tube: Green Park

30 Green's Restaurant and Oyster Bar ★★★$$$ Here is a dining spot that has the ambience of a gentlemen's club and seems to be filled with typical Bertie Wooster clones (however, the serving staff aren't as deferential and all-knowing as Jeeves). It has a bar with booths for the secretive and an open eating area for rubberneckers. Choose from a mountain of lobsters, crabs, and oysters, all fresh, simply prepared, and outstanding. In addition to favorites like salmon fish cakes and Dover sole, chef Patrick Williams offers such dishes as sea bass with broccoli and sautéed halibut with fresh peas. If you come here for lunch, resign yourself to eating in a very crowded room. The oyster bar is cheaper. ♦ British ♦ Restaurant: daily lunch and dinner Oct-Easter; M-Sa lunch and dinner, Su lunch Easter-Sept. Oyster Bar: daily lunch and dinner. Reservations required. 36 Duke St (between Ryder and Jermyn Sts). 930.4566. Tube: Green Park

31 Quaglino's ★★★★$$$ "Tables to kill for" was the verdict of food critics when Sir Terence Conran opened this beautiful restaurant in 1993 (named for a smart-set club that flourished here in the 1930s). This opulent place is a welcome addition to his restaurant empire (four places at Butler's Wharf and **Bibendum** in Kensington, among

others) and a further tribute to his talents. On the street level, the discreet Q logo seems to adorn a minimalist delicatessen; there's a bar inside (overlooking the main attraction below) with a small eating area and a snack menu offering Thai-spiced tuna salad and grilled tuna. However, a sweeping grand staircase leads to a huge subterranean restaurant that's as large and resplendent as a luxury ocean liner. Romantically lit with an artificial skylight ceiling, it has walls of mirrors and large urns filled with fresh lilies. And the food lives up to the surroundings. For appetizers, try the scallops in onion cream sauce, pan-fried foie gras with prosciutto, or squid with hummus and chickpeas and harissa. Main courses include peppered beef, duck confit with baked chicory and apple, and entrecôte with béarnaise sauce. Diners rave about such desserts as white chocolate torte with raspberries, Sauternes-flavored custard with Armagnac prunes, and bread-and-butter pudding with chocolate sauce. The fine wine list offers international labels within a reasonable to expensive price range. Adding to the festive ambience, there's a jazz trio in the bar area Friday and Saturday nights; a pianist plays Monday through Thursday and also on Sunday. ♦ Modern British ♦ Daily lunch and dinner. Reservations required. 16 Bury St (between Ryder and Jermyn Sts). 930.6767. Tube: Green Park

32 Favourbrook Fabulous-looking silks, velvets, and damasks are used in fashioning the waistcoats (vests), luxurious smoking jackets, frock coats, and tasseled fez-style smoking hats sold here. In fact, the character played by Simon Callow in the film *Four Weddings and a Funeral* wore one of the shop's creations—a waistcoat hand-painted with an angel. Although the decadent English fop look is at odds with the conservative tastes reflected in the rest of the street, the style has become so popular that **Favourbrook** moved its menswear collection to these premises from its Piccadilly Arcade location around the corner. ♦ M-Sa. 55 Jermyn St (between Piccadilly Arcade and St. James's St). 493.5060. Tube: Green Park. Womenswear only is sold at 18 Piccadilly Arcade (between Jermyn St and Piccadilly). 491.2337. Tube: Green Park

32 Wilton's ★★$$$ When the restaurant moved from nearby Bury Street in 1982, it brought along its glass screens, Edwardian dining-room alcoves, polished mahogany, and clubby atmosphere so that the regulars would feel as if they hadn't

WILTONS

moved at all. It remains a favorite with politicians, businessmen, and the "old school tie" brigade who appreciate the stalwart, simple Englishness of such excellent dishes as smoked salmon, oysters, and game. The menu offers modern flourishes as well, such as grilled sea bass on a bed of zucchini, and pasta with sweet red peppers. For dessert, have the lemon-and–passion fruit syllabub. ◆ British ◆ M-F, Su lunch and dinner. Reservations required; jacket and tie required. 55 Jermyn St (between Duke and St. James's Sts). 629.9955. Tube: Green Park

33 Turnbull & Asser The name is familiar to Americans who wear English custom-made shirts, especially now that there's a **Turnbull & Asser** club in New York as well as department stores in the States that take appointments with their tailors. But those experiences aren't the same as coming into this solemn, dark, wood-paneled shop where the person next to you could be a duke or a salesman. The store's made-to-measure service takes six weeks, with a minimum order of six shirts after you approve the first. There are a lot of decisions to make: the shape of the collar; the length of the points, pockets, and monograms; the shape and color of the buttons; a two- or three-button cuff. You also must be patient—and it helps if you're as much a stickler for detail as the shirtmakers themselves. First you are measured; then a sample shirt is made and sent to you. Next you must write a set of fastidious notes and return the shirt, which is then remade and again returned to you for approval. This routine can go on for quite some time before you get a shirt that is perfect. The shop truly reflects Jermyn Street's Beau Brummell legacy faithfully: The famous Regency dandy could not resist fine craftsmanship, simple lines, and daring colors.

The store also has a large selection of ready-mades, and it sells blouses and shirts to women, including Candice Bergen, Lauren Bacall, Jacqueline Bisset, and model Naomi Campbell. ◆ M-Sa. 71-72 Jermyn St (at Bury St). 930.0502. Tube: Green Park. Also at: 23 Bury St (between Ryder and Jermyn Sts). 930.0502. Tube: Green Park

34 St. James's Street The elegant street serves as a compass for this royal and aristocratic quarter. At the bottom of the street is Henry VIII's gatehouse to **St. James's Palace,** with a sentry or two on duty. Pall Mall joins the street just in front of the palace, where the tradition of gentlemen's clubs continues, although the 18th-century clubs here are considered even more social, snobbish, and arrogant than the clubs farther along Pall Mall. There are no signs to indicate which club is which—if you're a member, you know, and if you aren't, you don't need to know. ◆ Between Pall Mall and Piccadilly. Tube: Green Park

34 White's London's oldest, most famous, and still most fashionable club was founded in the 1690s as **White's Chocolate House** (a meeting place where bitter hot chocolate was drunk). Built by **James Wyatt** in 1788, this is where Evelyn Waugh sought "refuge from the hounds of modernity" and where Prince Charles had his stag party the night before he married Diana. The gaming room here was called "Hell" in the previous century. This club is exclusive indeed: Even if you are sufficiently well connected to be proposed and accepted for membership, there is a waiting list of eight years (though Prince Charles probably didn't have to wait that long). Not surprisingly, it is not open to the public. ◆ 37-38 St. James's St (between Jermyn St and Piccadilly). 493.6671. Tube: Green Park

35 Davidoff Using three recipes for flavor, Zino Davidoff has created a cigar and pipe smoker's heaven. He purveys the finest Havana cigars, and there is a walk-in humidor. The shop has an ineffably masculine pull, with the handmade wooden humidors, the matchboxes, the cigar cases in leather, the cigar holders, and many other smoking accessories, as well as Cognacs. The sweet smell of unsmoked cigars evokes a sense of prosperity and sedate virility. ◆ M-Sa. 35 St. James's St (at Jermyn St). 930.3079. Tube: Green Park

36 Boodle's John Crunden's beautiful building, completed in 1765, is one of the best examples of club design in London, with a central arched Venetian window in the upper room. **Boodle's** has a long history of being *the* club for fashionable men-about-town (members have included Beau Brummell and the Duke of Wellington). It is closed to the public. ◆ 28 St. James's St (between Ryder and Jermyn Sts). 930.7166. Tube: Green Park

37 Economist Building Alison and Peter Smithson's complex is considered a fine example of successful modern architecture in London. In 1964, the architects designed a group of buildings that are compatible with the 18th-century scale of St. James's Street but still maintain their 20th-century integrity.

The complex provides a public open space, offices for *The Economist* magazine, a bank, and apartments. In the front court and in the foyer are sculptures that are part of changing exhibitions of modern works. The building is not open to the general public. ♦ 25 St. James's St (at Ryder St). 830.7000. Tube: Green Park

LONGMIRE

CUFFLINK JEWELLER

38 Longmire Acclaimed as "the king of custom cufflinks," Mr. Longmire boasts the world's largest selection, whether new, antique, gold, enameled, or set with precious gems. Initials, corporate logos, heraldry, racing colors, cars, and dogs, among many other subjects, can be immortalized in made-to-order enamel designs. He maintains a heraldic reference library and has three Royal Warrants. The shop also makes brooches, pendants, earrings, and buttons; vintage jewelry is also available. ♦ M-F Jan-Oct; M-Sa Nov-Dec. The shop is closed most of August. 12 Bury St (at Ryder St). 930.8720. Tube: Green Park

39 J.J. Fox & Robert Lewis Discerning cigar smokers flock to this Dickensian tobacco shop in droves. They follow in the footsteps of Robert Lewis's most famous customer, Sir Winston Churchill; he opened an account here on 9 August 1900 and placed his last order on 23 December 1964, a month before his death. James Fox also runs the tobacco departments at **Harrods** and **Selfridges.** ♦ M-Sa. 19 St. James's St (between King and Ryder Sts). 493.9009. Tube: Green Park

40 Brooks's Inveterate gambler Charles James Fox was a famous member of this club, founded in 1762 but built 16 years later by **Henry Holland.** The renowned Beau Brummell won £20,000 in one night when this was a great gambling club for Whig aristocrats. It's closed to the public. ♦ 60 St. James's St (at Park Pl). 493.4411. Tube: Green Park

"We spent our honeymoon in London, my favourite city, in a quiet little hotel in Chelsea. It's nice to see big, grand hotels, but I wouldn't want to stay in them. The English are the friendliest people I've ever met and when I'm in London I feel in some way connected to the past through the architecture. Everything is so new in America."

Gene Wilder,
interviewed in the *Sunday Times* (1996).

Restaurants/Clubs: Red   Hotels: Blue
Shops/ 🍴 Outdoors: Green   **Sights/Culture: Black**

41 St. James's Club $$$$ There is something special about staying at your own club. Current members here must propose you for membership and second your nomination if you want to belong to this exclusive, 59-room club, its pretty facade gracing a quiet cul-de-sac. However, you can get a taste of its luxury before applying; you're allowed to stay once as a temporary member to see if you like it. When Hollywood stars come to London—including Steven Spielberg, Liza Minnelli, and Dudley Moore—they often choose to stay here, enjoying the traditional English decor, including wood paneling and floral upholstery. Although there's a bar lounge and dining room, service can be more discreet, with a butler bringing a dining trolley to your room. There is also an exercise room, sauna, and steam bath. Note that the club maintains reciprocal arrangements with 450 clubs worldwide, including the **American Express Centurion Club.** ♦ 7 Park Pl (off St. James's St). 629.7688, 800/877.0447; fax 491.0987. Tube: Green Park

42 Stafford Hotel $$$$ Also in a quiet cul-de-sac, this hotel is virtually a club with a country house feel. Travelers who have stayed at too many anonymous international luxury hotels will find this very English accommodation a delightful respite. The 80 rooms are large and comfortable. English businesspeople often come for the delectable midday meal served in the dining room, and the wine list resembles that of a fine club—200 labels are housed in the cellars that once belonged to **St. James's Palace.** Don't miss afternoon tea here—one of London's best, served in a room filled with antiques, silver teapots, and Wedgwood china. ♦ 16-18 St. James's Pl (off St. James's St). 493.0111, 800/525.4800; fax 493.7121. Tube: Green Park

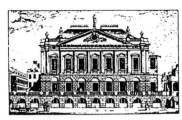

43 Spencer House The entrance to this remarkable Palladian mansion (pictured above) faces St. James's Place, but its finest facade is opposite **Green Park.** The house was begun in 1756 by **John Vardy,** who designed it for John, Earl of Spencer, an ancestor of Princess Diana. **James Stuart** took over its (mainly interior) construction in 1758; **Stuart** was nicknamed "The Athenian" for his love of classical architecture, and his anglicized Greek influence can be seen throughout. When completed in 1766, the house was considered one of the finest London residences. "I know not of a more beautiful piece of architecture," wrote Arthur Young after seeing it in 1772. The J. Rothschild Group of Companies acquired the building in 1985 and has restored its original splendor. On Sunday, visitors may enter (by guided tour only) to see **Vardy**'s dining room with its elaborate gilt-wood furniture, **Stuart**'s Neo-Classical state rooms, and Lady Spencer's private drawing room. Tours are given every 20 minutes. Before going in, look across the road at the building's austere neighbor, a concrete apartment block built by **Sir Denys Lasdun** in 1959-60 in the stark style he also used to design the **National Theatre.** Although not harmonious with its graceful surroundings, this apartment house has been lauded for its strong, modern design on a human scale. ♦ Admission. Su Feb-July, Sep-Dec. 27 St. James's Pl (off St. James's St). 499.8620. Tube: Green Park

DUKES HOTEL

43 Dukes Hotel $$$ This fine hotel stands in a gaslit courtyard. It's a kind of miniature palace with 64 rooms, 12 suites, and an elevator that descends with the dignity of an elderly duchess. The guest rooms are beautifully decorated with Edwardian furnishings, silk curtains, and marble bathrooms. The hotel's clubby atmosphere suits the neighborhood, while its loyal clientele relishes the location and the staff's impeccable courtesy. Late at night, taxis turning around in the cul-de-sac are audible, so ask for a quiet room in the back. Fine English food is served in the small dining room (residents only). Tea is served to the general public until 5:30PM. ♦ 35 St. James's Pl (off St. James's St). 491.4840, 800/381.4702; fax 493.1264. Tube: Green Park

44 Hugh Johnson Collection
The pretty shop, owned by the eponymous wine critic, sells elegant wine accessories (some antique), including corkscrews, decanters, glasses,

ice buckets—and wine. Books and videos about wine are also carried here. ♦ M-F. 68 St. James's St (between Little St. James's St and St. James's Pl). 491.4912. Tube: Green Park

44 Carlton Built in 1827 by **Thomas Hopper,** this club for Conservative politicians is a male domain, though Lady Margaret Thatcher can still enter; her larger-than-life portrait (as prime minister) hangs at the top of the double staircase. W.E. Gladstone was once told here that he should be "pitched out of the window in the direction of the **Reform Club.**" It is closed to the public. ♦ 69 St. James's St (between Little St. James's St and St. James's Pl). 493.1164. Tube: Green Park

44 Suntory ★★★$$$$
This is one of 10 restaurants worldwide owned by the Suntory Japanese Whiskey Company, and its standards are as high as the prices. Watch the chefs in the basement *teppanyaki* room dissect beef and seafood with mesmerizing skill. The

showplace perfection of the formal main dining room—stark white walls punctuated by black timber beams, eating spaces divided by paper screens, and well placed fine paintings and ceramics—appeals to Japanese businesspeople on expense accounts. The *dobin-mushi* (soup with such morsels as prawns, whitefish, chicken, shiitake, and gingko nuts) is superb. Other, seasonal specialties include fresh sardine tempura, elaborate arrays of sushi, and grilled sea eel with sweet soy sauce, served beautifully in a lacquered box. ♦ Japanese ♦ M-Sa lunch and dinner, Su dinner. Reservations recommended. 72-73 St. James's St (at Little St James's St). 409.0201. Tube: Green Park

45 King Street This street's claim to fame was once the **St. James's Theatre,** completed in 1835, which premiered Oscar Wilde's *Lady Windermere's Fan* and *The Importance of Being Earnest,* Arthur Pinero's *The Second Mrs. Tanqueray,* and, later, Terence Rattigan's *Separate Tables.* Unfortunately, the theater was demolished in 1959, even though Vivien Leigh interrupted a Parliamentary session in an attempt to save it. It stood at the passageway to Angel Court. Note the other narrow passages opening onto this street, vestiges of a bygone era when streets were no more than pedestrian thoroughfares. Saunter down Crown Passage, which leads to Pall Mall and has some interesting shops, cafes, and restaurants. ♦ Between St. James's Sq and St. James's St. Tube: Green Park

46 The Golden Lion ★$ The heavy theatrical curtains reflect this cozy pub's close links with the old **St. James's Theatre;** the upstairs bar had been connected to it and was patronized by theatergoers. Though the pub has been licensed since 1732, it was rebuilt in 1898 and given a flamboyant facade. There is still an upstairs bar, where you'll find such typical pub fare as lamb stew. ♦ British ♦ M-F lunch and sandwiches to 11PM; Sa lunch. 25 King St (at Angel Ct). 930.7227. Tube: Green Park

47 Christie, Manson and Woods Ltd. Better known simply as **Christie's,** this is one of the world's leading auction houses. In the art and antiques trade, **Sotheby's,** the largest auction house, is said to be run by businessmen trying to be gentlemen, while **Christie's** is run by gentlemen trying to be businessmen. Founded in 1766 on Great Castle Street, this firm has been located here since 1823, except for a period during and after World War II when the building was damaged during the Blitz.

If you arrive in the morning (when sales are generally held), you may see millionaires battling over a van Gogh or Picasso, an emerald necklace, or a famous pop star's worldly goods. If very important paintings are being auctioned, representatives from the world's museums will be here, and the atmosphere will resemble a cross between a Broadway opening and an operating room, with the auctioneer as leading actor and surgeon. Items to be sold are on view in the rooms and galleries around the auction room; perusing them is like exploring an informal museum, with the bonus that if you lose your head over the 17th-century carpet or the sentimental Victorian watercolor of the girl and the rabbit, you can attend the sale and bid on it. This auction house also offers wine for sale, and it purveys vintage motorcars, tribal art, photographs, and stamps. Its many experts specialize in icons, non-masterpiece artwork, furniture, and carpets. Glossy catalogs are for sale in the front shop. ♦ M-F; during a sale, also Tu 9AM-8PM, Su 2-5PM. 8 King St (at Bury St). 839.9060. Tube: Green Park. Also at: 85 Old Brompton Rd (between Sumner and Cranley Pls). 581.7611. Tube: South Kensington

48 Spink & Son Founded in 1666, this firm of art dealers is reputed to be the oldest in the world, specializing in coins, medals, Asian and English art, and militaria. The small rooms have a museumlike atmosphere, and the fine-art section exhibits exceptional 19th- and 20th-century paintings. ♦ M-F. 5-7 King St (at St. James's St). 930.7888. Tube: Green Park

49 Lobb's Five generations of Lobbs have shod the rich and famous since John Lobb walked from Cornwall to London to set himself up as a shoemaker. The list of distinguished feet served here is considerable: those of Queen Victoria, Mountbatten, King George VI, the current royals, Cecil Beaton, Winston Churchill, Laurence Olivier, Groucho Marx, Frank Sinatra, Cole Porter, and Katharine Hepburn.

In the basement of the shop, 15,000 wooden lasts of customers' feet are kept until they die—and some for long after that. The shoemakers draw an outline of each of your feet in their book, examine it from every angle in search of peculiarities, and then, on a long slip of paper, take a series of measurements, which are marked by snips in the paper. This is translated into wooden models of your feet, around which the leather is molded. After you've been walking the streets of London for a few days, the four-figure price may even sound appealing to get shoes that fit perfectly ♦ M-Sa. 9 St. James's St (between Pall Mall and King St). 930.3664. Tube: Green Park

"Right now London is a hip compromise between the non-stop newness of Los Angeles and the aspic-preserved beauty of Paris, sharpened to a New York edge . . . the coolest city on the planet."

Stryker McGuire and Michael Elliott, *Newsweek*

Henry VIII is engraved on the memory as a man who had six wives—and went to extensive lengths in order to do so. A truer picture is of a brilliant, gifted, scholarly, athletic, musical, and devout man who was handsome in youth—over 6 feet tall with blond hair—and who had a great appetite for life. Sir Thomas More described him as "a man nourished on philosophy and the nine muses." He is also the monarch who, more than any other, created the look of central London.

49 The Avenue ★★$$$ Chic minimalist decor has finally arrived in staid St. James's with this showy restaurant (formerly a bank): White walls are set off with a black video screen displaying art scenes, a long black bar with a shiny metallic-yellow counter, and lots of black-and-white drawings. Attracting a well-heeled, trendy clientele, the restaurant creates imaginative dishes with a Mediterranean flair, such as a cold tomato, red pepper, and pesto soup for an appetizer, and such entrées as fillet of beef with artichokes and French beans, and herb roast pork on tomato mash. For dessert, there's a Port-glazed fig tart with praline ice cream. ♦ Modern British ♦ Daily lunch and dinner. Reservations suggested. 7-9 St. James's St (between Pall Mall and King St). 321.2111. Tube: Green Park

49 Lock & Co. The house of **Lock** has been covering heads since 1676; it moved into this building in 1759. Lord Nelson's cocked hats were made here, and the Duke of Wellington, Beau Brummell, and all the American ambassadors to the Court of St. James's also purchased hats from this shop. The first bowlers were produced here in 1850 for the gamekeepers of a man named William Coke, and the shop still refers to the style as a Coke. There are about 16,000 hats in stock, but you can have one custom-made with the French *conformateur* that has been used to determine head measurements for 150 years. The flat tweed caps are popular with English country-lovers such as J.P. Donleavy and Prince Philip. The shop has extended its services to selling ladies' hats and even has a designer on the premises for custom-made commissions. It has two Royal Warrants. Paul McCartney shops here, as does that Englishman personified, Sir Alec Guinness. ♦ M-Sa. 6 St. James's St (between Pall Mall and King St). 930.5849. Tube: Green Park

L'ORANGER

49 L'Oranger ★★★$$$ Behind the bow window is a transformed lovely restaurant (replacing the old-fashioned **Overton's**) with lots of mirrors, wood paneling, and gleaming wood floors, and a carpeted, glass-ceilinged area in back overlooking a courtyard. Michelin-starred chef Marcus Wareing offers only fixed-price menus, but they feature such delights as marinated tuna rolled in crushed black pepper with white radish, and loin of pork and Toulouse sausage with mustard sauce. The wine list is strong on French labels, presented with a suitably reverential air by the sommelier. ♦ Modern British ♦ M-Sa lunch and dinner; Su dinner. Reservations recommended. 5 St. James's St (between Pall Mall and King St). 839.3774. Tube: Green Park

50 Berry Bros. and Rudd A wonderful, Dickensian structure with exquisite, strangely shaped black windows, this wine shop looks much as it did in the 18th century. The long, dark room contains a large oval table, chairs, antique prints, a few bottles of wine, and a pair of enormous scales embossed with "The Coffee Mill," acquired from the grocer who originally occupied the site. From the 1760s, clients used to weigh themselves on the huge scales, and their weights are recorded in the shop's ledgers. Weight watching was serious business even in the days when corpulence signified prosperity. The Duke of York, who led his men up the hill and down again, weighed 14.5 stone (one stone is 14 pounds), but the weight of his brother, King George IV, famous for his large girth, is not recorded.

The wine, however, is what marks this shop for posterity. The distinctive black-and-white labels have been appearing on bottles of claret for more than 200 years, and the cellars contain bottles that would fill many a Frenchman with awe. The shop also offers a wide selection of single-malt whiskies (including its own Cutty Sark brand). ♦ M-Sa. 3 St. James's St (at Pickering Pl). 396.9600. Tube: Green Park

50 Pickering Place Timber wainscoting still lines this 18th-century alleyway. Halfway along the street is a plaque, "The Republic of Texas Legation 1842-45," commemorating the days when Texas was an independent republic and this was its embassy. It was rented to the Texans by the **Berry Bros. and Rudd** wine shop during a serious slump in the business of vintners. At the end of the alley is a court surrounded by houses that looks more like a cul-de-sac in a cathedral town than in the center of London. ♦ Between Crown Passage and St. James's St. Tube: Green Park

51 House of Hardy This is considered London's finest shop for fishing tackle. Queen Mary had a **Hardy** rod, as has every Prince of Wales this century. The shop once developed a big-game reel for the American novelist Zane Grey. It also sells quality country clothing, especially the Barbour line, and it offers computerized bookings for, say, salmon fishing on the River Tweed in Scotland. ♦ M-Sa. 61 Pall Mall (between Crown Passage and St. James's St). 839.5515. Tube: Green Park

52 Red Lion ★★$$ Dating back 400 years, this picturesque, timber-fronted pub may have been one of the first to hang out the popular "Red Lion" insignia, and was once used for the assignations of Nell Gwyn and Charles II. There is a small wood-paneled bar where you can order sandwiches, and a pleasant upstairs room in which to partake of hearty home-cooked food. Tuck into fish-and-chips or a steak-and-ale pie. ♦ Pub ♦ Daily lunch. Crown Passage (between Pall Mall and King St). 930.4141. Tube: Green Park

53 Schomberg House A rare example of Queen Anne architecture, this house was built around 1698. The warm brown-red brick, tall Dutch windows, and human scale come as a relief from the imposing Italianate stones and stucco that dominate this area. Gainsborough spent his last years here, dying in 1788 after finally reconciling with his old friend and rival Joshua Reynolds. His parting words were, "We are all going to Heaven and Van Dyck is of the company." After World War II, the house was gutted and filled with modern offices. Next door is the site of a house that was owned by the charming actress Nell Gwyn, mistress of Charles II. All the property on Pall Mall belongs to the Crown, with the exception of **No. 79,** because Gwyn refused to live in a house she didn't own. The blue plaque here spells her name as Gwynne but it appears as Gwyn or even Gwynn in the many references to this memorable royal mistress. Neither of the premises is open to the public. ♦ 82 Pall Mall (between Carlton Gardens and Marlborough Rd). Tube: Green Park

54 Oxford and Cambridge Club This club is more democratic and less misogynistic than the others on Pall Mall, although true equality has not yet arrived. Out of a total membership of 4,500, women number only 550. This is a private club for people who have been admitted as members of a college at the **Universities** of **Oxford** or **Cambridge.** It has arrangements with some 125 clubs overseas, including many university clubs in the US, and lodging in one of the club's 42 rooms costs a fraction of the rates at hotels. Behind the impressive facade, the rooms are decorated and arranged in the manner of a large town house of the early 19th century. The dining rooms aren't fancy, but the wine lists are. **Sir Robert Smirke** and **Sydney Smirke** built this headquarters in 1837. ♦ 71 Pall Mall (between St. James's Sq and Pall Mall Pl). 930.5151. Tube: Green Park

55 St. James's Palace The whole St. James's area owes its development to the **Palace of St. James's** (whose name comes from the Augustinian hospital for leprous women that stood on this site in the 13th century). Henry VIII purchased the land in 1532 to build a small royal palace—initially a hunting lodge (he also enclosed some 300 acres to the south) and later his third royal residence. After the fall of Cardinal Wolsey, Henry switched his allegiance to **Whitehall Palace.** Even so, he regarded the rambling brick mansion called **St. James's Palace** (shown left) with affection. Feminine appreciation for the palace is suggested in its history of royal births—Charles II, James II, Mary II, and Queen Anne were all born here in the 1600s. Charles II never liked **Whitehall,** so he spent time, energy

St. James's Palace

and money building up this palace; however, it did not become the official residence of the sovereign until 1698, when **Whitehall Palace** burned down. It remained the monarch's London residence until Queen Victoria ascended to the throne in 1837 and moved the court to **Buckingham Palace.** Yet **St. James's** maintains a presence in modern British life; Prince Charles not only has his office here, he also now resides in rooms here during the week. To this day, all foreign ambassadors present their "credentials" to the **Court of St. James's** before riding in the Glass Coach to **Buckingham Palace.** The palace originally had four courts, but fire, rebuilding, and time have cut the number in half. The state rooms, which can be glimpsed over the wall facing The Mall, were rebuilt by **Sir Christopher Wren** in 1703. The most charming surviving part of the Tudor palace is the gatehouse, with its octagonal clock tower, which faces St. James's Street. This four-story building of worn redbrick sits astride a pair of vast old gates. The turrets crowned with battlements and the sentry box manned by a soldier from the Guards seem too "Gilbert and Sullivan" to be true but are a reminder of the pomp for which this palace exists. ♦ Pall Mall (at St. James's St). Tube: Green Park

At St. James's Palace:

Chapel Royal This lovely chapel, west of the gatehouse at **St. James's Palace,** was built by Henry VIII in 1532. It is one of the great gems of Tudor London, with a coffered ceiling painted by Hans Holbein. Married beneath it were William III and Mary II (1677), Queen Anne (1683), George IV (1795), Queen Victoria (1840), and George V (1893). What stirs the heart most though is not the royal weddings, but Charles I, the sad, brave king who received communion in the chapel on the morning of his execution, 30 January 1649. This is one of five **Chapels Royal** in London, and as such, it is not subject to a bishop but owes its allegiance directly to the sovereign. Visitors can attend services in the chapel every Sunday from October to Easter. Since the chapel is within the palace complex, there is strict security, with a policeman on duty at a sentry box. Services start promptly. ♦ Su 8:30AM, 11:15AM Jan-Easter and Oct-Dec. Ambassadors' Ct (at Stable Yard Rd)

55 Friary Court Every new sovereign is proclaimed from the balcony in this courtyard, and it was from here that the cheers of her subjects reached the ears of 18-year-old Queen Victoria, causing her to weep. The **State Apartments,** reached through the door in the northeast corner, are open only on special occasions, usually when royal gifts are on display, and the wait can be considerable. The **Armoury Room** is lined with ancient weapons, and the **Tapestry Room** with pictorial textiles

woven for Charles II. The last person to have a hand at decorating these rooms was William Morris in the 1860s. ♦ Off Marlborough Rd

56 Queen's Chapel This 17th-century architectural gem by **Inigo Jones** was the first church built in the Classical style; like **Banqueting House** in Whitehall, also by **Jones,** the interior is a perfect cube. The chapel was built for the Spanish Infanta Maria, the intended bride of Charles I. The arrangement didn't work out, however, and Charles eventually married another woman, Henrietta Maria, here. Now it is one of five **Chapels Royal** in the city. The gold-and-white coffered ceiling is original. On summer Sundays, the chapel is marvelously lit by the sun through the wide Venetian window, which occupies the entire east wall. Visitors can enter the church for Sunday services. ♦ Su 8:30AM, 11:15AM Easter-July. Marlborough Rd (between the Mall and Pall Mall). Tube: Green Park

MICHAEL STORRINGS

57 Marlborough House Sir Christopher Wren built this residence (shown above) for John Churchill, first Duke of Marlborough, between 1709 and 1711—though it was more for the duchess than for the duke. Formidable, turbulent, brilliant, and beautiful, Sarah Churchill, first duchess of Marlborough and lady-in-waiting as well as intimate friend of Queen Anne, laid the inscribed foundation stone that survives within the house. The duchess hated the monumental palace of Blenheim (which Queen Anne had created for the duke after his victory at the Battle of Blenheim), so she instructed **Wren** to make her London mansion strong, plain, and convenient. The Crown acquired the house in 1817. Unfortunately, its pure simplicity has been disguised by the additions and enlargements made in the early 1860s by **Sir James Pennethorne.** Edward VII lived here while he was Prince of Wales, George V was born in the house, and his consort, Queen Mary, lived here during her widowhood. In 1959, Queen Elizabeth presented the **Marlborough House** to the nation so that it could become the **Commonwealth Conference Center.** It is still used for meetings today, but is closed to the public.♦ Pall Mall (at Marlborough Rd). 839.3411. Tube: Green Park

58 Clarence House This house was built for the Duke of Clarence, later King William IV. Until Queen Elizabeth's accession to the throne in 1952, she and Prince Philip lived here. Now it is the dwelling of the queen mother, who comes to the gate to greet the public on her birthday, 4 August. On that day a lone bagpiper plays in the garden at 9AM, a gentle Scottish alarm clock for one of the best-loved members of the royal family. Diana Spencer and Sarah Ferguson stayed here on the eves of their weddings. The house is closed to the public, and it is not possible to get close to it; it is the cream-colored building visible from the Mall. ◆ Stable Yard Rd (off the Mall). Tube: Green Park, St. James's Park

59 Lancaster House In 1825, **Benjamin Dean Wyatt** started construction of this house in light Bath stone for the Duke of York, who commissioned the extravagant home but died before paying for it, whereupon it was sold to the Marquess of Stafford (hence the structure was first called **York House** and then **Stafford House**). **Sir Robert Smirke** completed it in 1840, and **Sir Charles Barry** designed the interior. Chopin played for Queen Victoria in the **Music Room,** and the Duke of Windsor lived here when he was the Prince of Wales (from 1919 to 1930). Since being restored from war damage, the building has been a venue for state banquets and conferences. The Louis XV interiors are sumptuous. It is closed to the public. ◆ Stable Yard Rd (at Stable Yd). Tube: Green Park, St. James's Park

60 St. James's Park In the 16th century, Henry VIII enclosed this, the oldest and most perfect of royal parks. Today it comprises 93 acres and is an enchantment of water, birds, views, gaslights, and Englishness. It is a royal park in the best sense of the word: monarchs have lavished their wealth and ingenuity on it, making it a graceful, contemplative place. Henry VIII drained the marshland between **St. James's** and **Whitehall Palaces** to make a forest and deer-hunting park. Charles I created the ceremonious walks, and he strode bravely across the park to his execution. His son, Charles II, created what you see today; he hired French landscape gardener André Le Nôtre and, shortly after the Restoration, opened this exotic oasis of trees, flowers, ducks, geese, and pelicans to the public. In 1827, George IV enlisted **John Nash** to reshape the canal and create the meandering lake, spanned by a bridge that grants a magical view of **Buckingham Palace.** Daily at 3PM the distinguished pelicans appear for an afternoon tea of whiting and other aquatic delicacies; they are direct descendants of the pair given to Charles II by a Russian ambassador. On the south side of the park runs **Birdcage Walk,** named for the aviaries Charles II established here for his amusement. ◆ Bounded by Horse Guards and Spur Rds, and Birdcage Walk and the Mall. Tube: St. James's Park

61 Buckingham Palace The royal palace is the most looked-at building in London, not because of its magnificence or its age, but because of the appealing mystique of the monarchy—and as Maude declared to her young lover in *Harold and Maude,* "We [Americans] may not believe in monarchy, but we miss the kings and queens."

This is the oldest monarchy in the world, and it resides in the last country where monarchy exists on a grand and sanctified scale, with religious processions and backed-up by a titled aristocracy that transcends nationality, social class, and party affiliation.

Her Most Excellent Majesty Elizabeth the Second, by the Grace of God, of the United Kingdom of Great Britain and Northern Ireland and of her Realms and Territories Queen, Head of the Commonwealth, Defender of the Faith, Sovereign of the British Orders of Knighthood, is the 40th monarch since the Norman Conquest, descended from Charlemagne and King Canute. Her accession in 1952 coincided with the beginning of the end of the British Empire, and she has presided over its dissolution with noble leadership. She is probably one of the best-informed diplomats alive today, having had continuous access to world leaders for more than 40 years. She has known Khrushchev, Eisenhower, de Gaulle, Kennedy, Brezhnev, Reagan, and Gorbachev, and is acquainted with every current major head of state around the globe. On Tuesday nights when Queen Elizabeth is in London, the prime minister goes to **Buckingham Palace** for a talk with her. The queen's concern, excellent memory, and sharp insight have been appreciated by almost all the prime ministers of her reign.

Will she retire and turn the business over to her eldest son? The answer is no. Elizabeth is queen for life, having been anointed during what is considered to be the sacrament of coronation; the monarchy's continuity and survival depend on adherence to its spiritual laws. Under the hereditary system, the last intake of breath by the dying sovereign coincides with the next intake by the living sovereign, hence the ancient cry, "The king is dead. Long live the king."

When the queen is in residence at **Buckingham Palace,** the royal standard flies overhead. The tourist's viewpoint is the rather dour eastern facade (see page 63), completely rebuilt by **Sir Aston Webb** in 1913. The front western facade, visible only to visitors to the palace, is by **John Nash,** the palace's first architect (**Nash** began the building in 1820, and **Edmund Blore** finished it). The main building is flanked by two Classical pavilions and overlooks an immense sweep of lawn, 45 acres of private gardens, woodlands, giant trees, more than 200 species of wild plants, a lake graced with pink flamingos, a leafy border, and tennis courts. This is where the queen's garden parties are held each summer.

The original redbrick house, built for the Duke and Duchess of Buckingham in 1702-5, was bought by George III some 60 years later for his beloved Queen Charlotte, who filled it with children and made it into a family home, which became known as **Queen's House.** George IV commissioned **Nash** to make it into a residence worthy of a monarch, but the plans became grander and more difficult to execute with time. The transformation process had many of the elements of a Laurel and Hardy film, not the least being the scheme to surround the palace with scaffolding to disguise the fact that a new palace was being constructed, as Parliament had granted permission only for renovations and repairs. When the king died, an investigation into the palace's spiraling costs revealed financial irregularities. **Nash,** who had transformed London into an elegant city, was dismissed by an outraged Parliament. Publicly disgraced, he died five years later, in 1835. George IV died before the palace was finished, and his successor, William IV, preferred to live in **Kensington Palace** until his death. **Buckingham Palace** became the official London residence of the sovereign in 1837, when Queen Victoria moved in. Building work began soon after: There were not enough bedrooms or nurseries, and the kitchens were old-fashioned and badly planned. Yet the royal standard flew as repairs were made, and the queen and her consort, Prince Albert, extended the palace, also building the **State Supper Room** and the **Ball Room.** The queen had the **Marble Arch** removed from the front of the palace and placed at its present site on the north side of **Hyde Park.** By 1843, Victoria had written in her diary that she was very happy here. **Webb,** architect for George V and his popular wife, Mary of Teck, transformed

the palace's facade, replacing the flaking Caen stone with Portland stone and adding the French-inspired pilasters. George V also saw the 1911 unveiling of the **Victoria Memorial** in front of the palace: A wedding cake of a sculpture by Sir Thomas Brock, it shows a seated, 13-foot-high Queen Victoria facing the Mall, surrounded by the figures of Truth, Justice, and Motherhood—all dear to her heart. At the top, Victory is attended by Constancy and Courage. **Buckingham Palace** is open to the public during August and September (when the royals are vacationing). Tickets can now be bought in advance—they go on sale at 9AM in a ticket office erected each summer beside **Green Park** in **The Mall.** Beginning at 9:30AM, time-specific tickets (for that day only) gain visitors entry to a palace entrance on Buckingham Palace Road. The admission price goes toward the restoration of the fire-damaged **Windsor Castle.** The 18 rooms on view include the **State Rooms,** the **Throne Room,** the **State Dining Rooms,** and the **Music Room.** Many works in the nonpareil **British Royal Collection** can be seen as well (also see the **Queen's Gallery,** below). A gift shop in a hut at the garden exit sells specially commissioned gifts that are only available here. The Changing of the Guard ceremony is held inside the palace gates at 11:30AM from early April through early August, usually every 48 hours (call for information about the schedule or check *The Times*) and varies the rest of the year. ♦ Admission. Daily Aug-Sept. At the end of The Mall. 839.1377. Information on the Changing of the Guard ceremony: 0839/123411 (premium rate call); www.royal.gov.uk. Tube: St. James's Park, Victoria, Green Park

62 Queen's Gallery This royal treasure chest, built by **John Nash** in 1831, was originally a conservatory and in 1843 became a chapel. In 1962, Her Majesty established it as a gallery to show artworks from the **Royal Collection,** one of the world's greatest art collections. Only a small fraction of the hundreds of

Buckingham Palace

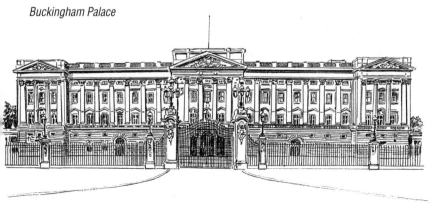

Crown Commodities: The Royal Family Talks Shop

Although it may be hard to picture them doing so, members of Britain's royal family have been known to go shopping. Whether the baskets and bags are filled by the sovereigns or their servants is a matter for speculation; however, finding out where the ruling class spends its cash is simple—look for a Royal Warrant, a coat of arms that represents one of four members of the royal family: the queen, the queen mother, the Duke of Edinburgh, or the Prince of Wales. When a supplier holds a Royal Warrant, it means that it provides goods to one of the "Big Four" by appointment. The privilege is worth having, since the supplier can then advertise to all and sundry that "royalty shops here"—not a bad way to drum up business. Like much of English heritage, the tradition began in the Middle Ages. Henry VIII gave his approval to a "King's Laundresse"; his daughter, Elizabeth, had her own "Operator for the Teeth." In order to qualify for royal approval today, a business must have supplied goods or services to the royal household for three years running. At last count, there are around 1,000 Royal Warrant holders.

Some are easy to identify and fairly obvious. There is **Harrods,** of course, with all four Royal Warrants;

ROLANDO CORUJO

Hatchards, the bookseller, and **Lobb's,** the shoemaker, both hold three. **Twinings,** on the Strand, has the honor of supplying all the royal tea, the **House of Hardy** claims to have sold fishing rods to every Prince of Wales this century, and **Lock & Co.** serves as hatter to the Duke of Edinburgh. You can play "spot the Warrant" throughout **St. James's** and **Piccadilly** (the insignia are usually displayed over or near the shop's door)—since these two areas are convenient to **Buckingham Palace,** they contain possibly the largest concentration of Royal Warrant holders in London.

The other way to find out what the royals use is simply to look at the goods. With this method, you can tell which marmalade the queen prefers (it's probably sold at **Fortnum & Mason,** "the Queen's Grocer") and what cologne Prince Charles uses (from **Floris**). Every roll of Andrex brand toilet paper proudly displays the Royal Warrants of the queen and the queen mother, an advertising coup for Scott Limited, the supplier that proclaims itself "by appointment. . . manufacturer of disposable tissues" to these two royal shoppers.

---

paintings, sculptures, furnishings, and drawings in the collection can be shown at any one time. Exhibits (which change every 18 months) focus on a particular subject or theme, such as royal children, animal paintings, British soldiers, specific old masters such as Gainsborough or Leonardo, or heirloom silver, cutlery, and furniture. There is also a gift shop, excellent for souvenirs from the royal homes such as pungent lavender scent from Prince Charles's country house Highgrove. ♦ Admission; a single admission ticket covering both the **Queen's Gallery** and the **Royal Mews** (see below) is also available. Daily Mar-Dec. Buckingham Gate (between Birdcage Walk and Buckingham Palace Rd). 839.1377. Tube: Victoria, St. James's Park

63 Royal Mews All seven state carriages and coaches from all periods are on display in this circa-1826 building by **John Nash;** this is probably the finest and most valuable collection of state coaches in the world. Here is the State Coach acquired by George II in 1762 that is still in use today. It looks like the enchanted coach from *Cinderella,* with

elaborate carvings representing eight palm trees, branching at the top and supporting the roof, and three cherubs, representing England, Scotland, and Ireland. It is 24 feet long, 8 feet wide, and 12 feet high; it weighs 4 tons. This is also the home of the royal horses, which may sometimes be seen pulling carriages in **Hyde Park.** ♦ Admission. W noon-4PM Oct-Mar; Tu-Th noon-4PM Apr-July; M-Th noon-4PM Aug-Sept. Buckingham Palace Rd (at Lower Grosvenor Pl). 839.1377. Tube: Green Park, St. James's Park, Victoria

The Goring Hotel

64 Goring $$$$ Just behind the queen's home is another family-run dwelling, albeit on a smaller scale. The Goring family has owned this revered hotel since 1910 and regularly receives plaudits for its high standards and modern-day comforts. There's a beautiful private garden, and the 75 stylishly furnished rooms boast marble bathrooms. The classically decorated lobby areas have a welcoming atmosphere. ♦ 17 Beeston Pl (at Eaton La). 396.9000; fax 834.4393. Tube: Victoria

Within the Goring:

Goring Restaurant ★★$$$ The meals live up to reasonable standards with some flair. Try the grilled Dover sole or lobster thermidor. Clarets and coffee are served. ♦ British ♦ Daily lunch and dinner. 396.9000

65 Royal Mint Sovereign Gallery Beautiful British coins, newly minted, are on display but a historical exhibition concentrates on the sovereign, a coin first introduced by Henry VII. It achieved icon status within the British trading empire; in India, gold sovereigns were used in jewelry worn by aristocratic families to show off their spectacular wealth. The sovereign is no longer in circulation but special editions are minted to sell to coin collectors. These are

on sale along with other, reasonably priced souvenir editions of British coins. ♦ Daily. 7 Grosvenor Gardens (between Beeston and Lower Grosvenor Pls). 828.8724. Tube: Victoria

66 Westminster Cathedral Coming across this distinctive red-and-white structure is a sweet surprise amid the thundering traffic of this area. Its hidden location is a shame, since the cathedral is the principal Roman Catholic church in England. By London standards, it came on the scene relatively late—the cathedral was designed and built in 1894 by **John Bentley** at the behest of Archbishop Herbert Vaughan, who demanded something entirely different from **Westminster Abbey.** The archbishop got what he wanted: **Bentley** mixed Romanesque and Byzantine influences, just as he mixed redbrick with white Portland stone. The result is somewhat Venetian. Within, side chapels are decked with glowing mosaics, and there is a bronze by Elizabeth Frink. The view from **St. Edward's Tower,** a 273-foot bell tower, is stunning. Every second Tuesday from mid-June to mid-September, the cathedral hosts concerts of classical music played on its organ, which is one of the finest such instruments in Europe. ♦ Admission for concerts and the bell tower. Daily. Ashley Pl (between Ambrosden Ave and Morpeth Terr). 798.9055. Tube: Victoria

Bests

John Ruler
Travel Writer and Broadcaster, Ruler Editorial Services

Watching the sun set over the **Thames** from the walkways of **Tower Bridge,** now open to the public.

Having afternoon tea and homemade cakes in the **Crypt Restaurant** at **St. Martin-in-the-Fields** close to **Trafalgar Square;** their sandwiches and hot snacks are pretty good too.

The scent of spring flowers, especially the daffodils, in the almost country-cottage setting of **Church Street, Chelsea,** still a village in so many ways.

Admiring **Buckingham Palace** from the bridge in the middle of **St. James's Park,** ready made for photographers looking for that distinctive shot.

Browsing through the specialist bookshops in **Charing Cross Road.**

Strolling along the **South Bank** away from the traffic—and with more than its fair share of sights—in either direction. Plenty of coffee and rest room stops, also novelty shopping at the **National Film Theatre** and the **Museum of the Moving Image.**

Feeling proud that at long last **Southwark,** the genuine heart of London, is being recognized, thanks to projects like the reconstruction of **Shakespeare's Globe Theatre,** and the conversion, by the year 2000, of the old **Bankside Power Station** into the **Tate Gallery of Modern Art.**

Listening to Shakespeare during the summer at the open-air theater, **Regent's Park;** mulled wine during the interval keeps out the evening chill. If it looks like rain, bring an umbrella and book a seat for *The Tempest.*

Horse-riding in **Rotten Row:** Go early when the Horse Guards are exercising. It's as extraordinary as riding in Central Park, New York. I have done both.

Taking the riverbus to **Greenwich Park** for a picnic and a tour round the splendidly ornate **Maritime Museum.**

Andrew Currie
Owner, Nomad Books/Whisky Distiller

Waterloo Bridge, October—Walking across at sunset to the **National Theatre.**

Royal Opera House, Crush Bar—Best bar staff in Europe.

Zen Central—Best Chinese food.

Putney Towpath—Running to **Hammersmith Bridge** past **Harrods Depository.**

Soho, Summer—6AM Sunday. Last night's detritus with new day.

Stamford Bridge, August—Watching new football season. Clean grass, clean shirts, bright hope.

Paddington Station, November, 7AM—good cappuccino. Leaving town as commuters arrive.

Mayfair/Piccadilly

From its risqué beginning as the site of a ribald 17th-century festival, Mayfair has grown into one of the most desirable of London addresses. Bordered to the north and east by celebrated shopping thoroughfares **Oxford Street** and **Regent Street**, to the south by charismatic Piccadilly, and to the west by frenetic but fashionable **Park Lane,** this neighborhood is a playground for the wealthy. Such affluence grew from an initial half-dozen estates. The owners, landed aristocrats, laid out the rectangular area in orderly patterns of generous avenues and stately squares, and lined them with their elegant mansions—which, of course, were equipped with mews in back for horses and carriages. After the rich and famous came the suppliers to the rich and famous; soon the district contained elite merchants as well as their prosperous patrons.

Today, diplomats from **Grosvenor Square** and financial magnates from **Brook Street** have replaced the dukes and duchesses, but the aristocratic

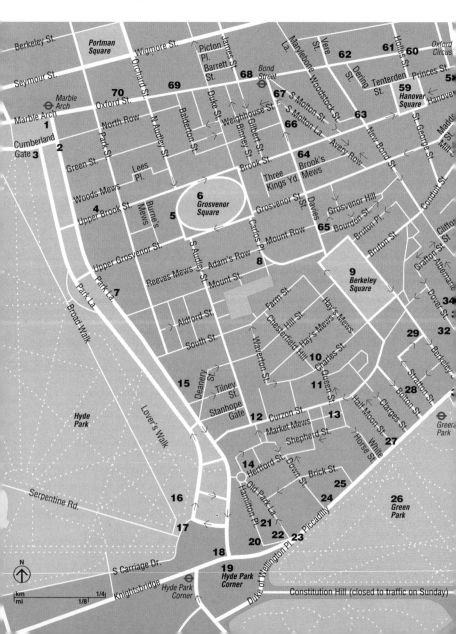

mbience lingers. Mayfair and Park Lane are still the most expensive, exclusive properties on Britain's Monopoly board, with the retail meccas of Oxford, **Bond,** and Regent Streets close behind. Dotted in between are some of the most luxurious hotels and restaurants the pound can buy. To the south lies the "Magic Mile" of Piccadilly, named for a fashionable 17th-century collar called a "picadil." The street begins at **Hyde Park Corner** in an atmosphere of respectability, then coasts past the verdant **Green Park;** the Ritz hotel, with its "romantic getaway" mystique; and tranquil **St. James's, Piccadilly.** But as Piccadilly approaches the beloved statue of **Eros,** a popular meeting place in the center of **Piccadilly Circus,** the grandeur diminishes. Piccadilly Circus, London's answer to Times Square, has consistently defied attempts to make it dignified. Confusion, traffic, and neon characterize the scene (no wonder they call it a circus), yet Londoners and visitors fiercely defend this traffic circle–cum–meeting place, flocking to the feet of the God of Love (meant to represent the angel of Charity).

The best time to see Piccadilly is on a weekday, when the English gentry is on the prowl for cashmere sweaters and other such necessities. You can also observe a few of the blue bloods' haunts: the headquarters of London's cafe society (**Langans Brasserie and Cafe Royal**), one of the most beautiful dining rooms in the world (the **Ritz Restaurant**), a Regency shopping center (the **Burlington Arcade**), what is probably the world's most opulent grocery store **(Fortnum & Mason)**, and one of London's most intriguing galleries (the **Royal Academy of Arts**). Head back to Mayfair for afternoon tea at **Brown's Hotel,** and you will have indulged for a time in the upper-crust experience, London-style.

City code 0171 unless otherwise noted.

1 Marble Arch Built in 1827 by **John Nash,** this version of Rome's Arch of Constantine was originally a gateway to **Buckingham Palace,** but when the front was redesigned, it was no longer appropriate so the arch was moved to a corner of **Hyde Park.** It rests on the former location of the Tyburn Gallows, London's main site for public executions until the 18th century. Only the royal family and the King's Troop Royal Horse Artillery may pass through **Marble Arch.** However, the incessant flow of traffic around it tends to negate its dignity. ◆ Oxford St and Park La. Tube: Marble Arch

2 Park Lane Once a narrow strip between a green oasis and prominent grand houses, this hectic four-lane thoroughfare runs past several high-rise hotels and offices. From the 18th century onward, the street has been associated with riches, though today's version concentrates more on conglomerate wealth than the private kind. Take a taxi ride here in the evening and you're likely to come across limos dropping off debutantes for a charity ball or powerful executives for a gala dinner; at any rate, you'll see a lot of slicked hair, tailcoats, and flowing gowns. ♦ Between Hyde Park Corner and Oxford St. Tube: Marble Arch, Hyde Park Corner

3 Speakers' Corner Oratory at the famous northeastern corner of **Hyde Park** dates back to 1872, when mass demonstrations at the site (against a proposed Sunday Trading Bill) led to the established right of assembly. The area is liveliest on Sunday afternoons, and hecklers are part of the show. ♦ Cumberland Gate (at Park La). Tube: Marble Arch

LE GAVROCHE

4 Le Gavroche ★★★★$$$$ *The Good Food Guide* regularly votes this among the top restaurants in London, and Michelin keeps giving it two stars. Having taken over from his father, the famous Albert Roux, the equally renowned Michel Roux produces divine dishes based on regional French recipes. Million-dollar deals are struck here as property developers bargain across the lunch table, while diplomats from the American Embassy speak softly in this opulent basement with its deep green walls edged in copper and lined with paintings. Appetizers include langoustines with pesto and balsamic vinegar, and one of the formidable main courses is pigeon on a bed of glazed turnips and rosemary-flavored risotto. The prices are just as formidable but, as in many expensive restaurants, the fixed-price lunch menu is better value. The wines are fabulously expensive. ♦ French ♦ M-F lunch and dinner. Reservations required; jacket and tie required. 43 Upper Brook St (between Park St and Park La). 408.0881. Tube: Marble Arch

5 American Embassy The design of **Eero Saarinen**'s bunkerlike embassy, completed in 1959, has few fans, especially since Georgian town houses were demolished for its construction. The Duke of Westminster still owns this land in the area known as "Little America," so even though it is the largest embassy in Britain (with 5.85 acres of floor space), it's also probably one of the only American embassies not to stand on "American" soil. Note the gigantic bald eagle on top; its wingspan is approximately 35 feet. ♦ 24 Grosvenor Sq (at S Audley St). 499.9000. Tube: Bond Street, Marble Arch

6 Grosvenor Square The largest square in London after Lincoln's Inn Fields, this was once the grandest address the capital could offer. In 1710, Sir Richard Grosvenor procured an act allowing him to build on his property, a group of fields in the area between Oxford Street and Park Lane. The entire estate was planned as a unit, with the architecturally imposing square at its heart. **Colen Campbell** designed the east side with uniform houses, but the rest grew up in a variety of Georgian styles, all overlooking a central formal garden said to have been laid out by William Kent. Today, fancy additions and rebuilding have erased the architectural consistency, and the garden is merely a swath of pleasant green, watched over by William Reid Dick's bronze statue of Franklin Delano Roosevelt. ♦ S Audley St (between Upper Grosvenor and Upper Brook Sts). Tube: Bond Street, Marble Arch

7 Le Méridien Grosvenor House Hotel $$$ The annual Grosvenor House Antiques Fair is held in this grand hotel, whose 453 luxurious bedrooms are desirable for the view over **Hyde Park** alone. There are also 140 apartments and a health club. The property's main draw, however, is the superb French food of **Chez Nico at 90 Park Lane** (see below). There is also an informal eatery, **Cafe Nico**, serving breakfast, lunch, and dinner. ♦ 90 Park La (between Mount and Upper Grosvenor Sts). 499.6363, 800/225.5843; fax 493.3341. Tube: Bond Street, Marble Arch

Within Le Méridien Grosvenor House Hotel:

Chez Nico at 90 Park Lane ★★★$$$$ In this romantically lit room with dark paneling, richly colored paintings, and fresh flowers galore, the self-taught and outspoken Nico Ladenis is the favorite chef of many London epicures. Some say this place (also known as **Nico at 90**) is the city's finest restaurant; its wonderful French food rates three Michelin stars. Appetizers include foie gras terrine with nuggets of poached pears. The veal cutlet with diced cèpes and garlic cloves is an excellent sample of the master's work, as is the caramelized lemon tart for dessert. The wine list is likewise superb. ♦ French ♦ M-F lunch and dinner; Sa dinner. Reservations required. 409.1290

Park Terrace ★★$$$ With its pale turquoise walls and carpet and huge windows overlooking Park Lane, this large, airy restaurant is a good choice for a light lunch or dinner. Dishes might include squid and chorizo salad for an appetizer and such main dishes as pan-fried brill on cabbage with a clam-and-bacon broth or roasted wood pigeon on an herb-and-potato pancake. ♦ International ♦ Daily breakfast, lunch, afternoon tea, dinner until 2AM. 499.6363

The Italian Restaurant ★★$$ A pleasant taverna with light beige walls and polished wooden floors, it replaces **Pasto Vino**. Chef Stefanio Savio produces regional Italian dishes based on seasonal offerings. Appetizers include duck prosciutto served with truffle-scented lentils and such main courses as parmesan-crusted fillet of veal with creamed spinach. ♦ Italian ♦ M-Sa lunch and dinner. 499.6363

8 Connaught $$$$ An opulent, exclusive atmosphere exudes from this Mayfair landmark. Enjoying discreet service and attention, guests feel like they're spending the night in a deliciously comfortable, English country mansion. All 66 rooms and 24 suites are decorated differently, with oil paintings, antiques, and flowers everywhere, and an open fire warms the sitting rooms. ♦ Carlos Pl (at Mount St). 499.7070, 212/838.3110 in New York City, 800/223.6800 elsewhere in the US; fax 495.3262. Tube: Bond Street

Within the Connaught:

Connaught Restaurant ★★★★$$$$ Chef Michel Bourdin's French haute cuisine exemplifies what a master can do. Try the *feuilletté* of scallops, langoustines, and sole *bonne femme* (sole with white wine sauce and mushrooms), or the filet mignon Stroganoff. The vintage Ports here are truly vintage, and the wine is expensive. The same menu is also available in the adjacent **Grill Room,** a smaller, less formal dining room with the ambience of a gentleman's club. ♦ French ♦ Restaurant: daily lunch and dinner. Grill Room: daily lunch and dinner. Restaurant and Grill Room: reservations required; jacket and tie required. 499.7070

9 Berkeley Square Like Grosvenor Square, this Georgian square is associated with the rich and famous. In the late 1890s, Waldorf Astor lived at **No. 54,** followed by department store tycoon Gordon Selfridge, whose legacy stands in Oxford Street. More recently, in the early 1970s, the elusive Lord Lucan played poker at the **Clermont Club (No. 44).** Accused of murder, he disappeared but is regularly "spotted" in some country or other. At **No. 45,** Lord Clive, better known as Clive of India, committed suicide in 1774. The **Clermont Club,** built by **William Kent,** is said to be the finest remaining example of a Georgian terraced house in central London. Centuries-old plane trees shade the west side of the square, where privileged young men and

women sip Champagne at the annual Berkeley Square Ball. ♦ At Bruton and Hill Sts, and Berkeley and Davies Sts. Tube: Green Park, Bond Street

10 English-Speaking Union (ESU) US Ambassador Charles Price II called the **ESU** "without doubt the most effective and vigorous private group linking the United Kingdom, the United States, and many other nations in a worldwide effort to improve mutual understanding." Its headquarters— draped with both the Union Jack and the Stars and Stripes—has been located in **Dartmouth House** since 1927. The house dates to 1757, and a number of British aristocrats, including the Earl of Dartmouth, have lived here. Today, in addition to providing an assortment of educational opportunities and exchanges, the building hosts cultural activities—concerts, readings, lectures, and dramatic events. ♦ M-F. 37 Charles St (between Hay's Mews and Chesterfield Hill). 493.3328. Tube: Green Park

11 Zen Central ★★$$$ This chic noshing hole serves nouvelle Chinese dishes in designer surroundings. Entrées include sea bass with black bean sauce and rice-wine–marinated chicken. The people watching is as good as the food. It is part of a chain of Zen Garden restaurants, all of which have Zen in the name. ♦ Chinese ♦ Daily lunch and dinner. 20 Queen St (between Curzon and Charles Sts). 629.8089. Tube: Green Park. Also at: 85 Sloane Ave (between Petyward and Ixworth Pl). 589.1781. Tube: Sloane Square, South Kensington

12 Les Saveurs de Jean-Christophe Novelli ★★★$$$ This well-known restaurant is now part of the growing group of dining places owned by Michelin-starred chef Jean-Christophe Novelli. The menu features set meals which are inexpensive by haute cuisine standards. Novelli is known for his daring combinations: cervelas of cured salmon and foie gras with a fine herb fromage blanc, lasagna of beef daube and shiitake mushrooms with leek puree and licorice sauce. The wine list is long and distinguished. ♦ French ♦ M-F lunch and dinner; Sa-Su dinner. Reservations recommended. 37A Curzon St (between Chesterfield Gardens and S Audley St). 491.8919. Tube: Green Park, Hyde Park Corner

13 Shepherd Market The best way to reach this tiny square, filled with small white houses, boutiques, restaurants, and pubs, is from Curzon Street, through the covered passage at **No. 47.** This is the site of the infamous **May Fair,** begun by Lord St. Albans in 1686 and described on a local shop wall as "that most pestilent nursery of impiety and vice." In 1735, Edward Shepherd obtained a grant from George II for a marketplace to be located on the former grounds of the revelry. Although the market sent most of the bawdiness elsewhere, upscale ladies of ill repute are still occasionally seen flitting from doorway to doorway like beautiful ghosts. ◆ Between White Horse and Trebeck Sts. Tube: Green Park, Hyde Park Corner

On Shepherd Market:

L'Artiste Musclé ★★$$ Nicknamed "The Muscley Artist" by the students and weary businesspeople who come here to regroup, this bistro feels like a Left Bank wine bar, complete with sullen French waitresses. Sit in the tiny upstairs dining room or at a bare wooden table in the wonderfully bohemian cellar; both areas fill quickly after 8PM. *Boeuf bourguignon* and salmon steak are good choices, and there's tiramisù for dessert. Wine is available at decent prices, but the service is annoyingly slow. ◆ French ◆ M-Sa lunch and dinner; Su dinner. 1 Shepherd Market (at White Horse St). 439.6150

Al Hamra ★★★$$ Many patrons think this eatery has the best Lebanese food this side of Beirut. The tabbouleh, hummus, and *f'ul medames* (broad beans sprinkled with parsley, olive oil, lemon juice, and garlic) are as well presented as they are tasty, and the lamb minced with pine nuts and onions cooked inside double layers of cracked wheat is delicious. The atmosphere is noisy and informal with recorded Lebanese music in the background. ◆ Lebanese ◆ Daily lunch and dinner. Reservations recommended. 31-33 Shepherd Market (at Trebeck St). 493.1954

L O N D O N

ON PARK LANE

14 London Hilton on Park Lane $$$$ This elegant property boasts traditional English decor. The 447 rooms feature plush upholstery and draperies in soft, rich colors, and the service is what you would expect from one of London's classier establishments. Amenities include a health club, a spa offering massages and other beauty treatments, a salon, and shops. Executive guest rooms on eight floors of the hotel receive a number of additional complimentary extras, such as continental breakfast, private check-in, a club room, a meeting room, and snacks and drinks throughout the day. Excellent French food is served in the **Windows Restaurant** on the top floor (see below), and **Trader Vic's** offers Polynesian food in the basement. ◆ 22 Park La (between Hertford St and Pitt's Head Mews). 493.8000, 800/HILTONS; fax 208.4142. Tube: Hyde Park Corner

Within the London Hilton on Park Lane:

Windows Restaurant ★★★$$$$ The best part of the **Hilton** is this paneled dining room on the 28th floor, which has a marvelous view across London, **Hyde Park,** and even into the queen's backyard at **Buckingham Palace.** Chef Jacques Rolancy's menu includes *cuisine bourgeoise légère,* which uses traditional methods but is "extra light" in that it is exceptionally low in fat, cholesterol, and calories. Start your meal with oysters with Champagne granita and fried shallots. Then try venison noisettes with sauce chinon and finish with pistachio savarin with kirsch ice cream. At lunchtime in summer, fans of the royals might glimpse a garden party. There is also dancing in the evenings Thursday through Saturday. ◆ French ◆ M-F lunch and dinner; Sa dinner; Su brunch. Reservations recommended; jacket and tie required for dinner. 208.4021

15 Dorchester $$$$ Opulence is the keynote of this 244-room hotel. The imposing foyer has a black-and-white marble floor, while the long, marble-pillared **Promenade** is one of the best places to have afternoon tea in London. Many of the bedrooms and suites, which are listed with English Heritage, have been returned to their original splendor (they were designed by **William Curtis Green** from 1928 to 1931), and some of the rooftop suites are spectacular. The luxurious bathrooms have white Italian marble and—a rarity in England—powerful showers. ◆ 53 Park La (between Deanery and South Sts). 629.8888, 800/727.9820; fax 409.0114. Tube: Hyde Park Corner

Within the Dorchester:

Grill Room ★★★$$$ Designed in 1931 to resemble an old Spanish palace, the opulent dining room boasts ornately carved walls, rich red drapes, and large framed mirrors. Under the direction of chef Willi Eisener, the emphasis here is on British food—such as roast beef with Yorkshire pudding, saddle of lamb, and shepherd's pie—stylishly served from beautiful carving trolleys. Follow a hearty entrée with some delights from the English cheese board. Health-conscious diners will be pleased to know there's a low-cholesterol menu, too. Breakfast here is superb: egg-and-bacon lovers should splurge on the traditional full English version, while those watching their fat intake can go for fruits and whole-grain cereals. ♦ British ♦ Daily breakfast, lunch, and dinner. Reservations recommended. 317.6328

Oriental Restaurant ★★★$$$ At this, London's only Michelin-starred Chinese restaurant, chef Kenneth Poon offers such delights as braised slices of abalone with black mushrooms, and, for a side order, stir-fried heart of mustard greens in a clear stock with dried ham. The décor is traditional Chinese. ♦ Chinese ♦ M-F lunch and dinner; Sa dinner. 317.6328

16 Statue of Achilles Behind **Apsley House** in **Hyde Park** is a memorial to the Duke of Wellington financed by the Ladies of England. The statue was cast by Sir Richard Westmacott in 1822 from French cannons captured at Salamanca, Vitoria, and Waterloo. At one time *Achilles'* flagrant nudity was a shock (a fig leaf was even added to protect Victorian sensibilities). ♦ SE corner of Hyde Park (near Park La). Tube: Hyde Park Corner

17 Queen Elizabeth Gate The name refers not to the present sovereign but to her mother, affectionately known as the "Queen Mum." The frilly wrought-iron gates, designed by **Giuseppe Lund,** were erected in 1993, along with sculpture by David Wynne. The installation has provoked controversy, but the queen mother herself seemed pleased. ♦ S Carriage Dr (at Serpentine Rd). Tube: Hyde Park Corner

Nº 1 LONDON

18 Apsley House (Wellington Museum) Although the austere facade of this building makes it appear permanently closed, and its location on a traffic island means it can be reached only via a maze of pedestrian tunnels, the effort is well worth it. Originally built in 1771-78 by **Robert Adam** for Henry Bathurst, Baron Apsley, the honey-colored stone house was enlarged and remodeled in 1828-30 by **Benjamin Dean Wyatt.** This was the home of Arthur Wellesley, the Duke of Wellington, sometimes known as the Iron Duke and forever remembered as the man who finally

defeated Napoléon. The Marquess of Douro, the heir to the present duke, lives on the top floor of the house, and the duke himself has an apartment on the ground floor.

The structure is a mix of flawless proportions and appended grandeur made possible by a gift of £200,000 to the duke from a grateful Parliament. Inside the house, Napoléon looms considerably larger than he did in life: a statue by Canova expands the French emperor to an idealized 11 feet and covers him not in medals but with a fig leaf. Napoléon commissioned the statue, then rejected it for failing to express his calm dignity—it depicts the winged figure of Victory turning away from him. It stayed packed away in the basement of the Louvre until 1816, when it was bought by the British government and presented by George IV to the Duke of Wellington, to whom Victory had eventually turned.

The museum contains an idiosyncratic collection of victors' loot, along with glorious batons, swords, and daggers. The grateful emperors and kings of the time presented the duke with magnificent dinner services of Sèvres, Meissen, and Berlin porcelain, plus silver and gold plate on display (including the ultimate extravagance: a silver-plated dinner service). The focal point of the china collection is the Sèvres service that Napoléon commissioned as a divorce present for Josephine (she refused to accept it). Together in a museum as they would never have been in life are the Duke of Wellington's sword and Napoléon's court sword (taken from his carriage after the Battle of Waterloo), along with flags, medals, and snuffboxes.

The **Waterloo Gallery,** designed by **Wyatt** in 1828, is the showpiece of **Apsley House.** A banquet was held in this vast 90-foot corridor each year on the anniversary of the great victory over the French at Waterloo. The room was designed to showcase the magnificent art collection, particularly the Spanish pictures presented to the duke by King Ferdinand VII of Spain in gratitude for the defeat of Napoléon.

The collection includes works by Rubens, Murillo (the beautiful *Isaac Blessing Jacob*), Correggio (*The Agony in the Garden,* which was the duke's favorite), and four outstanding pictures by Velázquez, including the early *Water Seller of Seville.* One of the two notable Van Dycks in the room is *St. Rosalie Crowned with Roses by Two Angels.* At the far end of the gallery is Goya's *Equestrian Portrait of Wellington.* But X-rays show the picture was originally of Joseph Bonaparte, Napoléon's brother. Last-minute political alterations called for the head to be replaced with the duke's; Wellington never liked the painting and kept it in storage in his country house at Stratfield Saye, Berkshire. But another portrait of the duke may be more familiar (at least to Britons): Painted by Sir Thomas Lawrence, this likeness of the duke appeared on the back of every £5 note until mid-1990, when it was replaced with a portrait of George Stephenson, inventor of the steam locomotive. The windows, which are fitted with sliding mirrors that at night evoke Louis XIV's Galerie des Glaces at Versailles, are almost as fascinating as the pictures. ♦ Admission. Tu-Su. 149 Piccadilly (at Park La). 499.5676. Tube: Hyde Park Corner

19 Hyde Park Corner "It is doubtless a signal proof of being a London-lover *quand même* that one should undertake an apology for so bungled an attempt at a great public place as Hyde Park Corner." That, at least, was Henry James's opinion, written at the turn of the century. Many decades, improvements, and embellishments later, this triangular patch remains lost in confusion and now suffers the ultimate indignity: it has become a traffic island (albeit a grand one). In order to reach it, you must go into a warren of underpasses, where you can probably find your way by following the forlorn sounds of an equally forlorn harmonica player.

On top of the arch is the beautiful and dramatic *Goddess of Peace*, depicted reining in the Horses of War. Placed on the corner in 1912 after the Boer War, the statue presents an almost identical profile from either side. Looking at her, you almost forget that 200 cars a minute are circling the corner. The sculptor was Adrian Jones, a captain who had spent 23 years as a cavalry officer. The chariot is a quadriga: it is pulled by four horses abreast. Sadly, World War I broke out two years after this monument to peace was placed here, and the memorials that surround the statue today are for the many thousands who died in the worldwide stampede of the Horses of War.

Few arches have been pushed around as much as the one here, which was designed by **Decimus Burton.** It was originally built as a northern gate to the grounds of **Buckingham Palace** and crowned with a statue of the Duke of Wellington; then it was aligned along the same axis as the neighboring Ionic **Hyde Park Screen,** which **Burton** also designed in 1825. The arch was placed here in 1828. In 1883, however, it was repositioned along the axis of Constitution Hill, and now it leads nowhere. It has been called **Wellington Arch** and **Green Park Arch,** but it's now usually referred to as **Constitution Arch.** A statue of David, with his back to the motorized world, commemorates the Machine Gun Corps. Designed by sculptor Francis Derwent Wood in 1925, it proclaims that "Saul hath slain his thousands but David his tens of thousands." Facing the **Lanesborough Hotel** is the

massive, splendid **Royal Artillery Monument,** designed by **C.S. Jaeger** in 1920. It bears the simple, sad inscription: "Here was a royal fellowship of death." Four bronze figures surround a huge gun aimed at the Somme, a battlefield in France where so many men of the Royal Artillery died during World War I. Finally, the statue facing **Apsley House** was created by Sir J.E. Boehm in 1888. It shows the Duke of Wellington on his beloved horse, Copenhagen, who bore his master nobly for 16 hours at the Battle of Waterloo. (When Copenhagen died in 1836, he was buried with full military honors.) ♦ Between Piccadilly and Knightsbridge. Tube: Hyde Park Corner

INTER·CONTINENTAL®
HOTELS AND RESORTS

20 Hotel Inter-Continental London $$$$ With glorious views over **Hyde Park** and Knightsbridge, this fine hotel has an enviable reputation and is understandably popular with international travelers. The smart marble foyer includes the recently upgraded, bright and comfortable **Observatory** lounge. All of the 458 rooms and suites feature mini-bars, marble baths, satellite TV, and in-room movies, and are luxuriously decorated with plush, upholstered chairs and sofas, artwork, silk-trimmed bed coverings, and hand-printed wallpaper. An excellent 24-hour business center has also been added, and there's a gym/sauna for fitness buffs. ♦ 1 Hamilton Pl (between Piccadilly and Park La). 409.3131, 800/327.0200; fax 493.3476. Tube: Hyde Park Corner

Within the Hotel Inter-Continental London:

Le Soufflé ★★★$$$$ With caviar and cool yellow-and-turquoise pastels, this hotel dining room exudes luxury. Aware that they're at one of London's top restaurants, diners sip their Champagne (choose from 15 on the wine list) with the nonchalance of film stars. This trend-setting restaurant is named for the specialty of chef Peter Kromberg, who is famous for bringing pizzazz to the traditional soufflé with his inspired flavor combinations, and for always featuring soufflés as appetizers, main courses, and desserts. So you'll eat it here first, then find it elsewhere. The menu changes completely every two weeks and also varies seasonally. Offerings may include smoked salmon-and-avocado soufflé with crème fraîche and chives to start, then fillet of lamb with citrus crust or Dover sole fillet with lobster and Champagne sauce. For the irresolute (and hungry), there's a fixed-price dinner menu with seven courses. The wine list is a labor of love, even though these prices are usually associated with things that last a bit longer than a meal. Have a look at the special sommelier's choice. ◆ French ◆ Tu-F lunch and dinner; Sa dinner; Su lunch. Jacket and tie required for dinner. 409.3131

Coffee House ★★$$ The *Times* rates breakfasts here as among the best in London. There's a choice of four: the basic continental; the healthy fruit-and-grain buffet; the classic English breakfast with kippers, kedgeree, kidneys, and so forth; and Japanese sushi or seafood. You can also order à la carte. Famous chefs congregate here from time to time. ◆ International ◆ Daily breakfast, lunch, and dinner. 409.3131

21 Four Seasons London $$$$ This super-luxurious property with 201 rooms and 26 suites is suffused with the elegance of past eras. The spacious rooms, prettily decorated in pastels, feature comfortable beds. The hotel's impressive wood-paneled lobby boasts an ornate staircase just right for making a dramatic entrance. In fact, a stay here is a bit like traveling first class on a 1930s ocean liner decorated with fabulous antiques. The hotel even has its own Savile Row tailor come to measure and fit clients. Starting at 3PM, afternoon tea is served in the ground-floor lounge, with harp or piano music in the background and views overlooking Park Lane. You'll enjoy the largest choice of teas in London, as well as a satisfying sequence of sandwiches, scones, and pastries. Should you wish to eat in **Hyde Park** on a summer's day, an excellent picnic lunch will be provided. ◆ Hamilton Pl (between Piccadilly and Park La). 499.0888, 800/332.3442; fax 493.1895. Tube: Hyde Park Corner

Within the Four Seasons London:

Four Seasons Restaurant ★★★$$$$ Chef Shaun Whatling brings innovation to classic dishes, which might include pan-fried duck with sweet-corn cake and an orange-and-coriander sauce or sautéed lamb cutlets with goat cheese and basil sauce. The decor and ambience are elegant and formal, with pink and white linen tablecloths and napkins, Wedgwood china, fine crystal glassware, chandeliers, and large windows overlooking a minute private garden. There's also an extensive wine list. Customers are asked to leave their portable phones with the manager. ◆ International ◆ Daily lunch and dinner. Reservations recommended; jacket and tie required for dinner. 499.0888

Lanes ★★$$$ Hearty English-style fare is served in this casual eatery for lunch and dinner; dishes include roast beef and Yorkshire pudding, fried cod with squid and saffron-mashed potatoes, and pasta. Also try the prix-fixe lunch buffet, which always features sushi, smoked salmon, terrines, king prawns, and a variety of salads. The restaurant boasts a bright yellow color scheme, flowering plants, and oil paintings; it is popular with pre- and post-theater diners. ◆ Modern British ◆ Daily breakfast, lunch, and dinner. 499.0888

22 Hard Rock Cafe ★★$$ People have been waiting in line to eat here for almost three decades, undeterred by rain, sleet, or snow. There is even a line at the souvenir shop at the side. For Americans, a meal here is a nostalgic trip home to the 1960s: Budweiser beer, **Chicago Bears,** hamburgers the size of a catcher's mitt, waitresses with name tags like Dixie and Cookie, and hot fudge sundaes. The best time to go is late afternoon, when the music isn't brain-damagingly loud and you may not have to wait. ◆ American ◆ Daily lunch and dinner. 150 Old Park La (at Piccadilly). 629.0382. Tube: Hyde Park Corner

23 Piccadilly Once the "Magic Mile" was simply a western route out of London, but when a 17th-century tailor named Robert Baker came on the scene, the street's name and image changed forever. Baker made his fortune selling the "picadil," a stiff, ruffled collar, to slaves of fashion at court. The mansion he built was called **Piccadilly Hall,** and the name stuck. Now Piccadilly (not to be confused with Piccadilly Circus) is lined with sights, some appealing, some overbearing. ◆ Between Piccadilly Circus and Hyde Park Corner. Tube: Hyde Park Corner, Green Park, Piccadilly Circus

THE ATHENÆUM HOTEL

24 Athenaeum Hotel and Apartments $$$$ Smaller than its modern neighbors, this property boasts 123 rooms and 33 apartments. Every room is luxuriously decorated, with a two-tone marble bath, hand-printed wall coverings, mahogany furnishings, a CD player, and a VCR. But the icing on the cake is the friendly staff, some of whom have worked here for more than 20 years. There's also a health spa with a gym, pool, steam room, and sauna, and a stylish dining room, **Bullochs** (see below). The hotel is a favorite stop on the international celebrity circuit, drawing such guests as Richard Dreyfuss, Charles Dance, Val Kilmer, and Patrick Bergin. ◆ 116 Piccadilly (at Down St). 499.3464, 800/335.3300; fax 493.1860. Tube: Hyde Park Corner, Green Park

---

Restaurants/Clubs: Red   **Hotels:** Blue
Shops/ ⌖ **Outdoors:** Green   **Sights/Culture:** Black

Within the Athenaeum Hotel and Apartments:

Bullochs ★★★$$$ Decorated in a red, blue, and green color scheme, this restaurant also has such charming touches as skylights and a stone floor. The food is well-prepared, traditional continental fare: rack of lamb with *Provençale* herbs, peppered fillet steak, and a combination seafood dish consisting of grilled scallops, sea bass, and salmon. Interesting desserts include sultana cheesecake with brown-bread ice cream and date-and-toffee pudding. The wine list includes selections from California, Australia, and South Africa as well as the Continent. ♦ Continental ♦ Daily breakfast, lunch, and dinner. 499.3464

25 Park Lane Hotel $$$$ Old, lovely, and full of character, this property isn't actually on Park Lane but rather on Piccadilly, overlooking **Green Park.** It is now part of the Sheraton Group, which has restored the hotel to its former glory. The 266 rooms are individually furnished, the 42 suites have their original 1920s decor and dreamy Art Deco bathrooms, and the clientele is fiercely loyal. The hotel's ballroom—a monument to the Art Deco period—regularly hosts debutante and charity balls. ♦ Piccadilly (between Brick and Down Sts). 499.6321; fax 499.1965. Tube: Hyde Park Corner, Green Park

Within the Park Lane Hotel:

Brasserie on the Park ★★$$ A 1980s Art Deco setting is teamed with French-style brasserie classics—including onion soup, steaks, salads, risottos, fish, and shellfish. ♦ French brasserie ♦ Daily lunch and dinner. 499.6321

Bracewells ★★★$$$ Louis XVI carved paneling (from the London home of American financier John Pierpont Morgan) makes this restaurant feel like a gentlemen's club, and the wine list has the vintages—and prices— that are usually found only in such privileged places. Dishes include lobster with crispy fennel salad to start and such entrées as fillet of sea bass with stuffed mushrooms and black bean sauce. For dessert, be sure to sample the pear-and-almond frangipane tart scented with pear liqueur. ♦ French/British ♦ M-F lunch and dinner; Sa dinner. 499.6321

26 Green Park Greener than emeralds from **Asprey,** these 60 acres of sable-soft grass offer the kind of luxury money can't buy in a city. The land was first enclosed by Henry VIII as a hunting ground, then made royal by Charles II, who established the **Snow House** in the center (now marked only by a mound) for cooling the royal wines. There are no flower beds in the park. Instead, ancient beech, lime, and plane trees spread their limbs like maps of the world. In spring, a tapestry of daffodils and crocuses is woven.

Renting one of the sloping canvas chairs costs a few pence; the chair collector will give you a little sticker as proof that you have paid. Near the gates by The Mall is a strikingly unusual fountain-cum-monument erected in 1994 to the one million Canadians who fought alongside Britain in both World Wars. Maple silhouettes are imbedded onto a slab lapped by constantly flowing water; somehow the effect is of falling leaves. ♦ Bounded by Queen's Walk and Duke of Wellington Pl, and Constitution Hill and Piccadilly. Tube: Green Park

27 Half Moon Street Poke around for a few minutes—this street is haunted by some very distinguished ghosts. Author and reluctant lawyer James Boswell resided here, recording his walks with Samuel Johnson and trying endless remedies for his gonorrhea, which he described graphically in his London journal. Novelist Fanny Burney also called the street home for a time, as did the essayist Hazlitt and the poet Shelley. Inside the world of fiction, this street was the address of P.G. Wodehouse's Bertie Wooster and his faithful valet Jeeves. ♦ Between Piccadilly and Curzon St. Tube: Green Park

Langan's Brasserie

28 Langan's Brasserie ★★★$$$ This Mayfair institution continues to thrive in its third decade. The beautiful, clever, rich, and promising still come here to see and be seen, and it is good luck for everybody that the food is as tasty as it is, thanks to chef and part-owner Richard Shepherd (another co-owner is Michael Caine). Dress glamorously and be sure to look at the pictures (interesting 20th-century British art, including works by David Hockney, hangs on the walls). The bourgeois classics like bangers and mash (sausage links and mashed potatoes) and bubble and squeak (fried pureed potatoes and cabbage) are cooked to perfection. Rumor has it that famous people get the best seats and the lesser known get what they're given; of course, this is rigorously denied by the restaurant, but don't let them put you at a table upstairs. ♦ British ♦ M-F lunch and dinner; Sa dinner. Reservations recommended. Stratton House, Stratton St (between Piccadilly and Berkeley St). 491.8822. Tube: Green Park

29 Mayfair Inter-Continental $$$$ This unassuming sister to the **Inter-Continental** down the street is an appropriate neighbor for **Langan's.** Photographs of celebrities who have stayed here—Neil Diamond, Billy Joel, and Stevie Wonder, to name only a few—line the walls of the bar where resident pianist Iain Kerr plays every evening. This 287-room hotel has 51 suites, 25 of which have bathrooms with Jacuzzis. There is a small health club with solarium, gym, and swimming pool. The rooms are comfortable and well equipped, with good service from the friendly staff, some of whom have been with the hotel for more than 20 years. An all-day snack service is available in the **Mayfair Cafe.** ♦ Stratton St (at Berkeley St). 629.7777, 800/327.0200; fax 629.1459. Tube: Green Park

Within the Mayfair Inter-Continental:

Opus 70 ★★$$$ To complement the hotel's ambience, chef Michael Coaker serves modern cuisine with Asian and European influences. Try his delicious Cajun red mullet with sugar snap peas or rack of lamb with whole-grain mustard crumble. ♦ Continental ♦ M-F, Su lunch and dinner; Sa dinner. Reservations recommended. 915.2842

30 Ritz $$$$ A more evocative word is hard to imagine. Such is its power that the name can be spelled in flashing neon and still look glamorous. The hotel, named for César Ritz, the Swiss hotelier who founded the **Savoy,** was built in the style of a Beaux Arts château with a Parisian arcade from the designs of **Mewes and Davis** in 1906. For ordinary, aspiring folk, this is an aristocratic world of elegance, beauty, and perfection that is rooted in the past, even if the Champagne era has little in common with the Perrier age. Applying gallantry to 20th-century service (and now managed by the Mandarin Oriental Hotel group), the 129-room property is dedicated to the memory of that bygone age when men and women once danced cheek to cheek while orchestras played; waiters were anonymous and moved like members of a corps de ballet; and hotels were an art, one of the civilizing forces in any capital city.

The afternoon tea ritual here, for a long time *the* social event of the city (and consequently hard to get into without planning way ahead) has become a bit less exclusive. Reservations are still recommended about two months in advance, but now it's possible for last-minute tea fanciers to enjoy tea at the **Ritz,** too. The room is also pleasant for early evening Champagne. The **Ritz** still puts on the ritz, so jackets, ties, and all such formality are required. ♦ 150 Piccadilly (between Arlington St and Queen's Walk). 493.8181, 800/526.6566; fax 493.2687. Tube: Green Park

Within the Ritz:

Ritz Restaurant ★★★★$$$$ A wonderful way to begin any day is with a stroll in **Green Park** followed by breakfast at the **Ritz.** The menu offers such English treats as Cumberland sausage, Lancashire black pudding, Finnan haddock kedgeree, and Scotch kippers. Yet dinner here is the restaurant's finest hour. The delicate murals of the world's grandest dining rooms, subtly illuminated at breakfast and lunchtime by dreamy London daylight, are transformed at night by resplendent chandeliers and gilt ornamentation. Chef Giles Thompson is taking the cuisine into the new millennium with such dishes as terrine of rabbit with foie gras and roast duck. Breakfast is casual here but no sneakers, please. ♦ British ♦ Daily breakfast, lunch, and dinner. Reservations recommended; jacket and tie required for lunch and dinner. 493.8181

31 Le Caprice ★★★$$$ Because the restaurant takes orders at midnight, London's chic set nibbles and chatters the night away, amid white walls, a black-tiled floor, and David Bailey's black-and-white photographs, while glancing around to see who else is here. The menu is always eclectic with such appetizers as sesame-oil–infused crispy duck salad and old favorites like haddock and chips with peas, or liver and bacon with colcannon (potatoes and cabbage). *The* place to go, it is located just behind the **Ritz.** ♦ Brasserie ♦ Daily lunch and dinner (last orders at midnight). Reservations essential. Arlington House, Arlington St (off Piccadilly). 629.2239; fax 493.9040. Tube: Green Park

CHEZ GÉRARD

32 Chez Gérard ★★$$$ Here you will find good food and wine at unpretentious prices, served efficiently in smart surroundings. Brasserie classics are on the menu: *moules marinières,* onion soup, chicken liver pâté, Chateaubriand, and the best *frites* in London. A bottle of Côtes du Rhône will enhance the meal, and either the excellent cheese board or a chocolate concoction from the dessert menu will bring it to a satisfying conclusion. ♦ French ♦ M-F lunch and dinner; Sa-Su dinner. Reservations recommended. 31 Dover St (between Piccadilly and Hay Hill). 499.8171. Tube: Green Park. Also at: 8 Charlotte St (between Percy and Windmill Sts). 636.4975. Tube: Goodge Street, Tottenham Court Road; First floor Opera Terrace, Covent Garden Central Market (facing Russell St). 379.0666. Tube: Covent Garden; 119 Chancery La (between the Strand and Carey St). 405 0290. Tube: Temple

33 Granary ★★$ Come for simple dishes such as avocado stuffed with prawns, spinach, and cheese or lamb casserole with lemon and mint. Or try one of the delicious English puddings. ♦ British ♦ Daily lunch and afternoon tea. 39 Albemarle St (at Stafford St). 493.2978. Tube: Green Park

Brown's Hotel

34 Brown's Hotel $$$$ There is no discreet plaque saying that Henry James stayed here, and he probably didn't, but there is something perfectly Jamesian about this 118-room hotel just off Piccadilly. It is favored by the kind of Anglophilic Americans who come to England once a year to look at pictures, visit their tailor, see a few plays, and socialize with friends they have known since the War. Theodore Roosevelt and Edith Carow honeymooned here in 1886 (they got married a few blocks away, at **St. George's, Hanover Square**), and Franklin D. Roosevelt spent his wedding night with Eleanor here in 1905. The hotel retains the intimate and democratic feel of an English country house, with such charming touches as inlaid armoires and Colefax & Fowler fabrics. Afternoon tea is served here daily from 3 to 5:45PM in one of the most quintessentially English settings in London. The rooms are intimate and lamp-lit, the sofas and chairs solid and comfy, and the sandwiches, strawberry tart scones, light shortcake biscuits, and rich eclairs are superb. There's also a smart restaurant serving English fare complemented by an impressive wine list. ♦ 30-34 Albemarle St (between Stafford and Grafton Sts). 493.6020; fax 493.9381. Tube: Green Park

35 Museum of Mankind You may find yourself in a Bengali village or with a primitive mountain tribe in Peru here. Built in 1866 by **Sir James Pennethorne** as the headquarters of **London University,** the building today is the ethnographic department of the **British Museum.** Children love the tribal skulls, sculpture, masks, weapons, pottery, textiles, and puppets from all over the world, especially the Native American war bonnets, bows and arrows, and peace pipes. The permanent collection (in **Room 8**) includes stunning Benin bronzes from Africa and a life-size skull carved from a piece of solid Mexican crystal. A special true-to-life exhibition is staged once a year; it might, for example, explore the Day of the Dead in Mexico, with spectacular memorials made of papier-mâché sculptures, sugar figures, fruit and vegetables perfumed with incense, and marigolds created for the day the dead return to greet the living. All this is in the heart of (but light-years away from) Piccadilly. The exterior of the museum is an example of High Victorian architecture, with statues of leaders in science and philosophy punctuating the sky; it is also a confusion of styles: from Classic to Italian Gothic. The bookshop carries replicas of artworks and artifacts. ♦ Free. M-Sa; Su 2:30-6PM. 6 Burlington Gardens (at Burlington Arcade). 323.8043. Tube: Green Park, Piccadilly Circus

Within the Museum of Mankind:

Cafe de Colombia ★$ Tuck into a light lunch or nibble on an excellent cake at teatime. They also know how to make good cappuccino here—a rare talent in London. ♦ Continental ♦ M-Sa lunch and snacks; Su snacks. 287.8148

36 Burlington Arcade This Regency promenade of exclusive shops, designed and completed in 1819 by **Samuel Ware,** might be considered a forerunner to modern shopping malls, even though they are quite dissimilar. Inspired by Continental models and built in the years after Waterloo for Lord George Cavendish, the arcade provided the gentry with a shopping precinct free of the mud splashed by carriages and carts on Piccadilly, and it prevented the locals from flinging their garbage into his back garden. The three cheerful top-hatted beadles who patrol the arcade today are the smallest police force in the world. Originally they were installed to protect prosperous shoppers from pickpockets and beggars. Now they will ask you not to whistle or run, and they lock the gates at 6PM Monday through Saturday. Though the promenade was badly damaged in the Blitz, it was rebuilt and today exudes an atmosphere of intimate but conceivable elegance, lined with shops abounding in luxury goods. Admire the glass roof as well as the iridescent green paintwork complemented by gold lettering on the delicately detailed shop fronts. The ostentatious facades were added in 1911. ♦ Between Piccadilly and Burlington Gardens. Tube: Green Park, Piccadilly Circus

Within Burlington Arcade:

Irish Linen Company Linen napkins that could sail a small ship, sheets that assume you use a professional laundry service, and special cloths for drying the Waterford crystal wineglasses that grace fine linen tablecloths can be found in this shop. ♦ M-Sa. Nos. 35-36. 493.8949

N. Peal Wise Englishwomen would rather be draped in cashmere than diamonds, and they stroll through the arcade on weekdays wearing the clothes to prove it. The two **N. Peal** shops in the arcade have the best cashmere in London—from the addictive kneesocks for women to the handsome capes. Remember when you enter these shops that you get what you pay for. ♦ M-Sa. Women's shops: Nos. 37-40. 493.9220; Men's shop: No. 71. 493.0912

The Sporting Life

he British people's love of what they call "sport"
the stuff of legend. The passion with which they
llow such popular sports as cricket, football
occer), and rugby can border on the fanatical—as
evidenced by news reports several years ago of
eople being trampled by overzealous crowds at FA
up Final matches. If you want to tap into this fever,
sit the sports arenas in and around London, all of
hich house museums or offer behind-the-scenes
urs that explain the nuances of the games.

occer, the most widely attended and followed
port in Great Britain, was originally called football.
ut after the establishment of rugby football in
e late 19th century, the game became known
s "association football" and was shortened
"soccer." No matter what you call it, Britons
e mad for it. London has five clubs (**Arsenal,
helsea, Tottenham Hotspur, West Ham United,
nd Wimbledon**), and it also boasts soccer's
timate temple: **Wembley Stadium** (Empire Way,
etween Wembley Hill Rd and Wembley Park Dr,
08/902.0902), where the **Football Association
up Final** is played every year. Daily tours
08/901.8833), for which there is an admission
narge, take in the playing field itself, and kids get a
nance to hold up a football in a victory clutch to the
mulated roar of the crowd at the **Royal Box** (where
e real FA Cup is always presented by a member
f the Royal family). Visitors also tour the players'
nanging rooms and the high-tech control room;
addition, a film is shown that details some of the
ost compelling moments in he stadium's history.
Wembley also hosts American football matches
spring and late summer; call the stadium for
formation.)

ugby, an offshoot of soccer, was invented in 1823
hen a schoolboy at the great English public school
ugby deviated from the rules by picking up the ball
nd running with it. This new form of the game was
dopted by other public schools, and it was formalized
1871. Eventually, it spread to the US and developed
to American football, which it still resembles;
ecause of that connection, rugby may seem
ore accessible to American visitors. The game's
ontrolling body, the **Rugby Football Union**, holds
l of its international matches at **Twickenham**
ate 7, Rugby Rd, at Whitton Rd, 208/892.8161);
so here is the state-of-the-art **Museum of Rugby**
208/892.2000), offering re-created rooms such as

baths with a smell of liniment in the air, computers that
provide statistical data about players and teams, and
a theater showing films of some of the best matches.
There are 75-minute guided tours of the stadium and
the grounds; they're very popular, so book ahead.
Separate admission is charged for the museum and
the tour but you can buy a combined ticket. The
museum is open Tuesday through Sunday; on match
days it is open only to ticket holders from 11AM to an
hour before kickoff (ticket holders also have to pay
admission). Tours are given Tuesday through
Saturday at 10:30AM, noon, 1:30PM, and 3PM, and
on Sunday at 2:30PM.

Though soccer and rugby may be more popular, the
game that is most strongly associated with England
is cricket. If you want to understand the English
character, which emphasizes good sportsmanship,
team spirit, skill, and endurance, nothing beats
spending a summer afternoon watching a match
at **Lord's Cricket Ground,** also known as the
Marylebone Cricket Club (St. John's Wood
Rd, between Wellington and Grove End Rds,
207/289.1611). While the pace of the game is
slow, at times the action can be explosive and
spectacular—not unlike baseball. Before you go,
though, it's a good idea to introduce yourself to
this complicated game by dropping into the **MCC
Museum** (on the grounds of the cricket club,
207/432.1033). Exhibits here include the various
paraphernalia used in cricket (bats, balls, caps,
etc.), videos about the game, and "The Ashes," the
much-sought-after trophy. The museum is open for
browsing on match days, and admission is charged;
otherwise, the only way to see the museum is on
behind-the-scenes tours, which are held daily (on
nonmatch days) at noon and 2PM, and there's a fee
(207/266.3825).

The sport that brings the most international attention
to the British Isles is probably tennis. This is because
the **All England Lawn Tennis Championship,** the
world's oldest professional tennis tournament, is
held in the London suburb of Wimbledon for two
weeks each summer. The Duke and Duchess of
Kent preside over the proceedings, and thousands of
fans turn out to watch the game's top professionals
scurry, charge, and leap across the lush grass courts
trying to hit, smash, lob, or ace a little yellow ball.
Wimbledon has been the playground for such tennis
legends as Bjorn Borg, Rod Laver, Chris Evert,
Martina Navratilova, Steffi Graf, and Billie Jean
King. The tournament's lengthy history, as well as
general information about the sport, are explored in
detail at the **Wimbledon Lawn Tennis Museum**
(Church Rd, between Somerset and Bathgate Rds,
208/946.6131), which displays tennis memorabilia,
a video theater that shows some of Wimbledon's
greatest matches, quizzes about the game on
computer screens, and other exhibits.
It is open Tuesday through Sunday
and charges admission; during the
tournament, only ticket holders are
admitted, and they must pay admission.

St. Petersburg Collection Living up to his illustrious name, Carl Fabergé's grandson, Theo, continues the family tradition of creating exquisite objets d'art and jewelry. The gallery also shows decorative antiques, Russian lacquer boxes, fine porcelain, and paintings. Surprisingly for such small premises, there are three stories to browse in. ♦ M-Sa. No. 42. 495.2883

Underwood This is the place to visit for a wide selection of handmade leather goods. Briefcases are a specialty here; other items include wallets, desk sets, and travel accessories. ♦ M-Sa. Nos. 54-55. 495.0677

Richard Ogden Come here for antique jewelry, including museum-quality pieces of Art Nouveau. ♦ M-Sa. Nos. 28-29. 493.9136

Map World All sorts of antique maps—including such oddities as "A New Mappe of the Romane Empire" by John Speed, created around 1626—are available for all sorts of prices. ♦ M-Sa. No. 25. 495.5377

Michael Rose Mr. Rose calls his shop "the source of the unusual." It specializes in handmade period and modern engagement and wedding rings ("the largest collection in Europe"), as well as all types of antique jewelry, including Fabergé. ♦ M-Sa. No. 3. 493.0714

W&H Gidden The smells in this shop are reminiscent of leather shops in Florence: rich and pungent. The high prices smack of Florence as well. The store has been the saddler to the sovereign since 1806; these premises, however, contain purses, wallets, portfolios, and various accessories. An older, larger branch, specializing in equestrian gear, is about a block away in Mayfair. ♦ M-Sa. Nos. 1-2. 495.3670. Also at: 15D Clifford St (at Cork St). 734.2788. Tube: Piccadilly Circus, Oxford Circus

Sandra Cronan Ltd

Sandra Cronan High-quality antique jewelry, especially from the Art Nouveau and Art Deco eras, are among the interesting wares on display. The staff are very knowledgeable about vintage jewelry, and the shop stages periodic themed exhibitions on such subjects as cufflinks through the ages or the changing look of paste jewelry. ♦ M-F. No. 18. 491.4851

Penhaligon's These very British and very special perfumes all carry the scent of an English country garden. Try "Bluebell" (people will whisper, "Where did you get that

fragrance?"). The labels are enchanting, whil the antique silver bottles are truly tokens of love. ♦ M-Sa. Nos. 16-17. 629.1416

ROYAL ACADEMY OF ARTS

37 Royal Academy of Arts, Burlington House The house on this site has undergone many changes since its construction in 1707 (see drawings on page 79). In 1717, the building was acquired by Richard Boyle, third Earl of Burlington, and he immediately commissioned architect **Colen Campbell** to remodel it. **Campbell** redesigned the rather unprepossessing structure in classical Palladian style, and it became a textbook example of the genre. The present staircase and other decorative features were added by **Samuel Ware** in 1815, when the house was purchased by Lord George Cavendish. In 1854, the government bought the building and made it the permanent home of the **Royal Academy of Arts,** which had been sited in various locations since its founding in 1768. **R.R. Banks** and **E.M. Barry** were hired to add new wings and side buildings, and later, in 1872, **Sydney Smirke** added a second story (spoiling the structure's classical Palladian look) and a number of exhibition galleries. **Sir Norman Foster** added the **Arthur Sackler Galleries** on the top floor in 1991. The complex's imposing grandeur is lightened by banners heralding the exhibitions inside.

In the courtyard stands *Sir Joshua Reynolds,* a statue of the first president of the academy. In the rooms along the quadrangle, learned societies have their headquarters: the Geological Society, the Royal Society of Chemistry, the Society of Antiquaries, and the Royal Astronomical Society.

The **Royal Academy** marked the recognition of the importance of art and artists in this country and, for better or worse, made artists members of the Establishment. Artistic temperament being what it is, many painters refused to exhibit at this "Official Marketplace for Art": George Romney, William Blake, Dante Gabriel Rossetti, and James Abbott McNeill Whistler declined, while Thomas Gainsborough exhibited for a few years but stopped because he was dissatisfied with the way his works were displayed. The division hasn't really healed with time—you can be certain that Francis Bacon was not part of the academy, yet David Hockney is. The initials "RA" after artists' names (meaning they are among the 80-odd Academicians) may add to the price of their works in the salesrooms but do not significantly affect their reputations in the art world.

In the center of the entrance hall are ceiling paintings by Benjamin West: *The Graces Unveiling Nature* and *The Four Elements.* There are two paintings by Angelica Kaufmann at each end: *Genius and Painting,* near the door to the **Friends Room** on the east, and *Composition and Design,* on the west. Above the central staircase is a circular painting by William Kent: *The Glorification of Inigo Jones.* The first floor includes the **Saloon,** the only surviving part of **Campbell**'s **Burlington House,** with a ceiling by William Kent.

Exhibitions of paintings, sculpture, and architectural drawings and models take place in the rooms on the first and second floors. The Summer Exhibition is the big event of the year at the academy and one of London's more important social occasions. Some 14,000 works by 4,000 artists are submitted, with 1,300 finally selected. The gala opening in June looks like a royal garden party with pictures. The academy's reputation now rests on its international art exhibitions. Parts of the permanent collection are on view in the **Private Rooms** on the first floor. Splendid pictures by Sir Joshua Reynolds,

From an engraving by Jan Kip after Leonard Knyff, 1707

After the changes made circa 1717

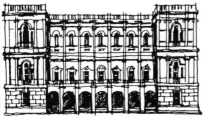

The present front, developed by Sydney Smirke, 1872-74

John Constable, Sir Henry Raeburn, Sir Alfred Munnings, and Walter Sickert may be seen, while sculptures by Sir Eduardo Paolozzi and Dame Elizabeth Frink are displayed around the building.

The second floor houses the award-winning **Sackler Galleries,** which are reached by a glass elevator. Here is the spacious sculpture gallery where the academy's most prized possession, Michelangelo's *Madonna and Child with the Infant St. John,* carved in 1505, is on permanent display. It is one of only four major sculptures by the artist outside Italy. ♦ Admission. Private Rooms: free tours Tu-F 1PM. Free public gallery talks W, Su 2PM. Daily. Piccadilly (between Albany Ct Yd and Burlington Arcade). 439.7438. Tube: Green Park, Piccadilly Circus

Within the Royal Academy of Arts, Burlington House:

Royal Academy Shop Jam-packed with wonderful items, this store offers easels, brushes, and paints, a framing service, jigsaw puzzles of paintings, a large collection of art books, catalogs from exhibitions abroad, original items by academy artists and silk scarves designed by them, plus the obligatory canvas museum bags. ♦ Daily. 439.7438

Royal Academy Restaurant ★★$
Big and cafeterialike, this eatery provides a welcome refuge from the nonstop glamour of Piccadilly. Women in tweed suits and sensible shoes, in town for the day, sit in the attractive paneled room, tranquilly sipping tea and indulging in cakes. Hot and cold meals are served at lunchtime, and there's a decent salad bar. ♦ International ♦ Daily lunch and afternoon tea. 439.7438

38 **Piccadilly Arcade** Thrale Jell built this extension of the **Burlington Arcade** a century later, in 1910. Today, its charming, casual row of shops connects Piccadilly to Jermyn Street. ♦ Between Jermyn St and Piccadilly. Tube: Green Park, Piccadilly Circus

Within Piccadilly Arcade:

Waterford Wedgwood These china specialists have a complete and tempting collection of Wedgwood and Spode. All the price lists include the import cost and the amount in dollars. ♦ M-Sa. No. 173 Piccadilly (at the arcade entrance). 629.2614

Favourbrook Sumptuous materials are used in fashioning waistcoats and Nehru-collar jackets for women only. ♦ M-Sa. No. 18. 491.2337. Menswear only is sold at 55 Jermyn St (between Duke and St. James's Sts). 493.5060. Tube: Green Park

New and Lingwood, Ltd. On the Jermyn Street side is one of the best and least-known shops in the arcade. It started as the London branch of the **Eton** shop, which has been outfitting Etonians for decades. The branch here has splendid, ready-made shirts and a small but choice selection of sweaters. The cotton shirts and lamb's-wool sweaters from this shop are worth every pound and penny. Shirts are also made to order. Upstairs is **Poulsen and Skone,** makers of fine footwear; a custom-made pair requires another serious investment, but the shoemakers share the burden, providing lifelong care and service. The ready-made shoes are quite wonderful, too. ♦ M-Sa. No. 53. 493.9621

FORTNUM & MASON

39 Fortnum & Mason Inside one of the world's most magnificent groceries and oldest carryout stores, crystal chandeliers reflect off polished mahogany, highlighting temptations of caviar, truffles, marrons glacés, hand-dipped chocolates, stilton cheeses, teas, honeys, Champagnes, and foie gras. On the hour, two mechanical figures emerge from the store clock's miniature doors: dressed in the livery of 18th-century servants, Mr. Fortnum and Mr. Mason turn and nod to each other while the bells chime sweetly. The clock was placed here in 1964, making it a relatively recent addition to this treasure house, which has been serving the privileged since 1707.

Those luxurious hampers filled with gourmet foods, always seen at Ascot and Glyndebourne, began in 1788 as packed lunches (known as "concentrated lunches") for hunting and shooting parties as well as for members of Parliament who were detained in chambers. The fortunate recipients would dine on game pies, boned chickens, lobster, and prawns. During the Napoleonic Wars, officers in the Duke of Wellington's army ordered hams and cheeses. Baskets were sent to Florence Nightingale in the Crimea, to Mr. Stanley while he was looking for Mr. Livingstone, and to suffragettes confined in London's **Holloway Prison,** who shared their hampers with fellow prisoners. You order the hamper the day before you want it, and choose among the cold delicacies, which include Parma ham and melon, smoked salmon cornets, fresh-roasted *poussin,* ox tongue, salad, profiteroles, cheeses, Champagne, and chocolate truffles.

If you are buying many items, you may choose to be assisted by gentlemen in morning coats, who will accompany you from department to department, write down your choices and requests, and offer advice with knowledge, patience, and charm. **Fortnum**'s blue-green tins of tea are as much a sign as a guarantee of good taste. The cakes and Christmas puddings are bought by those in the know (Lady Margaret Thatcher bought her

son's wedding cake here). Not only are he deluxe fruitcakes in a class of their own, they are (oddly) cheaper than those found in similar stores in London. Tastes are available in the cake shop's cafe at the back of the store. **Fortnum**'s has its own brand of marmalades. After purchasing teas, a game pie or two, a tin of English biscuits, a couple of crocks of stilton, and a jar of Gentlemen's Relish (a very special anchovy paste) decorated with pheasants, consider lunch at the **Fountain Restaurant** (see below). ♦ M-Sa 181 Piccadilly (at Duke St). 734.8040. Tube: Green Park, Piccadilly Circus

Within Fortnum & Mason:

Fountain Restaurant ★★★$$ The much-loved murals add charm to this excellent restaurant, a good place to stop for lunch or a pre- or post-theater dinner. The grills are first-class, the game, steak, and kidney pies excellent, and if you just want something light, the sandwiches are fit for Ascot. To accompany one of the famous ice-cream sundaes, fabulous coffee, espresso, and cappuccino are served at the counter. This is a favorite spot for tea, and a number of writers, artists, faded rock stars, and other local figures use this as a sort of club. It is without a doubt the best place in the area for breakfast, but if you have already eaten, come for what the English call "elevenses" (typically coffee and a Danish). The restaurant is located underneath **Fortnum**'s main shopping floors with a separate entrance on Jermyn Street, at Duke Street. ♦ British ♦ M-Sa breakfast, lunch, afternoon tea, and dinner. 734.8080

St. James's Restaurant ★★★$$ This fourth-floor restaurant is far less well known than the **Fountain;** hence, it is quieter and ideal for exchanging confidences over roast beef and Yorkshire pudding. Your neighbors will look like they have come to London to bid on a little something at **Christie's** or **Sotheby's**—very tweedy and proper. ♦ British ♦ M-Sa breakfast, lunch, and afternoon tea. 724.8040

Patio ★★$ A light snack here will keep you going after shopping around the store has roused your appetite. ♦ British ♦ M-Sa breakfast, lunch, and snacks. 724.8040

40 Albany Sir William Chambers built this residence for Viscount Melbourne in 1774. It looks like an English Palladian version of a Parisian *hôtel particulier* (mansion). Henry Holland converted its garden to chambers for bachelor gentlemen in 1803. This building has been the home of Lord Byron, Thomas B. Macaulay, Lord Gladstone, and, more recently, J.B. Priestley, Graham Greene, and 1960s British film star Terence Stamp (featured prominently in the campy 1994 film *The Adventures of Priscilla, Queen of the Desert).* ♦ Albany Ct Yd (off Piccadilly). Tube: Green Park, Piccadilly Circus

Booking It Through London

Although there's no substitute for an actual visit to London, you can get a good sense of this city's history, geography, and personality from the printed page. The number of books that have been published about London in the latter half of this century alone could fill several libraries, but the titles listed below are a fine place to start.

Behind the Blue Plaques of London by Alan Symons (Polo Publishing, 1994). Throughout the city, blue plaques mark the residences of the great statesmen, writers, musicians, artists, and soldiers who lived in London. This book relates the stories behind those plaques, giving a sense of individual personalities and idiosyncrasies.

Chelsea Past by Barbara Denny (Historical Publications, 1996). Scores of interesting characters from British history have called the **Chelsea** area home, ranging from saints (Thomas More) to sinners (Oscar Wilde) and from kings (Henry VIII) to villains (the criminal Aleister Crowley). Their stories are told in this fascinating volume written by a local newspaper reporter.

The Diaries of Samuel Pepys (HarperPaperbacks/S, 1995). These personal, often titillating journals were written between 1660 and 1669 by the most famous (some might say infamous) personality of his era. They offer a unique look at life in the capital during the tempestuous period following the Restoration, including such momentous events as the Great Plague and the Great Fire, although the reader is also told about Pepys's hangovers, parties, and flirtations. A fun browse.

Dickens' Journalism: Volumes 1 and 2 edited by Michael Slater (Dent, 1996). Most people know Charles Dickens as a great novelist, but he was also a crusading newspaper reporter, publishing vivid, sharply critical, and sometimes heartbreaking accounts of life in Victorian London, many of which are collected in this volume

The Great Plague of London by Walter George Bell (Bracken Books, 1994). This fascinating look at the medical disaster that hit the capital in 1665 also examines the lifestyle of Londoners during the Commonwealth and Restoration.

The Inns of Court by Jill Allibone and David Evans (Black Dog, 1996). The mysteries of London's legal enclave are explored in great detail in these essays, illustrated by many evocative black-and-white images by architectural photographer Helene Binet.

Lights Out for the Territory by Iain Sinclair (Granta, 1996). By walking around the city, observing and eaves-dropping on Londoners in their daily lives, Sinclair has produced an interesting book of odd vignettes and offbeat quotes.

London—A Companion to Its History and Archaeology by Malcolm Billings (Kyle Cathie Ltd, 1994). The capital's history is revealed through its archaeological finds, including the **Roman Wall,** the **Temple of Mithras,** and Celtic war artifacts.

London: A Guide to Recent Architecture by Samantha Hardingham (Ellipsis, 1995). This excellent, pocket-size guide contains pictures and descriptions of 100 modern building projects, from shops and bars to the megadevelopments in **Docklands.**

London as It Might Have Been by Felix Barker and Ralph Hyde (John Murray, 1982). What if **Sir Christopher Wren**'s original plans to re-create London after the Great Fire of 1666 had not been rejected? Barker and Hyde speculate on what the city would have looked like if this building plan, along with several others that were proposed and rejected throughout the years, had been carried out. The text is supplemented by drawings of the bridges, parks, monuments, and streets that never came to be.

London's Statues and Monuments by Margaret Baker (Shire Publications, 1995). Believe it or not, you can explore London's lengthy history without setting foot in a single museum. This book, organized into 20 districts (with clear maps), examines every statue and monument within the city limits, explaining the history behind each one in a light, readable style.

The Oxford Book of London edited by Paul Bailey (Oxford University Press, 1995). The London-born editor has collected off-the-beaten track descrip-tions of the capital that run the gamut from 12th-century monks' chronicles to current novels, interspersed with a variety of interesting quotes.

The Queen: a Biography of Elizabeth II by Ben Pimlott (HarperCollins, 1996). The many recent difficulties of the royal family add poignancy to this well-written, well-assessed portrait of the monarch, written by a history professor.

A Spy's London by Roy Berkely (Leo Cooper, 1994). The author describes some 21 walks through the streets of London, revealing the places where famous spies lived, rendezvoused, and sometimes were killed.

Walking London by Andrew Duncan (New Holland Publishers Ltd, 1991). The 30 walks described in these pages are a delight for visitors who enjoy exploring hidden corners of such well-known neighborhoods as **Kensington, Soho,** and **Bloomsbury.** The maps are excellent, the directions detailed, and the anecdotes enlightening.

41 Princes Arcade Right next to **Hatchards** is an arcade of genteel, smart shops that tends to get overshadowed by the more famous **Burlington Arcade** just down the road. But the stores here are just as noteworthy, including **Jones the Bootmakers, Jeremy and Guy Steel** for jewelry, **Richard Caplan** for cameras, **Prestat** for chocolates, and **N. Peal** for exquisite woolens. ♦ M-Sa. 192 Piccadilly (between Church Pl and Duke St). 437.0106. Tube: Green Park, Piccadilly Circus

41 Hatchards When this bookseller opened in the 18th century, it fostered a clublike atmosphere by laying out daily newspapers by the fireplace and putting benches outside for the customers' servants. The shop (now affiliated with the **Dillons** chain of bookstores) still has the rambling charm of that age, but it has made the transition to the paperback era with intelligence and style. One of the best-known bookstores in England, it currently holds three Royal Warrants. It is a veritable book emporium, with an excellent selection of children's books (third floor), art books (second floor), and reference volumes (first floor), including dictionaries, bibles, and the Oxford companions to music and literature. You can find the complete works of your favorite British writers here, as well as secondhand and rare books. As you enter, have a look at the latest hardcover fiction releases, or browse through the extensive biography department with its special royalty section. The literature department stocks a wide selection of leather-bound volumes. The charming shop assistants can trace any book you care to name if it's still in print and will ship it to you anywhere in the world. If books are your passion, this is paradise. ♦ Daily. 187 Piccadilly (between Church Pl and Duke St). 439.9921. Tube: Green Park, Piccadilly Circus

42 Sackville Street Take a quick look at this almost purely Georgian street, which radiates a confident modesty. ♦ Between Piccadilly and Vigo St. Tube: Green Park, Piccadilly Circus

On Sackville St:

Henry Sotheran Ltd. Row upon row of glorious antique leather-bound books greet you here, glistening like chestnuts. ♦ M-Sa. No. 2. 439.6151

Folio Society This bookshop in the basement of **Henry Sotheran Ltd.** makes handsome editions of all the favorite English

works. A beautifully bound and printed set of Jane Austen novels is a timeless treasure. ♦ M-Sa. No. 2. 629.6517

43 Midland Bank Built by **Sir Edwin Lutyens** 1922, this charming neighbor of **St. James's Piccadilly** is worth a glance. The architect kindly deferred to **St. James's** by creating a bank on a domestic scale in brick and Portland stone. ♦ 196A Piccadilly (between Church Pl and Duke St). Tube: Green Park, Piccadilly Circus

43 St. James's, Piccadilly Sir Christopher **Wren**, the man who gave London **St. Paul's Cathedral** and some 50 other churches, completed this place of worship in 1684. From the outside, the newly pointed brick, the replaced and restored spire, and the **St. James Craft Market** in the courtyard (see below) give no clue of the miracle within. But when visitors walk inside they are typically awestruck by the wide-open space, the barrel-vaulted roof, the rows of two-tiered windows, the Corinthian columns, the brass, the gilt, the paint. This has always been a fashionable church, especially designed for large weddings. The organ was built for James II. In 1757, William Blake was christened at the wonderful white-marble font whose figures of Adam and Eve and the Tree of Life were carved by **Grinling Gibbons**. Of this, his favorite church, **Wren** said, "There are no walls of a second order, nor lanterns, nor buttresses, but the whole rests upon pillars, as do also the galleries, and I think it may be found beautiful and convenient; it is the cheapest form of any I could invent." The church is also a moving tribute to its congregation. Almost completely destroyed the bombing of 1940, it was restored through determination and dedication. The spire was completed in 1968 by **Sir Albert Richardson**. This is an active church today, offering lunchtime concerts on Wednesday and Friday and running lectures on various aspects of faith most evenings. ♦ Daily. Services: Su 8:30AM, 11AM, 5:45PM. 197 Piccadilly (at Church Pl). 734.4511, concert box office 437.5053. Tube: Green Park, Piccadilly Circus

Within St. James's Yard:

The Wren at St. James's ★$ Come to this cheerful place for homemade vegetable soups (served with thick slices of whole-grain bread), herbal teas, and fresh salads, as well as cakes, fruit tarts, and coffee. ♦ Vegetarian ♦ M-Sa breakfast, lunch, and dinner; Su breakfast, lunch, and afternoon tea. No credit cards accepted. 35 Jermyn St (at Church Pl). 437.9419

St. James Craft Market This lively crafts market with some 30 stalls always attracts large crowds for its good and modestly priced assortment of pottery, hand-knit sweaters, carved wooden toys, and enameled jewelry. ♦ Antiques: Tu. Crafts: W-Sa.

Le MERIDIEN

PICCADILLY

44 Le Méridien Piccadilly $$$$ When it opened in 1908, this establishment was London's most elegant hotel. One of the leading Edwardian architects, **Norman Shaw**, combined dazzling opulence with architectural perfection in its design. Following a period of decline after World War II, the hotel is now once again a Piccadilly showpiece after receiving a generous physical and psychological face-lift. The harpist (a favorite on London's current hotel scene) welcomes you to late–20th-century notions of essential luxury: health club with squash courts, solarium, swimming pool, supervised gym, Turkish baths, sauna, Jacuzzi, beauty salon, and fitness-cuisine brasserie. The glamour is in the facilities; the 266 rooms and suites are comfortable, tasteful, and elegant. ♦ 21 Piccadilly (between Air and Swallow Sts). 734.8000, 800/225.5843; fax 437.3574. Tube: Piccadilly Circus

Within Le Méridien Piccadilly:

Oak Room ★★★$$$$ The original pale, oak-paneled elegance of this dining room illuminated with magnificent chandeliers looks like a set from "Edward and Mrs. Simpson." It is now the flagship of superchef Marco Pierre White's restaurant group, offering exquisite, albeit expensive, delights such as terrine of foie gras with prunes and spiced gelée followed by roast cod with herb crust, and a sublime blackberry soufflé to finish. ♦ French ♦ M-F lunch and dinner; Sa dinner. Reservations recommended. 437.0202

The Terrace Restaurant ★★$$$ This stunning brasserie in a conservatory retains an undiscovered feel; it's a nice place to begin the day or end a theater evening. The crab soup, served with gruyère and croutons, is savory. Parisian chef Michel Rostang, in his first London venture, devises a daily three-course table d'hôte, and afternoon tea is served from 3 to 5:30PM. Business London eats its power breakfasts here. ♦ French ♦ Daily breakfast, lunch, afternoon tea, and dinner. 734.8000

44 Cordings If London weren't a Dickensian tangle of ground leases, this shop would have been abolished and the grandeur of **Le Méridien Piccadilly** extended. Only the web of property laws enabled the ceremonial designs of **John Nash** to

be destroyed and this little store to remain. Located here since 1839, it has kept its character in an ever-changing world. You can get terrific raincoats, waterproof boots, country woolens, and tweeds, all high quality. ♦ M-Sa. 19 Piccadilly (at Air St). 734.0830. Tube: Piccadilly Circus

45 Tower Records A whole block and several floors of tapes, CDs, and videos draws countless customers through the glass doors of one of London's largest music stores. You'll find tunes with every kind of beat and from almost every country. The desk in the ground-floor foyer handles bookings for certain concerts. ♦ M-Sa 9AM-midnight; Su noon-6PM. Piccadilly Circus (at Regent St). 439.2500. Tube: Piccadilly Circus

46 Criterion Theatre Tawdry signs have long buried the French-château facade of this elaborately refurbished theater, designed in 1870 by **Thomas Verity.** Seating 598, it is London's only underground theater in the physical sense of the word: Patrons go down a series of steps, even for the upper circle. The lobby is decorated with Victorian tiles. ♦ Piccadilly Circus (at Piccadilly). 369.1747. Tube: Piccadilly Circus

46 Criterion Marco Pierre White ★★★ $$$$ Located on Piccadilly Circus, this restaurant (formerly **Criterion Brasserie**) was designed by **Thomas Verity** in 1870, along with the **Criterion Theatre,** when Piccadilly was the hub of the Empire. As the area declined, this eatery became a lowly cafeteria. Some five decades later, the now-regentrified area inspired the Forte hotel group to restore it and join forces with the charismatic chef Marco Pierre White. Beneath layers of plywood and Formica, grease and smoke, they struck gold, or the closest thing to it: shimmering, dazzling, gold-mosaic, Byzantine vaulted ceilings, and marble walls. Restored to its Victorian splendor, this is now one of the prettiest restaurants in London. The menu is interesting, with specialties such as roast port cutlet with marjoram jus and puree of mirabelle plums, and for dessert, bread and butter pudding or lemon tart. ♦ British ♦ Daily lunch and dinner. Reservations recommended. 224 Piccadilly (at Piccadilly Circus). 930.0488. Tube: Piccadilly Circus

---

"London—the smoky nest fated to be my favourite residence."
—Mendelssohn

You'll find no man at all intellectual, who is willing to leave London. No sir, when a man is tired of London, he is tired of life; for there is in London all that life can afford.

—Samuel Johnson

47 Eros The city's best-loved statue, depicting the God of Love, symbolizes London itself to people all over the world. It is a memorial to the virtuous Lord Shaftesbury, a tireless reformer and educator who lived from 1801-85. The sculptor, Alfred Gilbert, was no less idealistic; he believed Shaftesbury deserved a monument that would represent both generosity of spirit and love of mankind, and would symbolize, according to the sculptor, "the work of Lord Shaftesbury, the blindfolded Love sending forth indiscriminately, yet with purpose, his missile of kindness, always with the swiftness the bird has from its wings, never ceasing to breathe or reflect critically, but ever soaring onwards, regardless of its own perils and dangers." (According to legend, Gilbert also intended Eros's bow and arrow to be a pun on Lord Shaftesbury's name.)

Gilbert created his statue in aluminum, marking the first time the material had been used for such a sculpture. As a result, the eight-foot figure is so light that it sways in the wind. Gilbert was paid £3,000 for his work, even though it had cost him £7,000 to make it. His eventual and inevitable bankruptcy left him with little alternative but to leave the country, living first in Belgium and then in Italy. Lord Shaftesbury himself died lamenting, "I cannot bear to leave this world with all the misery in it." He would presumably have been sadder still to know how much misery had afflicted the artist who tried to honor him. Although the creator of *Eros* was rejected, the statue has an enduring place in the hearts of Londoners. ♦ In the center of Piccadilly Circus. Tube: Piccadilly Circus

48 Trocadero The history of the "Troc" on this site goes back to the 1740s, when it was a tennis court. During the 19th century, it served in turn as a circus, a theater, a music hall, and a restaurant. In the 1920s and 1930s, it flourished as the venue for Charles Cochran's "Supper Time Revues." In the 1970s, 1980s, and the early part of this decade, it was an entertainment complex of exhibits, shops, and restaurants. Now this building, along with the adjacent **Pavilion,** has been purchased by Burford, the Japanese video game/computer software corporation, which opened a £30-million indoor theme park, the largest in the world. Called

Segaworld, it offers mind-boggling rides that use virtual reality technology, computer software, and hydraulically powered platform to simulate action and adventure. **Aquaplane** is a collision with an underwater planet, **Gho Hunt** goes through a haunted house, and **Ma Bazooka** is set in a gladiatorial arena.

Also in the **Trocadero** is **Virtual World,** which offers a choice of two space travel adventure games for up to seven players. Recently added are the **Pepsi Max Drop,** the world's first and only indoor freefall ride with a 131-foot drop, and the **Pepsi Imax Theatre** which shows 3-D movies on a 49-foot-high screen. Several of the previous stores and exhibitions remain, including **HMV,** a link in the worldwide chain of record shops. ♦ Admission to Segaworld and Virtual World. Daily. 13 Coventry St (between Ruper and Windmill Sts). Segaworld: 734.2477; Virtual World: 494.1992; Pepsi Imax Theatre 494.4153; http://www.imax.com. Tube: Piccadilly Circus

48 Rainforest Café ★★$$$ This is Europe's first branch of the American-theme restaurant chain. For the uninitiated, expect regular thunderstorms and a cacophony of wildlife noises. Food is American/Caribbean with a jungle twist: treetop tenderloin, chicke monsoon, and Amazon flatbread are featured ♦ American/Caribbean ♦ Daily lunch and dinner. 20 Shaftesbury Ave (at Great Windm St). 434.3111. Tube: Piccadilly Circus

49 Piccadilly Theatre This large, comfortab theater has air-conditioning, which is fortunate given that it seats 1,213. It's a good venue for the less-hyped musicals. ♦ Denman St (at Sherwood St). 369.1734. Tube: Piccadilly Circus

50 Regent Street Signs of the grand designs of **John Nash** are apparent here, with Regent Street running southward to Waterloo Place and The Mall, and northward to Oxford Stree and **Regent's Park.** Unfortunately, what you see now is not what **Nash** created. **Nash** planned Piccadilly Circus as an elegant squa with a long arcade, very much like the Rue d Rivoli running alongside the Tuileries in Pari The Quadrant, an even larger version of the crescent at **Regent's Park,** was the essence of the scheme—so crucial that **Nash** finance its construction out of his own pocket, persuading his builders to accept leases instead of payment when his money ran out.

Completed in 1819, the Quadrant must have been very handsome indeed. Its destruction began in 1848, and it was completely obliterated by 1905. Since then planners hav tried with monotonous regularity to restore and re-create Piccadilly Circus. The latest attempt is the 1986 effort visible today: a precinct that one hopes won't succumb to th shabbiness to which the area has been prone

MICHAEL STORRINGS

Trocadero

Sightseers should go to Regent Street when the shops are closed; it is at its most attractive when deserted. Remember to look up: A lot of fine detail can be found at the tops of the buildings. For shopping, the street is somewhat deficient; considering its central location and length, it has more than its share of airline offices and ordinary chain stores. However, there are some notable exceptions. Start with **Aquascutum** (reputed to be Lady Margaret Thatcher's outfitter) at the Piccadilly Circus end, followed by **Garrard** (the queen's jewelers), and then walk purposefully up to **Mappin & Webb,** another high-class jewelry store. If you feel the urge to buy china, wait until you've seen the extraordinary department store **Liberty** (see page 88), which is much loved by the English gentry. Don't forget to look in **Hamleys** toy shop (see page 56), but be prepared to stay a long time if you bring your children—they'll never want to leave.

To the right of Regent Street (the bottom end) is Waterloo Place, presided over by the **Duke of York Column,** created in 1834 by **Benjamin Dean Wyatt.** This street was meant to mark the southern end of **Nash**'s triumphal way from Carlton House Terrace to **Regent's Park.** In the distance you can see the **Victoria Tower** of the **Houses of Parliament.** ♦ Between Piccadilly and Oxford Circuses. Tube: Piccadilly Circus, Oxford Circus

51 Cafe Royal The famed multiple rooms of the Cafe Royal, founded in 1865 by a French wine merchant, Daniel Nicholas Thévenon and long known as an elegant hangout for London painters and literati from Max Beerbohm and George Bernard Shaw to Dylan Thomas, are now mostly venues for private functions, except for a single splendid bar, **Daniels,** where the old atmosphere is carefully maintained. Light meals are also served. ♦ M-Sa. 68 Regent St (at Air St). 437.9090. Tube: Piccadilly Circus

52 L'Odéon ★★$$$ At this large brasserie, whose windows overlook the scuttling shoppers of Regent Street, natural wood and high-voltage reds and blues perk up the minimalist decor of the long curving room, which is divided into friendly spaces. There are fixed-price lunch and dinner menus, which, as always in restaurants with high-profile chefs, are better value than ordering à la carte. Try Anthony Demetre's roast salmon with spiced aubergine (eggplant) or roast neck of lamb with merguez and moussaka, and finish with mango *tarte tatin* and lemongrass ice cream. ♦ French ♦ Daily lunch and dinner; Su brunch. 65 Regent St (at Air St). 287.1400. Tube: Piccadilly Circus

---

Great Britain and the United States are nations separated by a common language.

Englishmen will never be slaves: they are free to do whatever the Government and public opinion allow them to do.

—George Bernard Shaw

Restaurants/Clubs: Red   **Hotels:** Blue

Shops/♥ Outdoors: Green   **Sights/Culture:** Black

Regent Street Shopping

OXFORD STREET

(west side)	(east side)
casualwear **Benetton**	**Shellys** shoes
womenswear **French Connection**	

PRINCES STREET

fine chocolates **Godiva**	**Bally** shoes
menswear **Reiss**	**Laura Ashley** womenswear
woolens **House of Scotland**	**Thorntons** chocolates
soaps/perfumes **Crabtree & Evelyn**	**Off the Cuff** shirts/ties
film processing **City Photo**	**National Westminster Bank**
menswear **Damart**	

LITTLE ARGYLL STREET

| woolens **London House** | |
| opticians **Dolland & Aitchin** | **Dickins and Jones** department store |

HANOVER STREET

building society **The Woolwich**	
Caffè Nero	
outdoor clothing **R.M. Williams**	

MADDOX STREET / GREAT MARLBOROUGH STREET

jewelry **Pravins**	**Liberty** designer department store
TVs/stereos **West Base Electronics**	
fabrics **Tops**	
hair/beauty **alan d.**	**Barclays Bank**
Cyprus Government Tourist Office	
woolens **Scottish Wear**	
Moroccan airline **Royal Air Maroc**	**The Gap** casualwear
shoes **Clarks**	

CONDUIT STREET / FOUBERT'S PLACE

shoes **Church's**	**Jaeger** classic clothes
The Pen Shop	**House of Chinacraft**
country and sportswear **Racing Green**	
menswear/womenswear **Thomas Burberry**	
sandwich/coffee shop **Hampers**	**Hamleys** toys
leatherwear **Harley-Davidson Motorcycles**	
fabrics/fine woolens **Court Textiles**	
Israeli airline **El Al**	

REGENT STREET

NEW BURLINGTON PLACE

womenswear **Viyella**	
Royal Jordanian Airlines	**Boss** menswear
House of Cashmere	**Warner Bros. Studio Store** clothes/gifts
Bureau de Change	
Saudi airline **Saudia**	**Levi Strauss & Co.** outdoorwear
tartans/woolens **Regent's**	**Episode** womenswear

NEW BURLINGTON STREET / TENNISON COURT

menswear **Bellini 077**	**Mappin & Webb** jewelry
classic clothing **Burberrys**	**Next** womenswear/menswear
gifts **Past Times**	**Waterford Wedgwood** fine china
The English Teddy Bear Company	**British Airways**
menswear **Cougar**	

BEAK STREET

| **The Woollen Centre** | **Lawleys** china/glass |

HEDDON STREET

Singapore Airlines	**Bally of Switzerland** shoes
Scottish clothing **Oxfords**	**Gap Kids** children's clothing
woolens **The Scottish Cashmere Co.**	**The Disney Store**
china **Rosenthal Studio House**	**The Cashmere Gallery**
Midland Bank	**Reject China Shop**
	Lloyds Bank

HEDDON STREET / REGENT PLACE

woolens **The Highlands**	**Boodle & Dunthorne** jewelry
	Watches of Switzerland
fabric **Fine Textiles**	**Tie Rack** ties/shirts/underwear
pen specialists **Pencraft Ltd.**	**Evans** womenswear
Bureau de Change	**Burton/Dorothy Perkins** clothing
	Garrard jewelry

VIGO STREET / GLASSHOUSE STREET

menswear **Austin Reed**	**Aquascutum** clothing
shoes **Kshoes**	**Dunn & Co.** menswear
The London Textile Company	**Moss Bros.** menswear

Map continues on next page

Regent Street Shopping, cont.

SWALLOW STREET

	REGENT STREET	
leatherwear **Cyril**		
shirts/ties **Off the Cuff**		
tartans/woolens **Clans of Scotland**		
opticians **Boots**		**Scotch House** woolens/tartans
handbags/gifts **Salisburys**		**Bella Ricco** shoes
Bureau de Change		**QUADRANT ARCADE**
cafe **Patisserie Valerie**		**British Designer Knitwear Group**
china/porcelain **Reject China Shop**		handmade sweaters
designer eyewear **Paris-Miki**		**Alexandra** sportswear/workwear
coffee shop **Whittard**		**Angus Steak House**

AIR STREET

socks/underwear **Sock Shop**	**Cafe Royal** cafe/bar
tartans/fabrics **Excellence of London**	**Paul & Shark** menswear
womenswear **Jigsaw**	**House of Cashmere**
ties/underwear **Tie Rack**	**Pringle** woolens
CDs/tapes/videos **Tower Records**	**Washin** opticians
	Travelbag luggage

PICCADILLY CIRCUS

53 Legends ★★$$ Tucked away on staid and sensible Old Burlington Street is a place where you can dance till you drop. A restaurant by day, this place becomes a glossy modern dance club Thursday through Saturday evenings, staying open until the wee hours. Live music is featured on some nights; call ahead to see who's appearing. Recommended dishes include salmon fishcakes and beef fillet. ♦ British/Continental ♦ Restaurant: M-F noon-3AM. Club: Th 10:30PM-3AM; F 10:30PM-4AM; Sa 10:30PM-5AM. 29 Old Burlington St (between Burlington Gardens and Clifford St). 437.9933. Tube: Piccadilly Circus, Oxford Circus

54 Savile Row Many of the tailors on this street, rightly famed the world over for their expertise, have been in this location for at least 200 years. It is benefitting from the resurgence of interest in British fashion, attracting young, flashy tailor/designers to open shops next to the traditional establishments. ♦ Between Vigo and Conduit Sts. Tube: Oxford Circus, Piccadilly Circus

On Savile Row:

Gieves & Hawkes Founded in 1785, this is the oldest tailor on the street (though it didn't actually get to Savile Row until the mid–19th century). Its representatives once followed the British fleet around the world, dressing such illustrious figures as Nelson, Wellington, Livingstone, and Stanley, not to mention the infamous Captain Bligh of the Bounty. ♦ M-Sa. No. 1 (at Vigo St). 434.2001

Ozwald Boateng One of the flamboyant new breed of tailors, Boateng is also a designer of men's suits and shirts. At 30, he was the youngest person ever to open his own shop here, in 1996. ♦ M-Sa. 9 Vigo St (at Savile Row). 734.6868.

Dege Four top tailors (including one that makes women's clothing) work under one roof at this shop, whose name is pronounced Deej. Customers for their suits and sports clothes include heads of state. ♦ M-Sa. No. 10 (between Vigo and New Burlington Sts). 287.2941

Henry Poole & Co. This establishment has tailored gentlemen's clothes since 1806. Originally their shop entrance was around the corner on Old Burlington Street; when the descendants of the first Henry Poole turned a back room into a new shop front, in 1846, they became the first ever tailor shop to grace Savile Row. In Victoria's day, it dressed the French aristocracy (or what was left of it), including Baron de Rothschild and Prince Louis-Napoléon. ♦ M-F. No. 15 (between Vigo and New Burlington Sts). 734.5985

Richard James This tailor is very much in the forefront of the fashion scene. His many clients in the creative professions appreciate the sharp cut and bold-colored fabrics of his made-to-measure and ready-to-wear men's suits, as well as his coordinated shirts. Famous shoppers here include Elton John and Tom Cruise. ♦ M-Sa. 31 Savile Row (between Burlington Gardens and Clifford St). 434.0605

Anderson & Sheppard The tailor here, Arthur Mortenson, is renowned for his ability to sew a Sholte shoulder, which is softer and deeper than the traditional English cut. One of the most discreet tailoring establishments in London, it considers merely being listed in shopping guides as vulgar advertising. Ironically, the now-over-the-top fashion genius Alexander McQueen, who presently heads Givenchy in Paris, started here and even made suits for Prince Charles. ♦ M-F. No. 30 (at Clifford St). 734.1420

Tom Gilbey The fabulous waistcoats designed by this tailor were once displayed in their own shop on Bond Street; now they're sold here along with his distinctively styled made-to-measure suits, which can include those fashioned from silks, velvets, and brocades to achieve that English dandy look straight from another era. The shop also has suits for rent. ♦ M-Sa. 2 New Burlington Pl (at Savile Row). 734.4877

55 Hamleys First established as the 18th-century "Noah's Ark" on High Holborn, the shop with the "infinite variety of toys, games, magical apparatus and sports goods" moved to Regent Street in 1881; shortly afterward, it introduced table tennis to London. Today, the variety of toys and games still seems limitless, spread out as it is over seven levels. Unless you have a strong constitution, avoid this store near Christmastime, when a one-way system is in operation to keep the aisles from getting jammed. Any other time of year, indulge the child in yourself. ♦ M-Sa; Su noon-6PM. 188 Regent St (between Beak St and Foubert's Pl). 734.3161. Tube: Oxford Circus. Also at: Unit 3, The Piazza, Covent Garden. 240.4646. Tube: Covent Garden

LIBERTY

56 Liberty Since the shop opened in 1875, its name has been synonymous with the best-quality printed fabrics money can buy. Founder Arthur Lasenby Liberty was a fan of the Orient, and his skill at importing and selling exotica actually helped foment the pre-Raphaelite movement (Ruskin, Rossetti, and Whistler were all regular customers). The remarkable Tudor-style building is worth experiencing for its architecture alone. Built in the 1920s, it is not authentic, but the beams and timbers came from two 19th-century ships, and the interior features linen-fold paneling, balustrades, oak staircases, stained glass, and Italian carving. A frieze on the Regent Street frontage, completed in 1925, shows goods being transported from Asia to Britain. Of course, the merchandise housed here also merits admiration. Rummage in the remnants section of the fabrics department for designer prints at bargain prices, and head to the basement to browse through an eccentric collection of china and gifts from all over the world. ♦ M-Sa; Su noon-6PM. 210-220 Regent St (at Great Marlborough St). 734.1234. Tube: Oxford Circus

57 Dickins & Jones At this fashionable department store, it's clothes, clothes, and more clothes plus personal shopping services, beauty salons, cosmetics, and perfume. Mostly womenswear is sold here, by such British designers as Amanda Wakely and Patrick Cox,

as well as Giorgio Armani. Menswear fashion on the lower ground floor, are designed by Kenzo and British stalwarts such as Jasper Conran and Paul Smith. The store features its own rather conservative label called House of Fraser. ♦ M-Sa; Su 11AM-5PM. 224-244 Regent St (at Great Marlborough St). 734.7070. Tube: Oxford Circus

58 Godiva Taste some of the best chocolate truffles in Europe, or simply rest your shopping-weary feet while sipping a cappuccino. ♦ M-Sa. Princes and Regent Sts 495.2845. Tube: Oxford Circus

59 Hanover Square This formal square was built in 1717 to reflect the Baroque style of King George I's German house of Hanover. Early residents included two of the king's mistresses. While the square's architect is unknown, **John James** designed the **St. George Hanover Square Church,** just south on St. George Street. Completed in 1724, it was the site of several famous weddings, including those of Percy Bysshe Shelley, Benjamin Disraeli, and George Eliot. ♦ At Hanover and Brook Sts, and St. George St and Harewood Pl. Tube: Oxford Circus

60 Oxford Street What was once a Roman road from Hampshire to the Suffolk coast was already a renowned commercial strip by the 19th century. It is said that some of the modern-day fruit and flower sellers are descended from the original traders who once pushed their barrows along this street, now home to two giant department stores: **John Lewis** (see below) and **Selfridges** (see page 95). An estimated 464,500 square miles of selling space lines the street, and not all of it is worth looking at. However, those who can tolerate crowds will want to give the bigger firms a try. Oxford Circus, at the junction of Oxford and Regent Streets, was part of **John Nash**'s grand plan, though it was rebuilt by **Sir Henry Tanner** in the early 1920s. ♦ Between Charing Cross Rd and Park La. Tube: Oxford Circus, Marble Arch, Bond Street

61 John Lewis Known for the quality of its merchandise, this department store is particularly good for fabrics and drapes. Its motto is: "Never knowingly undersold." *Note* The only credit card the store accepts is its own. ♦ M-Sa. 278-306 Oxford St (at Holles St). 629.7711. Tube: Bond Street, Oxford Circus

Favorite London Haunts

As you might expect from a city with such a long and distinguished history, London has a goodly number of spectral residents. Here are some of the most popular ghost stories floating around town:

Like many of their living counterparts, the dearly departed seem to enjoy hanging around pubs. For example, at the **Grenadier** (18 Wilton Row, off Old Barrack Yd), there's the spirit of a young military officer who was caught cheating at cards in the pub and subsequently beaten to death. He seems to favor the month of September, as that is when most of the alleged sightings have occurred. And the ghost of a Tudor maiden who was supposedly murdered and dumped in the **Thames** makes appearances at the **Silver Cross** (33 Whitehall, between Great Scotland Yd and Craig's Ct), a pub near **Trafalgar Square.** (Her portrait hangs over the fireplace, so you'll know her if you see her.)

The theatrical world has produced its share of spectral presences, the most famous of which is probably the Man in Grey. Wearing a three-cornered hat, a powdered wig, and a gray riding cloak, he favors the **Theatre Royal Drury Lane** (Catherine St, between Tavistock and Russell Sts); he has been seen walking along the back of the upper circle of seats. Rumor has it that he's the ghost of a man whose skeleton—with a dagger embedded between the ribs—was found in a hollow section of a wall during the 19th century. His appearances are usually welcomed because over the years they've been associated with successful plays. According to the legend, he was sighted during the London premieres of the hit musicals *Oklahoma!, South Pacific,* and *The King and I.*

At the **Theatre Royal, Haymarket** (Haymarket, between Suffolk Pl and Orange St), where Ibsen's *Ghosts* was performed in 1914, another ghost lingers, that of John Buckstone, who was the manager here from 1853 through 1878. Dressed in a black frock coat, he is usually sighted in the Royal Box occupying the chair he used when royal visitors attended a performance. And one of the dressing rooms at the **Adelphi Theatre** (Strand, between Southampton and Bedford Sts) is said to be spooked by Victorian actor William Terriss. He apparently had a part to die for—a rival actor stabbed him to death there.

Somerset House (Lancaster Pl, at Strand), where the **Courtauld Galleries** are now,

housed the Admiralty for a time after it was built in 1776, and it has a famous specter of its own. Admiral Horatio Nelson, with an empty sleeve where his arm is missing, has been seen walking across the old cobbled quadrangle here.

Ghost busters would find quite a few apparitions slipping through their fingers at the **Tower of London** (Tower Hill, at Tower Bridge Approach). Anne Boleyn appears on **Tower Green** near the scaffold where she was executed in 1536, as well as in the **Chapel Royal** inside the **White Tower.** (As an old song has it, "With her head tucked underneath her arm, she walks the bloody tower. . . at the midnight hour.") Henry VI has been seen in the chamber where he was stabbed to death just before midnight on 21 May 1471. According to legend, the sight of St. Thomas à Becket's ghost in the building over **Traitor's Gate** inspired Henry III to include a small chapel here (it was his grandfather, Henry II, who had caused Becket's murder in 1170 at **Canterbury Cathedral**). And Sir Walter Raleigh's ghost still takes his exercise along **Raleigh's Walk,** a stretch of wall beside the **Bloody Tower.** (The pitiful ghosts of two Little Princes who were brutally murdered to further their uncle Richard III's ambitions and who used to haunt the **Bloody Tower** disappeared after their bones were moved to **Westminster Abbey** in 1485.)

The spirits of two of Henry VIII's wives still linger at **Hampton Court Palace.** Jane Seymour, who died in childbirth a year after becoming queen, wafts through what is now called **Haunted Gallery,** clad in white and holding a candle. And Catherine Howard, executed for her adultery with the dashing Thomas Culpepper, is heard rather than seen: Her cries echo through the galleries, and her fists pound on the chapel door, just as they probably did when she pleaded with the king to spare her life.

Oxford Street Shopping

PARK LANE

Left side	Right side
music **Virgin Megastore**	**Cumberland Hotel**
	Kentucky Fried Chicken
	OLD QUEBEC STREET
	Evans *womenswear*
	Wallis *womenswear*
Pizza Hut	**Next** *womenswear/menwear*
	Cascade Shops *clothing/gifts*
	Benetton *woolens/women s and children s clothing*
department store **C&A**	**Littlewoods** *department store*
PARK STREET	**PORTMAN STREET**
electrical goods **Dixons**	**Roland Cartier** *shoes*
womenswear **Bay Trading Co.**	**Watches of Switzerland**
ties/shirts **Tie Rack**	**Baggage Co.**
outdoorwear **The Highlands**	**Russell & Bromley** *shoes*
menswear **Oakland**	**Boots** *chemist*
womenswear **Hennes**	**Etam** *womenswear*
Aberdeen Steak House	**Clarks** *shoes*
building society **Abbey National**	**H. Samuel** *jewelry*
clothing **Gap**	**Bally** *shoes*
House of Cashmere	
underwear **Knickerbox**	
woolens **House of Scotland**	
maternity and children s clothing **Mothercare**	
American Burger	**Marks & Spencer** *department store*
NORTH AUDLEY STREET	**ORCHARD STREET**
womenswear **Laura Ashley**	
denims **Jean Jeanie**	
jewelry **MacKenzie s**	
cashmere/woolens **London House**	
Churchill Gifts	
chemist **Boots**	
socks/stockings **Sock Shop**	**Selfridges** *department store*
Midland Bank	
BALDERTON STREET	
Angus Steak House	
Sunglass Hut	
gifts **The Oxford Street General Store**	
LUMLEY STREET	
clothing **Principles**	
menswear **Ciro Citterio**	

DUKE STREET

Left side	Right side
jewelry **Mappin & Webb**	**Barratts** *shoes*
tartans/woolens **Clans of Scotland**	**Jane Norman** *womenswear*
shoes **Bertie**	**Stylo Instep** *sports gear*
Carphone Warehouse	
BINNEY STREET	**BIRD STREET**
Lloyds Bank	**C&A**
Pizzaland	
GILBERT STREET	**JAMES STREET**
sportswear **Gap**	**Body Shop** *lotions/perfumes/toiletries*
clothing **Jeans West**	**Suits You** *menswear*
chemist **Boots**	**Bally** *shoes*
tartans/woolens **Oxford s**	**H. Samuel** *jewelry*
⊖ **Bond Street Tube Station**	**Woodhouse** *menswear*
assorted shops **West One Shopping Centre**	**Kooka** *womenswear*
clothing **Burtons/Dorothy Perkins**	**Lilley & Skinner** *shoes*

OXFORD STREET

Map continues on next page

90

DAVIES STREET
SOUTH MOLTON STREET

jewelry **Leslie Davis**
⊖ **Bond Street Tube Station**
croissants **La Brioche Durée**
menswear **Oakland**
gifts **Churchill**
gifts **Sedley Place Selection**
House of Cashmere
chocolates **Thorntons**
casualwear **Chainstore Discounts**

WOODSTOCK STREET
burgers **Wendy's**
snack bar **Café Zeynah**
cafe **Bonjour Paris**
gifts **Splash**
shoes **Dolcis**

NEW BOND STREET
womenswear **Next**

DERING STREET
sportswear **Gap**
watches **Swatch**
supermarket **Tesco Metro**
womenswear **New Look**
sports gear **Olympus**
shoes **Babers/Church**
shoes **Saxone**
ties/shirts **Tie Rack**
accessories **Accessorize**

HAREWOOD PLACE
McDonald's
optician **Vision Express**
Bureau de Change
Deep Pan Pizza
menswear **Cecil Gee**
chemist **Boots**
womenswear **River Island**
jewelry **Ernest Jones**
cafe **Le Baguette Parisienne**
JD Sports
womenswear **Richards**
opticians **For Eyes**
socks/stockings **Sock Shop**
Benetton
woolens/women's and children's clothing

STRATFORD PLACE

Sunglass Hut sunglasses
Art of Silk ties/waistcoats

MARYLEBONE LANE
Trustee Savings Bank
British Telecom
Off the Cuff ties/boxers

MARYLEBONE LANE

Debenhams department store

VERE STREET
Citibank
Smokers pipes/tobacco
Naf Naf fashion clothing
Sock Shop
K Shoes
D.H. Evans department store

OLD CAVENDISH STREET

John Lewis department store

HOLLES STREET
Wallis womenswear
Clinton cards
Body Shop lotions/perfumes
Ann Harvey womenswear
Monsoon womenswear
Jane Norman womenswear
Clarks shoes
BHS department store
H. Samuel jewelry
Ravel shoes
Bally shoes
Mister Byrite menswear

JOHN PRINCE'S STREET
Hennes womenswear

OXFORD STREET

REGENT STREET
fashions **Topshop**
Shellys shoes

62 D.H. Evans Women's fashions are this store's strength, and there is also an able hairdresser on the top floor. If you can fight your way past the ground-floor armies of salespeople eager to spray you with the latest fragrance, you'll have ample opportunity to browse for accessories. ◆ M-Sa. 318 Oxford St (at Old Cavendish St). 629.8800. Tube: Bond Street

63 Bond Street This is Fifth Avenue, Rodeo Drive, and the Faubourg St-Honoré rolled into one. Imperturbably chic, Bond Street leads from Piccadilly to Oxford Street and is paved all the way with American Express Gold cards (it might as well be, anyway). A little over a decade ago, the legendary shopping street celebrated its 300th birthday, but it cheated a little bit: while Old Bond Street was built in 1686, New Bond Street, which begins at Clifford Street, only dates back to 1721. You can blame the confusing street numbering system on Parliament, which, in 1762, forbade the use of hanging signs to identify shops (too many customers were being clobbered in high winds) and numbered the streets separately, first up the east side toward Oxford Street and then down again on the west.

Bond Street Shopping

OXFORD STREET

shoes **Dolcis**	**Next** clothing
womenswear **Warehouse**	
womenswear **Blazer**	**Berkertex** bridalwear
menswear **Cecil Gee**	
shoes **Grant**	

BLENHEIM STREET

	Bellini 077 clothing
shoes **Kurt Geiger**	**Cerruti 1881** menswear
shoes **Carvela**	**DERING STREET**
Royal Bank of Scotland	**Louis Féraud** womenswear
linen/lingerie **Frette**	**Timberland** clothing, shoes
womenswear **Betty Barclay**	**Jason** fabrics
shoes **Lanzoni**	**Liz Davenport** womenswear
Phillips Auctioneers	
countrywear/accessories **Proudfoot**	
shoes **Florsheim**	**Please Mum** children's clothing
shoes **Ivory**	**Robina** womenswear
womenswear **Laurel**	**Escada** womenswear
womenswear **Cerruti 1881**	
clothing **Gant**	**Guy Laroche** womenswear
designer menswear **Lanvin**	
shoes **Russell & Bromley**	**Dixon's** electrical goods

(NEW BOND STREET)

BROOK STREET

menswear/womenswear **Emporio Armani**	**Fenwick's** department store
Bond Street Silver Galleries	
antique jewelry arcade	
shoes **Bally**	**Calvin Klein** menswear/womenswear
menswear **Gieffeffe**	
menswear **Gianfranco Ferre**	
womenswear **Aigner**	
menswear **Vercace**	
designer clothing **Cecil Gee**	

LANCASHIRE COURT

Lane Fine Art	
44 shops **Bond St. Antique Centre**	**White House** linen/clothing
menswear **Herbie Frogg**	**Chappell** musical instruments
womenswear **Jigsaw**	**Bruno Magli** shoes
Midland Bank	**F. Pinet** women's shoes

GROSVENOR STREET — MADDOX STREET

leather accessories **Loewe**	**Avi Rossini** menswear/furs
menswear **Beale & Inman**	**Cashmere Shop** woolens
shoes **Church's**	**Mulberry** clothing/accessories
womenswear **L. Mugler**	**Smythson** stationers
menswear **Yves Saint Laurent**	

BLOOMFIELD PLACE

womenswear **Marie Claire**	
antique jewelry **S.J. Phillips**	**Pal Zileri** menswear
menswear **Zilli**	**Ermenegildo Zegna** menswear
art/fine furniture **Mallett**	**Fogal** hosiery
clothing **Polo/Ralph Lauren**	**Sotheby's** auctioneer
art/antiques **Partridge**	**Richard Green** paintings
fine art **Wildenstein & Co.**	**Fior** jewelry
The Fine Art Society	**Wana** womenswear
leather travel goods **Louis Vuitton**	**Tessier's** antique jewelry
shoes/womenswear **Joan & David**	**Russell & Bromley** shoes

(NEW BOND STREET)

BRUTON STREET — CONDUIT STREET

clothing **Hermès**	**Philip Landau** menswear
cashmere **Ballantyne**	**Moira** '30s antique jewelry
womenswear **MaxMara**	**Massimo** menswear
menswear/womenswear **Nicole Farhi**	**Moira** jewelry
womenswear **Miss V**	**Donna Karan NY** menswear/womenswear
fine art **John Mitchell & Son**	
ornaments **Lalique**	
shoes **Church's**	
Savoy Tailors Guild	

Map continues on next page

GRAFTON STREET

jewelry/gifts **Asprey**
womenswear **Caroline Charles**
jewelry **Collingwood**
jewelry **Bulgari**
womenswear **Chanel**
watches/jewelry **Cartier**
shoes **Fratelli Rossetti**
jewelry **Diancor**
clothing **Mikomoto**
jewelry **David Morris**
jewelry **Tiffany & Co.**
womenswear **Chanel**
womenswear **DKNY**

ROYAL ARCADE

chocolates **Charbonnel et Walker**
womenswear **Christian Lacroix**
shoes **Bally**
shoes **Pied à terre**
leather/clothing **Gucci**

STAFFORD STREET

clothing **Gianni Versace**
art gallery **Baccarat**
men's shirtmakers **Holland & Holland**
Lloyds Bank
art gallery **Noortman**
fine art **Thomas Agnew & Son**
art gallery **Thomas Gibson**
luxury goods **Isetan**

CLIFFORD STREET

Watches of Switzerland
Patek Philippe watches
Georg Jensen silver/porcelain
Chopard jewelry
Adler jewelry
Hennell jewelry
Philip Antrobus jewelry
Adèle Davis womenswear
Clough jewelry/pawnbroking
Ciro jewelry
Bentley & Co. jewelry
GRAFF jewelry
Watches of Switzerland
Richard Green art gallery

BURLINGTON GARDENS

Salvatore Ferragamo womenswear
Joseph womenswear
Chatila jewelry
Sulka menswear
Frost & Reed art gallery
Ricci Burns womenswear
Colnaghi Art Gallery
The Leger Art Galleries
Benson and Hedges tobacco
Anna Molinari womenswear
Cesare Paciotti shoes
Swaine Adeney umbrellas/leather goods
Ginza Yamagataya tailor
Ana House Takashimaya luxury goods
Gold Pfeil leather goods
MCM leather goods
Mayfair Carpet Gallery
E.B. Meyrovitz optician
Watches of Switzerland

OLD BOND STREET

PICCADILLY

Art galleries flourish on and around Bond Street: buy a Turner at **Thomas Agnew & Son,** or discover an unknown genius at **Sotheby's,** the world's largest auction house. If art is your interest, browse along Albemarle, Dover, and Grafton Streets—and don't overlook Cork Street, with its little upscale galleries that always seem to be showing works by the latest artists. Antiques lovers should turn into Burlington Gardens, then also explore a maze of backstreets crammed with the old, the opulent, and the unusual.

You can shop at an almost endless number of international fashion boutiques—including **Gucci, Hermès, Cartier, Louis Vuitton, Ralph Lauren,** and **MaxMara.** The designer district spreads into nearby streets: If Oxford Street is behind you, turn right onto Brook Street (it cuts across Bond) to find British designer **Margaret Howell.** Her shop (here and in Knightsbridge) specializes in a modern yet classic English look with well-coordinated clothes for men and women. Then stroll along South Molton Street to find many stylish shops. If you turn left onto Brook Street instead, you will come upon **Halcyon Days**—a darling little gift emporium filled with enamel boxes and knickknacks by Royal Appointment. ◆ Between Piccadilly and Oxford St. Tube: Bond Street, Green Park

On Bond Street:

SMYTHSON
OF BOND STREET

Smythson The leather address books and diaries sold here are highly coveted status symbols, and even though it's un peu pretentious, the address book divided into three sections and inscribed simply "London/New York/Paris" is truly useful for fortunate vagabonds. ◆ M-Sa. 40 New Bond St (near Maddox St). 629.8558. Also at: 135 Sloane St (between Sloane Sq and Cadogan Gardens. 730.5520. Tube: Bond Street, Green Park

---

Lady Astor to Sir Winston Churchill: If you were my husband, I would feed you poison.

Churchill: If you were my wife, madam, I would take it.

Mulberry For the traditional British look in menswear and womenswear, with matching accessories, this handsome shop is the place to visit. It's also known for its leather goods; home furnishings are found only here, at their flagship store. ◆ M-Sa. 41-42 New Bond St (near Maddox St). 491.3900. Also at: 11-12 Gees Ct (between Oxford and Barrett Sts). 493.2546. Tube: Bond Street; 185 Brompton Rd (at Beauchamp Pl). 225.0313. Tube: Knightsbridge

Nicole Farhi Always popular with conservatively fashionable women in their thirties and forties, this French-born designer (married to the playwright David Hare), makes beautiful clothes for women that reflect the season's trends. The flagship store is large, cool, and relaxed, with a chic basement restaurant. There's also a menswear collection and accessories. ◆ M-Sa. 158 New Bond St (between Grafton and Bruton Sts). 499.8368. Also at: 193 Sloane St (between Harriet St and Knightsbridge). 235.0877. Tube: Knightsbridge; 25-26 St. Christopher's Pl (between Barrett and Wigmore Sts). 486.3416. Tube: Bond Street; 11 Floral St (between James and Garrick Sts). 497.1813. Tube: Covent Garden

Asprey Allow the doorman to welcome you to England's most luxurious jewelry and gift shop, which specializes in the finest items, from crocodile suitcases to Fabergé frames. ◆ M-Sa. 165-169 New Bond St (at Grafton St). 493.6767

Charbonnel et Walker The fabulous chocolates come in boxes that are equally treasured. ◆ M-Sa. 28 Old Bond St (at Royal Arcade). 491.0939

SWAINE ADENEY
1750

Swaine Adeney One of London's oldest family-run businesses, this venerable establishment was a Piccadilly landmark for centuries until its move to Bond Street in 1995. Well settled in its new location, reminiscent of a baronial home, the shop boasts three Royal Warrants: whip and glove makers to the queen, umbrella makers to the queen mother, and supplier of leather goods to the Prince of Wales. Here, you can get the Rolls-Royce of umbrellas—the high-quality, handmade Brigg "brolly." Typical features of these long-lasting umbrellas include silver collars and nosecaps, black silk English covers, and hand-bent crooks, which can be made of a variety of woods—such as malacca, whangee, chestnut, cherry, hickory, or ash—as well as hand-sewn calf or crocodile. There is also a selection of unusual canes and sticks, some with built-in compartments for such items as flasks and measuring rulers. The extensive range of leather goods available includes handmade attaché cases, luggage, and accessories. A wide variety of fine country clothing is sold as well, from waxed rain jackets to elegant sportswear. ◆ M-Sa. 10 Old Bond St (between Piccadilly and Burlington Gardens) 409.7277

64 **Claridge's** $$$$ If the royal family favors one hotel above all others as a location for functions, it is this one. The service at this reassuringly traditional and unassuming establishment is always respectful (you would be respectful, too, if you dealt with governmental higher-ups and diplomats several times a day). Bell-pushes in each of the 197 rooms pay tribute to another era and allow guests to summon a waiter, maid, or valet. And there's nothing here so vulgar as a bar—drinks are brought to you at your table in the **Foyer** by a liveried footman. Creating an atmosphere evocative of the 1930s, a Hungarian quartet entertains here daily. Morning coffee and afternoon tea are served in the **Reading Room.** If you can afford to stay in one of the huge guest rooms with a real wood-burning fireplace and a separate dressing room, you'll learn why the queen is so fond of the place. Facilities include a hair salon and a health club for weight training, massages, facials, and aromatherapy. ◆ Broo St (at Davies St). 629.8860, 800/63.SAVOY; fax 499.2210. Tube: Bond Street

Within Claridge's:

The Restaurant ★★★★$$$ Basil Ionides's splendid 1926 Art Deco creation affords a beautiful setting for the meals produced by chef John Williams, whose menu features classic dishes with flair. Stalwart British offerings might include roasted sea scallops with braised turnips and watercress scented with horseradish or roast rack or saddle of lamb. Among the French dishes might be tartlet of crisp potatoes with smoked salmon and celery to start, then roast monkfish in a *Provençale* sauce. Desserts are served from a trolley with a choice of fresh fruit salads, cakes, and pastries. Dinner dances are held every Friday and Saturday night. ◆ British/French ◆ Daily breakfast, lunch, and dinner. Reservations required. 629.8860

The Causerie ★★★$$$ This green and cream room is one of the few places in London where it is possible to enjoy a first-class *smörgåsbord*. Sample the five types of herring, as well as the wonderful smoked beef. Other, more traditional dishes include medaillon of monkfish with fennel, chicken pie, and rosettes of lamb served with artichokes and wild mushrooms. Save room for dessert—the rum baba with *Chantilly* cream and fruit is fabulous. ◆ Scandinavian/Continental ◆ M-F lunch and dinner. Reservations recommended; jacket and tie required. 629.8860

65 Vivienne Westwood This most influential of British designers is still grabbing the headlines with her collections for men and women. Her couture clothes (Gold Label) are at this little shop. ◆ M-Sa. 6 Davies St (between Bourdon and Grosvenor Sts). 629.3757. Tube: Bond Street. The Man Collection and the less expensive range (Red Label) is at 44 Conduit St (between New Bond St and Savile Row). 439.1109. Tube: Bond Street, Oxford Circus. The affordable, street-style range with the young in mind is at 430 Kings Rd (between Park Walk and Limerston St). 352.6551. Tube: South Kensington

66 Grays Antique Market/Grays Mews About 180 antiques dealers display their wares at these two adjacent market areas, and if prices for the collectibles, fashion jewelry, and curios are not the lowest, they are at least reasonable. In addition, all items are backed up by a guarantee of authenticity. ◆ M-F. Market: 58 Davies St (at S Molton St). Mews: 1-7 Davies Mews (at S Molton La). 629.7034 (for both). Tube: Bond Street

67 Browns Stocking top designers' labels such as Georgina von Etzdorf, and Prada, this handsome store looks rather like a large house. It is divided into cozy rooms for its women's and men's departments. Other locations include **Browns Focus** which offers more affordable clothing than **Browns** (38 S Molton St, 491.7833) and **Browns Labels for Less,** which features the creations of established designers at a discount (62 S Molton St, 495.7301). ◆ M-Sa. 23-27 S Molton St (at Davies St). 491.7833. Tube: Bond Street

68 St. Christopher's Place Just off the hurly-burly noise and activity of Oxford Street, this narrow pedestrian alleyway is an oasis of smart shops and restaurants. The first little stretch is also called "Gees Court." Its many boutiques include **Nicole Farhi** (see page 94), offering women's clothing by the eponymous designer, and **Buckle-My-Shoe** (935.5589), which sells designer footwear for kids up to age 10. ◆ Between Oxford and Wigmore Sts. Tube: Bond Street

On St. Christopher's Place

Whistles Lucille Lewin, the astute owner of this chain of fashion shops, offers trendy clothes from the hottest young designers without the excruciatingly high price tags. ◆ M-Sa. Nos. 12-14. 487.4484

Paddy Campbell Creating understated but stylish clothes for women, this designer pays great attention to detail. Her collection, primarily daywear, includes chic suits and classic wool and linen dresses; she also provides a range of flattering evening wear. ◆ M-Sa. 8 Gees Ct. 493.5646. Also at: 17 Beauchamp Pl (between Walnut St and Brompton Rd). 225.0543. Tube: Knightsbridge

69 Selfridges Although this department store, which opened in 1909, has become a British institution, it is actually an American import, developed by a retail magnate from Wisconsin named Gordon Selfridge. Its display windows, situated between 22 Ionic columns, create sidewalk crowds at Christmas, its perfume counter is said to be the largest in Europe, and the food hall and stationery section are both great fun. This is the second-largest department store in London (next to **Harrods**)—it occupies nearly an entire city block. ◆ M-Sa; Su noon-6PM. 400 Oxford St (between Duke and Orchard Sts). 629.1234. Tube: Marble Arch, Bond Street

70 Marks & Spencer It is claimed that at any given time 8 out of 10 people in London will be sporting underwear from this decidedly British institution, often called "Marks & Sparks" or simply "M&S." While its undergarments are indeed good, so are its woolens, clothing for both sexes, coats, housewares, and famous food department, where the items under its own "St. Michael" label match up to those of **Harrods**—and are better priced. ◆ M-Sa; Su noon-6PM. 458 Oxford St (between Orchard and Portman Sts). 935.7954. Tube: Marble Arch

At Gonville and Caius College, Cambridge, graduating medical students traditionally crawl out onto the roof of the Porter's Lodge and place hats on the school's infamous (and many) resident gargoyles.

King's Road/Chelsea

Avant-garde King's Road, once synonymous with the swinging London of the 1960s, runs the entire length of the affluent riverside village known as Chelsea. A highway created by Charles II as his royal route to **Hampton Court Palace**, the street is now a stage set for an assortment of marginal, hip Londoners, in sharp contrast to the surrounding cosmopolitan village of upscale town houses (there are relatively few apartments in this area) inhabited by privileged professionals. Chelsea dwellers live on tree-lined streets in domestic tranquillity and endure the anarchy and decadence of King's Road with humor. In fact, they're more preoccupied with changes in their lifestyle (boutiques and antiques markets have replaced the local fishmonger, greengrocer, and baker) than they are with the eclectic parade of denizens along the borough's main route.

Cozying up to the **River Thames** southwest of **Westminster** and south of **Hyde Park**, this section of London is one of the most intimate in the city. The human-scale streets and architecture provide a counterpoint for the imposing

public buildings and monuments of other areas that dwarf pedestrians. Some Londoners consider **Christopher Wren**'s magnificent **Royal Hospital** here one of the most beautiful buildings in the city. Aesthetics aside, the building still functions as a hospital and residence for war veterans (mostly alumni of World War II), whose distinguished scarlet and blue uniforms are part of the iconography of Chelsea life.

It is here, in Chelsea, in houses that appear grand even by today's standards, that writers Oscar Wilde, Thomas Carlyle, and George Eliot, and painters James Whistler, John Singer Sargent, and J.M.W. Turner lived. Novelist Henry James and painters Augustus John and Dante Gabriel Rossetti were among the illustrious intellectuals, artists, and bohemians who resided in the neighborhood at one time or another. It doesn't take a vivid imagination to picture them walking these streets, which have changed so little since their tenure here.

Chelsea is known for its vitality, but also for trendsetting and juxtaposing styles. Until 1985, Lady Margaret Thatcher's private London address was here; but this is also where Mary Quant launched miniskirts, where the Rolling Stones lived once they'd gotten some satisfaction, and where punk began (and lingered long past its demise in less colorful quarters). The village is also home to the **Designers Guild**, a fabric, furniture, and interior-design shop where the latest trends are being set; and to **Sloane Square**, a small plaza that has become synonymous with a type of upper-class, inbred Londoners known familiarly as Sloane Rangers. "Sloanes" are preppy to the extreme: the women have a marked preference for pearls (even with sweatshirts), ruffles, and floral prints, especially in the country-style interiors of their homes. They favor phrases that brand them as Sloanes, and they have a distinctive accent.

The ideal day to visit Chelsea is Saturday, when King's Road is in full bloom, complete with archetypes, poseurs, newlyweds on their way to **Chelsea Town Hall** for the final formalities, Sloane Rangers, and tourists. To get a feel for the yin and the yang of the quarter, make sure you spend some time exploring side streets as well as King's Road. *Note:* The only underground station that serves Chelsea is **Sloane Square Station**, via the **District** and **Circle Lines**, though **South Kensington Station** is closer to the shops on the far end of King's Road. Also, to get to the far end of King's Road from **Sloane Square**, take bus *No. 11, No. 22,* or *No. 211.*

City code 0171 unless otherwise noted.

1 Sloane Square Chelsea begins here, under a tent of young plane trees. A running soundtrack of cars and taxis in the background drowns out the watery music of Gilbert Ledward's Venus fountain, presented to Chelsea by the **Royal Academy** in 1953. Nothing grows in the square save trees, but color is provided by the flower sellers who purvey fluorescent blooms here. The square was named after one of Chelsea's most distinguished residents, Sir Hans Sloane, a wealthy physician at the beginning of the 18th century who was also president of the Royal Society, an organization founded more than 300 years ago to further scientific knowledge. Sloane, who at one time owned practically all of the village of Chelsea, lived in Henry VIII's former manor house. His vast collection of plant specimens, fossils, rocks, minerals, and books, amassed over a lifetime, formed the foundation of the **British Museum**. ♦ At Cliveden Pl and King's Rd, and Lower Sloane and Sloane Sts

2 W.H. Smith This chain bookseller is a good place to acquire maps, guidebooks, writing paper, pens, magazines, newspapers, and paperbacks. There is also a large selection of international periodicals. ♦ Main shop: M-Sa. Newsstand: M-F. Sloane Sq (between Sloane Gardens and Lower Sloane St). 730.0351; fax 259.0242. Also at: Numerous locations in the city, including many British Rail stations

3 L'Incontro ★★$$$ A bit off the beaten track, this elegant restaurant attracts a lot of evening business, even on Sunday: Jason Robards often dines here, as do many other celebrities, including Mick Jagger. An army of Italian waiters eases dishes on and off your table with polished grace. Pasta made on the premises provides the base for wild mushroom or fresh crab sauce, and each bite of the baked monkfish in garlic and butter sauce dissolves delectably in your mouth. Scallops Venetian style, fish mousse with polenta, and baked artichoke are also popular. Be prepared to pay handsomely (the fixed-price lunches offering two or three courses are a better value), and wines aren't cheap, either; however, the selection of Italian vintages provides refreshing diversity and quality. ♦ Italian ♦ M-F lunch and dinner; Sa-Su dinner. Reservations recommended. 87 Pimlico Rd (between St. Barnabas St and Bloomfield Terr). 730.3663

3 Orange Brewery ★★$ Located in a Victorian building, this fine pub still boasts darkwood paneling and gaslight fittings. Best of all, it makes its own ale and beer—one of the few London pubs to do so. The three main house brews, concocted in the basement, are SW1 (the best-selling "bitter" (dark beer); SW2 (a stronger beer); Pimlico Porter (very dark, rich ale; porter was the most popular brew 200 years ago), and Victorian Lager—the only house-brewed lager in the country. The beer vats are actually visible from a barrel-shaped glass panel in the pub floor, giving patrons an idea of how the stuff they're quaffing came to be. Also, brewer John Horn conducts tours of the basement Monday through Friday by appointment only. Of the traditional pub grub served here, the favorite is bangers and mash (sausages with mashed potatoes). ♦ Brew pub ♦ Fee for tour of brewery, including tasting. Daily lunch and dinner. Reservations required for brewery tour. 37 Pimlico Rd (at St. Barnabas St). 730.5984

4 Ebury Wine Bar ★★$$$ One of the first wine bars to open in London in the 1970s, it is still one of the best. The bar in front leads to two dining areas; head for the back room, where murals line the dark green walls and lots of dark wooden furniture adds to the cozy air. Australian chef Josh Hampton produces good food with flavors of the Pacific and the Mediterranean plus such British basics as black pudding with potato cake, and also surprises like roast kangaroo. There is an excellent range of moderately priced wine. The place is humming weekdays. ♦ International ♦ Wine bar: daily; restaurant: daily lunch and dinner. 139 Ebury St (at Elizabeth St). 730.5447

4 Lime Tree Hotel $$ David and Marilyn Davies run this 26-room, superior bed-and-breakfast establishment. The cheerful rooms, most with bath or shower, have ivory walls set off with pastel spreads and floral curtains. They're comfortable, well maintained and, amazingly, for such a posh district, very reasonably priced. A full English breakfast is served in a pleasant room overlooking the handsome street, which is on the fringe of Chelsea and a useful link to Victoria, with its bus, train, and tube stations. ♦ 135-137 Ebury St (between Elizabeth and Eccleston Sts). 730.8191; fax 730.7865

5 Royal Court Theatre *Look Back in Anger* by John Osborne, an explosive 1950s drama whose kitchen-sink realism was unlike anything the class-conscious English theater had ever seen before, put this venue and its **English Stage Company** on the map. But it wasn't the first time the theater had shocked audiences: It had also produced the provocative early plays of George Bernard Shaw. The structure was originally designed by **Walter Emden** and **W.R. Crewe** in 1887-88 and was rebuilt once and remodeled twice. In 1988, the theater was closed for another, major refurbishment, while the company moved to two West End theaters, the **Duke of York's** and **Ambassadors**; it was expected to reopen as we went to press. ♦ Sloane Sq (between Holbein Pl and Bourne St). Information: 565.5000; www.royalcourttheatre.com

6 Oriel ★$$ This French cafe has most of the usual advantages of the genre: hot coffee and croissants served early in the morning, good wine by the glass, and attractive cane chairs pulled up to marble-top tables. This is the best place in the area for observing Sloanes and Chelsea poseurs. English specialties such as toasted tea cakes are served with panache by the predominantly French staff. French dishes include Toulouse sausages with lentils, pancetta, and mushrooms. Note that even without the **Royal Court**'s patrons (see above), the cafe has been getting pretty crowded. ♦ French ♦ Daily breakfast, lunch, and dinner. 50-51 Sloane Sq (at Cliveden Pl). 730.2804

7 David Mellor Outstanding contemporary designs for the kitchen and dining room are the hallmark of this inimitable store, whose offerings include handmade wooden salad bowls, pottery bowls, and glassware—the best from British craftspeople, along with a superb selection from France, Poland, and Spain. The specialty is the cutlery designed by Mellor. There are also lots of interesting deli-style food products in jars and bottles, especially the flavorful olives. ♦ M-Sa. 4 Sloane Sq (between Eaton Terr and Sedding St). 730.4259

7 Sloane Square Moat House $$$ Previously known as the **Royal Court Hotel**, the premises have been refurbished by the new owners who have, however, kept the relaxed atmosphere of a provincial English country hotel. The 105 rooms, decorated in pastels, blond-wood furniture, and framed modern prints, have all the modern comforts, including 24-hour room service. The traditional **Tavern** pub on the ground floor draws crowds, while the **Otto** bar, tucked away in the basement, is a more intimate watering hole. The doorman, with his gold-and-black braided uniform, has become a fixture in the square. ♦ Sloane Sq (at Sedding St). 896.9988; fax 824.8381

Within Sloane Square Moat House:

No. 12 ★$$ In this eatery, decorated with French tapestries and contemporary prints, diners can choose from a selection of good, reliable entrées such as salmon with asparagus or cutlets of lamb with a swede

(rutabaga) puree. The front part is an all-day cafe serving light meals and snacks. ♦ Cafe/Continental ♦ Cafe: daily breakfast, lunch, and dinner. Restaurant: daily breakfast, dinner. 896.9988

8 Sloane Street At the upper end of the street you'll find designer shops, enhanced by the prestige of being located next to **Harvey Nichols** (see page 133). The lower half is residential until Sloane Square with its array of chic stores.♦ Between Sloane Sq and Knightsbridge

9 Holy Trinity Despite the destruction of the vault over the nave by German bombs in World War II, this church, built between 1888 and 1890 by **J.S. Sedding,** remains a Gothic Revival homage to the 19th-century Arts and Crafts Movement. Among the pre-Raphaelite treasures are the stunning east window, designed by **Sir Edward Coley Burne-Jones** and made by William Morris, and the grille behind the altar. ♦ Services: Su 8:45AM, 11AM. Sloane St (between Sloane Sq and Sloane Terr). 235.3383

10 Wilbraham Hotel $$ One of the rare hotels to offer the shabby-genteel atmosphere of country England in the heart of London, this one does so at refreshingly low prices. The privately owned 50-room hotel, converted from three town houses dating from 1880, is unashamedly old-fashioned. Reflecting the Victorian era, the lobby has a grand wooden staircase, writing desks, and knickknacks tucked away in cozy corners. Ask for a largish room with your own bath and you will be pleased; otherwise beware—the single rooms are very small. There is a small restaurant on the premises. Since the hotel is nearly always full, book at least two months in advance. ♦ 1 Wilbraham Pl (at Sloane St). 730.8296; fax 730.6815

It is the proud perpetual boast of an Englishman that he never brags.

–D.B. Wyndham Lewis

Sloane Street Shopping

SLOANE SQUARE

Midland Bank	Lady Daphne *interior design*
Holy Trinity	General Trading Company *department store*
womenswear Emanuel Kenel	The Garden Restaurant
jewelry Cobra & Bellamy	India Jane *fine gifts*
sandwich bar Picola	Savills *real estate*
pharmacy Andrews	Hackett *menswear*
SLOANE TERRACE	Smythson *stationery*
dry cleaning Sketchley	Partridges *deli*
interior design Jane Churchill	Hilditch & Key *shirtmakers*
real estate Knight Frank & Rutley	Vidal Sassoon *hairdresser*
WILBRAHAM PLACE	Patrick Cox Wannabe *womenswear/shoes*
florist Moyses Stevens	Pulbrook & Gould *florist*
Cadogan Travel	Dollond & Atchison *optician*
Europa Food Stores	**CADOGAN GARDENS**
ELLIS STREET	
womenswear Pallant	
CADOGAN PLACE	**CADOGAN GATE**
	PAVILION STREET
	Cadogan Hotel

PONT STREET

	Royal Danish Embassy
	Ivor Gordon *jewelry*
	Stephanie Kélian *shoes*
	Pollini *leather goods/shoes*
CADOGAN PLACE	
bank Coutts & Co.	
restaurant Rib Room	
womenswear Jaeger	
COTTAGE WALK	
	Prada *womenswear*
	Giorgio Armani *menswear/womenswear*
	Emanuel Ungaro *womenswear*
	Walter Steiger *shoes*
womenswear Valentino	**HANS CRESCENT**
clothing Dolce & Gabbana	Yves Saint Laurent *womenswear*
formalwear Tomasz Starzewski	MaxMara *womenswear*
clothing Hermès	Chanel *womenswear*
womenswear Georges Rech	National Bank of Pakistan
womenswear Istante	Giannefranco Ferre *womenswear*
National Westminster Bank	Joseph *womenswear/menswear*
pub The Gloucester	Christian Dior *womenswear*
jewelry Cartier	Equipment *womenswear*
women's shoes Gina	Katherine Hamnett *womenswear*
	The Chelsea Hotel

(SLOANE STREET runs vertically through the center)

Map continues on next page

EST **GTC** 1920

THE GENERAL TRADING COMPANY

11 General Trading Company (GTC) Just off Sloane Square, this huge store epitomizes everything Sloane—and if you still aren't sure what that means, go in and look around. Once, nice young girls (pronounced *gels* in Sloane-speak) worked in florist shops in the hope that they might meet their prince. Now that the royal life has been found lacking, the *gels* work in estate agencies or the **GTC,** waiting for lords rather than princes to whisk

HARRIET STREET	SLOANE STREET	Gucci *leather/clothing*
menswear **Cecil Gee**		**Joseph** *womenswear*
womenswear **Nicole Farhi**		**Kenzo** *womenswear*
shoes **Fratelli Rossetti**		**Alma** *womenswear*
linens **Descamps**		**Sloane Brasserie**
luggage **Louis Vuitton**		**Cashmere Studio** *women's knitwear*
		Oilily *children's clothing*
womenswear **Designer Club**		**The Coach Store** *luggage*
Midland Bank		**Christian Lacroix** *womenswear*
hair advisory center **j.f. lazartique**		**Strenesse** *womenswear*
		Browns *womenswear*
		La Cicogna *maternity and children's clothing*
		Esprit *womenswear*
shoes **Bruno Magli**		**BASIL STREET**
		ilias LaLaounis *jewelry*
National Bank of Dubai		**Cashmere Stop** *women's knitted clothing*
		Bureau de Change
department store/restaurant **Harvey Nichols**		**Pied à terre** *women's shoes*
		Fogal *hosiery*
		Red or Dead *womenswear*
		Knightsbridge Tube Station ⊖

KNIGHTSBRIDGE

them off their feet. The store resembles a Sloane-size country house, with charming knickknacks that fit into English country life with a touch of London style. Check out the china department, the antiques (upstairs), the garden department, and the children's toy department. There's also a good selection of souvenirs and gifts. The cafe downstairs serves Sloanish foods like lasagna and salad, lemon syllabub, and chocolate cake. Although you can expect long lines at lunchtime, this is an excellent place to observe Sloanedom in general. ♦ M-Sa. 144 Sloane St (at Sloane Sq). 730.0411

12 Peter Jones Department Store Sloane Square's local emporium is a much acclaimed piece of modern design that still succeeds 60 years after it was built. The main architects—**Crabtree, Slater, and Moberly**—followed the curve of King's Road, and by 1938 had created a building that possessed the grace and shapeliness of an ocean liner. Both duchesses and secretaries shop here, and this is where Sloanedom buys school uniforms. The store carries great kids' stuff: well-made, classic English children's clothes at very reasonable prices. The china and glass department has a superb selection of English patterns, and the linen department offers beautiful Egyptian cotton sheets, Scottish woolen blankets, and Irish linen tablecloths and napkins. Fascinating vases and ornaments from all over the world are displayed on the ground floor. On the first floor, you'll find ladies' leather gloves lined in cashmere and sensible country shoes for a lot less than you would pay elsewhere. For antiques and rugs, take the lift to the fourth floor. Members of the helpful sales staff are all called partners (at the end of the year they get a share of the profits). The cafe on the fifth floor serves excellent food all day; there is also a restaurant on the fourth floor. *Note:* The only credit card the store accepts is its own. ♦ M-Sa. Sloane Sq (at King's Rd). 730.3434

13 Body Shop It's easy to get hooked on these beauty products made from appetizing natural ingredients: rosemary, jojoba, cocoa butter, honey, and orange blossom. They are sold in refillable plastic bottles at reasonable prices (much cheaper than their US branches, in fact), and are not tested on animals. The shop now offers a range of perfumes that resemble big-name fragrances, but these sell at everywoman prices. Their line of products include the Endangered Species and Trade Not Aid brands whose sales benefit animal welfare and developing countries. ♦ M-Sa; Su noon-4PM. 54 King's Rd (between Cadogan Gardens and Blacklands Terr). 584.0163. Also at: Numerous locations around the city

14 Duke of York's Headquarters Behind the iron railings lie the barracks of several London regiments of the Territorial Army. The handsome Georgian brick building with its central Tuscan portico (best viewed from Cheltenham Terrace) was originally built in 1801 by **John Saunders,** a pupil of **Sir John Soane,** as a school for the orphans of soldiers. Called the **Royal Military Asylum,** the school split into separate girls' and boys' academies, moving to Southampton and Dover, respectively. It is not open to the public. ♦ King's Rd (between Sloane Sq and Cheltenham Terr)

15 Admiral Codrington ★★$$ A haunt for both yuppies and Sloanes, the "Admiral Cod," as it's affectionately known, welcomes children in the restaurant and conservatory in back but not in the pub. Even if it's raining, the Plexiglas roof allows you to sit in a bright, cheery room, surrounded by hanging plants. Interesting dishes include chargrilled eggplant topped with goat cheese on ratatouille. Regulars here are pleased that Mel Barnett, the cheery publican who adds so much to the friendly atmosphere, has returned to manage the pub; he set it up as *the* place to be in Chelsea during the 1980s. ♦ Pub/Modern British ♦ Pub: M-Sa; Su noon-10:30PM. Restaurant: M-Th lunch and dinner; F-Su lunch. 17 Mossop St (between Draycott Ave and Lever St). 581.0005

16 Osteria Le Fate ★★$$ The proprietors (including chef Paolo Zanca) of this charming, wood-paneled restaurant offer such Italian dishes as panfried scallops with lemon and herbs, and fried John Dory fish with tomato and basil. Start with the fine minestrone and finish with a baked polenta-and-custard concoction studded with sultanas and pine nuts and sweetened with honey. ♦ Italian ♦ M-Sa lunch and dinner. 5 Dracott Ave (at Bray Pl). 591.0070

17 John Sandoe Books Just off King's Road, this is one of the best literary bookshops in London, beloved by readers and writers alike. The staff has a knowledge of books that would put many an Oxford don to shame. The shop, which allows writers to buy books on credit, has a devoted clientele of literate aristocrats, and will send your books to you anywhere in the world. ♦ M-Sa. 10 Blacklands Terr (between King's Rd and Bray Pl). 589.9473

18 English Garden ★★$$$$ A lovely plant-filled conservatory at the back of a dark, heavily draped front room provides the setting for a scrumptious and sometimes innovative menu. Try offbeat English dishes such as saddle of hare and raisin salad, cured salmon with coriander salsa, lemon bread-and-butter pudding, and the lavender shortbread, made with a dash of crushed lavender flowers. If you're watching your wallet, note that lunch here is a lot cheaper than dinner. ♦ British ♦ Daily lunch and dinner. 10 Lincoln St (at Bray Pl). 584.7272

Sir Winston Churchill's youth was anything but promising: the eldest son of Lord Randolph Churchill and an American, Jennie Jerome, the young Winston usually ranked last in his class in school, and spoke with a stutter.

Restaurants/Clubs: Red **Hotels:** Blue
Shops/ ♥ Outdoors: Green **Sights/Culture:** Black

19 Pret a Manger ★$ Excellent sandwiches are available at this location (part of a ubiquitous chain) as well as flavorful salads such as the chicken with bacon. Also worth trying are the croissants and coffee. ♦ International ♦ Daily breakfast, lunch, and dinner. 80 King's Rd (between Lincoln and Anderson Sts). 225.0770. Also at: Numerous locations throughout the city

20 Hobbs Comfortable shoes with great style and a look definitely the company's own are the stock-in-trade. The additional good news is that the footwear coordinates beautifully with the linen-mix suits, dresses, and cashmere-blend coats that appeal to young career women. ♦ M-Sa; Su noon-5PM. 84 King's Rd (between Lincoln and Anderson Sts). 581.2914. Also at: Numerous locations throughout the city

21 Chelsea Kitchen ★$ Cheap and honest, this eatery is an offshoot of the **Stockpot** chain of restaurants; after three decades, it has become a King's Road institution. Everything is fresh and homemade, including the breads, scones, and pastries. The menu changes twice daily and regulars play "name that cuisine," trying to identify whether the dish they order is Italian, Spanish, French, or English. This place is also good for English and continental breakfasts. ♦ International ♦ Daily breakfast, lunch, and dinner. 98 King's Rd (between Lincoln and Anderson Sts). 589.1330

Pied à terre

22 Pied à terre Look here for high-fashion French and Italian shoes in great colors and first-rate designs. In winter, the boots are handsome, indeed. This is just one of several outlets in London. ♦ Daily. 33G King's Rd (between Cheltenham Terr and Walpole St). 259.9821. Also at: 32 Neal St (between Shelton St and Shorts Gardens). 379.4224. Tube: Covent Garden; 9 S Molton St (between Brook and Davies Sts). 629.0513. Tube: Bond Street

22 Karen Millen This British designer caters to career women on the lookout for affordable smart suits and dresses but who also seek the occasional wilder outfit that's great for partying. The shop also carries sportswear. ♦ M-Sa; Su noon-6PM. 33 King's Rd (between Cheltenham Terr and Walpole St). 730.7259. Also at: Numerous locations throughout the city

23 Royal Avenue Originally intended to be a triumphal route connecting the **Royal Hospital** with **Kensington Palace,** this ambitious avenue, conceived by **Sir Christopher Wren** for William III, never got beyond King's Road. But the four rows of majestic plane trees, with 19th-century

houses as a backdrop, make a magnificent impression. The avenue is also James Bond's London address. Bram Stoker, writer of *Dracula,* lived at **No. 18 St. Leonard's Terrace** (just around the corner) between 1896 and 1906. To the south lies **Burton's Court,** a large playing field with an 18th-century gate that was the original entrance to the **Royal Hospital.** Open-air art exhibitions are held here some Saturdays in the summer.
♦ Between St. Leonard's Terr and King's Rd

24 Royal Hospital Guidebooks perpetuate the myth that Nell Gwyn, mistress of Charles II, was so moved when a wounded soldier begged for alms that she persuaded the king to build this hospital. It's more likely, however, that Charles, impressed and inspired by reports of Louis XIV's Hôtel des Invalides, decided to emulate him. In 1682, diarist Sir John Evelyn and army paymaster General Sir Stephen Fox drew up plans for a hospital and residence for army pensioners, and Charles II commissioned **Sir Christopher Wren,** who chose the magnificent river site, to build it. This building, finished in 1686, is considered one of **Wren**'s masterpieces, second only to **St. Paul's.** The glorious elders' home still provides shelter to 400 war veterans known as the Chelsea Pensioners, and there's a waiting list to get in.

In early June each year, the Pensioners celebrate Oak Apple Day, commemorating Charles II's escape from Cromwell's troops (he hid in an oak tree after the Battle of Worcester) by placing a wreath of oak leaves around the neck of the bronze statue of the king in the **Figure Court.** The statue was cast in 1676 by Grinling Gibbons. On Oak Apple Day, the Pensioners change from their blue winter uniforms, designed in the time of the Duke of Marlborough, to their scarlet summer tunics. This colorful ceremony is not open to the public, but throughout the year you can see the Pensioners proudly walking the streets of Chelsea resplendent in their red or navy blue uniforms. Some can be spotted watching the Changing the Guard ceremony at **Buckingham Palace,** where they often pose for photos with tourists.

The hospital consists of a central block, which houses the chapel and the main mall, connected by an octagonal vestibule. The Pensioners live in the twin galleries, or wings,

which run at right angles to the river. The small museum in the **Secretary's Office Block** on the east side of the hospital, designed in 1816 by **Sir John Soane,** contains prints, uniforms, medals, and photographs associated with the hospital and its history, including two large paintings in **Wellington Hall:** the *Battle of Waterloo* by George Jones, and Haydon's *Wellington Describing the Field of Waterloo to George IV.* The Pensioners have their meals in the **Great Hall** under the *Triumph of Charles II,* a huge painting by Antonio Verrio of the king on horseback crushing serpents, with the **Royal Hospital** in the background. Around the hall are portraits of British kings and queens from Charles II to Victoria. When Wellington was laid in state here in 1852, two mourners were trampled to death by the crowds.

The chapel is pure **Wren,** with his signature black-and-white marble floor, fine carved paneling by Gibbons, and Sebastiano Ricci's *Resurrection* over the altar. The glass case beside the altar contains a prayer book, placed there in 1690, opened to a prayer of thanksgiving for the Restoration (the reestablishment of the monarchy under Charles II in 1660), without which there would be no **Royal Hospital.** Visitors are welcome to attend services on Sunday. Although one of the Pensioners can be booked to show a group around, individual visitors should invest in the compact, inexpensive guidebook (available in the chapel).

In the 18th century, the vast **Ranelagh Gardens** of the hospital had a gilt rotunda and a site for eating, drinking, music, masquerades, fireworks, and balloon flights. Canaletto painted them, Mozart played in them, the royal family enjoyed them, and all levels of London society took pleasure in them—until 1803, when they closed their doors. Now the gardens and some of the **Royal Hospital** grounds are the site of the **Chelsea Flower Show,** and for four days in May some of the exuberance and pleasure of those early times is rekindled. The gardens are open to the public. ♦ Free. Grounds, chapel, and Great Hall: M-Sa 10AM-noon, 2-4PM. Museum: Su 2-4PM. Services: Su 8:30AM, 11AM, and noon. Royal Hospital Rd (between Chelsea Bridge and West Rds). 730.0161

Royal Hospital

25 National Army Museum The **Royal Hospital** doesn't feel like a hospital, nor does it exude military history, though many of the Pensioners are war heroes. Just next door, however, is this museum, which covers British Army history from the 15th century to the present, including the Falklands War of 1982. The museum's galleries have exhibits on the Peninsular War, the Victorian soldier, and World Wars I and II (with sections devoted to the Far Eastern campaign and the history of women in the army). There are lots of models and dioramas of battles, and the skeleton of Napoléon's horse, Marengo. The museum owns Hitler's telephone switchboard, which was captured in Berlin in 1945. On the board are direct lines to infamous people like Goebbels and Himmler. There is also a permanent exhibit of the Battle of Waterloo, which includes a 400-square-foot model of the battle itself, as well as a gallery with works by Sir Joshua Reynolds, George Romney, Sir Thomas Lawrence, and Thomas Gainsborough. Another permanent display is called *The Rise of the Redcoat: the British Army from Henry V to George III*. ♦ Free. Daily. Royal Hospital Rd (between West Rd and Tite St). 730.0717

26 Tite Street The favored haunt of artists and writers in the late 19th century, this street sheltered a number of celebrated people. The brilliant and eccentric Oscar Wilde lived at **No. 34** with his wife from 1884 until 1895. The study where he wrote *Lady Windemere's Fan, An Ideal Husband,* and *The Importance of Being Earnest* was painted buttercup-yellow with red lacquer accents. The dining room, in shades of ivory and pearl, exuded tranquillity, the one quality that permanently and fatally eluded Wilde. Convicted of sodomy and other "homosexual offences," the author was imprisoned from 1895 to 1897; while he was in Reading Jail, he was declared bankrupt and the house at **No. 34** was sold. When he was released, he moved to France, where he died in 1900. A plaque was placed on Wilde's former house in 1954, on the centenary of his birth, by Sir Compton MacKenzie, before an audience of Chelsea artists and writers.

The American artist John Singer Sargent lived at **No. 31** in a studio house that is pure Chelsea. Here he painted his portraits of the rich, famous, and often beautiful, including actress Ellen Terry, who lived nearby on King's Road, and the American writer who lived around the corner on Cheyne Walk, Henry James. Sargent died here in 1925.

The bohemian portrait painter Augustus John had his studio at **No. 33,** and **No. 13** is the former home of one of America's greatest painters, James Abbott McNeill Whistler. A libel suit he brought against critic John Ruskin left Whistler with huge and unpayable legal costs, and he was declared bankrupt in 1879.

No. 13 was his first permanent address after the lawsuit, but the disgruntled artist lived at total of nine Chelsea addresses before he die in Cheyne Walk in 1903. ♦ Between Chelsea Embankment and Tedworth Sq

27 Foxtrot Oscar ★★★$$ Despite its name, which is military jargon for a two-wor expletive that starts with the same initials, th restaurant, owned by an old Etonian, is very popular because of its grilled steaks, terrific large salads (such as seafood or Caesar), English classics like kedgeree and steak-and-kidney pie, a lot of burger choices, and the creative wine list. Its decor is a combination of a posh English club and a somewhat downtrodden Manhattan bistro, with bare brick and teak paneled walls, blackboard menus, cork tables, and wood chairs. It's always full of Sloanes and London's glitterati wearing bright colors and suntans, and talkin loudly. When they get very noisy, the English nickname them "Hooray Henrys." But ignore them: This place is so reasonably priced and relaxed that it is well worth putting up with th diners at the next table. ♦ British ♦ Daily lunc and dinner. Reservations required. 79 Royal Hospital Rd (between Paradise Walk and Tite St). 352.7179

28 Japanese Peace Pagoda If you walk down the streets off Royal Hospital Road (such as Tite Street or Swan Walk) to the Chelsea Embankment, you can see this pagoda across the Thames in **Battersea Park** the latest addition to the London riverside. Th 100-foot bronze and gold leaf Buddha, starin out over the river, was inaugurated in May 1985. This temple of peace was built in 11 months by 50 monks and nuns, mainly from Japan. Much to the amazement of locals, the pagoda is tended by several Buddhist monks who actually live in a small wooded area nearby. It is the last great work of the Most Venerable Nichidatsu Fujii, the Buddhist leader who died at the age of 100, one month before his noble and majestic temple was completed. ♦ Daily 7:30AM-dusk. Terrace Walk (off Carriage Dr N). 0181/871.7530

If one must have a villa in summer to dwell, oh, give me the sweet shady side of Pall Mall.

—Charles Morris

The well-bred Englishman is about as agreeable a fellow as you can find anywhere—especially, as I have noted, if he is an Irishman or a Scotchman.

—Finley Peter Dunne

29 Gordon Ramsay ★★★★$$$$
Formerly **La Tante Claire** (which has moved to Wilton Place—see page 135), this is the new culinary wonder of Gordon Ramsay, who masterminded the success of **Aubergine.** With two Michelin stars and eager to add a third, he offers an incredibly reasonable fixed-price lunch; dinner is also fixed-price, but more expensive. Highlights, which more than compensate for the plain decor, include roast scallops on cauliflower puree with white raisin vinaigrette, salad of pig's trotters with calf's sweetbreads, divine turbot poached in red wine, and, if you can manage them, delicious desserts like terrine of citrus fruits with sorbet. ♦ French ♦ M-F lunch and dinner. Reservations essential. 68-69 Royal Hospital Rd (between Swan and Paradise Walks). 352.4441

30 Chelsea Physic Garden Swan Walk, with its row of 18th-century houses, is edged on one side with a brick wall containing handsome iron gates. Behind them is the second-oldest surviving botanical garden in England. Founded by the Worshipful Society of Apothecaries in 1673 (100 years before **Kew Gardens**), the garden occupies four acres of land belonging to Charles Cheyne (pronounced *Chain*-ee). In 1722, Sir Hans Sloane, apothecary and physician to George II and Lord of the Manor, granted a continuous lease, requiring the apothecaries to present 50 plant species a year to the Royal Society (an organization founded in 1660 to further scientific knowledge) until some 2,000 had been acquired. Sloane was a member and eventually succeeded Isaac Newton as president of the Royal Society. After the invention of the Wardian case, a container for carrying plants that prevented them from perishing, the staff here became instrumental in distributing the world's staple crops. In 1722, the first cotton seeds were exported from the South Seas to a garden in the US state of Georgia. Robert Fortune, a curator of the garden, carried tea to India from China, and Malaya got its rubber from South America. The garden opened its doors to the public in 1983 for the first time in 300 years. Now, under the watchful eye of Sir Hans Sloane himself (depicted in a statue by Michael Rysbrack), you can examine some of the 7,000 specimens of plants that still grow here. The magnificent trees include the pomegranate and the exotic cork oak. Plants and seeds are for sale. ♦ Admission. W 2-5PM, Su 2-6PM Apr-Oct. 66 Royal Hospital Rd (between Chelsea Embankment and Swan Walk). 352.5646

31 Chelsea Embankment This unbeatably beautiful strip of land along the river, part of **Sir Joseph Bazalgette**'s dual sewage/roadway system, suffers from the noise of the relentless traffic it was built to support. Still, it's worth making an effort to transcend the motorized roar to see this miraculously unchanged patch of London. The embankment begins at **Chelsea Bridge.** Built in 1934 by **G. Topham Forrest** and **E.P. Wheeler,** this graceful suspension bridge edges up to the massive and dramatic **Battersea Power Station.** The station's four chimneys are part of London's industrial archaeology. So far, the power station has been protected officially from demolition, even after the chimneys were retired. (In fact, only two ever functioned: The front pair were added purely for aesthetic reasons, to provide a sense of balance.) The power station currently stands empty after an abortive attempt to transform it into a leisure center. However, the plan is revived regularly by business investors and may yet succeed. ♦ Between Chelsea Bridge and Cheyne Walk

32 Cheyne Walk Where Royal Hospital Road and **Chelsea Embankment** converge, this elegant street begins. The embankment (somewhat) protects the single row of houses from traffic, and the lucky residents have a view of the Thames through a row of trees. Some of the happy few who have lived in these priceless Georgian brick houses include Rolling Stones guitarist Keith Richards and the benighted, sadly reclusive J. Paul Getty Jr. But residents from the more distant past haunt the high windows as well. George Eliot lived at **No. 4** for 19 days after her late-in-life wedding to John Cross; she was 61 at the time, and died only a few months later. The pre-Raphaelite painter and poet Dante Gabriel Rossetti lived at **No. 16,** then known as **Tudor House,** the finest residence on the street. He led an eccentric *vie de bohème* here while mourning the loss of his wife, Elizabeth Siddal (the model for Sir John Everett Millais's painting of the dying Ophelia and the deadly beauty in *Beata Beatrix* by Rossetti—both in the **Tate Gallery**). Rossetti's Chelsea menagerie included a kangaroo, peacocks, armadillos, a marmot, and a zebu, and he received frequent visits from fellow pre-Raphaelites William Morris and his wife, Janey, who inspired great passion in Rossetti. Today, **No. 16** is known as **Queen's House** because of the initials RC on the top of the iron gateway. Long assumed to stand for (Regina) Catherine of Braganza, Charles II's wife, the initials in fact stand for **Richard Chapman,** who built the house in 1717.

Opposite the house in the **Embankment Gardens** is the **Rossetti Fountain,** a memorial to the artist from his friends, including Millais and G.F. Watts, unveiled in 1887 by William Holman Hunt. The fountain is by J.P. Seddon, and the bust of Rossetti is by Ford Madox Brown. Unfortunately, the original bronze bust was stolen, so it was replaced by this fiberglass copy. The plaque on **No. 23** commemorates the site of Henry VIII's **Manor House,** which stood where **Nos. 19** to **26** are now. Henry VIII became fond of the Chelsea riverside during his many visits to his friend Sir Thomas More, and the year after More's death, he built a palace along the embankment. Before Henry died, he gave the house to Catherine Parr, his last wife. One hundred years later, the house was purchased by Lady Jane Cheyne—the Cheynes were lords of **Chelsea Manor** from 1660 to 1712 (in 1737, Sir Hans Sloane bought the Manor). More's house was demolished a few years later. The gateway by **Inigo Jones** was given to the Earl of Burlington, who erected it in the gardens of **Chiswick House,** where it still stands. ♦ Between Royal Hospital Rd and Old Church St

33 Cadogan Pier Every July, this pier is the finishing point of one of England's oldest contests, the Doggett's Coat and Badge Race. The race began in 1715 to celebrate the accession of George I to the throne, and was sponsored by Thomas Doggett, actor-manager of the **Drury Lane Theatre,** who awarded a coat and badge to the winner. A moving ceremony reenacting the final journey of Sir Thomas More from his home here on the river to the **Tower of London,** where he was imprisoned and executed, also takes place at the pier in July. ♦ Chelsea Embankment (just east of Albert Bridge)

34 Albert Bridge Lovers propose here and tired commuters refresh themselves looking at this bridge, the one Londoners love the most. Although it was strengthened in 1973, the bridge still has a weight limit, which means that red London buses and lorries never darken its tarmac. There is even a notice telling foot soldiers to break step when crossing. The latticework suspension bridge, built by **R.M. Ordish** in 1873, is painted in ice-cream pastels—pistachio and cream—and at night is illuminated with strings of lights. The best time to view the bridge is at dusk from **Chelsea Bridge** (downriver), when the sun sets behind it and the bridge takes on a fairy-tale quality. At night, see it from **Battersea Bridge** (upriver); the red lights of **Chelsea Bridge** glow behind it to lovely effect. ♦ Between Parkgate Rd and Chelsea Embankment

35 Carlyle's House It's a short walk up Cheyne Row to the former **No. 5,** now known as **No. 24** (pictured at right). One of the most fascinating homes in Chelsea, it is in the care of the National Trust. Set in a terrace of redbrick houses begun in 1703, this was the residence of the writer Thomas Carlyle and his wife, Jane. The rooms are almost exactly as they were 150 years ago when *The French Revolution* made its author famous, and Charles Dickens, Robert Browning, Charles Darwin, Alfred Lord Tennyson, and Frédéric Chopin were visitors. Most of the furniture, pictures, and books seen here today belonged

to the Carlyles— Thomas's hat is still on the hat-stand by the door. Go down into the kitchen and see the pump, the stone trough, and the wide grate where kettles boiled. Tennyson and Carlyle used to escape to the kitchen when they wanted to smoke without provoking Mrs. C. Examine the rooms upstairs, with their four-poster beds, piles of books, mahogany cupboards, and dark Victorian wallpaper (which covers 18th-century pine paneling). Look at the double-walled attic study, carefully (if unsuccessfully) designed to keep out the noises of the house and the street. The 19th-century painting, *A Chelsea Interior,* hangs in the ground-floor sitting room and shows how little the house has changed.

24 Cheyne Row, Chelsea

The tombstone in the small garden behind the house marks where Mrs. Carlyle's dog Nero lies buried. Carlyle was a famous Chelsea figure: the "sage of Chelsea" took solitary walks along these streets throughout his life. A bronze statue of Carlyle (by Boehm and erected in 1883) in the **Embankment Gardens** of Cheyne Walk is said to look very much like him. Here the essayist and historian sits surrounded by a pile of books and gazes sadly at the river through an invasion of Mack trucks. ♦ Admission. W-Su Apr-Oct. 24 Cheyne Row (between Cheyne Walk and Upper Cheyne Row). 352.7087

36 King's Head and Eight Bells ★★$$ It's worth coming in for a drink just to raise your glass to a pub that's 400 years old, though the decor and engravings of Chelsea in bygone days only date to the 18th century. Thanks to the Embankment, it is not right on the riverbank anymore. You'll find such traditional fare here as steak-and-ale pie and fish-and-chips. ♦ Pub ♦ Daily lunch and dinner. 50 Cheyne Walk (at Cheyne Row). 352.1820

37 Justice Walk This narrow footpath is a relic of the days when Chelsea was a real village rather than a trendy enclave of London. Note the pub sign, "The Courthouse," which remains over the advertising business at **No. 9.** Both the street and the sign here recall the memory of John Gregory, a justice of the peace who once lived here. ♦ Between Lawrence and Old Church Sts

38 Chelsea Old Church Also known as **All Saints,** this church was founded in the middle of the 12th century. In spite of the heartless traffic that passes it daily and the German bombs that flattened it in 1941, this lovely old church is spiritually intact, a glorious monument to its former parishioner, Sir Thomas More. Hans Holbein the Younger, a friend of More's, contributed to the restoration and redesign of the chapel in 1528. The atmosphere resonates with the deep sadness of the gentle, pious man whose conscience would neither allow him to recognize his friend Henry VIII as head of the Church of England nor sanction the king's divorce. More, who wrote his own epitaph (against the south wall to the right of the altar) two years before his death in 1535, paid for his conscience with his life. The remains of the saint are believed to be buried at Canterbury, but a Chelsea legend holds that More's daughter, Margaret Roper, made her way back here with her father's head and placed it in the Gothic tomb inside the church.

The ornate tomb with the urn in the chapel is the burial place of Chelsea's next best-known citizen, Sir Hans Sloane. The half-dozen chained books (before books were mass-produced, hand-inscribed manuscripts were chained to desks to avoid theft) include the 1717 edition of the *Vinegar Bible,* which contains a printer's error that converted the parable of the "vineyard" into the parable of the "vinegar." These volumes are the only such books still found in a London church. The square tower, which has since been carefully rebuilt, was the casualty of a German air raid in 1941. Off to the left side is the **Lawrence Chapel,** where Henry VIII is supposed to have secretly married Jane Seymour a few days before their official wedding in 1536, a year after Sir Thomas More had ceased to be a conscience to the king. Today, the church is still the setting for weddings, and each July a sermon written by More is read from the pulpit. A memorial stone commemorates the American writer Henry James, who lived in Chelsea and died near here in 1916. ♦ M-F. Guided tours: Su 1:30-5:30PM. Old Church St (at Cheyne Walk). 352.5627

39 Roper Gardens This garden, created in the 1960s on the site of part of Sir Thomas More's estate, is named after Margaret Roper, More's beloved eldest daughter. It replaced a garden destroyed by German bombs. Note the stone relief of a woman walking against the wind by Jacob Epstein. ♦ Cheyne Walk (at Old Church St)

40 Crosby Hall Three hundred years after Sir Thomas More was executed, this splendid mansion he once owned was transported, stone by stone, from Bishop's Gate in the City to Chelsea. Originally built in 1466, the hall was then made into a royal palace by Richard III, and finally purchased in 1516 by More himself. For a time it was the dining room of the British Federation of University Women. Now privately owned, this building is no longer open to the public, which is unfortunate since the superb hammer beam roof, the stunning oriel window, the long Jacobean table (a gift from Nancy Astor), and the Holbein painting of the More family are all worth seeing. ♦ Cheyne Walk (between Danvers and Beaufort Sts).

41 Beaufort Street One of the busiest crossroads in Chelsea that connects the King's Road to Battersea Bridge, this street cuts across the site of Sir Thomas More's country house. The residence was demolished when Sir Hans Sloane acquired the estate in the 1740s. ♦ Between Cheyne Walk and King's Rd

42 Lindsey House Remarkable for its beauty and its survival against all odds, this large country house is the only one of its era (circa 1640-74) and size in Chelsea. The vast residence was built on the site of a farmhouse by Theodore Mayerne, the Swiss physician to James I and Charles I. In the 1660s, it was sold to Robert, third Earl of Lindsey, who purchased it and substantially rebuilt it. In subsequent years, the building was divided into several connected houses with separate addresses. The remarkable cast of residents in the 1770s included painter John Martin; engineer Sir Marc Brunel, who built the first tunnel under the Thames; and Brunel's son **Isambard Kingdom Brunel,** another engineer, who built many of England's suspension and railway bridges and lived at **No. 98. (Brunel House,** 105 Cheyne Walk, is named after the father and son.) James Whistler lived at **No. 96** from 1866 to 1878 (one of his nine Chelsea addresses). It was here that he painted the famous portrait of his mother. Elizabeth Gaskell, the novelist, was also born here. The gardens connected to **Nos. 99** and **100** were designed by **Sir Edwin Lutyens.** ♦ 96-100 Cheyne Walk (between Beaufort and Milman's Sts)

42 Turner's House England's greatest painter, J.M.W. Turner, lived in this tall, narrow house during his last years. To remain anonymous, he adopted his landlady's surname—he was known locally as Admiral Booth. Turner died here in 1851, uttering his last words, "God is Light." ♦ 119 Cheyne Walk (between Beaufort and Milman's Sts)

43 Chelsea Harbour The western end of Cheyne Walk, where it becomes Lots Road, is now the site of this fashionable condominium development with some of the most expensive apartments in London. A much sought-after place to live, it has attracted British television, pop, and sports personalities with its luxurious surroundings and terrific views. Houses, offices, shops, restaurants, gardens, and the **Conrad London** hotel are all crushed into this tiny area set around a 75-berth yacht marina. Hoppa buses (the small red buses that supplement the regular bus system) from Earl's Court and Kensington High Street serve the area regularly. ♦ Lots Rd (off Cheyne Walk)

Within Chelsea Harbour:

THE CANTEEN

The Canteen ★★★$$ British superstar Michael Caine is famous for pulling in the glitterati to eat at his restaurants. After his success with **Langan's,** he teamed up with the imaginative and mercurial chef Marco Pierre White to open this 150-seat French place. The chef is now Tim Powell, who also produces innovative dishes, though in the Modern British style. The restaurant's name harks back to the Old West, where people played poker in canteens, and the decor reflects this history: Playing card symbols accent the mirrors and upholstered chairs, and the back of the menu is covered with red diamonds. Main courses might include roasted fillet of cod with fennel and *rösti* potatoes (shredded and browned) or grilled loin of pork and choucroute with a *jus* of apple and thyme. Meanwhile, Caine himself can gaze down on the grazers from his apartment in the adjacent complex. ♦ French/Modern British ♦ M-Sa lunch and dinner; Su dinner. 351.7330

43 **Conrad International London** $$$$ Overlooking the **Chelsea Harbour** marina and apartment block, this curved, modern building is a beautifully designed part of the complex. The 160 quiet, two-room suites are decorated in muted colors by well-known interior designer David Hicks and offer many deluxe amenities, such as color TV sets and VCRs, mini-bars, fax and modem hookups, 24-hour room service, complimentary daily newspaper, luxury toiletries, terry cloth robes, and slippers; some rooms also boast lovely views of the marina and river. Other features include a good alfresco restaurant overlooking the harbor, a lounge where afternoon tea is served, a bar, complimentary limousine service to **Knightsbridge,** a beauty salon with massage services, meeting rooms, and a fully equipped health spa with pool, steam room, sauna, and solarium. ♦ 823.3000, 800/HILTONS; fax 351.6525

44 **Furniture Cave** One of London's largest places to buy antique furniture, this market contains 17 dealers selling antiques from all over the world. ♦ Daily. 533 King's Rd (at Lots Rd). 352.4229

44 **Christopher Wray's Lighting Emporium** Actor-turned-shopkeeper (and later millionaire) Christopher Wray gave up the lure of the bright lights to make bright lights himself, restoring antique lamps, shades, and bulbs (and later manufacturing his own reproductions) to be snapped up by the style-conscious middle class. His once-tiny shop is now the largest center of its kind in Europe, selling restored antique and reproduction Georgian, Victorian, Art Deco, and Tiffany lamps and light fittings. For the Tiffanys, he imports handmade opalescent glass from America. The shops themselves are Victoriana personified, with old-fashioned cast-iron–and-glass awnings. ♦ M-Sa. 591-593 King's Rd (near Lots Rd). 371.0077

45 **Chelsea Bun Diner** ★$ Named after an English cake, this cafe serves good, simple food like salads, spaghetti bolognese, and fish-and-chips, all dispensed quickly at affordable prices. It offers full English breakfasts (bacon, eggs, etc.) or American-style fare (waffles or pancakes with maple syrup). Sip coffee or eat a full meal. ♦ British ♦ Daily breakfast, lunch, and dinner. 9A Lamont Rd (between King's Rd and Langston St). 352.3635

46 **Johnny Moke** Facing you at the sharp bend in the King's Road known as World's End is a men's and women's designer shoe shop that's been here since the 1960s. The chap with the glasses is Johnny, who often serves you himself. He makes divine high-fashion shoes that show up in all the right magazines and on the feet of fashion editors and models. ♦ M-Sa. 396 King's Rd (at Park Walk). 351.2232

47 **Man in the Moon** ★$ This pub marks the sharp turn where King's Road suddenly veers south. It entices crowds for more than drinks: The pub doubles as a first-rate theater club, presenting mostly modern plays. Beautiful engraved glass and real ale, as well as lunchtime fare, add to the appeal. Dishes include chicken curry and ham-and-

mushroom tagliatelle. Recent redecoration has made it nicer than ever, and the theater has been doubled in size. There's also a new basement bar featuring live music. ♦ Pub ♦ Daily lunch and dinner. 392 King's Rd (at Park Walk). 352.5075, theater 351.2876

47 Cafe Rouge ★★$$ The French food at this bistro (one branch of a popular chain) is down to a fine art with such specialties as Toulouse sausages with sautéed potatoes, and grilled calf's liver. The look is also French, with fresh flowers adorning sturdy wooden tables and art posters on the beige walls. ♦ Brasserie ♦ Daily lunch and dinner. 390 King's Rd (between Beaufort St and Park Walk). 352.2226; Also at: Numerous locations throughout the city

48 Le Shop—the Véritable Crêperie ★★$ Formerly called **Asterix,** after the French comic hero (the comic book's publishers asked the owners to change the name), this was London's first creperie and has spawned dozens of imitators. The savory crepes are made with buckwheat flour. Smoked salmon, chicken, mushroom, and corn varieties are especially appetizing, or try the mozzarella and spinach. The irresistible dessert crepes round out the meal (and, alas, the waistline). ♦ French ♦ Daily lunch and dinner. 329 King's Rd (between Beaufort and Milman's Sts). 352.3891

49 Ed's Easy Diner ★$$ Chic teenagers and devotees of 1950s Americana congregate in this chrome-plated New York–style diner that could substitute for a film set. Offered here are delicious hot dogs, burgers, shakes, beer, and other diner food—all, believe it or not, in an Anglo-American way. ♦ American ♦ M-F lunch and dinner; Sa-Su breakfast, lunch, and dinner. 362 King's Rd (between Beaufort St and Park Walk). 352.1956. Also at: 12 Moor St (at Old Compton St). 439.1955. Tube: Leicester Square, Tottenham Court Road

50 Dôme ★$$ Open all day, this authentic brasserie, part of the citywide chain, serves very good French bistro classics: salade niçoise, *croque monsieur* (grilled ham and cheese), crudités, *assiette de charcuterie* (plate of mixed meats), *mousse au chocolat,* espresso, and *citron pressé* (lemonade). In the morning, you can order coffee and a croissant or a full English breakfast. Yes, this place is crowded and lively, but there's no need to book in advance. ♦ Brasserie ♦ Daily breakfast, lunch, and dinner. 354 King's Rd (between Beaufort St and Park Walk). 352.2828. Also at: Numerous locations throughout the city

51 Rococo Chocolates Good taste and imagination are the two prime ingredients in the most eccentric chocolate shop in the world. This art gallery for chocoholics indulges both the eye and the palate with its displays of Baroque and contemporary-style

Belgian chocolates, ranging from sardine-shaped chocolates to Nipples of Venus (mounds of white chocolate topped with coffee beans), the delicacies that Salieri offers to Mozart's wife in the film *Amadeus.* ♦ M-Sa. 321 King's Rd (at Beaufort St). 352.5857

52 Bluebird Sir Terence Conran, London's self-appointed style and gourmet food guru for the last four decades, has cast his eye on this end of King's Road and recently transformed the 1920s garage building on this site to another of his "Gastrodrome" complexes. (There is one beside Tower Bridge on the south bank.) In fact, this locale is particularly significant for Conran, who in 1956 opened one of his first restaurants just a couple of hundred yards away. In any new Conran enterprise, an important consideration is that the location be in an architecturally significant building. The former garage here is a rare survivor of an unusual building type, with the upper floor having a navelike appearance enhanced by a skylight running through its entire length. The tiled frontage boasts floor-to-ceiling windows, and it has all been carefully restored. The building's new features include a fruit and vegetable market in the courtyard; delicatessen shops for gourmet food, prepared deli dishes, and bread; a cooking equipment shop; a cafe; and a restaurant/bar. Thanks to Conran's development, this tired-looking end of King's Road should benefit from a welcome injection of style as other shops spring up in order to bask in its inevitable fashionability. ♦ Daily. 350 King's Rd (between The Vale and Beaufort St). 559.1000

OSBORNE & LITTLE
FABRICS & WALLPAPERS

53 Osborne & Little The location is conveniently across the street from the **Designers Guild** (see page 110); if you like one shop you will probably like the other. The wallpaper and fabric in florals, and clever trompe l'oeil marbles and stipples, are all in excellent taste. The shop has a range of Italian 15th century–style wallpaper in subtle autumnal shades, complete with golden stars like those in Juliet's house in Verona. ♦ M-Sa. 304-308 King's Rd (between Old Church St and The Vale). 352.1456

MANOLO BLAHNIK®

54 Manolo Blahnik This museum of a shoe shop often displays one priceless shoe in the window. Many a Sloane Ranger can be seen wearing Blahnik heels. Glamorous women in London have long sported this designer's beautiful footwear. The impeccably made shoes arrive from Italy in very limited numbers (12 to 15 pairs of each design), and are worth every pound of the considerable price you will pay for them. ♦ M-Sa. 49 Old Church St (between Paultons St and King's Rd). 352.3863

55 Old Church Street A spate of early 19th-century terraced houses surround this rambling stretch of pavement to the west of Carlyle Square. **No. 127** was home to potter/novelist William de Morgan, while **No. 141A** was the last London address of writer Katherine Mansfield. A small plaque on the wall of **Bolton Lodge,** at **No. 143,** announces the address of the elusive and exclusive **Chelsea Arts Club,** founded in 1891. Inside its comfortably shabby surroundings, modern creators strive to follow in the footsteps of early members such as James Whistler, W.R. Sickert, and Wilson Steer. ♦ Between Cheyne Walk and Fulham Rd

56 Designers Guild Sofas, rugs, and fabrics that are modern, timeless, and country-house comfortable all at the same time are the specialty of Tricia Guild's boutique. She designs and produces exquisite fabrics, which look like brilliant Impressionist watercolors of English gardens. Other patterns, based on African and Italian art, will appeal to those who shun florals; and the stunning accessories, especially the pottery, baskets, and lamps, will make you want to move into a bigger home. If you're at a loss as to how to coordinate the fabrics, there's an interior design service. ♦ M-Sa; Su noon-5PM 267-271 and 275-277 King's Rd (between Bramerton and Old Church Sts). 351.5775

56 Green and Stone Here's one of the original shops on King's Road that hasn't gone trendy or upscale. These dealers in art supplies carry beautiful sketchbooks and a prismatic selection of oils and watercolors. A tempting assortment of old and new silver and leather frames, and a very good framing service, are available for those who have a masterpiece to hang. The shop also stocks materials for creating your own decorative wall finishes, as well as for gilding and frame restoration. ♦ M-Sa. 259 King's Rd (between Bramerton and Old Church Sts). 352.0837

57 Chelsea Antiques Market Of the various antiques markets on King's Road, this one comes closest to the look and feel of a flea market; it's also the most likely to yield a bargain and claims to be the oldest in London. The stall owners are a friendly lot who

specialize mainly in books. **Harrington Bros.** with an emphasis on travel books, maps, natural history, and children's books, is one of the best. ♦ M-Sa. 253 King's Rd (between Bramerton and Old Church Sts). 352.5689

57 Joanna Booth One of the nicest shops on King's Road, this establishment carries a fine collection of tapestries, Elizabethan and Jacobean furniture, and wood carvings. Boot is patient and knowledgeable, and her shop speaks of taste, simplicity, and imagination. One whole wall is lined with antiquarian book for sale. ♦ M-Sa. 247 King's Rd (between Bramerton and Old Church Sts). 352.8998

58 Designers Sale Studio Former **Browns** buyer Andrea von Tiefenbach Savaricas scouts the design warehouses for canceled orders and classic end-of-line clothing, including those by such major designers as Giorgio Armani and Moschino. ♦ Daily. 201 King's Rd (between Oakley St and Glebe Pl). 351.4171

59 Givans This shop is a reminder that King's Road was not always Trend Central. The Irish linen sheets, luxurious terry cloth bathrobes, and damask table linens are typical of the high-quality merchandise here. ♦ M-F. 207 King's Rd (at Oakley St). 352.6352

59 Henry J. Bean's Bar and Grill ★$ Fifties freaks, trendies, and the occasional punk join tourists and nuclear families in this Chelsea branch of yet another chain that combines American-style fast food and retro ambience. Here is an English pub converted into an American saloon, with 1950s and 1960s rock 'n' roll as aural background. The all-star cast includes potato skins, nachos, hamburgers, hot dogs, chili, pecan pie, cheesecake, ice cream, brownies, and ice-cold American beer. The huge garden out back makes this a sunny-day favorite on King's Road and there is a marquee (tent) in winter. ♦ American ♦ Daily lunch and dinner. 195-197 King's Rd (between Chelsea Manor and Oakley Sts). 352.9255

60 Chelsea Farmer's Market This collection of small food shops, open-air cafes, delicatessens, and restaurants, some of which stay open all night, is a popular stop for Chelsea residents, who drop in for a cappuccino before zipping into the **Chelsea Gardener** (352.5656) to replenish their window boxes and the greenery on their tiny patios. Other stores here include **Neal's Yard**

Remedies (351.6830), a homeopathic apothecary; **Non-Stop Party Shop** (351.5771), selling balloons, party supplies, and gifts; and the **Monkey Bar** wine merchants (823.3878). For lunch and snacks, you can get delicious sandwiches, hot pizzas, cold beer, or wine by the glass. Sit in the piazza and enjoy your repast in the English sun. ♦ Daily. 125 Sydney St (at King's Rd)

61 Heal's Opened in 1997, this small branch of a major furniture and home furnishings store in the West End makes for cozier browsing than its main outlet. Still a family business, the firm has been known for good design since it was founded in 1810, particularly because it was involved in the Arts and Crafts Movement of the 1920s. The gift department features stylish glassware, including vases and candle holders. ♦ M-Sa. 234 King's Rd (at Sydney St). 349.8411. Also at: 196 Tottenham Court Rd (between Alfred Mews and Torrington Pl). 636.1666. Tube: Goodge Street

62 Chelsea Town Hall On Saturday, busy shoppers trek in for the antiques fairs and jumble sales that are regularly held here. A stream of wedding parties—brides in long white gowns with their grooms and retinue—wends in and out of the **Chelsea Registry Office** throughout the day. Formal wedding photographs are usually taken on the steps outside the hall, slowing traffic to a standstill. ♦ King's Rd (between Chelsea Manor and Oakley Sts)

63 Habitat Sir Terence Conran began his career in style by founding the first **Habitat** stores for home furnishings. He is no longer involved in the company but it continues to cater to young Londoners who want affordable yet handsome furniture and accessories. There's also a large selection of gift items and knickknacks for souvenirs. ♦ M-Sa; Su noon-6PM. 208 King's Rd (between Burnsall and Chelsea Manor Sts). 351.1211. Also at: Several locations throughout the city

Within Habitat:

King's Road Cafe ★★$ This chic, spacious, and airy cafe reflects the good design for which **Habitat** is famous. The menu changes daily to offer freshly made, delicious dishes such as rigatoni served in a tomato and ricotta sauce or spinach omelettes. There are excellent cakes, cheesecakes, and fruit tarts to have with coffee or tea. A cream tea (with scones, jam, and clotted cream) is served all day. Sandwiches, bagels, and croissants are also on the menu. ♦ Cafe ♦ Daily lunch and snacks. ♦ 351.1211

64 Basia Zarzycka Custom-made clothes for fancy occasions are the specialty of this pretty shop. Bridal gowns and other formal wear are the mainstay of the business, but

there are also fabulous one-of-a-kind accessories such as hats, shoes, and antique handbags and jewelry. The clients include foreign royalty and celebrities such as the Rolling Stones, Bob Geldof, Tom Cruise, and opera singer Jane Anderson. The staff is used to dealing with rush orders by telephone and shipping items to the US. ♦ M-Sa. 135 King's Rd (between Shawfield and Flood Sts). 351.7276

64 Antiquarius This is one of the earliest and best-known antiques hypermarkets, and still one of the best. You'll get agreeably lost in the maze of over 120 stalls, but you can find wonderful Georgian, Victorian, Edwardian, and Art Nouveau jewelry, antique lace, superb antique clocks, pictures, prints, and tiles; and if you shop carefully, you can expect to pay less than in an antiques shop. One of the longtime dealers, **Trevor Allen,** has irresistible antique jewelry and a good selection of Georgian and Victorian rings and earrings to offer. When your energy's flagging, slide into a seat in the cafe. ♦ M-Sa. 131-141 King's Rd (between Shawfield and Flood Sts). 351.5353

65 Chelsea Potter ★$$ After major refurbishment, this famous King's Road pub attracts more of the lively crowd, which likes to gather behind the big window frontage or outdoors on warm days. Dishes include steak-and-kidney pie and vegetable curry. ♦ Pub ♦ M-Sa lunch and dinner; Su lunch. 119 King's Rd (at Radnor Walk). 352.9479

66 The Pheasantry A beautifully restored building with a facade that dates to 1769, it was once a dance school at which Dame Margot Fonteyn was a pupil. Until January 1997 it housed the **Toad Hall** restaurant but is now a private club. ♦ 152 King's Rd (between Markham St and Jubilee Pl)

George Bernard Shaw offered Winston Churchill tickets for the first night of *St. Joan* for himself and a friend "if you have one." Churchill replied that he was sorry he would not be able to attend and asked for tickets for the second night, "if there is one."

When a proud mother said her baby looked like Churchill, he replied: "Madam, all babies look like me."

Bessie Braddock, MP (to Winston Churchill): *Sir, you are drunk.*

Churchill: *And you, madam, are ugly, but I shall be sober in the morning.*

Kensington/ Knightsbridge

Cromwell and **Brompton Roads**
gently embrace in front of the
flamboyant Baroque **Brompton
Oratory**, the first important Roman
Catholic church built in London
after the Reformation, uniting at
an almost imperceptible angle: two
roads, two villages (Kensington and
Knightsbridge), and two worlds.
Victorian, high-minded **South
Kensington**, with its nexus of
museums, is evidence of the high
regard that one man—Prince Albert—
had for the educational and moral
value of art; while luxurious and
high-spirited Knightsbridge is the
province of the chic, sophisticated,
and fashionable. It seems an
improbable union, but the two
adjoining neighborhoods bring
out the best in each other, and
a day spent in the company of
both is unimaginably satisfying.

Together, these areas encompass
everything from exhibits of dinosaurs
and their living descendants to a
quarter of a million butterflies, a
launch pad and the *Apollo 10* space
capsule, an enormous bed for weary
travelers that was mentioned in
Twelfth Night, 15 acres of fabulous
furniture and other highly desirable
goods (which you can buy if you like),
and 10 acres of the greatest collection
of antique furniture and decorative
art in the world (which you can't).

Begin at the **Natural History
Museum**, a grandly Victorian
building that looks more like an
ecclesiastical railway station than
a museum housing more than 50
million items from the natural world.
As you continue along **Exhibition
Road**, you'll see several monuments
to the purposeful Prince Albert,
including the **Science Museum**,
the **Victoria and Albert Museum**,
and the **Royal Albert Hall**, presided
over by the **Albert Memorial**. Then
again, there are those two shrines to

consumerism that sum up the area: **Harrods**, whose motto is "Omnia, Omnibus, Ubique (All Things, For All People, Everywhere)"; and **Harvey Nichols**, the fashion designer department store.

If a morning of museum-going has filled your mind with things cultural but left you craving the outdoors, you can enjoy the refreshing greenery of **Hyde Park** and **Kensington Gardens**. In the morning you might also see the queen's horse-drawn carriages travel down **Serpentine Road**; in May or June, you can watch soldiers practicing with their horses on **Rotten Row** for the Trooping the Colour ceremony. The **Hyde Park Hotel** is a worthy shrine for any Anglophile pilgrim who thinks tea in the late afternoon is a necessity for those who consider themselves civilized. Nearby is one of London's best wine bars, **Le Metro**, and a unique pub, the **Grenadier**, which was once the **Officer's Mess** for the Duke of Wellington's soldiers. If you're more gourmet and art lover than shopper, a perfect lazy Sunday in London might begin with lunch at a fashionable restaurant (try the excellent **Bibendum**), followed by visits to the museums (a particularly good rainy day itinerary).

City code 0171 unless otherwise noted.

1 Natural History Museum If you take a taxi into London from **Heathrow,** this twin-towered, terra-cotta–and–slate-blue museum is the first real feast that greets the eye. Designed between 1873 and 1880 by **Alfred Waterhouse,** the Romanesque building looks superb in

THE NATURAL HISTORY MUSEUM

sunlight and breathtaking when lit up against a night sky. Animal figures grace the outside, while painted panels of wildflowers decorate the high, curved ceiling inside. As you enter the navelike central hall, you expect to see a high altar (or a diesel engine). But in this holy terminus dedicated to the wonders of Life and Earth, rising high above the ordinary human figures below, is the 85-foot-long skeleton of *Diplodocus carnegii,* the 150-million-year-old dinosaur believed to be the largest plant-eating land animal to have ever existed.

Formerly part of the **British Museum,** this institution houses the national collections of zoological, entomological, paleontological, mineralogical, and botanical specimens—a long-winded way to describe a fun place that makes you appreciate the wonders of nature. It is divided into the **Life** and **Earth Galleries.** The museum has an often crowded self-service cafeteria that offers lunches, snacks, and afternoon tea. A free guide gives an overview of the museum's collections and exhibitions. ♦ Admission. Free M-F from 4:30PM; Sa-Su from 5PM. Daily. Cromwell Rd (between Exhibition Rd and Queen's Gate). 938.9123; www.nhm.ac.uk. Tube: South Kensington

Within the Natural History Museum:

Life Galleries In addition to the *Diplodocus* the ground floor houses life-size robotic models of other dinosaurs plus displays about marine invertebrates and "creepy crawlies"—spiders and insects. In the whale hall you can see the skeleton of a blue whale, while the bird gallery displays extinct dodos and flightless emus. If you'd like to know how a plant converts the sun's energy into food, step into the "Leaf Factory" and find out. The first floor presents displays on the origin of the human species, including specimens from Darwin's historic voyage on the *HMS Beagle.* The mammals exhibition shouldn't be missed. See the rare white rhinoceros and especially the giant panda Chi-Chi, who, having confounded early attempts at glasnost by refusing to mate with the Moscow Zoo's An-An in the 1960s, died of old age at the **London Zoo** in 1972. She's now shown permanently munching bamboo.

Earth Galleries A £12-million redevelopment program for these galleries is in progress (the first opened in 1996) to make the study of Earth even more fascinating. An escalator takes visitors through the center of a revolving globe, giving them the sensation of traveling from Earth's molten core to mountain peaks. And the new "Power Within" exhibition includes an earthquake experience—an audiovisual look at the earth's crust falling apart—plus a re-creation of an emergency evacuation when a volcano is about to erupt. The "Restless Surface" exhibition treats the causes and effects of tidal waves, tornadoes, hurricanes, landslides, and avalanches. Hands-on exhibits allow visitors to experiment with gravity (can you avoid triggering a landslide as you come to grips with erosion?).

Natural History Museum Shops These are terrific! The postcards in the first shop are the best bargain in town, with gentle gorillas, gory bugs, lavish butterflies, and fleas in costume. The shop next door carries dime-store items (plastic dinosaurs and the like), while the gift shop has more deluxe merchandise, including fossils, jewelry, minerals, replicas of skulls, and crystal goblets etched with images of endangered species. A new **Earth Galleries Shop** offers an interesting range of jewelry, minerals, and appropriately themed gifts. However, the best shop by far is the bookstore, which has an excellent collection of gardening books, beautifully illustrated guides to wildflowers, and, more specifically, Hugh Johnson's *Encyclopaedia of Trees,* the *Catalogue of the Rothschild Collection of Fleas* in five weighty volumes, and a replica of Darwin's journal of the *HMS Beagle.* ♦ Daily. 938.9123

2 Science Museum

Although the museum itself was founded in 1857, the present building, designed by **Sir Richard Allison,** dates only from 1913. This inspired tribute to science couldn't be more appropriately located than in the nation that gave the world Newton, Darwin, Davy, Huxley, Thomson, Rutherford, and Fleming. A visit here leaves you with the inevitable realization of just how many fundamental scientific discoveries have been British. The museum is especially enjoyable for the young, who can push, pull, and operate the countless knobs, buttons, and gadgets on display. Just like scientific theories, exhibitions change regularly, so check at the information desk to see what's currently being displayed and for the events of the day. The ticket you purchase is actually a leaflet with a map, to give you an overview.

The basement area, divided into three spaces, is heaven for curious toddlers, filled with such items as a burglar alarm to test and a periscope for spying on the floor above. The space called "The Garden" has a giant kaleidoscope at the end of a "noisy, feely tunnel"; "The Secret Life of the Home" is loaded with ingenious gizmos and gadgets; and "Things" shows how everyday objects work. There are also "explainers"—museum staff in green shirts—to help the kids enjoy the exhibits.

The emphasis on the ground floor is on power, transport, and exploration, with the **Foucault Pendulum** demonstrating the rotation of the earth on its own axis. Also on display are *Puffing Billy,* which, dating from 1813, is the oldest locomotive in the world; the Boulton and Watt pumping engine,

designed in 1777; a full-scale model of a moon lander; and, most popular of all, the actual *Apollo 10* capsule.

The "Launch Pad" section dominates the first floor. This hands-on gallery is where kids from 6 to 60 can test the scientific principles behind the modern technology used every day. Get a special ticket at the gallery entrance before you start your visit; it's very popular. You will also find everything you ever wanted to know about mapmaking, time measurement, iron, steelmaking and glassmaking, agriculture, meteorology, and telecommunications. You'll swallow nervously as you enter "Food for Thought" in the **Sainsbury Gallery,** which reveals how science tinkers with food.

The second floor deals with the more instructive subjects of chemistry, physics, nuclear power, and computers. Be sure to see the larger-than-life models of cells and how they work and the living molecules showing the work of seven Nobel Prize winners.

The art of aeronautics, from the hot-air balloon to jets, is explored in the flight gallery on the third floor. Of special interest is the *De Havilland Gipsy Moth,* used by Amy Johnson on her flight to Australia in 1930; a replica of the craft built by Orville and Wilbur Wright in 1903; and World War II aircraft. The aeronautics section shares the floor with areas devoted to a history of photography and cinematography from 1835 and health and medicine in the 20th century.

The fourth and fifth floors deal with medical and veterinary history, incorporating items collected between 1896 and 1936 by Sir Henry Wellcome, and now called the **Wellcome Museum of the History of Medicine.** It shows objects from important (if now primitive-looking) developments in medical history: trepanning (cutting out a circular core of the skull) in neolithic times and open-heart surgery in the 1980s. Clever, often spine-chilling displays cover tribal, Oriental, classical Greek, Roman, medieval, and Renaissance medicine. The vast collection of curiosities includes Florence Nightingale's moccasins, Dr. Livingstone's medicine chest, and Napoléon's beautiful silver toothbrush. Don't miss the **King George III Collection,** otherwise known as "Science in the 18th Century," which shows just how many advances in knowledge were made during the sovereign's reign.

The museum shop has nifty toys—gyroscopes, kites, Escher puzzles, etc.—for the gadget-minded. The *Guide to the Science Museum* (small charge) is excellent if you're in a hurry and want to find your way around easily. **Dillons the Bookstore** has a branch here with educational books for children and souvenir gallery guides on specific themes.

There is a new **Museum Cafe** in high-tech decor on the ground floor, and the museum also offers the **Megabite Picnic Area** if you want to bring your own refreshments. In the kids' basement is the **Eat Drink Shop** for snacks, cold drinks, and ice cream as well as souvenirs. ♦ Admission; free from 4:30PM. Daily. Exhibition Rd (between Cromwell and Imperial College Rds). 938.8008. Tube: South Kensington

3 Ognisko Polskie ★★$$ This popular Polish hangout, whose name translates to "Polish Hearth," is the supposedly secret haunt of many South Kensington bohemians and intellectuals. The high-ceilinged room housing the bar and restaurant is set off with chandeliers, patterned rugs, gilt chairs, and portraits on the paneled walls. The food is of the *zrazy* (beef rolls stuffed with bacon, mushrooms, and onions), *kasza* (boiled buckwheat), and pierogi variety, and the atmosphere is unbeatable. The fixed-price lunch and dinner often includes stuffed goose and *bigos* (chopped beef or pork, cabbage, sauerkraut, and onions simmered in a spicy sauce). Wash it down with one of the lethal Polish vodkas. ♦ Polish ♦ Daily lunch and dinner. 55 Princes Gate, Exhibition Rd (at Watts Way). 589.4635. Tube: South Kensington

4 Royal College of Music Inside this elaborate building, designed by **Sir Arthur Blomfield** in 1894, is a remarkable collection of more than 500 musical instruments, ranging from the earliest known stringed keyboard instruments to some wonderfully bizarre creations of the 19th and 20th centuries. Here, Handel's spinet rests amiably with Haydn's clavichord. There's also a collection of portraits (seen by appointment only) in various media, including more than 100 paintings and several thousand engravings and photographs. ♦ Admission. Music collection: 2-4:30PM Sept-July. Portrait collection: M-F by appointment only. Prince Consort Rd (between Exhibition and Callendar Rds). Museum: 591.4346; Department of Portraits: 591.4340. Tube: South Kensington

5 Royal Albert Hall This stupendous piece of Victoriana is a memorial to Prince Albert, ordained and encouraged by Queen Victoria. Oddly enough, it was designed not by architects but by two engineers: Captain Francis Fowke and Major-General H.Y. Darracott Scott, who used Roman amphitheaters as their inspiration. The redbrick elliptical hall with its 135-foot glass-and-iron dome can hold about 7,000 people, and its acoustics are superb. Apparently the prince approved of the design (although he had wanted this site for another **National Gallery**), and it is a fitting climax to the cultural complex honoring the education of the mind and spirit in which he so strongly believed.

Still operating under a Royal Charter, the hall is the venue for sporting events, beauty contests, pop concerts, military exercises, and most famous of all, the annual Henry Wood Promenade Concerts, performed daily between mid-July and mid-September. Known as the "Proms," these performances of classical and popular pieces have an informal atmosphere and are packed with true music-lovers. Most of the seats are sold well in advance, but there are always inexpensive standing-room tickets available on the day of the performance (sold from 6:30PM). The last night of the Proms is famously emotional, and tickets are so much in demand that they are sold by lottery. Wildly popular is a wide-screen showing of the last night to delighted spectators in adjacent **Hyde Park.** ♦ Kensington Gore (between Exhibition Rd and Jay Mews). 589.3203, box office 589.8212, 24-hour event information 0891/500252. Tube: South Kensington

6 Royal College of Organists This eccentric, four-story building was designed in 1874-76 by **H.H. Cole**, a lieutenant in the Royal Engineers whose architectural experience had been limited to scholarly publications on the buildings of ancient India (more to the point, his father was Sir Henry Cole, mastermind of the high-minded Victorian development of South Kensington). The building delights passersby with its euphoria of decoration and colors and its frieze of musicians. What's missing from this picture? Well, there is no organist—nor is there an organ. In fact, the College left the building in 1991 for premises at the guild church of St. Andrews, Holborn, and it is now a private residence. ♦ Kensington Gore (at Jay Mews). Tube: South Kensington

7 Albert Hall Mansions The warm, brick mansions, built between 1879 and 1886 by **Norman Shaw,** were among the earliest blocks of flats in London. If they weren't so utterly English—the style is Queen Anne Revival with oriels, gables, dormers, and arches—they would seem almost European in their scale and grandeur. The flats are extremely desirable because of their superb location and palatial rooms. They are occupied by an appreciative elite: The late English designer Jean Muir decorated her flat entirely in white. ♦ Kensington Gore (between Exhibition Rd and Jay Mews). Tube: South Kensington

8 Royal Geographical Society Gables and chimneys are features of the former **Lowther Lodge,** which became the home of the **Royal Geographical Society** in 1913. The building was designed by **Norman Shaw** between 1873 and 1875, and the statues outside are of two notable explorers: Sir Ernest Shackleton, who commanded three expeditions to the Antarctic

and discovered the location of the south magnetic pole in 1909; and David Livingstone, who discovered the Zambezi River, Victoria Falls, and was attempting to find the source of the Nile when he was famously rescued by the journalist H.M. Stanley. Inside is the outstanding **Map Room** with a collection of more than 900,000 maps, an extensive library, a photographic collection, and the **Expedition Advisory Centre,** which offers information, training, and advice to expeditions conducting geographical research overseas. Only the **Map Room** is open to the public (professional researchers preferred). The society's official name now includes "with The Institute of British Geographers" to show its recent link-up with that organization.
♦ M-F. 1 Kensington Gore (at Exhibition Rd). 591.3000. Tube: South Kensington

9 Kensington Gardens and Hyde Park Of all the features that make London the most livable city in the world—the innate courtesy of the English, the civilized lay of the land with its squares and humane, domestic architecture, the thick layers of sympathetic history—it is the parks, the vast oases of green, that give the city an almost unique supply of urban oxygen and humanity. It is inconceivable to know London without spending time in its parks, and for many residents and visitors, the vast, natural wonderland of **Hyde Park** and **Kensington Gardens** is not only a favorite part of the city but a compulsory stopover.

Even a half hour here is like a day in the country—a carpet of grass, the shelter of trees, a soundtrack of birdsong. Then there is the cast of exuberant dogs and their placid owners, joggers, pinstriped executives, nannies with baby carriages the size of economy cars, children briefly angelic in their school uniforms, and lovers who stroll in their own pool of private peace. The English, unlike the French and the Italians, don't look very impressive walking along city streets. But in their parks they become distinguished, their features enhanced by the blue of the sky, the green of the grass. They thrive in natural settings, even those surrounded on every side by busy roads and the relentless noise and movement of city life. **Kensington Gardens** is the Eliza Doolittle of London parks: elegant, charming, and romantic, merging seamlessly into the larger green of **Hyde Park.** The difference between the two parks and just where they do merge is a mystery to many. But true lovers of London earth and sky can define perfectly the area of the gardens, beginning at **Kensington Palace** and extending to **Alexandra Gate** on the south and **Victoria Gate** on the north, with the connecting The Ring as the boundary.

The gardens, which were in large part laid out by Queen Anne, were originally the private property of **Kensington Palace,** and they still have a regal air, enhanced by the presence of the royal home. They were opened by George III to the public in the 19th century—"for respectably dressed people" on Saturday only—and Queen Victoria opened them fully in 1841, after which they became a fashionable venue for promenades. Many English writers, among them Thackeray and Matthew Arnold, have praised their "sublime sylvan solitude," as Disraeli put it. The **Round Pond,** constructed in the 18th century, was originally octagonal, and the **Broad Walk** was once lined with magnificent elm trees. Today, there are occasional skateboarders and rollerskaters, while the **Round Pond** plays host to young skippers.

Neighboring **Hyde Park**'s 390 acres are, by contrast, an informal swath of green. Once yet another hunting ground for Henry VIII, it was given to the public by James I. Rotten Row, which runs along the south side, is thought to be a corruption of "Route du Roi" (French for "Road of the King"). ♦ Bounded by Park La and Palace Ave, and Knightsbridge, Kensington Rd, and Bayswater Rd. Tube: South Kensington, Marble Arch, Hyde Park Corner, Knightsbridge, Lancaster Gate, High Street Kensington, Queensway

Within Kensington Gardens and Hyde Park:

Albert Memorial Slightly west of where the **Crystal Palace** (which housed the Great Exhibition of 1851) once stood is the **Albert Memorial,** which for the last four years has been undergoing an £11-million restoration— £50,000 alone was spent on a double layer of 23-karat gold leaf.

Albert Memorial

MICHAEL STORRINGS

The monument portrays Prince Albert holding the catalog of the Great Exhibition of 1851 and gazing down on the museums, colleges, and institutions that his vision, energy, and endeavor inspired (profits from the Great Exhibition funded most of the museums in this area). The memorial earned its creator, **George Gilbert Scott,** a knighthood. Albert's throne, crowned by a spire of gilt and enameled metal that ends in a cross rising 180 feet, is an imposing piece of Victorian art made lovable by its sheer excess. The monument was commissioned by the prince's mournful widow, Queen Victoria, and unveiled by her in 1876. Below the bronze statue of the prince consort are marble statues of animals representing the four continents, while allegorical figures representing Agriculture, Commerce, Manufacture, and Engineering stand at the four angles. Nearest the top of the 175-foot-high monument rest figures of Faith, Hope, Charity, and Humility. On the pedestal is a magnificent procession of reliefs of the greatest artists, writers, and philosophers of the Victorian era.

Strangely, for many years the monument was denounced as an example of the worst of Victorian sentimentality and ugly excess. But a new appreciation of Victorian architecture has brought the memorial into deserved veneration, along with the prince it honors.

Serpentine Gallery Once the **Kensington Gardens Tea House,** the beautiful building is now the ideal art gallery, ambitiously providing a setting for monthly exhibitions of contemporary art. Gallery talks are given Sundays at 3PM. ♦ Free. Daily. 402.6075

 Serpentine This 41-acre artificial lake was formed in 1730 by damming the Westbourne, a stream that no longer exists. The resulting riverlike lake (the name comes from its winding shape) is home to a vast range of waterfowl. In 1816, Harriet Westbrook, the first wife of the poet Shelley, committed suicide by drowning herself in this lake. The swimming hole, the **Lido,** has been closed due to pollution (although members of the Polar Bear Club take a dip in the water here every New Year's Day). There is a small paddling pool for kids in summer. Nearby is the **Boathouse,** where rowboats may be hired by the hour for a perfect afternoon, as depicted by Renoir. Along the **Long Water,** that part of the lake that is located within **Kensington Gardens,** stands Sir George Frampton's *Peter Pan,* the most enchanting figure in the park. The statue, erected overnight in 1912, has been rubbed nearly smooth by adoring little hands. Just beyond him are the **Tivoli Gardens,** four ornate shimmering fountains bedecked with flowers that are more characteristic of Italy or France than of London.

THE KENSINGTON PARK
A THISTLE HOTEL

10 Kensington Park Thistle Hotel $$$ It's large but elegant, spacious yet quiet, and what's more, the location, tucked away just off the southwest corner of **Kensington Gardens,** puts the museums of Cromwell and Exhibition Roads within walking distance. There are 323 bedrooms and 10 suites, all of which are stylishly furnished, and you can choose from light meals at the glass-topped **Moniques Brasserie** or more formal, traditionally British food in the paneled **Cairngorm Grill.** Oddly enough, summer is not the high season for this hotel; it tends to fill up more from September to Christmas. ♦ 16-32 De Vere Gardens (at Kensington Rd). 937.8080, 800/847.4358; fax 937.7616. Tube: High Street Kensington, Gloucester Road

11 Kensington Palace If this building (pictured on page 119) looks more like a grand English country house than a palace, it's because that is exactly what it once was. Known in royal circles as "KP," it is very much a living palace. The late Princess of Wales occupied the largest apartment, with three floors on the north side. Current residents include Prince and Princess Michael of Kent; the Duke and Duchess of Gloucester and their three children, with 35 rooms at their disposal; and Princess Margaret, who has a mere 20 rooms but the best views. The Prince of Wales used to live here, but now he resides at **St. James's Palace** during the week and Highgrove on weekends. The queen decides who lives in the palace, and the residents don't pay rent, though they are responsible for alterations and decorating and pay their own electricity, telephone, and heating bills.

The palace's historical claims are quite considerable, dating back to 1689, when William III commissioned **Sir Christopher Wren** to build a palace out of the existing **Nottingham House,** away from the damp conditions of **Whitehall Palace,** which aggravated his asthma. Past residents include six monarchs: William and Mary, Anne, George I, George II, and William IV. This nonpalatial palace, formerly known as **Kensington House,** was Queen Victoria's birthplace, and it was here that she was awakened with the news that she was queen. In 1899, on Queen Victoria's 80th birthday, the **State Rooms** were opened to the public; in 1975, more rooms followed.

Tours start in the more intimate rooms, finishing with the grand ones. The **Queen's Staircase** leads to the **Queen's Apartments,** which look much as they did when **Wren** decorated them for William and Mary. Next door to the **Queen's Gallery,** with fine

---

Restaurants/Clubs: Red   **Hotels:** Blue
Shops/ ♦ Outdoors: Green   **Sights/Culture:** Black

carvings by Grinling Gibbons, is the **Queen's Closet,** which is anything but a closet. It was here that Queen Anne and her lady-in-waiting, the Duchess of Marlborough, had the angry quarrel that ended their longstanding friendship.

After you pass the **Queen's Bedchamber** with its tempting four-poster bed, the rooms become grander. The **Privy Chamber** has Mortlake tapestries by William Kent on the ceiling and overlooks the state apartments of Princess Margaret; beyond are the **Presence Chamber** and the **King's Staircase.** One of the most stunning rooms—looking even more splendid after its refurbishment—is **King William's Gallery,** designed by **Wren,** with wood carvings by Gibbons and an Etruscan ceiling painted by Kent. This room leads into the Duchess of Kent's drawing room and its anteroom, which contains Queen Victoria's Georgian dollhouse and her toys. But perhaps the favorite room is **Queen Victoria's Bedroom,** where the young princess received the news of her accession. It is now filled with mementos of the long-reigning queen, including the curtained cradle where her babies, and those of Queens Alexandra and Mary, slept. A collection of dresses worn at court is displayed in the costume gallery.

The trim palace garden and the **Orangery,** where morning coffee, lunch, and tea are served, reflect the taste of Queen Anne, who relied on both **Nicholas Hawksmoor** and **Sir John Vanbrugh** to help her change the previous formal Dutch-style layout to a more natural appearance. The queen spent much of her time here, and eventually died here from an attack of apoplexy due to overeating. ♦ Admission. Daily. Palace Ave (off Kensington Rd). 937.9561; evening activities and private tours: 376.2452. Tube: High Street Kensington

12 Thistle Hyde Park $$$ Squirrels wanting to be fed nuts will run up to you as you stroll along the North Flower Walk toward Lancaster Gate. Here, just across Bayswater Road, is one of London's most exclusive yet virtually unknown hotels (formerly **Whites Hotel**); with 54 rooms and suites, it is a shade less expensive than the **Savoy** and the **Four Seasons London,** two hotels with which it has been favorably compared. The building looks like the London home of an earl, and the interior wouldn't disappoint him, either, as it's decorated with crystal chandeliers, white marble, and the shades of old English roses. The Jeeves-like service is impeccable, and the **Grill** restaurant is rather delightful, too. ♦ 90-92 Lancaster Gate (between Bayswater Rd and Leinster Terr). 262.2711; fax 262.2147. Tube: Lancaster Gate, Queensway

13 Park Court Hotel $$ Part of the International Mount Charlotte Hotels Group, this property boasts 390 rooms, many of which have views of adjacent **Kensington Gardens.** The hotel has its own well-landscaped grounds as well, where, in fine weather, you can sit and enjoy a drink, and eat alfresco at one of the popular summer barbecues. The rooms are kitted out with such niceties as tea- and coffee-making machines and in-house movies. The staff is friendly as well. ♦ Lancaster Gate (at Leinster Terr). 402.4272, 800/847.4358; fax 706.4156. Tube: Lancaster Gate, Queensway

Kensington Palace

14 London Toy and Model Museum Calling all the young at heart: Here's a museum that features toys from (and for) all ages, from turn-of-the-century mechanical banks to a 2,000-year-old Roman gladiator doll. It has 20 themed galleries with plenty of knobs to push and mechanical toys to set in motion. In one gallery, visitors can walk onto the deck of a simulated boat and operate a steering wheel; another has a model of a working coal mine. In addition, the garden features a vintage 1920s carousel and a miniature railway. There are changing exhibitions. ♦ Admission. Daily. 21 Craven Hill (at Craven Hill Gardens). 706.8000. Tube: Bayswater, Queensway, Lancaster Gate

15 Texas Lone Star West ★★$ It's loud and raucous, but the ribs are cooked right and the accompanying cocktails are authentic and cheap (for London, anyway). If you get a hankering for enchiladas and chimichangas along with live country and western music, this is your place. ♦ Tex-Mex ♦ Daily lunch and dinner. 117-119 Queensway (between Bayswater and Moscow Rds). 727.2980. Tube: Queensway, Bayswater. Also at: 154 Gloucester Rd (at Harrington Gardens). 221.9235. Tube: Gloucester Road

16 Portobello Road Market A milelong stretch of this street erupts with about 1,500 dealers on Saturday, creating one of the largest open-air markets in London. It bills itself as the world's largest antiques market, and it's easy to see why. From 6AM until late afternoon, thousands of tourists and bargain and antiques hunters congregate in search of unique souvenirs or a silver teapot. Although it's packed with ethnic panache, there's loads of junk and kitsch, but then, the fun is in the search. With some dedicated rummaging, it is possible to find desirable items at reasonable prices, particularly in the surrounding shops and arcades. An information booth, open 9AM-2PM, offers guides to the specialist dealers. If you can't get there on Saturday, go during the week; many shops are open, and there are plenty of places to eat and drink and just watch the scene. Portobello Road is the main shopping street but there are dealers in adjoining streets, too. You'll find shops for other goods, such as the excellent **Portobello China and Woolens** at **No. 89** (727.3857), a factory outlet for quality Scottish cashmere and knitwear; it also carries the big names in china. ♦ Market: Sa. Shops: M-Sa. Between Chepstow Villas and Golborne Rd. 229.8354 Tube: Notting Hill Gate, Ladbroke Grove

17 Geales ★★$$ This fish-and-chips spot has been here for almost 60 years, and its cottage dining room and rustic furniture remain loved by all who come here. The fish is fresh from Billingsgate and Grimsby, and the batter that coats it is made with beer. Try the crab soup before tucking into a large cod and chips, and then finish with the apple crumble for dessert. Beer, wine, and Champagne are available, but oddly, you must pay your waitress immediately for alcoholic drinks, which is a bit inconvenient. Some say service can be rather slow. ♦ Fish-and-chips ♦ Tu-Sa lunch and dinner. 2 Farmer St (between Hillgate Pl and Notting Hill Gate). 727.7969. Tube: Notting Hill Gate

18 Kensington Place ★★★$$$ At the top of a street brimming with antiques and history, the residents favor the minimalist bare-wood–and-glass look in this London brasserie, which keeps retaining its "most fashionable" reputation despite a lot of competition from newcomers. Start with the delicious griddled scallops with pea puree and mint vinaigrette, followed by steak and chips or confit of duck. For dessert there's zabaglione, or *Mont Blanc* (chestnut puree) with chocolate sauce. ♦ Modern British ♦ Daily lunch and dinner. 201 Kensington Church St (at Kensington Pl). 727.3184. Tube: Notting Hill Gate

19 Boyd's Restaurant ★★★$$$ Boyd Gilmour, a self-taught chef and former professional percussionist, runs a greenhouse-style restaurant where locals dine on a regular basis, sampling starters like chargrilled goat cheese on a garlic crouton or the Indian-spiced carrot and parsnip soup, followed by main courses such as roast breast of pheasant with wild mushroom stuffing or chargrilled chicken with tarragon on vegetables. The fish of the day—often monkfish, salmon, or brill—is always a good choice. Save room for the divine iced chocolate and hazelnut soufflé. The set lunch is an excellent value, the wine list first-rate, and the surroundings serene and sophisticated. ♦ Modern British ♦ M-Sa lunch and dinner. Reservations required. 135 Kensington Church St (at Peel St). 727.5452. Tube: Notting Hill Gate

> "The passion for crowds is nowhere feasted so full as in London. The man must have a rare recipe for melancholy who can be dull in Fleet Street."
> Charles Lamb, 1802

> "The English winter—ending in July to recommence in August."
> Lord Byron

20 Clarke's ★★★$$$ The restaurant categorizes itself as European, but the food (and wine list) has decidedly Californian overtones. Whatever you call it, it seems that owner/chef Sally Clarke can do no wrong, thanks to such touches as her wonderful breads, which appear promptly at your table; everything is freshly baked (she has a bakery shop next door). Her formula is simple: a different four-course dinner menu is offered daily with no choices, so call in advance to check it out. You might start with chilled beetroot-and-vine-tomato soup followed by chargrilled lamb with tarragon and baked Sicilian-style ricotta tart to finish. Chocolate truffles, accompanying the coffee, add a final flourish. The fixed-price three-course lunch menu offers some choices. ♦ European ♦ M-F lunch and dinner. Reservations required. 124 Kensington Church St (between Berkeley Gardens and Kensington Mall). 221.9225. Tube: Notting Hill Gate

21 Hype DF Young, fashionable shoppers come to this sleek, up-to-the-minute fashion store, a "junior Harvey Nichols," looking for something different in the way of clothes, jewelry, accessories, and cosmetics. They find it here among the creations by up-and-coming designers in a cavernous space with loud music blaring. There's also a restaurant. ♦ Daily. 48-52 Kensington High St (between Old Court Pl and Kensington Church St). 937.3801. Tube: High Street Kensington

22 Linley Sambourne House This Victorian house and its contents—even the letters in desk drawers—have been left intact since the owner, Sir Linley Sambourne, a cartoonist for the satiric magazine *Punch,* lived there from 1874 to 1910. A visit here is a perfect, personal way to step into the Victorian era. ♦ Admission. W, Su March-Oct. 18 Stafford Terr (between Argyll Rd and Phillimore Gardens). 937.0663. Tube: High Street Kensington

THE COMMONWEALTH EXPERIENCE

22 Commonwealth Experience The newly opened galleries at the **Commonwealth Institute** have displays about 53 countries, from Antigua to Zimbabwe, that were once part of the British empire. One interesting exhibit is the "heliride," which uses simulator technology to give visitors a helicopter ride over Malaysia. There are also interactive computer facilities and changing art exhibitions, plus a cafe and a picnic area. ♦ Admission. Daily. Kensington High St (between Holland Walk and Melbury Rd). 371.3530. Tube: High Street Kensington

22 Leighton House A flamboyant home and studio built in 1866 by **George Aitchison** for the pre-Raphaelite artist Lord Leighton (1830-96), it is a wonderful extravaganza of high Victorian art. All the intricately decorated rooms reflect Leighton's opulent vision of living in a private palace devoted to art. Displays include his own paintings as well as those of William Burne-Jones and John Everett Millais. The centerpiece is the **Arab Hall,** designed to display his Islamic tiles and Walter Crane's gilt mosaic frieze. ♦ Free. M-Sa. 12 Holland Park Rd (between Melbury and Addison Rds). 602.3316. Tube: High Street Kensington

23 Victoria and Albert Museum If you have a curious mind and a receptive heart, and if you like *stuff,* this fascinating institution will become one of your favorite places on earth. It is one of the most addictive and rewarding museums in the world, covering 12 acres with items of enchantment and delight. The museum is the prodigious offspring of the **Great Exhibition of 1851,** opening a year later as the **Museum of Manufactures,** with a collection of objects purchased from the exhibition. The initial intent was to display *manufactured* art, but when great works of art were bequeathed to the museum (including the permanent loan of the **Raphael Cartoons** and the largest collection of Constable drawings in the world), the scope expanded and the intention and name were changed to the **Museum of Ornamental Art.** In her last major engagement, Queen Victoria laid the foundation stone for the buildings that face Cromwell Road in 1899, and at her request the museum was renamed once again. The **Victoria and Albert Museum,** affectionately known as the **V&A,** is eclectic, idiosyncratic, and immense, yet accessible and gracious—a museum that is truly worthy of the vision and energy of its founders.

Expect to see building work at the **V&A** on a new gallery, designed by **Daniel Libeskind** and scheduled to open in 2004. This avant-garde building will be an irregular shape and look as if huge triangles have been stacked up somehow. Called the **Spiral,** it will be devoted to modern design and craftsmanship and will provide a high-tech information center.

If there is such a thing as the "South Kensington Style," the **V&A** structure is its finest example. The massive building is a construction of redbrick, terra-cotta, and mosaic, with assertions of Victorian confidence towering beside equally Victorian gloom. Sir Henry Cole, the museum's first director, preferred engineers and artists to architects. The resulting cast-iron and glass structure with corrugated-iron facings—built by **William Cubitt** in 1855—looked like a decorated factory and quickly became known as the "Brompton Boilers." It was moved eastward in 1867 to form the **Bethnal Green Museum of Childhood.** The buildings that make up the main quadrangle of the museum began in 1857 with Captain F. Fowke's **Sheepshanks Gallery** along the east side, followed by the **Vernon and Turner Galleries** in 1858, and the **North, South,** and **East Courts** between 1861 and 1873.

A succession of craftsmen were responsible for further additions, among them **Godfrey Sykes, James Gamble, Frank Moody,** and **Reuben Townroe. Sir Aston Webb**'s Cromwell Road facade, begun in 1891 and completed in 1909, evokes the Victorian ethos of pomp and imperial importance. It is flanked by statues of Queen Victoria and Prince Albert by Alfred Drury, and Edward VII and Queen Alexandra by W. Goscombe John. On top of the great central tower is the figure of Fame resting upon a lantern shaped like an imperial crown.

Entering the museum is like embarking on a great, extravagant, and wonderful expedition. There are seven miles of galleries: the **Art & Design Galleries** contain masterpieces grouped around a style, nationality, or period, while **Materials & Techniques** galleries revolve around a type of object, like glass or ceramics. The enormous collection is constantly being added to and new permanent exhibitions created, such as the **Silver Galleries,** which show the national collection of English silver from 1300 to 1800. And don't miss the **Frank Lloyd Wright Gallery** (Level B, **Henry Cole Wing**), which displays a re-creation of the 1936 office of Edgar J. Kaufmann's Pennsylvanian department store—it is the only complete interior of **Wright**'s exhibited in Europe.

You will get lost in the more than 150 rooms, but don't despair. The **V&A** is the best place in town to be lost: Every cul-de-sac is a treasure trove of discovery. And the museum tries to help visitors by displaying color-coded banners to indicate directions. It also publishes a guide that gives museum-goers a taste of its displays by introducing 100 of the most significant and spectacular things to see. The collections are vast, so be warned: You shouldn't attempt to see everything in one visit.

You may want to take advantage of the free, hourlong guided tours that leave from the main (Cromwell Rd) entrance, or special tours announced daily to specific areas of the collection. There are also free gallery lectures that often focus on one particular topic, such as furniture or 18th-century British landscape artists. It is pleasant to visit on Wednesday evenings 6:30-9:30: Selected galleries are open. There are gallery talks and live music, plus a special menu in the restaurant. ◆ Admission; free after 4:30PM. M noon-5:50PM. Tu-Su. Guided tours: M 12:15, 2PM, and 3PM; Tu-Sa 11AM, noon, 2PM, and 3PM. Special tours: M 1:30PM; Tu-Su 11:30AM,

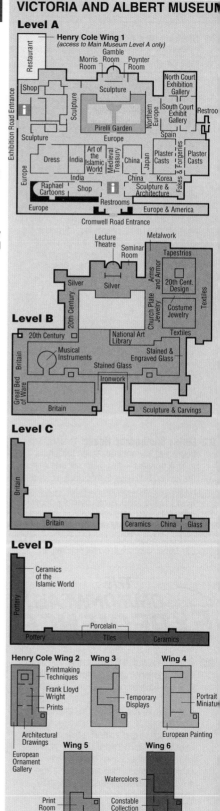

VICTORIA AND ALBERT MUSEUM

1:30PM. Gallery lectures: daily 2:30PM. Exhibition and Cromwell Rds. 942.2000; www.vam.ac.uk. Tube: South Kensington

Within the Victoria and Albert Museum:

Great Bed of Ware This huge Elizabethan bed, circa 1590, was said to have been occupied by 26 butchers and their wives on 13 February 1689. In the 1830s, Charles Dickens tried to purchase the bed from the innkeeper who owned it, but was outbid. This is easily the most famous bed in the world, mentioned by Shakespeare in *Twelfth Night* and by countless other writers and historians. It is nearly nine feet high, 11 feet long, and 10.5 feet wide, a size that sometimes distracts from the beauty of the carved, painted, and inlaid decoration. ♦ Room 54

Raphael Cartoons This gallery's treasures have been restored recently. The cartoons, works of art in their own right, were drawn with chalk on paper and colored with distemper by Raphael and his scholars in 1516 as designs for tapestry work for Pope Leo X. The tapestries are still at the Vatican. Three of the cartoons are lost; the others are here because Rubens advised Charles I to buy them for the newly opened tapestry factory at Mortlake. One of the tapestries made here is part of the display now. After Charles's death, Cromwell bought the cartoons for £300, and they remained at **Whitehall Palace** until William III moved them to **Hampton Court.** They have been on permanent loan to the **V&A** since 1865. ♦ Room 48A

Glass Gallery The national collection of 7,000 glass objects tells the story of glass from ancient Egypt to the present day. The range includes commemorative pieces as well as tableware. ♦ Room 131

Morris, Gamble, and Poynter Rooms The museum's original tearoom, cafe, and restaurant occupied this space until 1939; they almost knock you sideways with longing for those aesthetically elaborate and civilized days. The **Green Dining Room,** decorated for the museum by William Morris and Philip Webb, features Burne-Jones stained glass and painted panels representing the months of the year. The wallpaper and furniture are by Morris. The chimney piece in the **Gamble Room** came from **Dorchester House** on Park Lane. It is surrounded by pillared and mirrored ceramic work and a ceiling of enameled iron plates that incorporates a quotation from *Ecclesiastes.* The dazzling materials were chosen not so much for their beauty, but because they are fire-resistant and easy to clean! The **Grill Room,** designed by Sir Edward Poynter, still has the original grill, set in Minton blue-and-white tiles representing the seasons and the months. The three rooms present a first-class example of Victorian design. ♦ Level A

Dress Collection This room houses a collection of fashion dating from around 1580 to the present, and draws more crowds than any other exhibition in the **V&A.** The English and continental male and female fashions, with outfits from the 1960s and early 1970s, are strangely exotic and, some say, still eminently fashionable. ♦ Room 40

Fakes and Forgeries Even the floor of this gallery has criminal undertones; it was laid by the female inmates of Woking Prison. The best fakes of their kind are housed here from the hands of master forger Giovanni Bastianini, whose work is displayed among a host of other bogus objects purporting to be something they are not. ♦ Room 46

Sculpture During the Italian Renaissance, Donatello breathed life into stone in his marble relief, the *Ascension of Christ with the Giving of the Keys to St. Peter.* Few can match his mastery, though Rodin does with his *St. John the Baptist,* which also can be seen here. ♦ Rooms 11-21A, 51, Exhibition Rd entrance

British Art and Design, 1900-60 Huge sealed glass rooms were built to house the objects that trace British design from the Arts and Crafts movement, started by William Morris in the 19th century, to the new functionalism of the 20th. At press time, these galleries were being expanded and redisplayed; they probably won't be finished until November 2001, so expect some disruption in these rooms for quite some time. The redone galleries will show decorative and fine art by such artists as Grinling Gibbons, Robert Adam, and Thomas Chippendale. ♦ 20th-Century Exhibition Gallery

Henry Cole Wing This splendid wing houses the **Constable Collection,** which was presented to the museum by the artist's daughter. It provides a trip to the English countryside through the eyes and genius of one of England's most beloved painters. This artist, like no other, has captured this pastoral region the way the English would like to believe it still could be. ♦ Exhibition Rd entrance

V&A Restaurant ★★$$ One of the best museum restaurants in town, with imaginative salads and tasty hot foods, all freshly made, it also presents food themes, so you might be able to sample sushi during a Japanese exhibition. On Wednesday, a special menu is themed to reflect the subject of that evening's lecture and is accompanied by live music. This is a lovely spot for lunch, snacks, or afternoon tea; there's a jazz brunch on Sunday. ♦ Cafeteria ♦ Daily lunch and tea; Su brunch. 581.2159

V&A Shop Located to the left of the entrance is the main shop, run as a separate entity, but the profits are all poured back into the museum. There is also a small shop near the restaurant. On sale are replicas of individual works of art displayed in the **V&A,** including the *Statue of Shakespeare* in terra-cotta and the ceramic alphabet tiles from the **Gamble Room,** known as the *Kensington Alphabet;* in addition, there is an impressive array of stationery, diaries, and William Morris needlepoint cushions. The postcards, books, and other publications are outstanding, as are the ornaments at Christmastime. Just inside is the **Crafts Council Shop,** a showcase for British craftspeople, with original jewelry and objects in pottery, silver, gold, and glass—future treasures for the museum itself. ◆ Daily. 938.8434

24 Hoop & Toy ★$ The name of this pub refers to the game of metal hoop and wooden stick, which is now featured only in illustrated children's books. Rather well-worn, the pub has the atmosphere of days gone by, with dark wood and polished brass, Edwardian drawings on the walls, and a menu with 18th-century dishes like beef-and-ale pie. You'll also find a large choice of beers and seven real ales. ◆ Pub ◆ M-F breakfast, lunch, and dinner; Sa-Su lunch and dinner. 34 Thurloe Pl (at Cromwell Pl). 589.8360. Tube: South Kensington

25 Daquise ★$$ Regular visitors to the **V&A** often stop by this Polish cafe for lemon tea and apple strudel. The quality of the food varies and the surroundings are dingy, but the atmosphere's the thing. Nothing has changed since World War II: not the look of the Polish waitresses, nor the menu of *golubcy* (stuffed cabbage), *kasza* (boiled buckwheat), and *zrazy* (beef rolls stuffed with cucumber, bacon, and mushrooms). Polish émigrés meet here for morning coffee, lunch, afternoon tea, or dinner. ◆ Polish ◆ Daily lunch and dinner. 20 Thurloe St (between Thurloe Sq and Cromwell Pl). 589.6117. Tube: South Kensington

26 Rembrandt Hotel $$$ This 197-room hotel facing the **V&A** has welcomed guests since the turn of the century. Part of the Sarova group, it offers the kinds of facilities that some travelers (especially Americans) find very reassuring: fax services, direct-dial telephones, and 24-hour food and porterage service. The jewel in the hotel's crown, however, is access (at extra cost) to the incredibly posh **Aquilla** health club, located

within the hotel. The club is a conscious attempt to re-create a Roman spa, with a marbled world of tiles, pillars, arches, and murals; inside are a gymnasium, a 50-by-20-foot pool with a Jacuzzi, a fountain, music, a grotto, a sauna, a solarium, and a salad bar. The hotel itself is more down-to-earth and contemporary, and features two restaurants **Masters** serves a buffet lunch and an à la carte dinner (with hotel dining room classics like tournedos and scampi), while the **Conservatory** offers light meals and sandwiches and afternoon tea. You can get a traditional English breakfast here, including grilled kidneys, kippers, and smoked haddoc. ◆ 11 Thurloe Pl (between Brompton Rd and Thurloe Sq). 589.8100, 800/424.2862; fax 225.3363. Tube: South Kensington

Felton & Sons Ltd

27 Felton & Sons Ltd. One of the many joys of life in London is that flowers don't cost a small fortune. This florist has been here since 1900 and is known for its sumptuous and rare blossoms, as well as pretty posies and even Belgian chocolates to accompany floral gifts. ◆ M-F; Sa to noon. 220 Brompton Rd (at Thurloe Pl). 589.4433. Tube: South Kensington

28 Brompton Oratory (London Oratory of St. Philip Neri) Built between 1880 and 1893 by **Herbert Gribble** and officially named the **London Oratory of St. Philip Neri,** this was the first important Roman Catholic church to be constructed in London after the Reformation. Of the few beautiful Catholic churches in London, this one is sensational. The smell of incense greets you upon entering the High Roman oratory, with domes and vaults, a domed nave, and Italian ornaments and statues. Included are Carrara marble statues of the apostles carved by Giuseppe Mazzuoli, a disciple of Bernini, which stood for 200 years in Siena Cathedral, and the altar in the **Lady Chapel,** constructed in 1693 by Francis Corbarelli and his sons Dominic and Antony, which came from Brescia, Italy. In ecclesiastical and liturgical terms, an oratory is a congregation of secular priests living together without vows. The Fathers of the oratory are not monks, and thus are not bound together by the three religious vows but by the internal bond of charity and the external bond of a common life and rule. St. Philip founded the Institute of the Oratory in Rome in 1575.

The Oratorian movement in England came about as the result of John Henry Newman, a Victorian whose conversion to Catholicism shook the Anglican establishment. It was Father Faber who bought the site for this building in 1853, despite protests from his fellows of it being in "a neighborhood of second-rate gentry and second-rate shops." Don't miss the triptych paintings of saints Thomas More and John Fisher (and their execution at Tyburn Gallows) by Rex Whistler in **St. Wilfred's Chapel,** and the dome, designed by **G. Sherrin,** with wooden ribs faced with 60 tons of lead. At 11AM on Sunday, the church is packed with nearly 2,000 people, both parishioners and visitors, for Latin High Mass with a full choir after the Italian manner (family mass is at 10AM). It also holds concerts. ◆ Daily. Mass: M-Sa 7AM, 7:30AM, 8AM, 10AM, 6PM. Benediction: Tu, Th 6:30PM. Family Mass: Su 10AM. Latin High Mass: Su 11AM. Brompton Rd (at Cottage Pl). 589.4811. Tube: South Kensington

29 Sun and Snow The name heralds a snazzy sportswear shop, with the latest in fashionable ski gear, including an ample selection for kids. In summer, it carries everything you need for squash, tennis, swimming, and running. ◆ Daily. 229 Brompton Rd (between Egerton Terr and Egerton Gardens). 581.2039. Tube: South Kensington

30 Brasserie St. Quentin ★★★$$$ The food served here is excellent most of the time. Don't expect to find nouvelle cuisine; at this dining spot, classic food is in. The *boeuf bourguignon* and steak au poivre deserve every star available. The decor is traditional brasserie, with a long zinc bar, mirrors, brass, chandeliers, glass, and waiters who dress the part. The tables along the banquette are uncomfortably close together, however, so you can hear every word of every diner's conversation. The best value is the two-course set menu (available for lunch and early dinner) that offers such tasty items as fish soup, terrine of eggplant, rump steak with horseradish sauce, and fillet of mackerel. ◆ French ◆ Daily lunch and dinner. 243 Brompton Rd (at Egerton Gardens). 589.8005. Tube: South Kensington

31 The Collection ★★★$$$ The latest place for the fashionable set to see and be seen, this huge restaurant was once a designer's warehouse. It is almost hidden from the street, but an illuminated walkway gives the entrance some drama. The skylit ground floor bar has an amazingly long counter, fluted iron pillars, brick walls, and a showy staircase leading to the balcony-style restaurant. You can get reasonably priced snacks at the bar, while the restaurant serves trendy dishes such as chicken breast chermoulah with tabbouleh and dukkah yogurt, and for dessert, steamed mango and pineapple with chocolate and coconut sauce. ◆ International ◆ Daily lunch and dinner. 264 Brompton Rd (between Pelham St and South Terr). 225.1212. Tube: South Kensington

31 La Brasserie ★★$$ A permanent London fixture, this restaurant has been here for 25 years and looks just like the type of brasserie you'd expect to find in Paris, right down to the imported waiters. In addition to the substantial main menu there is a weekly changing regional menu. It's a great place for noshing and watching London's glamorous residents gird their loins for an onslaught on **Harrods** and Beauchamp Place. The service is efficient even when the place gets busy. ◆ French ◆ Daily breakfast, lunch, and dinner. 272 Brompton Rd (between Pelham St and South Terr). 581.3089. Tube: South Kensington

32 Betty Jackson For two decades, this British designer has been producing understated, stylish yet classic clothes that suit women who like to feel comfortable. Her clothes include dresses, coats, separates, and knitwear at mid-range prices. ◆ M-Sa. 311 Brompton Rd (between Draycott Ave and Egerton Crescent). 589.7884. Tube: South Kensington

33 Number 16 $$ Even though the Victorians did everything in the grand manner, when four Victorian houses are smacked together it doesn't necessarily mean that the resulting hotel is large or spacious. This elegant but somewhat cramped 36-room property is a case in point; however, nostalgia buffs will probably forgive the occasional tiny guest room because, from the pretty morning room onward, all are lovingly furnished with antiques. In summer, it's sheer bliss to sit in the conservatory out in the garden. There is no restaurant. ◆ 16 Sumner Pl (between Fulham Rd and Onslow Sq). 589.5232; fax 584.8615. Tube: South Kensington

33 Five Sumner Place Hotel $$ This small, privately owned hotel, cited as one of the best bed-and-breakfasts in the greater Kensington area, is part of an impressive Victorian terrace built around 1848. The hotel has been faithfully refurbished to re-create the style of a bygone era. After registration you are given your own front door key so you can come and go as you please. All 11 bedrooms have TV, radio, and telephone. ◆ 5 Sumner Pl (between Fulham Rd and Onslow Sq). 584.7586; fax 823.9962. Tube: South Kensington

34 Butler & Wilson The late Princess Diana sometimes used to nip into this shop for a little bauble to match a designer ensemble. It's the best place for fake antique and gemstone jewelry. The range of costume jewelry is also sold at **Harrods.** ♦ M-Sa. 189 Fulham Rd (between Stewart's Grove and Sydney St). 352.8255. Tube: South Kensington. Also at: 20 S Molton St (between Brook and Davies Sts). 409.2955. Tube: Bond Street

T

35 Theo Fennell The owner is both a silversmith and a jeweler who enjoys fashioning novelty souvenir miniatures such as a London phone booth or mailbox. Well known as the unstuffy alternative to the likes of Cartier and Garrard, he works from his new five-story flagship store. He also will custom-design a piece of jewelry to your specifications. Some of his designs are for sale at **Harrods.** ♦ M-Sa. 169 Fulham Rd (between Bury Walk and Pond Pl). 591.5000. Tube: South Kensington

36 Au Bon Accueil ★★$$$ Come here for the kind of delicious, unpretentious French cooking you'd expect to get in the heart of the French countryside. Standard classics include snails in garlic butter, onion soup, and *boeuf bourguignon*. The dining room is decorated simply and tastefully, with banquette seats, pictures and prints of London and Paris scenes, pink tablecloths and napkins, bright lighting, and mirrors; in summer, there are also outdoor tables. ♦ French ♦ M-F lunch and dinner; Sa dinner. 19 Elystan St (at Ixworth Pl). 589.3718. Tube: South Kensington

37 Zen ★★$$$ Popular for many years, this large, cozy eatery was the first of the Zen group's restaurants that became well known for the nouvelle approach to Chinese cooking. The food is good and beautifully presented. Peking duck is a favorite, and the seafood dishes are excellent: Try the lobster and prawns on noodles or the steamed sea bass in black bean sauce. Elegant napery, large windows, Chinese astrological signs etched on the windows, and a lively ambience give the place a formal but friendly character. ♦ Chinese ♦ Daily lunch and dinner. Chelsea Cloisters, 85 Sloane Ave (between Makins St and Ixworth Pl). 589.1781. Tube: South Kensington. Also at: 20 Queen St (between Curzon and Charles Sts). 629.8089. Tube: Green Park

38 Bibendum ★★★$$$$ This restaurant is set in a spectacular Art Deco building once owned by the Michelin Tire Company, whose unlikely mascot is Bibendum, a bespectacled chap made entirely of white tires. The image of "the Michelin Man" can be seen everywhere you look in the large dining room. This is a showpiece in the group of diverse, but always stylish, restaurants run by Sir Terence Conran. Besides the main restaurant, there is the ground-floor **Oyster Bar** for great seafood in a beautiful Art Deco–tiled room. Unfortunately, you can't book here, and the line can be discouraging, but it is also a cafe in the mornings, so maybe a coffee stop is the answer to enjoy the atmosphere. Upstairs, the overall effect of the restaurant is stylish, light and elegant. As for Matthew Harris's cooking, each of the dishes on the ever-changing menu is prepared perfectly using the best ingredients. Offerings include herring marinated in yogurt and tarragon, chicken leg in a Thai-style ochre broth, and blueberry-and-almond tart. ♦ Modern European ♦ Restaurant: daily lunch and dinner. Oyster Bar: daily breakfast, lunch, and dinner. Reservations required in the restaurant. Michelin House, 81 Fulham Rd (at Sloane Ave). 581.5817. Tube: South Kensington

38 Conran Shop Above, around, and to the side of **Bibendum** is this emporium, Sir Terence Conran's personal apotheosis. A legend in his lifetime, Conran has been bringing style to London since the 1960s. You can buy everything here, from leather-encased pencil sharpeners to bedspreads and furniture, including items from the newly launched Conran Collection, boasting more than 1,000 pieces by Conran's in-house designers. ♦ Daily. 81 Fulham Rd (at Sloane Ave). 589.7401. Tube: South Kensington. The complete Conran Collection is at 12-13 Conduit St (between New Bond and St. George's Sts). 399.0710. Tube: Piccadilly Circus

39 Joseph Joseph Ettedgui's two-floor department store contains a selection of everything that is designer chic in clothing: It sells his own collection and those of other designers for both men and women. ♦ M-Sa, Su noon-5PM. 77 Fulham Rd (at Sloane Ave). 823.9500. Tube: South Kensington. The Joseph Collection only is sold at 26 Sloane St (between Hans Crescent and Basil St). 235.5470; a smaller boutique on the same stretch of road sells more exclusive Joseph clothes as well as those of other designers: 16 Sloane St. 235.7541. Tube (for both): Knightsbridge. His new flagship store is at 23 Old Bond St (between Piccadilly and Burlington Gardens). 629.3713. Tube: Piccadilly Circus

40 Joe's ★★$$$ Owned by Joseph Ettedgui (of **Joseph** shops fame), this remains a style-conscious restaurant following a major renovation from minimalist black and white to trendy beige and brown. Try the smoked goat cheese–and–apple tart with fruit relish and the blackened cod with prawn and chili sticky rice. ♦ Modern British ♦ M-F lunch and dinner; Sa late breakfast, lunch, and dinner; Su late breakfast and brunch. Reservations required on weekends. 126 Draycott Ave (at Walton St). 225.2217. Tube: South Kensington

41 Walton Street Only the elegant window displays on the rather bare facades of the buildings at the lower end of the street reveal the array of goods inside. Restaurants such as **Ma Cuisine** and **San Martino** have loyal followings, and **The Enterprise,** once a pub and now a trendy restaurant, is a Walton Street landmark. New shops spring up along the street to join the old favorites. As you wander toward Beauchamp Place, the street's domestic side becomes apparent. The shops are less frequent, turning into noble, neatly formed town houses guarded by iron gates at the more affluent end of the street. ♦ Between Draycott Ave and Beauchamp Pl. Tube: South Kensington, Knightsbridge

VAN PETERSON designs

41 Van Peterson A bijou shop on a bijou street, it sells charming, elegant jewelry, created by a husband-and-wife team. It is all of fine quality and not overly expensive. ♦ M-Sa, Su noon-5PM. 194-196 Walton St (between Draycott Ave and First St). 584.1101. Tube: South Kensington

42 San Martino ★★$$ Here's another much-loved, busy, and friendly Italian restaurant. For fun, why not try the spaghetti cooked in a paper bag? ♦ Italian ♦ Daily lunch and dinner. 103 Walton St (between Draycott Ave and First St). 589.3833. Tube: South Kensington

ALASTAIR LOCKHART
Limited

43 Alastair Lockhart Fans of luxurious writing paper love this special boutique that stocks Crane's 100-percent-cotton paper in a wide spectrum of colors. The paper can be printed to your specifications, as can visiting cards, invitations, and announcements. ♦ M-Sa. 97 Walton St (between Draycott Ave and First St). 581.8289. Tube: South Kensington

44 Monogrammed Linen Shop This is where the cognoscenti come to buy monogrammed Irish linen sheets, duvet covers, dressing gowns, and handkerchiefs. If you like, all the items can be tastefully embroidered with your initials. ♦ M-Sa. 168 Walton St (between Draycott Ave and Glynde Mews). 589.4033. Tube: Knightsbridge, South Kensington

44 Jo Malone The fashion crowd love Jo Malone's sleekly packaged fragrances. You'll find soap, oils, creams, and candles. The most popular scent is the lime, basil, and mandarin. There's even a delivery service called Sent-a-Scent and the shop does ship to the US. ♦ M-Sa. 154 Walton St (between Draycott Ave and Glynde Mews). 581.1101; mail order

720.0202. Tube: Knightsbridge, South Kensington

The English House

45 English House ★★$$$$ When you walk in, it feels as if you're in a private room in someone's home, gazing at mirrors, floral wallpaper, and objets d'art. Chef David Clouston aims for traditional British cooking with a modern slant. Dishes include braised ham hock with apple polenta, perhaps followed by rhubarb and honey crumble with whisky cream. ♦ British ♦ Daily lunch and dinner. Reservations recommended. 3 Milner St (at Hasker St). 584.3002. Tube: South Kensington

46 Dragons This enchanting shop is for grownups who want to give their youngsters the childhood they never had. The exquisite, hand-painted children's furniture is made for royal children and other fortunate little ones; there are children's fabrics, tiny seats, and even some toys (to keep the kiddies amused while their parents browse). ♦ M-Sa. 23 Walton St (at Hasker St). 589.3795. Tube: South Kensington

46 Tapisserie This well-established shop sells hand-painted canvases (for making tapestries), all designed exclusively for sale here. You can also commmission, or even design your own evening, clutch, or tote bag. ♦ M-Sa. 54 Walton St (between Glynde Mews and Ovington Square). 581.2715. Tube: South Kensington

47 Grill St. Quentin ★★$$$ First-rate cooking is offered here, straight from the chargrill in a brightly lit basement. Chef Nigel Davis devises refreshingly uncomplicated French dishes, and there are always fish choices and oysters. ♦ French ♦ Daily lunch and dinner. 3 Yeoman's Row (at Egerton Gardens Mews). 581.8377. Tube: Knightsbridge

48 Patisserie Valerie ★$ Like its older sister in Soho, this busy cafe (the largest in the group) offers such pleasant main dishes as roast chicken, sausages, and pasta; and the cakes, eclairs, pastries, and buns are quite scrumptious. The afternoon tea here is particularly good. ♦ Cafe ♦ Daily breakfast, lunch, afternoon tea, and early dinner. 215 Brompton Rd (between Yeoman's Row and Egerton Terr). 823.9971. Tube: Knightsbridge. Also at: 44 Old Compton St (between Frith and Dean Sts). 437.3466. Tube: Piccadilly Circus, Leicester Square; 105 Marylebone High St (between St. Vincent and Moxon Sts). 935.6240. Tube: Baker Street, Bond Street

Walton Street Shopping

DRAYCOTT AVENUE

British restaurant **Waltons**	**Sara Davenport Gallery** antique pet paintings
women's shoes **Azagury**	**Andrew Martin** interior design
perfumes **Santa Maria Novella**	**Figure Shapers** beauty salon
cocktail bar **Barfly**	**Andrew Martin** interior design
dried flowers **Martin Robinson**	**Van Peterson Designs** jewelry
interiors/knitwear **Nordic Style/Moussie**	**Walton Street Garage**
Italian restaurant **San Martino**	**Bentley's** leather goods
lamps **Besselink & Jones**	**Walton Contemporary Art**
stationery **Alaistair Lockhart**	**Percy Bass Ltd.** eccentric interiors
jewelry **Cox & Power**	**Anne McKee & Co.** estate agents
modern art **The Blue Gallery**	**Merola** jewelry
gifts **The Wedding List Co.**	**Özten Zeki Gallery**
French restaurant **Turner's**	**Butterscotch** children's clothes
Lightning Dry Cleaners	**Bon Chic Bon Genre** womenswear
kids' interior design **Nursery Window**	**The Monogrammed Linen Shop**
corporate apartments **Peerman**	**John Campbell** framing/restoration
maternity designerwear **Maman Deux**	**Maria Andipa Icon Gallery**
jewelry **Kiki McDonough**	**The Room** gifts/glassware
sleepwear **Lawrence Tavernier**	**Arabesk** African jewelry
hairdressers **Ellishen**	**Jo Malone** perfumes
silver/jewelry **Benney**	**The Orientalist** antiques
estate agents **Janet Osband**	**Le Salon** hair
womenswear **Liola**	**Ainslie Design Associates** interior design

(WALTON STREET — running vertically between the two columns)

FIRST STREET

restaurant **The Enterprise**
jewelry **Marie Storms**

HASKER STREET

kids' toys and furniture **Dragons**
tiles **Walton Ceramics**
kids' designs **Patrizia Wigan**
antique prints **Stephanie Hoppen**
interior design/furnishings **Louise Bradley**
antiques **Port of Call**

OVINGTON STREET

wine merchant **Wine Rack**
interior design **Nina Campbell**
curtains/fabrics **Chelsea Textiles Design**
deli **La Picena**
Italian restaurant **Scalini**

LENNOX GARDEN MEWS

Italian restaurant **Totos**

GYNDE MEWS

La Réserve wine merchant
Tapisserie sew-it-yourself tapestries
Wm. Hawkes & Son silversmith, jeweler
Concorde of Knightsbridge dry cleaners
Baker & Spice bakery/deli

LENNOX GARDENS   **OVINGTON SQUARE**

49 Bunch of Grapes ★$$ Once upon a time, glass partitions separated the six bars in this authentic Victorian pub, which has kept some of the screens, etched glass, and wood carving. Homemade pub grub, such as fish-and-chips and steak-and-kidney pie, is served at lunch and snacks are served until 9PM; all are accompanied by real ale. ◆ Pub ◆ Daily lunch and snacks. 207 Brompton Rd (at Yeoman's Row). 589.4944. Tube: Knightsbridge

50 Crane Kalman Gallery This gallery sells the works of established 20th-century British and European artists such as Calder, Léger, Degas, Dufy, Nicholson, Moore, and Sutherland, to name a distinguished few. Even if you're not planning to buy, stopping in here is like visiting a small museum. ◆ M-Sa. 178 Brompton Rd (between Montpelier St and Cheval Pl). 584.7566. Tube: Knightsbridge

51 Paul Costelloe With several boutiques in his native Ireland, Costelloe uses linen, silk, and wool to create simple, elegant womenswear. This is his first branch in England. ◆ Daily. 156 Brompton Rd (between Montpelier St and Cheval Pl). 589.9480. Tube: Knightsbridge

51 Past Times Here you'll find gifts inspired by English arts and crafts, encompassing everything from Celtic times to the early 20th century. There are Gothic playing cards, books, and jigsaws; Celtic, Tudor, and Stuart jewelry; and scarves and tapestries for ladies of the manor. ◆ M-Sa. 146 Brompton Rd (between Montpelier St and Cheval Pl). 581.7616. Tube: Knightsbridge. Also at: 155 Regent St (between Heddon and New Burlington Sts). 734.3728. Tube: Piccadilly Circus, Oxford Circus; 179 Kensington High St (between Adam and Eve Mews and Allen St). 795.6344. Tube: High Street Kensington

52 Bonham's Founded in 1793, but not as internationally famous as **Sotheby's** or **Christie's**, this auction house is nevertheless well worth checking out for its oil paintings, watercolors, carpets, clocks, porcelain, furniture, wine, silver, and jewelry. The firm, which has a sixth-generation Bonham on staff, normally has set days for certain items, so call ahead for sale details. When special events are held in London, such as the **Chelsea Flower Show** or the **National Cat Show,** the house usually holds a paintings auction to match. ◆ M-Sa; Su 11AM-4PM. Montpelier St (between Brompton Rd and Cheval Pl). 393.3900. Tube: Knightsbridge.

53 Emporio Armani This Italian designer's store operates on the grand scale, with sections for every kind of clothing—men's, women's, and *bambini,* together with every accessory they'll need to go with the suits and sportswear. It has a smart **Express** cafe to indulge in a healthy lunch of seared salmon with saffron and herb risotto, followed by *semifreddo* (soft ice cream) and a cup of steaming hot java. The place can get really hopping: The coffee machine makes up to 400 cups an hour! ◆ M-Sa. 191 Brompton Rd (between Beaufort Gardens and Beauchamp Pl). 823.8818. Tube: Knightsbridge. Also at: 57-59 Long Acre (between Bow St and Hanover Pl). 917.6882. Tube: Covent Garden; 112a New Bond St (at Brook St). 491.8080. Tube: Bond Street

Reject China Shops

53 Reject China Shops The name is from the 1960s, when bargain hunters snapped up the seconds it stocked then. Now high-quality china is carried, as well as the best crystal. But with a policy of offering special promotions, the shops keep prices lower than comparable stores. You can still pick up some reasonably priced seconds, as well as oddly shaped novelty teapots and mugs that might make amusing souvenirs. Everything is spread out in two shops. ◆ M-Sa; Su noon-5PM. 183 Brompton Rd (at Beauchamp Pl) and 2 Beauchamp Pl (between Walton St and Brompton Rd). 581.0739. Tube: Knightsbridge. Also at: 134 Regent St (between Regent Pl and Beak St). 434.2502. Tube: Oxford Circus

53 Janet Reger If you're looking for the kind of silk lingerie that the finest fantasies are made of, this is the only address you'll ever need. The brassieres are brilliantly designed, amplifying or diminishing with seductive perfection. ◆ M-Sa. 2 Beauchamp Pl (between Walton St and Brompton Rd). 584.9360. Tube: Knightsbridge

53 Anvers If you want style at affordable prices then try this Belgian import featuring classically understated clothing for women of all ages. The pieces stand on their own or mix seamlessly with your wardrobe .◆ Daily. 193-195 Brompton Rd.(between Beaufort Gardens and Beauchamp Pl). 581.3737. Tube: Knightsbridge

54 Beauchamp Place Temptations are many on this Regency street (pronounced *Beech-*um), where you can easily spend a whole day or a whole week browsing in the boutiques and smart shops. You will find the best of British designer clothes, old maps and prints, antique silver, made-to-measure shoes, and lingerie fit for royalty. While struggling to resist the many covetables on the street (or not), you can eat delectable food in restaurants that are equally stylish and fun. ◆ Between Walton St and Brompton Rd. Tube: Knightsbridge

55 Map House Antique, rare, and decorative maps, botanical prints, lithographs, and aquatints line every inch of this tiny town house and at honest prices. ◆ M-Sa. 54 Beauchamp Pl (between Walton St and Brompton Rd). 589.4325. Tube: Knightsbridge

CAROLINE
CHARLES
LONDON

55 Caroline Charles This top English designer sells only the finest silks and linens. Charles's style is very English, but it's flavored with her own brand of sophisticated elegance. She creates clothes that you will want to wear for a lifetime. ♦ M-Sa. 56-57 Beauchamp Pl (between Walton St and Brompton Rd). 589.5850. Tube: Knightsbridge

56 San Lorenzo ★★★$$$ At this elegant restaurant decorated in muted colors and featuring many potted plants, you might glimpse notables such as Mel Gibson, Naomi Campbell, Arnold Schwarzenegger, Lauren Bacall, or Eric Clapton. Discretion is a watchword. The staff seems to know all the glamorous hairdos and suits personally, but service to unknowns is just as attentive. This first-class Italian restaurant attracts the kind of people who appreciate carpaccio prepared three ways and fresh game in season. ♦ Italian ♦ M-Sa lunch and dinner. Reservations recommended; no credit cards accepted. 22 Beauchamp Pl (between Walton St and Brompton Rd). 584.1074. Tube: Knightsbridge

57 Bill Bentley's ★★$$ Sit at the basement wine bar, order a dozen oysters and a half bottle of Muscadet, and bask in the charming atmosphere of this friendly dining place. The restaurant on the ground floor serves British fish dishes such as Dover sole and such imaginative creations as grilled tuna with Mediterranean vegetables and pesto. ♦ Wine bar/British ♦ M-Sa lunch and dinner; Su lunch. Reservations recommended for dinner. 31 Beauchamp Pl (between Walton St and Brompton Rd). 589.5080. Tube: Knightsbridge

57 Floriana ★★★$$$ Executive Chef Fabio Trabocchi has worked in Milan, Washington, DC, and Marbella. Now he has the chance to show his talents in this new London restaurant. Treat yourself to one of his wonderful signature dishes: whole duck roasted with herbs or roast sea bass in cod puree with potato crumbs and black-truffle sauce. The set lunch is a very good value, while the à la carte dinner is expensive. ♦ Modern Italian ♦ M-Sa lunch and dinner. Reservations recommended. 15 Beauchamp Pl (between Walton St and Brompton Rd). 838.1500. Tube: Knightsbridge

58 Harrods In the past, the desire for greatness led to the creation of cathedrals and palaces. Today, it leads to department stores, and this one is Notre Dame, the Taj Mahal, and Blenheim Palace, all rolled into one. Even as as the silk-scarfed ladies of England vow that it has gone downhill, the fact remains that the cathedral of consumerism is hard to beat.

Behind the solid and elegant Edwardian facade built between 1901 and 1905 by **Stevens and Munt**, 4,000 employees in 230 departments stand ready to fulfill almost every request. You can book a trip around the world, reserve theater and concert tickets, and get your lighter repaired, your clothes dry-cleaned, and your nails polished. There's even a special long-hair department in the beauty salon. Four bagpipers in **Harrods** tartan play in the store daily.

Above all, don't miss the **Food Halls,** with their stunning mosaic friezes and fabulous displays of food. (The wet-fish display is a masterpiece!) **Harrods** began as a grocer's shop, and even now their food hampers are "musts" at posh picnic events like the Henley regatta and Wimbledon, and as Christmas presents (when 300,000 of them are sold). If you're afraid this palace of temptation will make you forget the limitations of your bank balance, plan to visit London just after New Year's Day, when **Harrods**' month-long January sale begins. The most famous shopping event of the year, it is a true test of consumer stamina, but those who are tenacious and strong will be rewarded with real bargains. **Harrods** has 13 restaurants and 5 bars, including a juice bar and a wine bar.

The store does have some quirks. Its dress code states that doormen will not admit customers "who wear ripped jeans, cropped tops, high-cut athletic shorts, or dirty and unkempt clothes. Men are not allowed to wear cycling shorts and footwear must be worn at all times." It also charges £1 to use the "luxury washrooms" unless "you are a **Harrods** account customer, you have used one of the restaurants, you are pregnant, or have small children, you are disabled, or you have spent £100." (So even if you only have coffee and a croissant, keep the receipt to show the attendant). ♦ M-Sa. 87-135 Brompton Rd (between Hans Crescent and Hans Rd). 730.1234, theater tickets 589.1101 Tube: Knightsbridge

Within Harrods:

Georgian Room ★★★$$$$ With their barrel-shape, ornate ceilings, huge windows draped in fringed green fabric, and chairs upholstered in pink silk, the cavernous dining rooms here look like a setting from a Merchant and Ivory film. Elegant, well-prepared English fare is on the menu for lunch, and at teatime, this place is *always* crowded with people enjoying traditional English brews, buns, pastries, salads, butters, creams, and jams. The **Terrace Bar** is also here, serving the same menu in a conservatory-style setting. ♦ British ♦ M-Sa lunch and afternoon tea. Reservations recommended for tea.

Beauchamp Place Shopping

BROMPTON ROAD

leather goods/luggage **Mulberry**	**Reject China Shop** china/porcelain
	Pasta Prego restaurant
Knightsbridge Furniture Co.	**Reject China Shop** china/porcelain
hairdresser **Naim**	**Janet Reger** lingerie
sandwiches **Prêt à Manger**	**Kruszyǹska** womenswear
jewelry **Domer & Hall**	**La Petite Difference** ceramics/jewelry
hair salon **Berte Blanch**	**Ninivah Khomo** fake fur/womenswear
jewelry **Kenneth Jay Lane**	**Pizza Express**
womenswear **Caroline Charles**	**McQueen's Flowers**
tanning parlor **Tanning Island**	**Kanga** womenswear
antique prints **The Map House**	**Patara** Thai restaurant
leather goods **The Bridge**	**Mozafarian** women's jewelry
jewelry **Annabel Jones**	**Shirin** cashmere
Italian restaurant **Ciro's Pizza Pomodoro**	**Sergio Rossi** shoes
women's formalwear **Rivaaz**	**13½** Italian restaurant
gifts **Museum Store**	**Arthur Morrice** optician
Portuguese restaurant **O Fado**	**Whistles** womenswear
womenswear **CiBi**	**Via Veneto** Italian restaurant
designer clothing **Bertie Golightly**	**Stanley Leslie** silver
Russian restaurant **Borshtch 'n Tears**	**John Boyd** women's hats
jewelry **Folli-Follie**	**Paddy Campbell** womenswear
pub **J.J. Murphy & Co.**	**Julie Loughnan** children's dresses/books/
leather goods **Osprey**	model horses
	Olympia Tours travel agency
handmade shoes/bags **Deliss**	**Ronit Zilkha** womenswear
Portuguese restaurant **Caravela**	**San Lorenzo** Italian restaurant
Lebanese restaurant **Maroush**	**Maison Panache** womenswear
womenswear **Hawa**	**Comicedici** shoes
menswear **Nejoud Boodai**	**Pamela Stevens** beauty salon
leather goods **Franchetti Bond**	**Scruples** womenswear
Oriental womenswear **Tian Art**	**Bruce Oldfield** womenswear
designer womenswear **Isabell Kristensen**	**McKenna & Co** jewelry
womenswear **Spaghetti**	**Margaret Howell** womenswear
wine bar/restaurant **Bill Bentley's**	**Verbanella** Italian restaurant

(BEAUCHAMP PLACE runs along the center)

WALTON STREET

---

59 L'Hôtel $$$ This charming hotel is really a small country inn—the kind you never seem to find anymore. There are only 12 rooms, so you have to book well in advance in order to enjoy the pine furniture, Laura Ashley fabrics, twin beds, color TV, and clock radios, all at reasonable prices. For the lone traveler, this is one of the best places to feel at home. A continental breakfast is included in the price. ♦ 28 Basil St (between Hans Crescent and Hooper's Ct). 589.6286; fax 823.7826. Tube: Knightsbridge

Within L'Hôtel:

Le Metro ★★★$$ The only drawback to this wine bar is that its justifiable popularity makes it very crowded at times. Although it's in the basement, its chic black-and-white minimalist decor gives it an airy look. The best of things French are served here—salad *frisée aux foies de volailles* (salad greens with chicken livers), cheeses that are fresh and ripe, savory soups, casseroles, and tarts, and a choice of first-rate, carefully chosen wines, with a special selection of important *crus* by the glass, made possible by a state-of-the-art machine. The place opens early in the morning for genuine espresso or frothy *café crème* and croissants or English breakfast, and it stays open in the afternoon to accommodate those who crave coffee and a *croque monsieur* (grilled ham and cheese sandwich). ♦ French ♦ M-Sa breakfast, lunch, and dinner. 589.6286

59 Capital Hotel $$$$ David Levin is a first-class hotelier, and when he decided to open his own establishment he went about creating the very best. This property is small, modern, sophisticated, personal, attractive, and one minute from **Harrods.** Nina Campbell designed the 48 luxurious rooms, packed with as many of the creature comforts as could fit into the rather small dimensions, including super king-size beds with Egyptian cotton sheets, bathrobes, toothbrushes, and a rose for every lady. ♦ 22 Basil St (between Hans Crescent and Hooper's Ct). 589.5171, 800/926.3199; fax 225.0011. Tube: Knightsbridge

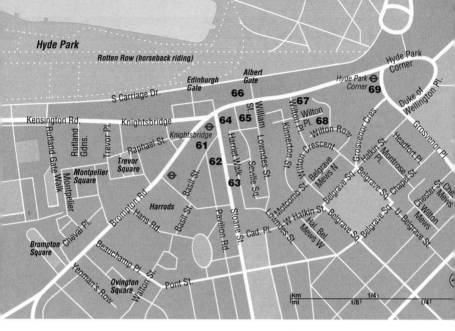

Within the Capital Hotel:

Capital Restaurant ★★★$$$ This one-Michelin-star restaurant has put the **Capital Hotel** on the map. Accolades for chef Philip Britten appear with delicious regularity in the British press (no pun intended). The room has been redecorated by Nina Campbell, using beige tones and introducing engraved-glass window shutters along with oil paintings. The menu, which changes every few months, features dishes such as crab and asparagus tulip with truffle vinaigrette and long-roasted duckling glazed in honey with cardamom and Vermouth. The set lunch is a real value, and the French wines draw serious oenophiles from far and wide. ◆ Continental ◆ Daily lunch and dinner. Reservations recommended. 589.5171

The Scotch House.

60 Scotch House If you want a cashmere sweater or scarf, you will do better here in terms of quality and price than at **Harrods.** The shop has a huge selection of the best Scottish woolens, including 300 tartans and a reference book that can match names with patterns. ◆ M-Sa. 2 Brompton Rd (at Knightsbridge). 581.2151. Tube: Knightsbridge. Also at: 84-86 Regent St (between Air and Glasshouse Sts). 734.0203. Tube: Piccadilly Circus

60 Mr. Chow ★★★$$$ The restaurant's popularity dates back to 1968, when owner Michael Chow decided to combine the style and exuberance of an Italian restaurant with the finest Chinese cooking. The decor is chrome and dimmed glass, and the inventive menu is explained in down-to-earth language. Try the velvet chicken or specialty noodles. ◆ Chinese ◆ Daily lunch and dinner. Reservations recommended. 151 Knightsbridge (between Brompton Rd and Knightsbridge Green). 589.7347. Tube: Knightsbridge

61 Basil Street Hotel $$$ Traditional English charm abounds at this 93-room hotel, which has been owned by the same family since it was built in 1910. An old-fashioned, antiques filled delight, the place rambles eccentrically from floor to floor. It has a loyal clientele of English country folk who make twice-yearly trips to London to shop and see plays. Afternoon tea here is an institution, and it's served in a lounge that looks like a setting for an Agatha Christie novel, untouched by the passage of time. The restaurant sticks to no-fuss, traditional fare such as salmon fish cake or roast beef. ◆ 8 Basil St (at Hooper's Ct). 581.3311; fax 581.3693. Tube: Knightsbridge

62 Katherine Hamnett Decorated with minimalist flair, this shop is a showplace for the eponymous designer's witty creations, whether it's a slinky party dress or a safari-style suit. There is menswear, too, and au courant shoe designs. ◆ M-Sa. 20 Sloane St (between Hans Crescent and Basil St). 823.1002. Tube: Knightsbridge

63 Tomasz Starzewski This London-born designer combines fun and elegance in his daywear, short sexy cocktail dresses, and bold evening gowns. His new flagship store has ready-to-wear clothes, including his Gold Label, exclusive to the shop, as well as couture and a bridal collection. ◆ M-Sa. 177-178 Sloane St (between Cottage Walk and Harriet St). 235.4526. Tube: Knightsbridge

ree For All in London

ndon, one of the most exhilarating cities to visit, is
so one of the most expensive. Pricey temptations
ound, from queenly lodgings and luxurious
staurants to exquisite antiques and trendy
utiques. Still, there are plenty of great things
do in this city that don't cost a king's ransom.
fact, the following activities are free to royals
d commoners alike.

Watch the traditional spectacles of the Changing
of the Guard at **Buckingham Palace** (in the
orning) and the Ceremony of the Keys at the
wer of London (at night).

Listen to the rabble rousers and soapbox
pontificators who address crowds at **Speakers'
rner** in the northeastern corner of **Hyde Park** on
nday mornings. It's a great bit of real-life theater.

Browse one (or all) of the great museums in
London that don't charge admission, including
e **British Museum**, the **National Gallery**, the
ational Portrait Gallery, Sir John Soane's
useum, the **Wallace Collection**, and the **Tate
allery.** Many of the other major institutions waive
eir admission charges for the last hour before
osing, including the **Natural History Museum**, the
cience Museum, the **Victoria and Albert Museum**,
d the **Museum of London**. And several smaller
useums also admit visitors gratis, such as the
ank of England Museum, the **National Postal
useum**, and the **Guildhall Clock Museum**.

Sit in the public galleries at the **Houses
of Parliament** and witness the intricate
achinations of British politics.

5 Stroll through the lovely small oasis of **St.
James's Park,** with its peaceful, tree-bordered
lake, flowers, ducks, geese, and even pelicans. From
the footbridge spanning the lake there's a fine view
of **Buckingham Palace.**

6 Check out original artworks and handicrafts (and
meet their creators) on Sunday in front of the
railings on **Bayswater Road,** near **Speaker's Corner.**

7 Attend the peaceful 8AM communion service
at **Westminster Abbey** and get a sense of this
beautiful church sans crowds of tourists.

8 Listen to sublime chamber or choral music at
St.-Martin-in-the-Fields at lunchtime concerts
held Monday, Tuesday, and Friday at 1:05PM.
(Call 207/839.8362 to reserve seats.) Also, some
of the small churches in the **City of London** present
lunchtime concerts during the week. (For details, call
or visit the **City of London Information Centre,** St.
Paul's Churchyard, 207/332.1456.)

9 Inspect the usually valuable and frequently
artistic possessions of other people by attending
the pre-auction displays at **Bonham's, Christie's,
Phillips,** and **Sotheby's.** It's like visiting a museum,
art gallery, and antiques shop in one go.

10 Picnic in **Hampstead Heath** on the verdant
lawn of historic **Kenwood House,** which
slopes down to a splendid ornamental lake. On most
summer weekends, strains of symphonic works can
be heard wafting from the concert bowl on the site.
And before or after your alfresco meal, see the
paintings of Gainsborough and Vermeer in the
Robert Adam–designed 18th-century house.

HARVEY NICHOLS

64 Harvey Nichols Like two guards at each
end of Sloane Street, the **General Trading
Company** at Sloane Square and **Harvey
Nichols** at Knightsbridge are the arbiters of
London's jet set chic. "Harvey Nicks," as it's
lovingly called, is a department store devoted
to fashion—you'll find only designer labels
here. (Britcom fans will recognize this place
as a favorite haunt of Patsy and Edina, the
debauched fashion mavens on the hit BBC
sitcom "Absolutely Fabulous.") Dior and
Giorgio Armani have been joined by such
innovators as Kenzo and Katherine Hamnett.
Menswear is in the basement, fashionable
accessories on the ground floor, big-name
designers on the first. On the fifth floor
is a trendy food hall. ♦ Daily. 109-125
Knightsbridge (at Sloane St). 235.5000.
Tube: Knightsbridge

Within Harvey Nichols:

The Fifth Floor Restaurant ★★$$
This chic barrel-vaulted restaurant, with
views of London as well as of the adjoining
cafe, is the perfect setting for the ultra-smart
shoppers who flock here. Chef Henry Harris's
specialties include oysters and lemon sole
with aioli (garlic mayonnaise) and crispy quail
with cashew nuts and coriander. For dessert
try the chocolate marquise with coffee sauce.
♦ Modern British ♦ Daily lunch and dinner.
Reservations recommended. 235.5250

Fifth Floor Cafe ★$$ You can't make
reservations at this trendy spot, so join the
line for the light lunch, which might include
twice-baked goat cheese soufflé or a salad.
Or you can pop in for cappuccino or tea—
and rest those tired feet. In the evenings
there is a fixed-price three-course menu.
Service can be brisk at lunch and during peak
shopping times. ♦ Modern British ♦ M-Sa
breakfast, lunch, snacks, and dinner; Su
lunch, snacks, and dinner. 235.5250

Yo!Sushi ★★$$ This is a smaller and
quieter branch of the Japanese restaurant
of the same name found on Poland Street.
With 100 different sushi items, it's an ideal
choice for a quick meal to revitalize you when
shopping at "Harvey Nicks." ♦ Japanese
♦ Daily lunch and dinner. 235.5250

65 Sheraton Park Tower $$$$ With a
modern silhouette that makes an impact on

the Knightsbridge skyline, this circular luxury hotel offers a marvelously egalitarian notion: 273 equal-size rooms (and 20 suites) with views. The higher up the 17 stories, the better the room *and* the view, and you can count on spacious comfort and reliable service. There is also a more expensive executive floor with such services as two-hour laundering and a valet to unpack your suitcase. Afternoon tea is served in the **Knightsbridge Lounge** (open to the public). ♦ 101 Knightsbridge (at William St). 235.8050, 800/334.8484; fax 235.8231. Tube: Knightsbridge

Within the Sheraton Park Tower:

Restaurant One-o-One ★★$$$ Facing Knightsbridge, this restaurant is within a conservatory, which gives it a commodious, airy feeling. Chef Pascal Proyart, from a Brittany coastal village, indulges his flair for the preparation of seafood, and *cuisine de la mer* is the theme here, although meat and vegetarian dishes are also served. Try the sea bass fillet in a caviar cream sauce. ♦ Continental ♦ Daily lunch and dinner. 235.6067

66 Mandarin Oriental Hyde Park Hotel $$$$ More a stately home than a hotel, this property (pictured above) is a Knightsbridge institution. Most people still refer to it as the "Hyde Park" although since 1996 the new owners have officially added their brand name. The splendor is Edwardian: marble entrance hall, gilded and molded ceilings, and Persian carpets the size of cricket fields leave you wondering how **Buckingham Palace** can hold a candle to it; at any rate, one suspects the service is far better here. Guests have included Winston Churchill, Madonna, the three famous operatic tenors—Pavarotti, Domingo, and Carreras—and Mahatma Gandhi, for whom a goat was milked each day. The hotel keeps adding luxury refurbishments with no expense spared. The 187 rooms and suites are country-house size, individually decorated, and furnished with antiques. There is also a fitness center. Adjoining the **Restaurant on the Park** is The

Lounge, open 24 hours for everything from coffee to snacks. ♦ 66 Knightsbridge (between Albert and Edinburgh Gates). 235.4552, 800/526.6566 in the US; fax 201.3619. Tube: Knightsbridge

Within the Mandarin Oriental Hyde Park Hotel

The Restaurant on the Park ★★$$$ This grandly proportioned, recently refurbished restaurant overlooks the greenery of **Hyde Park**'s Rotten Row. Underneath the crystal chandeliers, dishes from northern Italy and the Mediterranean reflect the trend to lighter meals and healthy eating. Chef David Nicholls and his team produce such innovative fare as cream of aubergine, pot-au-feu of lamb with spring greens, roast veal sweetbreads, and for dessert, raspberry crème brulée. This is also a wonderful venue for a grand afternoon tea: Choose from 12 kinds of sinfully delicious pastries, all to the accompaniment of a pianist. ♦ Continental ♦ Daily breakfast, lunch, tea, and dinner. Jacket and tie requested for lunch and dinner. 235.2000

The Bar Decorated with bookshelves, this library alcove also has sofas for relaxing. It serves drinks and snacks, and a pianist plays every evening. ♦ M-Sa; Su noon-10:30PM

The Restaurant Marco Pierre White ★★★$$$$ The controversial young chef Marco Pierre White regularly faces a combination of bouquets and brickbats from critics. His best creations, such as pig's trotter stuffed with veal and poached sweetbreads, are deemed brilliant; in other dishes, the ingredients are rated as too daringly mismatched. (The *Michelin Guide,* however, has been impressed enough to keep awarding the restaurant three stars—its highest honor.) The well-constructed set menu is a better value than the à la carte, but whichever you choose, dining here is expensive. ♦ Modern British ♦ M-F lunch and dinner; Sa dinner. Reservations recommended. 259.5380

THE BERKELEY

KNIGHTSBRIDGE LONDON

67 Berkeley $$$$ It is pronounced the "*Bark*-lee," and despite the pervasive theme of wealthy elegance, the hotel has a personality of its own. It is known for providing amenities to suit every whim, including a rooftop indoor/outdoor swimming pool and a health club with sauna, gym, steam room, and beauty treatment rooms. Such distinguished luxury is usually associated with things of the past, but this version of the hotel is relatively new, built in 1972 with a major refurbishment in 1995. The old **Berkeley,** which sat on the corner of

Berkeley Street and Piccadilly, wasn't left behind; the charming reception room, designed by a young and then-unknown architect named **Edwin Lutyens,** was re-erected here. It is this incredible attention to detail that makes the hotel one of the most popular in London. ♦ Wilton Pl (between Wilton Crescent and Knightsbridge). 235.6000, 212/838.3110 in New York City, 800/223.6800 elsewhere in the US; fax 235.4330. Tube: Knightsbridge, Hyde Park Corner

Within the Berkeley:

Berkeley Restaurant ★★$$$
Bartolozzi's 18th-century reproductions of the queen's Holbein collection adorn the paneled walls of this very English room furnished in Colefax and Fowler chintzes and lime-oaked paneling, with a portrait of Sir Thomas More observing the elegant surroundings. Chef Andrew Turner's food is very tasty, with skillful handling of veal, game in season, and fish. ♦ Continental ♦ Daily lunch and dinner. 235.6000

Minema Café ★$$ Named after the adjacent cinema, this brasserie serves Mediterranean-style lunches and dinners, as well as drinks and light snacks. ♦ Cafe ♦ Daily lunch and dinner. 235.6000

Vong ★★$$$ Although part of the hotel, this trend-setting restaurant with its own entrance has become popular for its exotic cuisine, a fusion of French and Thai that was introduced to London by the New York–based chef Jean-Georges Vongerichten, who also owns this place. The spare decor—natural stone tabletops, chunky wooden chairs, and a window into the kitchen—allows diners to see and be seen. Expect such dishes as red curry with baby vegetables and flat rice noodles and, for dessert, banana, kiwi, and passion fruit with white-pepper ice cream. ♦ French/Thai ♦ M-Sa lunch and dinner. Reservations recommended. 235.1010

La Tante Claire ★★★$$$$ This familiar name on the London restaurant scene has set up shop in a new location. Triple Michelin-starred chef Pierre Koffman's à la carte menu is predictably pricey, but the set lunch is a very good value. Delectable items include lobster risotto, roasted woodcock, and grilled Dover sole. ♦ French ♦ M-F lunch and dinner. Reservations recommended. Wilton Pl (between Wilton Crescent and Knightsbridge). 823.2003. Tube: Knightsbridge, Hyde Park Corner

68 Grenadier ★★★$$$ The atmosphere of this pub is as old and military-like as in the days when it was the Officer's Mess for the Duke of Wellington's soldiers, complete with a ghost of an officer who was beaten to death for cheating at cards. Both the bar and the restaurant are tiny, but the service is of the highest standard. So if you fancy a pint of the best bitter and a pub meal which is a cut above the rest, this is the place. ♦ British ♦ Daily lunch and dinner. Reservations recommended. Old Barrack Yard, Wilton Row (at Wilton Pl). 235.3074. Tube: Hyde Park Corner

69 Lanesborough $$$$ Overlooking the hurly-burly traffic chaos of **Hyde Park Corner,** this property was originally a hospital built in the Classical/Greek Revival style of Portland stone in 1829. Now it's a welcoming, self-indulgent place to stay where every detail has been thoughtfully considered. When billionaire Texan Caroline Rose Hunt acquired the property, she flew in the face of prudence by spending a reputed $1.7 million on *each* of the 95 guest rooms and suites—for a total of $161.5 million—despite the recession. Well, the *Times* heralded the result as "a sumptuous temple of luxury," and a stunning landmark was transformed. Inside are polished marble floors and Neo-Georgian furnishings; even the windows are triple-glazed against traffic noise. There is 24-hour butler service for all rooms on a complimentary basis, so you don't even have to unpack yourself (or iron the wrinkles from your clothes). Another nice touch is the personalized stationery. ♦ Hyde Park Corner (at Knightsbridge). 259.5599, 800/999.1828; fax 259.5606. Tube: Hyde Park Corner

Within the Lanesborough:

Conservatory ★★$$$ The setting is perfect for hot summer nights, with a high glass roof, giant potted palms, candlelight, and piano music setting a serene mood as you enjoy your meal. Chef Paul Gaylor's imaginative dishes include turbot roasted on the bone with rosemary *jus* or spice-roasted duckling with ginger and star anise. Good vegetarian choices include basil gnocchi with seasonal green vegetables. There is live music Monday through Thursday and jazz at Sunday lunch; on Friday and Saturday a full band provides the sound for dancing. ♦ International ♦ Daily breakfast, lunch, afternoon tea, and dinner. Jacket required at dinner. 259.5599

Library Bar This cozy room has solid bookshelves that cocoon you from the hectic world as you sip great cocktails or sample the impressive list of vintage whiskies and cognacs and enjoy the pianist's pleasantly paced music. ♦ M-Sa; Su noon-10:30PM. 259.5599

Which city in Europe is the friendliest and the best to live in? London, according to a survey of business executives and diplomats conducted by *Fortune* magazine.

Marylebone/ Camden Town

A sedate, almost feminine feel characterize this elegant section of London. Perhaps th charm should come as no surprise, si a woman, Margaret Harley, daughter of Edward Harley, the Earl of Oxford, originally inherited the land, which has frequently been owned by and passed on to women. J.M.W. Turner and Allan Ramsay were just two of the artists who exercised their talents on **Harley Street**, Elizabeth Barrett scribbled in secret while waiting for her true love, Robert Brow to whisk her away from nearby **Wimpole Street.** Today, enigmatic Marylebone displays a doppelgänger personality. On the one hand, it's cultured and refined: can stroll through the royal lawns at **Regent's Park**, take in Shakespeare at the C **Air Theatre**, or visit the **Wallace Collection**, a mansion containing a number o artistic treasures, including an astounding array of 18th-century French furnitur and Old Master paintings. On the other hand, the neighborhood is playful and whimsical: There's the **London Zoo, Madame Tussaud's, Lord's Cricket Grou** and **Baker Street,** home to the most famous detective (either real or make-believ ever to have sleuthed through London: Sherlock Holmes.

Northeast of Marylebone (a shortened version of the church name, **St. Mary by the Bourne**—Bourne being an alias for the **Tyburn River**) lies Camden Town, which also originally belonged to a woman—in this instance, the wife of the first Earl of Camden. Once pastures and coal wharfs, Camden Town is now a somewhat bohemian neighborhood, its cottages furnished to overflowing with antiques and cellular phones. When not converting Victoriana, the occupants, who range from novelists to spiritual seekers, wander down to **Camden Market**, one of London's most interesting street markets, and to the burgeoning artists' and craftsmen's colony of **Camden Lock.**

City code 0171 unless otherwise noted.

1 Cavendish Square It's always so cold and windy in this stately square that it's almost possible to feel the tears of Mrs. Horatio Nelson (who lived here in 1791) at being continually abandoned by her admiral husband. **John Prince** laid the square out in 1717, but it wasn't until 1761, when George II's daughter Amelia came to live at **No. 16,** that it really came into its own. You can see Jacob Epstein's sculpture, the *Madonna and Child*, standing among the trees. ♦ At Cavendish Pl and Wigmore St, and Holles and Harley Sts. Tube: Oxford Circus

2 All Souls Church John Nash designed this church (his only one in London) as an architectural landmark for the end of Regent Street and to mark the bend of the road westward that links up with Portland Place. Built in 1822-24, the church was much criticized then because it looked so unusual. **Nash** had given it a round portico, and the whole edifice was topped by a very sharp spire encircled with another round colonnade of pillars. Although his stagy mix of architectural styles was ingenious, Nash was publicly lampooned. A cartoon showed the architect impaled on the metal spike atop his steeple. Nash's reply was that criticism exalted him. The church is now the venue for musical events and some broadcasts for the nearby BBC. ♦ M-F, Su. Langham Pl (at Riding House St). 580.3522. Tube: Oxford Circus

3 Portland Place When **Robert Adam** laid out this thoroughfare between 1776 and 1780, it was considered one of the finest London streets in an architectural sense—that was part of the reason **John Nash** came here to add Regent Street to its southern end. ♦ Between Langham Pl and Park Crescent. Tube: Regent's Park, Oxford Circus

3 Broadcasting House On Portland Place, at the curve of Langham Street, stands the BBC's **Broadcasting House,** built by **George Val Myers** and **F.J. Watson-Hart** in 1931. Sculpture by Eric Gill decorates the outside, including the Shakespearean figures of Prospero and Ariel from *The Tempest;* this was Gill's way of showing Ariel, who has become the symbol of broadcasting, being sent out into the world. A visitors' center— **BBC Experience**—opened in late 1997, so now you can take a guided tour through the facility, see displays and hands-on exhibits about British TV and radio history, watch a radio show being recorded, and even try your hand at making a program yourself. There's also a gift shop and a cafe. ♦ Admission. Daily. Reservations required. Portland Pl (between Langham and Duchess Sts). 0870/603.0304

3 Villandry Now in a new location, this shop may have high white ceilings and automatic glass doors, but what it lacks in charm and character when compared to the original, it more than makes up for with a greater choice of goods—and there is an even larger restaurant attached. Delicacies, collected by foodie owner Jean Charles Carrarini, include a variety of breads—such as French, Italian, and Parisian sourdough—as well as jams and olive oils, original salads, picnic baskets, and special pastries baked on the premises. The shop also offers gourmet cheeses and chocolates, some made in Britain and others imported from the Continent. Neighborhood residents, dressed in their best tweeds, gather here every Wednesday when fresh produce arrives from Paris. ♦ M-Sa. 170 Great Portland St (at Weymouth St). 631.3131. Tube: Great Portland Street

Within Villandry:

Villandry Dining Room ★★$$
Deceptively plain-looking, with a warehouse-like floor, pale walls, and high ceilings, this new restaurant offers some first rate fare, including mussels with *rouille* and croutons, grilled sea bass with baby leeks and salsa verde, and risotto primavera. The desserts are equally excellent: chocolate cake, lemon ricotta cheesecake, and pear *tatin*. ♦ French ♦ M-F breakfast, lunch, and dinner; Sa brunch and dinner. 631.3131

4 Harley Street This area is one gracious band of stately Georgian houses, all designed with the eye for proportion and attention to detail that this era left as its architectural legacy. Artists such as J.M.W. Turner and Allan Ramsay lived here first; then, beginning in the 1840s, private doctors took it over, and today it is wall to wall with specialists catering to the ills of the wealthy. ♦ Between Cavendish Sq and Marylebone Rd. Tube: Regent's Park, Oxford Circus

---

Restaurants/Clubs: Red   Hotels: Blue
Shops/ 🍴 Outdoors: Green   Sights/Culture: Black

WIGMORE HALL

5 Wigmore Hall Friedrich Beckstein built this concert hall in 1901 as an afterthought to his spacious piano showrooms. Its near-perfect acoustics make it a regular venue for classical concerts, particularly those performed by chamber orchestras. Performances take place daily, including Sunday morning. ♦ Box office: daily. 36 Wigmore St (between Wimpole and Welbeck Sts). 935.2141. Tube: Bond Street

6 Button Queen This tiny, old-fashioned shop really lives up to its name: It is stocked with every kind of button you can imagine—from ordinary modern styles to antique military ones. The buttons are made of materials ranging from plastic and metal to leather and animal horn. ♦ M-Sa. 19 Marylebone La (between Wigmore and Hinde Sts). 935.1505. Tube: Bond Street

7 Wallace Collection This off-the-beaten-path museum houses one of the finest collections of French furniture and porcelain, Old Master paintings, and objets d'art in the world. It is arguably one of London's major museums—and it's also one of its best-kept secrets. But visiting this grand town house, built between 1776 and 1788, and seeing its owner's private art collection is a much more intimate experience than going to a museum. The rich and varied collection of 5,470 objects was acquired by successive marquesses of Hertford during the 18th and 19th centuries. The first marquess (1719-94) was partial to Canalettos; the second, who lived between 1743 and 1823, added Gainsborough's *Mrs. Robinson* and Reynolds's *Nelly O'Brien*. He acquired the lease on **Hertford House** (the name of the present building) in 1797. The third marquess (1777-1842) was a close friend of the Prince of Wales (later George IV), and collected French furniture and porcelain and 17th-century Dutch paintings. The fourth marquess (1800-70), an eccentric who lived most of his life in seclusion in Paris, collected a large number of 18th-century French paintings by Watteau, Boucher, Fragonard, and Greuze, as well as works by several old masters (including masterpieces by Rembrandt, Rubens, Poussin, and Velázquez). He also made lavish purchases of 18th-century French furniture by Boulle, Crescent, and Riesener, including the chest of drawers made for Louis XV's bedroom at Versailles and various pieces made for Marie Antoinette, not to mention what is now the world's richest public collection of Sèvres porcelain. Don't miss the exquisite gold boxes or the wrought-iron and gilt-bronze staircase balustrade, which was made in about 1720 for Louis XV's Palais Mazarin (now the Bibliothèque Nationale). It was sold around 1870 as scrap iron but rescued by Sir Richar Wallace, the fourth marquess's illegitimate son, who inherited the collection and brough it to **Hertford House,** adding the European arms and armor and medieval and Renaissance works of art. Just after Wallace death in 1890, his widow bequeathed the collection to the nation and it opened to the public in 1900. The museum plans to celebrate its centenary in June 2000 by opening a study center and new galleries in the now-unused basement for exhibitions, watercolors, and miniatures. ♦ Free. M-Sa; S 2-5PM. Manchester Sq (between Spanish Pl and Manchester St). 935.0687. Tube: Bond Street

Stephen Bull

8 Stephen Bull ★★★$$$ At this stylish restaurant, you'll find innovative culinary combinations: cod with Cumbrian ham or roast fillet of pork with apple chutney and thyme. The wine list, running to about 100 bottles, is superb. ♦ Modern British ♦ M-F lunch and dinner; Sa dinner. Reservations required. 5-7 Blandford St (between Thayer and Manchester Sts). 486.9696. Tube: Baker Street, Bond Street. Also at: 71 St. John St (near St. John's La). 490.1750. Tube: Farringdon

9 Marylebone Lane and Marylebone High Street An old village at heart, this area is full of expensive specialty food shops and boutiques that cater to the wealthy (and healthy) relatives of the ill who pay court to the good doctors of nearby Harley Street. Charles Dickens, who lived all over London, wrote 11 books when he resided here. ♦ Marylebone La (between Oxford and Thaye Sts); Marylebone High St (between Thayer St and Marylebone Rd). Tube: Baker Street, Bond Street

10 Patisserie Valerie at Maison Sagne ★★★$ This link in the popular chain of London tearooms has become a Marylebone institution. It is a gathering place of great cachet—everyone is someone at **Valerie's** or Saturday morning. Butterfly-light croissants and French cakes and pastries, and light salads and sandwiches are served for lunch. ♦ Cafe ♦ Daily breakfast, lunch, and afternoor tea. 105 Marylebone High St (between St. Vincent and Moxon Sts). 935.6240. Tube: Baker Street, Bond Street. Also at: 44 Old Compton St (between Frith and Dean Sts). 437.3466. Tube: Piccadilly Circus, Leicester Square; 215 Brompton Rd (between Yeoman's Row and Egerton Terr). 823.9971. Tube: Knightsbridge, South Kensington

11 Daunt James Daunt was a **Cambridge** graduate–turned–New York City banker before he started this travel bookshop, a place that makes it seem unnecessary to travel anywhere else. The shop takes you back in time to a turn-of-the-century galleried

Bloomsbury studio, where books are arranged by nation rather than by genre, with fiction, poetry, and nonfiction grouped together. ♦ M-Sa. 83 Marylebone High St (between Moxon and Paddington Sts). 224.2295. Tube: Baker Street

12 St. Marylebone Parish Church Built by **Thomas Hardwick** between 1813 and 1817, this church is splendidly ornate on the outside, with gold caryatids on the steeple. Halfway through its construction, plans shifted, turning what had begun as a chapel into a parish church. The resulting interior was therefore quite dramatic—much more like a theater than a church—but today its simplicity gives the place a tranquil atmosphere. Elizabeth Barrett and Robert Browning were married here. These days, the building doubles as an active holistic healing center. ♦ M-Sa. Marylebone Rd (between Marylebone High St and Nottingham Pl). 935.7315. Tube: Baker Street

13 Madame Tussaud's The queues are long here, but everyone thinks it's worth the wait. Forget whatever reservations you may have about waxworks—there is nothing ordinary about this place. A British institution since 1802, it continues to be extensively refurbished and keeps up-to-date with current world personalities.

Mme. T learned her trade making death masks in Paris during the French Revolution, and those of Louis XVI and Marie Antoinette are displayed on spikes beside the actual blade that beheaded them. The oldest surviving likeness, dating from 1765, is that of Mme. du Barry, also known as "The Sleeping Beauty." A mechanism hidden in the bodice of her dress allows the figure to "breathe." King Henry VIII is shown surrounded by all six of his wives, and there is a full re-creation of the royal family. The wax likenesses are most often modeled from life and are never displayed behind glass. They stand in small tableaux, grouped as figures from history, politics,

literature, sports, and entertainment, and new figures are added regularly, such as Pierce Brosnan after his first James Bond film.

One room is devoted to **Contemporary Heroes,** where Arnold Schwarzenegger and Bill Clinton share space with Oprah Winfrey, Elizabeth Taylor (this is her third model), magician David Copperfield, and Joanna Lumley (who plays Patsy in the hit BBC sitcom "Absolutely Fabulous"). Culture buffs can admire figures ranging from highbrow (Luciano Pavarotti) to down-to-earth (Dudley Moore). **Superstars and Legends** includes Elvis Presley and Marilyn Monroe.

The **Chamber of Horrors** has been completely revamped to create realistic sets and spine-tingling sound effects. Displays include "Visions of Hell" with Vlad the Impaler, and torture wheels with suspended victims. There is also Joan of Arc at the stake, a drowning pirate at his execution, and Newgate prisoners from the Victorian era. Serial killers start with Jack the Ripper. Elsewhere you can see James Dean and Humphrey Bogart on a Hollywood set.

The £11-million ride **Spirit of London** has visitors traveling in cars representing London taxis (the same firm builds both) through a dark tunnel. The city's heritage is brought to life by modern technology, as animated wax figures take you through London's great events. One of the most impressive is the figure of William Shakespeare, quill in hand, writing plays.

Even the cafe has entertaining things to do, thanks to its traditional amusement arcade machines. And the shop is furnished to represent different eras of shopping in London.

Also on the grounds is the **London Planetarium,** which has had a £4.5-million relaunch of its shows and keeps adding new ones like **Planetary Quest,** which uses state-of-the art 3-D computer and video effects to take you into the solar system as if you were a space traveler. You see Neptune's hurricane storms, the rings and moons of Saturn, whirling star fields, footsteps on the moon, a sky glow from Earth, and you even zoom through London. To avoid waiting in line for the museum, either visit the planetarium first and buy a combined ticket or book by credit card 24 hours in advance. ♦ Separate admissions to Madame Tussaud's and the planetarium (combined tickets also available). Daily. Marylebone Rd (between York Gate and Allsop Pl). 935.6861. Tube: Baker Street

---

It was the nation and the race dwelling all around the globe that had the lion's heart. I had the luck to be called upon to give the roar.

—Sir Winston Churchill

The Game's Afoot

For legions of visitors, a trip to London means a chance to steep themselves in the mystique of Sherlock Holmes, whereas Sir Arthur Conan Doyle is relegated to second place behind his creation. With societies devoted to the fictional hawk-eyed sleuth and fans continuing to write him, it's not surprising that the upper part of **Baker Street** (around the Baker Street tube) has become an enclave of Holmes enterprises. There's now the **Sherlock Holmes Museum**, kitted out with kitsch—deerstalker hat, cloak, fan letters—it's all there in a fine old house. The Victorian bobby standing guard outside completes the scene. (The address is faked—the "real" site of the fictional address was down the road at **No. 215**, home of the Abbey National Building Society.) Attached to the museum is the equally twee **Mrs. Hudson's Restaurant,** serving Victorian-themed dishes at lunch, afternoon tea, and dinner. If you're looking for better-quality souvenirs than the schlock Sherlock baubles at the museum, cross the street to the **Sherlock Holmes**

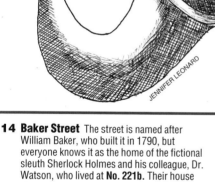

Memorabilia Company, where you'll find everything from tweed hats and T-shirts to playing cards and postcards.

For researchers and scholars, a small room at **Marylebone Library** (Marylebone Rd, at Upper Montagu St, 0171/798.1206) is devoted to a collection of books on both Holmes and Conan Doyle. The custodian, Catherine Cooke, is the person to contact for an appointment to view the collection.

Thirsty Sherlockians will want to quaff an ale at the **Sherlock Holmes Pub** (10 Northumberland Ave, at Craven Passage, 0171/930.2644), near **Trafalgar Square.** Located on the site of the **Northumberland Hotel** where Sir Henry Baskerville *(The Hound of the Baskervilles)* lived, the pub, like the museum mentioned above, is crammed with memorabilia about the great detective. Upstairs you'll see a replication of Sherlock's Baker Street sitting room, overflowing with mementos representing his famous cases—from footprint casts to handcuffs to a pistol. You can almost hear his violin and smell his pipe tobacco.

Recently, Sir Arthur Conan Doyle has started to get some recognition in his own right. Near Baker Street at **7 Upper Wimpole Street** (between Weymouth and Devonshire Sts) is a plaque put up by the **City of Westminster** and the Arthur Conan Doyle Society that reads: "Arthur Conan Doyle, Author 1859-1930, worked and wrote here in 1891." (Note that a block away, at **2 Devonshire Place,** corner of **Devonshire Street,** is a building called **Conan Doyle House**; the resident dentist who named it was hoping that the commemorative plaque would grace *his* building. Nice try, but your motives, dear dentist, were elementary.)

14 Baker Street The street is named after William Baker, who built it in 1790, but everyone knows it as the home of the fictional sleuth Sherlock Holmes and his colleague, Dr. Watson, who lived at **No. 221b.** Their house also was a fiction, but the Abbey National Building Society at **No. 215** is approximately at the right site, and it employs someone to answer letters still written to the great detective! (See "The Game's Afoot," above). ♦ Between Orchard St and Park Rd. Tube: Baker Street

14 Sherlock Holmes Memorabilia Company
Badges, chess sets, deerstalker hats, refrigerator magnets, key rings, pens, sweatshirts—whatever Sherlockiana you can imagine is for sale at this upscale shop. ♦ M-Sa. 230 Baker St (between Marylebone Rd and Allsop Pl). 486.1426. Tube: Baker Street

15 Sherlock Holmes Museum It's now possible to visit the fictional detective's "home"—at a fictional address, of course—in this fine Victorian house devoted to the supposed memorabilia of Holmes and Watson. The rooms are crammed with mementos, particularly the study, where you'll find souvenirs of the cases solved and letters written by the duo, along with Holmes's opium pipe and deerstalker hat. Kitschy details include the costumed "maid" who helps visitors take photos of the rooms. The basement shop sells mugs, ceramic figures, playing cards, and many other trinkets. ♦ Admission. Free entry to the shop only. Daily. 221b Baker St (between Melcombe St and Park Rd). 935.8866. Tube: Baker Street

Within the Sherlock Holmes Museum:

Mrs. Hudson's Restaurant ★$$$
Furnished like a Victorian dining room, the place is awash with knickknacks, plants, pictures, and china displays that supposedly belonged to Holmes's housekeeper. The food echoes the Victorian theme with such dishes

as bubble-and-squeak (cabbage and mashed potatoes), Baskerville game pie, and, for desserts, treacle pie or bread-and-butter pudding. ♦ English ♦ Daily lunch, afternoon tea, and dinner. 953.3130

16 Sea-Shell ★★$$ The wooden booths and communal tables of this famous fish-and-chips restaurant are always full—a testament to the tastiness of the varieties of batter-fried fish and the delectable chips (french fries). The prices, however, are a little higher than at most other eateries of this kind. A busy takeaway shop adjoins the restaurant. ♦ Fish-and-chips ♦ M-Sa lunch and dinner; Su lunch. 49-51 Lisson Grove (at Shroton St). 723.8703. Tube: Marylebone

17 Lord's Cricket Ground The gentle pop of a leather ball being hit by a willow cricket bat characterizes a game that remains a mystery to many Americans (and quite a few Brits as well). In England, if not around the world, this field beats at the very heart of the cricket scene, particularly once a year, when English teams attempt to overthrow the regular cricket dominance of Australia, Pakistan, and New Zealand. The current site was established in 1814, following a move by founder Thomas Lord from the Dorset Square area. You'll find the entrance to this hallowed ground farther along St. John's Wood Road, where the **W.G. Grace Memorial Gates** open onto the **Marylebone Cricket Club (MCC)**, the owners of this field, officially called **Lord's.** Guided tours of the grounds, including a museum of memorabilia dedicated to the sport, are now available daily year-round, except during matches. ♦ Admission for tours. Tours: noon and 2PM. St John's Wood Rd (between Wellington and Grove End Rds). 432.1033; www.lords.org. Tube: St. John's Wood

18 Regent's Park London is a city of parks and squares, and nowhere do nature and people coexist more gloriously than in this green space. The essence of **John Nash**'s original plan of 1811 to turn almost 500 acres of farmland into a park survived eight years of government commissions. His spectacular terraces, iced with stucco and lined with columns, surround the park, making it look like a gigantic wedding cake; the terraces are named after the titles of some of George III's children. **Cumberland Terrace** is the most splendid, with its magnificent pediment and 276-yard facade lined with Ionic columns;

Chester Terrace is the longest, stretching 313 yards with 52 Corinthian columns. The elegant **Clarence Terrace,** designed by **Decimus Burton** in 1823, is the smallest. The Neo-Georgian **Winfield House,** now the residence of the US ambassador, is located on the site of **St. Dunstan's Lodge,** designed in 1825 by **Burton;** the house was donated by F.W. Woolworth heiress Barbara Hutton, and now forms one of the few private areas of the park. The curiously shaped boating lake, reaching out in every direction and surrounded by ash groves, is undeniably romantic, as is the exquisite **Queen Mary's Garden,** which contains 40,000 rose bushes laid out in large beds, each with a different variety. **Regent's Canal** skirts the northern boundary of the park and runs for eight miles from Paddington to Limehouse and passes the animals at the **London Zoo.** ♦ Daily. Bounded by Outer Cir. Tube: Regent's Park

Within Regent's Park:

LONDON ZOO

London Zoo As the oldest zoo in the world, created in 1826, the gardens of the **Zoological Society of London** (the first society to shorten its name to "zoo") now spread over 36 enchanting acres of **Regent's Park.** Rather than being cooped up in depressing iron cages, most of the 6,000 animals roam in settings similar to their natural habitats—separated from the public by moats.

A large aquarium and a children's zoo were designed to make the animals more accessible, and the **Mappin Terraces** have been redesigned to house Asian mammals such as sloth bears. Ask on arrival about the schedule for feeding the lions, sea lions, and penguins, as well as washing the elephants. On Friday, see the snakes feeding on whole dead animals (ugh!). The zoo's focus is now on captive breeding of endangered species. There is a cafe, and fish-and-chips and pizza stalls. ♦ Admission. Daily. 722.3333

Open Air Theatre From May through early September, this delightful outdoor amphitheater, which seats 1,187, presents a season of Shakespeare works, as well as the occasional musical. For refreshments, there's a barbecue, cafe, and salad bar or you could opt to bring along a hamper from **Harrods** or **Fortnum & Mason.** That old adage "The show must go on" is taken as gospel here—it always does, despite rain, roaring jets, and hay fever. ♦ M-Sa May–early Sept. 486.2431

19 Primrose Hill Sixty-two acres seem inconsequential in comparison to **Regent's Park,** its larger neighbor to the south, yet this green space is beloved and well used by nearby residents for everything from kite flying to druidical ceremonies (seriously!). The grounds were once owned by **Eton College,** but in 1841, the site was made public, given in return for royal land closer to the school in Windsor. On a clear day, you can get a fantastic view from the top of the park— the summit measures around 219 feet—both of **Regent's Park** and of the whole vista of central London. No wonder Alan Bennett, V.S. Pritchett, and other celebrated literati have moved into the area. ♦ Bounded by Regent's Park, Prince Albert, and Primrose Hill Rds. Tube: Chalk Farm

20 Cecil Sharp House This is the headquarters of the **English Folk Dance and Song Society** and England's **National Folk Centre.** It was built in 1929 by **H.M. Fletcher** in honor of Sharp, who pioneered techniques of collecting and preserving folk songs. Inside, the **Vaughan Williams Memorial Library** houses more than 11,000 books on folklore, folk songs, and related interests, and more than 3,000 recordings. The center is busy, with dance and music sessions of all types taking place every day. If you'd like to learn morris dancing or clogging, or want to take part in a Celtic singers' night, you've come to the right place. The small shop inside sells tapes, books, folk instruments, and sheet music. A cafeteria and a bar are open during events. ♦ Shop: M-Sa. Library: M-F. 2 Regent's Park Rd (at Gloucester Ave). 485.2206. Tube: Camden Town

21 Camden Markets Camden Town markets just keep spreading and now cover several adjoining sites. The famous one is **Camden Market,** a huge weekend affair beginning in the northern reaches of Camden High Street where stallholders gather to sell fashion clothes and jewelry, as well as all sorts of artistic items. At Camden Lock Place is the **Camden Lock Market,** an area that is a crafts aficionado's paradise, with shops occupied by working artists who sell handmade furniture, rugs, pottery, baskets, and an abundance of high-quality gift items.

On the weekends, it changes its face, and the stallholders invade to lure tourists with everything from secondhand clothing to New Age crystals. Don't worry if you get lost; that's half the fun of experiencing Camden, since as long as you keep walking, you're bound to stumble onto something you simply can't resist purchasing. Be warned: It gets very crowded. ♦ Camden Market: Th-Su. Camden High St and surroundings. Tube: Camden Town. Camden Lock Market: Sa-Su; indoor stalls and shops Tu-Su. Camden Lock Pl (off Chalk Farm Rd). 284.2084. Tube: Camden Town

Within Camden Lock Market:

Jongleurs The comedy/cabaret show held in this nightclub inside **Ted's Bar** has spawned a wealth of famed British performers. Lenny Henry, Ben Elton, Ruby Wax, Stephen Fry, and Hugh Laurie (to name just a few) have all walked the boards here, and the club prides itself on providing the "Best of British Comedy." It is generally well worth the admission charge, which includes temporary membership, reserved seating, a drink from the bar, dinner, and entrance to the on-premises disco. The club is open only on Friday and Saturday.♦ Admission. F-Sa 7:30PM-2.30AM.Reservations recommended 924.2766. Also at: 49 Lavender Gardens (between Clapham Common North Side and Lavender Hill). 924.2766

22 Kennedy Hotel $$ Conveniently close to **Euston Station,** this is a modern property— not the place to stay if you're looking for traditional English ambience. While **Regent's Park** and **Madame Tussaud's** are nearby, the hotel also provides easy access to most of central London. All 360 rooms are equipped with hair dryers and tea- and coffee-making facilities. The informal **Spires Restaurant** within the hotel serves a wide range of items, from light snacks to international main dishes. ♦ 43 Cardington St (between Drummond St and Hampstead Rd). 387.4400 800/847.4358; fax 387.5122. Tube: Euston

23 Manatiy's ★★★$$$ Mary and Sabah Manatiy have done up this jazz supper club to look like a swanky watering hole of the 1950s with mirrors around the walls reflecting the opulent fabrics that robe the chairs in gold, red, or tiger-skin patterns. The 18-piece **Manatiy's Jazz Orchestra** plays on Monday night. Tuesday through Saturday night, guest artists are featured. Also, a DJ plays mellow music that reflects the style of American jazz/blues singers George Benson and Lionel Ritchie. The menu offers Mediterranean-style charcoal-grilled lamb, chicken, and fish dishes. The place swings in the evenings, and there's a cover charge; if you order a drink, you can get a table without having a meal. ♦ Supper club/Mediterranean ♦ Cover charge in the evening. M-Sa lunch and dinner to 3AM. Reservations recommended for dinner. 34-38 Eversholt St (at Doric Way). 388.6487. Tube: Euston

24 British Library The move from its location within the **British Museum** to a newly built £500-million home at St. Pancras is finally complete. In addition to this great library's 12 million volumes, a host of treasures— illuminated historical, musical, and literary manuscripts and maps— are on display in three galleries, including the large, firm signature of Elizabeth I on the order sentencing Robert Devereux, Earl of Essex, to death by beheading; two of the four surviving copies of the *Magna Carta* issued in 1215 by King John; the *Lindisfarne Gospels,* written and illuminated in 698; a Gutenberg Bible; the 15th-century *Canterbury Tales;* and a *First Folio* of Shakespeare's works. There are also a bookshop and a restaurant. ♦ Free. Daily. 96 Euston Rd (between Midland Rd and Ossulston St). 412.7000; www.bl.uk. Tube: King's Cross/St. Pancras

Bests

Adele D. Evans
Freelance Radio Broadcaster/Writer

Harrods Food Hall—A feast for all the senses. Still the biggest authentic foods paradise in the metropolis with impeccable service, and the sale bargains are definitely worth a detour.

Beauchamp Place—A little road in **Knightsbridge** full of designer boutiques—from **Deliss** and its bespoke shoe service to **Janet Reger** with her stunning lingerie and where it's always fun to watch the men shamefacedly returning their purchases for up- AND down-sizing.

Haymarket, Theatre Royal—Catch a glimpse of the infamous "woman in white" resident ghost in London's most magnificent auditorium complete with ceiling paintings. One of London's most elegant theatres—but then we are spoilt for choice!

Globe Theatre—Not the original Shakespeare one, of course, but a wonderful testament to Sam Wanamaker's tenacity and vision.

The **National Theatre** on the **South Bank**— anything!

Eurostar to Paris in 3 hours—Go there for lunch and back to London, the theater capital of the world, for a play/comedy/musical.

Chelsea Flower Show—Considered to be *the first event of the English summer social season.* Originally held in 1888 in the **Temple Gardens** on the **Embankment;** moved to the present site of **Sir Christopher Wren's Royal Hospital, Chelsea,** in 1913. Chat with the red-uniformed Chelsea Pensioners and be there on the last day, Friday, at 5PM when the plants are sold and the **Chelsea Bridge Road** becomes a sea of moving flowers. Witness the massacre at **Sloane Square** station when delphiniums get trapped in the tube doors!

Lamb & Flag pub, **Covent Garden**—Authentic, tiny, spit and sawdust 16th-century hostelry— don't forget to breathe in!

Walk everywhere—especially along **Pimlico Road** (just south of Sloane Square) to covet the contents of all the antiques and designer shops.

Lunch at the **National Gallery,** new **Sainsbury Wing**'s brasserie—A bird's-eye view across **Trafalgar Square** and excellent food—don't miss the fresh strawberry sabayon. If you run out of time because lunch is just too enjoyable, you can always claim, with reason, that you've "done a gallery." Or linger even longer and cross the road to **St. Martins-in-the-Fields** for a 7:30PM concert.

Do go to the **Royal Academy,** the largest contemporary art exhibition in the world with work by new and living artists.

Visit the **Royal Parks**—the lungs of London with more open spaces than any other capital in the world. **St. James's** is very romantic and the most ornamental—ducks, geese, and pelicans swim on the lake: You can feed them and have a bird's-eye view of "Buck House" too!

Take a boat to **Greenwich** and stand astride the Greenwich meridian.

Visit **Edward Stanford**'s bookshop in **Covent Garden** with its wonderful collection of travel guides and maps to plan your next trip, but always remember "when a man is tired of London, he is tired of life; for there is in London all that life can afford" (Samuel Johnson). I'm sure that he meant women too!

Matthew Saunders
Architectural Historian

Sir John Soane's Museum—An intense and idiosyncratic house-museum, created by England's most influential Neo-Classical architect.

Highgate Cemetery—Victorian bombast with Egyptian catacombs and Baroque tombs of the 19th century, set amid trees and foxes. Includes the grave of Karl Marx.

Bloomsbury—Set piece 18th-century townscape around the **British Musem**—the Georgian terrace was England's greatest gift to European architecture alongside Perpendicular Gothic.

St. Pancras—The hotel in front of the station on **Euston Road.** Freshly cleaned—looking just as it did when **Gilbert Scott** designed it in 1869-74.

St. Bartholomew's The Great—Glorious internally begrimed Romanesque—so unexpected in the **City.** Founded 1123.

Spencer House (Open on Sundays only except in August)—London's most spectacular reclaimed 18th-century interior.

Bloomsbury/ Holborn

Bloomsbury is the **Oxford** of London, a sheltered kingdom of scholars that is rule both by the past, in the form of the **British Museum**, and by the future, which is constantly being shaped i the halls of the **University of London**. Between these institutions lie spaciou squares filled with shade trees and rosebushes. Illustrious ghosts haunt the streets where Clive Bell struggled with literary criticism, W.B. Yeats struggled with poetic philosophy, and Virginia and Leonard Woolf struggled with themselves and each other—and with T.S. Eliot whenever he came to tea. Though a bookish air pervades the neighborhood, Bloomsbury is not devoid of everyday pleasures. Modern minds swap theories over a pint in the **Plough** head tutors munch chips in the **Museum Cafe**, and burgeoning novelists bu pullovers in **Westaway & Westaway**.

In striking contrast, Holborn is decidedly Dickensian, almost as if the author himself still resided at **Dickens House**. His footsteps are easy to follow through the ancient legal byways of two **Inns of Court**; into **Bleeding Heart Yard**, which is portrayed in *Little Dorritt*; and finally to the **Old Bailey** and th largest meat market in the world, **Smithfield**, with their grim atmospheres of crime and slaughter. Since this area covers so many miles of terrain, you should pick and choose your stops in keeping with your interests.

1 University of London In 1826, a group of enlightened sponsors decided to establish a center of higher learning that would not be tied to the Anglican Church and would offer a more liberal and wide-ranging curriculum than other universities. Opponents said it wouldn't last. But over the next 170 years, the "godless college in Gower Street" built a formidable reputation, and today it comprises 50 colleges. Currently, its full-time student body exceeds 75,000.

Although the university received its charter relatively late, it has made up for lost time, scoring a string of firsts over the years. Medical research in its facilities led in 1846 to the first use of ether and in 1867 to the first antiseptic surgery. In 1878, it became the first British university to admit women. Today, Princess Anne is its chancellor.

Many university buildings are in the area around Gower and Malet Streets. The best-known is **Senate House,** which was designed by **Charles Holden** in 1932. The huge Portland stone structure contains the university's massive library, with its specialist collections of Elizabethan books and music. ♦ Bounded by Bedford Way and Gower St, and Montague and Gower Pls. Tube: Russell Square, Goodge Street

Within the University of London:

46 Gordon Square Considered the birthplace of the Bloomsbury Group, this was the home of Virginia Woolf and her sister, Vanessa Bell, before they were married. Later Vanessa occupied the house with her husband, Clive Bell, until 1916, when John Maynard Keynes, the economist and another member of the group, took up residence. Now owned by the **University of London,** it's not open to the public. However, the garden at **Gordon Square** is, looking much as it did when Virginia Woolf described it in her memoir *Old Bloomsbury.* "It was astonishing to stand at the drawing room window and look into all those trees; the tree which shoots its branches up into the air and lets them fall in a shower; the tree which glistens after rain like the body of a seal." ♦ East side of the square (near Endsleigh Pl)

2 Russell Square The west side of London's second-largest square is lined with huge plane trees and houses once favored by lawyers and merchants. Readers of Thackeray's *Vanity Fair* may recognize this as the turf of the Sedleys and Osbornes. The square was laid out between 1800 and 1814 by **Humphrey Repton** and named after the Russells, Dukes of Bedford, who owned the land. The elaborate statue of Francis Russell, fifth Duke of Bedford, created in 1809 by Sir Richard Westmacott, portrays him leaning on a plow. Some of the original houses by **James Burton** remain, including **Nos. 25** to **29,** which now contain two branches of the **University of London:** the **Institute of Commonwealth Studies** and the **Institute of Germanic Studies.** The great law reformer Sir Samuel Romilly lived (and died by his own hand) at **No. 2.** Sir Thomas Lawrence had his studio at **No. 67** from 1805 until his death in 1830 (the building was later demolished). Here he painted his portrait series of princes, generals, and statesmen who helped bring about Napoléon's downfall; these works were painted for the **Waterloo Chamber** at **Windsor Castle.** Stop at the wooden coffee booth on the square's northern tip for a frothy cappuccino and enjoy it at one of the outdoor tables. ♦ At Guilford St and Montague Pl, and Southampton Row and Woburn Pl. Tube: Russell Square

HOTEL
RUSSELL
LONDON

3 Hotel Russell $$ This rambling Bloomsbury institution (now managed by the Granada hotel group) looks and feels as if it should be attached to the Great Western Railway. Built by **Charles Fitzroy Doll** in 1898, it tempers the Victorian appetite for size with modesty. The stairway is grand, but the 329 rooms are not (although they are prettily decorated). The best rooms are on the seventh floor. The **Fitzroy Doll's Restaurant** offers British dishes, and **Virginia Woolf's Restaurant** has burgers, pastas, and salads. ♦ Russell Sq (between Guilford and Bernard Sts). 837.6470, 800/225.5843; fax 837.2857. Tube: Russell Square

CARING FOR CHILDREN
SINCE 1739

4 Thomas Coram Foundation for Childre Also known as the **Foundling Hospital,** this museum owes its existence to sea captain Thomas Coram, who lived from 1668 to 175 and made his name by helping to colonize America. Returning to London, Coram was shocked at the number of abandoned infants He enlisted 21 noblewomen, 11 earls, and 6 dukes to petition George II for assistance in establishing a home for the foundlings.

William Hogarth was one of the original governors; he and his wife served as foster parents to the children. A major Hogarth wo the *March to Finchley* (1746), and the super portrait of a robust *Captain Coram* (1740) are two of the treasures in the museum's picture collection, which includes works by Gainsborough and Reynolds. The composer Handel was also an early benefactor. He not only donated a pipe organ and gave performances to raise money for the childre but also bequeathed his own copy of the manuscript for his *Messiah.* An unforgettabl collection is found in the lovingly preserved 18th-century **Courtroom.** Mothers often left mementos in the baskets of their abandoned infants, and many of these are displayed her coral beads, locks of hair, a section of a map of England, earrings, watch seals, coins, a crystal locket, a single lace glove, and the letter "A" cut in metal. These tokens were the foundlings' only clues to their personal histories. ♦ Admission. By appointment only 40 Brunswick Sq (off Hunter St). 278.2424; fax 837.8084. Tube: Russell Square

5 St. Margaret's Hotel $$ Friendly, small, and quiet (for central London, anyway), this establishment is part of a Bloomsbury estate owned by the Duke of Bedford and has been managed by the same Italian family for 45 years. Although some of the 64 rooms are small, all are sparkling clean and have TVs and phones. Prices include a full English breakfast, but if you want a private bath or shower, book well in advance. If you're flying into **Heathrow,** you can take the **Piccadilly** line straight to the nearby underground stop (although those with heavy bags may need a taxi; it's a six-minute walk from both **Russell Square** and **Holborn** tube stations). ♦ 26 Bedford Pl (between Great Russell St and Russell Sq). 636.4277; fax 323.3066. Tube: Russell Square, Holborn

---

Restaurants/Clubs: Red   Hotels: Blue
Shops/♥ Outdoors: Green   **Sights/Culture: Black**

BRITISH MUSEUM

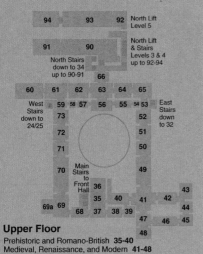

| | 94 | 93 | 92 | North Lift Level 5 |

North Lift & Stairs Levels 3 & 4 up to 92-94

91 90

North Stairs down to 34 up to 90-91   66

60 61 62 63 64 65

West Stairs down to 24/25   59 58 57 56 55 54 53   East Stairs down to 32

73   52

72   51

71   50

70 Main Stairs to Front Hall 36   49

35 40 41 42   43

69a 69 68 37 38 39   44

47 46 45

48

Upper Floor

Prehistoric and Romano-British **35-40**
Medieval, Renaissance, and Modern **41-48**
Western Asiatic **53-59**
Egyptian **60-66**
Greek and Roman **68-73**
Coins and Medals **69a**
Prints and Drawings **90**
Oriental **91-94**

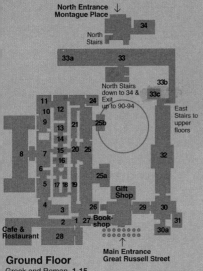

North Entrance
Montague Place ↓

34

North Stairs

33a   33

33b

North Stairs down to 34 & Exit up to 90-94   33c

East Stairs to upper floors

11 24 25b
10 12
9   13 21
14
15 20 25   32
8   7 16
6
5 17 18 19   25a

Gift Shop

4
3   26   29 30
2 1 27 Book-shop 31
Cafe & Restaurant   28   30a

Main Entrance
Great Russell Street ↑

Ground Floor

Greek and Roman **1-15**
Western Asiatic **16-24, 26**
Egyptian Sculpture **25**
British Library (until 1999) **29-32**
Oriental **33**
Ethnographic Collections **33c**
Islamic Art **34**

West Stairs up to 12

78 77
80 79
86 Lecture Theatre
81
82 87 Stairs up to 16
83 85 88
84 89 Stairs up to 17

Basement

Greek and Roman **77-85**
Western Asiatic **88**

Objects of Special Interest

Assyrian Lionhunt Reliefs **17**
Egyptian Mummies **60, 61**
Elgin Marbles **8**
Indian Sculpture **33**
Lewis Chessmen **42**
Lindisfarne Gospels **30a**
Lindow Man **37**
Magna Carta **30**
Mildenhall Treasure **40**
Portland Vase **70**
Rosetta Stone **25**
Sutton Hoo Treasure **41**

5 The Montague on the Gardens $$$
A stone's throw from the **British Museum**, this elegant addition to London's hotel scene boasts 95 rooms and 9 suites, all decorated in a traditional English style. You can even book a Nordic Spa room complete with your own in-room exercise equipment! Amenities include the **Terrace Bar** and the **Blue Door Bistro**. ♦15 Montague St (between Russell Sq and Great Russell St). 637.1001; fax 637.2516. Tube: Russell Square, Holborn

6 British Museum Ennui, wrote the lyricist of an old song, was the day when "the British Museum had lost its charm." For those still excited by history, this institution is as charming as ever; the only problem is managing to see the exhibitions through the crowds.

When physician and naturalist Sir Hans Sloane died in 1753, his will allowed the nation to buy his vast collection of art, antiquities, and natural history for £20,000—less than half of what it cost to assemble. With the additions of Robert Cotton's library and antiquities and the manuscripts of Robert Harley, Earl of Oxford, the collection grew, and when George II's 12,000-volume library was dedicated in 1823, it filled **Montagu House,** where it had been on display since 1759. A decision was then made to build new quarters for the burgeoning national collection. **Sir Robert Smirke** designed a large quadrangle with an open courtyard behind **Montagu House,** then surrounded it with a fine Neo-Classical facade. When the renovation and roofing of the Great Court is completed (estimated date September 2000), this will open up the museum's inner court for the first time in 150 years. In 1847, he added an Ionic colonnade and a pediment decorated with Sir Richard Westmacott's figures representing the progress of civilization. The architect's brother, **Sydney Smirke,** began the courtyard's conversion into the beautiful, blue-domed **Reading Room** in 1852 according to a plan by Sir Anthony Panizzi, the principal librarian. Space problems were alleviated in the 1880s, when the natural history exhibitions moved to the **Natural History Museum,** and in 1970, when the ethnographic exhibitions were moved to the **Museum of Mankind.** Start with the **Egyptian Sculpture Gallery (Room 25)** on the ground floor. The massive granite figures can be seen over the heads of any number of people. To the left of the door is the **Rosetta Stone,** not so much fascinating in itself (it is an irregularly shaped, tightly inscribed piece of black basalt) as in the way it changed our understanding of history. Written in Greek and in two forms of ancient Egyptian script, the Greek translation on the stone provided the key to hieroglyphics undeciphered for 1,400 years and finally made sense of all the previously mysterious symbols found on so many monuments. In the rest of the gallery, enormous sculptures, intricate pieces of jewelry, and carvings give an overwhelming introduction to the ancient Egyptians. There is a haughty bronze cat from 600 BC, sacred to Bastet (an Egyptian deity); a large reclining granite ram with a tiny figure of King Taharqa tucked beneath his chin; and from the Temple of Mut in Thebes, carved in about 1400 BC, are four huge granite representations of the goddess Sakhmet, with the body of a woman and the head of a lion. The rest of the Egyptian exhibitions are on the upper floors **(Rooms 60-66).** The Etruscans, the Italian civilization that reached its peak of power in the seventh and sixth centuries BC, were fine metalworkers and potters. Here their achievements in jewelry and ornamentation are revealed; some of the pieces are so intricately wrought that modern jewelers cannot copy them **(Room 71).** Before climbing the stairs, visit **Rooms 1** through **15,** which hold the museum's collection of Greek and Roman antiquities, including the hotly contested Elgin Marbles **(Room 8),** sculptures from the Parthenon and the Erechtheum that Lord Elgin brought to England in 1816 and which the government of Greece is seeking to have returned. Mostly fragments, they are described in the diary of an attendant, John Conrath, who helped move them into the museum and was assigned to the gallery where they were displayed. This diary can be seen in the **British Library.** "Northside," he

wrote, describing the frieze that had been inside the great colonnade, "a young man almost naked, putting a Crown on his head, another ready to mount, attended by his grooms, around the west corner a single person, a magistrate or director, two Chariots . . . South frieze, Seven more Bulls, a man Crowning himself." Although the eroded and broken state of the marbles disappointed some early visitors, they also attracted such illustrious fans as the Grand Duke Nicholas, later Czar Nicholas I of Russia, who spent two days looking at the marbles in 1817.

At the head of the stairs in **Room 37,** the well-preserved body of Celtic Lindow Man (discovered in a Cheshire bog) lies in an airtight chamber; even the brutality of his death as a religious sacrifice cannot detract from the gleaming artistry of the golden torques in the rest of the Celtic collection. The upper floors also hold "Medieval and Later Antiquities from Europe" **(Rooms 41-48),** with lethal bronze weapons and the extraordinary Lycurgus Cup, a Roman goblet carved from a single block of green glass that shows the tortured face of the Thracian king Lycurgus, imprisoned by the tendrils of a vine. The rooms also contain remarkable displays of jewelry. The **Gallery of Clocks and Watches (Room 44)** exhibits a range of timepieces from the Middle Ages to the beginning of this century.

At press time, with the move of the **British Library** to its new St. Pancras headquarters (see page 143) complete, renovation and roofing on **Smirke**'s **Great Court** had begun, opening up the museum's inner court for the first time in 150 years. When it is finished (projected date September 2000), visitors will once again have access to the famed **British Library Reading Room,** with its domed ceiling, which has been used by readers as diverse as Marx, Lenin, Gandhi, George Bernard Shaw, and Thomas Carlyle. The reading room will become a study center, surrounded by the **Great Court,** redeveloped to provide visitor facilities including bigger shops and restaurants.

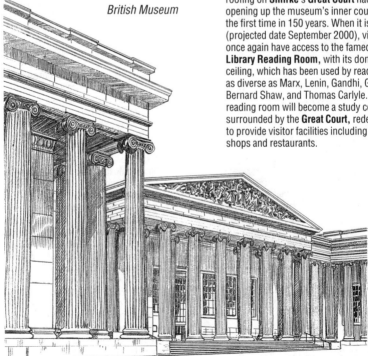

British Museum

The **British Museum** occupies the site of the first Duke of Montagu's house. Needing to replenish a fortune ravaged by the extravagances of building this mansion, he set out to win the hand of the extremely rich (and quite mad) second Duchess of Albemarle. The duchess, who insisted that she would marry only a crowned head of state, happily offered her hand when the duke convinced her that he was the Emperor of China. The ghost of the erstwhile empress is probably roaming contentedly through the collection of Oriental antiquities, in **Room 33** on the ground floor and **Rooms 91** through **94** on the upper floor.

Ask at the information desk on the ground floor for details of free museum gallery talks and lectures. For a fee, there are daily 90-minute guided tours of the highlights of the collections. ♦ Free. M-Sa; Su 2:30-6PM. Great Russell St (between Montague and Bloomsbury Sts). 323.8599, recorded information 636.1555. Tube: Russell Square, Holborn, Tottenham Court Road

Within the British Museum:

British Museum Shop There are two excellent shops—one for books and cards, left of the main entrance; the other for replicas, jewelry, and coins, left of the **Reading Room** entrance. You won't need a degree in archaeology to take home fabulous pieces of (well-replicated) antiquity. There is a special stall for children beside the book shop. ♦ M-Sa 10AM-5PM; Su 2:30-6PM. 323.8613

Museum Cafe $ Sometimes the temperature in the museum seems hotter than the Egyptian deserts, and following in the footsteps of Howard Carter is hungry and thirsty work. Refresh yourself with delicious snacks, soups, and soft drinks in this informal cafe. ♦ International ♦ Daily lunch and afternoon tea. Ground floor. 323.8599

Museum Restaurant ★$ A self-service cafeteria, it is open for a buffet lunch of quiches, salads, hot dishes, and tea. Too small for the size of the museum, it tends to get crowded. ♦ Cafeteria ♦ Daily lunch and afternoon tea. 323.8599

7 **Bloomsbury Workshop** Specializing in the literature and art of the Bloomsbury Group, this little gallery and shop carries an extensive range of books and even rare first editions by Virginia Woolf, Lytton Strachey, and E.M. Forster. The gallery features changing art exhibits showcasing work by the writers' descendants, such as the textile designs of Cressida Bell and the paintings of her brother, Julian (Vanessa's grandchildren), as well as others connected with the famous group. ♦ M-F. 12 Bury Pl (off Bloomsbury Way). 404.7433. Tube: Holborn, Tottenham Court Road

8 **Westaway & Westaway** London's most reliable and most affordable dealer in woolens carries scarves, blankets, hats, and socks—everything for keeping warm. The variety of Scottish cashmeres, woven in Scotland from the wool of cashmere goats in China, gives you a better selection here than in Scotland. ♦ Daily. 62-65 Great Russell St (at Bury Pl). 405.4479. Tube: Holborn, Tottenham Court Road. Also at: 92-93 Great Russell St (at Bloomsbury St). 636.1718. Tube: Tottenham Court Road; 26 Henrietta St (between Southampton and Bedford Sts). 497.5060. Tube: Covent Garden

9 **Print Room** Specializing in prints of London, prints by Hogarth, and caricatures of the 18th and 19th centuries, the shop also has a large, tempting, and reasonably priced collection of botanical prints. Its staff is friendly and helpful. ♦ M-Sa. 37 Museum St (between Gilbert Pl and Great Russell St). 430.0159. Tube: Holborn, Tottenham Court Road

10 **Plough** ★$ The feel of Bloomsbury lingers in this literary pub, perhaps because it has remained popular with publishers and writers for so long. They appreciate its coziness in winter and the outdoor tables in summer, as well as the bar lunch menu and wide selection of ales. ♦ Pub ♦ Daily lunch and dinner. 27 Museum St (at Little Russell St). 636.7964. Tube: Holborn, Tottenham Court Road

11 **L. Cornelissen** This is an old-fashioned shop with old-fashioned and very special art supplies—its own brand of violin varnish (with the imaginative name of Dragon's Blood), cobalt blues, British and French gold leaf, pure squirrel-mop brushes, and quill brushes. At the back of the store, you will find "His Nibs," Philip Poole, who had to move from his beautiful shop in Drury Lane several years ago because of rent increases. The white-haired Poole still runs the spectacular scribbler's emporium himself, selling every make and age of fountain pen, many collected when Biros (ballpoints) first became fashionable, as he was convinced they were a passing fad. Every kind of ink is available, along with pencils, paper, and objects related to aesthetic writing. ♦ M-Sa. 105 Great Russell St (between Bloomsbury St and Adeline Pl). 636.1045. Tube: Tottenham Court Road

12 **Central Club Hotel (YWCA)** $ An affordable option for anyone who doesn't mind basic, no-frills accommodations, these **YWCA** facilities are clean, well located, and much like a hotel. Most of the 104 rooms have TV sets, radios, telephones, and tea- and coffee-making facilities (but none have private baths). You can opt for room only, room and breakfast, or half board (breakfast and either lunch or dinner). Public areas include a lounge and a launderette; also on the premises are a hairdressing salon, a gym, and a solarium. In addition, there's a coffee shop serving fresh salads, health food, and vegetarian fare. ♦ 16-22 Great Russell St (between Dyott St and Adeline Pl). 636.7512; fax 636.5278. Tube: Tottenham Court Road

On the Trail of London's Literati

The streets of London have long echoed with the footsteps of the many British novelists, essayists, and poets who lived there at least part of the time and drew inspiration for their immortal works. Happily, it is still possible to soak up the literary atmosphere by visiting the haunts of such leading lights as Virginia Woolf, Samuel Johnson, and Charles Dickens, among others (see "Shakespeare's Globe Comes Full Circle," on page 196).

Bloomsbury conjures up the eponymous group of writers and artists centered around Virginia Woolf and Lytton Strachey during the early 1900s. It was here that the friends, many opposed to Victorian restrictions, wrote and painted, conducted their passionate affairs, discussed art, literature, and society, and deeply influenced the British avant-garde. In this lovely tree-shaded neighborhood of pleasant Georgian squares, behind the **British Museum,** you'll find **Gordon Square,** with its clutch of houses displaying blue plaques to show where members of the circle lived until World War II. Their central meeting place was **No. 46,** the home of Virginia and her sister, Vanessa. Nearby (in a building that no longer exists), Virginia and Leonard Woolf ran the Hogarth Press from 1925 to 1939 and published several of her works, including the classic feminist essay *A Room of One's Own* and the acclaimed novel *The Waves.* Bloomsbury aficionados won't want to miss the **Bloomsbury Workshop,** a little gallery and shop that stocks many first editions of the Bloomsbury writers.

Another London literary denizen was Dr. Samuel Johnson, whose traces remain in **Westminster Abbey** (a bust of the essayist, poet, and scholar is near his grave in **Poets' Corner**), and **St. Paul's Cathedral,** where his statue stands beneath the dome. There's also a statue behind his parish church, **St. Clement Danes,** in the **Strand:** With book in hand, his figure gazes toward the **Fleet Street** he found so convivial and stimulating. In fact, Johnson lived mostly around **Fleet Street** in at least 13

addresses, but the one place open to visitors is **Dr. Johnson's House** (17 Gough Sq, at Pemberton Row, 0171/353.3745), where he resided from 1748 to 1759 and compiled his famous *Dictionary.* Nearby was, and still is, **Ye Olde Cheshire Cheese,** his favorite watering hole, where he met with local wits who called themselves the Literary Club; his favorite armchair still sits in the **Chop Room.** There's now a large **Johnson Bar** on the first floor, where a display case holds a huge seventh edition of his dictionary. Johnson's acerbic humor is evident in such entries as "Oats—a grain, which in England is generally given to horses but in Scotland supports the people."

And then there's Charles Dickens, a literary great whose spirit totally pervades London. In fact, this author, possessed of feverish energy, seems to pop up everywhere: in the same **Ye Olde Cheshire Cheese,** mentioned in *A Tale of Two Cities;* in **The George,** near **Southwark Cathedral,** cited in *Little Dorrit;* in the **George & Vulture** on **Cornhill,** where he wrote part of *The Pickwick Papers.* However, the best place to immerse yourself in Dickensiana is at the much-visited **Dickens House** (48 Doughty St, between Roger and Guilford Sts, 0171/405.2127), a charming 18th-century building on a lovely Georgian street. During the two years Dickens lived there (1837-39) he was remarkably prolific, working on *The Pickwick Papers, Oliver Twist,* and *Nicholas Nickleby;* he also composed over 500 letters and even began *Barnaby Rudge.* It was here, too, that tragedy struck the household when the author's cherished sister-in-law, Mary, died in 1837 at age 17.

The house is chockablock with memorabilia, and the restored study and first-floor drawing room vividly evoke the author's presence. Among the house's treasures are the author's desk, his good-luck china monkey and other personal relics, first editions, autographed letters, and portraits and illustrations. In fact, you will come across Dickens's well-recorded footsteps throughout the pages of this guide: He was the ultimate chronicler of London.

13 Museum Street This narrow, friendly street is lined with some of the best antique-print dealers and bookshops in London. ♦ Between Bloomsbury Way and Great Russell St. Tube: Holborn, Tottenham Court Road

On Museum Street:

MUSEUM STREET CAFE

Museum Street Cafe ★★$$ This tiny, rather cramped restaurant enjoys a wonderful reputation with local gourmets. The

atmosphere is country-style and informal (rustic wooden tables and paper napkins), the breads are freshly baked, the meats and fish, such as seared salmon, are char-grilled to perfection, the ice cream is homemade, and the British cheeses come from **Neal's Yard Dairy** in Covent Garden. No wonder the place is always packed to the rafters. Each day the set menu offers either two or three courses of simple, freshly cooked dishes. ♦ British ♦ M-F breakfast, lunch, and afternoon tea. Reservations recommended; no smoking. 47 Museum St (between Bloomsbury Way and Little Russell St). 405.3211

S.J. Shrubsole A distinguished dealer in old English silver, this shop offers outstanding pieces of old Sheffield plate at honest prices. ♦ M-F. 43 Museum St (between Bloomsbury Way and Little Russell St). 405.2712

14 Stefania's Delicatessen ★$ Order sandwiches, lasagna, and pizza to go. ♦ Italian deli ♦ M-Sa breakfast, lunch, and snacks. 184 Drury La (at Stukeley St). 831.0138. Tube: Holborn, Covent Garden

15 New London Theatre Built in 1973 by **Michael Percival,** this 1,106-seat theater is on an old foundation, a place of entertainment that's been here since Elizabethan times. The theater is ultramodern, with movable seats, lights, walls, and stage—all surrounded by lots of glass. Andrew Lloyd Webber's feline phenomenon, *Cats,* opened in 1981; at press time it was still playing—the longest-running musical in British theater history. ♦ Drury La (at Parker St). Box office: 405.0072. Tube: Holborn, Covent Garden

16 Bhatti ★★$$ Highly recommended by the Curry Club of Great Britain, an organization for fans of Indian cooking, this restaurant occupies a 17th-century "listed building" that retains its original paneling, stenciling, and fireplaces (because listed buildings have been deemed important to England's heritage, they cannot be knocked down nor can the structure of the interiors be altered). Try the lamb *pasanda* (lamb fillet sliced thinly, marinated in spices and yogurt, and cooked with herbs) or the chicken *jalfrezi* (boneless chicken pieces cooked with tomatoes, onions, peppers, and a blend of spices, including ginger). Also a fine value is the vegetarian *bhojan*—that's simply the Gujarati word for "meal." The set lunch and the popular pre-theater menu are good bargains. ♦ Indian ♦ Daily lunch and dinner. Reservations recommended. 37 Great Queen St (between Drury La and Newton St). 831.0817. Tube: Holborn, Covent Garden

17 Freemason's Hall The imposing headquarters of the United Grand Lodge of England, built by **H.V. Ashley** and **F. Winston Smith** in 1933, boasts a central tower rising 200 feet above the street. The Art Deco building was conceived as a memorial to Masons who died in World War I. Today, it houses an exhibition on the history of English Freemasonry, which may help to dispel the suspicion surrounding the "funny handshake brigade." This is the largest collection of Masonic regalia, medals, art, and glassware in the world, though few of the sect's secrets are divulged. Look for angels and pyramids, both Masonic symbols. Guided tours are given several times a day (visitors on Saturday are admitted only on the tours). Free. M-F 10AM-5PM; Sa 10AM-noon. 60 Great Queen St (at Wild St). 831.9811. Tube: Holborn, Covent Garden

18 Great Queen Street This once-fashionable thoroughfare, named in honor of Henrietta Maria, the devoted wife of Charles I, is now lined with restaurants along one side. Though similar in feel to the **Covent Garden** area, of which it is an extension, this neighborhood has lost some of its cozy charm due to the presence of a conference center and the **Freemason's Hall.** ♦ Between Drury La and Kingsway. Tube: Holborn, Covent Garden

19 Sir John Soane's Museum Go out of your way to visit this museum. **Sir John Soane,** the official architect of the **Bank of England** for 45 years, chose the largest square in central London for the site of his house, which was actually three domestic residences. He required an appropriate setting for his enormous collection of international antiquities and art, and the result is a fascinating dwelling that is unique in London. Moving through rooms of unusual proportions, built on varying levels with cantilevered staircases and hundreds of mirrors, you will feel that time has been suspended and that you are experiencing the mind of a brilliant and eccentric master builder. Incorporated within the house are a sculpture gallery, a crypt, and a mock ruin of a medieval cloister. The colored glass in the skylights (which was bombed out during World War II) was replaced, re-creating the ingenious lighting effects so beloved by **Soane.** In the **Picture Room,** you can see William Hogarth's two famous series: *The Rake's Progress* and *The Election;* the latter is cleverly mounted so that the first paintings pull away from the wall to reveal hidden panels with subsequent paintings. Other "secret" panels hold **Soane**'s architectural drawings for this house. A well-known highlight of the collection, found in the **Sepulchral Chamber,** is the magnificent **Sarcophagus of Seti I.** Discovered at Thebes in 1815, it dates from 1300 BC—**Soane** snapped it up when it was passed over by the **British Museum.** The collection contains unpredictable juxtapositions of fragments salvaged from various buildings (such as the original **House of Lords**) destroyed during **Soane**'s lifetime. Glancing through a window into the court known as the **Monk's Yard,** it is possible to glimpse a huge melancholy tomb inscribed, "Alas, Poor Fanny"—a monument to **Soane**'s favorite dog.

The **Shakespeare Recess** features a bust of the playwright and several paintings by Henry Howard depicting some of his most famous characters. The new **Soane Gallery,** designed by **Eva Jiricna,** stages two exhibitions annually and features works from the museum's 30,000 architectural and decorative drawings.

Guided tours are given Saturday at 2:30PM; 22 tickets are distributed on request from 2PM, so go early to avoid disappointment. ♦ Free. Parties of more than six must book in advance, and a donation is requested. Tu-Sa; first Tuesday of month 10AM-5PM and 6-9PM. 13 Lincoln's Inn Fields (north side, between Newman's Row and Gate St). 405.2107, recorded information 430.0175. Tube: Holborn

20 Lincoln's Inn Fields When property developer William Newton won the right to build here in 1620, angry lawyers appealed to the **House of Commons.** They won, and the space was left open. Adjacent to **Lincoln's Inn,** the largest rectangular square in central London is surrounded by tennis courts, flower beds, and a bandstand, and is graced by many distinguished houses, including stately **Lindsey House (Nos. 59-60),** which may have been based on plans by **Inigo Jones,** and its imitative younger neighbor **(Nos. 57-58)** by **Henry Joynes.** The queen's solicitors are at **No. 66. Canada Walk** commemorates the Royal Canadian Air Force, which was based here during World War II. ♦ At New Sq and Sardinia St, and Portsmouth and Gate Sts. Tube: Holborn

21 Lincoln's Inn Of the four great **Inns of Court (Lincoln's Inn, Inner Temple, Middle Temple,** and **Gray's Inn),** this is the most unspoiled and the only one to have escaped World War II without major damage. The inns were formed in the Middle Ages to provide lodgings for solicitors, barristers, and law students. They now belong to barristers' societies, which control the admission of students to the bar, finance, law reform, legal education, and the maintenance of professional standards for lawyers.

This inn was established on the site of the Knights Templars' tilting ground after the dissolution of the order in the early 14th century. Reflecting the times when a great majority of highly educated people became lawyers, the rolls of the inn contain famous names: Sir Thomas More, John Donne, Oliver Cromwell, William Penn, Horace Walpole, William Pitt, Benjamin Disraeli, William Gladstone. The brick-and-stone buildings, arranged in a collegiate plan, date from the 15th century.

There is a sentry box and an entrance in the southeast corner of **Lincoln's Inn Fields,** or you can enter through the gatehouse, facing Chancery Lane, which dates from 1518 and bears the arms of **Lincoln's Inn:** a lion rampant. The Tudor redbrick **Old Buildings** date from the early 16th century, and the **Old Hall,** built around 1491 and approached through the archway and small courtyard, contains a superb wooden roof, linen-fold

paneling, and William Hogarth's painting, *St. Paul Before Felix,* completed in 1748. The hall was the **Court of Chancery** from 17?? to 1883; the fictional case of Jarndyce vs. Jarndyce in Charles Dickens's *Bleak House* was tried here. **Henry Serle**'s 1697 **New Square,** which faces toward **Lincoln's Inn Fields,** is a tranquil and pretty courtyard of solicitors' offices; this is where the 14-year-old Dickens was once employed as a clerk. Built in the 1840s, **Philip Hardwick**'s redbric **New Hall** contains a vast mural by G.F. Watt *Justice, a Hemicycle of Lawgivers.* With nearly 100,000 volumes, **Hardwick**'s library is the oldest and most complete law library in England. The rebuilding of the Gothic chapel was finished in 1623. John Donne laid the foundation stone and gave the first sermon. The buildings themselves are closed to the public, but the chapel and gardens may be visited. ♦ Chapel and gardens: M-F 12:30-2:30PM. Chancery La (between Bishop's Ct and High Holborn). 405.1393. Tube: Chance Lane

22 London Silver Vaults English silver, marked with the emblem of the British lion, deserves its rich reputation: the silver content is the highest in the world, and the tradition of design has been consistently strong. Unless you're familiar with hallmarks, makers, and dealers however, buying silver is bound to be an unnerving experience, and coming to this subterranean site in **Chancery House,** with 3 silver vaults and shops containing the greate concentration of silver dealers in London, certainly won't set you at ease. You have to make your way through a lot of junk, and on you come upon desirable silver, you'll find it hard to interact with the taciturn dealers. If you persevere, though, and have a clear idea of what you want, you will eventually find prices lower here than elsewhere. Study a simple hallmark card, the guide to hallmarks (on sale here), or the hallmark plaques on the wall before making a major purchase. ♦ M-F; Sa 9AM-1PM. 53-64 Chancery La (at Southampton Bldgs). 242.3844. Tube: Chancery Lane

23 Cittie of Yorke ★★★$ One of the largest pubs (with the largest bar) in London this 17th-century establishment must have served most of Holborn in bygone days. A capacious three-sided fireplace and little cubicles keep the place warm and intimate. The bar food is excellent, and the real ales ar much appreciated by the legal clientele. ♦ Pu ♦ M-Sa lunch and dinner. 22-23 High Holbor (between Gray's Inn Rd and Warwick Ct). 242.7670. Tube: Chancery Lane

COURTESY OF CHARLES DICKENS HOUSE, LONDON

Dickens House
Doughty Street

24 Dickens House The sheer quantity of Dickensiana crammed into this row house (shown above) is all the more amazing because the structure is one of four Dickens houses open to the public. (The others are outside London, although he did live and work at other city addresses.) The author lived here from 1837 to 1839, writing the last part of *The Pickwick Papers,* most of *Oliver Twist* and *Nicholas Nickleby,* and the beginning of *Barnaby Rudge.* He also penned some 550 letters here. In the sitting room, Dickens's 17-year-old sister-in-law, Mary, died in his arms, a blow from which he never recovered. Visitors can see the writer's desk, the china monkey he kept on it for good luck, and the family Bible, as well as portraits, illustrations, autographed letters, and other personal relics. The first-floor drawing room has been reconstructed to appear as it did in Dickens's time, as have the study and basement. ♦ Admission. M-Sa. 48 Doughty St (between Roger and Guilford Sts). 405.2127. Tube: Russell Square

25 Gray's Inn In the 14th century, the manor house of Sir Reginald le Grey, Chief Justice of Chester, was located here. By 1370, the grounds had developed into a hostel for law students, which was expanded during the Tudor period. Unfortunately, the inn was badly damaged during World War II; despite much restoration, it lacks the authentic feeling of **Lincoln's Inn,** its neighbor to the south. But be sure to walk through the passage in the southwest corner of the 17th-century **Gray's Inn Square** (off Gray's Inn Rd). Laid out by Sir Francis Bacon in 1606 and known affectionately as "The Walks," these sloping, tree-filled lawns delighted Samuel Pepys, who noted "fine ladies" promenading there, while Charles Lamb called them the "best gardens of the Inns of Court." The square and the chapel here are the only parts of the inn open to the public. In addition to the main entrance, there is a narrow passageway into the inn off High Holborn (between Gray's Inn Rd and

Fulwood Pl). ♦ Gray's Inn Square: daily noon-2:30PM May-Sept. Chapel: M-F. Gray's Inn Rd (between High Holborn and Theobald's Rds). Tube: Chancery Lane

26 Staple Inn Buildings A pure, domestic remnant of Elizabethan London, this pair of houses (one of which is pictured at right) dates from 1586 and displays black-and-white timber and plaster, gables, overhangs, and oriels. Badly damaged by a bomb in 1944 and then carefully restored, the inn now comprises offices and Old World shops, including the **Institute of Actuaries,** which is one of the **Inns of Chancery** affiliated with **Gray's Inn.** Dr. Samuel Johnson moved into **No. 2** in 1759, following his wife's death and his departure from Gough Square. The silver griffin on the stone obelisk in front marks the boundary of the City of London. ♦ Off Holborn (between Furnival St and Southampton Bldgs). Tube: Chancery Lane

27 Barnard's Inn On the south side of Holborn lies the City of London's oldest surviving secular building, which incorporates the remains of the **Inn of Chancery** where Pip and Herbert Pocket shared rooms in *Great Expectations.* The 14th-century hall has 16th-century paneling and fine heraldic glass. From 1894 to 1958, this was the hall of **Mercer's School.** ♦ Off Norwich St (between Fetter La and Furnival St); the passage to the hall is beside Nos. 20-23 Holborn (between Fetter La and Furnival St). Tube: Chancery Lane

28 Prudential Assurance Building This is an example of what the late Sir John Betjeman, poet laureate and longtime resident of the neighborhood, admired, defended, and fought to save: high Victorian architecture. Also known as "The Pru," the Gothic redbrick immensity, built by **Alfred Waterhouse** between 1879 and 1906, no doubt infuses passersby with confidence in this large insurance company. It stands on the site of **Furnival's Inn,** where Charles Dickens lived and wrote part of *The Pickwick Papers.* Only the structure's facade remains. The building is closed to the public. ♦ 142 Holborn (between Leather La and Brooke St). Tube: Chancery Lane

"Nearly all people in England are of the superior sort, superiority being an English ailment."
D.H. Lawrence, *The Last Laugh*

29 Leather Lane Market You can reach this lunchtime street market via a passage down the east side of the **Prudential Assurance Building.** Shop for new clothes at bargain prices—lamb's-wool sweaters, shoes, and jeans. Some plants, fruit, vegetables, and glassware are also sold. However, the only leather that can be found is at a stall that sometimes offers genuine chamois. ♦ M-F 10:30AM-2PM. Between Greville St and Clerkenwell Rd. Tube: Chancery Lane, Farringdon

30 Quality Chop House ★★$$ With the opening of the **Quality Fish Bar** next door, the menu (which is the same in both restaurants) has been extended to include fish in a big way. There's everything from jellied eels to Sevruga caviar. Gaslight enhances the historical ambience. ♦ British ♦ M-F, Su lunch and dinner; Sa dinner. Reservations recommended. No credit cards accepted. 94 Farringdon Rd (at Exmouth Market). 837.5093. Tube: Farringdon

31 Bleeding Heart
★★$$ Bleeding Heart Yard, where this wine bar and restaurant are located, is featured in Charles Dickens's *Little Dorrit.* Bookshelves with the author's first editions line the walls. The spooky wine bar basement room is also lined with bottles of wine—which may explain why the wine list is a book in itself and offers more than 400 vintages. Try the *gigot d'agneau aux flageolets* (roast leg of lamb with kidney beans) or a simple *omelette avec frites;* then consider the excellent *tarte au citron* (lemon tart) for dessert. As one would expect, the restaurant is a little pricier than the wine bar. In summer, there is a terrace with a menu that combines the restaurant and wine bar specialties, but you'll be jostled by lots of City workers. ♦ French ♦ M-F lunch and dinner. Reservations recommended for lunch. Bleeding Heart Yard, off Greville St (between Saffron Hill and Hatton Garden). 242.8238; fax 242.2056. Tube: Farringdon

32 Hatton Garden Named for Elizabeth I's chancellor, Sir Christopher Hatton, the center of the diamond trade isn't what it used to be. Office blocks have descended and ascended, and most of the shops look so vulgar or so impenetrable that you'd have to be an expert shopper to take them on. Behind the walls of the impressive building that houses the London Diamond Club at **No. 87** (which is not open to the public), dealers buy and sell the precious gems to jewelry shops on a commission basis. ♦ Between Holborn Circus and Clerkenwell Rd. Tube: Chancery Lane, Farringdon

33 Ely Place A watchman in a small gatehouse still guards this charming cul-de-sac of 18th-century houses. As the land belongs to Ely Cathedral in Cambridgeshire, the street remains legally under the jurisdiction of the Bishops of Ely, meaning London police cannot automatically enter—perhaps a more useful edict now that the lovely doorways by the **Adam** brothers lead to lawyers' and accountants' offices rather than to private houses. Sadly, as with many other parts of historic London, the developer's ax threatens to fall here. ♦ Off Charterhouse St (between Farringdon Rd and Holborn Circus). Tube: Chancery Lane, Farringdon

On Ely Place:

St. Etheldreda (Ely Chapel) This church, once the chapel to **Ely Palace,** is all that is left of the building, which belonged to the bishops of Ely. When it was built in 1290, it was, of course, Catholic, and like all churches in England during the Reformation, it became Protestant. In 1874, the Roman Catholics bought it back and named it **St. Etheldreda,** making it the first pre-Reformation church to return to the fold. This masterpiece of the 13th-century Early Decorated style has a mood of great antiquity and quotidian warmth thanks to **Sir Giles Gilbert Scott**'s sensitive restoration in 1935. The windows at the east and west ends are noted for their superb tracery; the west window, which dates from around 1300, is one of the largest in London. Modern stained-glass windows by Charles and May Blakeman depict English martyrs. Very much a living church, it is active in the community and in such organizations as Amnesty International. The vaulted crypt, dating from about 1252, serves as a nicely chaotic combination of meeting room, Sunday school, and storage area.

34 Statue of Prince Albert The almost whimsical statue of Prince Albert on a horse in the middle of a traffic island is unworthy of the man who worked tirelessly for his adopted country, left a legacy of great museums, and introduced the Christmas tree to Britain. The monument was created by Charles Bacon in 1874 and heralds the beginning of **Holborn Viaduct.** ♦ Holborn Circus (at Holborn Viaduct and Holborn, and St. Andrew St and Hatton Garden). Tube: Chancery Lane, Farringdon

35 Ye Olde Mitre Tavern ★★$ Just to the south of the church, down a little passageway is this atmospheric pub built in 1546 for the Bishop of Ely's servants. In the corner of the front bar is an unusual relic: A five-foot section of trunk from the cherry tree around which Elizabeth I once danced is preserved in a glass display case. Pub food includes sausages and sandwiches. ♦ Pub ♦ M-F lunch and dinner. No credit cards accepted. Ely Ct (between Ely Pl and Hatton Garden). 405.4751. Tube: Chancery Lane, Farringdon

36 St. Andrew Holborn Sir Christopher Wren built his largest parish church in 1690, on the remains of a church founded in the 13th century. In 1704, he refaced the medieval tower of the original church, which miraculously survived the five bombs that destroyed its interior during World War II. In the 1960s, the furnishings were replaced with treasures from the **Foundling Hospital Chapel** in Bloomsbury, including the gilded 18th-century organ that Handel gave to the hospital and the 18th-century font and altar rails. The church records show the 1770 burial of Thomas Chatterton, the poet who committed suicide by poison at the age of 18 after despairing over his poverty and lack of recognition (he later became a symbol of the Romantic movement). Essayist William Hazlitt was married here in 1808, with Charles Lamb as his best man and Mary Lamb as a bridesmaid. The Jewish-born prime minister Benjamin Disraeli was baptized here in 1817 at the age of 12. And the tomb of Captain Coram, founder of the **Foundling Hospital**, withstood the bombing of World War II; a weeping cherub watches over the good man. ♦ Holborn Circus (at St. Andrew St). Tube: Chancery Lane, Farringdon

37 Holborn Viaduct The world's first overpass, 1,400 feet long and 80 feet wide, was constructed between 1863 and 1869 by William Haywood to bridge the valley of the River Fleet and to connect Holborn with Newgate Street. The cost was 4,000 dwellings and £2.5 million. Its elaborate cast-iron work is best seen from Farringdon Street. Four bronze statues representing Agriculture, Commerce, Science, and Fine Art grace the north and south sides of the bridge section, and at the corners are four City heroes: Henry FitzAilwin, first lord mayor of London; Sir Thomas Gresham, founder of the Royal Exchange; Sir Hugh Myddelton, who brought fresh water to London; and finally antihero Sir William Walworth, who fatally stabbed rebellion leader Wat Tyler. Before the viaduct was built, the steep banks of this part of the river were very difficult to negotiate. Steps lead down to Farringdon Street and **City Thameslink Station,** a small railway depot that serves commuters to the southern counties. ♦ Between Giltspur St and Holborn Circus. Tube: Farringdon, St. Paul's

38 Magpie and Stump ★★$ The original pub faced the gallows of **Newgate** jail and rented out its upper floors for all-night parties before an execution. Today's incarnation, built after the recent redevelopment of this corner, is modern, complete with air-conditioning and an elevator. The three-story structure also houses a wine bar and a restaurant. All serve stuffed potato skins and pizzas with such cutesy names as Probationary, Sentence, and Community Service. The pub's special brew is called Well Hung. ♦ Pub/Pizza ♦ M-F lunch and dinner. 218 Old Bailey (at Bishop's Ct). 248.5085. Tube: St. Paul's

39 Old Bailey (Central Criminal Court) The figure of Justice, holding scales but neither blind nor blindfolded, stands atop the dome, a bronze-gilded prelude to countless TV and film thrillers. The carved inscription over the main entrance, "Defend the Children of the Poor and Punish the Wrongdoer," proves as difficult a combination today as it was when Fagin went to the gallows on this very site in Chapter 52 of *Oliver Twist.* "Old Bailey" is the more familiar name for the **Central Criminal Court,** which serves Greater London and parts of Surrey, Kent, and Essex; it's where the most serious, dramatic, and celebrated criminal cases are heard. A medieval gatehouse where murderers and thieves were imprisoned originally stood on this site. It was part of **Newgate Prison,** which for centuries played an important and dreadful role in London life, especially during the late–18th and 19th centuries when it was the city's chief penitentiary. Methods of execution were particularly horrible, including death by pressing. The conditions, despite numerous extensions and the installation of a windmill on the roof to improve ventilation, were just as notoriously barbaric. In 1750, a plague of "gaol fever"—actually a nasty strain of typhoid—swept through the prison, killing more than 60 people, including the lord mayor, jury members, and three judges. This was the origin of a tradition still honored today whereby judges carry nosegays on the first day of each session to protect against vile smells and diseases.

The first **Old Bailey** (or **Sessions House**) was built in 1539 for trials of the accused. Those tried here include the men who condemned Charles I in 1660; Oscar Wilde (for "homosexual offences") in 1895; and famous 20th-century murderers Dr. Crippen, J.R. Christie, and Peter Sutcliffe (the Yorkshire Ripper). In 1973, a terrorist bomb went off in the building during a trial of members of the Irish Republican Army, which led to fortresslike security during IRA trials. Public executions were held outside this building from 1783 until 1868, replacing **Tyburn Gallows.** The road was widened to accommodate the large number of spectators.

The present building with an elaborate Edwardian frontage (built in 1907) and its extension (built in 1972) accommodate 19 courts. Ten of them are in the old building, entered on Newgate Street, which has a very unassuming door with the words "Ring bell hard" written above the doorbell; the other nine courts are in the newer building. Visitors watch trials from the public gallery; few experiences are more fascinating than seeing the English judiciary at work, with the judge and barristers in their traditional white wigs and the accused in the dock. Major trials held in courts one through four attract large numbers, so you may have to wait in line. ◆ Free. M-F (court opening times vary). No children under 14, cameras, tape recorders, large carryalls, or bags allowed. Old Bailey (at Newgate St). 248.3277. Tube: St. Paul's

The Viaduct Tavern

40 Viaduct Tavern ★★$ This fascinating pub was named for **Holborn Viaduct.** Built in 1869 over the debtors' cells of the old **Newgate Prison,** it's a Victorian extravaganza, its interior lavished with gold mirrors and large paintings. The proprietor arranges tours of the cells now and then. ◆ Pub ◆ Daily lunch and dinner. 126 Newgate St (between King Edward and Giltspur Sts). 606.8476. Tube: St. Paul's

41 Holy Sepulchre Often referred to as "St. Sepulchre's," the spacious church was originally dedicated in 1137 to King Edmund (who ruled East Anglia in AD 841-870). It was rebuilt in the 15th century, restored after the Great Fire (possibly by **Sir Christopher Wren**), heavily Victorianized in 1878, and sensitively repaired after World War II. Known as the "Musicians' Church," it has a long tradition of memorial services for composers and singers, a **Musicians' Chapel** with windows dedicated to opera singer Dame Nellie Melba and composer John Ireland, and exquisite kneelers with names of great musicians, bars of music, and musical instruments in fine needlepoint. Sir Henry Wood, the founder of the Promenade Concerts, was baptized here, became assistant organist when he was 12, and is remembered in Gerald Smith's central window of the north chapel, which is also dedicated to St. Cecilia, the patron saint of music. Every year on St. Cecilia's Day (22 November), a festival is held, with the choirs of **Westminster Abbey** and **St. Paul's.** American associations with the church inspired the south aisle's stained-glass window of Captain John Smith, of the expedition to Virginia that began in 1606. Taken prisoner by Native Americans, he is said to have been saved by the chief's daughter, Pocahontas, just as he was about to be killed. The English captain became president of the colony, and the princess married another settler, John Rolfe, who brought her to England. Sadly, Pocahontas's

health declined quickly, and she died a year later. Smith is buried here, but the resting place of his rescuer is at the appropriately named town of Gravesend in Kent.

To the right of the altar, a small glass case encloses a hand bell that was tolled outside the cell of a condemned man at midnight on the eve of his hanging. The bellman recited the following verses: "All you that in the condemned hole do lie; Prepare you, for tomorrow you shall die; Watch all and pray; The hour is drawing near; That you before the Almighty must appear; Examine well yourselves; in time repent; That you may not to eternal flames be sent; And when St. Sepulchre's Bell in the morning tolls, Lord have mercy on your souls." All this, including the ringing of the great bell of St. Sepulchre on the morning of the execution, was arranged and paid for by an endowment of £50 made by parishioner Robert Dowe in 1605. ◆ M-F. Holborn Viaduct (at Giltspur St). 248.3110. Tube: St. Paul's

42 Bishop's Finger ★★$ This pub used to called the **Rutland,** but Bishop's Finger is the name of one of the beers made by the brewe Shepherd Neame, to which the pub is tied, and the name stuck. Meat carriers from the market, doctors and medical students from **Bart's,** lawyers and reporters from the **Old Bailey,** and moneymakers from the City all drink in the two bars, which spill over into the park opposite on sunny days. The place serves traditional pub grub at lunch and sandwiches and meat pies at dinner. ◆ Pub ◆ M-F lunch and dinner. 9-10 W Smithfield (at Hosier La). 248.2341. Tube: Barbican, St Paul's

43 St. Bartholomew's Hospital When Wat Tyler was stabbed by Sir William Walworth during the 1381 peasants' confrontation with Richard II, he was brought to **Bart's,** as this institution is commonly called, and died in the "emergency room." Though still treating patients and considered part of the **University of London,** it faces closure due to the government's privatization of health care— despite the fact that it's the oldest hospital in London and the only one of London's medieval foundations to remain on its original site. Like **St. Bartholomew the Great** (see page 157), the hospital was founded in 1123 by Thomas Rahere, although Henry VIII is regarded as a kind of second founder after he dissolved the adjacent priory during the Reformation and granted a royal charter refounding the hospital in 1546. The gateway built in 1702 by Edward Strong the Younger, is topped by a statue of Henry VIII by Francis Bird. The collegiate-style buildings inside the great quadrangle were added by **James Gibb** between 1730 and 1770. There are weekly guided tours of the hospital's historic sights, including *The Pool of Bethesda* and *The Goo*

Samaritan, two large murals painted in 1737 by William Hogarth, a governor of the hospital. They line the staircase that leads to the **Great Hall.** The **Medical School,** which is a vital part of the hospital, is the oldest in London, founded in 1662. There's also a small museum. ♦ Free. Hospital: Guided tours on Friday 2PM. Museum: Tu-F. W Smithfield (between Little Britain and Giltspur St). Guided tours 837.0546, museum 601.8152. Tube: Barbican, Farringdon, St. Paul's

Within St. Bartholomew's Hospital:

St. Bartholomew the Less This octagonal chapel is the parish church of **St. Bartholomew's Hospital** and was founded in the 12th century, rebuilt 300 years later (two 15th-century arches survive under the tower), rebuilt again in 1789 and 1823, and restored in 1951 following damage suffered during World War II. The register dates back to 1547 and indicates that **Inigo Jones** was baptized here in 1573. ♦ Open to tourists daily for services and prayers. Open 24 hours for friends and families of hospital patients 601.8888, ask for the church

44 St. Bartholomew the Great
For lovers of antiquity and lovers of London, this church is a shrine. It's the oldest parish church in London (only **St. John's Chapel** in the **Tower of London** exceeds it in age) and the city's only surviving Norman church. Thomas Rahere, a favorite courtier of Henry I, built it as a priory in 1123, along with **St. Bartholomew's Hospital,** as an act of gratitude after he had a vision during a fever in which St. Bartholomew saved him from a monster. The building's simple majesty and ancient beauty quicken the hearts of all who enter: An inexplicable power comes from the stones, the strong pillars, the pointed windows, the tomb of Rahere, and the miracle of survival to which the church is witness. Today's visitors do not see it quite as Rahere, first canon and first prior, saw it. The massive nave was the choir of the original church; the original nave is now part of the courtyard; and the 13th-century entrance gate was originally the west entrance to the south aisle. But the choir and vaulted ambulatories, crossing, chancel with apse, two transepts, and at least one bay of the nave have changed little since Rahere's time. The music sung during the choral service on Sunday seems to reach back in time, forming a heavenly connection among

stones, centuries, saints, and angels.

The restored **Lady Chapel** dates from the 14th century and contains the only medieval font in the City; William Hogarth was baptized here in 1697. The five pre-Reformation bells in the tower peal before Evensong on Sunday. The crypt and cloister have been restored, and the large chamber is dedicated to the City of London squadron of the RAF, which holds a memorial service here each year.

During the Reformation, the church was sold and fell upon hard times. The cloisters became a stable, the crypt was used for storing coal and wine, and the **Lady Chapel** became a printer's office where a young Benjamin Franklin worked in 1725. There was a blacksmith's forge in the north transept.

In the 1860s, architect **Sir Aston Webb** began the Parliament-funded restoration of the church. With the assistance of his colleague, **F.L. Dove, Webb** saved both the reality and the spirit of the structure. The gateway has been restored in memory of the two architects—notice their coats of arms. The wooden figure of Rahere was carved from a beam taken from the church and placed here in memory of **Sir Aston**'s son, Phillip, who was killed in action in France during World War I.

Film buffs might like to know that it was the location for the wedding that didn't happen in the movie *Four Weddings and a Funeral.* ♦ M-F, Su; Sa 10:30AM-1PM; closed Monday in August. Services: Su 9AM, 11AM, 6:30PM. W Smithfield (at Little Britain). 606.5171. Tube: Barbican

45 Cloth Fair This street in the heart of old London retains the style that the whole City of London had before it was destroyed by money, the Great Fire of 1666, and World War II. **No. 41** is the only house in the City built before the fire. Sir John Betjeman, a beloved poet laureate, once resided at **No. 43.** Now the short terrace of the 18th-century houses is owned by the **Landmark Trust,** a charity that rescues minor buildings in distress before they are knocked down by vandals or developers. **Nos. 43** and **45A** are available for short holiday rentals; to book, contact the **Landmark Trust** (Shottesbrooke, Maidenhead, Berkshire, SL6 3SW, 0162/882.5925) a year in advance. ♦ Between King St and Little Britain. Tube: Barbican

"Courtesy is not dead; it has merely taken refuge in Great Britain."

—Georges Duhamel

Englishman—a creature who thinks he is being virtuous when is only being uncomfortable.

—George Bernard Shaw

46 Fox and Anchor ★★$ Bleary-eyed medical students, young doctors and nurses, and butchers from **Smithfield Market** come here in the morning to enjoy huge platters of eggs, bacon, sausages, black pudding, baked beans, and fried bread (but you can get a vegetarian breakfast if you prefer). The special early morning market license that allows alcohol to be served between 7 and 9AM to market workers now applies to all diners. The facade is Art Nouveau, and the interior has been refurbished to match, but the ambience and the food are the real attractions—best appreciated after working up a hearty appetite. The pub is popular with office workers, so it is essential to book on weekdays. ♦ Pub ♦ M-F breakfast, lunch, and dinner 7AM-9PM. Reservations required for early breakfast and lunch. 115 Charterhouse St (between Charterhouse Sq and St. John St). 253.4838. Tube: Barbican, Farringdon

47 St. John Street An off-the-beaten- path "in" place for high-flying City workers, this street is attracting innovative chefs to open stylish restaurants. It is part of **Clerkenwell,** an interesting area that is fun to explore. ♦ Between Charterhouse St and Clerkenwell Rd

48 Stephen Bull's Bistro & Bar ★★$$ Young men and women from the City gather at this trendy canteen to see who else is here and to sample the daily soups, salads, and pastas. The brown sugar meringue with fudge sauce is divine. ♦ Modern British ♦ M-F lunch and dinner; Sa dinner. 71 St. John St (between St. John's La and Clerkenwell Rd). 490.1750. Tube: Barbican, Farringdon

The Sir Loin Restaurant

49 Sir Loin ★$ This is the only other Smithfield Market venue besides the **Fox and Anchor** (see above) for hearty English breakfasts, sometimes downed with Champagne. Lunch dishes include leek-and-potato soup, roast pork loin, and lamb cutlets. The restaurant is a no-nonsense, oak-paneled room above the rather basic **Hope Pub,** which offers hefty sandwiches at lunch. ♦ English ♦ M-F breakfast 7AM-9.30AM, lunch. Reservations required. 94 Cowcross St (between Charterhouse St and Farringdon Rd). 253.8525. Tube: Barbican, Farringdon

50 Smithfield Market At midnight, the vans start arriving at the oldest and largest "dead meat" market in Europe. Covering 10 acres and two miles of shop frontages, this wholesale market is still on its original medieval site. Unloading, weighing, cutting, marking, and displaying all take place before selling begins at 5AM. Starting the day at dawn amid the orderly bustle of city life makes you feel like both an honorary and an ordinary citizen, no matter where you come from.

When you stroll through the market, surrounded by white-coated butchers and "bummarees" (porters) effortlessly conveying pink, red, purple, and brown carcasses, you may feel like a background figure in a surreal painting; you'll see calves by Georgia O'Keeffe, piglets by Mother Goose, rib cages by Francis Bacon. Feathered chickens, geese, and turkeys hang alongside furry rabbits. A pervasive sense of the history of this trade allows guilt and nausea to recede: Life depends on markets, markets depend on death.

Signs announcing beef from Australia, New Zealand, and Scotland hang between the shining hooks. The arches, pillars, ornaments and swirls of ironwork that adorn the trading halls are worthy of a City church. Though the animated atmosphere is pure Gothic, the long iron-and-glass building, modeled on **Sir Joseph Paxton**'s **Crystal Palace,** is mid-Victorian; designed by **Horace Jones,** it opened in 1868 with a meaty banquet for 1,200 people. With typical Victorian high-mindedness, a small park was built in the center of **Smithfield** where the bummarees could rest, but they choose now, as they chose then, the pubs in the area, which have special licenses to serve liquor in the early morning.

The site has far more sinister associations than the slaughter of animals for consumption. Originally, it was a grassy "smooth field," or level, just outside the City walls for citizens' entertainment and exercise (hence the name, a corruption of "Smoothfield"). Executions were held here as early as 1305, when Scottish patriot William Wallace (whose life is depicted in Mel Gibson's 1995 film *Braveheart*) was put to death on St. Bartholomew's Day. Roger Mortimer, who murdered Edward II and loved his queen, was executed here on the orders of Edward III, and it was here, in 1381, that the confrontation over a poll tax took place between Wat Tyler with his band of revolutionaries and the 14-year-old Richard The young king calmed the angry mob and promised them mercy and justice. The crowd took him at his word and peacefully dispersed but Richard II delivered neither justice nor mercy, and Tyler, stabbed by Sir William Walworth during the confrontation, died a few hundred yards away at **St. Bartholomew's Hospital.** From the 15th century onward, **Smithfield** was the execution place for all who were convicted of heresy, including the Catholics set ablaze by Henry VIII and most of the 277 Protestant martyrs who also were burned alive for their faith during the reign of Mary I. **Smithfield**'s history is not entirely grim, however. The great St. Bartholomew's Fair was held here every August, from Henry II's time until 1855. The three-day event was the most important cloth fair in England, expanding as the export of wool and fabric grew. The Royal Smithfield Show (now held at Earl's Court) began here in 1799, and as far back as medieval times there was a large horse-and-cattle market; live animals were herded across the streets of London to reach it. The days of great fairs have passed, but the area has been kept vital by the remarkable and ironic juxtaposition of its two principal institutions: the meat market and the hospital. Both are under threat, however. The former may be moved elsewhere, while the latter is struggling against government cutbacks and privatization of medical services. ♦ M-F 5-10:30AM. Bounded by Lindsey St and

Farringdon Rd, and W Smithfield and Charterhouse St. Tube: Barbican, Farringdon

Within Smithfield Market:

Bubbs ★★$$$ Tucked on the outskirts of **Smithfield Market,** this bistro is a series of connecting rooms packed with City ladies and gents. The fish specials change daily, but meat lovers should stick with the entrecôte béarnaise. And if you're still hungry, there are several delicious desserts to choose from, like chocolate truffle mousse and ice-cream nougat served with raspberry sauce. ♦ French ♦ M-F lunch. 329 Central Market (between W Poultry Ave and Farringdon Rd). 236.2435

Bests

Mark Taylor
Director, Museums Association

As the global village gets smaller, the experiences available in the world's greatest cities are disturbingly similar. Here are a few suggestions that are uniquely British and leave you in no doubt you are in London:

Happy visitors march on their stomachs—London does high-class food very well:

Lunch at the **Design Museum** at **Butler's Wharf** with great food and an even better view of the **River Thames** and **Tower Bridge.**

The food halls at **Fortnum and Mason's** in **Piccadilly** and **Harrods** in **Knightsbridge**—specialist food beautifully presented and horrifyingly priced. Get there early in the morning.

Even earlier in the morning, visit **Smithfield Market,** a fascinating hive of activity with pubs, shops, and cafes surrounding the Market and all "jumping" at 6AM. A great venue for a proper English breakfast—not for vegetarians.

Take tea, as only the English can, at the **Basil Hotel** in **Knightsbridge** or the **Cadogan Hotel** in **Sloane Street.**

For art galleries that present art in an intelligent but unpatronizing way, try the **National Gallery** in **Trafalgar Square** (the evening openings are fun) or the **Tate Gallery** on **Millbank.** For a more noisy, interactive time visit the **Science** and **National History Museums** in **South Kensington** or the **Museum of the Moving Image** at **Waterloo.**

Residents forget it, but London is beautiful—particularly the River Thames and its parkland. First thing on a summer morning, the following places can do nothing but raise your spirits:

The view of the Thames from **Blackfriars Bridge.**

Canary Wharf and the new business center at the **Isle of Dogs.**

The north end of **Regents Park.**

The view toward **Buckingham Palace** from **St. James's Park.**

Hampden Court from the River.

The climb to the **Royal Observatory** and the view from the top.

Mark Rylance
Actor and Artistic Director of Shakespeare's Globe

Swimming in **Brockwell Lido** on Sunday morning over breakfast.

Riding my bicycle anywhere late at night.

Walking from **Poets' Corner** via the **Temple** to **Shakespeare's Globe** with a book of sonnets.

Sitting in the **Temple** church after walking around the Temple.

Looking at the river.

Smelling the smell of fresh carved oak and new thatch at the **Globe.**

Looking at the birds in **St. James's Park** at night.

Standing on **Parliament Hill.**

Wandering aimlessly in the **West End.**

Having a bagel late at night on **Brick Lane.**

Talking with angels and lunatics impersonating Londoners.

Carol Ripka
Manager, City Information Centre

It's a delight wandering round the streets of **Hampstead,** full of character, old world charm, beautiful architecture, hilly streets, etc.

Hampstead Heath and **Golden Hill Park, Kenwood**—all near each other offering beautiful scenery and excellent outdoor cafes. **Kenwood House** itself.

Enjoying a free jazz concert at the **National Theatre** before attending a play—all of which are excellent.

Strolling round the **Temple** area of the **Strand,** peaceful and architecturally beautiful.

Listing to a lunchtime concert in one of the churches in the **City.**

Soho/Covent Garden

The whole of Covent Garden revolves around the **Piazza**, an open square with a covered arcade modeled on Italian lines by **Inigo Jones**.

But of the 1631 original, only **St. Paul's, Covent Garden**—the church that **Jones** built between 1631 and 1633—survives. By 1830, it was fashionable for the rich to mingle in the square alongside farmers and flower girls, and this is where George Bernard Shaw got his inspiration for *Pygmalion*. Walk along these streets, once haunted by the poor, and you will tread in the footsteps of kings and actors. Nowadays, designers, ad execs, and PR people make their living in this area, and they are the clientele that so many excellent restaurants here strive to impress (all the better for visitors to London, who are typically drawn to the warren of boutiques, colorful street stalls, and sidewalk entertainment in Covent Garden). The quaint streets of this tiny area are packed and noisy, vibrant with the goings-on of locals and the comings and goings of visitors. Fashion buffs shop in **Floral Street**, **Neal Street**, and **Long Acre**.

West of Covent Garden is Soho, a neighborhood that began as a royal park but gradually deteriorated into squalor, slums, and sex shops. (Incidentally, the neighborhood's name comes from the ancient hunting cry of "So-ho!" that rang out in this area when it was a game preserve for Henry VIII.) Since the beginning of the 1980s, however, the relatively cheap rents here have attracted a more fashionable sort: filmmakers, whose releases are screened in the giant cinemas on **Leicester Square**; music companies, whose employees hang out in **Denmark Street**, London's answer to Tin Pan Alley; and designers, whose clothes are displayed in the side-street boutiques. Catering to these trendy residents is a variety of excellent restaurants and brasseries, including the huge number of Oriental eateries flourishing in Chinatown. Sit down at virtually any table in these parts and you may find yourself staring at a TV producer, a pop singer, or even a movie star.

City code 0171 unless otherwise noted.

1 Theatre Royal Drury Lane The present theater (shown at right) is the fourth on the site since 1663; two were destroyed by fire and one was demolished. "What, sir," said owner Sheridan, as his life's work went up in flames, "may a man not warm his hands at his own fireside?"

Few London theaters have so illustrious or lengthy a past as this one. Nell Gwyn made her debut in *Indian Queen* in 1665, with King Charles II, her future lover, in the audience. King George II was shot at in the theater in 1716, and his grandson George III was shot at here in 1800. One of Gainsborough's favorite models, Mary Robinson, was discovered here by the Prince of Wales while she was playing Perdita in *A Winter's Tale* in 1779, and this is where the Duke of Clarence, later William IV, first saw Dorothea Jordan, the Irish actress who became his mistress and mother of 10 of his children. The theater was also the scene of riots over admission prices and impromptu duels that spilled over from the pit onto the stage.

Today, it is the safer home of musicals, most recently *Miss Saigon*. **Benjamin Dean Wyatt** modeled the present theater, which seats 2,237 people, after the great theater at

Theatre Royal Drury Lane

Bordeaux in 1811. The portico was added in 1820, and the pillars came from **John Nash**'s quadrant on Regent Street. The interior was reconstructed in 1921. ♦ Catherine St (between Tavistock and Russell Sts). 494.5060. Tube: Covent Garden

2 Fortune Theatre The immortal line "There is a tide in the affairs of men which, taken at the flood, turns on to fortune" is embossed on a highly polished brass plaque in the foyer of this theater. Though it was built after World War II, the delightful marble-and-copper foyer shows little evidence that money and materials were scarce. This lovely, intimate theater (with 440 seats) puts on a wide

selection of plays. When ordering tickets, be sure your view of the stage isn't blocked by one of the pillars in the stalls. ♦ Russell St (between Bow St and Crown Ct). 836.2238. Tube: Covent Garden

3 Taste of India ★★$$ The vegetarian *thali* or the fashionable Bangladeshi entrées are the dishes to try in this bustling Indian restaurant. There's also a set buffet lunch that provides a choice of curries, freshly made onion *bhajis,* and *pilau* rice for a very reasonable price. A wine bar downstairs serves food from the main kitchen. ♦ Indian ♦ Daily lunch and dinner. 25 Catherine St (between Tavistock and Russell Sts). 836.2538. Tube: Covent Garden

4 Luigi's ★★$$ After the show, this Italian bistro becomes crowded with actors and opera singers, many of whom are represented by signed photographs lining the walls. The atmosphere is lively and the food authentic, especially the cannelloni. ♦ Italian ♦ M-Sa lunch and dinner. Reservations required for post-theater dinner. 15 Tavistock St (between Wellington and Catherine Sts). 240.1795. Tube: Covent Garden

LE CAFE DU JARDIN

4 Le Cafe du Jardin ★★★$$ Although the ground floor is on the smallish side and feels like a foyer, the basement is spacious and has its own bar and pianist. The menu is eclectic and features dishes such as warm salad of spicy sausage, black pudding, spinach, bacon, and mushroom; and as an entrée, roast leg of rabbit stuffed with chorizo on a pearl-barley risotto. There is a pre- and post-theater prix-fixe menu. ♦ Modern European ♦ Daily lunch and dinner. Reservations advised for lunch. 28 Wellington St (at Tavistock St). 836.8769. Tube: Covent Garden

5 Christopher's ★★★$$$ Owner Christopher Gilmour once lived in Chicago, where he fell in love with American cuisine (i.e., clam chowder, Maine lobster, and New York strip steak). So here you can sample Maryland crab cakes and grilled rib eye steak, and vegetables such as red cabbage with apple or mashed potatoes with nutmeg. The wine list includes a good American selection, and the desserts are a sure cure for homesickness. Sunday brunch is a good value. ♦ American ♦ M-F lunch and dinner; Sa dinner; Su brunch. Reservations required. 18 Wellington St (at Exeter St). 240.4222. Tube: Covent Garden

6 Joe Allen ★★$$ This is one of London's favorite American restaurants, known for its big burgers and salads, good cocktails, and an extensive blackboard of unchanging favorites, including chili. It has become a London institution and is particularly popular with the theater crowd, so you should book ahead. ♦ American ♦ Daily lunch and dinner. Reservations recommended. 13 Exeter St (between Wellington and Burleigh Sts). 836.0651. Tube: Covent Garden

7 Orso ★★$$$ Much beloved by those in the know, this flourishing first-class trattoria (run by the same group that owns **Joe Allen**) is a haven for good food and attentive service. As well as good pasta, interesting dishes feature here include fried courgette (zucchini) flower filled with wild mushroom, ricotta, and basil; and grilled scallops with artichokes and new potatoes. Some excellent Italian wines add to the pleasant dining experience. ♦ Italian ♦ Daily lunch and dinner. Reservations required. 27 Wellington St (between Exeter and Tavistock Sts). 240.5269. Tube: Covent Garden

8 London Transport Museum Housed in a former flower market hall, this fun museum has lots of hands-on exhibits, videos, and touch-screen displays. Old-fashioned buses, trams, trolley buses, and trains demonstrate how London's transport system works both above- and below-ground. Look for the original horse-drawn bus of 1829 (and learn, among other facts, that 1,000 tons of horse dung were being deposited on London street each day by the end of the 19th century). Londoners will add (with tongue firmly in cheek) that some of the exhibits are still in use on the **Northern Line.** There are also many talks, films, and special tours (ask at the information desk). The shop has great souvenirs for kids and a wide choice of charmingly nostalgic transport posters. There is a cafe. ♦ Admission. M-Th, Sa-Su; F from 11AM. 39 Wellington St (between Tavistock and Russell Sts). 379.6344. Tube: Covent Garden

By appointment to
HRH The Duke of Edinburgh
Manufacturers of Toilet Requisites
Penhaligon's Limited London

By appointment to
HRH The Prince of Wales
Manufacturers of Toilet Requisites
Penhaligon's Limited London

PENHALIGON'S

Perfumers Established 1870

8 Penhaligon's Straight from the world of *Brideshead Revisited,* this shop is filled with silver mirrors and dressing-table treasures. The bottles are exclusive and as exquisite as the scents; you won't find them elsewhere "Bluebell," in particular, is divine. ♦ M-Sa. 41 Wellington St (between Tavistock and Russell Sts). 836.2150. Tube: Covent Garden

THEATRE MUSEUM
NATIONAL MUSEUM OF
THE PERFORMING ARTS

9 Theatre Museum The 20-foot-high golden statue of *Gaiety* that dominates the ground

floor of this museum gives a hint of what's to come. Here Britain proudly displays her theater collections, showcasing the history of her stage from Shakespeare to today, with regularly changing performing arts exhibitions. (This neatly complements **Shakespeare's Globe Exhibition** in Southwark, where theater history is chronicled up to Shakespeare's era.) Theater memorabilia includes costumes, paintings, photographs, and stage models. An interactive display, "SLAP," traces the history of makeup, including special effects from *The Phantom of the Opera*. You can see theater, ballet, circus, opera, mime, puppetry, rock, and pop. Visit the costume workshop and try on a costume—there's no charge. There is a gift shop and a tiny theater. You can also book tickets for the **Barbican,** West End shows, concerts, and the **Royal National Theatre.** ♦ Admission. Tu-Su. Russell St (at Wellington St). 836.7891. Tube: Covent Garden

10 Covent Garden Market Covent Garden once produced fruits and vegetables for a 13th-century abbey in Westminster, and a market was established here in the 1700s. Immortalized by the first scene of George Bernard Shaw's *Pygmalion*, in which Cockney flower girl Eliza Doolittle sold violets to rich operagoers leaving the nearby **Royal Opera House,** the market today has more in common with the luxurious tastes of Henry Higgins. It is nonetheless a brilliant example of urban survival: The restored central market is a picturesque structure of iron-and-glass roofs covering a large square, which was designed in 1831 by **Charles Fowler.** The market's revitalization has dramatically altered this part of London, providing shops, restaurants, cafes, and pubs. At the same time, it has freed the area of the wholesale fruit and flower market that, for all its sentimental charm, clogged the surrounding streets. Although the shops in the **Piazza** are mainly boutique-size branches of existing chain stores, the surrounding stores are often one-offs (merchandise that is sold in one shop only, for a limited period). There is an antiques market within the Piazza on Monday, a crafts market Tuesday through Saturday, and occasional fairground amusements. ♦ At Russell and Henrietta Sts, and Southampton and James Sts. Tube: Covent Garden

Within Covent Garden Market:

Chez Gérard ★★$$ Facing the Piazza from the second level of the market, this glorious glass restaurant (formerly **Opera Terrace**) provides a lovely escape from the crowds in spring and summer. A branch of the steak-and-frites mini-chain of restaurants, it features crudités as a light starter or *moules marinières* (marinated mussels), followed by grilled meat dishes served with *pommes frites* (french

fries). A bottle of Côtes du Rhône enhances the food, and either the excellent cheese board or a chocolate concoction from the dessert menu rounds out the meal. ♦ French ♦ Daily lunch and dinner. 45 E Terr. 379.0666

Culpeper Mrs. C.F. Leyel founded this herbal remedies firm in 1927, naming it after Nicholas Culpeper, an herbalist from 1616-52. The products, which include lotions, soaps, and the like, are made of natural ingredients and are not tested on animals. ♦ Daily. Unit 8. 379.6698. Also at: 21 Bruton St (between New Bond St and Berkeley Sq). 629.4559. Tube: Green Park, Bond Street

Cabaret Mechanical Theatre This space is filled with playthings both old and new, including a fascinating selection of "mechanicals"—wind-up toys—many of which are fashioned by hand from wood. ♦ Daily. Unit 33. 379.7961

Market Cafe ★$ Situated at the western corner of the market, this creperie's terrace and outside tables afford fine views of the Piazza; the only problem is that when the sun is out you may not want to move for the rest of the day. There *are* tables downstairs, but the dark interior is decorated in varying shades of pink, which may detract from the otherwise tasty meal set before you. This is one of the few places in London to find an excellent selection of crepes—both sweet and savory. ♦ French ♦ Daily lunch and dinner. Unit 21. 836.2137

Museum Store Here you'll come across a bizarre collection of the best items from museum shops around the world. Sissinghurst watering cans, statues of Egyptian cats, and Mackintosh cards and prints compete for space. ♦ Daily. Unit 37. 240.5760

"The Victorian middle-classes thought the theatre was only one step removed from the brothel . . . Audiences at the ordinary theatres were too rough for the queen . . . so command performances were arranged for the court at Buckingham Palace, Windsor, and even Balmoral."

Graham Norton, *Victorian London*

Beauty or Blight: The Modern Face of London

The classical look is what appeals to British architecture's most famous outspoken critic, Prince Charles, who firmly stated, "There's no doubt in my mind that something like a spire or a dome, something which gives an inspired finish to the top of the building, has the effect of raising one's spirit in a remarkable way."

These days, informed critics disagree, disdaining buildings that they see as a pastiche of an earlier era. They speak out for architects to forge a truly modern look. Increasingly, most people concur, especially in recent years when they have been regaled with bold new buildings like the copper-clad **Ark** office block in west London (Talgarth Rd, between North End and Fulham Palace Rds). Designed jointly by **Lennart Bergstrom Architects** and **Rock Townsend Architects,** it is indeed ark-shaped and presents a distinctive silhouette.

When **Docklands** was redeveloped in the 1980s (see "The Docklands: Vibrant Revival," on page 174), it set the tone for this new spirit of adventurous building. The policy there was to save and refurbish small-scale housing, restore old warehouses, and create new buildings of glass and steel. The rest of London now reflects this approach. Perfect Georgian streets are conserved gems to come across in any stroll, but so are modern buildings erected with flourish and dynamism.

It was primarily the stark look of buildings erected in the 1960s and 1970s that set many people against what they saw as architecture that didn't belong in London and that even entailed the demolition of Victorian and Georgian buildings. Prince Charles publicly singled out the **Royal National Theatre** (South Bank Centre, Upper Ground, at Waterloo Rd), by **Sir Denys Lasdun,** saying it looked like "a concrete bunker." He further deplored a proposed **Sainsbury Wing** extension to the **National Gallery,** maintaining that it would be "like a carbuncle on the face of a much loved and elegant friend." His opinions carried some weight. Plans were scrapped and the Philadelphia firm **Venturi, Scott Brown & Associates** designed a new building faced with Portland stone to blend with the Neo-Classical original gallery. The result is considered a modern architectural success. Prince Charles himself laid the foundation stone in 1988.

The structures below exemplify the new spirit of building in London today:

Lloyd's of London Building (1 Lime St, at Leadenhall St) is the capital's most famous piece of modern architecture—and possibly one of its most controversial. Designed in 1979 by **Sir Richard Rogers** (creator of the Pompidou Center in Paris), the building shows all of its structural details, such as service pipes, metal flooring, and glass. Once maligned, it is now regarded as a striking landmark.

The **Broadgate** complex (bounded by Liverpool Street rail station and Wilson St, and Eldon and Sun Sts) is chockablock with contemporary buildings, the most striking of which is **Broadgate Arena.** The circular, open-air structure, designed by **Arup Associates,** is made of granite and glass and boasts several tiers of terraces bedecked with greenery, slanted glass windows, and modern sculptures.

The design of **Minster Court** (Mark La, at Great Tower St) echoes the look of a Gothic cathedral, complete with mock buttresses, vestige towers, and granite panels, some of which are a story high. Built in 1991 by the **GMW Partnership,** the building contains the offices of several London insurance companies, as well as shops and restaurants.

Looking ahead, the **Millennium Dome** in Greenwich by architect **Sir Richard Rogers,** was scheduled to open as we went to press, and will become the largest domed structure in the world—encompassing the equivalent of 13 **Albert Hall**s or 2 **Wembley Stadium**s. The **Dome** will contain 14 vast themed zones offering attractions and exhibits such as live theater performed six times a day. Other changes in the skyline: the **Millennium Wheel,** a giant silver-and-white Ferris wheel on the **South Bank** in **Jubilee Gardens;** a new bridge over the **Thames,** and the new **Tate Gallery of Modern Art** designed by Swiss architects **Herzog and de Meuron** in the former Bankside Power Station in Southwark (see page 42). Ironically, the gallery will be a neighbor of the new **Globe Theatre,** rebuilt as a replica of the original, using 16th-century techniques.

Lloyd's of London

Benjamin Pollock's Toy Shop Traditional toys, including hand-stitched teddies like the one you had as a child, can be found in this gem of a shop, as well as miniature, paper-cut model theaters. ♦ Daily. Unit 44. 379.7866

11 Jubilee Market Pay a fraction of the price you would in a regular shop for homemade silk lingerie, hand-knit sweaters, pottery, hand-carved wooden salad bowls, and other items. It takes time and patience to poke around the 180 stalls, but the merchandise here is worth it. The prices seem particularly good after shopping at the smart boutiques in the area. There are even a few fruit and vegetable stalls for old time's sake. There's also an antiques section, offering small items such as glassware, knickknacks, china, pottery, jewelry, and clothing. ♦ Daily. Tavistock St (between Wellington and Southampton Sts). Tube: Covent Garden

12 St. Paul's, Covent Garden When the thrifty fourth Earl of Bedford was developing **Covent Garden,** he asked **Inigo Jones** to design an economical church not much bigger than a barn. **Jones** complied, creating what he called the handsomest barn in Europe. The redbrick church features a pitched roof, overhanging eaves, and a famous Tuscan portico; the interior is now frequented by artists and actors, while the portico serves as a backdrop for many of the street performers who play here, especially during summer. Gutted by fire in 1795, the church was carefully restored by **Philip Hardwick.** Today, it is known as "the Actors' Church" because of its close association with the theater; numerous plaques inside commemorate actors and playwrights. ♦ The Piazza (between Henrietta and King Sts). Tube: Covent Garden

13 Rules ★★★$$$ Founded in 1798, London's oldest restaurant has always been a museum of London's literary and theatrical beau monde, and it still is today. The Prince of Wales (later Edward VII) and his mistress Lillie Langtry drank Champagne behind a special door on the first floor, and Dickens had a regular table across the room. With the arrival of game season in autumn, this spot becomes irresistible—an ideal location for a leisurely lunch. Chef David Chambers's specialties include whole roasted widgeon (wild duck) with pureed parsnips; roast partridge with foie gras, and pease pudding (split peas) with thyme sauce. ♦ British ♦ Daily lunch and dinner. Reservations required. 35 Maiden La (between Southampton and Bedford Sts). 836.5314. Tube: Covent Garden

14 Porters ★★$$ Owned by Richard, the seventh Earl of Bradford, this restaurant serves English fare: pies, sausages, and delicious nursery puddings like apple and blackberry crumble, bread-and-butter pudding, spotted dick (a sponge cake baked with currants or raisins), and Sherry trifle. The prices are honest and it's fun for babies and toddlers, too. ♦ British ♦ Daily lunch and dinner. 17 Henrietta St (between Southampton and Bedford Sts). 836.6466. Tube: Covent Garden, Charing Cross

15 TGI Friday's ★$$ Tiffany lamps hang in this cavernous place. You can munch on a big burger or chunky chicken wings and choose a cocktail from a long, impressive list. There is also a special children's menu. ♦ American ♦ Daily lunch and dinner. 6 Bedford St (at Chandos Pl). 379.0585. Tube: Covent Garden, Charing Cross

16 O'Neills ★$ Formerly **P.J. Malloy and Sons,** this Irish theme pub is decorated to look like an old-fashioned draper's shop that just happens to sell alcohol (a familiar combination in rural Ireland). Dishes include Irish stew with colcannon (mashed potatoes with spring onions and shredded cabbage) and blarney ginger cake. An Irish band plays Thursday and Sunday from 8:30PM. ♦ Irish pub ♦ M-Sa lunch; drinks M-Sa, Su noon-10:30PM. 14 New Row (between Bedford St and Bedfordbury). 836.3291. Tube: Leicester Square. Also at: Numerous locations throughout the city

17 Garrick Club Dickens, Trollope, Millais, and Rossetti met actors and "men of education and refinement" in this gloriously ornate gentlemen's club, founded in 1831 and named in honor of Shakespearean actor David Garrick. The portraits of famous British stage actors that hang on the walls are said to comprise the best collection of theatrical paintings in the country. Unfortunately, the club is closed to the general public. ♦ 15 Garrick St (between New Row and St. Martin's La). Tube: Leicester Square

18 Lamb & Flag ★★$ The cobbled courtyard of this lovely and extremely popular pub (ca. 1627) is always filled with office workers. But it wasn't always so nice. The back room was called the "Bucket of Blood"' after the bare-knuckle fights held there and in 1679 the poet John Dryden was badly beaten up in the alley for writing nasty things about Charles II's mistress. ♦ Pub ♦ Daily lunch and dinner. 33 Rose St (at Garrick St). 497.9504. Tube: Covent Garden, Leicester Square

---

Restaurants/Clubs: Red	**Hotels:** Blue
Shops/ 🌳 Outdoors: Green	**Sights/Culture:** Black

19 Moss Bros. An upscale store that caters to England's gentry, it offers plenty of top designer menswear, as well as a department that rents formalwear to Ascot attendees, the charity ball set, bridegrooms, and best men. ♦ M-Sa. 27 King St (at Bedford St). 497.9354. Tube: Covent Garden, Leicester Square

20 Calabash ★$$ African food is served in a laid-back, slightly seedy dining room in the **Africa Center,** making a change from the hectic tourism of Covent Garden. Masks, headdresses, and batik cloths decorate the walls and tables. Choose from Ghanaian groundnut stew, Tanzanian beef stew with green bananas and coconut cream, vegetarian couscous, and excellent Zimbabwean and Algerian wines. It's been going strong since the 1960s. ♦ African ♦ M-F lunch and dinner; Sa dinner. 38 King St (between Covent Garden Market and Garrick St). 836.1976. Tube: Covent Garden, Leicester Square

20 Palms Pasta on the Piazza ★★$ The food at this light, airy dining spot is usually delicious. Fresh pasta is a specialty here: Try the spaghetti with mussels or the penne salvatore (creamy spinach and chicken sauce). The grilled salmon on spinach in parsley sauce is also excellent. To finish, there's banoffi pie (sliced bananas in pie crust topped with toffee) and homemade ice cream. The set meals are good value. The restaurant doesn't take reservations, so get here early for lunch or after 2PM; it's a good idea to come early on Friday and Saturday nights as well. ♦ Italian ♦ Daily lunch and dinner. 39 King St (between Covent Garden Market and Garrick St). 240.2939. Tube: Covent Garden, Charing Cross

21 agnès b. White walls and pine floors showcase a collection of practical French clothing for men, women, and children. ♦ M-Sa; Su noon-5PM. 35-36 Floral St (between Banbury and Conduit Cts). 379.1992. Tube: Covent Garden

21 Tintin Shop The Belgian cartoon character is emblazoned on every item in the store, including mugs and T-shirts. The books featuring the character are also sold here. ♦ Daily. 34 Floral St (between Banbury and Conduit Cts). 836.1131. Tube: Covent Garden

22 Sanctuary This spa for women only is an idyllic and essential indulgence. Restore your spirits and health in the sauna, Turkish steam room, swimming pool, and Jacuzzi, or make use of the sun bed. Shampoo, conditioner, towels, soap, body lotion, and cologne are provided free. Indulge further with top-to-toe beauty treatments, including massage and facial, and a healthy lunch at the food bar. ♦ Daily membership fee (beauty treatments extra); evening rate available from 5-10PM. M-Tu, Sa-Su; W-F 10AM-10PM. 12 Floral St (between James and Rose Sts). 420.5151. Tube: Covent Garden

23 Paul Smith Even restrained men go wild in this shop, trying on stylish suits, sportswear, sweaters, and shoes. Combining the timeless and the trendy is Smith's specialty; he describes his clothes as "classic with a twist." Women's fashions and kid's clothes are sold next door. ♦ M-Sa. 40-44 Floral St (between Langley and Banbury Cts). 379.7133. Tube: Covent Garden

24 Long Acre Once the medieval market garden for **Westminster Abbey** (where monks grew crops such as potatoes or apples for sale), this street became the center of both coach- and furniture-making by the middle of the 18th century. It's easy to imagine Thomas Chippendale walking to his workshop here from his home in St. Martin's Lane. ♦ Between Bow St and St. Martin's La. Tube: Covent Garden

24 Blazer Preppy clothing for men, British style, can be purchased here at reasonable prices. ♦ Daily. 36 Long Acre (between James St and Langley Ct). 379.6258. Tube: Covent Garden. Also at: Numerous locations throughout the city

24 Dôme ★$ Part of a citywide chain, this eatery offers good snacks and croissants, as well as coffee, tea, and wine. Good main-course options include the meat casseroles and salads. ♦ Brasserie ♦ Daily breakfast, lunch, and dinner. 32 Long Acre (between James St and Langley Ct). 379.8650. Tube: Covent Garden. Also at: 354 King's Rd (between Beaufort St and Park Walk). 352.2828. Tube: South Kensington

25 Royal Opera House Three theaters have stood on this site since 1732. The great dome you see today is **E.M. Barry**'s 1858 design, capable of seating 2,096. The frieze under the portico, *Tragedy and Comedy* by Flaxman, was salvaged in 1855 from a fire at the theater. In 1946, **Covent Garden** became the home of the **Royal Opera** and, for a time, the **Royal Ballet.** At press time, the theater was closed for an extensive renovation; it is scheduled to reopen in December 1999 as the home once more of both the opera and ballet companies, as well as a basement studio theater and small dance performance space upstairs. ♦ Box office M-Sa 10AM-8PM. Bow St (at Floral St). 304.4000; www.royaloperahouse.org.uk. Tube: Covent Garden

26 Bow Street This street really is shaped like a bow. **Covent Garden**'s cafe society reads like a Who's Who of English history and literature. But most of it happened in just two spots: the **Garrick Club** on Garrick Street (see page 165) and the long-departed **Will's Coffee House** on Bow, where you could expect to meet Pepys, Dryden, Pope, Swift, Johnson, Boswell, Sheridan, and Henry Fielding—though not all at the same time. This area was poor and dangerous in the late 18th century, and eventually things got so unruly that Fielding, who was a local magistrate, established the forerunners of today's police force to catch thieves; they were called the "Bow Street Runners." There is still a **Bow Street Magistrates' Court.** ♦ Between Russell St and Long Acre. Tube: Covent Garden

THE FIELDING HOTEL

27 Fielding $$ This is a rare hotel in London: small, relatively inexpensive, and quiet. It attracts performers from the **Royal Opera House,** a stone's throw away, and media and arts clientele, who are drawn by the discreet charm and perfect location. The 24 rooms are modest and small—all have showers instead of baths—and there's no restaurant, but the pedestrians-only street outside spares you from the sounds of cars at night. The hotel is named after Henry Fielding, the author of *Tom Jones.* He was also a magistrate at **Bow Street Court** nearby. ♦ 4 Broad Ct (at Crown Ct). 836.8305; fax 497.0064. Tube: Covent Garden

28 Cafe des Amis du Vin ★★$$ This elegant, popular restaurant with a distinctive apricot interior features French cuisine with Italian, British, and Thai influences. Start with boiled quail's eggs on prosciutto or scallop *boudin* with crab coleslaw. Then move on to corn-fed chicken with wild-mushroom polenta or traditional sirloin steak and french fries. For dessert try the iced Calvados parfait with

glazed apples and cinnamon sauce. There's a pre- and post-theater menu. ♦ French ♦ M-Sa lunch and dinner. Reservations recommended. 11-14 Hanover Pl (between Floral St and Long Acre). 379.3444. Tube: Covent Garden

29 Emporio Armani Everyone who is anyone flocks here for *très chic* men's and women's clothing, accessories, jeans, and casual wear. ♦ M-Sa; Su 11:30AM-5:30PM. 57-59 Long Acre (between Bow St and Hanover Pl). 917.6882. Tube: Covent Garden. Also at: 191 Brompton Rd (between Beaufort Gardens and Beauchamp Pl). 823.8818. Tube: Knightsbridge

30 Magno's ★★$$ Hidden away at the end of Long Acre, this restaurant is a favorite of theater buffs, who come for coq au vin or roquefort in puff pastry. There's a spectacular wine list, and a set menu at lunch (a better value, as otherwise vegetables are charged à la carte). ♦ French ♦ M-F lunch and dinner; Sa dinner. Reservations recommended. 65a Long Acre (between Hanover Pl and James St). 836.6077. Tube: Covent Garden

31 Neal Street East Everything Asian is sold here, from Afghan tribal jewelry to tiny Chinese pincushions. ♦ M-Sa; Su noon-6PM. 5 Neal St (between Long Acre and Shelton St). 240.0135. Tube: Covent Garden

31 Tea House If you like London policemen, you can buy a ceramic one here and he will pour your tea forever. The shop is packed with eccentric and absurd teapots and a vast array of teas, from decaffeinated and jasmine blends to spiced Christmas teas. ♦ M-Sa; Su noon-6PM. 15a Neal St (between Long Acre and Shelton St). 240.7539. Tube: Covent Garden

31 Natural Shoe Store It seems like this shop has been here forever, selling well-made traditional English shoes for men and women. They also do "Jesus boots": healthy shoes with thick soles and straps for people who believe that comfort comes before looks. ♦ M-Sa; Su noon-5:30PM. 21 Neal St (between Long Acre and Shelton St). 836.5254. Tube: Covent Garden. Also at: 325 King's Rd (at Beaufort St). 351.3721. Tube: South Kensington

"I have often amused myself with thinking about how different a place London is to different people."

James Boswell

There are about 750 employees of the Royal Household in Buckingham Palace, Windsor, Holyrood House, and St. James's Palace. Housemaids and footmen earn £9,000-£11,000; secretaries, administrators, and clerks, £14,500-£18,000; middle managers and chefs, £20,000-£25,000; and senior managers, £43,000-£53,000.

Small Wonders

The most famous museums in London—the **British Museum,** the **National Gallery,** the **Tate,** the **National Portrait Gallery,** and the **Victoria and Albert Museum**—are far too large to be fully appreciated in a single visit. At these grand behemoths, the most you can hope to do is get a sense of all the riches they contain. But London also boasts a number of small, special museums that are far less daunting. Most of them focus on one particular theme, and they can be easily seen in an hour or so. Here are some of the best.

Bank of England Museum Although the fortress-like bank that houses the nation's gold supply is off-limits to visitors, the on-site museum tells the history of its monetary maneuvers and offers money-minded gawkers vicarious satisfactions with its display of gold bars and coins and even surprisingly good forged notes. ♦ Free. M-F. Bartholomew La (between Threadneedle St and Lothbury). 207/601.5792.

Carlyle's House The 18th-century house in **Chelsea** where the writer and historian lived with his wife, Jane, for 47 years has been faithfully preserved in Victorian splendor, including the authentic furnishings, books, portraits of the Carlyles, oil lamps—even Carlyle's hat, still hanging on the hat stand by the door. ♦ Admission. W-Su Apr-Oct. 24 Cheyne Row (between Cheyne Walk and Upper Cheyne Row). 207/352.7087.

Florence Nightingale Museum Appropriately located in **St. Thomas's Hospital,** at which the renowned nurse inspired Britain's first nursing school in 1860, this museum documents the life and career of the "lady with the lamp." Among the items displayed here are Nightingale's prescription book, medicine chest, and the famous lamp she carried during the Crimean War. ♦ Admission. Tu-Su 2 Lambeth Palace Rd (at Westminster Bridge Rd). 207/620.0374.

Freud Museum Set in the house in **Hampstead** where the Viennese "father of psychoanalysis" lived from 1938 until his death in 1939, the museum contains antiques and Freud-related books, but the main attraction is the actual couch on which his patients reclined while he delved into their psyches. ♦ Admission. W-Su noon-5PM. 20 Maresfield Gardens (between Fitzjohn's Ave and Nutley Terr). 207/435.3471.

Keats House John Keats, author of such evocative poems as "Ode on a Grecian Urn" and "The Eve of St. Agnes," lived in this Regency house from 1818 to 1820. He wrote "Ode to a Nightingale" while sitting under a plum tree in the garden. On display in the house are letters, manuscripts, books, and other memorabilia of the tragically short-lived romantic English poet. ♦ Free. M-F 10AM-1PM and 2-6PM, Sa 10AM-1PM, Su 2-5PM Apr-Oct; M-F 1-5PM, Sa 10AM-1PM and 2-5PM, Su 2-5PM Nov-Mar. Keats Grove (between South End Rd and Downshire Hill). 207/435.2062.

Museum of Garden History A special treat for visitors who share the English passion for gardening, this museum, located in the deconsecrated 14th-century church of **St. Mary's-at-Lambeth,** explores the subject at length with display panels showing how gardening evolved from monastic herb cultivation to country cottage profusion. There's even a little garden of plants that are labeled to show when they were introduced to England, such as the then-exotic irises (1373), geraniums (1375), lungworts (1525), and lilies (1634). ♦ Free. M-F, Su Mar-Dec. Lambeth Palace Rd (at Lambeth Rd). 207/401.8865.

Post Office Archives The history of Britain's postal service is lovingly chronicled here. Among the exhibits transferred here in 1999 from the old **National Postal Museum** on King Edward Street are stamps, postal documents, drawings, letter boxes, and a bit of rock 'n' roll memorabilia—the postal album belonging to the late Freddie Mercury, philatelist and lead singer of the band Queen. Free. By appointment, M-F. Freeling House, Phoenix Place, Mount Pleasant Complex. 207/239.2570.

St. Bride's Church In this grand church designed by **Sir Christopher Wren,** the crypt contains a museum dedicated to the history of the printing process and **Fleet Street** journalism. Displays include examples of 18th- and 19th-century pamphlets and news-papers as well as photographs showing Fleet Street in its heyday. ♦ Free. Daily. Bride La (off Fleet St). 207/353.1301.

Thomas Coram Foundation Accessible only by appointment, this museum, founded by sea captain and philanthropist Thomas Coram, displays several paintings by Hogarth, Gainsborough, and Reynolds. Another precious item here is Handel's original manuscript of the *Messiah.* ♦ Admission. By appointment only. 40 Brunswick Sq (off Hunter St). 207/278.2424

Keats House

32 Belgo Centraal ★★$ This is the best place for *moules* this side of Brussels, so if you can't make it to the Continent, come here. The restaurant is large and boisterous but people flock here for the beer hall atmosphere and the Belgian beer, flavored with fruit juices like raspberry and blueberry. Dishes include wild boar sausages with *stoemp* (mashed potatoes). ◆ Belgian ◆ Daily lunch and dinner. Reservations required. 50 Earlham St (at Neal St). 813.2233. Tube: Covent Garden. Also at: 72 Chalk Farm Rd (between Ferdinand and Belmont Sts). 267.0718. Tube: Chalk Farm

33 Thomas Neal's Like a modern **Burlington Arcade,** this is a barrel-vaulted brick mall on a diminutive scale with more than two dozen small, idiosyncratic specialty shops, a restaurant, and a theater. ◆ Shorts Gardens (between Neal and Monmouth Sts); another entrance is on Earlham St (between Neal and Monmouth Sts). Tube: Covent Garden

Within Thomas Neal's:

Luna Nuova ★★$$ Good for a quick bite while spending a day shopping, or before or after the theater, the conventional menu features reasonably priced pizzas and pasta plus a strong wine list. Pre- and post-theater menus are available. ◆ Italian ◆ Daily lunch and dinner. 836.4110

Lunn Antiques Risk the temptation of dreamy antique lace nightdresses and blissful christening gowns lovingly made by someone's grandma a long time ago. Textiles, clothing, and costumes from the 19th century to the early 1960s are plentiful in this little shop. ◆ M-Sa. 379.1974

Changing Room Drop in here for a wide selection of women's clothes by designers from Britain and the Continent. The staff is friendly and helpful. ◆ M-Sa; Su 12:30-5:30PM. 379.4158. Also at: 10a Gees Ct (between Oxford and Barrett Sts). 408.1596. Tube: Bond Street

Donmar Warehouse Refurbished in 1992, this 252-seat venue now hosts all sorts of theater. This is where Nicole Kidman took London by storm in her first stage appearance in *The Blue Angel.* ◆ Entrance on Earlham St (between Neal and Monmouth Sts). 369.1732. Tube: Covent Garden

33 Space NK Apothecary Known as the "coolest" beauty shop in London, this place pioneered the non-intimidating, help-yourself school of selling cosmetics. Beauty labels such as Stila (makeup-artist cosmetics) and Philosophy are the stock in trade. ◆ 379.7030. Also at: 307 Kings Rd (between Old Church St and The Vale). 351.7209. Tube: South Kensington; 307 Brompton Rd (between Draycott Ave and Egerton Crescent). 589.8250. Tube: South Kensington

34 Food for Thought ★$ This tiny restaurant classes itself for "gourmets on a budget." There's often a line to get in, especially at lunch (it also has takeaway food), but if you don't mind being hurried and eating practically in someone else's lap, try the carrot, orange, and ginger soup, or penne pasta Milano. The menu changes each day, but stir-fried vegetables with brown rice and quiche are constants. And try the scrunch, a legendary dessert with a thick oat base topped with fruit, yogurt, cream, and/or honey. No alcohol is sold but you can bring your own wine for evening meals. ◆ Vegetarian ◆ M-Sa breakfast, lunch, and dinner; Su lunch. No credit cards accepted. 31 Neal St (between Earlham St and Shorts Gardens). 836.0239. Tube: Covent Garden

35 Neal Street Restaurant ★★$$$$ Brick walls hung with abstract art and wild mushrooms, which are displayed in profusion near the entrance, have added to this restaurant's popularity. The famous celebrity chef here is Antonio Carluccio; try his delicious carpaccio of beef with truffle cheese. But tread carefully through the menu, for it can become quite pricey. ◆ Italian ◆ M-Sa lunch and dinner. Reservations required. 26 Neal St (between Shelton St and Shorts Gardens). 836.8368. Tube: Covent Garden

36 Diana's Diner ★$ Here's a great place for cheap and good (if unimaginative) British/Italian cafe grub. The hearty food will weigh you down, so complete the day's sightseeing before you come here. If you're into British food, feast on the liver and bacon with chips followed by one of the filling desserts; otherwise, opt for spaghetti carbonara, lasagna *al forno* (baked lasagna), or cannelloni. You'll have to adjust your waistband, but your wallet will remain relatively unscathed. ◆ British/Italian ◆ M-Sa breakfast, lunch, and dinner; Su breakfast, lunch, and afternoon tea. 39 Endell St (between Shelton St and Shorts Gardens). 240.0272. Tube: Covent Garden

37 Rock & Sole Plaice ★★$ Reputed to be the oldest surviving fish-and-chips shop in London, this place is clean, inexpensive, and rather small. In fine weather, you can sit outside, munching on delectable plaice or cod fried in a crisp, golden batter and accompanied by "mushy peas" and wedge-shaped chips. ◆ British ◆ M-Sa lunch and dinner. 47 Endell St (at Shorts Gardens). 836.3785. Tube: Covent Garden

38 Ajimura ★★$$ Japanese food in London can be very expensive, but this casual spot has kept its prices reasonable. This versatile and relaxed restaurant offers sashimi, sushi, tempura, sukiyaki, *shabu-shabu,* and an endless variety of set meals and menu specials. ♦ Japanese ♦ M-F lunch and dinner; Sa dinner. Reservations recommended for dinner. 51-53 Shelton St (between Drury La and Endell St). 240.9424. Tube: Covent Garden

39 Arthur Beale The shop's founder, yacht chandler Arthur Beale, could trace his origins back to a company of 16th-century rope makers on the Fleet River. Dream of the sea as you look at the bright-yellow macs and boots sold here. It looks so nautical and shipshape that fashion shoots for magazines often get their props here. ♦ M-F; Sa 9:30AM-1PM. 194 Shaftesbury Ave (at Monmouth St). 836.9034. Tube: Tottenham Court Road

40 Mysteries New Agers and the wholly holistic dip in to buy their crystals, books, a new tarot pack, or to get in touch with the future—and the shop's resident clairvoyants, palmists, and crystal ball gazers are happy to help. ♦ M-Sa. 9-11 Monmouth St (between Neal's Yard and Neal St). 240.3688. Tube: Tottenham Court Road

41 Kite Store Drop in here for kites, Frisbees, boomerangs, and anything else that flies. ♦ M-Sa. 48 Neal St (at Shorts Gardens). 836.1666. Tube: Covent Garden

41 Equinox At this astrology shop quasi-scientific horoscopes can be prepared while you wait, or you can rummage among the astrology books, cassettes, videos, and prints. ♦ M-Sa. 78 Neal St (between Shorts Gardens and Monmouth St). 749.1001. Tube: Covent Garden

As recently as World War II, Nazi war criminal Rudolph Hess was a prisoner in the Tower of London.

The world's largest diamond, the Cullinan, was mailed third class from South Africa, considered the safest way to get it to London.

Restaurants/Clubs: Red   **Hotels:** Blue
Shops/ 🌳 **Outdoors:** Green   **Sights/Culture:** Black

41 Janet Fitch Featured here is contemporary jewelry from some of Britain's top designers Simon Day, Meital Hillel, Faith Tavender, and Jessica Briggs. Most of the pieces are sterling silver, but there are some in gold and gold plate. ♦ M-Sa; Su 1-6PM. 37a Neal St (at Shorts Gardens). 240.6332. Tube: Covent Garden. Also at: 25a Old Compton St (at Dean St). 287.3789. Tube: Leicester Square; 188a King's Rd (between Chelsea Manor and Oakley St). 352.440l. Tube: South Kensington Sloane Square

42 Neal's Yard This quaint little courtyard is jammed with tiny shops specializing in top-quality food popular with the health conscious. ♦ Between Shorts Gardens and Monmouth St. Tube: Covent Garden

Within Neal's Yard:

Neal's Yard Dairy Everything is British here, from the blue sheeps' cheeses to the little round goat cheeses and the well-matured cheddars. It's like walking into an edible map of England: caerphilly, red leicester, sage derby . . . all with their own names and from those parts of the country that provided them. Move over France, the British cheesemakers are here. ♦ Daily. 379.7646

Neal's Yard Bakery and Tearoom ★$ Soups, pizza, and salads can be eaten in the upstairs tearoom, while the shop sells wonderful breads, organic vegetable juice, and Indian vegetarian curries to take away. ♦ Vegetarian ♦ M-Sa early lunch and early dinner. 836.5199

Neal's Yard Remedies Catering to New Age health enthusiasts, this apothecary sells herbal medicines packaged in old-fashioned blue-glass jars and bottles. ♦ Daily. 379.722.

43 Mon Plaisir ★★$$ An authentic bistro and pre-theater stalwart, this eatery presents good food with service to match. Garlic-laden escargots and coq au vin star on the French classics menu, along with vegetarian options. There's also a convenient prix-fixe pre-theater menu. ♦ French ♦ M-F lunch and dinner; Sa dinner. 21 Monmouth St (between Seven Dials and Neal's Yard). 836.7243. Tube: Covent Garden

43 Monmouth Coffee House Taste the delicious freshly ground coffee along with Danish pastries in the tiny cafe in the back of this store, and then buy some coffee beans to take home. There is a limited range of top-quality coffees like Colombian Medellí Kenyan, and Papua New Guinea mild. ♦ M-Sa. Su 11AM-2PM, 2:45-4:30PM. 27 Monmouth St (between Seven Dials and Neal's Yard). 836.5272. Tube: Covent Garden

44 Mountbatten $$$$ Theater lovers flock to this 127-room Radisson property named after Lord Louis Mountbatten of Burma, the much beloved uncle of Prince Charles who was killed tragically in a 1979 terrorist bombing.

The Edwardian-style hotel could almost be Broadlands, the family seat, it's so full of Mountbatten memorabilia, comfy sofas, chandeliers, and marble. There's also a restaurant. ♦ 20 Monmouth St (at Seven Dials). 836.4300, 800/333.3333; fax 240.3540. Tube: Covent Garden

45 Seven Dials A tall column stood in the center of this junction of seven streets, and each of the column's seven faces contained a sundial—hence the name. The area was once a notorious thieves' quarter—Dickens described it in *Sketches by Boz,* published in 1834—and when word got out that the column was built by Thomas Neale, Master of the Mint (where British coins are struck), a legend grew that treasure was buried at the bottom of the column. It was actually dug up in 1773, but nothing was there. The pillar was sent to Weybridge in Surrey at the time, and it wasn't until 1989 that some locals banded together to pay for a replacement. ♦ At Monmouth and Mercer Sts. Tube: Covent Garden

46 St. Martin's Lane Furniture builder Thomas Chippendale once lived here, but that didn't stop the city from knocking down the buildings to make way for **Trafalgar Square.** Unfortunately, they didn't renumber the street, so it starts at No. 29! ♦ Between William IV and Litchfield Sts. Tube: Leicester Square

46 Beotys ★★$$ A **Covent Garden** favorite and one of the oldest Greek restaurants in town (it opened the year World War II ended), this comfortable, informal place decorated in a blue and white color scheme is known for its charming, competent waiters, delicious dolmas, and succulent lamb. The restaurant also offers some French and Portuguese dishes, but you're better off sticking to the Greek-Cypriot side of the menu. ♦ Greek ♦ M-Sa lunch and dinner. 79 St. Martin's La (between Great Newport and Litchfield Sts). 836.8768. Tube: Leicester Square

47 Edward Stanford The largest collection of maps, guides, charts, atlases, and travel books in the world is located in this Edwardian shop, built in 1901. David Livingstone had his maps drawn here. ♦ M-Sa. 12-14 Long Acre (between Slingsby Pl and Upper St. Martin La). 836.1915. Tube: Leicester Square

48 Photographer's Gallery This is probably the best gallery for photographic art in London, usually running three exhibitions by international photographers at a time. It is split into two venues a couple of doors apart, with a cafe at **No. 5.** There are free gallery tours as well as admission-only lectures; times vary. ♦ Free. Admission for lectures. M-Sa. 5. 8 Great Newport St (between Upper St. Martin's La and Charing Cross Rd). 831.1772. Tube: Leicester Square

48 Unicorn Arts Theatre Founded in 1948, London's oldest professional children's theater has adventurous plays, concerts, and entertainments for 4-to-12-year-olds. In the evenings, there are shows for theatergoers 16 and over. ♦ 6-7 Great Newport St (between Upper St. Martin's La and Charing Cross Rd). 836.3334. Tube: Leicester Square

49 Sheekeys ★★★★$$$ Started in 1896, this is among London's oldest and best-loved seafood restaurants, tucked away on St. Martin's Court alongside two theaters—**Wyndham's** and **Albery.** Arranged as a series of rooms, the restaurant has a traditional and somewhat formal atmosphere, with mahogany-paneled walls, antique reproductions, and lots of photos of actors, directors, and other theater people who have eaten here over the years (including Laurence Olivier, Maggie Smith, Vanessa Redgrave, and Christopher Plummer). Expertly prepared lobster, potted shrimps, flambéed scallops, Dover sole—you name it, they serve it. Even the humble fish cake tastes dreamlike here. Have a dozen oysters with a bottle of house wine or a full meal at the long oyster bar. Pre-theater dinners and set lunches offer the best value. While you're here, take a look at a genuine Van Gogh—the artist's painting *The Indian Maiden* is displayed prominently on one wall. ♦ Seafood ♦ M-Sa lunch and dinner. Reservations recommended on Saturday. 28-32 St. Martin's Ct (between St. Martin's La and Charing Cross Rd). 240.2565. Tube: Leicester Square. Also at: 11 Queen Victoria St (at Queen St). 489.8067. Tube: Bank

50 Browns ★★$$ This brasserie, one of a chain that began in Oxford and Cambridge, is

housed in a grand building formerly occupied by local magistrates' courts. Where once crimes and sentences were duly considered by judges and lawyers, now reasonably priced meals are served in a handsome, spacious room with enormous mirrors, brown leather banquettes along beige walls, black lacquer-topped tables, and lots of plants. English and French dishes are featured, such as country chicken pie or gigot of lamb. ♦ English/French ♦ Daily lunch and dinner. 82-84 St. Martin's La (between St. Martin's Pl and Cecil Ct). 497.5050. Tube: Leicester Square. Also at: 47 Maddox St (between St. George and New Bond Sts). 491.4565. Tube: Oxford Circus; 114 Draycott Ave (between Donne Pl and Walton St). 584.5359. Tube: South Kensington

51 Giovanni's ★★$$$ Pictures of the West End stars who pop across after they're finished for the night fill this good old-fashioned Italian restaurant that offers about 60 traditional dishes on its menu. It seems like Giovanni has been here forever. Its location is a bonus—a gem of a passageway lined with charming 17th-century houses. ♦ Italian ♦ M-F lunch and dinner; Sa dinner. 10 Goodwin's Ct (at Bedfordbury). 240.2877. Tube: Leicester Square

52 Coliseum This 2,356-seat theater is the home of the **English National Opera,** which sings only in English. It has a very splendid interior, complete with chariots, granite columns, and 20 boxes. The globe on top was designed to revolve, but an obscure 1904 legal ordinance prevented this; the flashing lights on the globe are the next best thing. ♦ St. Martin's La (between Brydges Pl and Mays Ct). 632.8300. Tube: Leicester Square

53 Royal Court Theatre Downstairs at the Duke of York's This mouthful of a theater name is due to the transfer here of the **English Stage Company,** which normally performs at the **Royal Court Theatre** in Chelsea. The company will continue its original and avant-garde productions in this 647-seat venue until its own theater is completely refurbished. (The studio theater has its own temporary home at the **Ambassadors Theatre,** see page 173). ♦ St. Martin's La (between St. Martin's Pl and Cecil Ct). 565.5000. Tube: Leicester Square

53 Droopy & Browns This dreamy wedding gown, party dress, and ball gown designer set

up shop here with opera- and ballet-goers in mind. As you leave the **Coliseum** opposite, next week's "opening night outfit" beckons from window displays. Lace, velvet, satin, an silk—all are available at a price. ♦ M-Sa. 99 St. Martin's La (between St. Cecil Ct and St. Martin's Pl). 379.4514. Tube: Leicester Square

54 Dance Books This shop sells volumes, videos, CDs, cards, and pictures covering all aspects of dance and movement. ♦ M-Sa. 15 Cecil Ct (between St. Martin's La and Charing Cross Rd). 836.2314. Tube: Leicester Square

54 David Drummond at Pleasures of Past Times Showtime is captured forever in the books sold here—plays, star biographies, and other theatrical books. You also can buy printed Victoriana—the greeting cards are a real find. ♦ M-F 11AM-2:30PM and 3:30-5:45PM. On the first Saturday of the month, open 11AM-2:15PM. 11 Cecil Ct (between St Martin's La and Charing Cross Rd). 836.1142 Tube: Leicester Square

54 Bell, Book and Radmall This shop is reserved for the dedicated bibliophile only. Expensive first editions reside in locked glass cabinets tended by a knowledgeable staff. ♦ M-Sa. 4 Cecil Ct (between St. Martin's La and Charing Cross Rd). 240.2161. Tube: Leicester Square

55 Murder One Budding supersleuths will have a field day in this brightly lit bookshop, with its volumes of mysteries and all sorts of crim fiction. If you're looking for tips from the grea detectives, you can find Sherlock Holmes, Hercule Poirot, and Miss Marple lurking among the shelves. There are also huge areas devoted to horror, science fiction, fantasy, and romance. ♦ M-Sa. 71-73 Charing Cross Rd (between Little Newport St and Shaftesbury Ave). 734.3485. Tube: Leicester Square

56 Quinto and Francis Edwards Bookshop Look at the glorious leather-bound first editions and antiquarian books here, or study the impressive collection of old military maps and prints. There are secondhand books, too. ♦ Daily. 48a Charing Cross Rd (at Great Newport St). 379.7669. Tube: Leicester Square

56 Charing Cross Road Books It's a wonder the floors don't give way under the myriad ancient books crammed into every conceivable cranny. There's a super-cheap bargain basement where you'll pay pennies (as little as 40p!) for a book, and a vast selection on the ground floor, where you can wax lyrical over the poetry and history, or grow hot under the collar in the political section. ♦ Daily. 56 Charing Cross Rd (between Great Newport and Litchfield Sts). 836.3697. Tube: Leicester Square

56 Any Amount of Books Here you'll find just what it says—this bookstore catches the overflow from nearby **Charing Cross Road Books.** ♦ Daily. 62 Charing Cross Rd (between Great Newport and Litchfield Sts). 240.8140. Tube: Leicester Square

57 Shipley Specialist Art Booksellers This specialist art bookseller is just up the road from the **National Gallery** and, as might be expected, they've got fine art books as well as titles on every kind of working art: graphics, design, fashion, architecture, photography, interior design, and furniture. ♦ M-Sa. 70 Charing Cross Rd (between Great Newport and Litchfield Sts). 836.4872. Tube: Leicester Square

57 Zwemmer Arts Bookshop Picasso, Mondrian, Warhol, Gainsborough . . . this art historians' mecca sells fabulous, opulent books on art and architecture. It's the leading shop of its type in Britain—possibly in Europe. There's a second branch a few yards away that concentrates on photography, design, film, and graphic arts books. ♦ M-Sa. 24 Litchfield St (at Charing Cross Rd). 240.4158. Also at: 80 Charing Cross Rd (at Litchfield St). 240.4157; 72 Charing Cross Rd (between Litchfield and Great Newport Sts). 240.1559. Tube (for all): Leicester Square

58 Ivy ★★★$$ There are many artistic touches—mirrors, wood panels, stained glass, and diamond lattice windows—in this utterly trendy, upmarket brasserie. This spot is a favorite with stage and screen stars and the food is as appealing as the decor. You can eat anything here from bacon and eggs to caviar. Good menu choices include the kedgeree with smoked haddock, salmon, and wild mushrooms and salmon cakes served on spinach with sorrel sauce. ♦ Modern European ♦ Daily lunch and dinner. Reservations required at least one month in advance. 1 West St (at Litchfield St). 836.4751. Tube: Leicester Square

59 St. Martin's Agatha Christie's *The Mousetrap,* the world's longest-running play (as listed in the *Guinness Book of Records*), transferred to this 550-seat venue from the nearby **Ambassador** in 1974. The play premiered in 1952 and, since everyone who sees it is sworn to secrecy, the whodunit factor has remained an attractive draw. A popular show with families, it is well worth the cost (discount tickets are unobtainable). ♦ West St (between Litchfield St and Cambridge Circus). 836.1443. Tube: Leicester Square

59 Royal Court Theatre Upstairs at the Ambassadors Much of the experimental and new drama that used to appear in the studio-size **Theatre Upstairs** at the **Royal Court**'s real home in Sloane Square will be presented here until refurbishment of that building is completed. (The main house productions are taking place at the **Duke of York's,** see page 172) This theater has been rearranged to allow the acting company three different spaces for performances. ♦ West St (between Litchfield St and Cambridge Circus). 565.5000. Tube: Leicester Square

60 No. 84 Charing Cross Road This address (which no longer exists) used to be the site of the **Marks & Co.** bookshop. In 1945, American bibliophile Helene Hanff began writing letters to the shopkeeper. The two corresponded for years and developed a close, long-distance friendship, although they never actually met in person. In 1987, the story was made into a film starring Anne Bancroft and Anthony Hopkins, but by then, the bookshop no longer existed. ♦ At Cambridge Circus. Tube: Tottenham Court Road

60 Sportspages Books, videos, magazines, and T-shirts are sold at this busy shop, a relative newcomer to this book-laden street. ♦ M-Sa. Caxton Walk, 94-96 Charing Cross Rd (between Cambridge Circus and Phoenix St). 240.9604. Tube: Tottenham Court Road

61 Foyles Walt Disney and George Bernard Shaw were just two of the illustrious customers of this British institution. It's chaotic and crammed from floor to ceiling with books, and a particular title can be as hard to find as a knowledgeable assistant. Don't knock it, though, as the British defend this oddity to the hilt. ♦ M-Sa. 119 Charing Cross Rd (between Manette St and Goslett Yd). 437.5660. Tube: Tottenham Court Road

---

Originally a stately home, Kensington Palace was bought by William III, an asthma sufferer, who wished to escape the stuffiness and pollution of the Thames by Whitehall Palace.

The Docklands: Vibrant Revival

The Docklands area is bursting with energy and regeneration, and its spirit will rub off on visitors who elect to spend an afternoon or evening here. It's a wonderful place to walk, feast, sightsee, relax, shop, and enjoy an unparalleled look at the luminous **Thames** from a Docklands pub or restaurant.

Once a bustling crossroads of merchant ships trading goods from around the world, the area declined when the shipping trade dried up. By the 1960s the docks had become a riverside wasteland. Then, 15 years ago, the government and private developers teamed up to revitalize the area. High-tech industries and newspaper offices began moving in. Restaurants, shops, and pubs sprang up. Old warehouses were converted to smart residences, and the small brick dwellings were restored and now stand proudly alongside some of the most innovative architecture in London.

The 8.5-square-mile patch of Docklands, which lies just east of **Tower Bridge**, is divided into four areas: **Wappping** and **Limehouse**, the **Isle of Dogs**, the **Royal Docks** (awaiting development), and the **Surrey Docks** (south of the Thames and stretching well into the heart of London, with such attractions across from the **Tower of London** as the **Design Museum**, the **Bramah Tea and Coffee Museum**, the *HMS Belfast*, and the **London Dungeon**—for more information, see "The City/The Thames").

The **Docklands Light Railway** (**DLR**; 363.9700) runs a frequent service to the Docklands (except the Surrey Docks) starting at **Tower Gateway**, a minute's walk east from the **Tower Hill** tube station, and ending at **Island Gardens.** Part of the Underground system (see a tube map for stops), the **DLR** accepts tube tickets and Travelcards. The trains are automated, but at certain times guides are aboard to present a running commentary about sites along the route. Trains with guides leave on the hour 11AM-4PM from Easter through October and 10AM-2PM from November to Easter. You can also buy a "Sail and Rail" ticket allowing you to travel to Island Gardens on the **DLR** and to return by riverboat to **Westminster Pier.**

First-time visitors should head for the **London Docklands Visitor Centre** (3 Limeharbour, just north of the **Crossharbour DLR** station, 207/512.1111); it's open daily. Ask questions, get free maps and leaflets directing you to the best sights, and watch a video dramatizing how this area was transformed from a virtual ruin to a vibrant urban space.

On the **Isle of Dogs**, Docklands' proud centerpiece is also Britain's tallest building—the 50-story **One Canada Square,** also called the "Canary Wharf Tower" (at Churchill Pl). Designed by American architect **Cesar Pelli,** the distinctive pyramid-topped dome dominates London's eastern skyline. The building, part of **Canary Wharf,** the commercial heart of the Docklands, has offices on the upper floors and a shopping mall on the two lower floors. You'll also find such pubs as the **Corney & Barrow** (9 Cabot Sq, at West India Ave, 207/512.0397), an ultraslick watering hole with tiled walls and chrome tables, attracting a stylish crowd; and the fun **Cat and Canary** (14 Wren Landing, between Cabot Sq and Fishermans Walk, 207/512.0397) with its mock-Victorian decor, including furnishings from former churches.

The **DLR**'s last stop, **Island Gardens,** a small, grassy park by the **Thames,** affords the best view of the palatial skyline of **Greenwich,** scarcely changed since Canaletto painted it in 1775. From here, it is only a 10-minute walk to Greenwich via the **Greenwich Foot Tunnel,** beneath the Thames. Lined with 200,000 tiles, the nine-foot-high tunnel (with two elevators) was built in 1902.

You may also wish to stroll along the Thames on the Docklands side. *Thames Path,* a free leaflet available at the visitors' center, shows the route. The path goes through Limehouse and Wapping, taking in some atmospheric pubs. You can enjoy great fish-and-chips at **The Grapes** (76 Narrow St, at Duke Shore Stairs, Limehouse, 207/987.4396), with its creaky wooden veranda overhanging the river. The cozy Victorian pub **The Town of Ramsgate** (63 Wapping High St, 207/488.2685) is sited beside the eerie-looking **Wapping Old Stairs,** which condemned pirates descended, to be chained to a post in the river and drowned as the tide rose. Also in Wapping is the beautiful riverside **Prospect of Whitby** (57 Wapping Wall, between Glamis Rd and Garnet St, Wapping, 207/481.1095), which began as **The Devil's Tavern** in about 1520 when it was a haunt of thieves and smugglers. A lovely finish to a Docklands visit would be a meal at the **Prospect**'s famous restaurant, from which you'll enjoy the same views over the Thames that inspired the paintings of Whistler and Turner.

Canary Wharf

61 Waterstones This chain store is eminently refined and sensible—in other words, it's packed with all the latest books, and they're easy to find. ♦ Daily. 121-129 Charing Cross Rd (between Manette St and Goslett Yd). 434.4291. Tube: Tottenham Court Road. Also at: 193 Kensington High St (at Allen St). 937.8432. Tube: High Street Kensington

62 Soho Square Begun in 1677 in honor of Charles II—that's his statue in the center—this was one of the first squares laid out in London. The Elizabethan hut in the middle is actually a folly tool shed built in 1870. Stargazers should keep their eyes open: Sir Paul McCartney occasionally visits his offices here. ♦ At Sutton Row and Carlisle St, and Greek and Soho Sts. Tube: Tottenham Court Road

63 Gay Hussar ★★$$$$ Famous for its old-fashioned, discreet service, this eatery is a bastion of Hungarian food; try the Transylvanian stuffed cabbage, veal goulash, or the chicken *paprikash*. Well-known politicians dive in here to gossip in private. ♦ Hungarian ♦ M-Sa lunch and dinner. Reservations required. 2 Greek St (between Manette St and Soho Sq). 437.0973. Tube: Tottenham Court Road

63 Au Jardin des Gourmets ★★$$$ In this haven of traditional French cooking, you can sample the best of this cuisine with dishes such as poached salmon with mussels flavored with orange and basil, or roast saddle of rabbit. The excellent wine list includes delicious older Clarets. ♦ French ♦ M-F lunch and dinner; Sa dinner. Reservations required. 5 Greek St (between Manette St and Soho Sq). 437.1816. Tube: Tottenham Court Road

---

I know I have the body of a weak and feeble woman, but I have the heart and stomach of a king, and a King of England, too.

—Queen Elizabeth I, addressing her troops on the approach of the Spanish Armada

---

64 L'Escargot ★★$$$ London's ad-land comes to this Soho institution to gossip in public, and be overheard. You can order snails or succulent duck confit in the brasserie downstairs, and a different but equally French selection in the more expensive, opulent dining room upstairs. ♦ French ♦ Restaurant: Tu-F lunch and dinner; Sa dinner. Brasserie: M-F lunch; Sa dinner. Reservations recommended. 48 Greek St (between Old Compton and Bateman Sts). 437.2679. Tube: Leicester Square, Tottenham Court Road

65 Pollo ★$ This is London's most famous budget restaurant. Pasta and risotto dishes are best. Claustrophobics beware: The place is small and crowded. ♦ Italian ♦ M-Sa lunch and dinner. 20 Old Compton St (between Charing Cross Rd and Greek St). 734.5917. Tube: Leicester Square, Tottenham Court Road

66 Maison Bertaux Don't be fooled by the spartan surroundings: This bakery has produced the lightest croissants in town since 1871—even during a five-year period when the ovens weren't working well. Only fresh butter and cream are used, so cholesterol counters should avoid the scrumptious French cream cakes and meringues. Try to stop in when the owners dress up to celebrate Bastille Day on 14 July. ♦ Daily. No credit cards accepted. 28 Greek St (between Romilly and Old Compton Sts). 437.6007. Tube: Leicester Square, Tottenham Court Road

66 Coach & Horses Most of Soho's pubs are hot, smoky, and cozy but have nothing much to distinguish them from one another. This one, however, has cartoons all over the walls. It's a well-known atmospheric Soho drinking place—in fact, it no longer serves food. The pub was immortalized in the West End because it was the setting for the play *Jeffrey Bernard Is Unwell*. ♦ Daily. 29 Greek St (at Romilly St). 437.5920. Tube: Leicester Square, Tottenham Court Road

66 Ed's Easy Diner ★★$ This is the perfect 1950s retro-diner, with very good, genuine American-style diner fare, including decent doughnuts. It's *the* place to be seen eating fast food. ♦ American ♦ Daily lunch and dinner. 12 Moor St (at Old Compton St). 439.1955. Tube: Leicester Square, Tottenham Court Road. Also at: 362 King's Rd (between Beaufort St and Park Walk). 352.1956. Tube: Leicester Square, Tottenham Court Road; The Trocadero, 13 Coventry St (between Rupert and Windmill Sts) 287.1951. Tube: Piccadilly Circus

67 Kettners ★$$ Once Oscar Wilde's favorite club, it then became Frank Sinatra's. The dining rooms and piano bar are beautifully decorated, but the fare is fairly standard: pizzas, hamburgers, and salads. Don't let them put you upstairs, or the food will be cold by the time it gets to you. Young, glittery advertising types froth and flutter in the Champagne bar here, swallowing copious quantities of Champagne cocktails. This room gets unbearably noisy and crowded at lunchtime and from 6:30 to 7:30PM. ◆ Pizzeria ◆ Restaurant: daily lunch and dinner. Champagne bar: M-Sa. 29 Romilly St (between Greek and Frith Sts). 734.6112. Tube: Leicester Square, Tottenham Court Road

68 Ming ★★$$ Pekingese recipes inspired by the Ming dynasty and geared to Western tastes are the specialty in this pale-blue restaurant. Its special menu highlights fresh vegetables from the market and many fish dishes. ◆ Chinese ◆ M-Sa lunch and dinner. 35 Greek St (between Shaftesbury Ave and Romilly St). 734.2721. Tube: Leicester Square

69 Shaftesbury Avenue Named after the beloved seventh Earl of Shaftesbury, whose *Eros* memorial stands in Piccadilly Circus, this avenue opened up in 1886. Almost immediately, a host of London theaters sprang up, and many of them are still here. For a British playwright to get a play "in the West End" is considered the pinnacle of success. ◆ Between Piccadilly Circus and New Oxford St. Tube: Leicester Square, Tottenham Court Rd, Piccadilly Circus

69 Palace Theatre This theater is as grand as its name, which is understandable because it was designed by **Collcutt and Holloway** in 1891 as the home of the **Royal English Opera.** This is where Sarah Bernhardt played the title role in *Cleopatra,* and where Pavlova made her London debut in 1910. In recent years, the 1,400-seat venue has hosted megahits such as *Les Misérables* (which is still playing here). The theater is now owned by Andrew Lloyd Webber. ◆ Shaftesbury Ave (at Cambridge Circus). 434.0909. Tube: Leicester Square

70 Cork & Bottle ★★$ The location— Central London's slightly sleazy Leicester Square area—hasn't stopped lots of locals from frequenting this basement haunt since 1971. It still gets very crowded. The food is simple, good, and plentiful. Try a wedge of the ham and cheese pie with a glass of New World or French wine. ◆ Wine bar ◆ Daily lunch and dinner. 44-46 Cranbourn St (between Charing Cross Rd and Bear St). 734.7807. Tube: Leicester Square

71 Capital Radio Cafe ★★$$ This huge, modern establishment (formerly **Man Fu Kung**) is a theme restaurant with a difference It's the workplace for the disk jockeys of London's popular radio station **Capital FM.** There's a real studio in the center with either an in-house DJ or one of the celebrity DJs doing a show on the air. Music is always playing, and banks of high-tech screens sho pop group videos and London scenery. You can even book tickets for a show or concert a the same time as you order your food. Texas born chef Harry Azima offers a trendy menu that includes crunchy coconut shrimp with a sweet mango and horseradish chutney, Thai grilled salmon on mixed greens with a spicy dressing, steaks, and hefty sandwiches. The radio station occupies the whole seven storie of this 1930s building, which now presents an artfully lit facade onto Leicester Square. ◆ International ◆ Daily lunch and dinner. Reservations for lunch only M-F. 29-30 Leicester Sq (at Irving St). 484.8888. Tube: Leicester Square

72 Poon's ★★$$$ This is the posh version of its cheaper sibling around the corner; here the look is elegant and contemporary, with white tablecloths and napkins and attractive wood furniture, while the less chic version has wind-dried ducks, sausages, and bacon hanging from the window. Typical main courses include fried bean curd with mincemeat and chili. ◆ Chinese ◆ Daily lunch and dinner 4 Leicester St (between Leicester Sq and Lisle St). 437.1528. Tube: Leicester Square. Also at: 27 Lisle St (betwee Newport Pl and Wardour St). 437.4549. Tub Leicester Square

73 Mr. Kong ★★$$ A foodie's Chinese restaurant crushed into three little floors, this dining spot offers innovative combinations and attracts many Western customers who enjoy dishes like sautéed chicken with fresh mango and asparagus. ◆ Chinese ◆ Daily lunch and dinner. Reservations recommended. 21 Lisle St (between Newport Pl and Wardour St). 437.7341. Tube: Leicester Square

74 New World ★★$ With 700 seats, this Chinese restaurant stakes a claim as London largest. Dim sum is the specialty. ◆ Chinese

Restaurants/Clubs: Red   **Hotels:** Blue

Shops/ 🌳 Outdoors: Green   **Sights/Culture:** Black

♦ Daily lunch and dinner. 1 Gerrard Pl (between Gerrard St and Shaftesbury Ave). 734.0677. Tube: Leicester Square

75 Dean Street In 1763, Mozart's father wanted to publicize the child prodigy's sight-reading ability, so the seven-year-old Wolfgang and his four-year-old sister gave a performance on Dean Street at **Caldwell's Assembly Rooms, No. 21.** Karl Marx lived at **No. 28.** ♦ Between Shaftesbury Ave and Oxford St. Tube: Tottenham Court Road, Piccadilly Circus

76 French House ★$ Originally called the **York Minster,** this pub picked up the affectionate nickname "The French House" because of M. Gaston, its French owner. After Gaston gave up the property, the new owners changed the name officially. It was the official headquarters of the Free French in World War II. General de Gaulle wrote his historic declaration of defiance to the Nazis in the room above the bar. There are still signed photos of famous French people on the walls. Typical pub food is served. ♦ Daily lunch and dinner. 49 Dean St (between Romilly and Old Compton Sts). 437.2799. Tube: Piccadilly Circus, Tottenham Court Road

Within the French House:

French House Dining Room ★$$
Situated over the pub, this dining room serves a mixture of traditional and contemporary British food, including stuffed quail with mashed celeriac, potato-and-squid stew, and butternut squash stuffed with wild rice and red onion. It's a tiny room with a jolly atmosphere, so be sure to book ahead. ♦ Modern British ♦ M-Sa lunch and dinner; Su lunch. Reservations recommended. 437.2477

77 Patisserie Valerie ★$ It's fabulous, fattening, and full of artsy Soho wannabes and cussing regulars squashed for space— they all come for the cakes. Try the chocolate-truffle cake, but be prepared: There is never a time, day or night, when this cafe/pastry shop isn't packed. Like the other members of this chain, it also serves good, light salads and sandwiches for lunch. ♦ Cafe ♦ Daily breakfast, lunch, and afternoon tea. 44 Old Compton St (between Frith and Dean Sts). 437.3466. Tube: Piccadilly Circus, Tottenham Court Road. Also at: 215 Brompton Rd (between Yeoman's Row and Egerton Terr). 823.9971. Tube: Knightsbridge; 105 Marylebone High St (between St. Vincent and Moxon Sts). 935.6240. Tube: Baker Street

78 Frith Street Mozart and his papa lived at **No. 20** from 1764 to 1765. Later, in 1926, John Logie Baird brought the street into the 20th century when he gave the first public demonstration of television at **No. 22;** the original equipment is now on display in the **Science Museum.** ♦ Between Shaftesbury Ave and Soho Sq. Tube: Leicester Square, Tottenham Court Road

On Frith Street:

Ronnie Scott's This club is one of the best-known jazz venues in the world. Ella Fitzgerald, Sarah Vaughan, George Melly, and Maynard Ferguson are just some of the names who have played here, not to mention the late legendary Ronnie Scott himself. It's a good place to kick back, relax, and enjoy the rhythm. There's even a menu of steaks, burgers, pasta dishes, and salads, though you don't have to eat here (but you must book a table in advance). ♦ Admission. Shows: M-Sa 8:30PM-3AM (starting times vary, so call ahead). Reservations required. 47 Frith St (between Old Compton and Bateman Sts). 439.0747

Alastair Little ★★★$$$$
Another haunt of London foodies, here is a restaurant where people go for serious eating. The decor is stark and minimalist, but there's an ever-changing menu of modern continental dishes, featuring such entrées as grilled tuna with tomato sauce and risotto with morels. There's also a fixed-price menu. ♦ Continental ♦ M-F lunch and dinner; Sa dinner. Reservations recommended. 49 Frith St (between Old Compton and Bateman Sts). 734.5183. Modern British cuisine is served at 136A Lancaster Rd (between Portobello and Ladbroke Rds). 243.2220. Tube: Ladbroke Grove

Frith Street Restaurant ★★★$$
The chef and co-owner of this new restaurant is Stephen Terry, one of the ever-growing number of superstar British chefs. Only fixed-price menus are offered, but they range from two to six courses. The spartan decor is offset by such delights as salmon set in jelly topped with crème fraiche, jellied borscht, salad of roast wood pigeon, pig's trotter and smoked bacon with caper and raisin butter, and ravioli of braised beef with roasted squash. Desserts include vanilla *panna cotta* with sweetened tomato. ♦ Modern British ♦ M-F lunch and dinner; Sa dinner. Reservations recommended. 63-64 Frith St. (between Old Compton and Bateman Sts). 734.4545

79 Gopal's Soho ★★$$ Chef N.P. Pittal (nicknamed Gopal) worked at the best Indian restaurants before opening his own place in the late 1980s. Try the fish in coconut curry, the chicken *jalfrezi* (boneless chicken), or the delectable king prawns with spring onions. The wine list is good. ◆ Indian ◆ Daily lunch and dinner. 12 Bateman St (between Frith and Dean Sts). 434.1621. Tube: Leicester Square, Tottenham Court Road

80 Red Fort ★★★$$$ The restaurant was named after the red sandstone fort built by Emperor Shah Jahan, and its cooking is definitely fit for a Mogul king. They will tandoori anything, and the ambience is swank and elegant, with patterned tapestries and rugs, cream-colored walls, and soft Indian music playing in the background. There are regular food festivals highlighting regional Indian food and entertainment. ◆ Indian ◆ Daily lunch and dinner. 77 Dean St (between Meard St and Richmond Bldgs). 437.2525. Tube: Piccadilly Circus, Leicester Square

81 Berwick Street Market Lots of cheap fruits and vegetables are on sale in this traditional London street market. Its lower end leads into Rupert Street, where there are stalls with clothes, records, and miscellanea. There's been a market here since the 1700s. ◆ M-Sa 9AM-3:30PM. Between Peter and Broadwick Sts. Tube: Piccadilly Circus

82 Fratelli Camisa/Lina Stores Soho's Italian delis go on forever, selling delicious fresh pasta, hundreds of cheeses, and panettone. Salamis hang from the ceilings, while breads are stacked in baskets on the floor. ◆ M-Sa (both stores). Fratelli Camisa: 1a Brewer St (between Wardour and Rupert Sts). 437.7120. Lina Stores: 18 Brewer St (between Wardour and Rupert Sts). 437.6482. Tube: Piccadilly Circus

82 Café Fish ★★$$ Relocated from Panton Street, this restaurant occupies two floors. The ground floor offers a "canteen menu" with ten very reasonably priced dishes, while the menu upstairs offers a wider selection and is pricier. Try deep-fried spiced squid with *gribiche* sauce or the creamy kedgeree. For dessert there are honey and apple, and Poire William (pear liqueur)–flavored ice creams. ◆ Seafood ◆ Daily lunch and dinner. 36-40 Rupert St (between Coventry St and Shaftesbury Ave). 287.8989. Tube: Leicester Square, Piccadilly Circus

83 Waxy O'Connor's ★★$$ This loud, fun, Irish-themed pub/restaurant gets incredibly packed on the weekends. Of the five bars, each on its own floor, one is actually decorated like a church. Mussels, oysters, and Irish fare are served. ◆ Irish pub ◆ Daily lunch and dinner. 14-16 Rupert St (between Coventry St and Shaftesbury Ave). 287.0255 Tube: Piccadilly Circus

84 Jade Garden ★★$$ This elegant mirrore restaurant offers a wide range of stir-fried, steamed, and roasted meat dishes served in clay pots. At lunchtime, try dim sum (perhaps paper-wrapped king prawns or steamed beef and ginger dumplings). At night, go for the noodles with squid and giant prawns. ◆ Chine ◆ Daily lunch and dinner. 15 Wardour St (between Coventry and Lisle Sts). 437.5065. Tube: Piccadilly Circus, Leicester Square

84 Chuen Cheng-Ku ★★$$ Though it seats 400, this restaurant still gets crowded. Opt for dim sum at lunch, or try the lemon-sauce roast duck in the evening. ◆ Chinese ◆ Daily lunch and dinner. 17 Wardour St (between Coventry and Lisle Sts). 437.1398. Tube: Piccadilly Circus, Leicester Square

85 Comedy Store The pioneer of the avant-garde comedy scene in London, this club for improvisational and stand-up comedy was founded by Don Ward in 1978. At the time, it was such a new concept that *Time Out* magazine did not have a category for it; today, there are more than 50 similar clubs throughout the city. This venue, however, is still the top spot for seeing stand-up comedians, revues, improvisational comedy and open-mike sessions. Although you may never have heard of any of them before, the performers are bright, energetic, talented, and above all, funny. (That's particularly true of the **Comedy Store Players,** who are well-established as individual performers; they play here on Wednesday and Sunday.) Many performers have gone on to work for the BBC and **Channel 4,** and a couple have appeared in movies as well (Mike Myers in the *Wayne World* and *Austin Powers* movies). The lines of people waiting to get in can be formidable but some tickets are available in advance through **Ticketmaster.** However, if you do wait in line, you'll find it great for people watching; this corner of Leicester Square has attracted such theme restaurants as **Planet Hollywood** and **Fashion Cafe,** which draw the occasional celebrity. ◆ Tu-Su. Haymarket House, Oxendon St (at Coventry St). 344.0234 for information, bookings 344.4444. Tube: Piccadilly Circus

86 Melati ★$ Cheap and cheerful (and popular with people who are long on fine food but short on cash), this restaurant offers Indonesian cuisine. Try the *ayam perc* (grilled chicken in spicy coconut sauce) or the excellent *tahu goreng* (fried bean curd and vegetables covered in peanut sauce). You can book a table, but you'll probably still wait (especially on weekends). ◆ Indonesian ◆ Daily lunch and dinner. 21 Great Windmill (between Archer and Brewer Sts). 437.2745. Tube: Piccadilly Circus

87 Just Games For a variety of old favorites, including Scrabble or chess, plus the largest selection of European games outside the Continent, visit this shop. They're all board games and therefore more suitable for older children and teenagers. ♦ M-Sa. 71 Brewer St (between Great Windmill and Sherwood Sts). 437.0761. Tube: Piccadilly Circus

88 Global Cafe ★$ For Internet users, this cafe is one of the roomiest and most modern. Located opposite the London ad agency Saatchi and Saatchi, it attracts smooth-talking executives as well as mere fanatics. The decor is fashionable with high-tech furnishings, art on the walls, and music in the background for those who just want to tuck into smoked salmon open sandwiches or a salad and a glass of wine. ♦ Continental ♦ M-Sa lunch, snacks, and dinner. 14 Golden Sq (between Lower James and Lower John Sts). 287.2242. Tube: Piccadilly Circus

89 Andrew Edmunds ★$ This wine bar/restaurant is a homey little place with a friendly staff serving hearty soups, casseroles, and tiramisù. Beware, it's hard to get a seat at lunch (reserve well in advance). ♦ British ♦ Daily lunch and dinner. Reservations required for lunch. 46 Lexington St (between Brewer and Beak Sts). 437.5708. Tube: Piccadilly Circus

90 John Snow In 1854, Londoners were dropping like flies from cholera until Dr. John Snow figured out that the bacteria was carried by water. The water pump he turned off, thereby saving countless lives, was near the site of this pub. There's a model of a steam train named after the doctor and all sorts of memorabilia in the rather shabby pub. ♦ M-F 11AM-11PM; Sa-Su noon-2:30PM. 39 Broadwick St (between Lexington and Marshall Sts). 437.1344. Tube: Oxford Circus

91 Contemporary Ceramics This stunning gallery and shop in **William Blake House** has been doing a brisk trade in Soho since 1960, selling the pottery and ceramics created by members of the Craft Potters Association. Throw out your ideas of quaint pottery; what's on sale here is exquisite and infinitely collectible. ♦ M-Sa. 7 Marshall St (at Broadwick St). 437.7605. Tube: Oxford Circus

91 Cranks ★$ This branch of the 10-store chain has vegetarian take-out and sit-down meals, and there's a shop for whole-foodies. ♦ Vegetarian ♦ Restaurant: M-Sa breakfast, lunch, and dinner. Shop: M-Sa. 8 Marshall St (between Broadwick St and Foubert's Pl). 437.9431. Tube: Oxford Circus

92 Carnaby Street During the 1960s, this street was a center of modern fashion. Its shops full of flared jeans and psychedelic patterns attracted scores of hippies and some celebrated personalities such as The Beatles and Mary Quant. Today, it's laden with shops selling touristy kitsch, but some smarter shops have appeared and the area promotes itself as West Soho. ♦ Between Beak St and Foubert's Pl. Tube: Oxford Circus

93 Shampers ★★$$ Very popular with media types, this dimly-lit wine bar/brasserie has about 200 different wines available and some 20 Champagnes. The wine bar features a short menu of salads and hot dishes; specialties include ham and cheddar pie in puff pastry, and squid salad. In the basement is the full-service brasserie, offering homemade sausages, calf's liver and bacon, and several seafood dishes such as fried tiger prawns. The food is good and plentiful. The eatery is located on an off-beat little street that looks like an alleyway except for the crowded pubs lining both sides. ♦ Wine bar/Brasserie ♦ M-F lunch and dinner; Sa lunch Jan-July, Sept-Dec. Reservations recommended. 4 Kingly St (between Beak and Ganton Sts). 437.1692. Tube: Oxford Circus

94 Soccer Scene These are two shop branches very close to each other where soccer fans go to buy their team's logo on just about anything: cigarette lighters, coasters, scarves, and shirts. It stocks the authentic, approved uniforms worn by all the teams in the **British Premiership League** (and some from teams on the Continent). ♦ Daily. 30-31 Great Marlborough St (at Carnaby St). 439.0778. Also at: 17 Foubert's Pl (at Carnaby St). 437.1966. Tube (for both): Oxford Circus

95 London Palladium On Sunday nights during the 1950s and 1960s, most people in Britain tuned in to the TV show "Sunday Night at the London Palladium," broadcast from this luxurious 1910 music hall. With a seating capacity of 2,286, it remains the home of great variety shows such as the *Royal Variety Performance,* which is presented especially for the queen, as well as the occasional musical. ♦ Argyll St (between Great Marlborough St and Oxford Circus). 494.5020. Tube: Oxford Circus

96 100 Club Smoky and slightly seedy, this underground nightclub is not famed for its decor (plastic tables and hard chairs), but for its musicians—Charlie Parker, Earl Hines, and George Lewis have played here. The club emphasizes jazz, swing, blues, and rhythm and blues, and rock 'n' roll bands perform here, too—including the Rolling Stones and the Sex Pistols. There's live music every night, and the atmosphere is especially lively on Fridays and Saturdays, when there's dancing. ♦ Cover charge. M-Th, Su 7:30PM-midnight; F 7:30PM-3AM; Sa 7:30PM-1AM. 100 Oxford St (between Newman and Berners Sts). 636.0933. Tube: Tottenham Court Road

The Strand/ Fleet Street

For the curious, the city lover, the history-minded, and the Dickensian-spirited, the treasures of the Strand and Fleet Street are many. This seamless thoroughfare that runs parallel to the **River Thames** has connected the center of government (the **City of Westminster**) to the center of finance (the **City of London**) for more than a thousand years and through 16 reigns.

Fleet Street also served as London's journalistic hub for more than 250 years. William Caxton's printing press was set up here, and England's first daily newspaper, *The Daily Consort,* was issued from **Ludgate Circus** around 1702. Today, however, all of the major British press organizations have moved from their Fleet Street locations. Veteran journalists sometimes return to their old watering holes and gaze at the buildings they once occupied, now more likely to be home to financiers and stockbrokers.

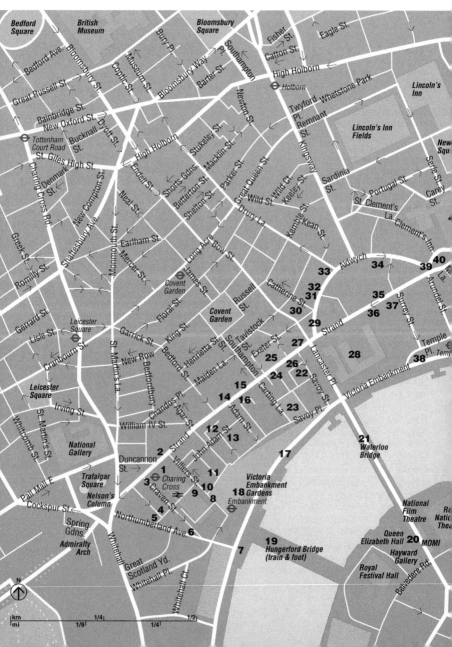

Long gone, however, are the days when the mansions of wealthy bishops, surrounded by gardens that led down to the river's edge, lined the Strand. Gone too are the days of elegance, when magnificent hotels, sophisticated restaurants, and glamorous theaters reflected in the glory of the newly opened Charing Cross Station. Although the Strand survived the Reformation, when aristocrats, not bishops, lived in the great houses, it failed to triumph over another type of reformation: the building in 1867 of the **Victoria Embankment**, which reclaimed land from the Thames (and removed its stench) but resulted in the isolation of the Strand from the river. Happily, the revitalization of **Covent Garden** to the north and a thriving theater scene kept the many massive office blocks from dehumanizing this well-used thoroughfare.

Those who stroll down the Strand and Fleet Street follow in the footsteps of an impressive list of walkers and talkers: Sir Walter Raleigh, William Congreve, Richard Brinsley Sheridan, Samuel Johnson, James Boswell, Samuel Taylor Coleridge, Charles Lamb, Henry Fielding, William Thackeray, Mark Twain, and the omnipresent Charles Dickens.

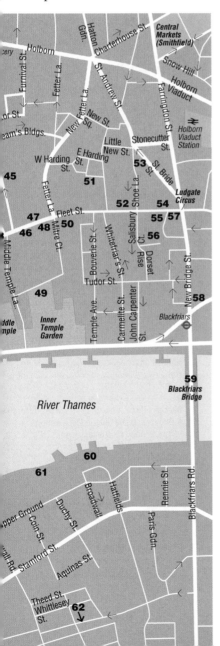

Along the way, stop for a port in London's oldest wine bar **(Gordon's)**; have lunch in a 17th-century pub **(Ye Olde Cheshire Cheese)**; peek in on the **Law Courts**; examine the building in which the first English dictionary was written **(Dr. Johnson's House)**; buy tea from the shop that supplies the queen **(Twinings)**; visit the best Impressionist collection this side of Paris (at the **Courtauld Gallery**); catch a show at the venue that helped make Gilbert and Sullivan famous (the faithfully restored **Savoy Theatre**); or attend a concert, play, or movie just across the river at Western Europe's largest arts complex **(South Bank Centre)**, which also offers one of the best vantage points from which to gaze at the stretch of London that Henry James called "a tremendous chapter of accidents." Indeed, all the best views of London are from the south side of the river, whether from its walkways or the increasing number of attractions and restaurants, particularly the wonderful **Oxo Tower Wharf**, a £20-billion riverside project combining residential and business developments with designer workshops and restaurants.

City code 0171 unless otherwise noted.

1 Charing Cross Station With the arrival of the railway at this huge station in 1863, the Strand became the busiest street in Europe, lined with enormous hotels, restaurants, and theaters built in the euphoria of the age. **British Rail** has reconstructed the cobbled driveway to the station and rebuilt the exterior walls as they were originally, adorned with 21 cast-iron lanterns. In the station yard stands what is known as an Eleanor Cross (see **Charing Cross Monument** below). ♦ Strand (between Villiers and Craven Sts). Tube: Charing Cross

1 Charing Cross Monument In 1290, a bereaved King Edward I placed 12 Eleanor Crosses along the route of the funeral cortege of his beloved consort, Queen Eleanor, from the north of England near Lincoln to **Westminster Abbey.** The final stopping place was a few yards from here, where the statue of Charles I now stands looking down Whitehall. But the octagonal Charing Cross placed here was torn down by Puritans in 1647; today, a replica stands in this spot, surrounded by eight statues of Eleanor. The cross you see in the forecourt of **Charing Cross Station** was designed by **E.M. Barry** in 1865; it is a memorial, not a replica of the original Charing Cross. ♦ Strand (between Villiers and Craven Sts). Tube: Charing Cross

1 Thistle Charing Cross Hotel $$$ The hotel, designed by **E.M. Barry** and built from 1863 to 1864, sits over the train tracks of **Charing Cross Station** and houses its waiting room. Railway hotels have a certain mystique, appealing to writers with vagabond souls and melancholy hearts. An extensive redevelopment has completely revamped the interior. The redesign means that this 222-room hotel now has a leisure club with a swimming pool, Jacuzzi, gym, and sauna. The rooms, many of them spacious, have been redecorated; deep red and blue predominate in the curtains, bedspreads, and wallpaper, and they have satellite TV and tea- and coffee-making equipment. The refurbishment of the **Strand Bar** and the **Strand Terrace Restaurant** has also been completed, and there is a new **Buckingham Wing**, where guests enjoy 24-hour butler service—the butlers, dressed in tails, oversee room service, laundry, shoe cleaning, and the purchasing of theater tickets. The air-conditioned rooms (in the **Buckingham Wing** only) with double-glazed windows have the latest electronic facilities including voice mail in five languages. Breakfast is served in the elaborately renovated **Betjeman Room.** ♦ Strand (between Villiers and Craven Sts). 839.7282, 800/847.4358; fax 839.3933. Tube: Charing Cross

2 Coutts Bank The bank of the royal family, established in 1692, has occupied this block of **John Nash**–designed buildings since 1904. In a daring and skillful act of restoration in 1979, **Sir Frederick Gibberd & Partners** created an ultramodern interior behind **Nash's** Neo-Classical stucco facade and pepper-pot corner cupolas. ♦ 440 Strand (between Agar and Adelaide Sts). Tube: Charing Cross

3 Craven Street The street forms the western border of **Charing Cross Station,** with Villiers Street on the east, and reaches down to the Embankment. Its greatest claim to fame is that Benjamin Franklin lived at **No. 36** from 1757 to 1762 and then again from 1764 to 1772; a recent effort to create a Franklin museum failed. Today, the street is a row of dilapidated buildings with officially protected facades waiting to be developed. ♦ Between Northumberland Ave and Strand. Tube: Charing Cross

4 Sherlock Holmes Pub ★★$$ Stuffed to the gills with memorabilia from the Sherlock Holmes Society, including a re-creation of the great detective's study, this flower-bedecked pub is where Holmes supposedly met his adversaries from the underworld. Although the place seems to cater to tourists, its eccentricity also attracts local office workers. There's a small restaurant serving British fare upstairs, and bar meals are available in the pub. The restaurant keeps up the theme by naming all its dishes after Sherlock Holmes stories and characters. In Arthur Conan Doyle's day, this was the site of the **Northumberland Hotel,** which appears in *The Hound of the Baskervilles.* Holmes and Watson used the Turkish bath next door (colorful tiles from the bath house can be seen on the side wall of **Barclays Bank,** now on the site). ♦ Pub/British ♦ Daily lunch and dinner. Reservations recommended for the restaurant. 10 Northumberland St (at Northumberland Ave). 930.2644. Tube: Charing Cross, Embankment

PLAYERS' THEATRE

5 Playhouse Theatre In 1987, Londoners blinked in surprise when this theater lit up again after 12 years of darkness. Founded by Sefton Parry in 1882, the venue's first production, George Bernard Shaw's *Arms and*

the Man, was staged in 1894. Tragedy struck 11 years later, when an arch above the tracks of **Charing Cross Station** collapsed onto the theater, killing six people. Actress Gladys Cooper ran the playhouse until 1933, and it was taken over by the BBC as a radio sound studio from 1951 to 1975, with the Beatles, among others, broadcasting from here. Now the 800-seat French Baroque–style theater has again established itself as a home of quality drama. There is a restaurant, so you can buy a show ticket and book a meal at the same time. ♦ Restaurant: daily lunch and dinner. Northumberland Ave (at Northumberland St). 839.4401. Tube: Charing Cross, Embankment

6 Cabman's Shelter This Victorian green wooden hut, with a gingerbread-style roof still lined with its original shingles, is a cafe for drivers of the officially licensed black cabs only. It is one of 13 structures dotted around London, the only ones left from the original 64. Built by such philanthropists as Lord Shaftesbury (whose memorial is the famous *Eros* statue), the shelters were designed to offer the cabbies (who were reputed to be heavy drinkers) cheap meals and hot, nonalcoholic drinks. These little buildings are now maintained by the English Heritage, a preservation organization. ♦ Northumberland Ave (at Craven St). Tube: Embankment, Charing Cross

7 Sir Joseph Bazalgette Statue It's sad that a man who had such a profound effect upon London and its people should be so totally forgotten, but such is the fate of the chief engineer, depicted in this statue by George Simonds. It was under Bazalgette that the solid granite **Albert, Victoria,** and **Chelsea Embankments** were built between 1868 and 1874. The project reclaimed 32 acres of mud and cost a cool £1.55 million, but unlike most new developments, was welcomed. Bazalgette had an even more important role, however: He built London's original sewer system between 1858 and 1875, saving the citizens from utterly disgusting conditions, including an overpowering stench, regular sewage floods, and cholera epidemics. ♦ Embankment Pl (at Northumberland Ave). Tube: Embankment

8 Villiers Street The road was named for George Villiers, Duke of Buckingham, whose immense **York House** was built in 1626 on a piece of land occupying both this site and Buckingham Street. It has a feeling of the past, with flower, fruit, and newspaper sellers, as well as two special attractions: the **Players' Theatre** and **Gordon's Wine Bar** (see below for both). Villiers was a clever opportunist, but not quite clever enough. A favorite of James I and his son Charles I, the duke progressed in less than 10 years from being plain George Villiers to viscount, marquis, and, finally, Duke of Buckingham. His ruthless behavior led to his assassination in 1628 and probably set the stage for Charles I's estrangement from Parliament, the Civil War, and the king's own execution. ♦ Between Embankment Pl and Strand. Tube: Embankment, Charing Cross

9 Players' Theatre This was once the site of Craven Passage, immortalized in the Flanagan and Allen song "Underneath the Arches" and in George Orwell's *Down and Out in Paris and London.* The 250-seat **Players' Theatre** was built in its place as part of the massive rebuilding program at Charing Cross.

It is a club with an annual membership fee but visitors can see a performance by paying admission. This is Victorian music hall entertainment at its best, with the same high-spirited sense of humor and fun that delighted audiences in the days before radio, television, and canned laughter. There are two bars and a supper room, and drinks and snacks are served during the performances. How civilized! Above the station complex is **Embankment Place,** a giant and appropriately tunnel-like glass and concrete landmark occupied by offices and shops. ♦ Admission (members free). Tu-Su at 8:15PM. The Arches, Villiers St (between Hungerford La and Strand). 839.1134. Tube: Charing Cross, Embankment

10 Gordon's Wine Bar ★★★$ Even though this wine bar looks every day of its 300 years, it feels very 1940s, like a film set of wartime London, with dim vaults stretching back beneath the street. The bottles are stored behind a locked grill; the tables and chairs don't match; and the food is basic but good, laid out the way it must always have been, as a buffet, with freshly made terrines, smoked hams, roasts, casseroles, fish dishes, and a large choice of fresh salads as well as first-class English and foreign cheeses. Sherries, ports, and Madeiras poured by the glass straight from the cask are impressive, as are the house wines chosen from the best districts and producers. ♦ British ♦ M-Sa lunch and dinner. 47 Villiers St (at Watergate Walk). 930.1408. Tube: Charing Cross, Embankment

11 Buckingham Street The street runs parallel to Villiers Street and is named for the same Duke of Buckingham, whose mansion was built here in 1626 on land formerly occupied by the Bishops of Norwich and York. One of the street's most famous residents, philosopher Francis Bacon, was evicted by Buckingham during his expansionist building program. Yet many other well-known people have stayed here, among them Samuel Pepys, Henry Fielding, Jean-Jacques Rousseau, and Samuel Taylor Coleridge. In place of the duke's mansion stands **Canova House,** an 1860s Italian-Gothic structure with redbrick arches built by **Nicholas Barbon.** ♦ Between Watergate Walk and John Adam St. Tube: Charing Cross, Embankment

Child's Play

Although London may seem like a grand, serious, even forbidding city at first (especially to children), there are lots of fun things for families to see and do. These 10 suggestions are just the beginning.

1 Feed the ducks, geese, and pelicans in **St James's Park.**

2 Create the perfect toothbrush on the computer at the **Design Museum.**

3 Explore the *HMS Belfast*, a real World War II battleship, from stem to stern.

4 Read the news or do an interview—and then watch yourself on TV—at the **Museum of the Moving Image.**

5 Get some hands-on knowledge of starfish, and other sea creatures at the **London Aquarium.**

6 Operate the automated wood and metal sculptures at the **Cabaret Mechanical Theatre.**

7 Play the stock market on the computer at the **Bank of England Museum**—and afterward, take a look at some real gold bricks.

8 Fly an airplane (well, a simulated one, anyway) at the **Science Museum.**

9 Whizz through 2,000 years of history at the **Tower Hill Pageant** ride—and then visit the **Tower of London** next door for a look at where a lot of that history was made.

10 Ride the old-fashioned merry-go-round and set mechanical toys in motion at the **London Toy and Model Museum.**

RSA

12 Royal Society of Arts (RSA) This is easily the most interesting building in the maze of streets that once comprised **The Adelphi**. Completed by **Robert Adam** in 1754, it has all the noble tranquillity, purity, and order that epitomize **Adam** architecture, complete with a Venetian window with a scalloped stone arch and acanthus leaf capitals. The society was founded in 1754 with the aim of encouraging art, science, and manufacturing, and it employed talented artists and craftspeople of the day. The fine hall is decorated with ten vast paintings by James Barry depicting the progress of civilization. Barry is regarded by some art critics as the first Impressionist and a source of inspiration for Turner. The pictures were cleaned as part of a £1.3-million program to restore the building to its full Georgian splendor. To see them, apply to the society librarian after 9:30AM. ◆ Free. 8 John Adam St (between Adam and Durham House Sts). 930.5115. Tube: Charing Cross, Embankment

13 The Adelphi Parallel to the Strand is John Adam Street, the site of the late, lamented **Adelphi,** a stunning architectural and engineering achievement and London's first grand speculative housing development. It was built between 1768 and 1774 by the **Adam** brothers, **William, James,** and **Robert,** with John as economic adviser. With brilliant vision and dreamy optimism, the brothers leased the land between the Strand and the Thames and built a quay above the river, with four stories of arched brick vaults for warehousing. On top of this structure they created four streets— Adelphi Terrace, John Adam Street, Robert Street, and Adam Street—and a terrace of 11 four-story brick houses that faced the river, inspired by the fourth-century Palace of Diocletian on the Adriatic coast, as well as by Pompeii and Athens.

The scheme was a testament to fraternal genius (and was named accordingly— *adelphos* is the Greek word for brother), but proved a financial disaster. The project almost ruined the **Adam** brothers, and the houses were eventually occupied by a £50-per-ticket lottery sponsored by Parliament in 1773. In the 19th century, **The Adelphi** was popular with artists and writers, and it became home for such literary celebrities as Thomas Rowlandson, Charles Dickens, John Galsworthy, Thomas Hardy, Sir James Barrie, H.G. Wells, and George Bernard Shaw. Richard D'Oyly Carte lived at **4 Adelphi Terrace** while producing the comic operas of Gilbert and Sullivan. In 1936, most of the development was demolished, a wanton act still lamented by architects and lovers of fine buildings. The legacy of the visionary speculation consists of the streets that the **Adam** brothers named after themselves, as well as a few fragments: **1-3 Robert Street,** with the honeysuckle pilasters that were the trademark of **The Adelphi; 7 Adam Street,** which is pure **Adam** in style; and **4-6 John Adam Street,** which still contains features of the original scheme. Undaunted, the **Adam** brothers went on to design and build Portland Place, north of Oxford Street. ◆ John Adam St (between Adam and Robert Sts). Tube: Charing Cross, Embankment

13 The Nell Gwynne Tavern ★★$ If you walk along the Strand from the direction of Charing Cross toward the **Adelphi Theatre,** just before you reach the theater turn into **Bull Inn Court** and you'll find one of the friendliest pubs in London. It has been squeezed into this narrow passage since 1623. Every tourist's picture of an old London pub, it is warmly lit and richly Victorian. It's also very small, so there is no room for a kitchen, but sandwiches are brought in from a nearby Italian restaurant. ♦ Pub ♦ M-Sa lunch and dinner. 2 Bull Inn Ct (off the Strand). 240.5579. Tube: Charing Cross

14 Adelphi Theatre Paternal devotion created this theater. In 1806, local tradesman John Scott built it to help launch his daughter's acting career. From 1837 to 1845, many of Charles Dickens's novels were adapted into plays and performed here. But a real drama took place out front in 1897, when actor William Terris was shot by a lunatic. The theater's simple interior, with its straight lines and angles and deep-orange paneling, dates from the extensive remodeling job by **Ernest Schaufelberg** in 1930. Today the 1,478-seat venue is the home of popular musicals. ♦ Strand (between Southampton and Bedford Sts). Ticketmaster 344.0055. Tube: Charing Cross

15 Vaudeville Theatre Opened in 1870, this structure was completely refurbished in 1969 and is now one of the most delightful theaters in the city, with an elegant gold-and-cream decor, plum-covered seats, and a beautiful chandelier in the foyer. Built by **C.J. Phipps,** the 1,067-seat theater has many long runs to its credit, including the first performances of Ibsen's *Hedda Gabler,* Barrie's *Quality Street,* and Julian Slade's *Salad Days* (which ran from 1954 to 1960—a London record at the time). ♦ Strand (between Southampton and Bedford Sts). 836.9987. Tube: Charing Cross

15 Stanley Gibbons International Since Stanley Gibbons opened this place in 1874, it has become the largest stamp shop in the world and, quite naturally, *the* source of British and Commonwealth stamps. Two huge floors are filled with stamps, albums, hinges, magnifying glasses, and stamp catalogs. Stamp auctions are held regularly. ♦ M-Sa. 399 Strand (between Southampton and Bedford Sts). 836.8444. Tube: Charing Cross

16 Shell-Mex House Beyond Adam Street, the vista is changed dramatically by the cold, white bulk of this structure. The immense building, designed by the **Messrs. Joseph** architectural firm in 1931, stretches from the Strand all the way to the **Embankment.** The frontage of redbrick and stone is all that remains of the 19th-century, 800-room **Hotel Cecil,** once the largest property in Europe, which was demolished in 1930 to make way for this Deco-style office block. The front is best seen from the other side of the river on the South Bank, a favorite view for theatergoers during intermissions at the **National Theatre,** thanks to its clock, which is larger than **Big Ben.** ♦ Strand (between Carting La and Adam St). Tube: Charing Cross

17 Cleopatra's Needle Rising 68 feet high and weighing 180 tons, this pink-granite obelisk is one of a pair created around 1500 BC by Thothmes III in Egypt on the edge of the Nile. It was in Cleopatra's reign that the obelisk was moved from Heliopolis to Alexandria (her royal city) during the Greek dynasty, whence apparently the name; though it wasn't actually set up there until 18 years after her death and the end of her dynasty. It was given to Britain by the viceroy of Egypt in 1819, but not collected by its new owners until 1877, in a barge, also called the *Cleopatra,* and under fairly dramatic circumstances (the barge got detached from its mother ship in a gale in the Bay of Biscay and was lost, along with the lives of six seamen, then finally found and towed into port by a Glasgow steamer). The obelisk was placed here by the river in 1879, and its companion is now in New York City's Central Park. ♦ Victoria Embankment (between Hungerford and Waterloo Bridges). Tube: Embankment

18 Victoria Embankment Gardens During summertime, office workers and tired tourists relax in deck chairs, children sprint along the grassy slopes, and bands play in this secluded riverside garden with a cafe. This is excellent picnic territory, with a population of 19th-century statues among the dolphin lamp standards and camel and sphinx benches. One of the best statues is of Arthur Sullivan, Gilbert's writing partner. The statue's inscription "Is life a boon?" is from their opera *Yeoman of the Guard.* Another favorite is the World War I memorial to the Imperial Camel Corps, complete with a fine miniature camel and rider. ♦ Victoria Embankment (between Hungerford Bridge and Savoy St). Tube: Embankment

Within Victoria Embankment Gardens:

York Water Gate Located in the western corner of the garden, this is a fairly ironic monument to George Villiers, the corrupt Duke of Buckingham. Built in 1626 in the Italian style with the duke's motto in Latin, *Fidei Coticula Crux* (which means "The Cross is the Touchstone of Faith"), and his coronet, the gate stands at the point where the Thames reached before the Embankment was built. It also marks the Duke of Buckingham's entrance to his gardens from the Thames at the bottom of the street.

Embankment Underground Station For the best route to **Hungerford Bridge,** walk into the station from Villiers Street, out the other side, turn right, and go up the flight of stairs to the bridge. ♦ Villiers St (at Embankment Pl)

19 Hungerford Bridge Built in 1863 by **John Hawkshaw,** this bridge replaced the 1840s one by **Isambard Kingdom Brunel.** A handsome red tapestry of trussed iron across the Thames, it is the only bridge in central

London for trains and people and is a useful walkway to the concert hall and theaters on the South Bank. Make sure to pause on your way across to appreciate the stunning views toward the City and Waterloo Bridge. ♦ Between Belvedere Rd and Victoria Embankment. Tube: Embankment

20 South Bank Centre At the eastern end of **Hungerford Bridge** sits the largest arts center in Western Europe. The center's massive structures have been described by Prince Charles as a "concrete bunker." ♦ Tube: Embankment, Waterloo

Within South Bank Centre:

Royal Festival Hall The first building you'll encounter is the **Royal Festival Hall,** which, in addition to hosting performances by visiting musicians, singers, and the like, is the permanent home of the **London Philharmonic Orchestra.** Jazz, rock, pop, and folk music are also performed here. Inside the hall is a **Farringdons** record shop (620.0198), the ever-wonderful **Books Etc.** bookstore (620.0403), and the buffet food stations where you can eat lunch or have a drink to the strains of free music in the foyer. TV chef Gary Rhodes has devised menus for its **People's Palace** restaurant (928.9999), which is in a renovated space with fabulous river views. There is also the **Voicebox** (960.4242), used mainly for literary events, and the **Poetry Library** (921.0943), Britain's largest public collection of 20th-century poetry and poetic ephemera. Browse through 60,000 books, magazines, tapes, and videos, including ones for kids. Next door is the smaller **Queen Elizabeth Hall** and the **Purcell Room. ♦** Daily. Belvedere Rd (between Hungerford Bridge and Waterloo Rd). 921.0809, box office 960.4242

Hayward Gallery The separate concrete structure that houses the art gallery is one of the largest and most versatile art exhibition spaces in Britain. The gallery focuses on retrospectives of individual artists' work, historical themes and artistic movements, and contemporary artists exploring new directions. To coincide with exhibitions, there are workshops, tours, lectures, and special publications. Also within is a permanent cafe and an art bookshop. ♦ Daily during exhibitions. Belvedere Rd (at Waterloo Rd). 928.3144, recorded information 261.0127. Tube: Embankment, Waterloo

bfi on the South Bank

Museum of the Moving Image (MOMI) Londoners and tourists alike rave about this museum, which showcases everything from pre-cinema experiments, European cinema, and cartoons to the technical wizardry of a modern TV studio. Visitors can be interviewed, fly across the Thames, read the news, and see how special effects are created, all with the help of guides who are actors by trade. Allow at least two hours for a visit. There's a shop, riverfront cafe, and a restaurant. ♦ Admission. Daily. Upper Ground (at Waterloo Rd). 401.2636

Royal National Theatre

Royal National Theatre The world-famous **National Theatre Company** was created in 1962 under Sir Laurence Olivier and opened with Peter O'Toole starring in *Hamlet* at the **Old Vic.** In 1971, construction of a new concrete cultural headquarters for the company, designed by **Sir Denys Lasdun,** was started on the South Bank, and the curtain was finally raised in 1976, with Sir Peter Hall as artistic director and Olivier as proud papa of the company. Under one vast roof are three theaters; eight bars; **The Mezzanine** restaurant (928.3531); the **Terrace Cafe** (401.8361); a bookshop; modern workshops; paint rooms; wardrobes; rehearsal rooms; and advanced technical facilities. The theaters differ in design, but all have first-class acoustics and good seats, and the tickets are reasonably priced, with the added bonus of magnificent views from their foyers of the Thames, the **Houses of Parliament,** and **St. Paul's.** The **Olivier** seats 1,160 people in its fan-shaped auditorium. The dark-walled, rectangular **Cottesloe** (named after Lord Cottesloe, the chairman of the South Bank Board and Council) is the smallest and most flexible, with removable seating for 400. Experimental plays and fringe theater are performed here. The 890-seat **Lyttelton** is a proscenium theater, with roughly finished, shuttered concrete walls for better acoustics.

Insightful tours of the three theaters and the backstage area can be arranged for a nominal fee at the information desk in the **Lyttelton.** Tickets for plays can be purchased in advance either at the main box office or by phone. In addition, if you join the mailing list (either by mail, phone, or in person at the box office), you can reserve seats from anywhere in the world—usually before tickets are sold to the general public (if writing, include international reply coupons and a self-addressed envelope: Mailing List, Royal National Theatre, South Bank, London SE1 9PX). The theater also offers tickets for same-day sale. Forty cheap "day" seats (20 on press nights) are available for the **Olivier** and **Lyttelton**—the line forms by 8:30AM (the box office opens at 10AM); only two tickets per person. Friday and Saturday nights are usually sold out, but inexpensive standby seats are often available for the rest of the week. These go on sale two hours before performances at the **Olivier** and **Lyttelton,** 45 minutes before performances at the **Cottesloe.** Live music, including folk and jazz, is presented free in the foyers of the **Olivier** and **Lyttelton** before evening performances, usually from 6 to 8PM and before Saturday matinees, from about 1 to 3PM. *Platforms* is a program of talks, dialogues, interviews, readings, debates, and panel discussion by playwrights, directors, and actors, as well as poets and authors that are held in all three theaters. Some discussions focus on the plays currently being shown. Events usually start at 6PM and reasonably priced tickets can be purchased at the box office or by phone. ◆ M-Sa. Upper Ground (at Waterloo Rd). Box office: 452.3000. Backstage tours: 452.3400

National Film Theatre More than 2,000 screenings and events a year take place in three cinemas. ◆ Daily. Off Upper Ground (at Waterloo Rd). Box office 928.3232

The BFI London IMAX Cinema A second IMAX cinema for London, opened in June 1999, is the biggest screen in Europe—ten stories high. It shows IMAX 2-D and 3-D films every hour. There are also a shop and cafe in the foyer area. ◆ Daily 11:30AM to 10PM. South Bank (by Waterloo Station). 902.1234. Tube: Waterloo

21 **Waterloo Bridge** Designed by **Sir Giles Gilbert Scott,** and completed by 1942 (but not opened until 1945 because of the war), this bridge replaced a Regency river crossing that opened on the second anniversary of the Battle of Waterloo. The original design was supposed to have been more elegant than **Scott**'s cantilevered concrete construction. But no one can deny the splendor of both City and Westminster views from the bridge itself. On the right of the bridge is the only floating police station in London, manned by the Thames Division, which patrols the 54-mile precinct of river in police-duty boats 24 hours a day. ◆ Between Waterloo Rd and Victoria Embankment. Tube: Waterloo, Temple

22 **Queen's Chapel of the Savoy** This haven of tranquillity belongs to the Duke of Lancaster, who is in fact the queen (the reigning monarch—whether male or female—keeps this title, which goes back to Henry IV, who was Duke of Lancaster before he usurped the throne from Richard II). Erected in 1505 in the late Perpendicular style on the grounds of the **Savoy Palace,** the chapel has been used by royalty since the reign of Henry VII. The present building is almost entirely Victorian, rebuilt by **Sir Robert Smirke** in 1820 and restored by his brother **Sydney Smirke** after a fire in 1864. The original chapel was once part of the Order of St. John (1510–16), and since 1937, it has been part of the chapel of the Royal Victorian Order, one of the orders of chivalry. The heraldic plaque in the vestibule is made of gilded marrow seeds crushed into the seductive forms of the leopards of England. The stained-glass window commemorates Richard D'Oyly Carte (1844–1901), and another window is in memory of Queen Mary, who died in 1953. The window with heraldic designs of the Royal Victorian Order was designed in part by King George VI. ◆ Tu-F 11:30AM–3:30PM Oct-July. Savoy St (at Savoy Row). Tube: Embankment, Temple

The Savoy

23 **Savoy Hotel** $$$$ In 1246, Henry II presented Peter, Earl of Richmond, with a splendid piece of land overlooking the Thames. Here the earl, who was also the Count of Savoy, built a magnificent palace where he entertained beautiful French women, organized politically advantageous marriages into the Anglo-Norman aristocracy, and created a feudal center of considerable power. The grand manor came into the hands of Simon de Montfort, one of the founders of the **House of Commons,** and the man who led the barons in revolt against Henry III. The illustrious past of this palatial site reached a fiery climax when a mob of angry peasants under the leadership of Wat Tyler stormed the palace, destroying everything of value, ripping tapestries into shreds, flattening the silver and gold, and, finally, burning the palace to the ground. The flames were watched from the **Tower of London** by 14-year-old Richard II, who was planning a swift and ruthless repression of the peasant revolt. But the site seems to have been ripe for palaces, and in 1889, a luxurious hotel was built by entrepreneur Richard D'Oyly Carte, discoverer of Gilbert and Sullivan, for whom he built the still-existing **Savoy Theatre** on the same plot of land.

The seven-story building took five years to complete and combined American technology with European luxury—the concrete walls, electric lights, and 24-hour elevators were all new to hotel construction in England. Tiny, bearded Carte outdid Peter of Savoy: he persuaded César Ritz to be his manager and Escoffier his chef (his pots and pans are still at the hotel). Johann Strauss played waltzes in the restaurant and Caruso sang. After having tea here, Arnold Bennet was inspired to write *Grand Babylon Hotel,* a lighthearted novel.

Whistler stayed here with his dying wife, sketching her and the river from his room. They say that the first martini in the world was mixed in the **American Bar** here; certainly the bar popularized cocktails in London.

The hotel has fully recovered from its decline of the 1950s and 1960s. Today, it wins guests' hearts with its 200 individually decorated rooms and suites, Art Deco marble bathrooms with dazzling chrome fixtures, and afternoon tea in the **Thames Foyer.** Particularly special accommodations can be had in the Edwardian riverside apartment suites, which are filled with antiques, arched mirrors, fine plasterwork, Irish linen sheets, and a gracious atmosphere that even kings and queens can't resist.

Several years ago, the front hall was restored to its 1924 splendor. The Savoy's extensive archives were scoured for original drawings, and the labyrinthine cellars were searched for woodwork with the original period detail that had been removed over the years. Rare veneers and marbles were matched and replaced, and experts were commissioned to restore the crystal chandeliers.

The hotel also has a health club with swimming pool, sauna, and two exercise rooms. Luminaries who have lived in these apartments include Noel Coward and Elaine Stritch; and Liza Minnelli, Goldie Hawn, and Kurt Russell stay here regularly. ♦ Strand (at Carting La). 836.4343, 800/63.SAVOY; fax 240.6040. Tube: Charing Cross, Covent Garden

Within the Savoy Hotel:

River Restaurant ★★★$$$ With fine views through the trees to the Thames, this spacious salmon-peach room rates as one of the prettiest places to dine in London. The elegant setting is matched with worthy cuisine, and if you have *le déjeuner au choix* (the set lunch) you can expect to eat well, feel rather grand, and survive the arrival of the bill. You'll be surrounded by businesspeople and media folk at lunchtime. Under the auspices of chef Anton Edelmann, the menu features plenty of choices, including a menu *de régime naturel* (simply cooked food), smoked salmon, and decaffeinated coffee. At dinner, the menu changes and the prices rise, but you can work off your anxiety about the cost while dancing to a live band. One way to feel truly right with the world is to have breakfast in this sumptuous setting: freshly squeezed fruit juices, prunes, eggs, bacon, kippers, toast and marmalade, and the famous **Savoy** coffee in the company of cabinet ministers, opera singers, tycoons, and movie stars. This is *the* place for a business breakfast in London. Book your reservation at least a day or two in advance. ♦ French ♦ Daily breakfast, lunch, and dinner. Reservations required; jacket and tie required. 836.4343

Grill Room ★★★$$$ Some French food critics give this dining room a thumbs down—probably because its food is so veddy British. However, if you're looking for classic English dishes prepared with a delicate touch and rare imagination, you won't go wrong here. Served in a traditional paneled room, the daily lunch specialties include bangers, mash, and onions (farmhouse sausages, creamed potatoes, and fried onions), shepherd's pie, Irish stew, and roast beef and Yorkshire pudding. At dinner, the menu is more expensive, richer, and just as traditional, with native oysters, Dover sole, pheasant, partridge, and steak Diane flambéed tableside. The cooking is everything that you would expect from one of the premier hotels in the world. There are some excellent wines, although they aren't cheap, and special pre- and after-theater dinner menus that are a good value for this part of town. ♦ British ♦ M-F lunch and dinner; Sa dinner. Reservations required; jacket and tie required. No children under 14 allowed. 836.4343

Upstairs ★★★$$ This informal brasserie situated on a balcony overlooking the **Grill Room** features dishes like cod and salmon kedgeree. You can choose between sitting at table along the balcony or at the long, marble topped bar. ♦ British ♦ M-F lunch and dinner; Sa dinner. 836.4343

24 Savoy Theatre Londoners feared this revered venue would never open its doors again after it was destroyed by fire in 1990. Built in 1881 by **Richard D'Oyly Carte,** it was the first public building in the world to be lit by electricity, providing audiences with opulence and comfort. The theater also became famous for staging Gilbert and Sullivan's wonderful comic operas. Happily, the 1,158-seat theater has arisen from the ashes, with a re-creation of its 1929 Art Deco interior by **Basil Ionides** Chinese lacquerwork, a five-shade color scheme, and aluminum-leaf fluted walls. If you're in the mood for a worthwhile splurge, book a pre- or post-theater supper at the **Grill Room** (see above). Note that Savoy Court is the only road in Britain where driving must keep to the right as allowed by a special Act of Parliament to provide easier access for carriages delivering their passengers to the theater. ♦ Savoy Ct (at the Strand). 836.8888 Tube: Charing Cross, Covent Garden

In 1840 the "penny post" was introduced to replace the old system under which the recipient of a letter had to pay heavily for its delivery. Under the new rule, a letter could be delivered anywhere in the British Isles for a penny; the "penny black" was the world's first adhesive stamp.

"Christopher Wren went to dine with some men. 'If anyone calls, say I'm designing St. Paul's.'"

Anonymous

25 Strand Palace Hotel $$$ Opposite the **Savoy**, this property is more hotel than palace, but the location is hard to beat. Originally built as an Art Deco showpiece, the hotel has 783 elegantly decorated rooms, and a **Club Floor** with a private lounge. There also are three restaurants and three bars. ◆ 372 Strand (at Exeter St). 836.8080, 800/225.5843; fax 836.2077. Tube: Covent Garden, Charing Cross

SIMPSON'S
IN-THE-STRAND

26 Simpson's-in-the-Strand ★★★$$$$ Only a meal at **Eton** or **Harrow** could be more English than this, with tables arranged in long rows, dark-wood paneling, and, at lunchtime during the week, a sea of dark-suited men watching as joints of beef and lamb are wheeled to their tables on elaborate silver-domed trolleys and carved to their specifications. Roast beef served with cabbage and roasted potatoes, saddle of lamb, and Aylesbury duck are classic British meals, and the waiters who bring them to your table are like old family retainers. The daily consumption averages 25 loins of beef, 23 saddles of lamb, and 36 ducklings. Approach a meal here as an authentic English experience, and finish it off with stilton cheese, treacle tart, and house claret. The restaurant has added hearty, full breakfasts as well as another English institution—afternoon tea. ◆ British ◆ M-F breakfast, lunch, afternoon tea, and dinner; Sa-Su lunch and dinner. Jacket and tie required. 100 Strand (between Savoy St and Savoy Ct). 836.9112. Tube: Charing Cross, Covent Garden

26 Thorntons Established in 1911, this firm still makes its chocolates, fudge, and boiled sweets in the north of England, which it then transports to its several London shops. Another delicacy to try here is the fresh, homemade ice cream. ◆ M-F. 104 Strand (between Savoy St and Savoy Ct). 424.9202. Tube: Charing Cross, Covent Garden. Also at: Unit 2, Main Hall, Covent Garden Market (at Russell and Henrietta Sts, and Southampton and James Sts). 240.9202. Tube: Covent Garden; 353 Oxford St (between New Bond and Woodstock Sts). 493.7498. Tube: Bond Street

26 Smollensky's on the Strand ★★$$$ Michael Gottlieb must have designed this with his tongue firmly in cheek—its exterior is exactly the same as **Simpson's-in-the-Strand** just up the street. Although it's actually located underground, the eatery is on the side of a steep hill with a view of the delightful **Queen's Chapel of the Savoy**, which is sometimes lit up at night. This large Prohibition Era Deco–themed restaurant offers hearty American-style food, steak sandwiches, steaks, and corn-fed chicken, with informal, friendly service. Finish off with a chocolate-peanut cheesecake or chocolate mousse, and, on Saturday evenings, you can dance off all the added calories on the spot to live jazz; a pianist plays on the other nights. Another **Smollensky's** location is especially noted for its Sunday brunch; kids love the party atmosphere—clowns, Punch and Judy shows, face-painting, magicians, and bedlam (1 Dover St, at Piccadilly; 491.1199. Tube: Green Park).◆ American ◆ Daily lunch and dinner. 105 Strand (between Savoy St and Savoy Ct). 497.2101. Tube: Charing Cross, Covent Garden

27 Lyceum Tavern ★★★$ The tap room downstairs pours real ale; the ground floor serves good salads, terrines, and tarts; and the bar upstairs has views over the Strand. ◆ British ◆ Daily lunch and dinner. 354 Strand (at Wellington St). 836.7155. Tube: Charing Cross, Covent Garden

27 Lyceum Theatre Splendidly renovated for £14.5 million to the ornate look of its Victorian heyday, when Henry Irving and Ellen Terry appeared most frequently in elaborate dramas, this 2,000-seat theater was reopened in late 1996 and is a venue for big-production musicals like Andrew Lloyd Webber's *Jesus Christ Superstar* and Disney's *The Lion King*. ◆ Wellington St (at the Strand). 656.1803. Tube: Charing Cross, Covent Garden

MICHAEL STORRINGS

28 Courtauld Gallery/Somerset House Architect **Sir William Chambers** designed this Georgian stronghold (illustrated above) from 1776 to 1786 to replace the 16th-century Renaissance palace that occupied the site. As one of London's premier Neo-Classical buildings, it stands facing the Thames east of Waterloo Bridge and is one of the few Georgian buildings still gracing the riverside. Like the old **Adelphi, Chambers's Somerset House** rose out of the Thames before the construction of the **Embankment.** The great palace of the Protector Somerset (1547-72), with its magnificent chapel by **Inigo Jones** and riverside gallery by **John Webb,** originally stood on this site and was lived in by Elizabeth I when she was a princess, as well as by the queens of James I, Charles I, and Charles II.

The present building had suffered a less-than-illustrious existence, housing administrative offices and institutions and the Registry of Births, Deaths, and Marriages (which have moved to Islington, north London, as the Family Records Centre, 0181/392.5300). Since 1990, the building has been home to the **Courtauld Institute of Art** and the recently reopened **Courtauld Gallery.** The restoration work focused on the **Fine Rooms** and the **Great Room,** designed between 1776 and 1780 by **Chambers** and among the most important 18th-century interiors in London. The original inhabitants of this block were the Royal Society, the Royal Academy of Arts, and the Society of Antiquaries, who finally left in 1850 and were replaced by the Registrar General until the 1970s. The rooms then remained empty for 20 years.

The **Courtauld** is one of the galleries that most people mean to visit but don't quite get around to, yet it has the best Impressionist and post-Impressionist collection in Britain, not to mention a fabulous Classical collection. The major collections were assembled by Samuel Courtauld and Viscount Lee of Fareham (the British counterpart of the Guggenheims), who founded the institute in 1931.

Resist all temptations to use the lift and take the magnificent spiral staircase instead, dubbed the "Rowlandson" after a painting by Thomas Rowlandson, showing revelers falling down it at a party. The works to see include the **Prince's Gate Collection** of Italian Renaissance and Dutch art from the 15th and 16th centuries that were given to the institute in 1978 by Count Antoine Seilern. The range of art is extraordinary, from Palma Vecchio's lush *Venus in a Landscape* and Van Dyck's *Portrait of a Man in an Armchair* to Botticelli's *Holy Trinity* and Albertinelli's *Creation.* There is also Rubens's spectacular Baroque work *Descent from the Cross,* which was the model for the altarpiece in Antwerp Cathedral. Other works are from the Rubens school, including *The Bounty of James I Triumphing Over Avarice,* a *modello* for the ceiling corners at **Banqueting House,** Whitehall. The haunting *Landscape by Moonlight,* at one time owned by Sir Joshua Reynolds, inspired both Sir Thomas Gainsborough and John Constable.

The Impressionist works are so familiar and frequently reproduced that they seem almost like icons of a world religion called 19th-century art. The surprise is that all the major Impressionist and post-Impressionist artists are here, beginning with Boudin, Daumier, Manet, Monet, Degas, Renoir, Pissarro, Sisley, Cézanne, Gauguin, van Gogh, Seurat Bonnard, Vuillard, and Modigliani.

Exhibitions change regularly, but don't miss the following:

Cézanne's *Mont Ste-Victoire.* Cézanne was t artist who inspired Braque and Picasso duri their Cubist periods. In this painting, the green, gold, and blue of the landscape form a geometric pattern so exquisite that you fee you could step into the frame and walk away

Renoir's *La Loge,* with a man staring at the stage through opera glasses while the viewe stares with equal intensity at his voluptuous companion, her neck wound round with crystal beads and her boldly striped opera cloak falling open to reveal a rose tucked between her breasts.

Manet's *A Bar at the Folies-Bergère.* Manet was an inspiration to the Impressionists, an this is his last major work. His blond barmai is instantly recognizable, and after looking a this work, no tawdry barroom can ever be quite the same again.

Van Gogh's *Peach Blossom in the Crau* and *Self-Portrait of the Artist with a Bandaged Ear,* which together sum up van Gogh at his happiest and his most despairing. Van Gogh left Paris for Arles in 1888, and almost immediately the orchards of Provence becar a foaming cascade of blossom. Here, he spe the happiest eight months of his brief life. Nearby is the tragic self-portrait, painted a fe months earlier when he was recovering from a fit during which he had attacked Gauguin, then cut off his own ear.

Gauguin's *Nevermore.* Paa'ura was Gauguin 14-year-old mistress, and this naked South Sea beauty somehow sums up his reaction against Impressionism. This painting and his *Te Rerioa* (The Dream), also here, will make you want to cut loose and fly to the islands.

Monet's *Vase of Flowers,* full of pink and mauve, is so evocative of summer light that it cuts through the grayest London day.

Modigliani's *Female Nude,* which even thousands of reproductions have failed to spoil.

There is also Gainsborough's portrait of his wife, as well as paintings by Allan Ramsay, George Romney, Roger Fry, and the Omega Workshop's collection, along with Oscar Kokoschka's huge *Prometheus Triptych.* The 19th- and 20th-century works include such artists as Walter Sickert and Ben Nicholson.

The gold treasures from the Italian and Netherlands collections of the 14th, 15th, and 16th centuries are tiny, gold-ground panel paintings such as the *Madonna* by Fra Angelico's workshop and the *Master of Flemalle Deposition,* an exquisite triptych by Bernardo Daddi from 1338.

The **Courtauld Collection** also contains magnificent old master drawings by Michelangelo, Rubens, and Rembrandt on the ground floor. You must make arrangements in advance to view some of the 25,000 old master prints. ♦ Admission; free after 5PM. M-Sa 10AM-6PM; Su noon–6PM. Lancaster Pl (at the Strand). 848.2526. Tube: Temple

29 **Aldwych** The crescent, identified mainly by the name on the street wall, sweeps around an immense stone fortress occupied by **Australia House, India House,** and **Bush House,** the latter decorated with symbolic figures of England and America. The street is named after the Danish word meaning "an outlying farm." Its familiarity is enhanced by also being the name of a theater, the **Aldwych.** ♦ Off the Strand. Tube: Covent Garden, Temple

30 **Duchess Theatre** This 475-seat theater, though one of the smallest in the West End, is one of the best designed in London, with excellent views from every seat. ♦ Catherine St (between Aldwych and Tavistock St). 494.5075. Tube: Covent Garden

31 **Strand Theatre** The **Strand** and **Aldwych** theaters sit like bookends on either side of the mighty **Waldorf Méridien Hotel.** Built as a pair, both are quite magnificent. The proscenium above the arch in the 1,067-seat **Strand** depicts Apollo in his horse-drawn chariot, with goddesses and cupids, and the whole is so ornately decorated that it's almost wanton to ignore it and rush out for that interval drink. ♦ Catherine St (at Aldwych). 930.8800. Tube: Covent Garden

32 **Waldorf Méridien Hotel** $$$ Old World charm, excellent service, and a pleasing interior, with marble floors, coral-and-white walls, crystal chandeliers, and palm trees and ferns, characterize **A. Marshall Mackenzie**'s jewel box of a hotel, built between 1907 and 1908. The 292 rooms and suites have been opulently decorated in Edwardian style, with heavy, patterned drapes, chandeliers, and large tubs and sinks in the bathrooms. Tea in the **Palm Court** is one of London's greatest treats. Tea dancing takes place Saturday and Sunday between 3:30PM and 6:30PM. Jacket and tie are required for the tea dancing; otherwise, smart dress is requested (no jeans, sneakers, or shorts). The **Palm Court** also serves daily lunch, dinner, and Sunday jazz brunch; an additional restaurant is the cosmopolitan **Aldwych Brasserie.** ♦ Aldwych (between Catherine St and Drury La). 836.2400, 800/378.7878; fax 836.7244. Tube: Covent Garden

33 **Aldwych Theatre** Slums between Drury Lane and **Lincoln's Inn** were razed to make room for Aldwych and Kingsway Roads, and in 1905, this theater, along with the **Strand,** was among the first to take up residence. Designed by **W.G.R. Sprague** for Charles Frohmant, the 1,180-seat Georgian structure is handsome and ornate, uncomfortable yet wonderful. This was the home of the **Royal Shakespeare Company** from 1960 until the troupe moved to the **Barbican** in 1982. ♦ Aldwych (at Drury La). 836.6404. Tube: Covent Garden

34 **Bush House** Namesake American Irving T. Bush wanted to erect a trade center with shops and marbled corridors, but it didn't work out that way. Since 1940, the **BBC World Service,** one of the most important broadcasting institutions in the Western World, has used the building for its transmissions. "To the Friendship of English Speaking Peoples" is carved into the stonework of this vital building erected in 1935 by **Harvey W. Corbett.** The entrance for both office workers and shoppers is opposite **St. Mary-le-Strand.** Inside is **Penfriend** (836.9809), a rather splendid pen shop offering the kind of personal service you just don't get in department stores. If you have a penchant for early radio recordings, television scripts, or videos, stop by the **BBC TV and Radio Shop** (257.2576). Access is to the shopping arcade only. ♦ Strand (between Melbourne and Montreal Pls). Tube: Temple

35 **St. Mary-le-Strand** St. Mary-le-"Stranded" is the sadder, more apt name for this jewel of a church once half surrounded by houses on the north side of the Strand but, since 1910, isolated by the widening of roads. Built between 1714 and 1717, this is the first major work of Scottish architect **James Gibbs.** It is essentially a Baroque church with its half-domed porch and numerous vertical pediments. As though in a self-fulfilling prophecy, the upper order contains the windows, while the lower order is solid to keep out the noise from the street. The entire structure was restored a few years ago, and the splendid five-stage steeple, weakened by wartime bombing, pollution, traffic vibration, and rusting iron clamps that bind the Portland stone, was dismantled stone by stone and then rebuilt. The barrel-vaulted building has ornate plasterwork and a coffered ceiling. Thomas à Becket was lay rector of the medieval church that originally stood on the site, and the parents of Charles Dickens were married here. Poet laureate Sir John Betjeman made it his life's work to save this beautiful church from demolition. Who can blame him? Hours can vary, and there are sometimes lunchtime concerts. ♦ Strand (between Aldwych and Montreal Pl). 836.3126. Tube: Temple

36 **King's College** Founded in 1829 by the Duke of Wellington, several archbishops, and 30 bishops of the Church of England, this college adjoins the east wing of **Somerset House** and has formed part of the **University of London** since 1898. ♦ Strand (at Surrey St). Tube: Temple

37 Roman Bath Tucked away down Strand Lane along the east side of **Somerset House** under a dark archway, this 15-foot enigma is considered by many to be Roman; others say it is possibly Tudor, but more likely 17th century. Built over a tributary of the River Fleet, a small underground stream that flows into the Thames, it fills each day with 2,000 gallons of icy water that drain into a pipe and down into the Thames. David Copperfield used to take cold plunges here, but now the bath belongs to the **National Trust** and can be seen by appointment (book a week in advance). However, it's mostly visible from the pathway through a specially arranged window that has a light switch which illuminates the whole bath. ♦ Admission. W 2–5PM by appointment only. 5 Strand La (off Temple Pl). 641.5264. Tube: Temple

38 Statue of Isambard Kingdom Brunel Son of the equally famous Marc Isambard Brunel, he was the brilliant engineer who designed the **Great Western Railway** and built the *Great Eastern,* the first steamship to make regular voyages between Britain and America. His statue by Baron Marochetti dates from 1871. ♦ Victoria Embankment and Temple Pl. Tube: Temple

39 Statue of W.E. Gladstone The statue designed by Sir Hamo Thornycroft in 1905 looks out bravely onto the sea of uncaring traffic from the middle of the roadway where the Strand is rejoined by the Aldwych. Gladstone, a liberal statesman, was prime minister four times. He introduced educational reform in 1870, the secret ballot in 1872, and succeeded in carrying out the Reform Act of 1884. But he failed to gain support for home rule in Ireland, which would no doubt have made the history of the 20th century in these islands more tranquil. This statue shows him robed as Chancellor of the Exchequer with Brotherhood, Education, Aspiration, and Courage represented at the base. ♦ Strand (at Aldwych). Tube: Temple

40 St. Clement Danes Now the official church of the Royal Air Force, **Sir Christopher Wren**'s oranges-and-lemons church (so called after the nursery rhyme "Oranges and lemons, say the bells of St. Clemens") was built from 1680 to 1682, blitzed during World War II, and skillfully rebuilt by **W.A.S. Lloyd** in 1955. (The steeple, added in 1720, was designed by **James Gibbs**.) The floor is inlaid with slabs of Welsh slate carved with the 735 units of the RAF, and the rolls of honors contain the 125,000 men and women of the RAF who died in World Wars I and II. The original pulpit by Grinling Gibbons was shattered in the bombing and painstakingly pieced together from the fragments. The organ was a gift from members of the US Air Force, and there is a shrine to the USAF under the west gallery. Each March, oranges and lemons are

distributed to the children of the parish in a special service. Samuel Johnson worshiped here and is now depicted in bronze behind the church, where he gazes nostalgically down the street he believed to be unequaled Fleet Street. ♦ Strand (between Bell Yd and Clement's Inn). Tube: Temple

MICHAEL STORRINGS

41 Royal Courts of Justice Better known as the **Law Courts,** this dramatic Gothic ramble buildings (illustrated above), with a 514-foot frontage along the Strand, was built in a peri of Victorian reorganization of the legal syster and opened by Queen Victoria in 1882, with the power and glory of the law architecturally proclaimed. The main entrance is flanked by twin towers and slate roofs. Solomon holds temple above the entrance on the left, and on the right is the founder of English law, Alfred the Great. The lofty **Great Hall** (238 feet long and 80 feet high) contains a monument to th original architect, **G.E. Street,** who, in the Victorian tradition of tutelage, was a pupil of **Sir George Gilbert Scott** and teacher of **Phil Webb** and **William Morris**.

"You ask, what was that song they sang at the opening—that's 'God Save the King.' You thought it was 'Sweet Land of Liberty'? So it is. You Yankees took it from us and put new words to it. As a matter of fact we took it from the Ancient Britons—they had it, England-may-go-to-hell—and the English liked it so much they took it over and made it 'God Save the King.'"

Stephen Leacock,
Welcome to a Visiting American

Restaurants/Clubs: Red   **Hotels:** Blue

Shops/ ☂ Outdoors: Green   **Sights/Culture:** Blac

The buildings house 64 courts spread over seven miles of corridors and 1,000 rooms. They are reached by way of the hall, and when the courts sit, the public is admitted to the back two rows of the courtrooms. Take time out for a visit if you're at all interested in seeing the English justice system at work, visually enhanced by the wigged presence of judges and barristers and undisguised solicitors. Read the *Daily Lists* in the central hall to decide what appeals to you in the still faintly Dickensian world of probate, bankruptcy, and divorce. These days, there are many libel cases. You're free to enter any court except those marked "court in camera" or "chambers." (Note that criminal cases are tried in the **Old Bailey**.) ♦ M-F. Strand (between Bell Yd and Clement's Inn). 936.6000. Tube: Temple

42 R. Twining & Co. Chinese Mandarins guard the Georgian entrance to London's narrowest shop and oldest business still to stand on its original site. (The store has been paying taxes longer than any other business in Westminster.) Thomas Twining opened the shop in 1706 as **Tom's Coffee House,** and it has been selling tea ever since it became the national drink. Alas, you can't drink a cup of tea here; you can only buy it or find out about it in the small museum in the back. ♦ M-F. 216 Strand (between Middle Temple La and Devereux Ct). 353.3511. Tube: Temple

Wig and Pen Club

42 Wig and Pen Club As the name indicates, this used to be an exclusive club for lawyers and journalists; it then became a restaurant, and now has gone back to being a private club. It is located in two adjoining timber-framed buildings, one of which dates to the early 17th century and escaped the Great Fire of London in 1666. The second story juts out over the street. ♦ 229–230 Strand (between Middle Temple La and Devereux Ct). Tube: Temple

43 Fleet Street This lively, congested street has a glorious and eclectic mix of styles and levels and a tremendous skyline defined by the tower and pinnacles of the **Law Courts,** the tower of **St. Dunstan-in-the-West,** and the dome of **St. Paul's Cathedral,** best seen from the north side of the street. Sadly, the last of the editorial offices of the nation's newspapers left Fleet Street in 1989. ♦ Between Ludgate Circus and Middle Temple La. Tube: Temple, Blackfriars

43 Temple Bar Monument This spiky dragon (which is definitely *not* a griffin), created in 1880 by Horace Jones, stands on the site of **Sir Christopher Wren**'s three-arched gateway, which was here from 1672 to 1878. (The gate was dismantled because it obstructed traffic and was moved to Theobald's Park in Hertfordshire.) The dragon is a mythical beast famous for its voracious appetite and, appropriately, it marks the boundary between the City of Westminster, impelled by restraint, and the City of London, inspired by acquisition. The dragon here also marks the end of the broad, dozy Strand and the beginning of Fleet Street. The figures on either side of the dragon are Queen Victoria and the Prince of Wales, later Edward VII. ♦ Fleet St (at Strand). Tube: Temple

44 Royal Bank of Scotland Founded in 1671, this is the oldest bank in London, and it was the inspiration for Tellson's Bank in Dickens's *A Tale of Two Cities.* The nonfictional list of customers includes Charles II, the Duke of Marlborough, Nell Gwyn, Samuel Pepys, Oliver Cromwell, and John Dryden. ♦ 1 Fleet St (between Middle Temple La and Devereux Ct). Tube: Temple

45 Public Record Office (PRO) Once a favored haunt of genealogists for the records that were stored here, this building is now a business office and is not open to the public. The **PRO** has moved to a huge modern complex at Kew Gardens (see page 220). ♦ Chancery La (between Fleet St and Bream's Bldgs)

46 Prince Henry's Room Located above the archway leading to the **Temple,** the timbered house containing **Prince Henry's Room** was built in 1610 as a tavern with a projecting upper story. The great treasure inside is the

Jacobean ceiling, one of the finest remaining enriched plaster ceilings of its time in London, with an equally enriched set of stories to go with it. The most persistent tale claims that the initials P.H. and the **Prince of Wales's Feathers,** which decorate the ceiling, commemorate the 1610 investiture of Henry, eldest son of James I. The prince died two years later, and the title passed to his younger brother, who would become the luckless King Charles I. The room also contains mementos of diarist Samuel Pepys, who was born in 1633 in nearby Salisbury Court, Fleet Street, was baptized in nearby **St. Bride's Church,** and lived most of his life close by Tower Hill. His remarkable shorthand diary, recording the period between 1660 and 1669, fills many volumes and is the liveliest and fullest account of London life ever written, including the Plague of 1665 and the Great Fire of 1666. The wide oriel windows overlooking Fleet Street and across to Chancery Lane manage to frame London's timelessness the way one longs to see it. ♦ Free. M-Sa 11AM–2PM. 17 Fleet St (at Inner Temple La). 583.5968. Tube: Temple

46 Ye Olde Cock Tavern ★★$$ Another illustrious roll call of former regulars—Pepys, Goldsmith, Sheridan, Dickens, and Tennyson—once drank in this small tavern when it was located across the road. It was moved here in 1887 with many of the original building's fittings. Unfortunately, a fire several years ago destroyed a number of the details,

The Temple

but the building has been re-created as completely as possible. It still offers traditional ambience, an excellent bar lunch, and delicious roasts and puddings in the dining room. ♦ Pub ♦ M-F lunch. Reservations recommended for the restaurant. 22 Fleet St (between Mitre Ct and Inner Temple La). 353.8570. Tube: Temple

46 Hoare's Bank The only private bank left in London is still as old fashioned, discreet, and attractive as when it was founded in 167 It's well worth a peek inside. ♦ 37 Fleet St (between Mitre Ct and Inner Temple La). Tube: Temple

47 St. Dunstan-in-the-West This architectural gem—London's Romanian Orthodox patriarchal church—is beautifully situated on the north side at the curve in Flee Street. Designed by **John Shaw,** the Victoria church, with its octagonal tower, openwork lantern, and pinnacles, was built in 1831 at the beginning of the Gothic Revival moveme on the site of an earlier church whose great treasures were saved when it was demolishe to widen Fleet Street.

The church is unusually placed, with the tower and entrance on the south and the brick octagon of the sanctuary and altar on the north. Treasures from the original churc include the communion rail carved by Grinlir Gibbons and the old wooden clock dating from 1671, with two wooden giants that stri each hour. In 1830, the Marquis of Hertford bought the clock for his house in **Regent's Park.** Viscount Rothermere, a British newspaper proprietor, later purchased the clock and returned it to the church in 1935 to commemorate King George V's Silver Jubilee. The statue of Elizabeth I over the do (believed to be the oldest outdoor statue in London) and the statues of King Lud and his sons came from the Ludgate when it was tor down in 1760. The bronze bust of Lord Northcliffe, who lived from 1865 to 1922 and was newspaper proprietor and founder of the *Daily Mail,* was sculpted by Lady Scott in 1930. ♦ Fleet St (between Fetter and Chancery Las). Tube: Temple, Chancery Lane, Blackfriars

48 The Temple An oasis of calm between the traffic of the **Embankment** and the bustle of Fleet Street, this structure was originally the headquarters of the Knights Templar, a monastic order founded in 1119 during the Crusades to regain Palestine from the Saracens for Christianity. They settled here in 1160, but were suppressed by the pope, and all that remains of their monastery is the **Temple Church** and the **Buttery.** Since the 14th century, the buildings have been leased to lawyers. Today, they house two of England's four **Inns of Court (Inner Temple** and **Middle Temple),** the voluntary legal society that has the exclusive privilege of calling candidates to the bar. Visitors are free to stroll through the warren of lanes, courtyards, and gardens and to admire the buildings, each composed like an **Oxford** or **Cambridge** college, with chambers built around steep stairways, communal dining halls, libraries, common rooms, and chapels. The tranquillity of the setting is disrupted by the speed with which the lawyers—either wearing their gowns or carrying them over their arms, and loaded down with books and papers—race between their chambers and the **Law Courts,** the vast Gothic world that stretches from **Temple Bar** to the Adlwych.

The **Temple Church,** located within the precincts of the **Inner Temple,** was badly damaged during the Blitz, but has been skillfully repaired. The beautiful round nave, completed in 1185, is modeled after the Church of the Holy Sepulchre in Jerusalem. It's the only circular nave in London, and one of the only five in England, all connected with the Knights Templar. The chancel was added in 1240, and the rib vaulting within the Gothic porch is original.

The **Middle Temple Hall,** also painstakingly restored after the Blitz, is a handsome Elizabethan building with a splendid double–hammer beam roof and carved-oak screen. Here, aspiring barristers are called to the bar upon passing their examinations. Daily lunch and dinner are served in the hall, and though residence at the inns has become vestigial, the students must eat three dinners during each term here. Shakespeare's *Twelfth Night* was performed in the hall in 1602, and the round pond amid the mulberry trees outside the **Fountain Court** was featured in Dickens's novel *Martin Chuzzlewit.* The **Inner Temple Gateway,** leading back to the Strand, is a half-timbered three-story house that looks suspiciously like a stage set, but it is genuinely

17th-century, with **Prince Henry's Room** (see page 193) on the top floor. ♦ Bounded by Victoria Embankment and Strand, and Mitre Ct and Essex St. Tube: Temple

49 El Vino's ★$ Whoever said "in vino veritas" didn't hang out at this historic wine bar opened in 1879. A lot of history (some truthful, some apocryphal) was written over bottles of wine here when this place was the haunt of boozy journalists. What started as a piece of gossip, idle speculation, or a mischievous rumor would become an item in the *Standard Diary* or an article in *Private Eye,* and sometimes progress to "something worth checking out" by more serious writers. Throughout most of its life, the bar has been a masculine institution (women weren't allowed to drink here until 1982). These days, it is packed daily with lawyers and City businesspeople. The wine list is long, as you might expect, and the menu in the small basement restaurant consists of simple British foods such as Scottish salmon and steak-and-kidney pie. Sandwiches are served at the bar. No jeans, leggings, track suits, or shorts are allowed. The bar also operates as a wine merchant and delivers orders to its customers all over Britain. ♦ Wine bar ♦ Bar: M-F. Restaurant: M-F lunch. Reservations recommended. 47 Fleet St (between Bouverie St and Mitre Ct). 353.6786. Tube: Temple, Blackfriars

50 Dr. Johnson's House This great English city is full of the houses of famous English men and women. Many of these historic homes have been lovingly bought and preserved, restored, rearranged, and revitalized in the spirit of the departed. They usually possess an orderliness that the former inhabitants would find astonishing, especially if they were writers. Among the most tempting for the London lover is the house of Samuel Johnson, one of his London residences and the place where he produced the first complete dictionary of the English language, published in 1755. Until he moved to Gough Square, Johnson had lived in miserable lodgings, taking whatever literary hackwork he could find. But with the advance he was given to write the *Dictionary,* he leased this house in 1748. On the day he signed the contract to write the *Dictionary,* he composed the following prayer: "Oh God, who hast

Shakespeare's Globe Comes Full Circle

Shakespeare buffs, rejoice! After 400 years, the "Wooden O" is back! The famous thatch-roofed, half-timbered, open-air Globe Theatre has been authentically reconstructed about 200 yards from the original spot in **Southwark,** on the south bank of the **Thames.** Since its grand opening in 1997 (with productions of *Henry V* and *The Winter's Tale*), aficionados have been flocking to see the Bard's plays performed very much as they were in his day: A thousand spectators sit in three galleries of the amphitheater while 500 "groundlings" stand in the yard of the open arena in front of the stage. (Elizabethan theatergoers who watched performances from the pit were called groundlings because they had only the ground for a floor.)

The history of the original Globe was set in motion in 1576 when the actor James Burbage built an amphitheater to stage plays in the **Shoreditch** area of London. Before then, actors had been traveling players performing in courtyards of inns like the **George** or in great halls such as the one at **Middle Temple.** Burbage simply called his new structure **The Theatre;** there wasn't any other. When the Shoreditch building was torn down, the timber frames were used in the building of the Globe in 1599. There Shakespeare presented and acted in many of his plays. Performances took place in natural light and sometimes in the rain. The groundlings had a boisterous time. They walked around, talked loudly, ate fruit—and threw some of it at the actors during performances. Theater people had to put up with a lot in those days; it was a risky business in which all the members of a company were shareholders. Not only was there no guarantee that a new play would ever see more than one performance, periodic outbreaks of plague meant that large gatherings were forbidden.

Southwark was where Shakespeare played as well as worked. The red light district of its day, it was full of bear-baiting pits, brothels, taverns—in fact, it welcomed all the entertainment the City merchants banned in their own neighborhood, though they didn't mind crossing London Bridge to enjoy the delights on offer. Shakespeare and his cronies drank at the first incarnation of **The Anchor.** He worshiped at **Southwark Cathedral,** which now holds a marble effigy of him, looking thoughtful. Above the statue, a stained-glass window depicts many of his characters.

Shakespeare and his players did cross the Thames for special performances. In the gorgeous **Middle Temple Hall** (Middle Temple La, between Victoria Embankment and Crown Office Row), where lawyers still dine today, they performed *Twelfth Night* in 1602. The gardens outside were immortalized in *Henry VI, Part I* in connection with the plot

that began the War of the Roses. Lord Suffolk says, "Within the Temple Hall we were too loud/The garde here is more convenient." Then the characters pluc first a white and then a red rose to indicate which side they back. Visitors can still admire the garden from the park benches in Fountain Court outside the hall.

The Globe burned down in 1613: A spark from a stage cannon that was fired to announce the entran of King Henry VIII ignited the thatch roof. The same fire also caused the original Anchor to go up in smoke. And Shakespeare died three years later. It's interesting to note that his favorite pub was rebuilt twice—the atmospheric, creaky-boarded **Anchor** of today dates from 1760—but the rebirth of his theat had to wait 400 years, and then it was American actor/director Sam Wanamaker who sparked its revival.

When Wanamaker came to London in the 1950s he was dismayed to find nothing of the Globe remainir the only reference was a dusty plaque on a disused warehouse on a derelict street. Wanamaker's disbelief that the world's greatest playwright had nc suitable tribute in the city in which he wrote his play led him to embark on a 40-year crusade to re-create the original theater. Finally, in 1970 he established the Globe Playhouse Trust, and the Southwark Council offered the trust a 1.2-acre site near the original theater. Unfortunately, Sam Wanamaker di in 1993 before the new theater was completed. It is appropriate that a memorial to him adjoins the one to Shakespeare in **Southwark Cathedral.**

Costing $47 million, the re-created theater is the first thatch building to be erected in London since tl Great Fire of 1666. Its materials include green oak, willow, and sand mixed with lime and goat's hair to create plaster for the walls In fact, it's the Wooden O Shakespeare would recognize—except that this one has a sprinkler system hidden within the thatch.

hitherto supported me, enable me to proceed in this labour, and in the whole task of my present state; that when I shall render up, at the last day, an account of the talent committed to me, I may receive pardon. For the sake of Jesus Christ, amen." Johnson installed his assistants in the huge attic, and for the next nine years, they worked at their task. In 1759, when his beloved wife, Tetty, 15 years his senior, died, he left this house, melancholy and impoverished, and went to live in one of the **Staple Inn Buildings**. ♦ Admission. M-Sa. 17 Gough Sq (at Pemberton Row). 353.3745. Tube: Blackfriars

Ye Olde Cheʃhirē Cheeʃe

51 Ye Olde Cheshire Cheese ★★★$$ This 17th-century hostelry is probably the most profitable institution on Fleet Street and one of the few remaining of its kind in London. "The House," as it's also known, has witnessed 16 reigns and hardly changed since it was rebuilt after the Great Fire of 1666. The 14th-century crypt from **Whitefriars** monastery is beneath the cellar bar, and is available for private parties. The sawdust on the floor, changed twice daily, and the oak tables in "boxes" with benches on either side enchant foreigners who long to visit an England frozen in time. Considering the unrivaled popularity of the place (which can sometimes cause culinary neglect), the food is pretty good, although the famous pudding of steak, kidney, mushrooms, and game, which celebrated its bicentenary in 1972, no longer feeds 90 people nor requires 16 hours to cook. Nor does it contain oysters and lark, as it once did, but it's still sustaining and flavorful. The biggest pies now serve up to 35 people with steak, kidney, venison, and game packed under a delicious pie crust. Rich game puddings are served in autumn and winter. Follow the pudding with stilton cheese or lemon pancakes and relish the Englishness of it all. ♦ British ♦ Bar: daily. Restaurant: M-Sa lunch and dinner. Su lunch. Reservations recommended. 145 Fleet St (between Shoe La and Hind Ct). 353.6170. Tube: Blackfriars

51 Daily Telegraph Building This massive, modernish Neo-Greek structure, designed in 1928 by **Elcock, Sutcliffe, and Tait,** once housed London's most sensible, conservative paper. The *Telegraph* was the capital's first daily penny paper, founded in 1855. The paper moved to Docklands, but the building's facade

remains. The building is now occupied by offices. ♦ 135 Fleet St (between Shoe La and Hind Ct). Tube: Blackfriars

52 The Cartoonist ★★$ A Fleet Street "local" and headquarters of the Cartoonist Club of Great Britain, every square inch of wall space in this pub and restaurant is covered in framed original cartoons. Journalists return here for nostalgic reunions with former Fleet Street colleagues over typical pub grub (beef stew, chili, sausages, meat pies). ♦ Pub ♦ M-F lunch and dinner. 76 Shoe La (at St. Bride St). 353.2828. Tube: Blackfriars

53 Daily Express Building Nicknamed the "Black Lubyanka" because of the glossy appearance of its facade, this building's black-glass tiles and chrome represent one of the finest examples—inside and out—of Art Deco in London. It was designed by **Ellis Clarke and Atkinson,** with **Sir Owen Williams,** and built in 1932. The *Daily Express* departed for a building on Blackfriars Bridge in 1989, and the building now houses offices. ♦ 121–128 Fleet St (at Poppins Ct). Tube: Blackfriars

54 Old Bell Tavern ★★$ **Sir Christopher Wren** built this intimate, warm pub in 1678 to house and serve the workmen rebuilding **St. Bride's** nearby after it was destroyed in the Great Fire. Sandwiches, sausages, and other traditional pub fare are served. Like other Fleet Street pubs that catered to journalists in the newspapers' heyday, it's now crowded with lawyers and bankers. ♦ Pub ♦ M-F lunch and dinner. 95 Fleet St (between Bride La and Salisbury Ct). 583.0070. Tube: Blackfriars

54 The Punch Tavern ★★$ This splendidly Victorian pub is closely associated with the humor magazine *Punch,* which was founded in 1841. (After having ceased publication for a few years, the magazine started up again in 1996.) This was the watering hole for the staff of the first *Punch* and for decades of journalists afterward. Major refurbishment in 1997 enhanced its historic features, including a display of original cartoons and caricatures from early copies of the magazine. The new owners have also found artifacts related to Punch and Judy, the traditional English puppet show characters—it was the irascible Punch puppet who inspired the magazine's title. The lunch menu includes scampi-and-chips and baked potatoes with a choice of fillings. ♦ Pub ♦ Daily lunch. Drinks: M-F 11AM–11PM; Sa-Su noon–4PM. 99 Fleet St (at Bride La). 353.6658. Tube: Blackfriars

55 St. Bride's Church Wedged in between the ponderous buildings that used to house newspaper offices is **Sir Christopher Wren**'s "madrigal in stone," one of his grander creations, with the tallest of his steeples (226 feet) resting on a plain, squarish nave—the origin and inspiration of the traditional wedding cake. Damaged in the Blitz, the church was beautifully restored in the 1950s. Optimistic journalists still marry and attend memorial services for fellow journalists here. The crypt—established in memory of Lord Beaverbrook—is now a museum about the history of Fleet Street and printing. ♦ Free. Daily. Recitals: Tu-W, F 1:15PM, 1:45PM. Bride La (off Fleet St). 353.1301. Tube: Blackfriars

56 Reuter's Although its news department now works elsewhere, this famous international news agency is still headquartered in these two 1939 buildings, which are another example of the genius of **Sir Edwin Lutyens. Lutyens**'s last commercial buildings in London, they are next door to **Wren**'s beautiful **St. Bride's Church;** the Edwardian architect was wisely inspired by and respectful of the wedding cake–style structure, conceiving his L-shaped plan as a backdrop. One of the buildings is linked to the church by a high vaulted passage. The buildings are closed to visitors. ♦ 85 Fleet St (between Ludgate Circus and Bride La). Tube: Blackfriars

57 The Blackfriar ★★$ This wedge-shaped pub with a jolly friar statue over its doorway was built in Art Nouveau–style on the site of a Dominican monastery in 1875. Inside is a wealth of marble as well as murals depicting the monks pursuing their daily tasks and amusements. Bar snacks are served at lunch. ♦ Pub ♦ M-F lunch. 174 Queen Victoria St (at New Bridge St). 236.5650. Tube: Blackfriars

58 Blackfriars Bridge Built in 1869 by **Joseph Cubitt** and **H. Carr,** the bridge carrying cars and pedestrians has five handsome wrought-iron arches and on its north side, a statue of Queen Victoria, who officially opened the bridge. A smaller, railway-only bridge constructed in 1886 by **John Wolfe-Barry** and **H.M. Brunel** stands to the east. Between the two bridges is a curious architectural sight—a series of red cast-iron columns with water lapping around them but supporting nothing. And the massive pylons of the partly demolished bridge still stand on either bank. It seems that **Cubitt** and **F.T. Turner,** who had built it for the **London, Chatham and Dover Railway** in 1864, did their job so well that their old bridge couldn't be completely demolished to make way for **Barry** and **Brunel**'s bridge without making the riverbed unstable, so there the old pylons remain. This oddity is described by some imaginative tour guides as looking like a Victorian Stonehenge. ♦ Between Upper Ground and Victoria Embankment. Tube: Blackfriars

59 Oxo Tower Wharf A £20-billion development program has transformed a derelict eight-story building, the **Oxo Tower,** into a stylish shopping and eating venue with fabulous views over the Thames. Situated on its own wharf, the Art Deco building was once used as a cold storage warehouse for the Oxo bouillon-cube company, but it was always a distinctive landmark because the letters "OXO" are etched in dark brick on the building's tower. Also containing offices and apartments, the building is generating excitement because of its designer workshops—there are no mass-produced items here. Shoppers can talk to the designer as they work and also commission items. Offered here are etchings, collages, and handmade cards; hand-tufted rugs and wall hangings; scarves, wraps, and jewelry; and sculptures, lamps, and furniture. **Harvey Nichols,** the fashion department store of Knightsbridge, caused a stir by opening a stylish restaurant on the top floor with sweeping views of London's skyline across the Thames, as well as a free viewing gallery for the public.

The renovation of this wharf was an initiative by the Coin Street Community Builders, which set out to revive this riverside and has succeeded brilliantly. They also run a summerlong events program, the Coin Street Festival, from June through September. ♦ Shops: Tu-Su. Bargehouse St (off Upper Ground). 401.3610. Tube: Blackfriars, Waterloo

Within the Oxo Tower:

Oxo Tower Restaurant and Bar ★★★ $$$$ A fashionable crowd flocks to this stunning aerie where the view, especially at sunset, is marvelous. With sloping windows and a slanted ceiling, the restaurant resembles the interior of an ocean liner. Head chef Simon Arkless offers dishes such as grilled magret of duck breast with *girolles* (chanterelle mushrooms), asparagus and rosemary noisette potatoes; roast sirloin with Thai noodle salad; or poached John Dory (also known as St. Peter's fish) with shellfish. ♦ Continental ♦ Daily lunch and dinner. 803.3888

Oxo Tower Brasserie ★★★$$$ Linked by a terrace to the restaurant and bar, this more informal eatery features panfried lemon sole with fennel salad and green-olive butter and roast chicken breast with parmesan-and-herb polenta served with tomato sauce. There is a fixed-price pre-theater menu offering three courses. ♦ Mediterranean ♦ Daily lunch and dinner. Reservations required. 803.3888

60 Gabriel's Wharf Here is a tiny shopping enclave a short stroll from the **South Bank Centre** arts complex with designer clothing

stores, jewelers, restaurants, and crafts shops. Its location right on the Thames offers terrific views of the river and the city.

The restaurants with views are **Gourmet Pizza** (928.3188) and the **Southbank Brasserie** (620.0596). Other eateries include **House of Crepes** (401.9816), **Studio Six** (928.6243), and **Sarnis Sandwich Bar** (928.6654). ♦ Shops: Tu-Su. Restaurants: daily lunch and dinner. 56 Upper Ground (between Bargehouse St and Waterloo Rd). 401.3610. Tube: Embankment, Waterloo

61 Meson Don Felipe ★★$ Perch on stools at the high wooden bar or squeeze around one of the closely packed tables, but arrive early to be sure of a seat of some kind. Popular with businesspeople at lunchtime and theatergoers in the evening, the bar serves a wide assortment of delicious, traditionally cooked tapas, ranging from Spanish omelettes to peppers stuffed with chicken and herbs in a cream sauce. The *pan Catalán* (a do-it-yourself toasted bread with garlic, tomatoes, and olive oil) is highly recommended. To experience true Spanish style, don't miss the *fino* or *oloroso* Sherry, served chilled, as it should be. The final flourish is a flamenco guitarist who plays nightly from 8:30PM. ♦ Spanish ♦ M-Sa

lunch and dinner. 53 The Cut (at Short St). 928.3237. Tube: Waterloo

61 Livebait ★★★$$ Dark green–and–white-tiled walls are the background of this simply decorated fish restaurant with booth seating. The seafood tastes as fabulous as its showy display. Main dishes include halibut Wellington with kumquat ratatouille and grilled whole lobster with potato salad. For dessert try the sublime mango, pineapple and hazelnut turnover. ♦ Seafood ♦ M-Sa lunch and dinner. 41-45 The Cut (between Blackfriars Rd and Short St). 928.7211. Tube: Waterloo. Also at: 21 Wellington St (at Exeter St). 836.7161. Tube: Covent Garden

61 Old Vic From 1962 to 1976, this venue was the temporary home of the **National Theatre Company,** under the direction of Sir Laurence Olivier. Though the foundation stone, taken from the demolished **Savoy Palace,** dates from the theater's opening in 1818, the rest of the structure has changed interiors and owners many times, most recently in 1998, when it was saved at the last moment (it seemed doomed to become a theme park) by a nonprofit angel, the Old Vic Theatre Trust, who have made it once again a venue for some of London's finest and most challenging theater. ♦ Waterloo Rd (at The Cut). 928.2651. Tube: Waterloo

Bests

William Forrester
Registered Guide

Upper Crust Baguettes—Available at most rail stations. Brits suffer a culinary inferiority complex with the French—here is beautiful French bread with sandwich fillings and proof that a rail station snack really can be edible.

The Reading Room at the **British Library**—One of the world's great spaces. It'll soon be much more accessible to the general public when it becomes part of the **British Museum.**

Coffee at the **Cloister** of **Westminster Abbey**—American friends are annoyed that (sometimes) the Brits can do good coffee.

Evensong at **Westminster Abbey** or **St Paul's Cathedral**—An opportunity to hear one of the world's greatest choirs with one of the world's greatest acoustics *for free.* Ask to sit in the choir area.

Summertime band concerts in the parks—Or on Thursday, summer lunchtimes in **Westminster Abbey's** private gardens.

Sir John Soane's Museum—An eclectic collection given to the nation by this great architect and unaltered ever since. A real window into the mind of a 19th-century collector. Trust me and just see it!

Prêt à Manger's crème (without the brûlée). One branch under the Impressionists at the café in the **National Gallery**—just the thing to recover from cultural exhaustion.

The City/ The Thames

The love affair between England's capital and its main waterway dates back more than 2,000 years, when the origins of what is now the City of London took root on the banks of the river. The small area that now includes the site of the **Lloyds of London Building**, the **National Westminster Tower**, and other skyscrapers is often referred to as the Square Mile, or as just "the City."

Commerce gave birth to the city, and that commerce was possible mainly because of the Thames. What the Roman conquerors called "Londinium" in AD 43 had been a hub of trade between Britain and the Continent since the

ronze Age. Everything from spices and jewels to silks and tea arrived on the
harves of the river, brought to Britain by explorers and captains who forged
seafaring tradition for their island nation.

mid this incessant trade governed by a powerful merchant class, the river
lfilled another function: It was the highway of sovereigns, as well as of
1ose who served or displeased them. Barges plowed slowly through the
ark waters, ferrying monarch to castle, bishop to church, and prisoner to the
xecution block. They also ferried actors to theaters, for on the south bank the
kes of William Shakespeare and Richard Burbage were shaping the history of
nglish language drama in **Southwark.**

Today, the Thames is basking in a new appreciation by Londoners. More attractions are opening, especially on the south bank, where theater is flourishing again in Southwark, thanks to the rebuilding of **Shakespeare's Globe**. Next door a huge, windowless former power station is being converted to the **Tate Gallery of Modern Art**, which is expected to open in May 2000 (see page 42). Finance still rules the City, though computers in the **Stock Exchange** now clinch deals once made with handshakes in coffeehouses or on the docks. The **Docklands** area is still a center of commerce, but it no longer handles crates of tea. Instead, offices and tourist attractions are its mainstay. Finally, the merchant class's struggle for dominance (they jousted with the crown and the church for centuries) is still evident in the buildings of the **Bank of England,** the **Guildhall,** and the **Tower of London,** a prison for traitors in medieval times. In the midst of it all stands stately and solemn **St. Paul's Cathedral,** London's epicenter. **Sir Christopher Wren**'s splendid cathedral has weathered countless changes but has always managed to keep its soul intact, just as London itself has.

City code 0171 unless otherwise noted.

1 St. Paul's Cathedral The glimpses you'll have of this cathedral (illustrated on page 203) while walking up Ludgate Hill are inspiring, reassuring, and awesome. But when you're within a few yards, the building grows smaller, the road veers too close, and a statue of Queen Anne seems dumpy and distracting. It's worth stepping back a moment when you reach **Sir Christopher Wren**'s greatest masterpiece to try and see what the architect himself intended: the slight curve of the road; the scale, monumental in the context of the medieval perspective; the magnificent dome, second only in Christendom to St. Peter's in Rome; and the skyline, uncluttered and harmonious. Even as late as 1939, before the Germans chose **St. Paul's** as a primary bombing target, the cathedral stood in a tapestry of streets, courts, squares, and alleys, and medieval London was still recognizable.

Five churches have stood on this site. The first, founded by King Ethelbert of Kent for Bishop Mellitus in AD 604, was destroyed by fire and then rebuilt between 675 and 685 by Bishop Erkenwald. This church, in turn, was destroyed by a ninth-century Viking raid, but was rebuilt in 962. In 1087, this Saxon structure also burned, but rebuilding began almost immediately, at the behest of William Rufus, son of William the Conqueror. It was this great stone cathedral, unfinished until 1240, that became known as **Old St. Paul's.** But the magnificent cathedral, with one of the tallest spires in Europe, fell into desperate decay, and after the Great Fire of 1666, it lay in ruins. Six days after the fire, **Wren,** then 33, submitted his plan for rebuilding the City and the cathedral. It was rejected, but the architect remained undaunted. In May 1675, his design for the cathedral was approved, though his layout for the City never was. His master mason laid the first stone on 21 June 1675,

and the last was set by **Wren**'s son, 33 years later.

In his proposal, the architect managed to win an important concession that gave him the freedom to make "ornamental rather than essential" changes during construction. He took full advantage of the clause, modifying his design considerably—including deleting a tall spire—during the three decades he spent building the church. When it was complete, **Wren,** who was retired and living in **Hampton Court,** would still come and sit under the dome of his monument: "If I glory, it is in the singular mercy of God, who has enabled me to finish a great work so conformable to the ancient model."

The structure's splendidly Baroque style was enhanced by an exterior of Portland stone, and when it was cleaned in the 1960s, Londoners were astonished to discover a dazzling, honey-colored building. In front of the cathedral stands the statue of Queen Anne looking down Ludgate Hill. The original statue, carved in 1712 by Francis Bird, suffered from decay and occasional attacks—she lost her nose, orb, and scepter—and was removed to the grounds of a girls' school in East Sussex in 1884. The statue and the forecourt were originally inside a railing, which was sold at auction in 1874. At the same time, the road was expanded, bringing **St. Paul's** closer to the hellish stream of traffic en route to the City.

The spacious 78,000-square-foot interior accommodates tourist groups more readily than **Westminster Abbey** and, in spite of its three centuries and large population of statue and monuments, there is a lack of clutter, unique in cathedral design. The focal point is the huge dome-space at the crossing. The dome rises 218 feet above the floor and is supported by eight massive double piers with Corinthian capitals. There are actually three domes: a lead outer dome, a wooden one for support, and a painted inner one of brick and plaster. The spandrels under the **Whispering Gallery** contain 19th-century mosaics executed by Antonio Salviati, depicting the four Evangelists (Matthew, Mark, Luke, and John) and the four Prophets (Isaiah, Jeremiah, Ezekiel, and Daniel). The surface of the dome is decorated with eight large monochrome frescoes by Sir James Thornhill, depicting scenes from the life of St. Paul. The epitaph to **Wren,** who is buried in the crypt, is written in Latin on the pavement under the dome, and a plaque to Winston Churchill is also set into the floor here.

If you are sound of lung and limb, it is well worth inspecting the dome more closely. For a small fee, you can climb the 259 steps to the **Whispering Gallery,** thus named because if you stand at the entrance you can hear what is being said in a normal voice on the other side 107 feet away. The gallery offers spectacular views of the concourse, choir, arches,

clerestory, and the interior of the dome. If you're still feeling fit, climb the steeper spiral to the **Stone Gallery,** which surrounds the little dome outside. From here you can see all of London. For the heartiest, the **Golden Gallery** at the top of the dome takes you to the lantern and the golden ball.

The best place to start a tour of the cathedral is at the west entrance in the small **Chapel of All Souls,** a 1925 memorial to Field Marshall Lord Kitchener, who died in 1916, and "all others who fell in 1914-18." Behind the splendid ornamented wooden screen—carved by Jonathan Maine, one of **Wren**'s greatest craftsmen, in 1698—is **St. Dunstan's Chapel,** reserved for private prayer. Beyond the chapel in the main aisle are various monuments (though **Wren** himself did not want memorials in the cathedral). Most impressive is the monument to the Duke of Wellington, which fills the central bay. Painter and sculptor Alfred Stevens spent the last 20 years of his

St. Paul's Cathedral

life creating it, and it wasn't completed until 1912, nearly 40 years after Stevens's death. The equestrian statue on top was made by John Tweed. The third bay in the aisle contains an eerie Victorian monument to Lord Melbourne, Queen Victoria's first prime minister, who died in 1848. The inscription above the double doors guarded by two angels reads: "Through the Gate of Death we pass to our Joyful Resurrection."

The **North Transept Chapel,** also called the **Middlesex Chapel,** is reserved for private prayer and contains a large marble font carved by Francis Bird in 1726-27. Beyond the crossing is the **North Chancel,** with a memorial screen that lists the names of former **St. Paul's** choristers who died in the two World Wars. The carved paneling on the right is the work of Grinling Gibbons. The aisle ends in the **Altar of the Modern Martyrs,** where the names of all known Anglican martyrs since 1850 are recorded in a book kept in a glass-topped casket. Pass through the fine ironwork gate by Jean Tijou into the **American Memorial Chapel,** paid for entirely by contributions of the British people as a tribute to the 28,000 members of the American forces who lost their lives in Britain, or in active service from Britain, during World War II. The names fill 500 pages of illuminated manuscript, bound in a red-leather volume and presented to **St. Paul's** by General Eisenhower on 4 July 1951.

The choir is enclosed by a low screen made from the original altar rail by Jean Tijou, and contains the exquisite carved choir woodwork made in the 1690s by Grinling Gibbons. The carved oak baldachino (canopy) above the high altar was inspired from some of **Wren**'s unused drawings by Godfrey Allen and Stephan Dykes Bower. It replaced the reredos damaged in 1941. The high altar serves as Britain's memorial to the more than 324,000 men and women of the Commonwealth who died in the two World Wars.

The **Lady Chapel,** in the eastern end of the south choir aisle, contains the cathedral's original high altar. Nearby is a statue of John Donne, the poet who became one of the finest Anglican preachers ever and the most famous dean of **St. Paul's,** serving from 1621 to 1631. When Donne believed he was about to die, he called for sculptor Nicholas Stone the Elder to come and draw him in his shroud, and the artist used his sketch as the basis for the statue. It is the only effigy that survived the Great Fire intact.

On the second pillar in the south aisle hangs William Holman Hunt's most famous painting, *The Light of the World,* depicting a pre-Raphaelite Christ knocking at a humble door overgrown with weeds. The door has no handle and can only be opened from the inside; this is the door of the heart. Nearly life-size, it is the third and largest version of the painting Hunt produced and was presented to the cathedral by wealthy shipowner Charles Booth in 1908. It looks even more striking now after conservation work.

The **Chapel of the Order of St. Michael and St. George,** with its beautiful woodwork by Jonathan Maine and colorful banners, can only be entered via a 1.5-hour Supertour (which begins at the **Friends' Table** near the west door). The order is awarded to British and Commonwealth subjects for overseas service. The chapel was dedicated in 1906 by Bishop Henry Montgomery, with the stirring words: "You who represent the best of the Anglo-Saxon race at work beyond the seas are now made the guardians of the west door of the cathedral." As you leave the chapel and continue westward along the aisle, you will reach the **Geometrical Staircase** (only accessible on a Supertour), designed by **Wren** and built with a railing by Jean Tijou. Each stone step is set into the wall only a few inches, the weight at each level carried by the step below.

The crypt, entered from the **South Transept** and covering the whole length of the cathedral, is probably the largest in Europe. Many famous people are buried here, including Nelson in the elegant black tomb Cardinal Wolsey had built for himself before he fell out of royal favor, as well as Wellington, and **Wren** and his family. The artists' corner commemorates Van Dyck, Blake, Turner, Reynolds, Constable, and many others. Especially noteworthy are the memorials to John Singer Sargent, designed by the artist himself, and Sir George Frampton, which includes a small replica of the statue of Peter Pan he sculpted for **Kensington Gardens.** A welcome development is the cafe/shop in a section of the crypt that can also be reached by a separate entrance next to the tombs. Here you'll find a warm, sheltering area containing a coffee stall, a huge shop selling postcards, slides, scarves, books, and other items related to the cathedral, rest rooms, and most recently a restaurant serving breakfast, lunch, and light afternoon tea to 5PM. At press time, a cafe/restaurant was in the works. Visitors may now rent audio guides, which are excellent for helping them pick out the highlights at the cathedral. Also, concerts and organ recitals are often given. ♦ Admission. Daily. Tours: 11AM, 11:30AM, 1:30PM, 2PM. St. Paul's Churchyard (at Ludgate Hill). 246.8348. Tube: St. Paul's, Blackfriars

2 Balls Brothers ★★$ Judiciously avoid the sandwich bars near the front of **St. Paul's.** The sandwiches and coffee are okay, but the meals are everything that you'd expect from cafes that cater to masses of tourists. Instead, go around the back of the cathedral to what looks like an insurance office. Here, you'll find this underground wine bar, where huge sandwiches are served (they boast at least three ounces of meat). On the ground floor is a traditional-style bar, with wooden paneling, glass screens, and bric-a-brac. There is outdoor seating. ♦ Wine bar/Sandwiches ♦ M-F lunch and dinner. 6-8 Cheapside (at New Change). 248.2708. Tube: St. Paul's. Also at: Numerous locations throughout the city

3 Postman's Park The City of London is long on big buildings and short on green spaces, so this tiny emerald enclave behind **St. Botolph's** churchyard is all the more welcome. The park is named for its proximity to the **London Chief Post Office** building across King Edward Street which served as the **National Postal Museum** from 1965 to 1998 (the collections can now be seen at the **Post Office Archives;** see "Small Wonders" on page 168); though the museum is gone, the name is unchanged. A long wall was dedicated in 1900 as a monument to those who died while rescuing others. Some of the plaques' inscriptions may bring tears to your eyes, such as this one, dated 12 July 1886: "William Fisher aged 9 lost his life on Rodney Road, Walworth, while trying to save his little brother from being run over." ♦ King Edward St (between Angel St and Little Britain). Tube: St. Paul's, Barbican

4 St. Botolph's Without Aldersgate One of four churches in London built in the 10th century for the spiritual comfort of travelers, this one is dedicated to St. Botolph, a 7th-century Saxon abbot who is the patron saint of travelers. It has been rebuilt twice, the last time by **Nathaniel Wright** in 1788-91. Despite its dull exterior, it is quite lovely inside because of its preserved 18th-century architecture, with big plaster rosettes covering the ceiling, three wooden galleries, barrel-vaulted roof, and exquisite stained-glass windows (including the *Agony in the Garden*). Methodists will love this church because, close by in Little Britain, John and Charles Wesley were converted back in 1736, a fact that is commemorated outside the church and on a big bronze scroll outside the nearby **Museum of London.** ♦ M-F. Services: Tu, Th 10:30AM. Aldersgate St and Little Britain. 606.0684. Tube: St. Paul's, Barbican

---

The English have an extraordinary ability for flying into a great calm.

—Alexander Woolcott

I love London. It is the most swinging city in the world.

—Diana Vreeland

museum of LONDON

5 Museum of London Two thousand years of London's history have been immortalized on this site, along the line of the old City wall. The Romans took up residence in AD 43 and built a wall that was 3.25 miles long with six main gates; this wall was demolished during the 18th century, although bits of it still survive. The explanation of how London came to be as it is today can be found here, starting with a splendid Roman gallery and ending with the newest gallery, **London Now,** which depicts how London has changed more in the last 50 years than in the previous 100.

A museum showpiece is the spectacular **Lord Mayor's Coach,** which is wheeled out on state occasions. There are four main themes. **Prehistoric and Roman** includes sculpture and artifacts from the **Temple of Mithras** (see page 207). **Medieval** spans a thousand years from the fifth-century Dark Ages to the 15th century. **Tudor and Stuart** contrasts those glittering eras against the Great Plague of 1665 and contains a re-creation of the Great Fire of 1666, which destroyed 80 percent of London, and, in turn, allowed **Sir Christopher Wren** his prolific church-building career. The **Modern** galleries cover the Georgian and Victorian periods and the 20th century. A painted line called the "Catwalk" leads visitors to computer screens for information and to display points where objects can be handled. It gets its name from the museum's logo, which shows Dick Whittington, a 15th-century lord mayor of London, followed by his cat. An outdoor attraction is the tiny **Nursery Garden,** which traces the development of the English garden from the Middle Ages to today by devoting each section to a particular nurseryman and displaying the plants he introduced. ♦ Admission; free after 4:30PM. Tickets are valid for unlimited admission for one year. M-Sa; Su noon-5:50PM. 150 London Wall (at Aldersgate St). 600.3699; www.museum-london.org.uk. Tube: St. Paul's, Barbican

Within the Museum of London:

Museum Restaurant ★$ In summer, do as the locals do and enjoy a bite to eat at one of the outdoor tables here—arrive by 12:30PM to get a spot. The sandwiches and salads are imaginatively done, the sun and fresh air a definite plus. ♦ Cafe ♦ Daily lunch, afternoon tea, and early dinner. 600.3699

Barbican Centre

6 Barbican Centre When Queen Elizabeth II opened this cultural center in 1982, she called it one of the wonders of the modern world, and, as usual, she was not exaggerating. Designed by the architectural firm **Chamberlin, Powell and Bon** on a site that was heavily bombed during the Blitz, this walled city within the City covers 20 acres, rises 10 levels, descends 17 feet below sea level, and caps it all with the largest unsupported dome roof in Europe.

The concert hall (on levels 5 and 6) is the permanent home of the **London Symphony Orchestra,** and visiting orchestras also present concerts here. In the foyers, the live music runs from chamber to folk. The art gallery (on level 3) stages major exhibitions, while the foyers mount more offbeat shows. The theater (levels 3 to 6) is the London home of the **Royal Shakespeare Company (RSC),** based at Straford-upon-Avon. The company also typically tours around Britain for several months a year. When it's not on tour, try to see at least one Shakespeare play by this brilliant company. There are usually some seats still available on the day of the performance. The theater has 1,166 seats, with raked stalls and three circles projecting toward the stage, putting every member of the audience within 65 feet of the action. The 109-foot, double-height fly-tower above the stage, used for scenery storage, is believed to be the tallest in the world. A remarkable stainless-steel safety curtain descends during intermissions. Small productions of Shakespeare, revivals, and new plays are performed in the **Pit,** which is a rehearsal space that was redesigned as a flexible auditorium seating 200 people. The **Barbican** complex also includes a library, cinema, and bookshop. There is a cafeteria and coffee stalls, but the good news for regulars is that talented chef Richard Corrigan is now in charge at **Searcy's Brasserie** (level 2; 588.3008), producing his trademark robust British dishes in two- or three-course set menus at affordable prices. The area around the **Barbican** is slowly acquiring restaurants and cafes, but it's still pretty much a windy wasteland at night. Getting here can be a drag, too. ◆ Daily. Silk St (at Whitecross St). 638.8891. Tube: Barbican, Moorgate

7 Guildhall The city's first lord mayor, Henry FitzAilwin, was installed here in 1192. The Gothic porch, which is still the entrance to the hall from Guildhall Yard, was finished in 1430; the main structure was finished in 1439. The most extensive medieval crypt in London today still exists beneath the hall and it has one of the finest vaulted ceilings in the city. London's second-largest hall (after **Westminster Hall**), the building was once used for treason trials, such as that of Lady Jane Grey. Nowadays, it is used for state occasions. It survived the Great Fire but was bombed out in World War II; it was repaired by **Sir Giles Gilbert Scott,** who also worked on the **Houses of Parliament,** among a host of other projects (he was even responsible for the design of the celebrated British red telephone box). The newer buildings east of the **Guildhall,** designed by **Sir Giles Scott Son & Partners,** seem to put a 1960s twist on the Gothic Classical look of the original structure. Before you visit, call ahead to check whether a state occasion is scheduled. The newly built **Guildhall Art Gallery** (expected to be open by late 1999) showcases the City of London's many artworks. ◆ Free. Daily May-Sept; M-Sa Oct-Apr (except during state occasions). Basinghall St (between Gresham St and Aldermanbury Sq). 606.3030. Tube: St. Paul's

Within the Guildhall:

Guildhall Library Dick Whittington, thrice lord mayor of London, left enough money to start this library in 1423. The entire contents were pilfered by the Duke of Somerset in 1549 and recovered in 1824. The library is the greatest source of information on England's capital, with genealogical histories, parish registers, and heraldic histories of important Londoners. ◆ M-Sa

Within the Guildhall Library:

Clock Museum This museum in the library's precincts contains clocks from many centuries, as well as books dating back to 1814. There are 700 exhibits under one roof (including a pocket watch said to have belonged to Mary, Queen of Scots), making it one of the foremost horological museums in the country. ◆ Free. M-F

8 St. Lawrence Jewry On the wall of this church is one of the few remaining blue police phone boxes in London. The building suffered great damage during World War II, losing its **Christopher Wren** features; nevertheless, it was restored and is pleasant enough for the lord mayor and corporation to worship here. ◆ Gresham and King Sts (at Guildhall Yard). Tube: St. Paul's

9 St. Mary-le-Bow It's said that every true Cockney is born "within the sound of Bow Bells." The church, which has stood on this spot since 1091, has a very bloody history: The tower collapsed sometime in the 12th century, killing 20, and people seeking sanctuary here got short shrift and usually death, too. **Sir Christopher Wren** rebuilt it in 1670, and the exterior is rather stunning. In the garden, note the splendid statue of Captain John Smith, who played a famous role in the settlement of Jamestown, Virginia. As with many churches in the City, where weekends are only for tourists, there are no Sunday services ♦ M-F (services offered several times daily). Cheapside (at Bow La). 248.5139. Tube: St. Paul's, Mansion House

Within St. Mary-le-Bow:

The Place Below ★★$$ What a find! In the crypt of the church, this restaurant serves lots of coffee, tea, and lashings of homemade lemonade throughout the day. Muffins and muesli cereal are offered at breakfast, and the lunch menu features delicious soups, salads, and a hot dish that changes daily. ♦ Vegetarian ♦ M-F breakfast, lunch, and afternoon tea. 329.0789

10 Bow Lane and Watling Street This is one of the oldest parts of London. Watling Street was first mentioned in 1230, but it is believed to have been part of the main Roman road between Dover and St. Albans, built nearly 1,000 years earlier. The tiny streets here show graphically just how chaotic the City is, lacking any formal plan. After the Great Fire of 1666 (which destroyed 80 percent of London's buildings), Londoners were desperate to get back to work and to make money. **Sir Christopher Wren,** among many others, drew up spectacular plans for a beautiful city. But changing the street plan would have taken a long time and cost a lot of money, so the medieval plan remains to this day. The only difference is that the buildings are made of stone, not wood. Today, Bow Lane is quaint and kitsch. Still, ancient pubs like **Ye Olde Watling** (built from ships' timbers by **Wren** in 1668) and **Williamson's Tavern and Library Bar** (an old lord mayor's house dating back to the 17th century) are still intact, as are the **Bow Wine Vaults,** the haunt of City businesspeople. ♦ Tube: St. Paul's, Mansion House

11 Temple of Mithras This is an archaeological showpiece of Roman London, with the remains of the brick walls neatly reconstructed to show the layout of a pagan temple that was built around AD 200. The temple was dedicated to Mithras, a sun god who appealed to Roman soldiers because he symbolized bravery, virility, strength, and action. It looks rather small and out of place next to a large office complex, but it was the construction of the complex in 1954 that led to the discovery of the temple. The statues, tiles, and artifacts that were excavated are now displayed in the **Museum of London.** A plaque explains the site's layout. ♦ Queen Victoria St (at Garlick Hill). Tube: Mansion House, Bank

12 Mansion House Lord mayors in London serve just one year in office, so they have a mere 365 days to live and work in the splendor of this Palladian mansion,

constructed between 1739 and 1753 by **George Dance the Elder.** There are a series of superb state rooms leading to an Egyptian banqueting hall with giant columns along each side on the first floor and the ballroom on the second. Note the pediment frieze depicting London defeating Envy and bringing in Plenty. ♦ Open by appointment only. Free. Mansion House St (at Walbrook). 626.2500. Tube: Bank

13 St. Stephen Walbrook Behind the **Mansion House** is this gem of a church. Built in 1679, it has one of **Sir Christopher Wren**'s most celebrated interiors, although it is exceedingly plain on the outside except for an ornate tower. Inside, a marvelous spatial harmony is created by intricate crosses, squares, and arches leading up to a dome. There are services occasionally. ♦ M-Th; F 10AM-3PM. Walbrook (between Bond Ct and St. Stephen's Row). Tube: Bank

14 Bank of England Museum During a session of the **House of Commons** in 1797, Richard Brinsley Sheridan referred to this bank as "an elderly lady in the city of great credit and long standing," and it's still called the "Old Lady of Threadneedle Street" to this day. The institution looks after the nation's gold and the National Debt, issues banknotes, and acts as the government's and bankers' bank (it also handles a very small number of private accounts). A figure of a woman holding a model of the building on her knee rests above the portico.

The "Old Lady" is the bank itself, according to those who work there. Established in 1694, it moved to Threadneedle Street 40 years later, where architect **Sir John Soane** rebuilt it between 1788 and 1808. The bank itself cannot be visited, but on the premises is a small museum that holds gold bars, coins, interactive videos, and even Roman mosaics found beneath the site. There is also a re-creation of a Victorian banking hall. ♦ Museum: free. Museum: M-F. Bartholomew La (between Threadneedle St and Lothbury). 601.4387. Tube: Bank

15 Royal Exchange A building where merchants can meet and conduct business has been on this site since 1566 and received royal approval from both Queen Elizabeth I and, later, Queen Victoria. This Classical building, designed in 1844 by **Sir William Tite,** is the third to stand here; the other two were destroyed by fire. Financial landmarks like this used to be open to the public, but the era of terrorism put an end to that. These days, the receptionist won't even tell you what companies have offices here! However, there are several tony designer boutiques and jewelry shops clustered together on the side of the building. On the Threadneedle Street side, note the statues of Henry FitzAilwin, the city's first lord mayor, and of Dick Whittington, the famous City merchant who was elected lord mayor three times. The outside steps are traditionally used to proclaim a new sovereign. ♦ Threadneedle St and Cornhill. Tube: Bank

At the Royal Exchange:

George Peabody Statue William Wetmore Story's bronze statue of American philanthropist George Peabody was erected in 1869. Peabody spent most of his life in Britain building 5,000 homes for the poor, which still stand today, and he was the only American ever to be buried in **Westminster Abbey** (his remains are now reburied in Massachusetts, his native state).

16 Cornhill Once a grain market, this is the highest hill in the City. Today, it is packed with office workers, bankers, and stockbrokers; a century and a half ago, these streets were traversed by authors like Elizabeth Gaskell, Thackeray, and the Brontës. ♦ Between Gracechurch and Lombard Sts. Tube: Bank

17 St. Michael's Alley Here is one of the few places in London that make you draw in your breath, for it is Dickensian London as you will rarely see it anywhere else. There's no need to rush along this alley, though—it ends within eyeshot and becomes modern London again. Just two buildings, the **Jamaica Wine House** and the **George & Vulture**, face each other across the street, sharing experiences of days gone by. ♦ Off Cornhill, between Gracechurch St and Birchin La. Tube: Bank

Within St. Michael's Alley:

Jamaica Wine House ★★$$ This popular pub got its name from customers back in the 1670s who were trading in Jamaica. When it opened in the mid–17th century, it was the first coffeehouse in London. At one time, it served Jamaican rum; today, the brews on tap include beer and real ale. Big sandwiches are served, such as smoked chicken and lemon mayonnaise or brie and bacon. ♦ Pub ♦ M-F lunch. 626.9496

George & Vulture ★★$$ This is a restaurant, not a pub, and it's very popular, so make reservations the day before—at least. A live, caged vulture used to serve as the establishment's sign. Charles Dickens used the place as a setting in *The Pickwick Papers*. The brass plate outside is worn thin from its daily cleaning; inside, the place is just

as pristine. And everything is first-rate, from the excellent service to the rack of roast lamb stilton cheese, and port at the end of your classic English meal. It is full of stockbrokers bankers, and insurance magnates, and the wine list reflects its international clientele. ♦ British ♦ M-F lunch. Reservations required. 3 Castle Ct (at St. Michael's Alley). 626.9710

18 Leadenhall Market A very pretty area crisscrossed with glass-roofed alleys, this market was built in 1881 by **Sir Horace Jones** Intricately decorated iron-and-glass facades cover what is one of the few places in the City where Londoners can buy fresh food. Cheese butter, meat, fish, eggs, plants, and even books can be purchased here. ♦ M-F. Gracechurch St (between Fenchurch and Leadenhall Sts). Tube: Bank, Monument

19 Broadgate Within this modern office complex, built during the 1990s, is the notabl **Broadgate Square** with an amphitheater at its center. Containing shops and trendy wine bars and restaurants at ground level, the amphitheater surrounds an open-air arena that in winter becomes an ice rink, the only outdoor one in Britain. Skates are available for rent; note that opening times vary, so call for information. In summer, the arena is given over to musical events and other entertainment. Free leaflets describing the events are on display throughout the area. ♦ Shops and restaurants: M-Sa. Ice rink: daily Oct-March (call for times). Bounded by Liverpool Street rail station and Wilson St, an Eldon and Sun Sts. 382.9854. Tube: Liverpoo Street

20 Spitalfields Famous for its weekend markets, this raffish district has always been home to immigrants but the Huguenot churches have now become Bengali mosques On Sunday morning, the **Petticoat Lane Market** is noisy and cheerful, full of stalls purveying cheap clothes and snack bars selling salt beef (corned beef) sandwiches an bagels with smoked salmon. Also on Sunday morning, the nearby **Brick Lane Market** offers a mishmash of junk and cheap goods of all sorts. In addition, **Spitalfields Market**, the former indoor fruit and vegetable market, now houses crafts shops and food stalls. Some shops are open during the week but the place really bustles on the weekend. ♦ Brick Lane Market: Su 9AM-2PM; Spitalfields Market: Sa Su; Petticoat Lane Market: Su. Bounded by Brick La and Bishopsgate, and Middlesex, Whitechapel High, and Quaker Sts. Tube: Liverpool Street

21 Lloyd's of London Building If you liked his Pompidou Center in Paris, this building by **Sir Richard Rogers** will also amuse, as it is a much smaller version squashed into a confined space. Erected in 1986 around a central atrium and bedecked with oversize pipework, metal flooring, and glass, this zoo-style design allows the public to look inside and watch the office workers busying about their day (the building is otherwise closed to visitors). That such a traditional insurance company as Lloyd's should be housed in this flamboyant structure is a surprise in itself. Although the building was controversial when it was completed, it is now seen as a bold landmark in a city packed with building blocks. ♦ 1 Lime St (at Leadenhall St). Tube: Bank, Aldgate

22 Minster Court In contrast to **Lloyd's,** this modern building echoes the monumentality of a gothic cathedral but translated into a modern silhouette with mock buttresses and faux towers. Completed in 1992, it houses the London Underwriting Centre and a mall-like hall with shops and eating places. ♦ M-F. Mark La (at Great Tower St). Tube: Tower Hill

23 The Monument These days, it has become more difficult to see things from the top of this block of Portland stone, since it is now surrounded by taller structures; nevertheless, you can still get a pretty good view of neighboring churches, the **Docklands** area, and **St. Paul's.** Built by **Sir Christopher Wren** and city surveyor **Robert Hooke** between 1671 and 1677, the monument was commissioned by Charles II to "preserve the memory of this dreadful visitation" (i.e., the Great Fire). If the 202-foot column were laid down, it would touch the exact spot where the Great Fire began on 2 September 1666, in a baker's oven in Pudding Lane. ♦ Admission. M-F; Sa-Su 2-6PM Apr-Sept; M-Sa Oct-Mar. Monument St (between Pudding La and Fish St Hill). 626.2717. Tube: Monument

24 All-Hallows-by-the-Tower William Penn was baptized in this church in 1644, and John Quincy Adams was married here in 1797. Although the first church on the site was Saxon, there are Roman tiles and a tessellated pavement in the crypt. Samuel Pepys watched the Great Fire of London from the church's spire. After many centuries of rebuilding, it was extensively renovated in 1950 because of war bomb damage. ♦ Byward St (between Tower Hill and Lower Thames St). 481.2928. Tube Tower Hill

TOWER HILL PAGEANT

24 Tower Hill Pageant To the west of the **Tower of London** stands "London's first dark ride museum," as it calls itself. Run in conjunction with the **Museum of London,** this institution chronicles the 2,000-year history of the city. Visitors take a 15-minute ride in automated cars past scenes showing London life from its earliest Roman days right up to the present. The attraction also includes a display of waterfront archaeological artifacts dating from Roman, Saxon, and medieval times. ♦ Admission. Daily. Tower Hill Terr (at Tower Hill). 709.0081. Tube: Tower Hill

25 Tower of London Though the crowds can be as thick and forbidding as the grayish-brown stone, this medieval monument (pictured on page 210), with its displays of armor and exquisite **Crown Jewels,** must be seen at least once in a lifetime. Nine hundred years of fascinating, though brutal, history are embraced within these walls, and even though the tower's violent years are long past, an atmosphere of impending doom still lingers. The tower has been used as a royal palace, fortress, armory, treasury, and menagerie, but it is best known as a merciless prison. Being locked up here, especially in Tudor times, was tantamount to certain death. Anne Boleyn, Catherine Howard, Lady Jane Grey, Sir Thomas More, and Sir Walter Raleigh are but a few who spent their final days, and in some cases, years, in the tower.

The buildings of **Her Majesty's Palace** and **Fortress of the Tower of London,** as it is officially known, reflect almost every style of English architecture, as well as the different roles the tower has played. William the Conqueror started the **White Tower** in 1078, and it was completed 20 years later by his son, William Rufus (William II). Richard the Lionheart strengthened the fortress in the 12th century by building a curtain wall with towers, of which only the **Bell Tower** remains. Henry III and his son Edward I completed the transformation into the medieval castle that stands today.

The 120-foot-wide moat, now covered with grass, was kept flooded with water by a series of sluice gates until 1843; today, it serves as the village green for the 50 or so families who live on the tower grounds. Prisoners and provisions were brought in through the **Traitors Gate** when the Thames was still London's main highway. A gate in the **Bloody Tower** leads to the inner precincts. This tower acquired its unpleasant name after the Little Princes mysteriously disappeared from it in 1483. Controversy still rages over whether Richard III, their uncle and protector, had them murdered so he could secure the throne. Sir Walter Raleigh wrote *A History of the World* during his imprisonment in the **Bloody Tower** from 1603 to 1616. Almost every stone in **Beauchamp Tower** is covered with desperately scratched messages from prisoners—pathetic reminders of those who perished. Nearby is the **Chapel Royal of St. Peter ad Vincula,** built in the 12th century and restored by Henry VIII in 1520 after a fire in 1512. The chapel is the burial place of the

Duke of Somerset, the Duke of Northumberland, Anne Boleyn, Catherine Howard (two of Henry VIII's six wives), and Lady Jane Grey, all of whom were beheaded.

Glittering amid the historical doom and gloom are the **Crown Jewels,** the tower's most popular attraction. Dazzling and brilliant, the spectacular collection far exceeds its reputation. The jewels were housed in **Martin Tower** until 1671, when the audacious Colonel Blood came very close to making off with them. They are now displayed in the ground-floor strongroom of **Waterloo Barracks,** known as the **Jewel House.** Here, robes, swords, scepters, and crowns adorned with some of the most precious stones in the world are shown to about 20,000 people every day. Most of the royal regalia was sold or melted down after the execution of Charles I in 1649. Only two pieces escaped: the **Anointing Spoon,** probably first used in the coronation of King Henry IV in 1399, and the 14th-century **Ampulla.** The rest of the collection dates from the restoration of Charles II in 1660. **St. Edward's Crown** was made for Charles II, and has been used by nearly all of his successors, including Queen Elizabeth II. It weighs almost five pounds and is adorned with more than 400 precious stones. The priceless **Imperial State Crown,** originally made for Queen Victoria, contains some of the most famous stones in the world, including the 317-carat **Second Star of Africa,** the **Stuart Sapphire,** and the Black Prince's balas ruby. Monarchs have worn this crown when leaving **Westminster Abbey** after coronation ceremonies, at the State Opening of Parliament, and at other state occasions. The exquisite **Koh-i-noor** diamond adorns the **Queen Mother's Crown,** made especially for her to wear at the coronation of George VI in 1936 (she also wore it for Queen Elizabeth II's coronation in 1953). But even grander is the 530-carat **Star of Africa,** believed to be the largest cut diamond in the world, which is on the **Sovereign's Sceptre.** Most spectacular of the many swords is the **State Sword,** decorated with diamonds, emeralds, and rubies that form the national emblems of England, Scotland, and Ireland.

Tower of London

The imposing Kentish and Caen stone walls of the **White Tower** dominate the complex. Started in 1078 for William the Conqueror by a Norman monk, the walls are 15 feet thick at the base, 11 feet thick at the top, and 90 feet above ground level. In 1241, Henry III added a great hall and royal apartments and had the exterior whitewashed, hence the name. The **Royal Armory** was housed here until recently when the collection was moved to Leeds. However, some armor is still on display, mostly pieces that belonged to Henry VIII, who established a fine armor-making foundry here. **St. John's Chapel,** on the second floor of the **White Tower,** is one of the finest examples of early Norman architecture, with simple columns, roundheaded arches, and beautiful tunnel vaulting. It was here in 1503 that the body of Elizabeth of York, wife of Henry VII, lay in state surrounded by 500 candles, and here that Lady Jane Grey prayed before her execution in 1554.

The tower's great sense of history and tradition lives on through ceremonies that have been performed virtually unchanged for centuries. The most famous one is the Ceremony of the Keys, perhaps the oldest military ceremony in the world. Every evening at precisely 10 minutes to 10PM, the chief yeoman warder, wearing a large scarlet coat and accompanied by four soldiers, secures the main gates of the tower. As the clock strikes 10, a bugler sounds the Last Post. To attend the Ceremony of the Keys, write at least six weeks in advance to the Resident Governor, Operations Department, Waterloo Barracks, HM Tower of London, London EC3N 4AB. Enclose a self-addressed envelope with two international reply coupons. Only 70 people are allowed to watch each night, so make your request as far in advance as possible (and suggest alternative dates).

On 21 May of each year, representatives from **Eton College** and **King's College, Cambridge,** place lilies and white roses in the oratory of **Wakefield Tower,** where Henry VI, the founder of the two schools, was murdered on the orders of Edward IV in 1471. The ceremony is closed to the public. **Wakefield Tower** serves as one of the settings for a re-creation of the medieval palace that used to occupy this area. Costumed players representing courtiers, knights, and servants tell visitors about the details of daily life at the royal court. The re-creation takes place several times daily.

Another longstanding tradition is the daily feeding of the ravens who live within the tower walls. Since Charles II decreed there should always be at least six ravens at the tower, there have always been six with two reserves. In 1989, the tower managed to breed the birds successfully for the first time. Their wings are clipped to keep them here because legend has it that if they leave, the tower will fall and the monarchy with it. Watch out: Ravens are much bigger than crows and sometimes peck at the ankles of unsuspecting tourists.

The **Jewel House** is closed in January or February each year, when the jewels are given a thorough cleaning. Call and check before visiting during these months. ♦ Admission. Daily. Tower Hill (at Tower Bridge Approach). 709.0765. Tube: Tower Hill

26 St. Katharine's Dock   For about three hundred years, beginning in the 16th century, London's Docklands had a proud heritage as working dockyards, but in Victorian times the area became poor, and crime rampant. During World War II, the Docklands area was devastated by bombs and remained largely unrepaired until the mid-1980s, when attempts at revitalization began (see "The Docklands: Vibrant Revival" on page 174).

This dock was the pioneer of the entire redevelopment plan. Designed by **Thomas Telford** in 1828, the dock offers lovely views of small ships and boats in the marina, as well as several shops, pubs, and restaurants. Because its warehouses were built close to the water, thieving was minimal. Eventually, the dock closed because it was unable to accommodate large ships. Today, however, it's a thriving marina, playing host to the big oceangoing yachts of the wealthy, and several upscale jewelry and fashion boutiques flourish on the waterside. It is next to the **Docklands Light Railway,** whose trains travel deeper into the Docklands. ♦ St. Katharine's Way (off E Smithfield). Tube: Tower Hill

At St. Katharine's Dock:

Dickens Inn ★$$ This rambling pub looks like a Walt Disney World creation, but it's a genuine 18th-century spice house that has been overhauled and converted to the style of a 19th-century balconied inn. Inside, it's all wood tables and beams, and the most pleasant place for a drink in the whole of **St. Katharine's Dock;** the locals use it (always a good sign), and it fills up on a Friday night. Upstairs, two restaurants offer fish dishes, but the ground-floor **Tavern Bar** is really the main attraction here. ♦ Pub ♦ Daily lunch and dinner. 488.2208

Nauticalia   Stop in here for seafaring gear such as captains' lamps, caps, spyglasses, scrimshaw, and other marine accessories. Avoid it like the plague, however, if you dislike brass! ♦ Daily. 480.6805

Tower Thistle Hotel $$$ Sandwiched between the Thames and **St. Katharine's Dock** with its colorful yachts and shops, this vast, zigguratlike property offers guests four-star accommodations in 803 plush, refurbished rooms right around the corner from that "other" tower. The hotel seems designed for the business executive but plenty of tourists stay, too. The **Princes Room** offers superb views over **Tower Bridge** and a menu featuring international cuisine, while the **Carvery** stays closer to home with traditional roast joints. **Which Way West Cafe,** serving food throughout the day, metamorphoses into a nightclub in the evenings. ♦ 481.2575; fax 488.4106

27 Tower Bridge London's most famous bridge (shown below) has been a museum since 1982. The original hydraulic machinery that operated the bridge until 1976 is on display, along with exhibitions that explain the Victorian genius behind the design. Built in 1894 by **Sir Horace Jones** and **John Wolfe-Barry,** the Gothic towered bridge represents Victorian architecture and engineering at its best. The twin towers of steel encased in stone support the 1,000-ton weight of the bascules that were raised and lowered by hydraulic machinery located in piers at the base of the towers. At the peak of London's river traffic, and before steam replaced tall masts, the bascules rose as many as 50 times a day. Now they are operated by electricity and open only a few times a week. The glass-enclosed walkway, stretching across the London sky 145 feet above the Thames, offers splendid views in every direction. From here you can step back and see the architectural variety of the city, from the Portland stone office

buildings on Tower Hill to the brick and concrete of the postwar rebuilding to the glass and steel of the last 20 years. The **Tower Bridge Experience,** located inside the bridge, offers a high-tech exhibition recounting the history and function of the bridge. ♦ Admission. Daily. Between Tower Bridge Rd and Tower Bridge Approach. 407.0922. Tube: Tower Hill

28 Butlers Wharf Here, among the streets and alleyways, is the best place to capture the mood of the old Docklands. The spices that were once shipped in from the Orient are still sold here. Dickens had Bill Sykes from *Oliver Twist* meet his end on Shad Thames, which is now the home of restaurants. ♦ Shad Thames (off Tooley St). Tube: Tower Hill, London Bridge

Within Butlers Wharf:

Le Pont de la Tour ★★★$$$$ One of Sir Terence Conran's four restaurants in this area, it has a huge wall of windows that afford a striking view of the Thames. There's a dramatic arched ceiling in the spacious dining room and attractive dark-wood tables set with white linen tablecloths and napery. Chef Andrew Sargent's menu features *crèpe parmentier* (crepe with potatoes) with smoked salmon and caviar, lobster fricassee, or an elaborate roast truffled pigeon Rossini. ♦ Continental ♦ Daily lunch and dinner. Reservations recommended. 403.8403, bar 403.9403

Tower Bridge

Butlers Wharf Chop House ★★$$$

Despite all its chrome and glass, this eatery is traditionally English in its menu by chef Andrew Johns. Try the smoked haddock with poached egg and mustard hollandaise, and the steak and kidney pudding with or without oysters. ◆ British ◆ M-F lunch and dinner; Sa dinner; Su lunch. 403.3403

Cantina del Ponte ★★$$ A huge

mural of an Italian market running its entire length and terra-cotta floor tiles give this charming restaurant a friendly and informal atmosphere. Chef Jonathan Nicholson offers Mediterranean-inspired dishes such as Piedmontese peppers with a spiced aubergine (eggplant) salad or chargrilled vegetable bruschetta, grilled tuna with French beans, zampone sausage with lentils and salsa verde, and eight different pizzas. ◆ Italian ◆ M-Sa lunch and dinner; Su lunch; Su dinner Mar-Dec. 403.5403

Design Museum The pet project of Sir

Terence Conran, this trendy museum draws fashionable folks sporting designer gear, designer spouses, and, of course, designer children. But beyond the people watching, the museum is interesting in its own right. The **Review** gallery showcases international design, while the **Collection** shows design in its historical context. ◆ Admission. M-F; Sa-Su noon-6PM. 403.6933

Within the Design Museum

Blue Print Cafe ★★★$$ This smart

little Conran restaurant, with its fabulous river view, has stark white walls hung with colorful prints and red or blue vinyl-topped tables displaying blue vases, each with a single fresh flower. It's a charming backdrop for the flamboyant creations of chef Jeremy Lee. Expect such dishes as monkfish wrapped in pancetta or calf's liver with beetroot and horseradish relish. ◆ Modern British ◆ M-Sa lunch and dinner; Su lunch. 378.7031

28 Bramah Tea and Coffee Museum

Next door to the **Design Museum** is a former warehouse chock-full of displays that tell you everything you ever wanted to know about tea and coffee. The teapots, drinking cups, and tea- and coffee-making machinery have been collected by Edward Bramah, a former tea merchant who is delighted to answer questions. There's also a cafe in which to sample the beverages. ◆ Admission. Daily. The Clove Building, Maguire St (at Shad Thames). 378.0222. Tube: Tower Hill, London Bridge

29 Hay's Galleria A yellow brick–built dock,

now under a glass atrium, it's close enough to the City to be crowded during the day with bustling workers rushing to the delis, sandwich bars, and pretty shops. In summer, they eat outside, so get here early if you want to do the same. The fine **Horniman's** pub has a re-created Victorian interior and great waterfront views. Although the structure's design is hardworking Georgian warehouse architecture, its renovation has added charm. Watch out for David Kemp's *The Navigators,* a 60-foot-tall bronze moving sculpture with water jets and fountains. ◆ Tooley St (at Battle Bridge La). Tube: London Bridge

30 HMS Belfast This World War II cruiser

is now a floating museum with seven decks to explore. Visit the **Captain's Bridge,** the mess decks, the sick bay, and even the boiler room to get a feel for how the sailors lived. ◆ Admission. Daily. Morgan's La (off Tooley St). 407.6434. Tube: London Bridge

31 London Dungeon Opposite the more

refined pleasures of **Hay's Galleria** stand the gruesome delights of the world's first and only medieval horror museum—founded, as it happens, by a Chelsea housewife! Within its gloomy vaults beneath **London Bridge,** you can learn the finer points of hanging, drawing and quartering, boiling, and pressing people to death. Relive the Great Fire of 1666, and wander through the "Jack the Ripper Experience" exhibit. This rivals the **Chamber of Horrors** at the pricier **Madame Tussaud's,** especially because of the atmospheric setting in the arches under the railway. But be forewarned: It's *not* for the fainthearted—people have passed out in here. ◆ Admission. Daily. 28-34 Tooley St (between Stainer and Joiner Sts). 403.0606. Tube: London Bridge

32 The George Inn ★★$ This pub is a must-

see for great atmosphere. Eisenhower and Churchill are just two of the famous patrons who drank beer here. And as a child, Charles Dickens walked here every Sunday from Camden Town to visit his father in nearby **Marshalsea Prison;** you'll even find the inn mentioned in *Little Dorrit.* Rebuilt in 1676, this is an extraordinary survivor of bygone days—the last timbered, galleried inn in London. Before theaters like the **Globe** and the **Swan** were built, plays were presented in these inns, with "groundlings" standing in the courtyard and wealthy patrons seated on the balconies. The bar food is tasty and there's a fine range of beers. The upstairs restaurant serves more expensive food: steak-and-mushroom pie, stuffed chicken breast, and apple crumble with custard. ◆ Pub/English ◆ Daily lunch and dinner. 77 Borough High St (at Talbot Yd). 407.2056. Tube: London Bridge

33 London Bridge Imagination is required

here, since "London Bridge has fallen down" time and time again. Twenty yards or so downstream was the site of the first wooden bridge to cross the Thames, built during the first century at the behest of Roman emperor Claudius. A succession of wooden bridges followed until 1176, when Peter de Colechurch constructed a 10-arch stone bridge for Henry II; it was embellished with ramshackle wooden houses, and a few traitors' heads were spiked on for good measure. The heads were eventually removed, but the bridge remained until John Rennie erected a new one, 20 yards upstream, in 1831. This one was moved to Lake Havasu City, Arizona, in 1971, when the current cantilevered affair was constructed. ♦ Between Borough High St and King William St. Tube: London Bridge, Monument

34 Southwark Cathedral The fourth church on this site and the earliest Gothic church in London, this charming cathedral is not to be missed. The oldest oak effigy, dating from 1275, is of a knight, ankles crossed, one hand on his sword, and even the ravages of time can't erase the eerie feeling that he's just fallen asleep. John Harvard, founder of Harvard University, was born in Southwark in 1607 and baptized here. The reconstruction in 1907 of the Harvard chapel was paid for by the university. Among those buried here is John Gower, known as the "first English poet" because he wrote in English, not French or Latin. The **South Aisle** features a **Shakespeare Memorial**, and every year on 23 April, a service is held here in the Bard's honor. Touchingly, now beside the Bard is a memorial to the late Sam Wanamaker, the American actor/director whose dream of re-creating Shakespeare's theater has come true upriver.

Behind the cathedral, redevelopment hasn't entirely overtaken the ancient Georgian warehouses of **Borough Market,** where lorries laden with fruit and vegetables still draw up before dawn. This is how **Covent Garden** once looked. Four hundred years ago, this area was the haunt of Shakespeare, Marlowe, and other Elizabethan playwrights, as well as their audiences. ♦ Daily; call ahead for times of services. Montague Close (at London Bridge). 407.3708. Tube: London Bridge

35 Golden Hinde This galleon is an exact reproduction of the ship Sir Francis Drake sailed when he circumnavigated the globe in 1577-80. Now moored permanently, this little vessel, only 20 feet wide and 120 feet long, has also sailed Drake's route. Visitors can see the re-created living quarters, armory, and captain's cabin, but it's hard to imagine how the crew of 60, as well as 20 officers and gentlemen, lived in such a tight space. ♦ Admission. Daily. St. Mary Overie Dock (at Clink St). 403.0123. Tube: London Bridge

36 Clink Exhibition "In the clink" became a common expression to describe a jail term, thanks to the original jail in this alley. It now has display boards about the area's history, the brothels, the bull- and bear-baiting pits, and the theaters of its medieval and Tudor heyday. Ironically, the area was owned by the Bishop of Winchester, whose palace ruin is on this street. ♦ Admission. Daily. 1 Clink St (at Stoney St). 403.6515. Tube: London Bridge

37 Anchor ★★★$$ Dr. Johnson drank here, and Shakespeare imbibed as well, in an earlier version of this watering hole. Sam Wanamaker often ate here when his wonderf● **Globe** was in the planning. The fine old pub with creaking floorboards galore also has a minstrels' gallery, a riverside terrace with tables that enjoy a fantastic view of **St. Paul's** plus good bar snacks and a restaurant servin● such English fare as lamb hot pot and steak-and-ale pie. The place gets very crowded. ♦ Pub ♦ Daily lunch and dinner. 34 Park St (a● Bank End). 407.1577. Tube: London Bridge

38 Shakespeare's Globe Shakespeare lovers who have longed to see the Bard's plays performed as they were in the 16th century can now do just that. The new **Globe Theatre**—a thatch-roofed, half-timbered replica of the original open-air theater that premiered some of Shakespeare's plays—opened in June 1997 with Mark Rylance as artistic director. (See "Shakespeare's Globe Comes Full Circle" on page 196) From June to September, four plays are performed in repertory during the day and early evening in the open arena, including those of such other Elizabethan dramatists as Thomas Middleton and Beaumont and Fletcher. As of old, the actors enjoy a great rapport with the audience especially the "groundlings" who stand in the yard around the stage. (In the Elizabethan theater, those who watched performances from the pit had only the ground for a floor.) The rest of the spectators are seated in the three galleries of the amphitheater.

Part of an education charity project, the new **Globe** was born of American actor/director Sam Wanamaker's 40-year-plus struggle to re-create the theater near the original site. (Unfortunately, he died before construction began). The **Globe** complex also includes an exhibition center with displays about the theater's history, the building's restoration, and Shakespeare's works (including videos and slides). Guided tours of the center, included in the price of admission, explain the rise of Elizabethan theater, the playwright's links to this area, and the construction techniques of the time. There are also 40-minute guided walking tours starting at the exhibition and finishing at the site of the original theater. ♦ Admission to the exhibition Additional fee for tours. Performances: daily June-Sept; Tours: daily; call for times. Walking tours: F-Su every hour on the half hour 11:30AM-4:30PM Apr-June; daily June-Nov. New Globe Walk (at Bankside). 928.6406, box office 401.9919, tours 01689/838410. Tube: Blackfriars, Waterloo, London Bridge

In the Footsteps of Jane Austen

In such classic novels as *Persuasion, Pride and Prejudice, Sense and Sensibility,* and *Emma*—all of which have recently been adapted into successful and acclaimed movies or TV series—Jane Austen (1775-1817) demonstrated a sharp, satirical wit, keen powers of observation, and an innate understanding of human nature. Her specialty was the comedy of manners, and she delighted in pointing out the ironies and hypocrisies of upper-class society. While she spent most of her short life in the county of Hampshire, she has several links to London, **Bath**, and **Winchester**.

In London

Start your Austen tour by viewing the tributes to the author that reside in London's major institutions. For example, the only known likeness of Jane, a tiny portrait in pencil and watercolor by her sister, Cassandra, is displayed in the **National Portrait Gallery**. An Austen work called *A History of England by a partial, ignorant, and prejudiced historian,* which she wrote when she was 15, can be seen in of the **British Museum.** And **Poets' Corner** at **Westminster Abbey** holds a memorial plaque that simply reads "Jane Austen 1775-1817."

Other Austen associations around the city are a bit harder to find. On the building at **23 Hans Place** (between Pont St and Walton Pl) in **Knightsbridge** is a plaque stating that Austen lived with her brother Henry "in a house on this site." She and her brother also lived at **10 Henrietta Street** (between Southampton and Bedford Sts)**, Covent Garden,** but there's no plaque to mark it; the fine Georgian house has been converted into a men's shop called **Rohan.**

Although her novels appeared anonymously, most members of the literary community of the time knew that Austen was the author. Sir Walter Scott praised her work in the *Quarterly Review* in 1815. Even the prince regent (who later became George IV) kept a set of her novels in each of his residences, and in 1815, he invited her to visit his London palace, **Carlton House.** He was so impressed that he asked her to dedicate her next work to him—which turned out to be *Emma.* The palace, alas, was demolished in the mid-19th century; it was replaced by **Carlton House Terrace,** a long row of grand buildings opposite **St. James's Park.**

In Bath

Austen and her family lived in Bath for five years after her father retired from his Hampshire vicarage in 1801. She made good use of the time, focusing on the manners and mores of Bath's high society; her insightful observations are reflected in *Persuasion* and *Northanger Abbey.* The Austens lived in several different residences, including **No. 1 The Paragon** (at Lansdown Rd) and **4 Sydney Place** (between Beckford and Sydney Rds), which lies on the other side of the River Avon and is reached by crossing the charming, shop-lined **Pulteney Bridge**.

Austen set many scenes of her novels in various locations around Bath, including the **Abbey Church Yard** (next to Bath Abbey), where her characters would promenade in their fashionable attire to see and be seen; and the **Assembly Rooms** (Bennett St, between Oxford Row and Circus Pl, 01225/461111), the venue for grand balls; the rooms are now the site of the **Costume Museum**. It is believed that Austen also visited the **Pump Room** (above the Roman Baths, Abbey Church Yd, at York St, 01225/444477), where today's visitors may still lunch, take tea, or try the spa water; the Georgian **Theatre Royal** (Saw Close, at Barton St, 01225/448844), the major playhouse in the area; and **No. 1 Royal Crescent**, an elegant town house that is decorated and furnished as it was during Austen's era. Her letters described how much she enjoyed her rambles in the leafy hills that cradle the city.

In Winchester

On 18 July 1817, Jane Austen died of Addison's disease in Winchester. She had spent the last few months of her life in a house at **8 College Street** (between College Walk and Kingsgate St) so she could be near her doctor; today, a plaque on the side of the building honors her memory. The **City Museum** (The Square, at Symonds St, 01962/863064) displays several of her manuscripts, as well as some of her personal possessions, including two pretty little purses. And she is buried inside the 11th-century **Winchester Cathedral.** The gravestone mentions "the sweetness of her temper and the extraordinary endowments of her mind" but nothing about her books. When Emma Thompson won an Academy Award in 1995 for her screenplay adaptation of *Sense and Sensibility,* she spoke of coming here to visit Austen's grave and referred to the incomplete inscription: "I went to pay my respects . . . and to tell her about the royalties."

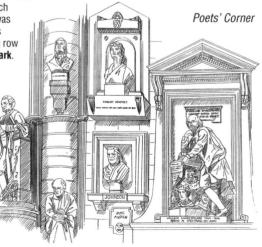

Poets' Corner

Day Trips

For all its myriad green spaces and riverbanks, London remains a city, with as much (if not more) chaos and traffic as downtown Manhattan. And while most visitors agree that every British experience has to include the city, few ever make it beyond central London, let alone into the historic towns and villages that lie within striking distance.

Just one or two hours' traveling out of London by car, bus, or train can take you to the spires of ancient **Oxford University**, to the quieter but no less impressive college town of **Cambridge**, to the Roman ruins of **Bath**, or the glorious cathedral at **Canterbury**. Faded Edwardian elegance resides on **Brighton**'s south coast, while the mystery of **Stonehenge** remains unsolved on **Salisbury Plain** to the southwest. Closer to home, one can stroll about bohemian **Hampstead** or trace part of Britain's lengthy maritime history at **Greenwich**. And those yearning for the full royal treatment may sail up the **Thames** to **Hampton Court Palace**, home to kings and queens from Henry VIII to Georgian times. If you have time during your visit to London, allow a day or two for a jaunt into the stunningly verdant countryside—the charms of rural England await.

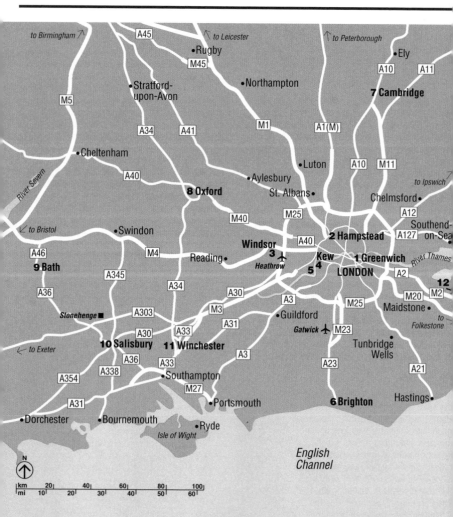

1 Greenwich Under Henry VIII (who was born here) and the Tudor royals, this Thames-side borough was the center of the world, and it still possesses the confidence and grandeur befitting that position. Greenwich Meridian (zero degrees longitude) and Greenwich Mean Time are still the standards by which the world sets its measures, and the vistas, elegant buildings, and parklands recall the long-lost British Empire.

The tall masts of the *Cutty Sark* (King William Walk, off Romney Rd, 858.3445), the last of the great 19th-century tea clippers that could sail 360 miles in a single day, loom over the streets. Now drydocked, the ship has been turned into a museum. Next to it is the smaller *Gipsy Moth IV*, which sailed around the world in 1966-67 with Sir Francis Chichester alone at the helm. Both ships are in the care of the Maritime Trust but only the *Cutty Sark* can be visited. ♦ Admission. M-Sa. Su noon-6PM Apr-Sept, noon-5PM Oct-May.

The domes and colonnades of the **Royal Naval College** (King William Walk, off Romney Rd, 858.2154), the triumphant achievement of three great architects— **Wren, Vanbrugh,** and **Hawksmoor**—preside magnificently over the River Thames. Inside, the paintings of Sir James Thornhill line the walls of the **Painted Hall.** The **Chapel** was redone with intricate detailing after a fire in the late 18th century. Only the **Painted Hall** and the **Chapel** are open to visitors. ♦ Free. M-W, F-Su 2:30-5PM.

The **National Maritime Museum** (Romney Rd, at Park Row, 858.4422), farther back from the river, houses the finest collection of globes in the world, along with marine paintings, navigational instruments, memorabilia about Lord Nelson, and more than 2,000 model ships. The centerpiece of the museum is the purely Classical **Queen's House,** designed by **Inigo Jones** in 1616-35. The great hall—a perfect cube—and the tulip staircase are both stunning. From the **Queen's House,** pass through **Greenwich Park,** with its delightful flower garden, to the buildings of the **Old Royal Observatory,** designed by **Sir Christopher Wren** for Charles II in 1675-76. Inside is a fascinating collection of telescopes and astronomical instruments. The park is free; one admission allows entry to the museum, house, and observatory. ♦ Daily.

The Millennium Experience at Greenwich is now a reality. The Dome, the largest construction of its kind in the world, is more than half a mile in circumference and covers over 250,000 square feet. The translucent roof—over 160 feet high at the center— is strong enough to support a jumbo jet. Two **Wembley Stadiums,** the **Eiffel Tower** (on its side), or even the great pyramids of Egypt could fit inside the Dome. The Dome contains 14 vast themed zones and a central performance area featuring a spectacular live show which includes live music, visual effects, and a cast of up to 200 performers. The site is off limits to cars, but accessible via the Tube—the new **North Greenwich** station on the **Jubilee Line**—and by riverboat from central London. There is a **Visitor Center** next to the *Cutty Sark*. ♦Daily. 0181/305.3456. Millennium Information Line: 0870/603.2000; www.mx2000.co.uk.

A riverside walk from the **Millennium Experience** takes you to the extraordinary **Thames Flood Barrier** (**Thames Barrier Visitors' Centre,** Unity Way, off Eastmoor St, Woolwich, 305.4188), constructed between 1975 and 1982 to the tune of £500 million and comprised of 10 enormous movable gates between river piers and abutments on either bank. ♦ Admission. Daily. It is possible to catch a boat to the **Thames Flood Barrier** from Greenwich pier. Or, if you go by train from London to **Charlton Rail Station,** it's a 20-minute walk.

Two restored early Georgian town houses contain a collection of more than 2,000 fans that date from the 17th century onward. The **Fan Museum** (12 Crooms Hill, at Burney St, 858.7879) hosts changing exhibitions on related themes. The fan motif even extends to the museum's cafe, the **Orangery**—you can gaze upon a fan-shaped parterre while enjoying tea or a snack here. ♦ Admission. Tu-Sa; Su noon-4:30PM.

Despite its grand buildings, Greenwich has a raffish air, never more so than on Sunday when there are several antiques and crafts markets. The **Greenwich Tourist Information Center** (46 Greenwich Church St, between Nelson Rd and College Approach, 858.6376) is open daily. ♦ The best way to reach Greenwich is by riverboat. Boats depart from **Westminster Pier** (Victoria Embankment, just north of Westminster Bridge, 0171/930.4097) every 30 minutes from 10:30AM to 5PM; the trip takes 45 minutes. The last boat leaves Greenwich at 5:45PM June through August and 3:45PM the rest of the year. Trains run from **Charing Cross** to **Maze** Hill every half hour and take 20 minutes. Bus *No.188* runs between Greenwich and **Waterloo Station,** making the journey in 35 minutes. If traveling by car, take the **A200** southeast.

2 Hampstead All the centuries of London's history converge in this little village—a must-see for architecture buffs—as houses and cottages of all shapes, styles, and periods ramble up and down the hills. This is one of the prettiest of London's villages, and the residents are wealthy enough to keep it that way. ♦ The best tube stations for **Hampstead** are Hampstead and **Belsize Park.** If driving, take the **A41** north from central London as far as Swiss Cottage, then the **B511** north from there to Hampstead.

In Hampstead:

Keats House The English Romantic poet John Keats (1795-1821) lived in this house on Wentworth Place from 1818 to 1820. Today, due in large part to American funds, the

Regency house is full of his letters, manuscripts, books, and other memorabilia. Keats composed "Ode to a Nightingale" in the garden here. ♦ Free. M-F 10AM-1PM and 2-6PM, Sa 10AM-1PM, Su 2-5PM Apr-Oct; M-F 1-5PM, Sa 10AM-1PM and 2-5PM, Su 2-5PM Nov-Mar. Keats Grove (between South End Rd and Downshire Hill). 0171/435.2062. Tube: Hampstead, Belsize Park

Freud Museum Sigmund Freud, the founder of psychoanalysis, moved to this house in 1938 and re-created his Vienna consulting rooms. Antiques, books, and his therapeutic couch are on display. ♦ Admission. W-Su noon-5PM. 20 Maresfield Gardens (between Fitzjohn's Ave and Nutley Terr). 0171/435.3471. Tube: Finchley Road

Above Hampstead, have a drink in the pleasant courtyard of the popular **Jack Straw's Castle Pub** (North End Way, between Spaniards Rd and Hampstead Way, 0171/435.8885), from which misty views of London can be glimpsed across **Hampstead Heath.** The heath has 802 preserved acres of grassland and woodland, providing great opportunities for exercise. For bird-watchers, 100 species are said to have been sighted here. There are plenty of walking and running trails, and the Bathing Ponds welcome open-air swimmers (though you have to be stouthearted—or masochistic—to swim here in cold weather). Farther along the top of the heath is the Spaniard's Inn (Spaniards Rd, at Hampstead La, 455.3276), an Elizabethan coaching inn, restaurant, and gateway to London rumored to have been a refuge for highwayman Dick Turpin. Avoid the heath at night.

At Hampstead Heath:

Kenwood House The grounds of this historic house, remodeled in 1767-69 by **Robert Adam,** are idyllic for picnics and for gazing across the beautiful heathland toward an ornamental lake and concert bowl where, most summer weekends, you can picnic to the strains of Vivaldi, Dvorák, and many others played by visiting symphony orchestras, with an occasional fireworks display to top things off. Inside is the **iveagh bequest,** a collection of works by such grand masters as Gainsborough, Reynolds, and Vermeer. The tearooms are wonderful, too. ♦ Free. Daily. Nightingale La (off Hampstead La). 348.1286

 Highgate Cemetery Located to the east of the heath, the grounds actually comprise two cemeteries. The western cemetery contains the haunting Egyptian Avenue, a walkway of family crypts dug deep into the ground and flanked by dark Egyptian columns. The eastern cemetery (where Karl Marx is buried) is an ordinary cemetery where people can enter unaccompanied, but the western cemetery is accessible only by guided tour arranged by a charitable trust called the Friends of Highgate Cemetery. ♦ Admission to western cemetery. Guided tours: M-F noon, 2PM, and 4PM; Sa-Su every hour on the hour between 11AM-4PM Mar-Nov; Sa-Su 11AM-3PM Dec-Feb. Swain's La (between Oakeshot Ave and South Grove). 340.1834

3 Windsor Home to a magnificent park, a famous boys' school, and **Windsor Castle,** which has been the residence of kings and queens for more than 900 years (and is the largest castle in the world still occupied by royalty), this town lies on a pretty bend of the Thames. The construction of **Windsor Castle** (01753/868286, ext 2235) started in 1078,

Windsor Castle

when William the Conqueror built a round keep made of timber here; over the centuries, successive monarchs have enlarged the castle and added new buildings. In the 1820s, Edward IV began **St. George's Chapel,** a fine example of Perpendicular architecture, with its elaborately carved stone vaulting. Henry VIII, his third wife, Jane Seymour, Charles I, and other monarchs are buried in the choir. **Windsor**'s ultimate accolade came in 1917, when George V declared that, henceforth, his family and descendants would take the surname Windsor. The **State Apartments,** used by the royal family when in residence, are decorated with paintings by Van Dyck and Rubens. Within the complex is Queen Mary's **Dolls' House,** designed by **Sir Edwin Lutyens** in 1921-24. Everything is a magical one-twelfth of life-size, with one-inch books by Kipling in the library.

In 1992, while Queen Elizabeth looked on in sorrow as **Windsor,** her favorite castle, went up in flames, her son Prince Andrew became a vital link in a human chain that saved almost all the priceless paintings and art treasures. Only the structure of the **Great Hall** was badly damaged. The following year, as part of the effort to raise funds for the restoration, the queen opened part of **Buckingham Palace** to the public for the first time, allowing visitors to tour 18 of the rooms (including the **State Rooms,** the **State Dining Rooms,** and the **Throne Room**) for two months during the summer. **Windsor Castle** has been undergoing restoration, and the newly refurbished **St. George's Hall** and the **Grand Reception Room,** which also suffered damage, have been reopened. On one side of the castle is the **Great Park,** which is equally fascinating, with 4,800 acres of lawns, trees, lakes, herds of deer, ruins, and Prince Charles—when he is playing polo on **Smith's Lawn.** ♦ Admission. Castle: daily. St. George's Chapel: M-Sa; Su 2-4:45PM.

The newest Windsor attraction, **Legoland** (Winkfield Rd/B3022, 2 miles from the center of Windsor, 0990/626375) is a theme park with 150 acres that spell fun, especially for the kids. Outdoor activities include adventure playground areas, rides, and plastic Lego cars that children can drive. Everyone can enjoy the costumed performers who put on street shows throughout the area. Indoor activities include theater spaces with circus acts and the chance for kids to join in or to try face-painting or magic tricks. There are also workshops with millions of bricks for the kids to build models. The site offers eateries as well as a lakeside picnic area. ♦ Admission. Daily March-Sept; Sa-Su Oct.

Another noteworthy attraction in Windsor is the **Household Cavalry Museum** (Combermere Barracks, St. Leonard's Rd, between Bolton and Osborne Rds,

01753/868222 ext. 5203), which houses equipment and other items dating from the reign of Charles II to the present. The swords and uniforms are particularly interesting. ♦ Free. M-F.

Across the cast-iron footbridge from Windsor, in the adjacent small town of **Eton,** is **Eton College** (01753/671177), the best-known public school in Britain, founded in 1440 by Henry VI. It is best to visit the school and its museum during term time (September through Christmas, January through Easter, and April through June), when you can see the 1,200 students in their wing collars and tails. Etonians exude an air of confidence that is unrivaled, and it is no surprise that 20 British prime ministers are among the alumni. ♦ Admission. Term time: daily 2-5PM; school holidays: daily.

The **Windsor Tourist Information Centre** (24 High St, between Sheet and Peascod Sts, 01753/852010) is open daily.

♦ Just 21 miles west of London, Windsor is 27 minutes by train from Paddington (change at Slough) or 50 minutes direct from Waterloo. Green Line buses (Nos. *700* and *702*) go from Hyde Park Corner or Victoria Coach Station (90 minutes). Driving takes one hour; take the M4 to the A332.

 Kew Gardens (Royal Botanic Gardens) What began as a hobby for Princess Augusta (mother of George III), back in 1759, has blossomed into the most famous collection of flowers and plants in the world. This garden is a botanical paradise of more than 40,000 varieties, set in 300 lush acres along the east side of the Thames. Officially called the **Royal Botanic Gardens,** it was given to the nation by the royal family in 1841 and is, for all its pleasure-giving, a scientific institution where plants are studied, classified, and cultivated. It offers a constantly changing display of flowers, as well as rock gardens and lakes with aquatic birds. Stunning paths down to the river afford a sublime view of **Syon House,** the stately home of the Duke of Northumberland, across the Thames. Amid the greenery are 18th-century garden follies designed by **Sir William Chambers** for Princess Augusta: classical temples, ruins of a Roman arch, a fanciful 10-story pagoda, and an orangery, now containing a shop and a restaurant.

The **Palm House,** with its sweeping curves of glass and iron, was built in 1844 by **Decimus Burton** and houses tropical plants from both hemispheres. All the greenhouses are masterpieces, as are the grand entrance gates on the corner of **Kew Green,** also built by **Burton.** Be sure to see **Queen Charlotte's Cottage;** the **Chinese Pagoda;** and, if you come in springtime, the **Rhododendron Dell.** **The Kew Gardens Gallery** (332.5618) has exhibitions year-round. ♦ Separate admissions for Queen Charlotte's Cottage and the Kew Gardens complex. Gardens: daily. Queen Charlotte's Cottage: Sa-Su Apr-Sept.

♦ The best way to get to Kew Gardens is either by riverboat (in summer only), a 90-minute trip from **Westminster Pier** (0171/930.4721) or by tube on the **District Line** toward Richmond. Trains leave from **Waterloo Station** for Kew Bridge (0345/484950). If driving from London, take the **A4** to the **M4,** Junction 1, then the **A205** south over Kew Bridge.

4 Maids of Honour ★★$$ The best tea shop in the area, this delightful spot is the original home of the tart of the same name. The story goes that it was invented by one of Henry VIII's maids of honor, and the king liked the pastry so much that he imprisoned her to ensure a constant supply. The recipe, which has been passed from generation to generation, is still top secret. This quaint, rambling cottage is a must for cream teas in true British tradition. You'll need patience—the queue for a seat can be quite long, especially on Saturday—but if you don't want to wait, you can also buy the cakes at the affiliated shop next door and eat alfresco in nearby **Kew Gardens** itself. ♦ Cafe ♦ M breakfast and early lunch; Tu-Sa breakfast, lunch, and afternoon tea. Reservations recommended for lunch. 288 Kew Rd (between Kew Gardens and Mortlake Rds), Kew. 940.2752. Tube: Kew Gardens

4 Public Record Office (PRO) Fascinating documents are filed away in this modern office complex, which holds the national archives of England and Wales. The pick of the bunch, including the 11th-century *Domesday Book,* William the Conqueror's survey of his newly acquired properties in England, were moved here in late 1996 when the **PRO**'s central London offices closed. At press time, plans were in the works for a small museum to open that will display such documents as the wills of Shakespeare and Jane Austen as well as George Washington's letters to George III. Until then, a facsimile of the *Domesday Book* is on display. ♦ Free. M-Sa. Ruskin Ave (off Mortlake Rd). 876.3444

5 Hampton Court Palace Not really out of town but 15 miles down the road from London (and better still, up the river), this special palace is a must as far as day trips go. The structure was begun in 1514 by Cardinal Thomas Wolsey, minister to Henry VIII. However, Wolsey's elaborately designed mansion and lavish lifestyle made him fear the envy of his king (and its possible deadly consequences)—so when the construction was almost complete in 1525, he presented the palace to Henry VIII in return for **Richmond Palace.** Henry VIII added a moat, a drawbridge, and a tennis court, plus new royal lodgings, galleries, and chambers. His third

queen, Jane Seymour, was married, gave birth, and died at the palace, and Henry lived there for a number of years with his sixth and last queen, Catherine Parr. Elizabeth I loved the palace, and Charles I lived in it both as king and as a prisoner of Cromwell.

When William and Mary came to the throne in 1689, they revamped the palace, with **Sir Christopher Wren** and **Grinling Gibbons** in charge. The south front was severely damaged in a fire in 1986, but luckily, most of the paintings and art treasures were saved and it has now been fully restored. Signs will help you find the **Renaissance Picture Gallery,** with works by Titian and Brueghel; the aromatic and evocative **Tudor Kitchen;** the **Great Hall,** site of Henry VIII's banquets and performances of Shakespeare's plays by the Bard's company; and the lower **Orangery,** featuring *The Triumphs of Julius Caesar,* a series of nine tempera paintings created from 1485-92 by Andrea Mantegna. The 50 acres of landscaped gardens are beautiful, and the maze is irresistible, but challenging—so leave plenty of time to explore it.

If you really enjoy the royal atmosphere here, you can choose to stay in one of two self-catering apartments at the palace. Each flat sleeps six to eight people and features a full kitchen and living room. Guests also have access to the rest of the palace during its normal operating hours. The price is actually quite reasonable for families or large groups. For more information about the flats, contact the **Landmark Trust** (Shottesbrooke, Maidenhead, Berkshire SL6 3SW, England, 01628/825925). ♦ Admission. Daily.

6 Brighton The first place to stop in this seaside community 53 miles south of London is the **Royal Pavilion** (Pavilion Parade, between Old Steine and Grand Parade, 01273/603005). Originally a modest 18th-century structure, the pavilion (shown on page 221) was rebuilt in grand fashion between 1815 and 1822 by **John Nash** for the prince regent, who later became George IV; the project cost £500,000 (a huge sum at the time). Its great onion-shaped dome, huge tentlike roofs, and small ornate pinnacles and minarets are so reminiscent of a fairy-tale Indian mogul's palace that you almost expect to see elephants filing past you carrying a rajah. Inside, it's pure chinoiserie, filled with ornate furniture and paintings that were chosen especially for this palace. A series of spectacular suites culminates in the **Banquet Room,** with brilliantly colored, gilt-painted walls and a ceiling like a huge palm tree with bedragonned chandelier. ♦ Admission. Daily

The rest of the town echoes the elegant proportions of Regency days with frequent and unexpected onion domes and roofs. For yet more inspiration, just behind the pavilion is the **Brighton Museum and Art Gallery** (Church St, at Marlborough Pl, 01273/

Royal Pavilion, Brighton

603005) with its Art Nouveau and Art Deco collections. ◆ Free. M-Tu, Th-Sa; Su 2-5PM.

Brighton has two piers, but only the **Victorian Palace Pier** is open to the public. This center of entertainment with amusement arcades and slot machines is well worth visiting during the week, but avoid it on weekends when it's crowded with day-trippers. Also, be sure to stroll through **The Lanes**—17th-century redbrick streets full of tiny shops selling every kind of antique imaginable. The area is heaven for browsers and connoisseurs alike, and there are even more restaurants than antiques shops. The **Brighton Tourist Information Centre** (10 Bartholomew Sq, in The Lanes, 01273/323755) is open daily. ◆ The nicest (and quickest) way to get to Brighton is by a 52-minute rail trip from **Victoria Station.** You also can go by coach from **Victoria Coach Station,** which will take 105 minutes. If driving, take the **M23**, then the **A23**; the journey takes about 1.5 hours.

Cambridge

7 Cambridge If you can manage only one excursion to the "palaces of privilege and academe," choose **Cambridge.** Established in the 13th century and a few decades younger than **Oxford,** it is architecturally more cohesive, more beautiful, and less interrupted by the city itself. The university is located in a part of England called East Anglia, on the edge of the River Cam, and the backs of the colleges face the river (hence the term "Backs"). The most interesting of the 31 schools are **St. John's Trinity,** founded by Henry VIII; **Clare; King's,** where the chapel has exquisite stained-glass windows, fan vaulting, and lofty spires; **Corpus Christi,** where the **Old Court** is worth a visit; **Queen's; Peterhouse;** and **Jesus.**

Also, be sure to visit the **Fitzwilliam Museum** (Trumpington St, between the Fen Cswy and Silver St, 01223/332900), one of the oldest public museums in the country. Founded in 1816, the institution boasts paintings by Delacroix, Renoir, Stubbs, Titian, and

Tintoretto; prints and drawings; Islamic and Far Eastern crafts and artifacts; music scores by Handel, Bach, Chopin, Britten, and Elgar; European and Oriental fans; and West Asiatic, Egyptian, Greek, and Roman antiquities. ◆ Free. Tu-Su.The ideal time to visit is May Week (which, is held in June), a 10-day period when graduating seniors receive their degrees. Festivities, including a rowing competition on the Cam, take place throughout the city. Plan your day to include Evensong at **King's College Chapel,** and however touristy it may seem, allow yourself to be punted on the River Cam along the Backs—it rivals the gondola in Venice in terms of sheer tranquillity.

The **Cambridge Tourist Information Centre** (Wheeler St, at Peas Hill, 01223/322640) is open Monday through Saturday; it's also open Sunday from April to September. ◆ Cambridge, 54 miles from London, can be reached by train direct from **King's Cross Station** in 55 minutes, from **Liverpool Street Station** in 80 minutes, by bus from **Victoria Station** in a little less than two hours, or by car on the **M11** in 90 minutes.

Fans of cathedral architecture might consider continuing their journey to **Ely,** 16 miles north of Cambridge. The crowning glory of this charming market town is the medieval **Ely Cathedral** (the Gallery, at Steeple Row), whose lantern tower can be seen for miles around. There is a stained-glass museum inside. ◆ Admission. Daily.

Oliver Cromwell, who was born in Cambridgeshire, had a family home in Ely. Called **Oliver Cromwell's House** (29 St. Mary's St, next door to **St. Mary's** church, 01353/662062), it has been beautifully restored in 17th-century style to house both the **Tourist Information Centre** and a Cromwell exhibition. ◆ Free. Daily Apr-Sept; M-Sa Oct-March. ◆ Ely is 70 miles from London. The Cambridge-bound trains continue to Ely (add another 20 minutes to the journey time). If you're driving, continue on the A10 from Cambridge

8 Oxford The university here has existed since the 1200s, making it the oldest institution of learning in England. The center of the city is dominated by the Gothic turrets, towers, and spires of the famed university's 30 colleges, all of which have unique charm. **St. Edmund Hall**, **Merton**, and **Balliol**, built in the 13th century, are the oldest colleges; **Christ Church**, whose august alumni include John Locke, W.H. Auden, and Lewis Carroll, and the academically distinguished **All Souls** probably are the best known. Bill Clinton attended **University College** as a Rhodes scholar. **Magdalen** (pronounced *Maud*-lin), whose 15th-century tower was used by Charles I as an observation post during his attack on the city in the civil war, has educated such notable students as Cardinal Thomas Wolsey and Oscar Wilde. Today, this is the central point of the May Morning festivities, a medieval celebration. A visit during the academic year (between mid-October and mid-May) is most interesting; during summer holidays, the colleges are deserted or filled with American students. Visiting times vary greatly: some of the colleges can be visited only in the afternoon during the school year.

Besides all of its other distinctions, this university also contains Britain's (and possibly Europe's) first public museum—the **Ashmolean Museum of Art and Archaeology** (Beaumont St, between St. Giles and St. Johns Sts, 01865/278000). Opened in 1863, it features an eclectic collection of art and antiquities, including Guy Fawkes's lantern; Powhatan's mantle; bronze works from China, India, Greece, and the Italian Renaissance; ceramic pieces from Asia, England, and Europe; and paintings by Dutch, Flemish, English, French, and Italian artists. There's truly something here for everyone. ♦ Free. Tu-Sa; Su 2-4PM (schedule varies during the Easter and Christmas holidays, so call ahead).

The **Oxford Tourist Information Centre** (**The Old School,** Gloucester Garden, at the bus

bays, 01865/726871l) is open Monday through Saturday. It's also open on Sunday from April to September. ♦ Oxford is 56 miles from London and can be reached by train from **Paddington Station** in an hour (trains leave hourly), or by bus from **Victoria Coach Station** in one hour and 45 minutes. If you're driving, take the **M40,** then the **A40** (the journey takes one hour).

9 Bath Elegantly laid out and proportioned, this ancient city is as perfect as a novel by Jane Austen—and why not, since the writer walked along the streets here, sipped the water in the **Pump Room,** and captured its grace, elegance, and usefulness in *Northange Abbey* and *Persuasion.* This city of terraces, crescents, and squares is the most famous spa in England (and the only one with hot springs); it's worth a visit for its Roman ruins glorious architecture, and gentle Austenesque atmosphere.

The Georgian perfection seen here today is largely the work of two 18th-century architects—a father and son, both named **John Wood**—but Bath existed long before that. The Romans, nostalgic for the warm waters of home, founded the city in AD 43 and stayed for four centuries. Bath declined rapidly after the Romans departed, and it wouldn't become fashionable again until the 18th century, when luminaries such as Gainsborough and Lord Nelson were regular visitors. The **Roman Baths** (Abbey Church Yd at York St, 01225/444477), among the most striking ruins in Europe, are still the major attraction here. Excavations nearby have unearthed relics ranging from coins to a sacrificial altar. You can sample water from the fountain in the **Pump Room** above the baths, which Charles Dickens said tastes like warm flatirons—he was right! ♦ Admission. Baths: daily. Pump Room: daily.

Magdalen College, Oxford

As for the modern architecture—well, just close your eyes and pretend it isn't there. After its heyday in the 18th century, the city went downhill. But the last two decades have brought new life to Bath. Today, Londoners come here for the city's cultural life the way they used to for the waters. If you're interested in art and antiquities, don't miss the **Holburne Museum** (Great Pulteney St, at Sydney Rd, 01225/466669), which houses one of the largest collections of silver in the country, along with porcelain and paintings by major British artists. ♦ Admission. Daily; Su from 2:30PM Feb-Dec.

The most elegant street is the famous **Royal Crescent** with its curved sweep of Georgian houses. To get an idea of life in a grand town house of this era, visit **No.1,** which has been restored using materials available in the 1700s. ♦ Admission. Tu-Su. 1 Royal Crescent (at Brock St). 01225/428126.

One of Bath's greatest achievements is the renovation of the **Theatre Royal** (Saw Close, at Barton St, 01225/448844), which hosts some of the country's top productions before they move on to London.

In a mansion on a hilltop a few miles outside Bath is the **American Museum in Britain** (Claverton Manor, A36. 01225/460503), the first museum of Americana outside the US. Its rooms are furnished to show domestic life in America from colonial times to the end of the 19th century. Opened in 1961, the museum was founded by Dallas Pratt and John Judkyn, two Americans with a deep appreciation of American arts who wanted to foster mutual understanding between Britain and America. ♦ Admission. Tu-Su 2-5PM. Take bus *No. 18* or *25* at the bus station at Newark and Dorchester Sts.

The **Bath Tourist Information Centre (Abbey Chambers,** Abbey Church Yd, at York St, 01225/477101) is open daily. ♦ Located 116 miles from London, Bath can be reached by high-speed train from **Paddington Station** in 70 minutes, by bus from **Victoria Station** in three hours, or by car, from the **M4** to **Junction 18** to the **A46** and the **A4,** in two hours.

10 Salisbury The country town of Salisbury in Wiltshire, 83 miles from London, rests on a plain where the Rivers Nadder and Bourne flow into the Avon, quietly expressing the calm beauty of this medieval town and its famous cathedral. The community is lucky: Because it's too far from London for commuters and bypassed by major roads, its old city center is virtually intact, utterly charming, and worth a wander round. Salisbury's other major asset is its convenient location—just 10 miles from **Stonehenge,** one of the most important prehistoric monuments in Europe.

Immortalized by John Constable (whose painting can be seen at the **National Gallery** if you can't make this trip), classic **Salisbury**

Cathedral (The Close, off North Walk), consecrated in 1258, is the pinnacle of English cathedral architecture. It was made even more beautiful by the addition of a majestic spire (circa 1320) rising above the water meadows beside the Avon. At 404 feet high, it is the tallest spire in England, enchanting the eye with its deceptively light appearance—in reality, the 6,400 tons of stonework have put such a strain on the four load-bearing columns that they are slightly bent. The Avon marks the western side of the cathedral's grounds, and a 14th-century wall of stone from Old Sarum, part of the city that was razed in 1331 to provide building materials for the Cathedral Close, borders the other three sides.

The interior of the cathedral is not as breathtaking as the exterior, due in part to the ruthlessness of **James Wyatt** 's renovations (1788-89), in which he removed the screens and chapels and rearranged the monuments in rows. Happily, the restoration by **Sir George Gilbert Scott** in 1859 minimized the damage. The cathedral contains tombs of the Crusaders and those who fought at Agincourt. Other treasures include exquisite lancet windows with patchworks of glass from the 13th and 15th centuries and a 14th-century wrought-iron clock that was restored to working order in 1956, and is now possibly the oldest working clock in the world. The Cloisters and the beautiful, octagonal Chapter House, built from 1364 to 1380, were modeled after those of Westminster Abbey. Many of the cathedral's treasures are displayed in the Chapter House, including one of four existing copies of the *Magna Carta,* brought here for safekeeping shortly after 1265. The Cathedral Close contains the medieval Bishop's Palace and Deanery. ♦ Admission. Daily.

Also in the Close and open to the public are **Malmesbury House,** built in 1327 and restored in 1749, and the 18th-century **Mompesson House**. Malmesbury House (01722/327027) features a Queen Anne facade and several rooms decorated with period furnishings, including a grand hall, a music room, and a drawing room. Part of the structure dates as far back as 1399. ♦ Admission. Tu-Sa Apr-Oct.

Mompesson House (01722/335659), operated by the National Trust, boasts an elegant oak staircase, antiques, a collection of china and glassware from the 18th century, and a lovely walled garden. ♦ Admission. M-W; Sa-Su.

The **Salisbury Tourist Information Centre** (Fish Row, at Queen St, 01722/334956) is open Monday through Saturday; it's also open Sunday from May to September.

In **Wilton Village,** easily reached by bus or car, is the splendid **Wilton House** (A30, 3 miles west of Salisbury, 01722/743115). The home of the Earl of Pembroke for more than 400 years, it features 17th-century staterooms by **Inigo Jones.** The incomparable art collection includes 16 works by Van Dyck, which are hung in the famous double-cube room (60 feet long by 30 feet high and 30 feet wide) where General Eisenhower viewed plans of the Normandy invasion. ♦ Admission. Daily Apr-Oct. Buses take the 18-minute journey from the station (Windsor Rd, off Fisherton St) to Wilton House every half hour; if you're driving, take the A30. ♦ Salisbury is 83 miles from London and can be reached by way of a picturesque, 90-minute railway journey, which leaves from **Waterloo Station** every hour. There are at least two bus trips daily from **Victoria Coach Station** that take three hours, but the bus service in the afternoon from Salisbury is often at awkward times—take the train! The station is a 10-minute walk from the center of Salisbury. If you're driving, take the **M3** and then the **A36.**

Near Salisbury:

Stonehenge This great, historic structure is one of the oldest and most important megalithic monuments in Europe, dating from between 1850 BC and 1400 BC, although the earliest signs of the Stone Circle date back to the Bronze Age, circa 3500 BC. Though the fence around the monument, added in modern times for its own protection, makes it look like a captive animal and takes away the initial impact, the sight of the long, eerie collection of stones is still breathtaking; and the way **Stonehenge** interacts with the sun on certain days of the year is astounding.

The stones are arranged in four series within a circular ditch 300 feet in diameter (see drawing below). The outer ring, with a diameter of 97 feet, is a circle of 17 sandstones connected on top by a series of lintel stones. The second ring is of bluestones, the third is horseshoe shaped, and the inner ring is ovoid. Within the ovoid ring lies the **Altar Stone,** made of micaceous sandstone. The great upright **Heelstone** is along the Avenue, the broad road leading to the monument. Some of the stones, weighing up to four tons each, come from the Preseli Mountains in Wales, a distance of some 135 miles.

Stonehenge was at one time believed to be a druid temple, a theory contradicted by the fact that the druids didn't arrive in Britain until circa 500 BC. In 1963, British astronomer Gerald Hawkins theorized that the collection of stones was a huge astronomical instrument used to accurately measure solar and lunar movements as well as eclipses. Avoid visiting during the two weeks preceding Midsummer Day (21 June), as security around the area is tightened because of the latter-day hippies and would-be druids who try to perform rituals at the monument at that time.
♦ Admission. Daily. Located 10 miles northwest of Salisbury. Take the **A345,** then the **A303.** 01980/624715

11 Winchester This is the ancient capital of England, graceful and unspoiled, and a perfect trip to combine with Salisbury and **Stonehenge,** only 20 miles away. Winchester was England's capital city for nearly 250 years, from 829 until after the Norman Conquest, when the Normans decided to move the capital to London. King Alfred the Great reigned here from 871 to 899, during the invasion of the Danes, and helped the city evolve into a great center of learning. The picturesque High Street, in the center of town, is lined with a charming medley of buildings dating from the 13th century. Near the end of the street is the **Great Hall** (1235), all that remains of **Winchester Castle,** which was demolished in 1644-45. An early fake **Round Table** (probably made in Henry VIII's time) of the legendary King Arthur stands in the hall, which was the scene of many medieval parliaments and notable trials, including that of Sir Walter Raleigh for conspiring against Elizabeth I.

The beautiful early Norman **Winchester Cathedral** (The Close, at Colebrook St) has the longest Perpendicular-Gothic–style nave in Europe (556 feet)—and it's made to seem even longer by its height (78 feet). The best view of the cathedral, emphasizing its setting in the city, is from Magdalen Hill, the road approaching Winchester from the east. Begun in 1079, consecrated in 1093, and partially rebuilt in 1346-66, it contains a wealth of treasures, most striking of which are the

Stonehenge

seven richly carved chantry chapels. **Bishop Wykeham's Chantry,** in the west end of the nave, contains an effigy of William of Wykeham, the great builder, statesman, and founder of nearby **Winchester College,** one of the oldest public schools in England (it dates from 1382), and of **New College, Oxford.** On the opposite wall are a brass tablet and window dedicated to Jane Austen (1775-1817), who is buried here. The bronze statues of James I and Charles I are by Hubert Le Sueur (1685).

Under the organ loft in the north transept is the **Chapel of the Holy Sepulchre** (12th century), with superb wall paintings (circa 1170-1205) of the *Life and Passion of Christ.* The oak screen separating the choir from the nave is by Sir Gilbert Scott, and the magnificent stalls (1305-10), with their misericords carved with human, animal, and monster motifs, are the oldest cathedral stalls in England, except for some fragments at Rochester. The **Library,** over the passage between the south transept and the old **Chapter House,** was built in the 12th century and reconstructed in 1668. It contains 4,000 printed books and rare manuscripts, the most important of which is the *Winchester Bible* (12th century), one of the finest existing medieval manuscripts.

If you walk about a mile south of the cathedral, you will come upon the ancient **St. Cross Hospital,** where the "wayfarer's dole" of a horn of beer and a portion of bread—once a handout to the needy—is still offered to visitors.

The **Winchester Tourist Information Centre** (**Guildhall,** Broadway, between Bridge and High Sts, 01962/840500l) is open Monday through Saturday; it's also open Sunday from April to September.♦ Winchester, 65 miles southwest of London, can be reached by train from Waterloo Station in 60 minutes, or by buses leaving Victoria Coach Station every hour for the two-hour journey. To get here by car from London, take the **M3;** from Salisbury, take the **A30** to the **A272.**

▮ 2 Canterbury This important ancient city in the county of Kent is the "cradle of Christianity" in England. It was here that St. Augustine landed in 597 to convert the locals and was welcomed by King Ethelbert, whose wife, Bertha, was already a Christian. The king and the local population duly became converts. Today the spiritual head of the Church of England is the Archbishop of Canterbury.

The interior of **Canterbury Cathedral** has an awesome beauty and a wealth of medieval stained glass. A site in a corner of the cathedral marks the martyrdom of St. Thomas à Becket in 1170 when King Henry II's knights took too literally his outburst "Who will rid me of this troublesome priest?" The Becket shrine attracted pilgrims for centuries, their journeys immortalized in Geoffrey Chaucer's *Canterbury Tales.*

The compact little town of Canterbury, nestled by the River Stour, still has substantial medieval stone walls with a walkway that allows visitors to stroll along the top. There are plenty of shops and restaurants, and the picturesque streets, with a wealth of thatch-roofed, half-timbered buildings, get quite busy, particularly as the town is close to Ramsgate, Dover, and Folkestone, the ferry ports for the Continent. Folkestone is also where the *Eurostar* train goes under the Channel Tunnel.

A large ruin just outside the town wall, **St. Augustine's Abbey** (Longport, at Lower Chantry La, 01227/767345) is now a museum with artifacts that were unearthed during excavations. Free interactive tours are offered. Visitors push the buttons of display panels throughout the abbey ruins that activate such sound effects as choral music, Gregorian chants, and anecdotes told by characters from its history. There's also a computer image that re-creates the abbey as it might have appeared at the various stages of its construction over the centuries. ♦ Admission. Daily.

In the center of town you'll find **The Canterbury Tales** (St. Margaret's St, between Watling and High Sts, 01227/454888), a display of tableaux with figures re-creating the stories told by Chaucer's famous characters. ♦ Admission. Daily.

The **Canterbury Tourist Information Centre** (34 St. Margaret's St, between Watling and High Sts, 01227/766567) is open Monday through Saturday; it's also open Sunday from Easter to September. ♦ Canterbury, 60 miles southeast of London, can be reached direct by trains from **Victoria** and **Charing Cross Stations** in 1.5 hours or by bus from Victoria Station in just over an hour. To drive, take the **A2/M2;** it takes just over an hour.

"Royalty is a government in which the attention of the nation is concentrated on one person doing interesting actions. A Republic is a government in which that attention is divided between many, who are all doing uninteresting actions. Accordingly, so long as the human heart is strong and the human reason weak, Royalty will be strong because it appeals to diffused feeling, and Republics weak because they appeal to the understanding."

Walter Bagehot

History

The dates given in parentheses after the names of the British monarchs are the years of their reigns.

55-54 BC Julius Caesar makes two expeditions into Britain, but following armed resistance, agrees to a peace settlement.

AD 43 The Romans conquer Britain led by Emperor Claudius and establish Londinium (London).

61 In a revolt against Roman rule, Boadicea, queen of the Iceni tribe, destroys London before her final defeat.

ca. 100 The first **London Bridge** is built.

200 The Romans build the first wall around London.

410 The Roman army withdraws from Britain to defend Rome from the Goths.

597 Christianity is introduced to Britain by the Benedictine monk Augustine.

829 Egbert King of Wessex (802-39) establishes the House of Wessex as the supreme ruling dynasty of England.

842 The Viking Danes invade Britain, sacking London.

886 Alfred the Great (871-899) defeats the Viking Danes and establishes himself and the royal court in London.

991 With renewed threats from the Vikings, Ethelred the Unready (979-1016) introduces a tax to buy off the invading armies.

1016 After Ethelred's death, Canute, the king of Denmark, marries Ethelred's widow and becomes king of England (1016-35).

1042 Edward the Confessor reestablishes the House of Wessex (1042-66).

1065 Edward's great building, the first **Westminster Abbey,** is consecrated at Christmas; he dies a few days later.

1066 The House of Normandy is established under William the Conqueror after he defeats Harold II at the Battle of Hastings. He is crowned at **Westminster Abbey,** establishing a tradition (1066-87).

1085-6 The *Domesday Book* is compiled, providing William with a complete record of his kingdom for taxation purposes.

1087 Fire destroys most of the **City** and St. Paul's Cathedral.

1097 William II (1087-1100) begins to build **Westminster Hall,** now the oldest part of the **Houses of Parliament.**

1135 After the death of Henry I (1100-1135), his nephew Stephen of Blois becomes king (1135-1154) but is challenged by Henry's daughter, Matilda. Civil war breaks out and lasts throughout his reign.

1154 Matilda's son, Henry II, is crowned king (1154-89) and establishes the Plantagenets.

1167 The expulsion of English students from Paris leads to the establishment of universities at **Oxford** (and a few decades later, at **Cambridge**).

1170 Thomas à Becket, Archbishop of Canterbury, is murdered at **Canterbury Cathedral** after his allegiance to the church causes disagreements with King Henry II (1154-89).

1176 Construction begins on **London Bridge,** the first stone bridge, which is completed in 1290.

1192 London establishes mayoral rule; Henry FitzAilwin is elected the first lord mayor.

1215 King John (1199-1216) signs the *Magna Carta* at Runnymede.

1269 The present **Westminster Abbey** is consecrated.

1280 Old **St. Paul's Cathedral** is completed; it is half as tall as the present building.

1337 Edward III (1327-77) claims the French throne and the Hundred Years War begins.

1338 Westminster becomes the regular meeting place of Parliament.

1348 Black death strikes Europe; about half of London's 50,000 citizens die.

1381 London bears the brunt of the Peasant Revolt, led by Wat Tyler against high taxes. It is quelled by Richard II (1377-99) and Tyler is stabbed to death.

1399 Henry IV (1399-1413) accedes to the throne, establishing the House of Lancaster.

1415 As the Hundred Years War continues, Henry V (1413-22) has a great victory at Agincourt.

1455 The War of the Roses begins.

1461 King Edward IV establishes the House of York.

1476 William Caxton's printing press is set up near **Westminster Abbey.** The first books in English are printed.

1483 The Little Princes disappear, probably murdered in the **Tower of London**. Their uncle, Richard III, becomes king (1483-85).

1485 Richard III is killed in battle, and with the accession of Henry Tudor as Henry VII (1485-1509) the House of Tudor is established.

1509 Henry VIII (1509-47) accedes to the throne and marries Catherine of Aragon. He starts to build **St. James's Palace.**

1530 The fall of Cardinal Thomas Wolsey occurs after he fails to secure an annulment of the king's marriage. Arrested for treason, Wolsey dies en route to London. Henry VIII moves into Wolsey's London residence, **York Place** (renaming it **Whitehall**); he has already taken over Wolsey's palatial country place, **Hampton Court,** five years previously.

1533 Henry VIII's marriage to Catherine of Aragon is declared void by the king's new archbishop, Thomas Cranmer. The king breaks with Rome, declaring himself the head of the Church of England. He marries Anne Boleyn.

1536 Anne Boleyn is executed for adultery at the **Tower of London.** Henry begins the dissolution of the monasteries (which continues until 1540).

37 Jane Seymour dies while giving birth to Edward.

40 Henry VIII marries Anne of Cleves; they divorce x months later, and the king marries Catherine Howard.

42 Catherine Howard is executed in the **Tower** for adultery. Henry VIII proclaims himself king of Ireland.

43 Henry VIII marries Catherine Parr, who outlives him.

47 Henry's son, Edward VI, age nine, succeeds him but lives only six years.

53 Mary I (1553-1558) marries Philip II of Spain and reinstates Catholicism. Protestant citizens are martyred at **Smithfield.**

58 Elizabeth I (1558-1603) accedes to the throne, restores Protestantism, and the Elizabethan Age begins.

68 Mary, Queen of Scots (executed 1587), flees to England. The Royal Exchange is set up.

85 Shakespeare arrives in London.

88 The Spanish Armada fails to invade Britain after being defeated in its coastal waters.

98 Timber beams from England's first theater in **Shoreditch** are taken apart and used to construct the **Globe Theatre** in **Southwark.**

03 Elizabeth I dies without an heir. James VI of Scotland becomes James I of England (1603-25) and establishes the House of Stuart.

05 The Gunpowder Plot, a Roman Catholic conspiracy to blow up the **Houses of Parliament,** fails. The participants, including Guy Fawkes, are executed.

20 Pilgrims sail on *Mayflower* from Plymouth and settle in New England.

25 Inigo Jones's **Banqueting House** is completed.

31 Covent Garden is laid out by **Inigo Jones.**

42-46 Quarrels between Charles I and Parliament lead to Civil War between the Royalists and Parliament. The king is forced to leave London and headquarters himself in **Oxford.** Civil war battles take place throughout England until the king is captured and imprisoned.

49 Charles I is executed at **Banqueting House,** the monarchy and the House of Lords are abolished, and the country is declared a republic.

53 The republic (Commonwealth) is headed by Oliver Cromwell, Protector (1653-58) and then by his son Richard Cromwell, Protector (1658-59).

60 The House of Stuart is restored when Charles II returns from exile in France.

65 In the year of the Great Plague, 100,000 die.

66 The Great Fire destroys half of London. It is described in the *Diary* of Samuel Pepys.

70-1723 Sir Christopher Wren designs and erects **St. Paul's Cathedral** and 52 other London churches during the rebuilding of London.

88 James II is deposed and exiled during the Glorious Revolution led by his daughter, Mary, and her husband, William of Orange. They reign as joint monarchs until her death in 1694; William reigns until 1702.

1694 The Bank of England is founded.

1698 Whitehall Palace is destroyed by fire.

1701 The Act of Settlement bars Roman Catholics (and anyone marrying a Roman Catholic) from the throne.

1714 The House of Hanover is established with the accession of George I (1714-1727).

1721 Sir Robert Walpole leads the Whigs in Parliament until 1742. He is known as the first prime minister.

1735 An act of Parliament is passed to purchase the extensive collections of Sir Hans Sloane to display to the public; this is the beginning of the **British Museum.**

1768 The Royal Academy of Arts is founded.

1772 The Adelphi is built by **Robert** and **John Adam.**

1776 America declares its independence from Britain.

1805 Lord Nelson dies at the Battle of Trafalgar and is buried in **St. Paul's Cathedral.**

1814 Gas lighting is installed in Piccadilly.

1815 The Duke of Wellington defeats Napoleon at Waterloo.

1816 John Nash lays out **Regent's Park, Portland Place, Regent Street**, and **The Mall.**

1824 The **National Gallery** is founded.

1829 The first police force is founded. The first London bus appears; it holds 18 passengers.

1835 Charles Barry and **Augustus Pugin** begin building the **Houses of Parliament;** they are completed in 1860.

1836 The **University of London** receives a Royal Charter.

1837 Victoria (1837-1901) accedes to the throne; **Buckingham Palace** becomes the permanent residence of the sovereign.

1838 London's first passenger railway opens, running from Southwark to **Greenwich.**

1843 Nelson's statue is erected in **Trafalgar Square. Isambard Kingdom Brunel's Rotherhithe Tunnel** (the first under the **Thames**) is built.

1851 The Great Exhibition in the **Crystal Palace** at **Hyde Park** shows off the masterpieces that can be created by machines.

1855 The first mailbox appears on the corner of **Fleet** and **Farringdon Streets.**

1861 The **Tooley Street** fire, the worst in London since 1666, destroys the whole waterfront south of the Thames.

1863 The first underground railway opens from **Paddington** to Farringdon Street station.

1877 Victoria is proclaimed empress of India.

1888 Jack the Ripper strikes for the first time in **Whitechapel.**

1889 The creation of the London County Council gives the city a comprehensive government for the first time.

1890 The first electric railway tube runs from the **City** to **Stockwell.**

1894 The **Tower Bridge,** with its double drawbridge, is opened.

1895 Westminster Cathedral is built.

1897 Queen Victoria's Diamond Jubilee is celebrated.

1914-18 During World War I, London is damaged by Zeppelin air raids.

1917 George V (1910-1936) renounces all German titles and adopts the name of Windsor for the royal family.

1918 The right to vote is given to all men over 21 and all women over 30.

1922 The British Broadcasting Corporation (BBC) is founded.

1929 The right to vote is given to all women over 21.

1936 Edward VIII abdicates because of his relationship with Wallis Simpson, an American divorcee. His brother, the Duke of York, becomes George VI (1936-1952).

1939-45 World War II puts England under siege. The Blitz destroys much of the City of London; **St. Paul's** stands among the ruins.

1945 The election of a Labour government brings about the nationalization of public service and major industries. The rebuilding of bomb-ravaged London begins.

1951 The Festival of Britain is staged as a symbol of its recovery from the war. **South Bank** is built as a cultural center.

1952 Elizabeth II accedes to the throne on the death of her father, George VI.

1953 The coronation of Elizabeth II is the first to be televised.

1971 Decimal currency is introduced, replacing the old pounds, shillings, and pence.

1972 The new **Stock Exchange** opens and the new **London Bridge** is completed.

1973 Britain joins the European Community.

1976 The **(Royal) National Theatre** opens.

1977 The Silver Jubilee of Queen Elizabeth II's reign is celebrated.

1979 Margaret Thatcher becomes the first female prime minister.

1981 The royal wedding of Prince Charles and Lady Diana Spencer takes place in **St. Paul's.**

1982 The **Thames Flood Barrier** is completed.

1984 The government establishes the London Development Docklands Corporation to regenerate the derelict docks in east London.

1986 The Greater London Council is abolished, leaving the capital without a central governing body. The *Times* is the first newspaper to move from Fleet Street to **Docklands.**

1989 The *Daily Express* is the last newspaper to leave Fleet Street.

1990 The Poll Tax is introduced. Prime Minister Margaret Thatcher is ousted from office by her own party in favor of John Major.

1992 The Prince and Princess of Wales separate, as do the Duke and Duchess of York. The long-divorced Princess Anne remarries. **Windsor Castle** catches fire. The **Canary Wharf Tower** is completed—Britain's tallest building at 800 feet. The Conservative Party wins the general election for the third time in a row. Betty Boothroyd becomes the first female Speaker of the House of Commons. The queen volunteers to pay income tax on her personal property and revenue.

1993 Women are ordained as priests in the Church of England for the fist time. The Irish Republican Army (IRA) attacks London's financial district.

1994 The **Channel Tunnel** (nicknamed the "Chunnel") is opened, linking Britain and France by a train route under the **English Channel.** In a TV interview, Prince Charles confirms that he had an affair with Camilla Parker-Bowles. A ceasefire is declared between Britain and the IRA.

1996 Terrorist bombings in London bring to an end the shaky peace between the IRA and the British government. Both Diana, Princess of Wales, and the Duchess of York are divorced. A fire on a freight train going through the **Channel Tunnel** stops service for several weeks.

1997 Prince William is confirmed into the Church of England. The Royal Yacht *Britannia* goes on her last voyage prior to being sold. Britain continues a lone battle against the introduction of a single currency for the countries within the European Community. The Labour Party wins the election with its biggest ever triumph and a majority of 179 in the House of Commons. Tony Blair, at 43, becomes the youngest prime minister since 1812. John Major steps down as leader of the Conservative Party in the wake of the party's most humiliating setback since 1832.

1997 Princess Diana is killed in a car accident in Paris. Millions watch the funeral procession in London, from **Kensington Palace** to **Westminister Abbey.** Princess Diana is buried at her ancestral home, Althorp Park, in Northampton.

1998 The various parties which have made Northern Ireland a war zone for the past two decades sign the so-called "Good Friday Agreement" which calls for an end to hostilities in the province. John Hume and David Trimble, the leaders of the two main factions, win the Nobel Peace Prize for their work on the peace negotiations.

1999 First elections are held for the new Scottish Parliament and Welsh Assembly, marking the beginning of the end of the United Kingdom as we know it. A series of mail bombs targeting various minority groups rip through the city.

Index

Index

Index

Index

Restaurants

Only restaurants with star ratings are listed below. All restaurants are listed alphabetically in the main (preceding) index. Always call in advance to ensure a restaurant has not closed, changed its hours, or booked its tables for a private party. The restaurant price ratings are based on the average cost of an entrée for one person, excluding tax and tip.

★★★★		An Extraordinary Experience
★★★		Excellent
★★		Very Good
★		Good
$$$$		Big Bucks ($21 and up)
$$$		Expensive ($17-$20)
$$		Reasonable ($12-$16)
$		The Price Is Right (less than $12)

Hotels

The hotels listed below are grouped according to their price ratings; they are also listed in the main index. The hotel price ratings reflect the base price of a standard room for two people for one night during the peak season.

$$$$ Big Bucks ($255 and up)
$$$ Expensive ($180-$250)
$$ Reasonable ($105-$175)
$ The Price Is Right (less than $100)

$$$$

$$$

$$

$

Features

Bests

Maps

ACCESS® Guides

Order by phone, toll-free: 1-800-331-3761

Name _____ Phone _____

Address _____

City _____ State _____ Zip _____

Please send me the following ACCESS® Guides:

☐ **ATLANTA** ACCESS® $18.50
0-06-277156-6

☐ **BOSTON** ACCESS® $19.00
0-06-277197-3

☐ **CAPE COD, MARTHA'S VINEYARD, & NANTUCKET** ACCESS® $19.00
0-06-277220-1

☐ **CARIBBEAN** ACCESS® $20.00
0-06-277252-X

☐ **CHICAGO** ACCESS® $19.00
0-06-277196-5

☐ **CRUISE** ACCESS® $20.00
0-06-277190-6

☐ **FLORENCE & VENICE** ACCESS® $19.00
0-06-277222-8

☐ **GAY USA** ACCESS® $19.95
0-06-277212-0

☐ **HAWAII** ACCESS® $19.00
0-06-277223-6

☐ **LAS VEGAS** ACCESS® $19.00
0-06-277224-4

☐ **LONDON** ACCESS® $19.00
0-06-277225-2

☐ **LOS ANGELES** ACCESS® $19.00
0-06-277259-7

☐ **MEXICO** ACCESS® $19.00
0-06-277251-1

☐ **MIAMI & SOUTH FLORIDA** ACCESS® $19.00
0-06-277226-0

☐ **MINNEAPOLIS/ST. PAUL** ACCESS® $19.00
0-06-277234-1

☐ **MONTREAL & QUEBEC CITY** ACCESS® $19.00
0-06-277160-4

☐ **NEW ORLEANS** ACCESS® $19.00
0-06-277227-9

☐ **NEW YORK CITY** ACCESS® $19.00
0-06-277235-X

☐ **NEW YORK RESTAURANTS** ACCESS®
$13.00 0-06-277218-X

☐ **ORLANDO & CENTRAL FLORIDA** ACCESS®
$19.00
0-06-277228-7

☐ **PARIS** ACCESS® $19.00
0-06-277229-5

☐ **PHILADELPHIA** ACCESS® $19.00
0-06-277230-9

☐ **ROME** ACCESS® $19.00
0-06-277195-7

☐ **SAN DIEGO** ACCESS® $19.00
0-06-277185-X

☐ **SAN FRANCISCO** ACCESS® $19.00
0-06-277169-8

☐ **SAN FRANCISCO RESTAURANTS** ACCESS®
$13.00
0-06-277219-8

☐ **SANTA FE/TAOS/ALBUQUERQUE** ACCESS®
$19.00
0-06-277194-9

☐ **SEATTLE** ACCESS® $19.00
0-06-277198-1

☐ **SKI COUNTRY** ACCESS®
Eastern United States $18.50
0-06-277189-2

☐ **SKI COUNTRY** ACCESS®
Western United States $19.00
0-06-277174-4

☐ **WASHINGTON DC** ACCESS® $19.00
0-06-277232-5

☐ **WINE COUNTRY** ACCESS® France $19.00
0-06-277193-0

☐ **WINE COUNTRY** ACCESS® California $19.00
0-06-277258-9

Prices subject to change without notice.

Total for **ACCESS**® Guides:	$
Please add applicable sales tax:	
Add $4.00 for first book S&H, $1.00 per additional book:	
Total payment:	$

☐ Check or Money Order enclosed. Offer valid in the United States only.
Please make payable to HarperCollins*Publishers*.

☐ Charge my credit card ☐ American Express ☐ Visa ☐ MasterCard

Card no. _____ Exp. date _____

Signature _____

Send orders to: HarperCollins*Publishers*
P.O. Box 588
Dunmore, PA 18512-0588

ACCESS®
Makes the World Your Neighborhood

Access Destinations

- Atlanta
- Boston
- Cape Cod, Martha's Vineyard, & Nantucket
- Caribbean
- Chicago
- Cruise
- Florence & Venice
- Gay USA
- Hawaii
- Las Vegas
- London
- Los Angeles
- Mexico
- Miami & South Florida
- Minneapolis/St. Paul
- Montreal & Quebec City

- New Orleans
- New York City
- New York Restaurants
- Orlando & Central Florida
- Paris
- Philadelphia
- Rome
- San Diego
- San Francisco
- San Francisco Restaurants
- Santa Fe/Taos/Albuquerque
- Seattle
- Ski Country Eastern US
- Ski Country Western US
- Washington DC
- Wine Country France
- Wine Country California

Pack lightly and carry the best travel guides going: ACCESS. Arranged by neighborhood and featuring color-coded entries keyed to easy-to-read maps, ACCESS guides are designed to help you explore a neighborhood or an entire city in depth. You'll never get lost with an ACCESS guide in hand, but you may well be lost without one. So whether you are visiting Las Vegas or London, you'll need a sturdy pair of walking shoes and plenty of ACCESS.

HarperResource
A Division of HarperCollins*Publishers*
http://www.harpercollins.com